IRAN BETWEEN TWO REVOLUTIONS

PRINCETON STUDIES ON THE NEAR EAST

IRAN
Between Two Revolutions

Ervand
Abrahamian

PRINCETON UNIVERSITY PRESS

PRINCETON, NEW JERSEY

TO THE MEMORY OF
Jess (Helen) Harbison

Contents

PART II. POLITICS OF SOCIAL CONFLICT

PART III. CONTEMPORARY IRAN

List of Tables and Figure

Preface

This work began in 1964 as a study on the social bases of the Tudeh party, the main communist organization in Iran. Focusing on the short period between the party's formation in 1941 and its drastic repression in 1953, the original work tried to answer the question why an organization that was clearly secular, radical, and Marxist was able to grow into a mass movement in a country noted for its fervent Shi'ism, traditional monarchism, and intense nationalism. The study, however, gradually expanded as I realized that the Tudeh success could not be fully assessed without constant references to the failures, on the one hand, of its many contemporary nationalistic parties; and, on the other hand, of its ideological predecessors, especially the Social Democrats of 1909-1919, the Socialists of the 1920s, and the Communists of the 1930s. The study further expanded as the 1977-1979 revolution unfolded, shattered the Pahlevi regime, and brought to the fore not the Tudeh but the clerical forces. Thus the study has evolved into an analysis of the social bases of Iranian politics, focusing on how socioeconomic development has gradually transformed the shape of Iranian politics from the eve of the Constitutional Revolution in the late nineteenth century to the triumph of the Islamic Revolution in February 1979.

The book is divided into three parts. Part I provides a historical background to the understanding of modern Iran, surveying the nineteenth century, the Constitutional Revolution, and the reign of Reza Shah. Part II analyzes the social bases of politics in the period between the fall of Reza Shah's autocracy in August of 1941 and the establishment of Muhammad Reza Shah's autocracy in August 1953. These thirteen years are the only major period in the modern era in which the historian can look below the political surface into the social infrastructure of Iranian politics, and thereby examine in depth the ethnic as well as the class roots of the various political movements. Readers who are not interested in the internal workings of the communist movement in this period are advised to skim Chapters 7 and 8, which examine in detail the class and ethnic bases of the Tudeh party. Finally, Part III examines contemporary Iran, describing the socioeconomic programs carried out by Muhammad Reza Shah, the political tensions aggravated by these programs, and eventually the eruption of the recent Islamic Revolution.

In working my way through the complex maze of Iranian politics, I have relied as much as possible on three important sources other social scientists have often overlooked: the gold mine of information in the British Foreign Office and India Office in London—especially the weekly, monthly, annual, and detailed survey reports sent from Iran between 1905 and 1949 by provincial consular officials as well as ministers, ambassadors, and special attachés in Tehran; the valuable material revealed in parliamentary debates, particularly from the time of the First Majles in 1906 to the Seventeenth Majles in 1953; these debates have been published under the title of *Mozakerat-i Majles-i Shawra-yi Melli* (The Proceedings of the National Consultative Assembly); and the equally valuable information found in the numerous Persian-language newspapers, journals, and periodicals published from 1905 until 1980 both inside the country and outside Iran. I have also used as much as necessary memoirs, histories, and articles written by active politicians, retired statesmen, and exiles living abroad after 1953. All these sources have their biases, of course. But the social scientist can still obtain a fairly objective picture of Iranian politics by taking into account their biases, double-checking the information with other primary materials, and using as many countervailing sources as possible. It is to be hoped that future historians will be able to test my findings by gaining access to the one major source left unused— the archives of the Soviet Union on Iran.

I would like to thank those who helped in the writing of this book: Professor Donald Zagoria for reading the original monograph; political activists who wish to remain anonymous for their patient interviews, rare documents, and valuable reminiscences; Nikki Keddie, Joseph Upton, E. P. Elwell-Sutton, Bozorg ʿAlavi, Hormoz Shahdadi, and the late T. C. Cuyler Young for commenting on earlier drafts of various chapters; and Shahen Abrahamian and Margaret Case for their meticulous editorial work.

I would also like to thank the following institutions for financial assistance: the Research Institute on International Change at Columbia University for Junior Fellowships from 1967 to 1969; the City University of New York for summer travel grants during 1972, 1974, 1976, and 1979; the Social Science Research Council for a postdoctoral grant in 1977; and Baruch College in the City University of New York for a sabbatical fellowship in 1979-1980 to complete the book. Finally, I would like to thank the Controller, H. M. Stationary Office in Britain, for permission to quote from unpublished Foreign Office documents at the Public Record Office and the India Office in London. Of course, neither these institutions nor the readers thanked above are responsible for any errors or political opinions found in the book.

For the sake of space, I have used footnotes only to cite quotations, to document controversial issues and to refer to highly important primary sources. Secondary works, however distinguished, as well as other important sources have been left for the concluding bibliography. Also for the sake of space, the footnotes contain only translations of article titles from Persian newspapers, journals, and periodicals. They do contain, however, the transliteration as well as the translation of Persian books and pamphlets.

The method of transliteration inevitably needs an explanation, since few linguists agree on a common system, some vowels are not written in Persian, and pronunciation varies greatly from one region to another within Iran. To ease these problems, I have modified the version devised by the Library of Congress. In my modified version, place names well known in the English-speaking world have been kept in their familiar form (e.g. Tehran, Isfahan, and Mashad); letters "o" and "e" have been introduced to denote their equivalent sounds in Persian; diacritical marks have been eliminated on the grounds that this is a work for social scientists, not linguists; and, for the sake of consistency but at the risk of appearing to be a metropolitan chauvinist, I have based my transliteration on the pronunciation of Persian as spoken in contemporary Tehran.

IRAN BETWEEN TWO REVOLUTIONS

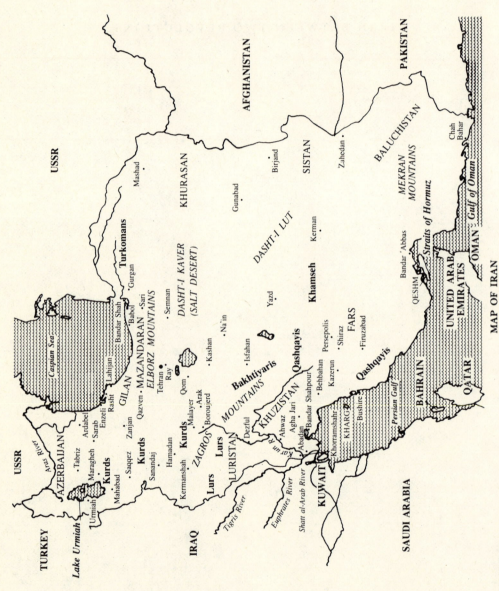

MAP OF IRAN

Introduction

Sociologists who have stopped the time-machine and, with a good deal of conceptual huffing and puffing, have gone down to the engine-room to look, tell us that nowhere at all have they been able to locate and classify a class. They can only find a multitude of people and different occupations, incomes, status-hierarchies, and the rest. Of course they are right, since class is not this or that part of the machine, but *the way the machine works* once it is set in motion—not this and that interest, but the *friction* of interests, the heat, the thundering noise. . . . Class itself is not a thing, it is a happening.

—E. P. Thompson, *The Making of the English Working Class* (London, 1968), p. 939.

In the last two decades, social scientists studying Western countries have developed a new discipline called political sociology. Disregarding the nineteenth-century premise that state and society were two separate and contradictory entities, modern social scientists have formulated a less grand but more precise perspective that sees state and society as intricately connected, and state politics as closely related to both political organizations and social forces. Equipped with this three-dimensional perspective, contemporary social scientists have produced not only perceptive theoretical frameworks on political sociology, but also many valuable empirical case studies of Western societies, analyzing the social bases of politics and on the complex relationship between state politics, political organizations and social structures.[1]

[1] For examples of empirical case studies on the social bases of politics in the West, see R. Bendix and M. Lipset, *Class, Status, and Power* (New York, 1960); L. Coser, *Political Sociology* (New York, 1966); S. Lipset, *Political Man* (New York, 1960); S. Lipset and S. Rokkan, *Party Systems and Voter Alignments* (New York, 1967); R. Rose and D. Unwin, eds., "Social Structure, Party Systems, and Voting," *Comparative Political Studies*, 2 (April 1969), 2-135; A. Stinchcombe, "Social Structure and Organizations," *Handbook of Organizations*, edited by J. March (Chicago, 1957), pp. 143-97. For an early example of such a case study, see K. Marx, "The Class Struggles in France," *Selected Works* (Moscow, 1958), vol. 1.

Whereas social scientists analyzing Western states have adopted the three-dimensional perspective of political sociology, however, social scientists examining non-Western states have tended to retain the nineteenth-century, two-dimensional outlook. Some, especially political scientists from the structural-functional school, have focused on the state: they have discussed how the state modernizes society, grapples with crises of legitimacy, and builds such new institutions as bureaucracies, armies, and one-party systems. Others, particularly anthropologists and political scientists from the behavioral school, have concentrated on society: the anthropologists on small communities, the political scientists on whole "political cultures" of "developing nations." Social scientists have thus written much on how political systems transform social systems, and social systems at times—through violence, riots, and alienation—disrupt the political systems. But they have produced little on how social struggles shape political conflicts, and how social forces, interacting with political organizations, affect the course of development in non-Western states.[2]

Similarly, few scholars have examined the social bases of Iranian politics. Whereas the past experts on Iran tended to write broad historical surveys—often stressing the impact of international affairs on internal affairs—contemporary experts focus on specific parts of either the political or the social systems. Some deal with such aspects of the political realm as nationalism, state building, land reform, and crises of legitimacy. Others write microstudies on small communities and major works on the "political culture" of the whole society. The last group argues that a national culture of individual insecurity, distrust, cynicism, rebelliousness, neurotic isolation, and psychological alienation explains the politics—especially the political instability—of twentieth-century Iran. Many analyze either the politics or the society of contemporary Iran; few study the political sociology of modern Iran.[3]

[2] Notable among the few that examine the social bases of politics in the non-Western world are Barrington Moore, *Social Origins of Dictatorship and Democracy* (Boston, 1967); M. Halpern, *The Politics of Social Change in the Middle East and North Africa* (Princeton, 1963); E. Wallerstein, *Africa: The Politics of Independence* (New York, 1961); K. Karpat, *Turkey's Politics: The Transition to a Multi-Party System* (Princeton, 1959); C. Geertz, ed., *Old Societies and New Nations* (Chicago, 1963); J. Bill and C. Leiden, *The Middle East: Politics and Power* (Boston, 1974); H. Batatu, *Old Social Classes and the Revolutionary Movements of Iraq* (Princeton, 1979).

[3] For a list of books on modern Iran, see the bibliography. Only two books can be described as studies on the social bases of Iranian politics: J. Upton, *The History of Modern Iran: An Interpretation* (Cambridge, Mass., 1968) and J. Bill, *The Politics of Iran: Groups, Classes, and Modernization* (Columbus, Ohio, 1972). The former, while explaining political instability in terms of foreign intervention, provincial insurrections, and the "national character" of "individualistic opportunism," also examines various forces competing within the society. The latter, focusing on power, authority, and methods

The present work intends to examine the politics of modern Iran by analyzing the interaction between political organizations and social forces. These forces can be categorized generally as ethnic groups and social classes. The book will use the phrase "ethnic group" to describe the vertical groupings of individuals with common ties of language, tribal lineage, religion, or regional affiliation. It will apply the term "social class" to the broad horizontal layers composed of individuals with common relationships to the means of production, common interactions with the mode of administration, and, in a developing environment, common attitudes toward economic, social, and political modernization.

Although the concept of social class has been employed, in slightly different forms, by such contrasting authorities as Marx and de Tocqueville, Machiavelli and Tawney, Weber and Dahrendorf, medieval ideologues and Muslim theologians, Roman censors and the American *Federalist Papers*, it has come under fire recently from diverse social scientists. Structural-functionalists have argued that societies are divided not into a few major classes but into many small occupational layers. These layers, they stress, are dependent upon each other because of the division of labor, but are differentiated from each other by various degrees of prestige, honor, and income.[4] Behavioralists have claimed that individuals in the developing countries attach themselves to ideologies rather than to members of their own socioeconomic class. Political forces, they emphasize, are created by competing ideas, not by conflicting classes. If Marx turned Hegel "right side up" with the formulation that man's consciousness is determined by his social being, the modern behavioralists have reversed Marx with the insistence that man's social being—at least in the Third World—is determined by his consciousness.[5] Students of political elites, meanwhile, have discarded the concept of social class by relegating

---

of modernization, answers in depth the reasons why the shah failed to win over the modern intelligentsia.

[4] T. Parsons, "Social Classes and Class Conflict in the Light of Recent Sociological Theory," *Essays in Sociological Theory* (New York, 1967); R. Merton, *Social Theory and Social Structure* (Chicago, 1957). For a discussion of whether Middle Eastern societies are divided into classes or occupational strata, see A. Perlmutter, "Egypt and the Myth of the New Middle Class," *Comparative Studies in History and Society*, 10 (October 1967), 46-65; M. Halpern, "Egypt and the New Middle Class," *Comparative Studies in History and Society*, 11 (January 1969), 97-108.

[5] L. Pye, *Aspects of Political Development* (Boston, 1966); G. Almond and S. Verba, *The Civic Culture* (Boston, 1965). For a study on the importance of ideology in Iranian politics, see L. Binder, *Iran: Political Development in Changing Society* (Berkeley and Los Angeles, 1962).

everybody else into an amorphous residue labeled the "masses."[6] At the same time, sociologists who have written on non-Western politics have also questioned the conceptual usefulness of class by arguing that the main conflicts in the Third World revolve around the ethnic divisions of tribe, race, caste, religion, and regional origins.[7] Classes, they conclude, exist in Europe and America but not in Asia and Africa. Finally, many social scientists in the Third World—together with some sympathizers of the Third World in the West—have tended to emphasize their external differences with the industrialized countries and gloss over their internal social antagonisms. National struggles, they insist, dwarf all social struggles, including class struggles.[8]

This book does not pretend to solve once for all the major theoretical problems of class versus elite, class versus stratum, social issues versus national ones, horizontal groups versus vertical divisions, and consensus versus conflict analyses. But it does intend to analyze the social bases of Iranian politics by examining the central class and ethnic conflicts of the last hundred years, the relationship between socioeconomic modernization and political development, the rise of new classes as well as the decline of old communities, and the social composition, together with the ideological outlook, of the main political parties. The book, in presenting a case study of the social bases of politics, hopes to throw some light both on major issues in political development—especially the role of ethnic conflicts in emerging countries—and on theoretical problems in political sociology—particularly the advantages, as well as the disadvantages, of class analysis. The underlying premise throughout the book will be E. P. Thompson's neo-Marxist approach that the phenomenon of class should be understood not simply in terms of its relation to the mode of production (as orthodox Marxists have often argued), but, on the contrary, in the context of historical time and of social friction with other contemporary classes.

[6] G. Mosca, *The Ruling Class* (New York, 1939); V. Pareto, *The Mind and Society* (London, 1935); C. Wright Mills, *The Power Elite* (New York, 1965); C. Van Nieuwenhuijze, *Social Stratification in the Middle East* (Leiden, 1965). For an elite approach to modern Iran, see M. Zonis, *The Political Elite of Iran* (Princeton, 1971).

[7] C. Geertz, "The Integrative Revolution: Primordial Sentiments and Civil Politics in the New States," in Geertz, ed., *Old Societies and New Nations*, pp. 107-57; L. Kuper, "Theories of Revolution and Race Relations," *Comparative Studies in History and Society*, 12 (January 1971), 87-107; A. Lewis, *Politics in West Africa* (London, 1965); J. C. Hurewitz, *Middle East Politics: The Military Dimension* (New York, 1969).

[8] These views are discussed by S. Lipset, "Issues in Social Class Analysis," in *Revolution and Counter-Revolution* (New York, 1970), pp. 157-201. For an interesting example minimizing the importance of internal conflicts in Iran while maximizing the significance of external crises with the West, see B. Nirumand, *Iran: The New Imperialism in Action* (New York, 1969).

PART I

Historical
Background

ONE

The Nineteenth Century

The king may do what he pleases; his word is law. The saying that "The law of the Medes and Persians altereth not" was merely an ancient periphrasis for the absolutism of the sovereign. He appoints and he may dismiss all ministers, officers, officials and judges. Over his own family and household, and over the civil or military functionaries in his employ he has power of life and death without reference to any tribunal. The property of any such individual, if disgraced or executed, reverts to him. The right to take life in any case is vested in him alone, but can be delegated to governors and deputies. All property, not previously granted by the crown or purchased—all property in fact to which a legal title cannot be established—belongs to him, and can be disposed of at his pleasure. All rights or privileges, such as the making of public works, the working of mines, the institution of telegraphs, roads, railroads, tramways, etc., the exploitation, in fact, of any of the resources of the country, are vested in him. In his person are fused the threefold functions of government, legislative, executive, and judicial. No obligation is imposed upon him beyond the outward observation of the forms of national religion. He is the pivot upon which turns the entire machinery of public life.

—G. Curzon, *Persia and the Persian Question*, I, 433.

Although the local officials are not formally elected, the voice of the people always points them out; and if the king should appoint a magistrate disagreeable to the citizens, he could not perform his duties, which require all the weight he derives from personal considerations to aid the authority of office. In small towns or villages the voice of the inhabitants in nominating their head is still more decided: if one is named of whom they did not approve, their clamour produces either his resignation or removal. These facts are important; for no privilege is more essential to the welfare of the people, than that of choosing or influencing the choice of their magistrates.

—J. Malcolm, *History of Persia*, II, 324-25.

SOCIAL STRUCTURE

"The past," R. H. Tawney once remarked, "reveals to the present what the present is capable of seeing."[1] Although the remark was made in reference to changing interpretations of

[1] R. H. Tawney, *Religion and the Rise of Capitalism* (New York, 1926), p. 3.

European history, it is particularly apt for twentieth-century perceptions of nineteenth-century Iran. The first generation of twentieth-century intellectuals, peering back through the narrow prism of the Constitutional Revolution, saw in the immediate past nothing but a corrupt state (*dawlat*) oppressing the people (*mellat*).[2] The second generation, struggling against religious conservatism, shunned the bygone era as a shameful age of dogmatism, fanaticism, and rampant clericalism.[3] The third generation, influenced by Marxism, dismissed the same era as the epoch of declining feudalism in which a handful of corrupt landlords had exploited the rural lower classes (*tabaqat*).[4] It was not until the contemporary generation that intellectuals have discovered the nineteenth century to be not merely an embarrassing prelude to the revolution, but an interesting age worthy of study on its own merits. The change from summary denunciation to analytical examination has been caused in part by a broader outlook attained through the passage of time; in part by a nostalgia for a bygone age; and in part by the gradual awareness that nineteenth-century Iran, despite its economic backwardness, was a land of infinite variety, of

[2] For elite/mass descriptions of nineteenth-century Iran, see *Mozakerat-i Majles-i Shawra-yi Melli* (The Proceedings of the National Consultative Assembly) (referred to below as *Parliamentary Proceedings*), First Majles (1906-1907). During this session, twenty deputies described their society as formed of a governmental elite (*dawlat*) and a national people (*mellat*). Only two deputies perceived it as divided into social classes (*tabaqat*). The word *tabaqeh* (class) was used loosely in this period—as in the Electoral Law in 1906—to describe any social category, such as the religious minorities, as well as the six main social orders: the royal princes (*shahzadegan*); the nobles (*ashraf*) and notables (*a'yan*); the clergy (*'ulama*); the merchants (*tujjar*); the guild members (*asnaf*); and the landowners (*malekin*).

[3] For anticlerical interpretations of nineteenth-century Iran, see "The French Revolution and the Promised Iranian Revolution," *Iranshahr*, I (April 1923), 282-93; H. Kazemzadeh, "Religion and Nationality," *Iranshahr*, 3 (December 1924), 1-45; A. Kasravi, "Islam and Iran," *Payman*, 1 (February 1933), 9-10; and A. Kasravi, "A Short History," *Parcham*, 29 February 1942.

[4] For class sketches of nineteenth-century Iran, see Malek al-Shua'ra Bahar, *Tarikh-i Ahzab-i Siyasi-yi Iran* (History of Political Parties in Iran) (Tehran, 1944), pp. 2, 320; "The Class War," *Mardom*, 23 April 1943; A. Qassemi, *Jam'ehra Beshenasid* (Get to Know Society) (Tehran, 1948); A. Ovanessian, "Class Cleavages," *Rahbar*, 30 October 1946; E. Tabari, "Concerning the Constitutional Revolution," *Mardom*, 2 (August-September 1948), pp. 1-8; H. Arsanjani, "Class Struggles in Iran," *Darya*, 18-22 July 1944; A. Khal'atbari, *Aristukrasi-yi Iran* (The Iranian Aristocracy) (Tehran, 1944); H. Hakim-Ilah'i, *Shahr-i Demokrat* (The Democratic City) (Tehran, 1946). The influence of the class perspective appeared even in the Majles among the conservative deputies. For example, during the Sixteenth Majles (1948-1958), in contrast to the First Majles, twenty-two deputies described their society as divided into conflicting classes; only two retained the old elite-mass dichotomy.

social complexity, and of regional diversity. It resembled, in the words of one recent work, a colorful mosaic and a complex kaleidoscope.[5]

The physical geography of the land laid the foundations for the social mosaic. A lack of navigable rivers and lakes, a marked shortage of rainfall—half the country's present 636,000 square miles receive less than ten inches of rain per year—a vast central desert surrounded by four formidable mountain ranges—the Zagros, the Elborz, the Mekran, and the Uplands—all served to fragment the population into secluded villages, isolated towns, and nomadic tribes. The villagers, forming over 55 percent of the total population of nearly ten million in the 1850s, lived in some 10,000 settlements: even a century later, when the ten million had almost doubled, the mean size of a village still reached no more than 250 inhabitants (see Table 1, note b). The urban population, constituting less than 20 percent of the country, resided in some eighty towns. Of these, only the following eleven contained more than 25,000 inhabitants each: Tabriz, Tehran, Isfahan, Mashad, Yazd, Hamadan, Kerman, Urmiah, Kermanshah, Shiraz, and Qazvin. Finally, the nomads, who formed as much as 25 percent of the population, were divided into sixteen major tribal groups, and each group was in turn divided into numerous tribes, subtribes, and migratory camps.

Many of these villages, tribes, and towns were on the whole isolated and economically self-contained, producing and consuming much of their own handicraft as well as agricultural goods.[6] Although there are a few anthropologists who claim that throughout Iranian history villages and towns have been remarkably interdependent,[7] the vast majority of historians and travelers have argued that until the rapid growth of commerce in the second half of the nineteenth century most villages and tribes remained virtually self-contained, practically self-sufficient, economically autonomous, and predominantly self-governing.[8] James Fraser, an Englishman traveling through Khurasan

[5] J. Bill and C. Leiden, *The Middle East: Politics and Power* (Boston, 1974), pp. 73-74, 255-58.

[6] F. Khamsi, "The Development of Capitalism in Rural Iran" (M.A. thesis, Columbia University, 1969).

[7] G. Goodell, "The Elementary Structures of Political Life" (Ph.D. dissertation, Columbia University, 1977). For a geographer stressing the same argument, see P. English, *City and Village in Iran* (Madison, Wisc., 1966).

[8] A. Lambton, *Islamic Society in Persia* (Oxford, 1954), p. 8; I. Harik, "The Impact of the Domestic Market on Rural-Urban Relations in the Middle East," *Rural Politics and Social Change in the Middle East*, edited by R. Antoun and I. Harik (Bloomingdale, Ind., 1972), p. 340; V. Nowshirvani and A. Knight, "The Beginnings of Commercial Agriculture in Iran" (paper delivered at a Yale University seminar, 1975), p. 2; N. Keddie, *Historical Obstacles to Agrarian Change in Iran* (Claremont, Cal., 1950), p. 5.

TABLE 1
Ethnic Structure of Iran

Total	1956[a] 18,945,000	%	1850[b] 10,000,000	%
Iranians	12,770,000	67	6,375,000	64
Persians	8,200,000		4,000,000	
Kurds	2,000,000		800,000	
Baluchis	500,000		264,000	
Mazandaranis	500,000		300,000	
Gilakis	500,000		300,000	
Bakhtiyaris	400,000		250,000	
Lurs	400,000		210,000	
Talleshis	75,000		50,000	
Hazars	10,000		5,000	
Afghans	10,000		5,000	
Others	175,000		126,000	
Turkic Speakers	5,130,000	27	2,900,000	29
Azeris	4,000,000		2,110,000	
Qashqayis	500,000		264,000	
Shahsavens	140,000		90,000	
Turkomans	200,000		100,000	
Timurs	30,000		20,000	
Afshars	200,000		150,000	
Jamshids	30,000		40,000	
Others—Qajars, Bayats, etc.	30,000		126,000	
Arabs	567,000	3	400,000	4
Non-Muslims	478,000	3	300,000	3
Assyrians	20,000		138,000	
Armenians	190,000		110,000	
Jews	60,000		32,000	
Zoroastrians	16,000		20,000	
Baha'is	192,000		—	

NOTES: a. Since the 1956, 1966, and 1976 censuses—the only nationwide censuses completed in Iran—do not give an ethnic breakdown of the population, these figures for 1956 are only vague estimates obtained mainly from the following "educated guesses": American University, *Area Handbook on Iran* (Washington, D.C., 1963); Foreign Office, "Handbook on Persian Minorities," *F.O. 371*/Eastern 1944/Persia 189-20219; S. Bruk, "The Ethnic Composition of Iran," *Central Asian Review*, 8:4 (1960), 417-20; S. Aliyev, "The Problem of Nationalities in Iran," *Central Asian Review*, 14:1 (1966), 62-70; M. Ivanov, "The Question of Nationalities in Iran," *Donya*, 12 (Spring 1971), 48-77; H. Field, *Contributions to the Anthropology of Iran* (Chicago, 1939), pp. 601-51.

b. The nineteenth century remains the dark age for Iranian statistics. Census data is nonexistent, tax assessments are highly unreliable, and travelers differ widely in their impressions. The total of ten million for the 1850s is a rough estimate obtained by projecting back the 1956 figures and taking into account the famines and bad harvests of 1853, 1857, 1860, 1866, 1872, and 1892. For a recent study on the nineteenth-century population, see G. Gilbar, "Demographic Developments in Late Qajar Persia, 1870-1906," *Asian and African Studies*, 2 (1976-1977), 125-56.

The estimates for the ethnic groups in the 1850s have been derived from nineteenth-century impressionistic calculations and from backward projections of the 1956 guesses. In these backward projections, consideration has been given to emigration as well as assimilation of smaller communities into the larger communities—especially the Persian and Azeri populations.

in the 1820s, found that even large villages grew mulberries and cotton to manufacture their own silk and cotton piece-goods. Henry Pottinger, another English visitor, noted that Baluchi women "attend to household affairs, milking, making butter, cheese and ghee, weaving carpets, flets, and coarse white cloth." Robert Binning, yet another Englishman, found that even prosperous peasants in the close vicinity of major towns grew much of their own food, and purchased from local markets only small amounts of salt, pepper, tobacco, and essential household goods. Similarly, Arthur Conolly of the East India Company discovered in the 1830s that the Turkoman tribes of Gurgan produced their own clothes and bought only a few luxury goods such as spices, sugar, and tobacco.[9]

Local self-sufficiency was reflected in, as well as reinforced by, poor communications. Since rural communities met their own needs and large towns obtained food from their agricultural suburbs, trade consisted predominantly of luxury goods either en route from one city to another or in transit through Iran to Europe. Edward Stack, a civil servant from British India, noticed that travelers were so rare even on the Tehran-Bushire road that their "sight throws others into commotion." Augustus Mounsey, a British diplomat touring northern Iran in the late 1860s, came across only one rider on the main road between Tehran and Rasht. He noted that the appearance of this rider "frightened many villagers into flight." Arthur Arnold, a contemporary English entrepreneur investigating the prospects of constructing railroads, found that the volume of trade was too little to justify any such projects.[10]

[9] J. Fraser, *Narrative of a Journey into Khurasan* (London, 1825), p. 405; H. Pottinger, *Travels in Beloochistan* (London, 1816), p. 73; R. Binning, *A Journey of Two Years' Travel in Persia* (London, 1857), II, 47-48; A. Conolly, *Journey to the North of India* (London, 1834), I, 165. Even in the last decade of the nineteenth century, many villages in the less accessible areas remained relatively self-sufficient. Isabella Bishop, a missionary traveling through the central highlands in the last decade of the century, noted that women in Bakhtiyari, Armenian, and Persian villages spun, wove, knitted, and dyed their own garments (I. Bishop, *Journeys in Persia and Kurdistan* [London, 1891], I, 365-66). Henry Landor, an English entrepreneur seeking new markets, found that Baluchi villagers still manufactured their own simple fabrics (H. Landor, *Across Coveted Lands* [New York, 1903], II, 61, 416). Percy Sykes, surveying Khurasan on behalf of the British Foreign Office, found to his surprise that some villages continued to produce their own food and clothes, even though many had started to grow commercial crops to pay their taxes in cash (P. Sykes, "Report on the Agriculture of Khorasan [1910]," reprinted in *The Economic History of Iran, 1800-1914*, edited by C. Issawi [Chicago, 1971], pp. 253-55). Likewise, a member of the British consular staff in Mashad during World War I was amazed to find that many villages in Khurasan remained economically self-sufficient and manufactured their own garments (F. Hale, *From Persian Uplands* [London, 1920], pp. 17-32).

[10] E. Stack, *Six Months in Persia* (New York, 1882), I, 160; A. Mounsey, *A Journey*

The little trade that existed was hindered by bad roads, rugged terrain, long distances, lack of navigable rivers, and frequent tribal upheavals. Sir John Malcolm, the first nineteenth-century envoy from Britain, discovered that muleteers were reluctant to cross the eastern mountains even in times of relative security. Sir Harford Jones Brydges, another British envoy, complained that he spent one whole week covering the two hundred miles between Isfahan and Tehran. Baron de Bode, a Russian visitor, traveling as lightly as possible, averaged no more than twenty-seven miles per day. Even at the end of the century, the important road between the southern port of Moham-merah (Khorramshahr) and Tehran was so slow that to get from the latter to the former it was quicker to travel from the Persian Gulf to the Black Sea by boat, from Erzerum to the Caspian by land, from Baku to Enzeli (Pahlevi) by boat again, and finally from Enzeli to Tehran by land. This lack of transport created periodic crises in which one region could starve from famine while a neighboring region was enjoying a good harvest.[11]

Paradoxically, improvements in transportation did not necessarily facilitate social communications. De Bode noted that the establishment of security on the Tehran-Tabriz highway had helped the tax collectors, and, thus, had encouraged the local peasants to resettle in more distant regions. "In Persia," he commented, "the richest villages are generally in some retired valley in the mountains or far from the main high roads." Sykes observed the same phenomenon: "The main roads are shunned by the villagers owing to the fact that Governors generally take supplies without payment." Likewise, a survey for the British Foreign Office reported: "There are large tracts of fertile land which remain waste owing to their proximity to the main roads, as no village having cultivators on such spots can possibly prosper or enjoy the least immunity from the pestering visits of Government officials, and thefts and robberies committed by the tribes."[12]

The geographical difficulties were compounded by ethnic differences. For Iran was, as it still is, a land of linguistic minorities. In the

through the Caucasus and the Interior of Persia (London, 1872), p. 320; A. Arnold, Through Persia by Caravan (London, 1877), II, 45.

[11] J. Malcolm, Sketches of Persia (London, 1854), p. 278; H. J. Brydges, An Account of the Transactions of His Majesty's Mission to the Court of Persia (London, 1834), p. 176; C. de Bode, Travels in Luristan and Arabistan (London, 1854), II, 321; A. Melamid, "Communications, Transport, Retail Trade, and Services," Cambridge History of Iran, edited by W. Fisher (London, 1968), I, 556; V. Chirol, The Middle East Question (London, 1903), p. 97.

[12] De Bode, Travels, II, 32; P. Sykes, Ten Thousand Miles in Persia (New York, 1902), p. 435; Great Britain, Foreign Office, "Report on Bushire (1880)," reprinted in The Economic History of Iran, 1800-1914 (edited by C. Issawi), pp. 227-31.

central plateau, the town population spoke Persian; the villagers Persian, Bakhtiari, Luri, or Armenian; the nomadic tribes Bakhtiari, Qashqayi, Baluchi, Arabic, or Mamasani. In the Caspian provinces, the peasantry used Gilaki, Taleshi, or Mazandarani; the townsmen Persian and the Azeri dialect of Turkish; the tribes Kurdish or the Turkoman dialect of Turkish. The inhabitants of Azerbaijan were predominatly Azeri-speaking; but the region also had pockets of Tat and Armenian settlements, and of Kurdish, Shahsaven, Turkoman, Afshar, and Qareh Daghi tribesmen. The western provinces consisted predominantly of Kurdish, Luri, and Arab tribes; and partly of Afshar, Azeri, Persian, Bayat, Gurani, and Assyrian settlements. Moreover, many of the Kurdish valleys had developed their own Kurdish dialects. The southeastern provinces contained Baluchi, Arab, Afghan, Afshar, Kurdish, and Nowshirvani tribesmen. Finally, the northeastern region was populated with Persians, Azeris, Turkomans, Kurds, Arabs, Shahsavens, Afshars, Jamshids, Tajiks, Afghans, Qajars, Hazaras, Bayats, and Baluchis.

The ethnic mosaic was further complicated by religious differences. In some areas, religious differences emphasized existing cleavages; in others, they created new ones. At times the religious differences were obvious; at other times, they were less obvious. The population as a whole was divided along three major lines. First, it was clearly separated into a Muslim majority and a non-Muslim minority. The latter included some 110,000 Armenians living in and near Isfahan, Tehran, Tabriz, Hamadan, and Arak; 138,000 Assyrians, both Nestorian and Catholic, concentrated in western Azerbaijan; 32,000 Jews residing in many of the major cities; and 20,000 Zoroastrians, remnants of the ancient religion of Iran, who congregated in Kerman, Yazd, and Tehran. Second, the Muslim population was divided, also clearly, into a Shi'i majority and a Sunni minority. The Sunnis consisted of tribes at the periphery, especially some of the Kurds, Turkomans, Arabs, Baluchis, and Hazaras.

Third, the Shi'i majority itself was divided, less obviously, among the main official branch sometimes known as the Mujtahedi Twelvers, and many small unofficial sects, schools, and factions scattered throughout the country. The Mujtahedi Twelvers, as Shi'is, considered the Prophet's legitimate heir to have been not his elected successor—the Sunni caliph, but his son-in-law Imam 'Ali. As Twelvers, they traced the line of descent from Imam 'Ali through his martyred son Imam Hussein to the Twelfth Imam, who had disappeared in the ninth century. This Hidden Imam, known also as the Mahdi, was expected to reappear in an age of extreme injustice to reestablish the reign of divine justice. As Mujtahedis, they believed that the Hidden

Imam had delegated the responsibility of interpreting the divine laws (*shari'a*) to the religious authorities (*'ulama*) in general and to the highest religious authorities (*mujtaheds*) in particular. This branch of Sh'ism thus had within itself a built-in tendency toward schism, for it not only rejected the notion of a structured church, but also endowed each high-ranking member of the 'ulama with the right to interpret and reinterpret the divine laws.

In the course of the nineteenth century, Shi'ism developed two major schisms: Shaykhism and Babism. The former was founded in the 1810s by an Arab preacher named Shaykh Ahmad 'Ahsa'i. A convert from Sunnism, the shaykh accepted wholeheartedly not only the orthodox Shi'i premise that the Imams were the true successors of the Prophet, but also the unorthodox teaching of Mulla Sadra, the seventeenth-century Sufi mystic who had argued that the Imams were divine, and that perfect believers could communicate directly with the Hidden Imam. The shaykh also added to these Sufi concepts the novel idea that the community was in constant motion toward improvement, and that God had given each generation a Perfect Shi'i—also known as the Bab (Gate)—to communicate with the Hidden Imam and to lead the way.[13] Although the mujtaheds denounced these ideas as heretical, the shaykh and his immediate successor, Sayyid Kazem Rashti, attracted numerous followers in the main cities, especially in Kerman, Yazd, and Tabriz. But after Rashti's death in 1843, their followers split into three rival groups.[14] The first group, formed predominantly of merchants and craftsmen in Tabriz, labeled itself the Shaykhis, and, while giving up the idea of the Bab, remained committed to the concept of social progress. The second group, led by a princely governor of Kerman named Hajj Karim Khan, gave up the concepts of both progress and the Bab, and turned highly conservative, preaching submission to the state and denouncing all reforms, including modern schools, as dangerous innovations. This group later adopted the label of Karimkhanis, and dominated the city of Kerman. The third group, headed by a Mulla Hussein Bushruyeh, remained true to the original teachings of the shaykh, advocating progress and reform, and expecting the imminent appearance of the Perfect Shi'i.

The expected messiah appeared in 1844 in the form of a young merchant turned theologian named Sayyid 'Ali Muhammad. After years of studying with Shaykhi theologians in Karbala, 'Ali Muhammad declared himself the Bab, and, winning over many former dis-

---

[13] M. Bayat, *Mysticism and Dissent: Socio-Religious Thought in Qajar Iran* (Syracuse, N.Y., 1982).

[14] For a brief history of the Shaykhis, see N. Fathi, *Zendiginameh-yi Shahid Shaykh al-Islam Tabrizi* (The Life of Martyr Shaykh al-Islam of Tabriz) (Tehran, 1974).

ciples of 'Ahsa'i, preached the need for social reforms, especially elimination of corruption in high places, purging of immoral clerics, legal protection for merchants, legalization of money lending, and improvement in the status of women. Not surprisingly, his message gained him both the enmity of the establishment and the support of some discontented traders, artisans, low-ranking clerics, and even peasants. Fearing the movement's rapid growth—especially in the Caspian provinces—the government in 1850 executed the Bab and initiated a bloody campaign against the Babis. Although persecution failed to destroy Babism, it succeeded in splitting the movement into two rival branches known as Baha'ism and 'Azalism. The former, headed by the Bab's chosen successor, Baha'ullah, gradually lost interest in radical reforms and eventually became a new apolitical religion outside the fold of Islam. The latter, led by Baha'ullah's brother, Subh-i 'Azal, remained true to its radical origins, and continued as a persecuted underground organization.

In addition to these new communities, nineteenth-century Iran still contained many old Shi'i sects. For example, scattered villages outside Yazd, Kerman, Mahallat, Nishapur, Qa'in, and Birjand adhered to the Isma'ili sect. As Isma'ilis, they believed that the Shi'i line of succession should have passed through a younger son of the Seventh Imam. Moreover, some villages on the western border practiced 'Ali-Ilah'i doctrines. These teachings denounced mosques, opposed polygamy, rejected the concept of ritual uncleanliness, permitted the consumption of pork and wine, and, most unorthodox of all, deified Imam 'Ali as the reincarnation of God. Furthermore, almost all the major towns were divided into two rival factions known as Ni'matis and Haydaris. The former took its name from Amir Nur al-Din Ni'mat Allah, a Sufi mystic and descendant of the Fifth Imam. The latter was named after Sultan al-Din Haydar, another Sufi mystic and ancestor of the Safavid dynasty that had transformed Iran into a Shi'i state. Explaining how towns became divided into Ni'mati and Haydari factions, Justin Sheil, the British minister to Iran from 1836 to 1853, commented, "it is strange that even well-informed people can give no real explanation for the original causes of these divisions."[15]

The religious lines appeared clearly in the towns, as the sects congregated in their own wards (*mahallat*). For example, Kerman, with 49,000 inhabitants, contained separate districts for Twelver Mujtahedis, Karimkhanis, Shaykhis, Sufis, Jews, and Zoroastrians. Shiraz was made up of five eastern Haydari quarters, five western Ni'mati

[15] J. Sheil, *Glimpses of Life and Manners in Persia* (London, 1856), pp. 322-23. For recent research on the topic see H. Mirjafari, "The Haydari-Ni'mati Conflicts in Iran," *Iranian Studies*, 12 (Summer-Autumn 1979), 135-62.

quarters, and one suburban Jewish quarter. Shustar, with fewer than 20,000 residents, consisted of four northern Haydari districts and eight southern Ni'mati districts. Tabriz, totaling 100,000, contained thirteen mahallat: one aristocratic suburb; one Armenian quarter; six agricultural districts farmed by Mujtahedi Twelvers—these orthodox Shi'is were known locally as Mutashar'is; three prosperous central wards—Khiaban, Nubar, and Amir-Khizi—populated with Shaykhi merchants, traders, and craftsmen; and two northern slums—Davachi and Sarkhab—crowded with Mutashar'i muleteers, laborers, porters, dyers, and carpet weavers.

The ethnic structure of Iran thus resembled an intricate mosaic in which each inlay differed in shape, size, and color. If any one term could describe the population, it would be "communal diversity." For there was diversity in the way of life among the villagers, the nomadic tribesmen, and the urban inhabitants. There was diversity in religious beliefs, particularly between Sunnis and Shi'is, Muslims and non-Muslims, Twelver Mujtahedis and other Shi'is. Moreover, there was diversity in languages and dialects, especially among Persians, Azeris, Turkomans, Kurds, Baluchis, Gilakis, and Mazandaranis.

COMMUNAL ORGANIZATIONS

The communal organizations reflected the social structure. Each community, whether tribal, peasant, or urban, contained its own local and separate networks. These networks, structured as small pyramids, were analogous to one another. At the base of the pyramid were the common people: the tribesmen (*iliyati*), the villagers (*dehqani*), and the townsmen (*shahri*). At the apex were the regional magnates: the tribal chiefs (*khans*), the local notables (*a'yan*), the large fief-holders (*tuyuldars*), the major landowners (*malekin*), the senior 'ulama, and the wealthy merchants (*tujjar-i 'amdeh*). At the intermediate stages were layers of local leaders, the most important of whom throughout much of the country were the tribal, the village, and the ward headmen (*kadkhudas*).

The primary social unit among the nomadic tribesmen was the migratory camp. These units, which usually consisted of families from the same clan (*tireh*), varied in size, depending on geography, from ten to one hundred households. The camps were headed by either formal leaders, the kadkhudas, or informal elders, known as the rish safids (white beards). The latter were senior members of the more prosperous households, the former were chosen initially by the elders and then confirmed in office by the tribal chiefs. These camp leaders, whether formal or informal, carried out the same two essential tasks.

They protected the external interests of their camp, especially in the frequent land and water disputes that flared up between their own followers and neighboring camps of the same tribe; thus they acted, and were accepted, as the group's representatives. And they maintained the internal peace of the camp, particularly in the recurrent quarrels that resulted from the temporary allocation of tribal land and water to individual households; thus they functioned as the group's arbitrators. As arbitrators, the camp leaders relied on persuasion, mediation, and group appreciation, for although they lacked the instruments of coercion, their followers had the option of "voting with their feet" and joining other camps. "The maintenance of the camp as a social unity," Fredrik Barth has written in his classic study of the Basseri tribe, "thus requires the daily unanimous agreement of all members on most vital economic questions."[16] The kadkhudas and rish safids, therefore, possessed authority rather than power, and their combination of local wealth and group allegiance signified the existence of a "rank" rather than a "simple egalitarian" or a "complex stratified" society.[17]

The subtribes (*tayifeh*) formed the second rung in the ladder of nomadic organizations.[18] They consisted of a number of camps (the number depended on the size of the tribe) and were headed by either khans or kalantars (bailiffs). The term *khan* was used freely for the heads of the leading clans; the title of *kalantar* was usually bestowed by the main chief, in consultation with the local khans, on the head of the leading clan. The functions of the khans and the kalantars were comparable to those of the kadkhudas and the rish safids: they protected their subtribe from other subtribes within their tribe, and they mediated disputes between different camps of their own subtribe.

The tribe (*il*), headed by its main khan, constituted the third rung in nomadic organizations. The number of tribes within the major nomadic populations varied. The Bakhtiyaris, for example, were divided into fifty-five separate tribes; the Qashqayis into thirty; the Mamasanis into four; the Boir Ahmedis, a Luri-speaking group in the south, into two; the Kurds of Luristan into six; the Baluchis into twelve; the Arabs of the southwest into thirty.[19] The role of the main

[16] F. Barth, *The Nomads of South Persia* (Boston, 1961), p. 26.

[17] For an elaboration of "rank," "simple egalitarian," and "stratified" societies, see M. Fried, *The Evolution of Political Economy* (New York, 1967).

[18] Some tribes, such as the Bakhtiyaris, interchangeably use the terms *tayifeh* and *tireh*.

[19] Tribes were termed *tirehs* among the Qashqayis and *tayifeh* among the Baluchis. Khans were called *shaykhs* by the Arabs, *sardars* by the Baluchis, and *aghas* by some Kurds.

khan within the tribe was similar to that of the kalantars within the subtribe and the kadkhudas within the migratory camps, but on a grander scale. Although the khan was by birth a member of the most important clan in the tribe, he was chosen to his position by the other prominent khans because of his ability. He protected the tribe against the outside world, whether against local villagers, government tax-collectors, or other tribes. In times of war, he was expected to be a general leading his warriors into battle; in times of peace, he was reckoned as a diplomat safeguarding the interests of his followers. Moreover, he ruled over the tribe, allocating land, leading the sem-iannual migrations, and most important of all, arbitrating feuds between subtribes and if necessary between camps, households, and even individual tribesmen. Thus he behaved as a grand judge who was bound not by civil and religious laws but by the need to attain tribal concensus. And his tent, known as the *darbar* (court), became a grand court in both the regal and the legal sense. If he failed in his tasks, rival relatives would sooner or later rally discontented khans to supplant him as the main khan.

Yet another level of organization existed among the Qajars, the Qashqayis, and the Bakhtiyaris. Each of these three groups, like other tribal groups, had its own dialect, its own common genealogy, however mythical, and its own aversion to the neighboring populations. But unlike other groups, each of these three also possessed its own central authority in the form of an ilkhan. The three thus were known as tribal confederations. The ilkhan, functioning as the supreme chief of the many chiefs with his confederation, delegated some of the internal responsibilities to an assistant called the *ilbeg*. Although the ilkhans and ilbegs were officially appointed by the central government, Malcolm correctly described them as "hereditary nobles," since they were first selected by their own khans and then confirmed in office as a matter of course.[20]

The village organizations were comparable to the nomadic organizations. Some villages, especially in the Kurdish, Lur, and Baluchi regions, were settlements of former nomads who had retained their tribal networks long after abandoning the nomadic way of life. Others were peasant communities that had evolved their own autonomous networks headed by kadkhudas. The village kadkhuda, who was often a small landowner elected by the community, carried out functions analogous to those performed by his namesake among the nomadic tribes. In larger settlements, he was often assisted by the rish safids and the local officials: the paykar, appointed to enforce the kad-

[20] J. Malcolm, *History of Persia* (London, 1829), II, 412.

khuda's decisions; the mulla of the mosque; the dastban, responsible for watching over village fields, crops, cattle, and fortifications; and the mirab, in charge of cleaning the intricate underground canals known as qanats. The informal method of electing village kadkhudas was described first hand by Edward Burgess, an Englishman who worked briefly in the 1830s as a government-appointed supervisor of state-owned lands in western Iran:

If a large majority are determined to have the *kadkhuda* out, not I nor even the Prince, nor the Shah himself, can prevent their doing so. . . . I give the term elections to this business because I have no other word for it, but they do not meet and vote. The thing is arranged amongst themselves, they meet and talk the matter over and whenever a large majority is in favor of one man the authorities can not resist their wish, if they did the people would stand upon their rights and would not pay taxes. If, as not infrequently happens, the governor is a tyrant, he might catch and punish two or three of the ringleaders, but he would get no good by his, and all men of sense find it better to let the village have its own way.[21]

Communal solidarity in villages was strengthened by plough teams called *boneh*s in some regions.[22] The members of these units of production included laborers as well as owners of oxen, seeds, water, and, at times, land. They pooled their resources to cultivate the fields, divided the annual produce, and jointly paid in kind the village blacksmith, coppersmith, barber, carpenter, and bath attendant, as well as the various village officials. Each member received a share corresponding to his contribution of labor, oxen, seed, water, and land. In villages where any of the latter four belonged to an absentee proprietor, a bailiff (*mubasher*) collected the landowner's share and controlled the peasant's dealings with the few accessible urban markets. Before the tremendous growth of the population in the second half of the twentieth century, customary residence entitled the villager to boneh membership; boneh membership, in turn, entitled the villager to a share of the produce and access to the village pastures, woods, and wells.

Communal solidarity was strengthened further in tribal areas by the clan networks. The sedentary Kurds of west Azerbaijan, for example, were divided into fifteen tribes, seventy-five subtribes, and nine hundred clans. Many of the clans constituted their own village or valley community and were headed by their own kadkhudas and rish

[21] C. and E. Burgess, *Letters from Persia*, edited by B. Schwartz (New York, 1942), p. 65.

[22] The units of production were known in other regions as *sarkars, sahras, paykal*s, *harash*s, and *pagav*s. See J. Safinezhad, *Boneh* (Production Teams) (Tehran, 1974).

safids.[23] Their settlements were thus analagous to the nomadic camps. And their village lands were still considered in theory to be communal tribal lands.

The villages, despite communal solidarity, economic self-sufficiency, and administrative autonomy, were sometimes owned by such absentee proprietors as tribal chiefs, fief-holders, large landowners, religious foundations (vaqfs), the state, and the royal family. Ann Lambton, in her major work on *Landlord and Peasant in Persia*, has argued that this external class was imposed upon the village communities during the ninth century.[24] In return for a share of the crop, the absentee landowners gave the peasants various forms of assistance: seeds after exceptionally disastrous harvests; financial help to repair the underground canals; and, most important of all, political protection against local nomads, rival villages, and threatening tax-collectors.

The social organizations were more complex in the urban centers. The ward kadkhudas, like the rural ones, were usually chosen by the more prosperous rish safids, and their main responsibility included mediating internal disputes and representing the ward in its external contacts. Their authority, however, was often complicated by the presence of state-appointed valis (governors), imam jom'ehs (leaders of Friday prayers), shaykh al-islams (clerical supervisors of the religious community), kalantars (overseers of the city kadkhudas), mirabs (water distributors), mobashers (bailiffs), darughehs (bazaar police-chiefs), and muhtasebs (overseers of prices, weights, and measures). The kadkhuda's authority was also complicated by the presence in the wards both of prominent residents, such as tribal chiefs, wealthy merchants, and influential mujtaheds; and of popular social centers, particularly mosques, qaveh khanehs (coffee houses), hammams (public baths), takiyas (passion play theaters), and zur khanehs (gymnasiums).

Closely attached to the zur khanehs were associations of wrestler-acrobats, who were known as lutis. These lutis, besides administering the gymnasiums, often worked in the bazaar as tradesmen, organized flagellation processions during the Shi'i mourning in the month of Muharram, patrolled the streets, and guarded the walls fortifying their wards. To strengthen their tightly knit associations, they wore special symbols, such as silk scarves from Kashan and notched chains from Yazd, joined local Sufi orders, and performed elaborate initia-

[23] For the Kurds of West Azerbaijan, see: British Consul in Tabriz, "Notes on Some of the More Important Kurdish Tribes," *F.O. 371*/Persia 1943/34-35093; idem, "Notes on the More Important Kurdish Tribes of W. Azerbaijan," *F.O. 371*/Persia 1944/34-40178.

[24] A. Lambton, *Landlord and Peasant in Persia* (London, 1953), pp. 1-8.

tion ceremonies. The central theme of the ceremonies was the vow to live by the luti code of ethics—personal honesty; occupational purity through avoidance of such "dishonorable" activities as laboring, cotton beating, and well digging; chivalry in defending the weak against the powerful; generosity by helping the poor and the orphaned; and, most important of all, bravery in protecting their ward against the outside world. Since, however, the line between self-appointed vigilantes and thugs often tends to be thin, lutis sometimes degenerated into racketeers terrorizing their own communities, threatening visitors, and raiding nearby localities. By the end of the century the word luti meant both a dangerous hooligan and a chivalrous folk-hero.

The communal organizations were further complicated in the large cities by the existence of occupational guilds (*asnaf*), especially among the skilled and well-to-do craftsmen. These guilds had their own kadkhudas, often elected by their own rish safids, and had elaborate methods for widening the external differences between themselves and other professions while narrowing the internal differences between their guild masters (*ustad*s), apprentices (*shagerd*s), and hired workmen (*kargar*s). They recruited apprentices only from their own families; resolved disputes within their own corporate courts; enforced professional standards on their own members; used their own favorite coffee houses, public baths, markets, mosques, gymnasiums, theaters, and even cemeteries; developed special rituals, symbols, and, in some cases, secret codes to preserve the mysteries of their own craft. These guilds were, in short, closed communities.

The multiplicity of ward, village, and nomadic organizations could be seen in the region of Isfahan.[25] The city itself, with a population of 50,000, contained twelve main wards. Each had its own kadkhuda, rish safids, and distinct communal character. The eight western wards of Chahar Sukh, Abbasabad, Shamsabad, Lunban, Juzban, Bidabad, Shish Bidabad, and Darb-i Kush were attached to the Haydari faction. The four eastern wards of Shahshahan, Yazdabad, Khuja, and Midan-i Mir were associated with the competing N'imati faction. Chahar Sukh was the residential quarter and the business center of money lenders from Shiraz. Abbasabad housed Azeri families that had been transported there from Tabriz at the beginning of the seventeenth century, when the Safavid dynasty had established its capital in Is-

---

[25] For descriptions of the Isfahan region, see Mirza Hussein Khan (Tahvildar-i Isfahan), *Jughrafiya-yi Isfahan* (Geography of Isfahan) (Tehran, 1963); Shaykh Jabari Ansari, *Tarikh-i Isfahan va Ray* (History of Isfahan and Ray) (Tehran, 1941); W. Ouseley, *Travels in Various Countries of the East, Particularly Persia* (London, 1819, III, 26-50; British Consul in Isfahan, "Report on the Isfahan Province," *F.O. 371*/Persia 1945/34-45476; idem, "Report on the Bakhtiari Tribe," *F.O. 371*/Persia 1944/34-40181.

fahan. Darb-i Kush was settled by a small southern Turkic tribe that now specialized in producing milk, mutton, and yogurt. Shish Bidabad was inhabited by the Kalianis, a Persian-speaking tribe from the south, who had first peddled odds and ends, but now, while retaining their original ward and particular dialect, controlled the city's lucrative trade with Istanbul. Lunban, Juzban, and Bidabad were crowded with Bakhtiyari migrants who scraped together a living as seasonal laborers, hired guards, and peddlers between the main market and their home tribes outside the city. In addition to these wards, there were two districts, Jubareh and Julfa-i Now, which were reserved for non-Muslims. The former housed the Jewish community, many of whom worked in the silk industry. The latter, with a separate council of elders, contained the Armenian minority; the Safavids had moved several thousand Armenians from old Julfa in the north to the new Julfa in Isfahan in order to encourage new industries in their recently established capital.

The many occupations in the central bazaar of Isfahan were organized into separate guilds. The city tax collector, in a detailed report for 1877, enumerated nearly two hundred different occupations.[26] Some, especially the skilled craftsmen such as engravers, miniaturists, coppersmiths, goldsmiths, silversmiths, gunmakers, bookbinders, saddlers, and carpenters, had well-structured and long-established guilds. Others, particularly the middle-income tradesmen such as grocers, confectioners, drapers, corn chandlers, tobacconists, opium sellers, haberdashers, and moneylenders, had less structured but nevertheless well-established associations. Yet others, particularly those in the unskilled, low-income occupations—porters, laborers, peddlers, bath attendants, and water carriers—had their own loosely structured but easily recognizable identities.

The nearby rural districts of Chahar Mahal, Fereidan, Pusht-i Kuh, Karvan, and Sehnahiyeh contained even more social organizations. Their peasant population was divided not only into some five hundred separate villages, but also into numerous linguistic and religious communities. Besides the many settlements that spoke various dialects of Persian and adhered to the official branch of Shi'ism, a substantial number spoke Azeri, thirty-six were Armenian, fourteen were Georgian, and one was Baha'i. Although the Azeris, Armenians, and Georgians had been transported there by the Safavids two centuries earlier—mainly to cultivate and guard the mountain passes—they still retained their cultural identity. A mid-twentieth-century visitor re-

[26] Mirza Hussein Khan, *Jughrafiya-yi Isfahan*, pp. 93-122.

ported that the Georgians, despite their conversion to Islam, tenaciously held onto their language, customs, and village organizations. And a late nineteenth-century traveler found that although the prosperous Baha'i village of Najafabad did not live up to its former fame as "revolutionary," as far as its neighbors were concerned it continued to bear a sinister reputation.[27]

The tribal population of the Isfahan region, on the other hand, was predominantly Bakhtiyari; pockets of Qashqayis, Arabs, Luri Kuhigiluyeh, and Boir Ahmedis also lived in the extreme southern districts. The Bakhtiyaris, although confederated under one ilkhan, were divided into two branches named the Haft Lang (Seven Feet) and the Chahar Lang (Four Feet). The tribesmen, perceiving the division in genealogical terms, as tribesmen invariably do, traced it to an ancient and probably mythical struggle for the chieftaincy between one claimant with seven sons and another with four sons. The townsmen, however, claimed that the division had resulted from an early property tax that had collected a seventh from the poorer tribes and a fourth from the wealthier ones. The two branches together totaled fifty-five tribes, each with its own ruling clan and khan. These tribes differed noticeably in size, wealth, importance, and sometimes even language. The Kianersi of the Chahar Lang, for example, declined from a position of predominance in the 1840s to one of insignificance in the 1860s as the result of dissensions within the ruling clan, migrations into Isfahan, and defections to the Kuhigiluyeh. The Zarrasvand of the Haft Lang, meanwhile, rose to dominance, pastured on the best Bakhtiyari lands, owned many non-Bakhtiyari villages, and even ruled a Turkic subtribe. The fifty-five tribes were segmented into one hundred thirty subtribes, many of which had their own khans and kalantars. These subtribes, in turn, were segmented into innumerable clans, each with its own kadkhuda and rish safids. Although most clans lived in migratory units, a few—particularly among the Janiki Sardir tribe of the Haft Lang and the Mahmud Saleh tribe of the Chahar Lang—had permanently settled in the districts of Chahar Mahal, Fereidan, and Sehnahiyeh. But having given up their nomadic way of life, these tribesmen had nevertheless retained their tribal networks. Thus they had introduced tribal organizations into a peasant region that was already studded with many small village organizations.

[27] British Consul in Isfahan, "A Tour in Bakhtiari, Chahar Mahal, Khumain, and Gulpaigan," *F.O. 371*/Persia 1944/34-40163; J. Bent, "Village Life in Persia," *New Review*, 5 (July-December 1891), 355-62.

COMMUNAL CONFLICTS

The modern observer, reacting against contemporary problems, could be tempted to portray traditional Iran as an idyllic society. The fear of uniformity, so real in the contemporary world, was inconceivable in an environment of such tribal, linguistic, and religious diversity. The problem of anomie, so prevalent in industrial nations, seldom appeared in a country of tightly knit clans, villages, guilds, urban wards, and religious communities. The politics of class conflict, so repugnant to some, rarely disrupted the close personal relations between tribal chiefs and tribesmen, village elders and peasants, guild masters and guild members, spiritual leaders and religious congregations. As one visitor from industrial Britain wrote, "there are no major cities in Persia, and likewise no major slums. There are no steam-driven industries, and therefore none of the mechanical tyranny that deadens the brain, starves the heart, wearies body and mind with its monotony. There is no gas and no electricity, but is not the glow of the oil-lamps pleasanter?"[28]

The idyllic picture, however, would leave out one marked feature of nineteenth-century Iran: communal conflict. Three interrelated pressures frequently transformed communal diversity into communal rivalry. First, the struggle for scarce resources, especially irrigated lands, rain-fed pastures, and underground water canals, tended to throw one community against another. Bishop, traveling through nomadic districts, observed that "most tribal feuds originate in quarrels over pasture lands." Forbes-Leith, a British officer working as a glorified bailiff for a northern landlord, commented that almost all major conflicts he observed under his jurisdiction "could be definitely traced to disputes about irrigation."[29] Second, the conventional notion that economies could not continually grow created the conviction that one could prosper only at someone else's expense. One group's profit was another's loss; one group's loss another's profit. Life appeared to be a zero-sum game. Third, the competition to fill local offices often pitted one community against its neighbor. This was particularly true in the towns, since the central government usually consulted local communities before appointing such important officials as mirabs, mubashers, muhtasebs, darughehs, kalantars, shaykh al-islams, and imam jom'ehs. These officials not only helped administer routine affairs, but also made crucial decisions that could determine the fate of each community—the quantity of water it received, the quality of

---

[28] Hale, *From Persian Uplands*, p. 30.
[29] Bishop, *Journeys in Persia and Kurdistan*, II, 10; F. Forbes-Leith, *Checkmate* (New York, 1927), p. 47.

justice it obtained in both state and religious courts, the number of men it contributed to the militia, and the amount of taxes it paid to the provincial governor. Thus communal diversity could easily turn into communal divisions; local integration into state disintegration; group collectivism into regional parochialism and political factionalism. As Lambton has stated, "factional strife, in one form or another, has remained a feature of Persian life down to modern times."[30]

European travelers in nineteenth-century Iran invariably noticed three forms of factional strife: the obvious religious strains between Muslims and non-Muslims, Sunnis and Shi'is; the age-old struggle between the nomads and the peasants—the "desert" and the "sown"; and the differences in language between the Iranian and non-Iranian populations. The last of these was emphasized by Europeans who had been influenced by their contemporary racial theories. Count Gobineau, for example, after a three-year residence in Tehran as the French representative, wrote in his famous *Inequality of the Human Races* that Iran was divided sharply into six "national" groups: Persians, Turks, Arabs, Kurds, Jews, and Zoroastrians. Edward Browne, the author of a monumental work on Persian literature, summarized the whole of Iran's history from legendary times to his own as a constant struggle between nothern Turks and southern Persians. "The old antipathy is well marked even today, as anyone who has taken the trouble to find out knows what the southern peasant thinks of the northerners, and how northerners regard the cradle of Persia's ancient greatness." Even the twentieth-century historian, Vladimir Minorsky, viewed the basic feature of Iran's past to be the continual conflict between the nomadic Turks and the sedentary Persians. He concluded that the two, "like water and oil," could not mix.[31]

These generalizations, however, oversimplify the complexities of factional strife by disregarding the multiple divisions within each major group: the tribal, regional, and religious divisions within the same "races"; the differences between neighboring communities within the nomadic, peasant, and urban populations; and the rivalries between the many sects, orders, and schools within the Shi'is. The history of nineteen-century Iran was more complex than a simple struggle between a few major groups: it was a history of multiple conflicts between innumerable small communities: of clan against clan, tribe against tribe, tribe against village, tribe against town, town against village,

[30] Lambton, *Islamic Society in Persia*, p. 16.

[31] J. Gobineau, *The Inequality of the Human Races* (London, 1915), p. 29; E. Browne, *A Year amongst the Persians*, London, 1893, pp. 99-100; V. Minorsky, *Tadkhirat al-Muluk* (London, 1943), pp. 187-88.

village against village, village against town ward, and town ward against town ward.

Conflict appeared in all levels of tribal organizations: from households of migratory camps to families of ruling khans. Some anthropologists have even argued that the tribe exists as a social organization only at times of strife: either during periods of external danger when it mobilizes for self-defense; or during periods of internal feuds, when each layer coalesces to mediate between its subordinate segments, and thus to prevent minor disputes from spreading through kinship ties into major disputes threatening the whole tribe.[32] For example, a quarrel between two households within the same camp can easily involve other relatives and thereby polarize the whole camp. In such a situation, the camp leader will be forced to mediate to preserve his camp. Similarly, a conflict between two households from different camps can quickly escalate into a confrontation between the two camps, and thus threaten the survival of the whole subtribe. In such an event, the chief of the subtribe will step forward to arbitrate, in order to preserve the existence of his subtribe. Likewise, a conflict between households from different subtribes can grow into a major confrontation between all the entire subtribes, and thus necessitate the intervention of the main chief. What is more, the main chief plays a leading role whenever disagreements between his own tribesmen and other communities escalate into explosive crises of "us" against "them." Western social scientists have coined the term "segmentary politics" to describe these escalating disputes.[33] Middle Eastern tribesmen, however, have a traditional saying to describe the same phenomena: "I against my brother. I and my brother against my cousin. I and my cousin against my tribe. I and my tribe against the world."

The tribal rivalries can best be seen in the armed forces and in the Bakhtiyari confederation. The armed forces, during much of the century, were formed of a royal bodyguard, a mass militia, a tribal cavalry, and a short-lived modern army known as the Nizam-i Jadid (New Order). The bodyguard, officered by Qajar nobles, contained 4,000 Georgian slaves. The militia, estimated on paper at over 150,000 men, was broken down into regional forces. Each force was recruited from the local Shi'i population, maintained by local taxes, and led exclusively by local officers. Malcolm, who as a wartime envoy took a special interest in military matters, reported that these part-time soldiers had "no further discipline than that of obeying their own leaders," and accepted as their leaders only "those of their own body they

[32] M. Sahlins, *Tribesmen* (Englewood Cliffs, 1968).

[33] For a detailed study of segmentary politics in the Middle East, see J. Waterbury, *The Commander of the Faithful: The Moroccan Political Elite* (New York, 1970).

deemed their superiors." The cavalry, the country's main fighting force with some 80,000 men, was formed by tribal levies: each levy was officered by its own tribal chiefs. Malcolm reported that the contingents were extremely reluctant to serve unless tempted by plunder or induced by having their own chief appointed commander of the whole campaign.[34] James Morier, a contemporary visitor, observed that the tribal contingents retained their separate identities even within the royal camp: "Since the army was mostly composed of men drawn from the different tribes, each tribe was encamped in separate divisions."[35] The Nizam-i Jadid, although initially designed to combat the tribalism of the traditional forces, eventually succumbed to the same problem because of its methods of recruitment. Its infantry in the capital, honored with the title of *janbaz* (literally, "those willing to sacrifice their souls"), was recruited predominantly from the Qajar tribes and certain clans from the mountains of Mazandaran. Its infantry in Azerbaijan, called *sarbaz* (literally, "those willing to sacrifice their heads"), was raised from various local tribes. Malcolm reported that "the different regiments are willing to be commanded by European officers but not by Persians of a different tribe." And Morier noted after speaking to some of these foreign officers, "the soldiers are in general taken from the wandering tribes of Aderbijan, who are bound to each other by the ties of clanship and are always ready to support each other upon the most trivial occasion. This produces a constant tendency for explosions."[36]

The Bakhtiyaris were faction-ridden throughout the century, not only because each tribe jealously guarded its migratory routes and each khan invariably detested the other khans, but also because the confederation was divided into the Chahar Lang versus the Haft Lang branches, and the ruling clan after the 1870s was split into the Hajji Ilkhani and the Ilkhani families.[37] In the 1840s, the chief of the Kianersi tribe, Muhammad Taqi Khan, revived the ancient feud between the two branches by uniting the Chahar Lang, defeating the Haft Lang, and claiming the title of ilkhan. But his success was short-lived: he was tricked into captivity by the government, and his family was supplanted by Jafar Quli Khan, the chief of the Zarrasvand tribe from the Haft Lang. Eliminating thirteen rivals, Jafar Quli Khan led the Haft Lang to victory over the Chahar Lang, and passed on his power

[34] Malcolm, *History of Persia*, II, 357.

[35] J. Morier, *A Journey through Persia, Armenia, and Asia Minor* (London, 1812), p. 214.

[36] Malcolm, *History of Persia*, II, 358; J. Morier, *Second Journey through Persia, Armenia, and Asia Minor* (London, 1818), p. 214.

[37] British Consul in Isfahan, "A Tour in Bakhtiari . . . ," *F.O. 371*/Persia 1944/34-40163; idem, "A Report on the Bakhtiari Tribe," *F.O. 371*/Persia 1944/34-40181.

to his son Hussein Quli Khan. And Hussein Quli Khan, during his thirty-year reign, confirmed Haft Lang supremacy by expropriating land from the Chahar Lang, expelling subtribes from the Kianersi, and securing the title as well as the power of ilkhan. By the 1880s, the Haft Lang-Chahar Lang conflict had ceased to be a burning political issue.

But the murder of Hussein Quli Khan by the government in 1882 initiated a bloody feud among his own relatives. One side of the family, headed by Hajji Imam Quli Khan—his brother—seized the title of ilkhan, and thus became known as the faction of Hajji Ilkhani. Meanwhile, another side of the family, led by his elder son Esfandiar Khan—who had been arrested when his father had been assassinated—denounced the Hajji as a usurper, and became known as the faction of the Ilkhani. The fortunes of the two sides were reversed within six years: Esfandiar Khan, on his release from prison, obtained armed support from the government, invaded the Bakhtiyari lands, rallied his supporters, and began a major civil war within the confederation. After a thirteen-year struggle, the two factions, growing fearful of tribal disintegration and of losing the family monopoly over the Bakhtiyari succession, agreed to share alternatively the two important posts of ilkhan and ilbeg. The open war had ended, but the family feud continued well into the twentieth century.

Conflict was also a common feature of the relationship between neighboring villages—between nontribal as well as tribal villages. I'timad al-Saltaneh, a court chronicler, came across whole districts in the southeast desolated by vicious local dissensions. Jahangir Mirza, another chronicler, related how one isolated valley in the south was totally divided into two parties, each headed by minor religious families, each fighting on behalf of its own candidate for regional governor, and each disguising its political interests with elaborate theological hairsplitting. Ahmad Kasravi, a leading historian of modern Iran, in his early work entitled *Tarikh-i Pansad Saleh-i Khuzistan* (Five Hundred-Year History of Khuzistan), has described how many rural regions of the southwest were torn apart by the Sunni-Shi'i, Haydari-Ni'mati, and other sectarian hatreds. He also noted in an autobiographical essay on the Ministry of Justice that rural judges, even in the twentieth century, devoted much of their time trying to settle land disputes between neighboring villages: "One group of peasants would claim a piece of land, another group would make a counterclaim, and the two would invariably confront each other in a bloody clash."[38]

[38] M. I'timad al-Sultaneh, *Mirat-i al-Buldan* (Mirror of Cities) (Tehran, 1877), IV, 252-54; Jahangir Mirza, *Narikh-i Now* (New History) (Tehran, 1946), pp. 271-72; A. Kasravi, *Tarikh-i Pansad Saleh-i Khuzistan* (Five Hundred-Year History of Khuzistan)

Village walls, especially in the central plateau, and watch towers, known as Turkoman towers in Khurasan, stood as permanent landmarks of these communal rivalries.

The towns also experienced communal conflicts. During his extensive travels, Malcolm found that

The divisions of the chief cities into wards, with the name of Haydaree and Neamatee, which one author has ascribed to Shah Abbas of the Safavid dynasty still exists, and continues to excite as much animosity as formerly. There is at all times a jealousy between these parties; and during the last three days of Muharram they attack each other with violence. If a mosque is decorated by one party, the other, if they can, drive them from it, and destroy their flags and ornaments. If they force their opponents from their houses, they make a mark on each door with a hatchet as a token of victory. These frays are often very serious, and many lives are lost.[39]

The Isfahan tax collector described how every year on the Shiʿi Day of Sacrifice (ʿAyd-i Qurban) thousands of Haydaris and Niʿmatis fought in the central square, often suffering numerous casualties. Hassan-i Fasaʾi, a Shiraz chronicler, recounted that the participants in these fights in his native city considered the casualties to be human "gifts" to God. Sheil, visiting Sarab, observed that the local Haydaris, led by the town mayor, would bring in reinforcements from nearby villages to strengthen their Muharram demonstrations vis-à-vis the Niʿmatis. Stack found that droughts in the small town of Khonsar near Gulpayegan had so intensified Haydari-Niʿmati rivalries that the local populations was sharply divided into two feuding sections. Kasravi, in his research on Khuzistan, concluded that Shustar, the provincial capital, had been torn apart during much of the nineteenth century by feuding between its four Haydari and eight Niʿmati wards. The two sides had competed to place their candidates in local offices, fought to expand their districts, and sought allies among the neighboring rural communities—the Haydaris had allied with the nearby Afshars, the Niʿmatis with the Arabs. Finally, ʿAli Shamim, a modern historian of the nineteenth century, has described how in his home town, Hamadan, the Muharram flagellation ceremonies would invariably end with violent street brawls between the Haydaris and the Niʿmatis.[40]

(Tehran, 1950), pp. 141-51, 240-42; A. Kasravi, *Zendigani-yi Man* (My Life) (Tehran, 1946), p. 301.

[39] Malcolm, *History of Persia*, II, 429.

[40] Mirza Hussein Khan, *Jugrafiya-yi Isfahan*, pp. 88-90; Hassan-i Fasaʾi, *History of Persia under Qajar Rule*, translated by H. Busse (New York, 1972), pp. 264-65; Sheil, *Glimpses of Life and Manners in Persia*, p. 325; Stack, *Six Months in Persia*, p. 111; Kasravi, *Tarikh-i Pansad Saleh-i Khuzistan*, pp. 131-51; ʿA. Shamim, *Iran dar Dawreh-i Saltanat-i Qajar* (Iran during the Qajar Dynasty) (Tehran, 1963), pp. 296-97.

The towns that were free of Haydari-Ni'mati divisions usually experienced other forms of communal conflicts. For example, Tabriz and Kerman divided into Mutashar'i and Shaykhi communities. The two groups, according to Kasravi, fought during Muharram, competed to fill local offices, refused to intermarry, and, segregating themselves within their own districts, avoided each other's homes, coffee houses, public baths, shops, theaters, gymnasiums, and even places of worship.[41] Mahabad and Mianduab both separated into Sunni and Shi'i wards. Bishop found that in the former town "religious conflicts were always eminent," and that in the latter the Sunni Kurds had been expelled because they had betrayed the town to the Ottomans in 1881.[42] And in Tehran, communal identity evolved not only around the mahallats but also around the Muharram processions and the takiya theaters. As I'timad al-Saltaneh described in his diaries, the city had over one hundred such theaters, and most small communities—whether occupational groups such as tanners and carpenters, or tribal migrants such as Afshars and Arabs, or ethnic groups such as former residents of Kerman, Tabriz, and the Persian Gulf—proudly patronized their own particular theater.[43]

These communal conflicts, despite their local focus, had far-reaching consequences. On the one hand, they reinforced the vertical connections between members of the same community. In the words of a traditional Persian proverb, "a man without a protector is like a dog howling in the wilderness." On the other hand, the same conflicts compounded the geographical obstacles, and, thus retarded the formation of horizontal ties between members of the same class—between merchants in one city and another, between nomads in one tribe and another, between wage earners in one locality and another, between peasants in one village and another. As one contemporary sociologist

[41] A Kasravi, *Tarikh-i Mashruteh-i Iran* (History of the Iranian Constitution) (Tehran, 1961), pp. 130-35, 171-73, 195-97, 490-94.

[42] Bishop, *Journeys in Persia and Kurdistan*, II, 209, 240.

[43] M. I'timad al-Saltaneh, *Ruznameh-i I'timad al-Saltaneh* (The Diaries of I'timad al-Saltaneh) (Tehran, 1967). In some towns, communal antagonisms involved the religious minorities. For example, in Barfarush (Babul), the town mullas often incited riots against the local Jews by claiming that the latter caused bad harvests and famines (see Mounsey, *A Journey through the Caucasus*, p. 273). In Yazd, local Jews were frequently persecuted and discriminated against. They had to pay high taxes; were obliged to wear special patches on their clothes; could not open shops in the bazaar; could not give evidence under oath in law courts; and were held jointly responsible for crimes committed by any of their members. Similarly, the Zoroastrians in Yazd were forbidden to wear eye glasses, rings, fine clothes, white socks, and any colors other than yellow, grey, and brown. They could not open shops in the bazaars or live in houses with more than one floor and rooms with more than four windows. (See M. Fischer, "Zoroastrian Iran between Myth and Praxis," Ph.D. dissertation, University of Chicago, 1973, pp. 430-43.)

of social conflict has stressed, group tensions tend to strengthen group cohesion and group leadership, and, concomitantly, weaken class identity and class consciousness.[44]

COMMUNAL CONFLICTS AND CLASS CONSCIOUSNESS

The term *class* has been used by social scientists in at least two different ways: first, as a simple sociological category to rank individuals with similar sources of income, similar amounts of revenue, similar degrees of influence, and similar styles of life; second, as a complex sociopsychological term to classify individuals who are not only located in parallel positions in the social hierarchy, but also manifest similar economic, social, and political attitudes. Marx aptly described the first as a class "in itself" but not "yet for itself"; the second as a class "for itself" as well as "in itself."[45] Similarly, sociologists have drawn a sharp distinction between, on one hand, socioeconomic, latent, and objective classes, and, on the other hand, sociopolitical, manifest, and subjective classes.[46] Obviously, all societies are stratified, to various degrees, into latent, socioeconomic, objective, sociological classes. Not all societies, however, are divided into manifest, sociopolitical, subjective, sociopsychological classes.

In early nineteenth-century Iran, classes existed in the first, but not in the second, meaning of the term. The general population can be classified into four major classes. The first, the landed upper class (*tabaqeh-i malek al-tava'if*), comprised a central elite and many local elites. The central elite included the Qajar dynasty, the royal princes (*shahzadegan*), the influential courtiers (*darbaris*), the large fief-holders (*tuyuldars*), the hereditary state accountants (*mustawfis*), the government ministers (*vazirs*), the princely governors (*farmanfarmas*), and the titled officials—al-Saltanehs (Pillars of the Monarch), al-Dawlehs (Aids of the State), al-Mulks (Victors of the Kingdom), and al-Mamaleks (Strengths of the Country). The local elites consisted of major notables (*a'yans*), provincial aristocrats (*ashrafs*), tribal chiefs (*khans*), and hereditary, titled, and invariably propertied, urban administrators (*mirzas*). Closely connected to the upper class were a few state-appointed religious officials: the imam jom'ehs; the shaykh al-islams, and the judges (*qazis*), presiding over the main low courts. These central and local elites later became known as the aristocracy (*aristukrasi*), the

---

[44] L. Coser, *The Functions of Social Conflict* (New York, 1969).

[45] K. Marx, *The Poverty of Philosophy* (Chicago, 1920), pp. 188-89.

[46] S. Ossowski, *Class Structure in the Social Consciousness* (London, 1963), pp. 69-87; R. Centers, *The Psychology of Social Classes* (Princeton, 1949), pp. 21-27.

magnates (*bozorgan*), the ruling cirlces (*hayat-i hakemeh*), and the ruling class (*tabaqeh-i hakemeh*).

The second major tabaqeh was formed of the propertied middle class. This included the urban merchants (*tujjar*s) as well as the many shopkeepers and small workshop owners (*pishevaran*). Since many of these businessmen, traders, and craftsmen financed the bazaar mosques, schools (*maktab*s), seminaries (*madrasheh*s), theaters (*takiya*s), and other charitable foundations (*vaqf*s), the commercial middle class was intricately connected to the ʿulama—the various preachers (*vaʿez*), Koranic teachers (*akhund*s), seminary students (*tullab*s), low-ranking clerics (*mulla*s), and even high-ranking theologians (*mujtahed*s). Often marriage reinforced this connection, as many sayyids (descendants of the Prophet), mullas, hojjat al-islams (middle-ranking clerics), and even ayatallahs (high-ranking clerics) had family ties with the bazaar merchants.

The third class was formed of urban wage-earners, especially hired artisans, apprentices, journeymen, household servants, porters, laborers, and construction workers. Finally, the fourth major class consisted of the vast majority of the rural population (*raʿiyat*)—the tribal masses (*iliyat*) as well as the landless and nearly landless peasantry (*dehqanan*).

Even though early nineteenth-century Iran had latent, objective, and socioeconomic classes, the predominance of communal ties retarded the formation of manifest, subjective, and sociopolitical classes. It was true that power and wealth were unequally distributed among the classes, and that most individuals were confined to the same class from the cradle to the grave. True, court ideologues argued that God had created these social divisions, and had assigned to the shah the duty of preserving class barriers by regulating clothes and headgear, punishing those disrespectful of the nobility, and creating various levels of knighthood.[47] True, class differences continually appeared in social snobbery and amazed even Victorian travelers such as Morier, who commented: "A description of etiquette in Persia would be of endless and trifling minutiae. They are such, however, and so recognized, and so easily observed by everyone from their youth and indeed so strongly marked the graduation of rank, that no person, even of the meanest condition, is ignorant of his proper situation and of the several etiquette attached to it."[48]

It was also true that social differences occasionally produced class antagonisms. Shamim writes that in the streets bazaar children mer-

[47] A. Piemontese, "The Statutes of the Qajar Orders of Knighthood," *East and West*, 19 (September-December 1969), 437-71.

[48] Morier, *A Journey through Persia*, p. 285.

cilessly teased the sons of the rich for dressing up like dandies. Arfaʿ al-Dawleh, a titled patrician, narrates in his autobiography how the aristocratic families were so contemptuous of trade that they forbade their sons even to contemplate careers in commerce. Landor reported that bazaar shopkeepers tried to avoid overcharging the poor but did their very best to cheat the rich.[49] Moreover, contemporaries such as Arfaʿ and Iʿtimad al-Saltaneh occasionally came across villages in revolt against exploitation and high taxation. Peasant dislike of land-lords is vividly described by Justine Perkins, a Protestant missionary active in western Azerbaijan:

I was once forcibly reminded of the depth of this hatred, by its development at the funeral of an aged khan, who like others of his rank, had grieviously oppressed his serfs. The villagers—all Nestorians (Assyrians)—came to the city, as is the custom, and assembled before the door of the deceased to make lamentations and tender their condolences to the family. One of our native helpers, who happened to be passing, related to me that they cried "The wicked oppressor is dead, and we are glad, he is receiving the reward of his iniquity and may his whole household soon follow him." The bereaved Mu-hammedan family did not understand the Nestorian language in which the villagers thus gave utterance to their sorrow, but were little disposed to ques-tion their sincerity, especially since the exclamations were accompanied with violent beatings of the breast as well as pious sobs and wailings.[50]

Despite these tensions between classes, it was even more true that they were fragmented by communal rivalries and thus prevented from becoming viable. Although landed aristocrats had no compunction about resorting to violence, they failed to combine to safeguard their mutual interests against the central government. Traditional Iran, in sharp contrast to feudal Europe, thus had no baronial rebellions, no magna cartas, no legal estates, and consequently no representative institutions. Although townsmen often took up arms, they fought not against the aristocracy but among themselves—invariably against the neighboring ward. Although tribesmen frequently rallied behind one khan against another, not once in all the annals of the nineteenth century did they rise up against the institution of khans. As Barth has written of the Basseri, nomads have respect for their chiefs since they depend on them in daily confrontations with formidable, confusing, and encroaching neighbors: "They explicitly recognize that without

---

[49] Shamim, *Iran dar Dawreh-i Saltanat-i Qajar*, p. 295; M. Arfaʿ al-Dawleh, *Iran-i Diruz* (Yesterday's Iran) (Tehran, 1966), pp. 6-7; Landor, *Across Coveted Lands*, I, 299.

[50] J. Perkins, *Eight Years in Persia* (New York, 1843), p. 284. The published literature from the nineteenth century gives only three incidents of village uprisings: Iʿtimad al-Saltaneh, *Ruznameh-i Iʿtimad al-Saltaneh*, p. 1148; Arfaʿ al-Dawleh, *Iran-i Diruz*, p. 152; and E. Collins, *In the Kingdom of the Shah* (London, 1896), p. 118.

their chiefs they would be helpless in a number of recurring situations.[51] Finally, although peasants were permanently exploited, they rarely rebelled; and when they did so, their rebellion took the form not of mass insurrection but of mass flight from one landlord to the "protective custody" of another. Whereas the nineteenth century sources give only three incidents of village uprisings, they frequently describe whole villages that had fled en masse to escape particularly oppressive landlords. In Fraser's words, "the seduction of peasantry from one district to another frequently caused bitter quarrels between adjacent magnates."[52] As Lambton has stressed, landowners and peasants, in spite of mutual suspicions, depended on each other since the former needed the latter for labor, whereas the latter relied on the former to ward off new hardships.[53] For many a peasant, exploitation by a landowner was a grievous burden, but a bearable one compared with the greater dangers posed by armed tribesmen, unsatisfiable tax collectors, and even land-hungry neighboring villages. In short, communalism stifled class consciousness.

Thus communal ties—especially those based on tribal lineages, religious sects, regional organizations, and paternalistic sentiments—cut through the horizontal classes, strengthened the vertical communal bonds, and thereby prevented latent economic interests from developing into manifest political forces. Insofar as numerous individuals in early nineteenth-century Iran shared similar ways of life, similar positions in the mode of production, and similar relations to the means of administration, they constituted socioeconomic classes. But insofar as these individuals were bound by communal ties, failed to overcome local barriers, and articulated no state-wide interests, they did not constitute sociopolitical classes. This absence of viable classes had far-reaching political consequences; for, as long as the central government was not confronted by statewide forces, the Qajar dynasty was able to dominate society in the typical manner of, to borrow a nineteenth-century term, oriental despots.

THE QAJAR DYNASTY

The Qajars, like many other Turkic tribes, migrated from Central Asia into the Middle East during the fourteenth century, but they did not appear on the political arena of Iran until the beginning of the sixteenth century. Allying with six other Turkic and Shi'i tribes known as the Qizilbash (Red Heads), the Qajars helped install the Safavid

[51] Barth, *Nomads of South Persia*, p. 80.
[52] J. Fraser, *A Winter's Journey from Constantinople to Tehran* (London, 1838), p. 289.
[53] Lambton, *Landlord and Peasant in Persia*, pp. 259-74.

family on the Iranian throne. The Safavids, although they invited the leading Qajar chiefs into the royal court in Isfahan, took the precaution of dispersing their tribes: some were sent to Georgia to protect the northern border; some to Khurasan to fight the Tartars; and some to Mazandaran to defend the city of Astarabad from the local Turkomans. Over the course of the seventeenth century, the first group merged with northern Afshars; the second disappeared from history; and the third, although sharply split into the Yukharibash (Upper Head) and the Ashshaqbash (Lower Head), survived to reappear in the early eighteenth century, immediately after the collapse of the Safavid dynasty.

With the Afghan invasion of 1722 and the subsequent collapse of the Safavids, Iran entered a long period of political and social chaos. While Bakhtiyaris, Qashqayis, Afshars, and Zands—a Luri tribe—fought for the central regions, Arab and Kurdish chiefs established their own petty shaykhdoms and emirates in the west, Turkomans and Shahsavens struggled over north Khurasan, and the Qajar Yukharibash battled the Qajar Ashshaqbash for Mazandaran. The period of chaos lasted until the end of the eighteenth century, when Aqa Muhammad Khan, the chief of the powerful Qoyunlu clan within the Qajar Ashshaqbash, made his successful bid for the Peacock Throne. Escaping from the Zand court in Shiraz, Aqa Muhammad Khan eliminated family rivals in Mazandaran, ironed out old differences with the Devehlu clan leading the Qajar Yukharibash, and forged alliances not only with the neighboring Turkomans and Kurds, but also with the Bakhtiyaris and Afshars in the central regions, and with Hajji Ibrahim, a powerful ward kalantar who governed Shiraz on behalf of the Zands. With the help of the latter, Aqa Muhammad Khan captured Shiraz, defeated the Zands, and, bringing much of the south under control, appointed his nephew Fath ʿAli Khan governor of the southern provinces. Refusing the crown on the grounds that he did not yet rule the whole of Iran, Aqa Muhammad Khan turned his attention to the north, moved the capital to Tehran, an obscure town near the Qajar territories, and then mustered a large expeditionary force to conquer the northeastern provinces. While leading this army into Georgia he was assassinated by two of his household servants.

After a brief struggle over the succession between rival Qajars, generals from the expeditionary force, and claimants from the Safavid and Afshar families, Fath ʿAli Khan—the crown prince—gained the support of the Qoyunlu and Devehlu clans, captured the crown jewels, and, winning over the Qajar governor of Tehran, entered the capital victorious. Until his victory, most communities tried their best to isolate themselves from these upheavals. For example, when one of the pretenders to the throne appeared before the gates of Qazvin, the local authorities closed the city and announced: "We know nothing of you and your title. Go to Tehran, possess yourself of the capital, and then the gates of Qazvin shall be open to the King."[54]

Although the Qajar dynasty was preserved, the style of rule changed drastically. Aqa Muhammad Khan had been first and foremost a tribal chief. He had sought, obtained, and consolidated power through tribal networks, tribal conquests, and tribal alliances. He had felt most at home either leading his men into battle or eating with them on the tent floor. Remaining to his last days uncomfortable in the royal palace, he had avoided the capital, reduced court etiquette to bare minimum, refused to wear the jeweled crown, and ordered his secretaries to communicate in "plain and simple language" instead of the traditional esoteric terminology only understood by fellow scribes.[55] Moreover, serving as his own minister of war, finance, justice, and foreign affairs, he had recruited only three high-ranking administrators from the previous Zand court: a state accountant (*mustawfi*), a military accountant (*lashkar-i nevis*), and a royal minister (*vazir*) in the person of Hajji Ibrahim.

His successors, however—Fath 'Ali Shah (1797), Muhammad Shah (1834-1848), and Naser al-Din Shah (1848-1896)—discarded the tribal style in favor of the ancient traditions of imperial shah-in-shahs. They tried to routinize their power by constructing a statewide bureaucracy; stabilize their position by creating an effective standing army; and legitimize their dynasty by imitating the court manners of previous emperors.

The attempt to construct a statewide bureaucracy failed. The Qajars learned the obscure terminology of their Persian scribes; recruited relatives into government service;[56] hired two hundred employees for the municipality of Tehran; provided each provincial governor (*farmanfarma*) with one minister (*vazir*) and two accountants (*mustawfis*); and expanded the three-man "tent" cabinet into a ten-man cabinet with a premier (*sadr 'azam*) and a finance minister (*mustawfi al-mamalek*). They also succeeded in compartmentalizing the large central palace into special sections for the royal treasury, mint, armory, store-

---

[54] Fraser, *Narrative of a Journey into Khurasan*, pp. 406-409.

[55] S. Nafisi, *Tarikh-i Ijtima'i va Siyasi-yi Iran dar Dawreh-i Mu'aser* (Social and Political History of Iran in the Contemporary Era) (Tehran, 1956), I, 72-74.

[56] The royal khans who accepted administrative positions added the title *mirza* after their names to differentiate themselves from the Persian scribes who placed the same title before their names. By the end of the century, the Persian mirzas were complaining that the Qajar mirzas were supplanting them from their rightful positions. 'A. Mustawfi, *Sharh-i Zendigani-yi Man* (My Life) (Tehran, 1943), II, 18-21.

houses, wardrobes, stables, guardrooms, and workshops. But, despite these successes, they failed to overcome financial hurdles to create an extensive and viable administration. Many of the cabinet ministers remained to the very end of the century without ministries, bureaus, or even permanent staffs. Moreover, most governors remained powerless outside the immediate vicinity of their provincial capitals. This was illustrated in an incident described by Perkins:

The King has just sent several orders to the Governor of Urmiah, which not a little embarrass him. One thousand soldiers, belonging to this province, deserted from the King's army four months ago and returned home. His Majesty now orders the Governor to exact from each of them thirty tomans, brand him on his forehead, and burn down his house. The order is written in the King's own hand. The Governor's authority is too weak to enable him to carry into effect the royal order, and he knows not what to do. There is little of quiet and comfort for either rulers or people in Persia. The local rulers are often given orders which they can not execute.[57]

The failure to create a centralized bureaucracy meant that local communities preserved their administrative autonomy. Lord Curzon, in his encyclopedic work on Iran, pointed out that the traditional system of self-administration could easily be mistaken for the modern method of political representation.[58] Similarly, Malcolm stressed that although in theory the monarch appointed the many officials, in practice the "voice of the people" pointed out the community leaders:

It is true, these magistrates cannot always screen the people from the hand of power, and are often compelled to become the instruments of oppression: still their popularity with their fellow citizens, which caused their elevation, continues to be their strength; and in the common exercise of their duties, they attend to their comfort, happiness, and interests. In every city or town of any consequence, moreover, the merchants, mechanics, and labourers, have each a head, or rather a representative, who is charged with the peculiar interests of his class, and manages all their concerns with the Governor of the town. He is chosen by the community he belongs to, and is appointed by the King. He is seldom removed, except on the complaint of those whose representative he is deemed.[59]

The Qajars were equally unsuccessful, for the same financial reasons, in building a viable standing army. Beginning the century with the backing of their formidable tribesmen, the Qajars ended the century having lost their nomadic warriors among the civilian population of Tehran—in the typical cycle of tribal "degeneration" outlined so

---

[57] Perkins, *Eight Years in Persia*, p. 322.
[58] G. Curzon, *Persia and the Persian Question* (London, 1892), I, 436-37.
[59] Malcolm, *History of Persia*, II, 324-25.

well by Ibn Khaldun—and having gained little substantial in return. For the cavalry contingents remained under the direct command of the independent tribal khans. As Mounsey noted, "each cavalry regiment is headed by a tribal chief and its men are recruited from a tribe. Consequently, he has the interests of his clan much more at heart than those of the Shah or army." The militias continued to be controlled by local officers. A British report in 1907 described its rank and file as untrained villagers "who have no more claim than others to be called soldiers." The artillery boasted five thousand men, but had no more than four batteries of guns. Finally, the Cossack Brigade, the only unit with a semblance of military discipline, had been formed in 1879 but numbered fewer than two thousand men in 1906. Moreover, while the government had failed to bolster its military, the smuggling of British rifles after the 1870s had strengthened the relative power of the tribes. As Sykes observed, the southern tribes had obtained modern rifles, were better equipped than the government troops, and consequently threatened to "hold the region in their mercy." Naser al-Din Shah did not exaggerate his precarious position when he complained to his chief minister, "I have neither a proper army nor the ammunition to equip a proper army."[60]

The Qajars also failed to recapture the full grandeur of the ancient shah-in-shahs. They soon gave up the simplicity of nomadic life, meticulously performed religious rites, financed holy shrines, patronized state-appointed imam jom'ehs and shaykh al-islams, girded the Safavid sword—the Shi'i symbol—sat on the Peacock Throne, and, as Morier observed, adopted the "elaborate paraphernalia of ancient emperors."[61] Despite the pomp and ceremony, however, the Qajars failed to obtain divine sanctity, for many of the mujtaheds openly claimed that the Hidden Imam had delegated the responsibility of guiding the public not to the temporal leaders but to the religious establishment. Although some members of the 'ulama, particularly the state-paid imam jom'ehs and shaykh al-islams were willing to identify with royal authority, most prominent mujtaheds remained aloof from the court and interpreted the early texts of Shi'ism to argue that the state was at worst inherently illegitimate and at best a necessary evil to prevent social anarchy. As Hamid Algar has succinctly noted in his work on *Religion and State in Iran*, many mujtaheds viewed

[60] Ibn Khaldun, *The Muqaddi mah* (Introduction to History), translated by F. Rosenthal (New York, 1958), 3 vols.; Mounsey, *A Journey through the Caucasus*, p. 143; British Military Attaché in Tehran, "Memorandum on the Persian Army," *F.O.371*/Persia 1907/34-2762; Sykes, *Ten Thousand Miles in Persia*, p. 295; H. Farmanfarmaian, ed., *Khatirat-i Amin al-Dawleh* (The Memoirs of Amin al-Dawleh) (Tehran, 1962), p. 77.

[61] Morier, *Second Journey*, p. 172.

the Shi'i state as a contradiction in terms. Similarly, Samuel Benjamin, the first permanent envoy from the United States, noted in 1887 that many of the senior mujtaheds assumed no outward pomp, but claimed the authority to unseat shahs, as well as princes and governors, if they transgressed the Islamic laws.[62]

Thus the Qajars were Shadows of the Almighty whose writ often did not extend beyond the capital; monarchs who considered themselves to be God's representatives on earth but were viewed by the main religious leaders to be usurpers of God's authority; sovereigns who sanctified the feet of their thrones but lacked the instruments for enforcing their decisions; shah-in-shahs who ruled not other kings, as they claimed, but through, and so with the kind permission of, "minor kings," such as tribal chiefs, local notables, and religious leaders. In theory, the shahs were omnipotent; in practice, they were politically impotent.

Having no military security, no administrative stability and little ideological legitimacy, the Qajars remained in power by systematically pursuing two concurrent policies: retreating whenever confronted by dangerous opposition; and, more important, by manipulating the many communal conflicts within their fragmented society. The Qajar dynasty ruled nineteenth-century Iran with neither the instruments of coercion nor the science of administration, but with the practice of prudent retreats and the art of manipulating all the possible variations in the complex web of communal rivalries.

The policy of retreat was implemented whenever stiff opposition appeared. When a popular mujtahed in Kashan demanded the recall of the city's unpopular governor and threatened massive protests against the "oppressive" government, Fath 'Ali Shah had no choice but to oblige.[63] When the 'ulama in Tehran demonstrated in outrage against the construction of a statue depicting Naser al-Din Shah, the government promptly removed the bust and admitted that such monuments violated the Islamic prohibition against three-dimensional representation of human beings.[64] And whenever the harvest was bad, the state lived in terror of urban revolts. William Ouseley, a private visitor, reported that "desperate" crowds in Shiraz forced the local

[62] J. Eliash, "Misconceptions Regarding the Juridical Status of the Iranian 'Ulama," *International Journal of Middle East Studies*, 10 (February 1979), 9-25; H. Algar, *Religion and State in Iran, 1785-1906* (Berkeley and Los Angeles, 1969), p. 5; S. Benjamin, *Persia and the Persians* (Boston, 1887), p. 441.

[63] M. Tunukabuni, *Qisas al-'Ulama* (A History of the 'Ulama) (Tehran, 1887), p. 93; cited by Algar, *Religion and State in Iran*, p. 57.

[64] M. I'timad al-Saltaneh, *Al-Ma'aser va al-Asar* (Memorials and Reminiscences) (Tehran, 1889), p. 107. Naser al-Din Shah had set up the statue after his views on royal grandeur had been reinforced by a visit to tsarist Russia.

shaykh al-islam to condone the lynching of profiteers, and thus brought down the price of bread. Edward Eastwick, a British diplomat, gave an eyewitness account of how angry mobs in Tehran pillaged the bakeries, nearly "thronged to death" the august imam jom'eh, dragged through the streets the dead body of the city kalantar, and broke through armed guards into the royal citadel: "Naser al-Din Shah commanded the prompt lowering of prices and so saved Tehran from a revolution by a hair's breadth." An Iranian official recounts in his memoirs that Naser al-Din Shah, years later, in appointing his favorite son governor of Tehran, warned him that he would be personally responsible if food prices rose: "You will hang on the public gallows so that everyone can see I am prepared to sacrifice my own son for the general good."[65] Thus the Qajar intervention in the market economy, especially through price controls and grain storehouses, was not a sign of their absolutism—as claimed by nineteenth-century liberal Europeans—but a direct product of their impotence in dealing with public disturbances.

The policy of manipulation took diverse forms. At most times, the Qajars balanced one community against another, one group of allies against another, one rebellious region against rival regions. The traditional enemies of a disloyal community invariably became the loyal and obedient friends of the shah; and with so many "friends," the Shah needed neither a bureaucracy nor a standing army to enforce royal authority. At other times, the Qajars encouraged internal dissensions to undermine a potential challenger. They thus exploited intracommunal as well as intercommunal rivalries. And at rare times when neither an internal rival nor an effective local ally could be found, the Qajars created such an ally by coalescing small disunited groups into a larger and more united counterbalancing force. They accordingly achieved an equilibrium even in regions where no equilibrium had existed.

"The Qajars," in the words of one British traveler, "ensured their own safety by nicely balancing and systematically fomenting mutual jealousies."[66] They preserved their presence in distant regions and placed their princes as provincial governors by continually taking advance of local rivalries—between Haydaris and Ni'matis in Shustar, Isfahan, Qazvin, Shiraz; between Shaykhis and Mutashar'is in Tabriz; between Karimkhanis and Mutashar'is in Kerman; between Shahsavens, Afshars, Kurds, Turkomans, and Persians in the northeast;

---

[65] Ouseley, *Travels*, II, 209-10; E. Eastwick, *Journal of a Diplomat's Three Years Residence in Persia* (London, 1864), I, 287-91; H. Qodsi, *Kitab-i Khatirat-i Man ya Tarikh-i Sad Saleh* (Book of My Life or History of One Hundred Years) (Tehran, 1963), I, 29-30.

[66] J. Kinneir, *A Geographical Memoir of the Persian Empire* (London, 1813), p. 45.

between Lurs, Afshars, Bakhtiyaris, Persians, and Arabs in the southwest. Malcolm observed with his perceptive eye that Iranian cities, unlike medieval European cities, failed to bargain for corporate privileges from the central government because they were so thoroughly factionalized into rival wards.[67] And Morier discovered in the southwest, soon after the region's conquest by the new dynasty, that

the particular interest which these changes might have excited in the people is swallowed up by the consideration that their new masters are Persian and that the rule of the Arabs is over. A feeling which naturally did not conciliate the Arab community to any successor to their Shaykh. The general impression was not ill-expressed by an old Arab whom we found fishing along the shore. "What is our Governor? A few days ago he was a merchant in the bazaar: yesterday he was chained by the neck in prison; today his is our Governor; what respect can we pay him? The Governor that is to be, was a few years ago a poor scribe; and what is worse, he is a Persian. It is clear that we Arabs shall now go to the wall and the Persians will flourish."[68]

This strategy of divide and rule was illustrated by Fath ʿAli Shah's handling of a major rebellion in 1814. In that year, one of the royal princes, taking advantage of his position as governor of Asterabad, formed an allegiance with the local Turkomans, armed the city fortress, and openly claimed the throne. Fath ʿAli Shah, having few contingents at his disposal, dispatched not troops but three proclamations: the first to the prince, pledging pardon if he laid down arms; the second to the city's religious leaders, promising them rewards and reminding them that the same prince had recently imprisoned some of them; and the third to the population of Asterabad, especially to the kadkhudas, warning that the presence of the Turkomans endangered their bazaar and claiming that their previous tax contributions had been too heavy. According to Morier, the last two letters had their desired effect.[69] As tensions increased, a large crowd of citizens, led by mullas and kadkhudas, closed the gates to the Turkomans, seized the rebel prince, and promptly delivered him to the shah. The city was duly rewarded, the Turkomans returned to their tribal territories, and the prince had his eyes taken out.

Moreover, the Qajars continually tried to keep alive and, if necessary, create communal rivalries. Burgess described how the central government used this "infamous way" to retain a semblance of authority in the western mountains: "It sets one chief intriguing against another, perhaps even appoints two rival chiefs governors of the same

[67] Malcolm, *History of Persia*, II, 429.
[68] Morier, *A Journey through Persia*, p. 27.
[69] Morier, *Second Journey*, p. 350.

district, and when, after spending half their fortunes in presents and bribes, they turn out their followers to fight, it fines both for not keeping the peace, and, at times, appoints a third man as the new governor." J. G. Lorimer, in his detailed *Gazetteer of the Persian Gulf*, wrote that the central government had few soldiers in the southwest but managed to use, on one hand, the Bakhtiyaris, Lurs, and Kurds against the Arabs, and, on the other hand, the Arab Ka'ab tribe of Fallahiyeh against the Arab Muhaisin tribe of Mohammerah. Sykes, Conolly, Landor, and Major Lovett—a British officer visiting Iran in the 1870s—each remarked that the Qajars, although generally disliked in the southeast, successfully played off the local Arabs, Kurds, Afghans, and Lurs against the Baluchis, and the Brahui Baluchis against the Nharui Baluchis. Similarly, Perkins wrote that the central government retained some influence in the region of Urmiah by relying on traditional Kurdish-Assyrian animosities.[70]

The Qajars also tried to prevent the development of dangerous situations by systematically weakening potential enemies. Malcolm found that the central government kept in check the ambitions of one important Kurdish dynasty by fomenting discontent within its ruling clan. De Bode remarked that the Tehran authorities secured Isfahan not so much through their own strength, but through Bakhtiyari civil wars for grazing lands and their "unquenchable thirst" for internal feuds.[71] Muhammad Shah weakened the Chahar Lang by imprisoning Muhammad Taqi Khan of the Kianersi and strengthened the Haft Lang by recognizing as ilkhan Jafar Quli Khan of the Zarrasvand. Naser al-Din Shah at first helped the Zarrasvand by granting it Kianersi lands as "fiefs," but later, feeling threatened, encouraged its internal feud between the Ilkhani and the Hajji Ilkhani families: in 1882 he imprisoned Esfandiar Khan of the former and nominated Imam Quli Khan of the latter faction as ilkhan; in 1888 he helped Esfandiar Khan depose Imam Quli Khan; and two years later he supported the deposition of Esfandiar Khan and the reinstatement of Imam Quli Khan. As Ann Lambton has appropriately stated, the Qajars systematically exploited the tribal families' "constitutional inability" to combine, and adopted the perpetuation of tribal feuds as instruments of state policy.[72]

[70] Burgess, *Letters from Persia*, p. 68; J. G. Lorimar, *Gazetteer of the Persian Gulf* (Calcutta, 1915), vol. I, part II, 1744-47; Sykes, *Ten Thousand Miles in Persia*, pp. 97, 404; Conolly, *Journey to the North of India*, p. 295; Landor, *Across Coveted Lands*, pp. 364-82; B. Lovett, O. St. John, and C. Evan Smith, *Eastern Persia* (London, 1876), pp. 5-8; Perkins, *Eight Years in Persia*, p. 6.

[71] Malcolm, *Sketches of Persia*, p. 287; De Bode, *Travels in Luristan and Arabistan*, II, 429.

[72] A. Lambton, "Persian Society under the Qajars," *Journal of the Royal Central Asian Society*, 48, (July-October 1961), p. 130.

In most regions, the Qajars were able to neutralize a dangerous opponent by finding either internal dissensions or existing rivals. But in the rare circumstance where neither could be found, they sought to create a counterbalancing force. This is typified by the formation in 1861-1862 of the Khamseh tribal confederation. During the first half of the century, the Qashqayis of Fars, united by a series of charismatic ilkhans and strengthened by an influx of smaller tribes that had supported the Zands, grew into a formidable force of over 120,000 armed horsemen.[73] At first the Qajars tried to check them by relying on the local Bakhtiyaris, the Boir Ahmedis, and the powerful family of Hajji Ibrahim—the same family that had played such an important role in the eventual downfall of the Zands. De Bode, after a tour of the region in the 1840s, described the local balance of power:

I found Shiraz divided into two rival camps. At the head of one is the *ilbeg*, whose elder brother, the *ilkhan*, resides in Tehran. At the head of the other was the *kalanter*, Hajji Mirza Ali Akbar, the son of the famous Hajji Ibrahim. . . . The power of the *kalanter* is greatest in the precincts of the town. His antagonist's is greatest among the nomadic tribes. The princely governor and his *vazir* hope to uphold their own authority by keeping alive the animosity between the two rival camps, and in this respect they only follow the policy pursued all over the empire, and that which appears to have been the system of government in Persia from time immemorial. It still happens oftener that the Prince, who is named governor of a province, embraces the cause of one party, while his minister sides with the adherents of the other.[74]

This balance, however, broke down in the 1850s. The five Niʿmati wards in Shiraz turned against the Hajji Ibrahim family, whose strength lay in the five Haydari wards, and formed an alliance with the Qashqayis. At the same time, the Bakhtiyaris and Boir Ahmedis, absorbed in internal feuds, ceased to deter the Qashqayis. The Qajars consequently resorted to other tactics. They awarded ʿAli Muhammad Khan, the grandson of Hajji Ibrahim, the title of Qavam al-Mulk and the governorship of Fars. They placed his relatives in crucial posts throughout the southern provinces. They encouraged him to ally five minor tribes—the Persian-speaking Basseri, the small group known locally as the "Arabs," the Turkic-speaking Nafar, Baharlu, and Ainarulu—all of whom were individually threatened by the expanding Qashqayis. And naming this confederation the Khamseh (Five Together), the Qajars nominated Qavam al-Mulk as its first ilkhan. The Khamseh was thus a purely pragmatic creation of five heterogeneous tribes headed by an urban notable who rarely appeared among his

---

[73] British Commercial Adviser in Bushire, "Report on the Qashqai Tribes," *F.O. 371/ Persia 1912/34-2843*.

[74] De Bode, *Travels in Luristan and Arabistan*, I, 180-81.

tribesmen and boasted no blood ties whatever to them; some even claimed that his fourteenth-century ancestor had been a Jewish merchant.[75] Yet the same confederation provided the Qajars with an effective counterforce against the Qashqayis, continued to be led by the family of Qavam al-Mulk, and even as late as World War II supplied the central government with valuable contingents to fight the pro-German Qashqayis. Royal fiat had achieved communal equilibrium.

The Qajars, in acting like grand manipulators, were helped by the collection of ordinary taxes, the infliction of extraordinary punishments, and the disposition of periodic rewards. The government obtained much of its revenue from taxes on land, cattle, shops, and houses. Each community paid according to its "presumed ability." The shah and his mustawfi al-mamalek determined how much each province and tribal confederation could afford to contribute. The governors and ilkhans, together with the provincial mustawfis, decided the sum each district and tribe was to collect. The district kalantars and tribal khans fixed the amount each kadkhuda was to raise. And the village, tribal, ward, and guild kadkhudas calculated the levy each household was to pay. The whole method was open to obvious abuse. Some communities, not surprisingly, were heavily overassessed; others, in the words of Curzon, were "ludicrously underassessed."[76] It was taxation with communal benefaction and communal discrimination. The same is true of extraordinary levies. For example, at the end of the century the city of Boroujerd was paying a special tax because at the beginning of the century it had been held responsible for the death of the shah's favorite horse. And Lur tribes were still burdened by an annual levy that had been placed on them in 1871, when Naser al-Din Shah, displeased by them, had commanded them to buy the diary of his travels in Europe. Curzon commented, "it was imposed as a means of simultaneously acquainting the subjects with the majesty of their sovereign, and the sovereign with the pecuniary resources of his subjects."[77] Obviously, much harsher punishments were inflicted on rebels. When, according to a court chronicler, the "ungrateful inhabitants" of Nishapur rebelled, the shah encouraged the local tribes to lay waste the city. Faced with a discontented but popular governor in Hudar, the monarch declared the whole city to be open booty for his loyal tribes. The same chronicler boasted that "the wealth which the inhabitants of the city had, in the course of so many years, collected

---

[75] British Military Attaché in Tehran, "Bibliographical Notices on Members of the Royal Family, Notables, Merchants, and Clergy in Persia *F.O. 881*/Persia," 1887/34-2658.

[76] Curzon, *Persia and the Persian Question*, II, 472.

[77] Ibid., p. 471.

and stored up, became in one instant the object of plunder and the subject of devastation."[78]

The Qajars, by playing off one section of the society against another, were able to stand over the whole society with such grandiose, but nevertheless significant, titles as King of Kings, Supreme Arbitrator, Shadow of God, Guardian of the Flock, Divine Conqueror, and Asylum of the Universe. Malcolm, visiting the court early in the century, concluded that the Iranian monarchy was unhampered by laws, institutions, and theories of checks and balances, and thus was "one of the most absolute monarchies in the world." When he tried to explain the constitutional limitations placed on the British king, the shah exclaimed, "your king then appears to be no more than a mere first magistrate. So limited an authority may be lasting but can have no enjoyment. I, on the other hand, can elevate and degrade all the high nobles and officers you see around me!"[79] For nineteenth-century Europeans, the Qajar dynasty was an epitome of ancient oriental despotisms; in fact, it was a failed imitation of such absolutisms. To European visitors, the Qajar state seemed to dominate society because it was all-powerful; in reality, the Qajar state dominated society not so much because it was itself strong, but because its society was remarkably weak.

As King of Kings, Protector of Subjects, and Supreme Arbitrator, the Qajar ruler defended the state against external dangers and mediated internal conflicts, in much the same way as communal leaders related to their own followers. In the words of a royal proclamation, authority had been structured hierarchically because society was formed of villages, tribes, and town wards, and each was protected from anarchy by its own chief: "These chiefs are known in villages and local districts as *kadkhuda*s; but the chief of the whole country is called the *Padishah* (Emperor)."[80] In order to defend the country against outside threats, the shahs alone had the power to determine foreign policy, to summon the army, to head—at least nominally—their subjects in war, and, in case of victory, to distribute booty among their warriors. As long as they effectively defended the kingdom, the communal leaders were obliged to serve them; but if they failed to provide this protection, the communal heads were morally at liberty to seek another wardship. In order to arbitrate internal conflicts, the shahs had the authority to sit in judgment not only over warring magnates, but also, if necessary, over squabbling town wards and their brawling street

[78] Quli Khan Dawnbali, *The Dynasty of the Kajars*, translated by H. J. Brydges (London, 1833), pp. 80, 89.

[79] Malcolm, *History of Persia*, II, 303, 435.

[80] Piemontese, "The Statutes of the Qajar Orders of Knighthood," p. 436.

lutis. The royal palace (*darbar*), consequently, functioned as the country's ultimate court of appeals: it handed down verdicts that were based not upon religious jurisprudence but upon political expediency; and it developed into a power center where major community leaders sought to place either official representatives (vakils) or unofficial "ears and voices." Fath ʿAli Shah made the second alternative possible by himself marrying 192 times, and marrying off 170 daughters and sons to the country's leading households. Any community that did not have access through the corridors of power to the royal palace invariably fell prey to rival communities that did. According to one contemporary, the Turkomans frequently resorted to arms because, being unrepresented at court, their rivals ("in the interests of their own pocket") had no difficulty in portraying them in an unfavorable light.[81]

The shahs, also as Shadows of God, Divine Conquerors, and Guardians of the Flock, exercised extensive authority over life, honor, and property. They claimed ownership of all land they had not previously granted. They possessed sole right to give concessions, privileges, and monopolies. They intervened in the economy, occasionally regulating production and prices, frequently buying, selling, and stockpiling food. They considered their word as law so long as it did not openly contradict the fundamentals of Islam. As one chronicler stressed, "wise men realize that when you have an opinion contrary to that of the Shah, you must make a sacrifice of your blood."[82] They moreover made and unmade all high officials: the famous Hajji Ibrahim was boiled in oil, another minister was strangled, yet another had his veins cut open, some were blinded, and many had their property confiscated. Fallen ministers so often lost their property that when one such minister did not, the court chronicler wrote in surprise, "I have never before known or heard of a shah dismissing a minister yet not confiscating his wealth."[83] Iʿtimad al-Saltaneh summed up the relationship between monarch and ministers when he approved Naser al-Din Shah's decision to bestow the office of a deceased court custodian to a common-born son over the aristocratic-born sons: "Your Majesty had exercised the absolutiness of royal power. You have shown once again that we are all your servants: that only you can elevate us to the highest positions: that you can hurl us down to the lowest depths;

[81] Quoted by Lambton, *Landlord and Peasant in Persia*, p. 161.

[82] Fasaʿi, *History of Persia under Qajar Rule*, p. 39.

[83] Mirza Muhammad Taqi al-Mulk, *Nasekh al-Tavarikh* (A Definitive History of Histories) (Tehran, 1960), III, 153.

that without your generosity we are all nothing—we are less than miserable dogs."[84]

The Qajars, finally, as Asylums of the Universe, claimed to channel unmanageable communal antagonisms into the ceremonious court, and thus transform them into manageable pressure groups. As they never tired of repeating, only they stood between communal tensions and total social anarchy. One court chronicler, while stressing that the Qajars derived their legitimacy from "divine origins" and "celestial rights of conquest," continually harped on the theme that the new dynasty had ushered in an "age of harmony" by ending the civil wars, by mediating between rival factions, and by directing political conflicts away from the battlefield into the peaceful setting of the royal court. The Qajar defeat of their opponents had supposedly saved the cities from tribal plunder. The return of Azerbaijan had ended a long period of poverty, "opened wide the portals of security," and ushered in an age of ease and quiet. The securing of law and order had preserved the population from the "evil" Kurds, the "barbarous" Arabs, and the "demoniacal" Afghans. And the establishment of a new order had brought a bright era in which the "people could repose in perfect tranquility."[85] These glowing descriptions may not have convinced many, but gave even the sceptical observer a justification for arbitrary rule. Malcolm, who was by no means a friend of autocracy, was nevertheless impressed when informed by a minor khan that his tribe no longer waged war against its rival tribe, as in the past, but instead safeguarded its interests through the royal court. Malcolm was doubly impressed when an old peasant admitted that if the Qajars "have done us no good, they have, at least, thank God, freed our village from the terrible ravages of local tribesmen."[86] And even James Fraser, whose travelogue reads like a long Victorian indictment of oriental despotism, concluded his tour with a Hobbesian justification for the Iranian version of the Leviathan: "Persia, to live secure from internal and external foes, requires the control of a warlike and determined sovereign. A weak or a pacific king, however good his disposition, will bring distress and ruin on the country. The sword must be ever ready in his hand to protect and punish."[87] Most contemporaries, both European and Iranian, would have agreed with Fraser's conclusion—that is, until the growth of the constitutional movement at the end of the nineteenth century.

---

[84] I'timad al-Saltaneh, *The Diaries of I'timad al-Saltaneh*, p. 834.
[85] Dawnbali, *The Dynasty of the Kajars*, pp. 46, 88, 147, 327.
[86] Malcolm, *Sketches of Persia*, pp. 156, 149.
[87] Fraser, *Narrative of a Journey into Khorasan*, p. 622.

TWO

The Constitutional Revolution

Warning. His Imperial Majesty has apparently forgotten that . . . he was not born by his mother possessed of crown and signet-ring, nor does he hold in his hand a warrant of absolute sovereignty from the Unseen World of the Spirits. He should remember that his sovereignty depends only on the acceptance or rejection of the People. The People that have elected him are also able to elect another in his place.

—A revolutionary proclamation reprinted in E. Browne, *The Persian Revolution of 1905-1909*, p. 169.

THE IMPACT OF THE WEST

The impact of the West during the second half of the nineteenth century undermined in two separate ways the fragile relationship between the Qajar state and Iranian society. First, Western penetration, especially economic penetration, threatened the many urban bazaars, and thereby gradually induced the scattered regional commercial interests to coalesce into one cross-regional middle class that was conscious for the first time of its own common grievances. This propertied middle class, because of its ties to the traditional economy and the traditional Shi'i ideology, became known in later years as the traditional middle class. Second, Western contact, particularly ideological contact through modern educational institutions, introduced new concepts, new aspirations, new occupations, and eventually a new professional middle class known as the intelligentsia. The world outlook of these modern educated intellectuals differed radically from that of the previous court intellectuals. They espoused not the divine right of kings but the inalienable rights of man. They promulgated not the advantages of royal despotism and political conservatism, but the principles of liberalism, nationalism, and even socialism. They venerated not the Shadows of God on Earth but the triumvirate of Equality, Liberty, and Fraternity. Moreover, they not only introduced into the vocabulary of contemporary Iran numerous Western words, such as *despot, fudal, parleman, sosiyal, demokrat,* and *aristukrat*; but also injected modern meanings into many old words. For example, *istibad* changed in meaning from "monarchy" to "despotic monarchy"; *mellat* from "religious community" to secular "nationality"; and *mardom* from the "people" without any political connotations to "The People" with its democratic and patriotic connotations. It was these radical concepts of the modern educated class, together with the antistate Shi'i ideas of the traditional middle class, that helped to bring about the eventual triumph of the Constitutional Revolution in 1905-1909.

The impact of the West began as early as 1800, and took the form of military pressure first from the Russians and then from the British. Moving through Central Asia and the Caucasus, the Russians, equipped with modern artillery, easily defeated Iran's faction-ridden tribal contingents, and imposed on Fath 'Ali Shah the humiliating treaties of Gulistan (1813) and Turkomanchai (1828).[1] Similarly, the British, eager to counterbalance Russian successes and to use Afghanistan as a buffer zone both against the tsars and against the Qajars, invaded southern Iran and extracted from the shah the Treaty of Paris (1857). As a result of these treaties, the Qajars regained Tabriz and southern Iran, and obtained international recognition as legitimate rulers of Iran; but lost Georgia, Armenia, and their Caspian navy, gave up all claims to Afghanistan, paid an indemnity of £3,000,000 to the tsar, and, most significant of all, granted a series of commercial capitulations to Russia and Britain. These capitulations enabled the two powers to open consular and commercial offices anywhere they wished, and exempted their merchants not only from the high import duties but also from internal tariffs, local travel restrictions, and the jurisdiction of shari'a law courts.

These diplomatic treaties initiated, as they were intended to, the economic penetration of Iran. During the course of the century, the total volume of foreign trade increased, in real terms, by as much as eight times.[2] Imports—especially mass-manufactured textiles, hardwares, glass, as well as sugar, tea, and spices—rose from £2,000,000 in 1830 to over £5,000,000 in 1900. Exports—mostly raw cotton, silk, wheat, rice, tobacco, hides, and carpets—grew in the same period from £2,000,000 to about £3,800,000. Whereas at the beginning of the century Iran had been isolated from the world economy, by the

[1] For descriptions of ethnic conflicts weakening the army during the two Russo-Iranian Wars, see: I'timad al-Saltaneh, *Mirat-i al-Buldan* (Mirror of Cities) (Tehran, 1877), I, 405; and Reza Quli Khan Hedayat, *Tarikh-i Rawzat-i al-Safa-yi Naseri* (History of Naser's *Rawzat-i al-Safa*) (Tehran, 1960), IX, 674-76.

[2] C. Issawi, *The Economic History of Iran, 1800-1914* (Chicago, 1971), pp. 130-51.

end of the century it was well on the way toward incorporation into the European network of international commerce.

Thus military defeats led to diplomatic concessions; diplomatic concessions produced commercial capitulations; commercial capitulations paved the way for economic penetration; and economic penetration, by undermining traditional handicrafts, was to cause drastic social dislocations. The Qajars responded to these challenges in two very different ways. During the first half of the century, they tried to initiate two ambitious programs for rapid, defensive, and statewide modernization. But having failed, they settled during the second half of the century for minor reforms. In these reforms they collaborated with rather than challenged the West, strengthened their state vis-à-vis their society rather than the society vis-à-vis foreign states, and introduced piecemeal, court-based rather than wholesale state-wide changes.

The first drive for modernization was led by Prince ʿAbbas Mirza. As heir apparent and thus governor of Azerbaijan, he discovered during the First Russo-Iranian War that the tribal cavalry—which he contemptuously dismissed as "the rabble"[3]—was no protection against the mobile artillery. He therefore modeled himself on the contemporary reformer of the Ottoman Empire, Sultan Selim III, and constructed in Azerbaijan his own version of the Ottoman Nizam-i Jadid (New Order). Six thousand troops constituted the core of this new order: they were equipped with mobile artillery and fairly up-to-date weapons, paid regularly by the state, dressed in uniforms, housed and drilled in barracks, and trained by European officers. To supply the new army, ʿAbbas Mirza established in Tabriz a cannon factory, a musket plant, and a translation office for military and engineering manuals. To safeguard it, he opened the country's first permanent missions abroad, in Paris and London. To insure its future, he dispatched Iran's first students to Europe: they were sent to study such practical subjects as military science, engineering, gun making, medicine, typography, and modern languages.[4] To finance all this, he cut court salaries, pensions, and extravagances; he also raised revenues through protective tariffs and decrees against the use of foreign cloth. And to prevent a repetition of the religious revolt that had destroyed Selim III, ʿAbbas Mirza obtained clerical pronouncements in favor of the Nizam-i Jadid. His friend the shaykh al-islam of Tabriz declared

[3] J. Morier, *Second Journey through Persia, Armenia, and Asia Minor* (London, 1818), p. 211.

[4] Mirza Saleh Shirazi, one of the eight students sent to Europe, returned in 1819 to open the first printing press, and to give, in his *Safarnameh* (Travel Book), the first description of constitutional governments in Persian.

that the army reorganization was in full accord with Islam, for had not the Koran stated that "Allah loveth those who battle for His cause in ranks as if they were a solid structure"? And his court chronicler argued that the prince, with his "penetrating mind," had rediscovered through the Europeans the military tactics invented by the Prophet: for while the Europeans had preserved these tactics, the followers of Islam had fallen victim to ignorance, laziness, pride, jealousy, and "uncoordinated battle-lines."[5] The new army was, thus, an indirect but nevertheless legitimate heir of the Prophet.

These opinions may have saved the Nizam-i Jadid from public outbursts, but they provided no protection against political intrigues. The austerity measures antagonized courtiers, pensioners, and tax collectors. The new tarrifs prompted Western protests: the commercial attaché from Britain complained that the "dogma" of protectionism was disrupting the natural laws of free trade.[6] The modern army aroused the fears of the provincial magnates. To allay these fears, the original plans were modified so many times that eventually each regiment became a tribal contingent officered by its own tribal chiefs. Moreover, the new army, by strengthening 'Abbas Mirza, aroused the hostility of his many brothers and half-brothers; some of these princes, who had refused to reconcile themselves to 'Abbas Mirza's nomination as heir apparent, spread rumors that the crown prince was dangerous, heretical, and even a "secret unbeliever."[7] Furthermore, the setbacks suffered by the new army in the Second Russo-Iranian War only served to confirm Fath 'Ali Shah's conviction that the best weapon was still the "ancestoral lance."[8] Consequently, 'Abbas Mirza saw the slow death of his Nizam-i Jadid long before he met his own natural death in 1833.

The second drive for modernization was initiated by Mirza Muhammad Taqi Khan Farahani, better known as the Amir Kabir (The Great Lord). Growing up in Tabriz, where his father was a cook in the household of 'Abbas Mirza's chief minister, he had attracted the attention of 'Abbas Mirza. Serving later as a special secretary for the army, he had admired the Nizam-i Jadid. When he was appointed special envoy to the Ottoman Empire, he had taken a deep interest in the Tanzimat reforms, and on his return had gradually won the confidence of the heir apparent, the future Naser al-Din Shah. As

[5] Dawnbali, *The Dynasty of the Kajars*, translated by H. J. Brydges (London, 1833), p. 308.

[6] Great Britain, Foreign Office, "Report on Commercial Negotiations," reprinted by Issawi, *The Economic History of Iran*, p. 78.

[7] J. Malcolm, *Sketches of Persia* (London, 1859), p. 135.

[8] M. von Kotzebue, *Narrative of a Journey into Persia* (London, 1819), pp. 160-61.

soon as the young prince ascended the throne in 1848, Amir Kabir was named Amir-i Nizam (Lord of the Army) and Sadr Aʿzam (Prime Minister), and was encouraged to implement extensive reforms. He revived the standing army, and established fifteen factories to supply this army and to cut foreign imports: factories for the production of cannons, light arms, uniforms, epaulets and insignias, woolens, cloths, calicoes, carriages, samovars, paper, cast iron, lead, copper, and sugar. He founded the country's first official newspaper, the *Ruznameh-i Vaqa-yi Ittifaqiyeh* (Newspaper of Current Affairs). And most important of all, he built the country's first secular high school, the Dar al-Fonun (Abode of Learning). The Dar al-Fonun offered its students, who were mostly sons of the aristocracy, classes in foreign languages, political science, engineering, agriculture, minerology, medicine, veterinary medicine, military sciences, and band music. To finance these projects, Amir Kabir reduced other expenses, especially court expenses, and raised government revenues through increases on import duties, a moratorium on sale of offices, scrutiny of tax collectors, and a new tax on fief holders that no longer contributed armed men for imperial defense.

These measures created an immediate reaction. The fief holders considered the new tax not a legitimate substitute for traditional dues but an unwanted extortion designed to strengthen the government at the expense of the provinces. The representatives from Britain and Russia were disturbed not only by the protective tariffs but also by the decision to seek technical assistance in France and the Austro-Hungarian Empire. The queen mother used her influence over the shah on behalf of courtiers who were hard pressed by the financial cuts. And as a final blow, the Babi revolt, which coincided with these reforms, created a general atmosphere of political instability. Amir Kabir was dismissed in 1851, banished to the provinces, and executed there soon after; his plans for the future were cast aside, and his industrial factories, despite heavy investments, were left to wither away. Thus ended the last nineteenth-century attempt at rapid, defensive, and statewide modernization.

Although Naser al-Din Shah, in eliminating Amir Kabir, scrapped the program of modernization, he did not by any means kill the whole process of modernization. Indeed, Naser al-Din Shah and his ministers, themselves brought about many innovations over a long reign that lasted until 1896.[9] But these innovations, instead of driving for rapid change, induced a slow drift toward change; instead of de-

[9] Some of the reforms were implemented by Naser al-Din's chief minister, Hajji Mirza Hussein (Sepahsalar), in 1871-1873.

fending the state against external enemies, they were aimed at buttressing the court against internal opponents; and, instead of protecting the economy, they sought to tempt Western interests further into the Iranian economy. Moreover, the decision to attract foreign trade coincided with two external trends: the British and Russian pressures to improve international communications, and the European, especially British, search for overseas ventures into which their surplus capital could be invested. Foreign investors launched their hunt for overseas concessions at about the same time as Naser al-Din Shah initiated his search for foreign investors.

The concession-hunting era was inaugurated in 1872 by what Curzon aptly described as an "international bombshell." Baron Julius de Reuter, a British citizen, purchased for £40,000 and 60 percent of the profits from a concession on the customs the exclusive right to finance a state bank, farm out the entire customs, exploit all minerals (with the exception of gold, silver, and precious stones), build railways and tramways for seventy years, and establish all future canals, irrigation works, roads, telegraph lines, and industrial factories. "The agreement," Curzon commented, "contained the most complete surrender of the entire resources of a kingdom into foreign hands that has ever been dreamed of, much less accomplished, in history."[10] The agreement, however, aroused so much opposition in Iran and Russia that it had to be canceled.

Although the Reuter concession was withdrawn, the sale of concessions continued. Reuter retained mining and banking privileges that developed later into the Imperial Bank of Persia. The British Department of Indo-European Telegraph, together with the British-owned Indo-European Telegraph Company, obtained contracts to extend the telegraph communications from Europe to India through Iran. Lynch Brothers, another British company, opened for shipping the Karun River as far as Shustar, and improved the road from Shustar to Isfahan. The Imperial Bank of Britain obtained monopoly over the printing of banknotes, permission to extend branches into the provinces, and rights to collect tolls on most southern roads. Meanwhile, the Russians acquired similar concessions. The Russian government bought the privilege to extend and administer the telegraph lines from its border to Tehran. Cie de la Route, a private Russian company, won contracts to dredge the port of Enzeli and pave the roads from Enzeli to Qazvin, from Qazvin to Tehran, from Qazvin to Hamadan, and from the northern border to Tabriz. These years

[10] G. Curzon, *Persia and the Persian Question* (London, 1892), I, 480.

have been described as the "paved road period" of Iran.[11] Another Russian company obtained a monopoly over the fishing industry in the Caspian Sea; and yet another a monopoly over the insurance of transport in the northern provinces. Moreover, the Russians, through shares in a Belgian company, also participated in the construction of a nineteen-mile railroad between Tehran and the quarries in ʿAbdul ʿAzim. Thus foreign investments increased during the second half of the century from almost nothing to over £12,000,000. Iran had been opened to European capital as well as to European trade.

The revenue derived from loans and concessions was used in various ways. As critics of the court loved to point out, some of it was wasted on conspicuous court consumption, and the mind-boggling Reuter concession was designed to finance Naser al-Din Shah's grand tour of Europe. But much of the revenue was used both to defray the heavy cost of inflation and to finance expensive modernization projects. The price rise, totaling nearly 600 percent between 1850 and 1900, was caused partly by government debasements of the coinage, but mainly by a drastic fall in the international market value of silver, the main metal used in Iranian coinage.[12] In addition to driving up the cost of imported goods, the fall of silver prices undermined confidence in the local currency and thereby further aggravated inflation.

Inflation had drastic effects on the state. Although government expenditures, especially on salaries, grain stocks, and military hardware, grew, government revenues, particularly from tax farms and out-of-date tax assessments, stagnated. For example, while prices rose sharply, the revenue from the land tax in Gilan rose only from 179,139 tomans in 1866 to a mere 202,100 tomans in 1892.[13] Caught between spiraling expenses and stagnating incomes, between the need to find additional revenues and the political dangers of levying new taxes, Naser al-Din Shah increasingly resorted to the sale of titles, patents, privileges, concessions, monopolies, lands, tuyuls (right to collect taxes on crown lands), and, most detrimental of all, high offices—judgeships, ambassadorships, governorships, and even ministries. As one

[11] Issawi, *The Economic History of Iran*, p. 157.

[12] The figure of 600 percent has been estimated from the following sources: Issawi, *The Economic History of Iran*, pp. 335-90; Curzon, *Persia and the Persian Question*, II; J. Bharier, *Economic Development of Iran, 1900-70* (London, 1971), pp. 2-20; M. Jamalzadeh, *Ganj-i Shayegan* (Abundant Treasure) (Berlin, 1956). In 1800 the English pound sterling was equivalent to 11 Iranian krans. By 1900, it was equivalent to 50 krans.

[13] R. McDaniel, "Economic Change and Economic Resiliency in Nineteenth Century Iran," *Iranian Studies*, 6 (Winter 1971), 36-49.

modern historian has commented, hardly a day passed in the court without the sale of something to someone for some price.[14]

Although much of the revenue from these sales went into court consumption, some of it was also used to finance new projects. The telegraph network, expanding to cover nine thousand miles by 1900, connected not only London with India, but also Tehran with the provinces, and thus the shah with his provincial administrators. The Cossack Brigade, growing to nearly two thousand men by 1896, provided the shah with a small but disciplined palace guard. At the same time, the capital obtained a regular police force, a municipal civil service, a host of road sweepers, a medical clinic, a central mint to replace the many provincial mints, and a network of paved streets, gas lanterns, and horse-drawn trams. Modernity, or at least its outward form, had at last reached Tehran.

Naser al-Din Shah also took intermittent but consequential interest in social, educational, and even administrative reforms. He banned the slave trade and promised to respect private property. He encouraged the cultivation of new crops, especially potatoes. He built prisons in the main cities to diminish the use of traditional punishments, particularly torture, live burials, and dismemberment of criminals. He set up, although briefly, an appointed Council of Advisers (Majles-i Maslahat Khaneh) and an elected Assembly of Merchants (Majles-i Tujjar) both in Tehran and in the main provincial cities. He instructed his governors to keep the ʿulama out of politics and to confine them within the realms of "praying, teaching, observing the shariʿa, and communicating with God."[15] He permitted Catholic and Protestant missionaries to work among Jews, Assyrians, and Armenians, and to open schools, medical clinics, and printing presses in Tabriz, Urmiah, Tehran, Isfahan, and Hamadan. Moreover, he expanded the Dar al-Fonun and sent forty of its first graduates to France.[16]

Finally, Naser al-Din Shah established two military colleges, two official journals—one for military matters and one for scientific subjects—a translation school, and a new government printing office. This printing office, together with the Dar al-Fonun and the older printing office in Tabriz, published in the course of the century over 160 titles.

[14] R. Sheikholeslami, "The Sale of Offices in Qajar Iran, 1858-1896," *Iranian Studies* 4 (Spring-Summer 1971), 104-18.

[15] Cited by F. Adamiyat and H. Nateq, *Fekr-i Ijtimaʿi va Siyas-i va Iqtesad-i dar Asar-i Montashernashudeh-i Dawreh-i Qajar* (Social, Political, and Economic Ideas in Unpublished Qajar Works) (Tehran, 1978), p. 182.

[16] A. Majd al-Islam Kermani, *Tarikh-i Inqilab-i Mashrutiyat-i Iran* (History of the Iranian Constitutional Revolution) (Isfahan, 1972), I, 79-87. Of these students, nine became army officers, seven civil servants, five teachers, five doctors, two portrait painters, one an optician, one a civil engineer, and five skilled craftsmen.

They included 88 military textbooks, language manuals, and medical handbooks; 4 biographies of famous Muslim leaders; 10 travelogues of the West, including Naser al-Din Shah's own account of his European tour; 10 translations of European classics, including Defoe's *Robinson Crusoe*, Molière's plays, Dumas's *Three Musketeers*, Verne's *Around the World in Eighty Days*, and Morier's famous satire on Iran, *The Adventures of Hajji Baba*; 10 histories of Iran, notably Malcolm's *History of Persia* and Markham's *Short History of Persia*—thus Iranians began to see their own past through the eyes of contemporary Europeans—and finally over 20 translations of European works on Western history: biographies of Napoleon, Nicolas I, Frederick the Great, Wilhelm I, and Louis XV; short histories of Rome, Athens, France, Russia, and Germany; and Voltaire's essays on Peter the Great, Alexander the Great, and Charles the Great of Sweden. The shah commissioned many of these translations to glorify the monarchy; but the same translations, by inadvertently drawing contrasts for the Iranian readers between their shahs and the most famous kings of Europe, between the poverty of Iran and the prosperity of Europe, tended to weaken the Qajar monarchy.

THE TRADITIONAL MIDDLE CLASS

The bazaars were the marketplaces, the workshops, the banks, the guild headquarters, the storehouses, the commercial hubs, and the religious centers of traditional Iran. It was in the bazaar that tradesmen sold merchandise, craftsmen produced commodities, businessmen built mosques, religious authorities preached, governments stored grain, moneylenders advanced loans, aristocrats, as well as some shahs, negotiated loans. But whereas the bazaars performed critical economic and social functions, the political influence of the commercial middle class was undermined by communal differences: geography isolated one city from another; and, within each city, sectarian, organizational, and linguistic rivalries separated one sector of the bazaar from another. Thus the traditional middle class existed as a socioeconomic entity, but not as a statewide political force.

All this was changed fundamentally by the Western impact and the Qajar response—or rather, the lack of a coherent response. In 1800, the middle class was sharply fragmented into small locally bound communities; by 1900, it was transformed into a broad statewide force conscious, for the first time, of its common political personality. The introduction of telegraph lines, the improvement of old roads, the building of new roads, the publication of newspapers, and the inauguration in the 1870s of a postal system, all facilitated communications, and thus narrowed distances between the urban centers. The integration of Iran into the world economy initiated the integration of local bazaars into the Iranian economy: the import of manufactured products increased internal trade; the export of agricultural goods—especially cotton, rice, tobacco, and hides—eroded the self-sufficiency of the local communities, began the commercialization of agriculture, and intensified contacts between town and country, between exporters and villagers, between moneylenders and farmers. The implementation of important economic decisions in Tehran, particularly the sale of concessions and the establishment in 1877 of a central mint, focused the attention of the many provincial towns onto the national capital. The influx of mass-manufactured products, especially textiles, undermined the traditional handicrafts, and consequently presented for the many bazaars a mutual enemy—the foreigner. As the tax collector of Isfahan noted in his report on the weavers' guild,

In the past, high-quality textiles were manufactured in Isfahan since everyone—from the highest to the lowest—wore local products. But in the last few years, the people of Iran have given up their body and soul to buy the colorful and cheap products of Europe. In doing so, they incurred greater losses than they imagined: local weavers, in trying to imitate imported fabrics, have lowered their quality; Russians have stopped buying Iranian textiles; and many occupations have suffered great losses. At least one-tenth of the guilds in this city were weavers; not even one-fifth have survived. About one-twentieth of the needy widows of Isfahan raised their children on the income they derived from spinning for the weavers; they have now lost their source of livelihood. Likewise, other important guilds, such as dyers, carders, and bleachers, have suffered. Other occupations have also been affected: for example, farmers can no longer sell their cotton for high prices.[17]

The refusal of the government to erect protective tariffs further antagonized the local manufacturers. One British report stated bluntly that although free trade was ruining many branches of native industry, the government was ignoring all requests for higher import duties.[18] The privileges granted to foreign merchants undermined not only local manufacturers but also the local merchants. For example, a European importer of cotton piece goods deposited at the border 5 percent duty, but an Iranian importer of the same goods lost another 7-8 percent in additional duties, bazaar taxes, local levies, and road tolls. A British commercial attaché warned that these exactions were

[17] Mirza Hussein Khan, *Jughrafiya-yi Isfahan* (Geography of Isfahan) (Tehran, 1963), pp. 100-101.
[18] British Consul in Tehran, quoted by Issawi, *The Economic History of Iran*, p. 259.

forcing native merchants to either abandon their trade or take up foreign citizenship.[19]

Inflation also weakened the competitive position of native merchants vis-à-vis European merchants. The international fall in agricultural prices, which started in 1871 and continued to the end of the century, brought insecurity to many Iranian exporters: as the price of a bushel of wheat declined from $1.50 in 1871 to $0.23 in 1894, the volume of wheat exported from Bushire increased by 80 percent but the realized value failed to rise significantly. Finally, the introduction of European capital and the capitulations granted to European businessmen created outside the bazaars a comprador bourgeoisie. Although this new group was reputed to be drawn from the non-Muslims, a British "Who's Who" indicated that it was not: of the fifty-three wealthiest businessmen active at the end of the century, one was a Zoroastrian, five were Armenians, but forty-seven were Muslims.[20]

The latter half of the nineteenth century, therefore, saw the division of the propertied middle class into two contrasting sectors. On the one hand, the growth of foreign trade stimulated the rise of a small but wealthy comprador bourgeoisie. On the other hand, the influx of foreign goods, capital, and merchants initiated the decline of the native bourgeoisie. And this decline—which hurt the Haydari as much as the Ni'mati, the Mutashar'i as much as the Shaykhi, the Shi'i as much as the Baha'i, the Tehrani as much as the Tabrizi, Isfahani, Shirazi, Kermani, Mashadi—together with improved communications, generated similar feelings of discontent throughout the country's bazaars.[21]

Many of the problems confronting the native bourgeoisie can be seen in a report written for Naser al-Din Shah by a government official visiting Bushire in 1882.[22] Having described how Bushire had grown during the last decade into a major port with the potential of becoming another Bombay, he listed the main reasons why the boom had not brought prosperity for Iranians. First, foreign governments, unlike the Iranian government, encouraged their own merchants: "English traders, for example, seek assistance from their diplomatic and commercial agencies in the Persian Gulf; these agencies, in turn, seek

[19] Ibid., p. 81.

[20] H. Picot, "Persia: Biographical Notices of Members of the Royal Family, Notables, Merchants, and Clergy," *F.O. 881*/Persia 1897/7028.

[21] For signs of decline in the bazaars, see: Issawi, *The Economic History of Iran*, pp. 41-42; N. Keddie, "The Economic History of Iran, 1800-1914," *Iranian Studies*, 5 (Spring-Summer 1972), 58-78; M. Malekzadeh, *Tarikh-i Inqilab-i Mashrutiyat-i Iran* (History of the Constitutional Revolution in Iran) (Tehran, 1949), I, 171-73.

[22] Mirza Taqi Khan Hakimbashi, "Report on Bushire," reprinted by I. Safa'i, *Asnad-i Nowyafteh* (Recently Found Documents) (Tehran, 1970), pp. 104-15.

assistance from Parliament in London; and Parliament invariably acts to further British interests." Second, local merchants using old sailing boats had to compete against European companies with modern steamships. Third, the Iranian government had failed to build storage facilities for its own citizens, whereas the British government provided for its merchants not only storage depots but also a medical hospital and a military garrison. Fourth, the Iranian merchants were handicapped by higher taxes, tariffs, and internal tolls: "The businessmen of Bushire often complain that Europeans pay in all 5 percent import duty but that they are forced to pay additional duties at Shiraz, at Isfahan, and at any other city they sell." The report concluded with the warning that Iranian merchants would be forced to buy British protection, and, with it, British citizenship in order to remain in business: "One of the most prominent merchants of Bushire recently became a citizen of the British Empire. This causes tax losses; it also threatens to encourage others to do the same. The government must take action to discourage this trend." On the back of the report, Naser al-Din Shah abused the merchants for being "selfish," praised the report for being "very interesting," but typically failed to prescribe any remedies.

THE INTELLIGENTSIA

Whereas the impact of the West coalesced the many bazaars into a propertied middle class, contact with the West—through travel, translations, and educational establishments—created modern ideas, modern aspirations, modern values, and, thereby, modern intellectuals. Although these intellectuals developed during the twentieth century into the salaried middle class, they constituted in the nineteenth century a mere stratum, for they were too few and too heterogeneous to form a social class: some were aristocrats, even royal princes, others civil servants and army officers, and yet others clerics and merchants. But, despite occupational and social differences, they formed a distinct stratum, for they shared a common desire for fundamental economic, political, and ideological change.

In coining the alternate terms *munaver al-fekr* and *rushanfekr* (enlightened thinkers) to describe themselves, the intelligensia revealed much about themselves. Western ideas, especially the French Enlightenment, convinced them that history was neither the revelation of God's will, as the ʿulama believed, nor the cyclic rise and fall of dynasties, as the court chroniclers endlessly described, but rather the continual march of human progress. Western history persuaded them that human progress was not only possible and desirable but also easily attainable if they broke the three chains of royal despotism, clerical dogmatism, and foreign imperialism. They abhorred the first as the inevitable enemy of liberty, equality, and fraternity; the second as the natural opponent of rational and scientific thought; and the third as the insatiable exploiter of small countries such as Iran. Moreover, Western education convinced them that true knowledge derived from reason and modern science, not from revelation and religious teaching. They thus claimed to be "enlightened" on the grounds not of quantative learning, since the traditional literati could boast more scholastic learning, but of qualitative savoir faire to construct a modern society.

The intelligentsia thus considered constitutionalism, secularism, and nationalism to be the three vital means for attaining the establishment of a modern, strong, and developed Iran. The first, they argued, would destroy the reactionary power of the monarchy. The second would eliminate the conservative influence of the clergy. And the third would eradicate the exploitative tentacles of the imperialists. But these three movements although aimed at the same goal, often created temporary shifts in immediate tactics. For the intelligentsia found itself at times allied with the shah against the ʿulama, at times with the ʿulama against the shah; at other times, with the shah against the imperial powers, and sometimes, as in the Constitutional Revolution, with the ʿulama against both the shah and the imperial powers. These tactical inconsistencies, as well as the general consistencies, can be seen in the life and works of the two most important members of the nineteenth-century intellectuals: Sayyid Jamal al-Din "al-Afghani" and Mirza Malkum Khan.

Sayyid Jamal al-Din was born in the late 1830s to a small landowning family in an Azeri-speaking village outside Hamadan. Although his father came from humble origins, family connections provided Jamal al-Din with a complete Shiʿi education, beginning in Qazvin and continuing in the prestigious seminary at Najaf. But during this conventional upbringing, Jamal al-Din's inquisitive mind led him to unconventional interests: first to Shaykhism, later to Babism, and eventually to India in search of the modern sciences. He later claimed that he had sought modern learning because he had obtained nothing from traditional learning. Reaching Bombay in 1857, he was deeply affected by the Indian Mutiny. On the one hand, the mutiny's initial success in inflaming the Muslims of India against Britain triggered his inquiry into the relationship between popular religion and political action. On the other hand, the mutiny's eventual failure reinforced his awe for modern technology, and thus intensified his quest for the new sciences. His thinking led him to three principal conclusions: that imperialism, having conquered India, now threatened the Middle East; that the East, including the Middle East, could prevent the onslaught of the West only by adopting immediately the modern technology of the West; and that Islam, despite its traditionalism, was an effective creed for mobilizing the public against the imperialists. Jamal al-Din retained these fundamental beliefs throughout his long career, although he often borrowed and discarded less fundamental views to fit immediate situations.

Leaving India, Jamal al-Din traveled through Arabia and the Persian Gulf to Afghanistan. As a guest of the conservative Afghan court, he concealed his reformist ideas, and instead concentrated on advising the king to ally with Russia against the more dangerous foreign threat—Britain. Moving on to the more advanced environment of Istanbul, he disguised his Shi'i background by labeling himself "the Afghan," and created a major scandal by publicly arguing that Muslims could regain their lost civilization if they were to seek knowledge through human reason as well as through divine revelation. This gained him the staunch admiration of reformers and the simultaneous opposition of religious conservatives. Deported to Cairo, he joined the local Freemasons, and called for political reforms to save the country from the British and their main collaborator, the Khedive. Deported once again, he spent the years between 1879 and 1886 traveling extensively in India and Europe.

In India, Jamal al-Din initiated polemical discussions with both religious and antireligious Muslims; he attacked the former for their reluctance to rejoin Hindu Indians in a national struggle; he criticized the latter for their inability to see that popular religion was an effective weapon in the fight against imperialism. His famous "Refutation of the Materialists"—which, ironically, gave him a reputation as a champion of Islam—stressed not the spiritual but the social aspects of religion; it argued that religion served the useful function of binding individuals, who were naturally lazy, greedy, and treacherous, into a community that was capable of withstanding the West.

In Europe, Jamal al-Din opened a dialogue with Orientalists who explained the decline of Islam in terms of the "unscientific" Arab mentality. He retorted that the true explanation lay not in race but in religious intolerance:

It is permissible to ask oneself why Arab civilization after having thrown such a live light on the world, suddenly became extinguished, why this torch has not been lit since, and why the Arab world remains buried in profound darkness. Here the responsibility of the Muslim religion appears complete. It is clear that wherever it became established, this religion tried to stifle science and was marvelously served in its design by political despotism. Al-Siuti tells that Caliph al-Hadi put to death in Bagdad 5,000 philosophers in order to extirpate sciences in Muslim countries up to their roots. . . . I could find in the past of the Christian religion analogous facts. Religions, whatever names they are given, all resemble one another. No agreement and no reconciliation are possible between these religions and philosophy. Religion imposes on man its faith and its belief, whereas philosophy frees him of it totally or in part.[23]

Jamal al-Din, departing from Europe in 1886, spent much of the next four years in his native Iran. At first, he tried to persuade Naser al-Din Shah to lead a campaign against the British. Failing in this, he turned to conservative clergymen and reforming intellectuals. To the former, he advocated a crusade against the heathen West. To the latter, he emphasized that reforms, especially political and educational reforms, would strengthen the country against the imperialistic West. These lectures attracted large and lively audiences, and thereby aroused Naser al-Din Shah's concern. Having taken sanctuary in ʿAbdul ʿAzim, Jamal al-Din was seized from the shrine and deported in chains to the Ottoman Empire. Although he had failed to expel the British and introduce reforms, he had succeeded in leaving behind in Iran many followers, especially among the ʿulama and the graduates of the Dar al-Fonun.

Jamal al-Din spent the last six years of his life in the Ottoman Empire. Finding the subject of political reform too dangerous a topic in Istanbul, he channeled his energies into safer activities. He urged the sultan to organize a pan-Islamic movement against the Russians, who now appeared more dangerous than the British. He continued to call for the reform of Islam, especially the adaption of Koranic principles to the discoveries of modern science, and the replacement of traditional knowledge with the new knowledge of contemporary Europe. Moreover, he continued to use both secular and religious arguments in his propaganda war against the shah of Iran:

Verily the King's character is vitiated, his perception is failing, and his heart is corrupt. He is incapable of governing, or managing the affairs of his people, and hath entrusted the reigns of government in all things great and small to the hands of a wicked freethinker, a tyrant and usurper, who revileth the Prophets openly, and heedeth not God's law. Moreover, since his return from the lands of the Franks [Europeans] he hath taken the bit between his teeth, drinks wine openly, associates with unbelievers and displays emnity toward the virtuous. Such is his private conduct; but in addition to this he hath sold

---

[23] Quoted in N. Keddie, *Sayyid Jamal ad-Din "al-Afghani"* (Berkeley and Los Angeles, 1972), p. 193.

the greater part of the Persian lands and the profits accruing therefrom, to wit the mines, the ways leading thereunto, the main roads, the river Karun and the guest houses which will arise on its banks. . . . Also the tobacco . . . with the chief centers of cultivation. He has similarly disposed of the grapes used for making wine, and the shops, factories and wine-presses; and so likewise soap, candles, sugar, and the factories connected therewith. Lastly there is the Bank: and what shall cause thee to understand what is the Bank? It means the complete handing over of the reins of government to the enemy of Islam, the enslaving of the people to that enemy, the surrendering of them and of all dominion and authority into the hands of the foreign foe. . . . In short, this criminal has offered Persia to auction amongs the Powers, and is selling the realms of Islam and the abode of Mohammad (on whom be greeting and salutations) to the heathen.[24]

However *bizarre* it may seem, it is nevertheless a fact, that after each visit of the Shah to Europe he has increased in tyranny over his people. The result is that the masses of Persia, observing that after each European tour the Shah becomes more intolerant and despotic, naturally ignorantly attributed their increased suffering to European influences, and hence their dislike of Europeans became yet more intense, at the very moment when . . . Persia stood in need of the kindling and liberalising influences of a wisely directed British statesmanship.[25]

On his death bed in 1897, Jamal al-Din expressed to a friend both hope and sorrow. Hope, because the "stream of renovation" flowing from West to East would inevitably destroy the "edifice of despotism." Sorrow, because he had wasted so much of his precious ideas on the "sterile soil" of royal courts: "would that I had sown the seeds of my ideas on the fertile ground of the people's thoughts."[26]

Malkum Khan was born of Armenian parentage in 1833 in the Christian quarter of New Julfa in Isfahan. His father, a graduate of a British school in India, taught English and French first in Isfahan and later at the royal court in Tehran. An enthusiastic admirer of Western civilization, he sent Malkum Khan to a French Catholic school in Isfahan, and then obtained for him a state scholarship to study engineering in France. While in Paris, Malkum Khan developed a keen interest in Freemasonary and contemporary political philosophy, especially in Saint Simon's school of social engineering and in Auguste Comte's controversial Religion of Humanity. Returning to Iran, Malkum Khan joined the recently opened Dar al-Fonun, impressed Naser al-Din Shah with scientific experiments, converted to Islam—probably to further his public career—and formed a secret society named the

[24] Ibid., pp. 342-43.
[25] Sheikh Djemal ed-Din, "The Reign of Terror in Persia," *Contemporary Review*, 60 (February 1892), 243.
[26] Keddie, *Sayyid Jamal ad-Din "al-Afghani,"* p. 419.

Faramushkhaneh (House of Oblivion), which was modeled on but not attached to the European Freemasons.

Having won the attention of the shah, Malkum Khan drafted for the court a *Daftar-i Tanzimat* (Book of Reform). Obviously inspired by the contemporary Tanzimat movement in the Ottoman Empire, the *Daftar* was one of the first systematic proposals for reform written in nineteenth-century Iran. It began with a general warning that the country would soon be engulfed by the foreign powers unless the shah immediately decreed laws for reform. Malkum Khan used the term *qanun* for these laws, to differentiate them from both the religious canons (*shari'a*) and the old state regulations (*'urf*). These new laws, Malkum Khan stressed, must be based on two fundamental principles: the improvement of public welfare, and the equality of all citizens. The book concluded with a list of specific recommendations: the separation of the government into a legislative council and an executive cabinet, both to be appointed by the shah; the acceptance of public opinion; the codification of the previous laws; the formation of a professional army; the creation of an independent tax department; the introduction of a comprehensive educational system; the building of new highways between the main towns; and the establishment of a state bank to finance economic development.

Naser al-Din Shah at first listened to the proposals, and even considered accepting the post of grand master in the Faramushkhaneh. But once the religious authorities in Tehran denounced the concept of qanun as a "heretical innovation" (*bid'a*) and accused the Faramushkhaneh of having connections to the "atheistic republican" Freemasons in Europe, Naser al-Din Shah banned the society, shelved the *Daftar-i Tanzimat*, and exiled Malkum Khan to the Ottoman Empire.[27]

It was probably during this period of exile that Malkum Khan wrote his satirical work on the traditional literati entitled *A Traveler's Tale*. In this work, he parodied on the one hand the court intellectuals, scribes, and poets for their obscure language, meaningless phraseology, obsession with trivia, and flattery for the powerful; and on the other hand, the religious authorities for their pomposity, ignorance, intolerance, distrust of modern science, use of incomprehensible Arabic, resort to esoteric mumbo jumbo, enflaming of sectarian passions, and financial exploitation of the faithful community. In addition to being one of the very first anticlerical satires to be circulated in Iran,

---

[27] I. Ra'in, *Faramushkhaneh va Framasuneri dar Iran* (The House of Oblivion and Freemasonry in Iran) (Tehran, 1968), I, 525. The religious authorities also spread rumours that the Faramushkhaneh was organizing "sex orgies" for the "beardless youth of the Dar al-Fonun."

A Traveler's Tale was also one of the first literary works to be written in clear Persian prose, free of the traditional decorative terminology.

While in exile in Istanbul, Malkum Khan befriended Mirza Hussein Khan (Sepahsalar), the liberally inclined ambassador from Iran, and obtained through him the post of consul general in Cairo. The years of exile ended in 1871, however, when Naser al-Din Shah, again toying with the possibility of reform, appointed Hussein Khan chief minister and named Malkum Khan special advisor with the title of Nizam al-Mulk (Regulator of the Realm). But no sooner had the new government cut the court budget, divided the administration into an executive cabinet and an advisory legislative council, and raised funds with the sale of the Reuter concession than it was confronted by an aristocratic and clerical reaction. Malkum Khan was sent off to London as ambassador, and after a brief period Hussein Khan lost his government position.

As ambassador in London, Malkum Khan continued to petition the shah for reforms, established contact with the exiled al-Afghani, and encouraged his colleagues in Tehran to seek further administrative improvements. After 1889, however, Malkum Khan turned more radical as soon as he lost his ambassadorship for refusing to share the spoils of a nonexistent gambling monopoly that he sold to a group of British concession hunters. The dismissal changed Malkum Khan from an insider petitioning for reform into an outsider advocating revolution, from a mild liberal seeking the protection of the shah against the ʿulama into an outspoken radical allying with the ʿulama against the shah; and from a royal administrator drafting proposals into a radical journalist presenting the ideas of modern Europe, especially Saint Simon's positivism and Auguste Comte's Religion of Humanity, in forms acceptable to traditional Iran. In a public lecture on Persian civilization delivered in London soon after his dismissal, Malkum Khan admitted that his main intention was to clothe the political philosophy of the West in the respectable terminology of the Koran, hadith, and the Shiʿi Imams.[28] Posing the question of why Iran was backward, he rejected the conventional European explanations based on race and religion. Instead, he placed the blame on political despotism and cultural insularity. To overcome the former, he advocated laws protecting life, liberty, and property; for without these three, there could be no security, and without security, there could be no progress. To overcome the latter, he proposed the introduction of modern concepts in terms palatable to conventional Islam.

[28] Malkum Khan, "Persian Civilization," *Contemporary Review*, 59 (February 1891), 238-44.

We have found that ideas which were by no means acceptable when coming from your agents in Europe were accepted at once with greatest delight when it was proved that they were latent in Islam. I can assure you that the little progress which you see in Persia and Turkey, especially in Persia, is due to this fact that some people have taken your European principles and instead of saying that they come from England, France, or Germany, they have said, "We have nothing to do with Europeans; but these are the true principles of our religion (and indeed, this is quite true) which have been *taken by Europeans!*" That has had a marvelous effect at once.

Malkum Khan founded the famous newspaper *Qanun* in order to carry his views from London to Iran. Although the paper was a sporadic one-man enterprise, it aroused considerable interest in Tehran: so much so that it was banned, its mere possession became a state crime, and it was later hailed as a major factor in the outbreak of the Constitutional Revolution. The first issue, published in 1890, set the tone for the following forty issues that appeared in the course of the next eight years. Headed by the slogan "Unity, Justice, and Progress," it began with a Muslim prayer in Arabic and continued with a long editorial in clear Persian stressing the need for rational laws:

God has blessed Iran. Unfortunately, His blessing has been negated by the lack of laws.

No one in Iran feels secure because no one in Iran is safeguarded by laws.

The appointment of governors is carried out without laws. The dismissal of officers is done without laws. The monopolies are sold without any laws. The state finances are squandered without laws. The stomachs of innocent citizens are cut open without laws. Even the servants of God are deported without laws.

Everyone in India, Paris, Tiflis, Egypt, Istanbul, and even among the Turkoman tribes, knows his rights and duties. But no one in Iran knows his rights and duties.

By what law was this mujtahed deported?

By what law was that officer cut into pieces?

By what law was this minister dismissed?

By what law was that idiot given a robe of honor?

The servants of foreign diplomats have more security than the noble princes of Iran. Even the brothers and sons of the shah do not know what tomorrow will bring—whether exile to Iraq or flight for dear life to Russia. . . .[29]

The following issues of *Qanun* described the type of laws that would establish security and thus stimulate social progress. They also advocated free discussion of all topics pertinent to public welfare; close alliance with the ʿulama; termination of sectarian conflicts, especially

[29] Malkum Khan, "God Has Blessed Iran," *Qanun*, No. 1 (February 1890).

between Sunnis and Shi'is, Shaykhis and Mutashar'is; ending of concessions to foreign "exploiters"; formation of societies that would propagate the principles of "Humanity" (*adamiyat*)—the principles of "Unity, Justice, and Progress"; and introduction of a national consultative assembly—this was one of the first appearances in Persian of the demand for a parliamentary government. Many of these issues were summed up in a short column in the sixth issue of *Qanun*:

A merchant from Qazvin writes: "By what laws does the government sell our national rights to foreign racketeers? These rights, according to both the principles of Islam and the traditional laws of Iran, belong to the people of our country. These rights are the means of our livelihood. The government, however, barters Muslim property to the unbelievers. By what law? Have the people of Iran died that the government is auctioning away their inheritance?" Dear Merchant, the government has mistaken our inaction for our death. It is time for the mujtaheds and other knowledgeable persons to arise and save the people of Iran. We propose two simple remedies to save Iran: law and more law. You may well ask, "where will the law come from?" The answer is again simple: the shah should call at once one hundred mujtaheds and other learned persons of the country into a national consultative assembly (*majles-i shawra-yi melli*); and this assembly should have full authority to formulate laws that would initiate social progress.[30]

Although Malkum Khan was one of the foremost proponents of constitutional government, infirmities of old age prevented him from actively participating in the actual Constitutional Revolution. Thus, while the revolutionaries in Tehran hailed him as their mentor, reprinted his works, and sought his advice, Malkum Khan remained in exile and died in Europe a few days after the outbreak of the civil war in 1908.

FROM PROTEST TO REVOLUTION (1800-1905)

Contact with the West, besides developing the modern intelligentsia and the traditional middle class, also created widespread social discontent. The intelligentsia, anxious for rapid progress, expressed increasing dissatisfaction with the slow pace of modernization and the high degree of court corruption. The traditional middle class, left defenseless against foreign competitors, gradually realized that the Qajars were interested more in strengthening the state against society than in protecting the society against the imperial powers. Meanwhile, the general population, especially the urban artisans and the rural masses, suffered a slight decline in their standard of living, partly because of Western competition, partly because of greater extractions,

[30] Malkum Khan, "A Letter from Qazvin," *Qanun*, No. 6 (July 1890).

and partly because the gross national product failed to keep pace with the gradual growth in population. In the eyes of Majd al-Islam Kermani, a typical late nineteenth-century intellectual, the corrupt Qajars, helped by the imperial authorities, bled the country dry by selling lands, concessions, privileges, and even peasants into slavery in the hands of Turkomans—"in short, the whole kingdom"—and by squandering the revenues on palaces, luxuries, pensions, presents, and foreign trips.[31]

There is little hard data on the economy, but there is impressionistic evidence to show that during the course of the century the average citizen's standard of living suffered a slight decline. Whereas early twentieth-century observers unanimously described rural life as abysmally poor and torturingly insecure, early nineteenth-century travelers had often found the peasantry enjoying fairly good conditions. For example, Sheil discovered in the villages "considerable air of substantial comfort which I often envied for my countrymen." "In a thinly populated country like Persia, it is in the interests of the landlord to conciliate his peasants and perpetuate their residence on his property. Thus the landlords treat their peasants well." Similarly, Benjamin found that laborers could ask for good wages since they were both mobile and in short supply. "The subjects of the Shah are not poor; there are few evidences of extreme poverty in his country." Likewise, Stack showed that the labor shortage strengthened the bargaining position of the peasant sharecropper. "On the whole it seems that the Persian tenant enjoys security of tenure so long as he pays his rent."[32] Finally, Fraser described rural life in terms that would be impossible to use a century later:

The cultivators of the soil . . . are those on whom the tyranny of their rulers fall the most heavily. Yet their houses are comfortable and neat, and are seldom found without a supply of good wheaten cakes, some mast or sour milk, and cheese,—often fruit makes its appearance, and sometimes a preparation of meat, in a soup or pillau. Their wives and children, as well as themselves, are sufficiently though coarsely clad; and if a guest arrives, there are few who cannot display a numed or felt carpet in a room for his reception. In fact, the high rate of wages proves that the profits of agriculture are high, while food is cheap; and we may be satisfied, that in despite of rapacity, enforced by torture, no small share of the gain is hoarded by the farmer.

[31] Majd al-Islam Kermani, *Tarikh-i Inqilab-i Mashrutiyat-i Iran*, III, 99-114.

[32] J. Sheil, *Glimpses of Life and Manners in Persia* (London, 1856), pp. 100, 390. A. Conolly stated that "in case of oppression, the ryots (peasants) are likely to remove themselves and resettle elsewhere." *Journey to the North of India* (London, 1834), II, 249; S. Benjamin, *Persia and the Persians* (Boston, 1887), pp. 173, 471; E. Stack, *Six Months in Persia* (New York, 1882), II, 205, 280.

Extortion and tyranny, like other things, become powerless after a certain point, and counteract their own efforts, although they never fail to beget deceit and falsehood. In spite of all discouraging circumstances, the peasantry possess activity and intelligence and, even among the modest, hospitality is seldom found wanting.[33]

There is also little statistical evidence on the intensity of social discontent, but there is enough documentary material to indicate that during the second half of the century the population, especially the urban population, increased its hostility toward the West, the Qajars, and the communities closely associated with the West. In the first half of the century, Europeans, such as Ouseley, Morier, and Sheil, freely attended mosque services, passion plays, and even Muharram flagellation ceremonies.[34] Moreover, Christian missionaries freely opened schools, printing houses, and churches without encountering major hostility from either the government or the Muslim population. One missionary even received thanks from the ʿulama for initiating a theological debate between Islam and Christianity. Western visitors experienced almost no public hostility. Conolly, after residing in the holy city of Mashad, wrote that he "experienced no ill usage": "I daily took my walks through all parts of the city and never was in the slightest degree insulted." Sheil found throughout the country "much agnosticism, deism, and freedom of religious expression." Monsieur Tancoigne, a French diplomat, reported that "I have never once received, even from the lower orders, epithets insulting to our religion."[35]

The mood, however, changed gradually as a result of the foreign war, and particularly after the humiliating Turkomanchai treaty. Immediately after the treaty, the tsar sent Griboyedov, a dramatist notorious for his contempt for all Asians, especially Iranians, to implement its degrading clauses.[36] After arriving in Tehran, Griboyedov permitted his Cossack bodyguards to roam drunk through the streets; insulted the court by refusing to take off his riding boots; and ordered his troops into private homes to "liberate" former Christians who were now Muslim slaves. The consequences were not surprising. While a

[33] J. Fraser, *Historical and Descriptive Account of Persia* (Edinburgh, 1834), p. 303.

[34] W. Ouseley, *Travels in Various Countries of the East* (London, 1819), II, 164-70; J. Morier, *A Journey through Persia, Armenia, and Asia Minor* (London, 1818), p. 197; Sheil, *Glimpses of Life and Manners in Persia*, pp. 322-25.

[35] H. Algar, *Religion and State in Iran, 1785-1906* (Berkeley and Los Angeles, 1969), pp. 99-102; Conolly, *Journey to the North of India*, I, 333; Sheil, *Glimpses of Life and Manners in Persia*, p. 200; M. Tancoigne, *A Narrative of a Journey into Persia* (London, 1820), p. 190.

[36] D. Costello, "Griboyedov in Persia in 1820," *Oxford Slavonic Papers*, 5 (1954), 81-93.

mujtahed proclaimed that Muslims had a duty to protect Muslim slaves, a large crowd from the bazaar assembled outside the Russian mission. Frightened by the assembly, the Cossacks fired, and thereby transformed the angry crowd into a violent mob that looted the mission and killed eighty of its staff.

Although the scale of violence expressed in the Griboyedov affair was not repeated, the sentiments underlying the violence continued during the rest of the century. Europeans no longer dared to venture into shrines, passion plays, and Muharram processions. Edwin Weeks, traveling in the 1890s, had to wear disguise to enter a mosque. Eustache De Lorey, a French contemporary, found that it was too dangerous for Christians to watch Muharram flagellations. Western missionaries lost their earlier freedom: they were forbidden to proselytize among Muslims; their schools, churches, and presses were tightly restricted; and no missionary in his right mind now contemplated debating the ʿulama. Benjamin wrote that it was too dangerous for Christians, especially missionaries, to attend religious ceremonies: "The population of Tabriz is exceedingly fanatical. Last year, foreigners were in some danger of being massacred during the holy frenzy of the religious festivals. In 1885, missionaries had to close down temporarily in the town because of the fear of massacres." Moreover, European tourists often encountered public hostility. As Landor noted, Westerners were considered adventurers and thieves: "They are rather tolerated than loved and a walk through the native streets is quite sufficient to convince one of that fact." European technicians now faced increasing public animosity. When an Iranian merchant hired foreign engineers to build a railway from Enzeli to Rasht, local muleteers combined to sabotage the whole venture. John Wishard, the director of the Presbyterian hospital in Tehran, commented that these muleteers, prodded by fanatical preachers, feared the loss of their livelihoods. Similarly, when Naser al-Din Shah contracted with a Belgian company to construct a railroad from Tehran to the shrine of ʿAbdul ʿAzim, cart drivers fearing cheap competition, mullas opposing foreign influence, and pilgrims shaken by the death of a fellow pilgrim under the steam engine joined hands to tear up the railway. Browne commented, "these innovations, so far as they are a source of wealth at all, are so, not for the Persian people, but for the Shah and his ministers on one hand, and for the European promoters of the schemes on the other hand."[37] By the end of the century, Western

---

[37] E. Weeks, *From the Black Sea through Persia and India* (New York, 1895), p. 62; E. De Lorey, *Queer Things about Persia* (London, 1907), p. 280; Benjamin, *Persia and the Persians*, pp. 113, 342, 379; H. Landor, *Across Coveted Lands* (New York, 1903), I, 116; J. Wishard, *Twenty Years in Persia* (New York, 1908), p. 144; E. Browne, *A Year amongst the Persians* (London, 1950), pp. 98-99.

visitors considered xenophobia and religious fanaticism to be in-grained aspects of popular culture in Iran. In fact, they were mostly recent and ironic byproducts of the Western impact on Iran.

The increasing public discontent erupted on a mass scale during the tobacco crisis of 1891-1892. The crisis was caused by Naser al-Din Shah's sale of yet another concession—this time to an Englishman named Major Talbot. In return for a personal gift of £25,000 to the shah, an annual rent of £15,000 to the state, and a 25 percent share of the profits for Iran, Talbot acquired a fifty-year monopoly over the distribution and exportation of tobacco. *Akhtar* (Star), a liberal Persian paper published in Istanbul, expressed the general concern of Iranian merchants:

It is clear enough that the concessionnaire will commence the work with a small capital and will purchase the tobacco from the cultivators and sell it to the merchants and manufacturers for higher prices, and all the profits will remain in the purse of the English. As the Persian merchants have no right to export tobacco from Persia, those who were formerly engaged in this trade will be obliged to give up their business and find some other work. The concessionnaire does not take into consideration how many merchants who were engaged in this business will be left without employment and will suffer loss in finding other occupations.[38]

The arrival of company agents in April 1891 was met with a shutdown of the bazaar in Shiraz, the main tobacco-growing region. The shut-down of the bazaar in Shiraz rapidly spread (thanks largely to the new telegraph system) into a general strike of the leading bazaars, particularly Tehran, Isfahan, Tabriz, Mashad, Qazvin, Yazd, and Kermanshah. The general strike, encouraged by a religious fatwa against the use of any tobacco, further spread into a state-wide con-sumers' boycott. The consumers' boycott, receiving support from the Russians, from the mujtaheds in Karbala, from Jamal al-Din in Istan-bul, from Malkum Khan in London, from menacing demonstrators in the streets of Tehran, and even from members of the royal harem, forced Naser al-Din Shah to annul the concession. The crisis revealed the fundamental changes that had taken place in nineteenth-century Iran. It demonstrated that local revolts could now spread into general rebellions; that the intelligentsia and the traditional middle class could work together; and that the shah, despite his claims, was a Titan with feet of clay. The tobacco protest, in fact, was a dress rehearsal for the forthcoming Constitutional Revolution.

In the years after the tobacco crisis, Naser al-Din Shah turned to-ward more political repression and away from dangerous innovation.

---

[38] Quoted by N. Keddie, *Religion and Rebellion in Iran: The Tobacco Protest of 1891-1892* (London, 1966), p. 49.

He sold few concessions; ended the growth of the Dar al-Fonun, forbade the opening of new schools, and turned a blind eye when a religious mob burned down a modern teaching establishment in Tabriz; outlawed *Akhtar* and *Qanun*; discouraged publications on the outside world; restricted government scholarships for study abroad; prohibited citizens, including relatives, from visiting Europe; boasted that he wanted ministers who did not know whether Brussels was a place or a cabbage; and, fearing antigovernment rumors, unsuccessfully tried to shut down the many teahouses of Tehran on the pretext that "storytellers and dervishes encouraged idleness and other vices among the lower classes."[39] Moreover, Naser al-Din Shah increasingly resorted to manipulating communal rivalries and using Babis as public scapegoats. As Mehdi Malekzadeh, the son of a leading martyr in the Constitutional Revolution, complained in his multivolume history of the Qajar downfall, "if the shah had been patriotic he would have built central institutions to control communal rivalries, especially tribal feuds. But since he was not patriotic, he mischeviously instigated one group against another, and thus threatened to down the whole ship of state in a sea of social chaos."[40]

This combination of repression, isolation, and manipulation—the hallmarks of the "Naser al-Din Shah Era"—ended abruptly in 1896. While preparing the celebrations for the fiftieth anniversary of his reign, Naser al-Din Shah was shot dead in ʿAbdul ʿAzim Mosque by a bankrupt trader who had studied under Jamal al-Din al-Afghani. His bullet not only ended the Naser al-Din era but also began the end of the Qajar regime.

The new monarch, Muzaffar al-Din Shah (1896-1906), inadvertently hastened the end of the regime by pursuing unpopular economic policies. He increased tariffs on native merchants, withdrew tax farms from their previous holders, and talked of increasing land taxes, decreasing court pensions, especially to the ʿulama, and tightening controls over vaqf holdings. Even more serious, he reopened the country to foreign entrepreneurs and again sought loans from abroad. He sold a monopoly to exploit oil in the whole of the central and southern provinces to an Englishman named D'Arcy; granted new road tolls to the Imperial Bank of Britain; and obtained a loan of £200,000 from a French company to buy arms, another of £3,000,000 from the Russian government to repay previous loans, and yet another £300,000 from the British government to finance his "medical" visit to London. At the same time, he contracted European companies to build a mod-

[39] De Lorey, *Queer Things about Persia*, p. 78.
[40] Malekzadeh, *Tarikh*, I, 139.

ern brick factory, a textile mill, a telephone system for Tehran, and to electrify the main streets of Tehran, Tabriz, Rasht, and Mashad. To guarantee security for these loans and investments, he appointed Monsieur Naus, a Belgian, as the country's director general of customs.

Even as he pursued these unpopular policies, Muzaffar al-Din Shah abruptly relaxed police controls—so much so that some staunch conservatives began to suspect him of being a secret Shaykhi.[41] He permitted the import of such liberal newspapers as *Habl al-Matin* (The Firm Cord) from Calcutta and *Parvaresh* (Education) from Cairo. He also lifted the ban on travel, appointed Malkum Khan as ambassador to Rome, and, most important of all, encouraged the formation of commercial, cultural, and educational associations.

In Isfahan a group of merchants formed the country's first statewide stock company by founding the Shirkat-i Islami (The Islamic Company). Their aim was to "preserve the country's independence by fostering such modern industries as textiles, and by protecting the traditional handicrafts, particularly the miniature arts."[42] In Tabriz, a circle of young intellectuals, whose knowledge of Turkish enabled them to follow cultural trends in the Caucasus and the Ottoman Empire, published an influential Persian-language journal entitled *Ganjeh-i Fonun* (Treasure of Knowledge).[43] At the heart of this circle were two men who were to play important roles in the forthcoming revolution: Mirza Muhammad ʿAli Khan "Tarbiyat" (Education), the owner of a secular bookstore that served as a meeting place for the group; and Sayyid Hassan Taqizadeh, who had first broken with his conservative clerical background to pursue his burning interest in Shaykhism, and later, on discovering the West, had turned to European languages and to the modern sciences of physics, medicine, and practical chemistry.[44]

A similar group of intellectuals in Tehran organized a Society of Learning (Anjuman-i Muʿaref) and pooled their books to form the country's first National Library (Ketabkhaneh-i Melli). With royal protection against the ultraconservative clergy, the Society of Learning was able to open fifty-five private secondary schools in Tehran during the brief period between its formation and the revolution. The leading personality in both the library and the society was a popular preacher named Hajji Mirza Nasrallah Malek al-Motakallemin. Despite his popularity and orthodox Shiʿi image, al-Motakallemin was a secret ʿAzali,

---

[41] Algar, *Religion and State in Iran*, p. 244.

[42] Malekzadeh, *Tarikh*, I, 175.

[43] M. Mujtahedi, *Tarikh-i Zendigani-yi Taqizadeh* (History of Taqizadeh's Life) (Tehran, 1942), p. 18.

[44] H. Taqizadeh, "My Life," *Rahenma-yi Ketab*, 13 (May-June 1970), 243-66.

a former colleague of al-Afghani, and a staunch advocate of modern civilization. In opening one of the new schools, al-Motakallemin summed up the main sentiments of his fellow educationalists:

It is education that separates humans from animals, useful citizens from useless ignoramuses, civilized beings from savage barbarians. Education generates light in an environment of intellectual darkness. Education shows us how to build power plants, steam engines, factories, railways, and other essential prerequisites of modern civilization. Education has enabled Japan to transform itself in one generation from a backward weak nation into an advanced powerful nation. Education, likewise, will enable Iran not only to regain its ancient glory but also to create a new generation that will be conscious of individual equality, social justice, personal liberty, and human progress. Education, in short, is a social factory that produces not material goods but responsible citizens and fully developed human beings.[45]

Muzaffar al-Din Shah hoped that his policy of liberalism would satisfy the political opposition. But by coinciding with intensified Western penetration, liberalism merely encouraged the opposition to form semiclandestine organizations. Of these organizations, the following five were to play important roles in the forthcoming revolution: the Secret Center (Markaz-i Ghaybi); the Social Democratic party (Hizb-i Ijtima'yun-i 'Amiyun); the Society of Humanity (Jama'-i Adamiyat); the Revolutionary Committee (Komiteh-i Inqilabi); and the Secret Society (Anjuman-i Makhfi).

The Secret Center was organized in Tabriz by twelve young radicals associated with the journal *Ganjeh-i Fonun*. The group was headed by a Shaykhi merchant, 'Ali Karbala-yi, who was nicknamed "Monsieur" because of his interest in French literature and French political philosophy. His colleagues included Tarbiyat's younger brother, three merchants who often traveled on business to Baku, two tanners, a civil servant, and a young linguist who had studied Russian, German, English, as well as French at the local French misionary school.[46]

The Social Democratic Party of Iran was formed in early 1904 in Baku by a handful of emigrés who had been active for some time within the Social Democratic Party of Russia. Opening a club named Hemmat (Effort), the party focused its activities among the some one hundred thousand migrant workers from Iran—mostly from Iranian

[45] Quoted in Malekzadeh, *Tarikh*, I, 153-54.

[46] Information on the Secret Center has been obtained from S. Javid, *Fedakaran-i Faramushshudeh* (Forgotten Heroes) (Tehran, 1966); 'A. Iqbal, "Sharifzadeh," *Yadgar*, 3 (May-June 1947), pp. 58-73; K. Taherzadeh-Behzad, *Qiyam-i Azerbaijan dar Inqilab-i Mashrutiyat-i Iran* (The Revolt of Azerbaijan in the Constitutional Revolution of Iran) (Tehran, 1953).

Azerbaijan—employed in the Baku oil fields. The party was headed by Narim Narimanov, an Azerbaijani school teacher who later became the president of the Soviet Socialist Republic of Azerbaijan. Almost all the other founders of the party were intellectuals from Iranian Azerbaijan. Their program, which was mainly a translation from the economic demands of the Russian School Democrats, called for the right of workers to organize and strike; an eight-hour day; old-age pensions; a progressive income tax; distribution of land among those who tilled it; housing for the homeless; free schools; reduction of consumer taxes; freedom of speech, press, and public meetings; and the toleration of all religions "acceptable to the *shari'a*."[47] The Secret Center, which soon established close ties with the Social Democrats, circulated the party program within Iran.

Whereas these two organizations were influenced by the revolutionary socialism of Russian Marxism, the Society of Humanity in Tehran was inspired by the radical positivism of Saint Simon and the liberal humanism of Auguste Comte. The society's founder, Mirza 'Abbas Quli Khan Qazvini, later surnamed Adamiyat (Humanity), was a close friend of Malkum Khan and a senior official in the Ministry of Justice. His son, Fereydoun Adamiyat, a well-known historian of the constitutional movement, wrote that the society had three main aims: to use social engineering to attain national development; to gain individual freedom so that human reason could blossom; and to obtain legal equality for all, irrespective of birth and religion, to secure dignity for all citizens.[48] Their secret initiation oath declared, "Equality in rights and duties is the only true foundation of human relations. Equality alone can create firm bonds of national solidarity. Equality alone can guarantee the individual his just rewards and obligations." The society drew its members mainly from the upper, but not princely, ranks of the central administration, for the demand of legal equality appealed to the civil servants' dislike of inherited privileges; the concept of social engineering promised them vital roles in the process of national development; the hope of liberty catered to their craving for personal security from arbitrary decisions; and the ceremonial secrecy, which was copied from the European Freemasons, protected them from the conservative authorities and the religious masses.

The Society of Humanity was cautious in its daily activities, but the

[47] "Concerning the Iranian S.D.P.," *Donya*, 5 (Summer 1966), 99-103; "The Regulations of the Iranian S.D.P.," *Donya*, 3 (Winter 1962), 76-80.

[48] F. Adamiyat, *Fekr-i Azad-i va Moqadimeh-i Nahzat-i Mashrutiyat-i Iran* (The Concept of Freedom and the Beginnings of the Constitutional Movement in Iran) (Tehran, 1961), pp. 206-17.

Revolutionary Committee was radical in both tactics and strategy. According to Malekzadeh, whose father, al-Motakallemin, headed the group, the committee was formed of fifty-seven "radical intellectuals" who frequented the National Library.[49] Meeting secretly in the suburbs of Tehran in May 1904, the fifty-seven drew up a plan for the "overthrow of despotism" and the establishment of "the rule of law and justice." The plan called for the exploitation of personal jealousies as well as political rivalries among the courtiers, ministers, and religious leaders, taking care to support the less conservatives against the more conservatives. It also called for the establishment of contact with "enlightened" religious leaders; the avoidance of all non-Islamic activities to allay the suspicions of the ʿulama, even though the committee accepted the principle of religious toleration as one of its main goals; and the use of sermons, lectures, newspapers, broadsheets, and translations to popularize the concepts of constitutional democracy among the Iranian masses. Malekzadeh commented years later that these secular radicals were obliged to seek the assistance of the religious authorities because the "lower class" was still dominated by the "ruling class" of royal princes, tribal chiefs, local magnates, and landed patrons.[50]

The composition of the Revolutionary Committee reflected both the ideological homogeneity and the sociological diversity of the early intelligentsia. The fifty-seven included fifteen civil servants, eight educators, four translators and writers, one doctor, fourteen clergymen who had some knowledge of modern sciences, one tribal chief, three merchants, and four craftsmen.[51] All were acquainted with Western civilization through the Dar al-Fonun, or the study of a European language, or the reading of recent translations, or the influence of al-Afghani and Malkum Khan. Many of the fifty-seven were in their forties and fifties. Three had been born into the Qajar aristocracy, twenty-one into ʿulama households, seven into civil-service backgrounds, and eight into bazaar families. Two were Zoroastrians, one was the leader of a Niʿmati order, at least five were secret ʿAzalis, and some others were suspected by the conservative clergy of being "freethinkers." Of the forty whose birthplace is known, thirty-five

[49] Malekzadeh, *Tarikh*, II, 5-18.

[50] M. Malekzadeh, *Zendigani-yi Malek al-Motakallemin* (The Life of Malek al-Motakallemin) (Tehran, 1946), pp. 148-149.

[51] Throughout this book biographical information has been obtained from contemporary newspapers, interviews, obituaries published in periodicals appearing between 1906 and 1980, the archives of the British Foreign Office, and M. Bamdad, *Tarikh-i Rejal-i Iran* (History of Iranian Statesmen) (Tehran, 1968), 6 vols.

came from the Persian-speaking cities of Tehran, Isfahan, Shiraz, and Kerman.

In addition to al-Motakallemin, the Revolutionary Committee included five important figures in the forthcoming revolution: Sayyid Jamal al-Din Isfahani, an eloquent preacher whose audacious advocacy of secular ideas had caused his expulsion from Isfahan; Hajji Mirza Yahya Dawlatabadi, also a refugee from Isfahan, who was a secret ʿAzali and a prominent leader in the movement to introduce modern education; ʿAli Quli Khan Sardar Asʿad Bakhtiyari, the head of the Ilkhani family, who while in prison after his father's execution in 1882 had translated a seventeenth-century English travelogue, and, after his release in 1896, had opened a modern school in Isfahan so that other khans could study, in his own words, the "advantages of constitutionalism and the disadvantages of despotism."[52] Also active in the committee were two brothers from the aristocratic, but academic, Iskandari family. Their ancestor, a son of Fath ʿAli Shah, had written the famous *Tarikh-i Now* (New History); their grandfather had published many of Dumas's popular novels; their uncle had translated Eugene Sue's dramatic social commentary entitled *Les Mystères du peuples*. The elder brother, Yahya Mirza, who became one of the first martyrs of the revolution, was a senior civil servant and active also in the Society of Humanity. The younger brother, Sulayman Mirza, was an outspoken admirer of Rousseau, Saint-Simon, and Comte. As a pupil at the Dar al-Fonun, he had helped organize the school's first student strike. And as a radical prince who had refused to attend the annual party for members of the royal family, he had been imprisoned briefly by Naser al-Din Shah. His career was to span three generations of radicalism in Iran. He survived the revolution to participate in the Democrat party of 1909-1919, to lead the Socialist party in 1921-1926, and to chair the Tudeh party in 1942.[53]

Whereas the Revolutionary Committee, the Society of Humanity, the Social Democratic party, and the Secret Center were organized by the modern intelligentsia, the Secret Society drew its members predominantly from the traditional middle class. Nazem al-Islam Kermani, a founding member, has described the society's formation in a detailed diary published under the title, *History of the Awakening of Iranians*.[54] Meeting in February 1905, the society formulated a code

[52] Malekzadeh, *Tarikh*, V, 203-204.

[53] The biographies published in Iran invariably overlook the importance of Sulayman Mirza Iskandari. For an informative sketch written by a former colleague, see Z. Qiyami, "Some Reminiscences of Sulayman Iskandari," *Donya*, 11 (Summer 1970), 40-47.

[54] Nazem al-Islam Kermani, *Tarikh-i Bidari-yi Iranian* (Tehran, 1967), 2 vols.

of conduct and a list of demands. The code, taken as a vow on the Koran, promised secrecy, opposition to oppression, respect for the ʿulama, prayers at the end of each session, and acceptance of the Mahdi as the one and only true protector of the society. The list of demands included a national code of justice and a House of Justice (ʿAdalatkhaneh), a survey for the registration of lands, a just tax structure, military reforms, guidelines for the appointment and dismissal of provincial governors, encouragement of internal trade, building of schools, reorganization of the customs, limitation on the power of state administrators, investigation into government salaries and pensions, and the implementation of the holy shariʿa. The program ended with the declaration that if the government accepted these proposals Iran would surpass within one generation the achievements of even Japan.

Having formulated a program, the Secret Society established contact with two of the three important mujtaheds living in the capital: Sayyid ʿAbdullah Behbehani and Sayyid Muhammad Tabatabai. Behbehani, who had earned himself the unsavory reputation of being pro-British by supporting the notorious tobacco concession, now opposed the court partly because of personal animosity toward the ministers and partly because of the increasing Russian influence within the customs administration. Tabatabai, however, enjoyed the reputation of being a moderate reformer, for he had worked closely with al-Afghani, opened one of the first modern schools in Tehran, and sent his son, Muhammad Sadeq Tabatabai, to Istanbul to study European languages. Muhammad Sadeq Tabatabai was to act as the main intermediary between the Secret Society, the bazaar, and the leading ʿulama in Tehran.

Thus Iran in 1905 was rapidly moving toward a political revolution. The traditional middle class, having coalesced into a statewide class, was now economically, ideologically, and politically alienated from the ruling dynasty. The modern intelligentsia, inspired by constitutionalism, nationalism, and secularism, was rejecting the past, questioning the present, and espousing a new vision of the future. Moreover, both the traditional middle class and the modern intelligentsia, despite their differences, were directing their attacks at the same target—the central government. Both were forming their own secret and semisecret organizations, societies, and political parties. Both were aware that the Qajar dynasty was not only financially bankrupt but also morally discredited, administratively ineffective, and, most important of all, militarily incompetent. The country awaited the final push to enter the revolution.

THE REVOLUTION (JUNE 1905-AUGUST 1906)

The final push came from the economic crisis of early 1905. A bad harvest throughout the country and a sudden disruption in the northern trade caused by a cholera epidemic, by the Russo-Japanese War, and by the subsequent revolution in Russia, led to a rapid inflation of food prices within Iran. During the first three months of 1905, the price of sugar rose by 33 percent and that of wheat by as much as 90 percent in Tehran, Tabriz, Rahst, and Mashad.[55] At the same time, the government, finding its customs revenues declining, its food costs rising, and its pleas for new foreign loans rejected, raised tariffs on native merchants and postponed loan repayments to local creditors.[56] This economic crisis promptly triggered three public protests, each more intense than the last, culminating in the revolution of August 1906.

The first protest took the form of a peaceful procession during the religious mourning of Muharram. Some two hundred shopkeepers and moneylenders meekly requested the government to dismiss Monsieur Naus, the Belgian customs administrator, and repay the loans it had borrowed from them. Receiving no reply, the petitioners closed their stores, aroused religious feelings by distributing a photograph of Naus dressed as a mulla at a fancy-dress ball, and proceeded, with a prominent scarf dealer at their head, to the sanctuary of ʿAbdul ʿAzim. Speaking to the correspondent of *Habl al-Matin*, a spokesman for the group summed up the main grievance: "The government must reverse its present policy of helping Russians at the expense of Iranian merchants, creditors, and manufacturers. It must protect our businessmen, even if their products are not yet as good as those of foreign companies. If the present policy continues, our whole economy will be ruined."[57] After two weeks of negotiations, Muzaffar al-Din Shah, anxious to leave for Europe and frightened by inflammatory leaflets, promised that on his return he would dismiss Naus, repay the debts, and establish a committee of merchants within the Ministry of Commerce. But these promises were never fulfilled. The committee received only advisory authority; the debts remained outstanding; and the Russians threatened "necessary measures" if the customs passed out of "secure" hands.[58]

The second protest erupted in December when the governor of

[55] *Habl al-Matin*, 2-23 March 1905.

[56] The shah rejected a Russian offer of a loan of £350,000 with the stipulation that a Russian officer should be placed in charge of the Iranian armed forces. British Minister to the Foreign Office, "Annual Report for 1905," *F.O. 371*/Persia 1906/106.

[57] *Habl al-Matin*, 19 June 1905.

[58] British Minister, "Annual Report for 1905," *F.O. 371*/Persia 1906/106.

Tehran tried to lower sugar prices by bastinadoing two of the leading sugar importers. One of the victims was a highly respected seventy-nine-year-old merchant who had financed the repair of the central bazaar and the building of three mosques in Tehran. He pleaded in vain that the high prices were caused not by hoarding but by the disruptions in Russia. The news of the beatings, according to one eyewitness, flashed like lightening through the bazaars.[59] Stores and workshops closed; crowds congregated in the main mosque; and two thousand merchants and theology students, led by Tabatabai and Behbehani, took sanctuary at ʿAbdul ʿAzim. From there, they sent the government four main demands: replacement of the governor; dismissal of Naus; enforcement of the *shariʿa*; and establishment of a House of Justice. The last was intentionally left vague for future negotiations. The government at first objected that such an institution would destroy all ranks—"even between princes and common grocers"—and told the protestors that if they did not like Iran they should emigrate to "democratic" Germany.[60] But after trying unsuccessfully for a full month to break the general strike in Tehran, the government finally gave in. The victorious protestors, on their return to the city, were greeted by huge crowds shouting "Long Live the Nation of Iran." Nazem al-Islam Kermani commented in his diary that the phrase "Nation of Iran" (Mellat-i Iran) had never been heard before in the streets of Tehran.[61]

The third protests broke out in the month of Muharram, during the summer of 1906. They were caused mainly by the failure of the shah to convene a House of Justice and dismiss Naus, and partly by the rash attempt made by the police to arrest a local preacher for his public denunciation of the government. This denunciation eloquently summarized the main issues of discontent:

O Iranians! O brethren of my beloved country! Until when will this treacherous intoxication keep you slumbering? Enough of this intoxication. Lift up your heads. Open your eyes. Cast a glance around you, and behold how the world has become civilized. All the savages in Africa and negroes in Zanzibar are marching towards civilization, knowledge, labor, and riches. Behold your neighbours (the Russians), who 200 hundred years ago were in a much worse condition than we. Behold them now how they possess everything. In bygone days we had everything, and now all is gone. In the past, others looked on us as a great nation. Now, we are reduced to such a condition that our

[59] H. Qodsi, *Kitab-i Khatirat-i Man ya Tarikh-i Sad Saleh* (Book of My Life or History of One Hundred Years) (Tehran, 1963), I, 99-100.

[60] Malekzadeh, *Tarikh*, II, 104.

[61] Nazem al-Islam Kermani, *Tarikh-i Bidari*, I, 124.

neighbours of the north and south already believe us to be their property and divide our country between themselves when they choose. . . . We have no guns, no army, no secure finances, no proper government, no commercial laws. In the whole of Iran we have not one factory of our own, because our government is a parasite. . . . All this backwardness is due to the autocracy and to injustice and to the want of laws. Also your clergy are at fault, for they preach that life is short and earthly honors are only human vanities. These sermons lead you away from this world into submission, slavery, and ignorance. The Monarchs, at the same time, despoil you with their power over your property, your freedom, and your rights. And with all this comes the strangers who receive from you all your money, and instead furnish you with green, blue, and red cloth, gaudy glassware, and luxury furniture. These are the causes of your misery, and the great luxury of Monarchs, some clerics, and the foreigners.[62]

The arrests of the preacher and other outspoken opponents prompted the secret societies to circulate angry broadsheets, and an emotional crowd of theology students to converge upon the city police station. In the ensuing melée, the police shot dead one of the demonstrating students who happened to be a sayyid. On the subsequent morning, thousands of students, shopkeepers, and guild members—many of them wearing white sheets as a sign of their willingness to die in a religious crusade—proceeded with the sayyid's body from the main bazaar to a public funeral in the central mosque. Outside the mosque, however, they were intercepted by Cossacks. The collision was brief but bloody: twenty-two lost their lives and over one hundred suffered injuries.[63] A river of blood now divided the court from the country. From that point on, some members of the ʿulama openly compared the Qajars to the notorious Yazid, the Sunni leader who had killed the Shiʿi martyr Imam Hussein.

The opposition reacted to the violence by organizing two large-scale demonstrations. Tabatabai, Behbehani, and other religious notables—with the exception of the state-appointed imam jomʿeh—led their families, retainers, and two thousand theology students to the holy city of Qum ninety miles south of Tehran. Even the ultraconservative but highly respected mujtahed Sayyid Shaykh Fazallah Nouri joined the protest. From Qum, the religious leaders proclaimed that the capital would be left without spiritual guidance—and consequently without judicial actions and legal transactions—until the shah fulfilled his earlier promises. The ʿulama had gone on strike.

[62] British Minister to the Foreign Office, "Translation of the Controversial Speech," *F.O. 371*/Persia 1907/34-301.

[63] *Habl al-Matin*, 28 September 1906. Nazem al-Islam Kermani claimed that over one hundred fifty were killed. See *Tarikh-i Bidari*, I, 246.

Meanwhile, two merchants, one of whom was a member of the Secret Society, approached the British representatives at their summer grounds in the village of Gulak a few miles north of Tehran. The British legation, in a memorandum to London, explained the events:

After the shootings, it appeared as if the Government had won the day. The town was in the hands of the troops. The popular leaders had fled. The bazaars were in the occupation of the soldiers. And there appeared to be no place of refuge. Under these circumstances the popular party had recourse to an expedient sanctified by old, and, indeed, immemorial custom—the rule of *bast*. It was resolved, failing all other resources, to adopt this expediency. . . . Two persons called at the Legation at Gulak and asked whether, in case the people took *bast* in the British Legation, the Chargé d'Affaires would invoke the aid of the military to remove them. Mr. Grant Duff expressed that he hoped that they would not have recourse to such an expedient, but he said it was not in his power, in view of the acknowledged custom in Persia, to use force if they came. . . . The following evening, fifty merchants and mullas appeared in the Legation and took up their quarters for the night. Their numbers gradually increased, and soon there were 14,000 persons in the Legation garden.[64]

The crowd, drawn predominantly from the bazaar, was organized by a committee of guild elders. This committee allocated space to the various guilds; one visitor reported that he saw more than five hundred tents, "for all the guilds, even the cobblers, walnut sellers, and tinkers, each had one tent."[65] The committee enforced discipline to safeguard property: the legation later reported that almost nothing had been damaged "although every semblance of a flower-bed had been trampled out of existence and the trees still bear pious inscriptions cut in the bark."[66] It organized women's demonstrations outside the royal palace and the legation. It also controlled the entry of new arrivals into the British grounds, admitting after the first week only students and faculty from the Dar al-Fonun and the schools of agriculture and political science. These new arrivals, according to Nazem al-Islam Kermani, converted the legation into "one vast open-air school of political science" by giving lectures on European constitutional systems and expressing ideas that had been too dangerous to express before in Iran.[67] According to another eyewitness, some of the students from

[64] Great Britain, *Correspondence Respecting the Affairs of Persia* (London, 1909), vol. I, no. 1, pp. 3-4.

[65] A. Kasravi, *Tarikh-i Mashruteh-i Iran* (History of the Iranian Constitution) (Tehran, 1961), p. 110.

[66] Great Britain, Correspondence, vol. I, no. 1, p. 4.

[67] Nezam al-Islam Kermani, *Tarikh-i Bidari*, p. 274.

the Dar-al-Fonun lectured even on the advantages of the republican form of government.[68] The committee, moreover, took the precaution of raising money from wealthy merchants to help the poorer workers who could not afford a prolonged strike. One participant wrote in his memoirs,

I clearly remember the day when we heard that the reactionaries were busy sowing discontent among the junior carpenters and sawyers. The former, angry at having been taken away from their work, demanded to know what they had to gain from the whole venture. The latter, being illiterate and irrational, were reluctant to accept any logical arguments. If these two irresponsible groups had walked out, our whole movement would have suffered. Fortunately, we persuaded them to remain in *bast*.[69]

Finally the committee, on the advice of modern educated colleagues, demanded from the court not just a House of Justice but a Constituent National Assembly.

At first the court dismissed the protestors as "a bunch of traitors hired by the British."[70] But confronted by a sustained general strike in Tehran and a flood of telegrams from the provinces in support of the protestors, it offered the less democratic-sounding "Islamic Assembly." But again confronted by the nonnegotiable demand for a National Assembly (Majles-i Melli), by telegrams from Baku and Tiflis threatening to send armed volunteers, by the widening gap between conservatives and moderates within the government, and by the "fatal announcement" that even the Cossacks were preparing to defect, the court eventually capitulated.[71] On August 5—three weeks after the first protestors took refuge in the legation—Muzaffar al-Din Shah appointed Mushir al-Dawleh, a senior official with liberal views, as his prime minister, and signed a proclamation convening a Constituent National Assembly.[72] The revolution was over; but the struggle for a constitution had only just begun.

[68] A. Tafresh-Husseini, *Ruznameh-i Akhbar-i Mashrutiyat* (A Diary of the Constitution) (Tehran, 1972), p. 40.

[69] M. Heravi-Khurasani, *Tarikh-i Paydayesh-i Mashrutiyat-i Iran* (History of the Genesis of the Iranian Constitution) (Tehran, 1953), p. 50.

[70] Recounted by Shaykh Yousef, *Parliamentary Proceedings*, 1st Majlis, p. 351.

[71] Many liberals suspected that the court intended to bar them from such an "Islamic Assembly" by denouncing them as "heretics"; see Nazem al-Islam Kermani, *Tarikh-i Bidari*, I, 329, 359. Most liberals in the court had been educated in the Dar al-Fonun; see H. Sayyah, *Khatirat-i Sayyah* (The Memoirs of Sayyah) (Tehran, 1966), pp. 565-66. Great Britain, *Correspondence*, vol. I, no. 1, p. 4.

[72] Mirza Nasrallah Khan, later titled Mushir al-Dawleh, had served in missions abroad and had translated law books from Russian and French.

THE STRUGGLE FOR THE CONSTITUTION (AUGUST 1906-JUNE 1908)

The Constituent Assembly convened hurriedly in Tehran to formulate an electoral law for the forthcoming National Assembly. The delegates were mostly merchants, clergymen, and guild elders from the Tehran bazaar. Not surprisingly, the electoral law reflected their social and regional backgrounds.[73] The electorate was divided into the following six "classes" (tabaqat): princes and Qajars; ʿulama and theology students; nobles (aʿyan) and notables (ashraf); merchants with a "definite place of business"; landowners with at least 1,000 tomans of property; and craftsmen-tradesmen from "recognized guilds" and with a shop whose rent was equivalent to at least the "average rent of the locality." The electorate was further divided into 156 constituencies; Tehran obtained 60 seats; the provinces together received only 96. Even Azerbaijan, with its large population, was allocated merely 12 seats. In addition, the parliamentary candidates were required to know how to speak, read, and write Persian. The elections in the provinces were to be carried out in two stages: each "class" in every district was to choose one delegate to the provincial capital; these delegates, in turn, were to nominate the provincial representatives to the National Assembly. The elections in Tehran, on the other hand, were to be carried out in one stage: the Qajars and princes would send four deputies; the landowners ten; the clergy and theology students four; the merchants ten; and the guilds as many as thirty-two. Before the elections, the guild elders were to group the 103 "recognized" guilds in Tehran into thirty-two related occupations, and allocate one seat to each of the thirty-two groups. Some low-paid occupations, such as porters and camel-drivers, were excluded from the electorate.[74]

These events of the summer—the convening of the Constituent Assembly and now the elections for the National Assembly—were catalysts for the development of political organizations and radical newspapers throughout the country. In the provincial capitals, the local populations, led by the bazaar people, rushed to form regional assemblies independent of, and invariably opposed to, the provincial governors. In the capital, over thirty proconstitutional societies (anjumans) appeared on the political arena. Some, such as the Society of Guilds (Asnaf), Society of Scribes (Mustawfian), and the Society of Theology Students (Taleb), were professional associations. Others, for

[73] Malekzadeh, Tarikh, II, 180. The translations of the constitutional laws have been reprinted by E. Browne, The Persian Revolution of 1905-1909 (London, 1910), pp. 354-400.

[74] Habl al-Matin, 12 November 1906.

example the Society of Azerbaijanis, the Society of Armenians, the Society of Jews, the Society of Zoroastrians, and the Society of Southern Iranians, were ethnic clubs.[75] Of all the anjumans, the most active and the largest, with a membership of three thousand, was the Society of Azerbaijanis. It was organized by merchants from Tabriz and a young electrical engineer from the Caucasus named Haydar Khan ʿAmu ʿUghli. Born into a family of doctors in Iranian Azerbaijan, Haydar Khan had been educated in Russian Azerbaijan, had joined the Russian Social Democratic party and, together with his elder brother and Narim Narimanov, had founded the Iranian SDP in Baku. While employed briefly as the manager of an electrical plant in Mashad, Haydar Khan had tried unsuccessfully to organize a branch of the SDP. As he wrote in his memoirs, he could not find recruits in the "immature" environment of Mashad.[76] Moreover, when the local ʿulama, feuding with the owner of the electrical plant, incited a religious mob to burn down the factory as a "heretical innovation," Haydar Khan moved on to Tehran, helped organize the Society of Azerbaijanis, and established within it the SDP's first cell inside Iran.[77]

The press was equally active. The number of papers and journals published within Iran jumped from six on the eve of the revolution to over one hundred during the ten months after the Constituent Assembly. Many carried such optimistic, nationalistic, and radical titles as *Taraqqi* (Progress), *Bidari* (Awakening), *Vatan* (Fatherland), *Adamiyat* (Humanity), *Ittihad* (Unity), *Umid* (Hope), and *ʿAsr-i Now* (The New Age). The most outspoken and popular were written by members of the secret organizations. Mirza Reza Tarbiyat and Sayyid Muhammad Shabistari, members of the Secret Center in Tabriz, edited the journals *Azad* (Free) and *Mujahed* (Freedom Fighter). Nazem al-Islam Kermani, of the Secret Society in Tehran, came out with *Nida-yi Vatan* (Voice of the Fatherland). Five members of the Revolutionary Committee, including Sulayman Iskandari, edited popular newspapers named *Huquq* (Rights), *Sur-i Israfil* (Trumpet Call of Israfil), *Musavat* (Equality), and *Ruh al-Qods* (Holy Spirit). It seemed that the intellectuals, after years of enforced silence, were now rushing to the printing presses to pour out all their newly acquired political ideas.

It was in the midst of this intense activity that the National Assembly opened in October. Predictably, the important role of the traditional middle class was reflected in the social composition of the assembly: 26 percent of the deputies were guild elders, 20 percent clergymen,

[75] *Habl al-Matin*, 4 August 1907.
[76] ʿA. Iqbal, "Haydar Khan," *Yadgar*, 3:4-5 (1946), 61-80.
[77] ʿA. Amir-Khizi, "Haydar Khan," *Donya*, 11 (Summer 1971), 89-96; Reza Rusta, "Haydar Khan," *Donya*, 3 (Spring 1973), 6-9.

and 15 percent merchants.[78] Its political complexion, also predictably, was apparent in the three loose but distinct groups (*maslak*) that gradually developed: the Royalists (Mostabed), the Moderates (Mo'tadel), and the Liberals (Azadikhaw). The Royalists, few in number and unpopular in the chamber, tended to stay away from the proceedings: they were drawn mostly from the ranks of princes, notables, and landowners. The Moderates, who formed the vast majority of the assembly, were headed by two wealthy merchants: Muhammad 'Ali Shalfurush (Scarf dealer), the leader of the peaceful procession to 'Abdul 'Azim in June 1905; and Amin al-Zarb, a former farmer of the royal mint and the main financier of the bast in the British legation, who, despite heavy exactions by Naser al-Din Shah, was still one of the wealthiest men in Iran. The Moderates also received valuable support from Tabatabai and Behbehani, who, although not actual deputies, frequently participated in parliamentary debates.

Whereas the Moderates drew their support mainly from the propertied middle class, the Liberals represented predominantly the intelligentsia. Led by Taqizadeh from Tabriz and Yahya Iskandari from Tehran, the Liberals advocated extensive social and economic as well as political reforms. Most of their twenty-one deputies belonged to the Revolutionary Committee, the Society of Humanity, or the Ganjeh-i Fonun. Some were elected by the Shaykhi community in Tabriz; some by the guilds in Tehran; and some by the assembly itself to fill vacancies caused by deaths and resignations. What the Liberals lacked in quantity, they made up in quality; for their determination to obtain a written constitution and their knowledge of Western constitutions made them, in the words of Edward Browne, the "salt" of the whole assembly.[79] Although the Liberals hoped for extensive reforms, even secular reforms, they were willing to soft-pedal their radicalism, for the time being, to work together with the Moderates to draft a satisfactory constitution.

The deputies began to draft the constitution by first safeguarding the role of Parliament. In a document that was later to be known as the Fundamental Laws, the National Assembly was granted extensive powers as "the representative of the whole People." It had "the right in all questions to propose any measure that it regards as conducive to the well-being of the Government and the People." It had final determination over all laws, decrees, budgets, treaties, loans, monopolies, and concessions. It was to hold sessions lasting two years, during

[78] Z. Shaji'i, *Nemayandegan-i Majles-i Shawra-yi Melli dar Bist-u-Yek Dawreh-i Qanunguzari* (Members of the National Consultative Assembly during Twenty-one Legislative Sessions) (Tehran, 1965), p. 176.

[79] Browne, *The Persian Revolution*, p. 146.

which period its members could not be arrested without the permission of the assembly. As a concession to the court, the shah was given the authority to nominate thirty senators to an Upper House of sixty senators. But the Lower House reserved the right to define at a later date the exact role of this Upper House. Having unanimously acclaimed the document, the deputies rushed it to the shah, who was on his deathbed. The shah, at the urging of his spiritual advisers and the more moderate of his ministers, ratified the Fundamental Laws on December 30, only five days before his death.

Muhammad ʿAli Shah ascended the throne determined to rule less like his father Muzaffar al-Din Shah and more like his grandfather Naser al-Din Shah. He slighted the deputies by not inviting them to his coronation. He tried, unsuccessfully, to retain Naus and to negotiate a new loan from Britain and Russia. He encouraged his ministers to ignore the National Assembly, and ordered his governors to disregard the provincial councils. He replaced Mushir al-Dawleh, the moderate premier, with Amin al-Sultan, a former conservative premier who now, as a result of a recent visit to Japan, argued that reforms could not be carried out without a strong, and if necessary an autocratic, central government. Muhammad ʿAli Shah also tried to weaken the opposition by reviving communal conflicts—especially between Shaykhis and Mutasharʿis in Tabriz, Karimkhanis and Mutasharʿis in Kerman, Muslims and Zoroastrians in Yazd, Persians and Azeris in Tehran, Haydaris and Niʿmatis in Qazvin, Shustar, Shiraz, and Ardabel.

But the main struggle between shah and National Assembly evolved around the future structure of government. The deputies, working with a translation of the Belgian constitution, formulated a parliamentary system of government. Their finished document, entitled the Supplementary Fundamental Laws, contained two main sections. The first was a "bill of rights" guaranteeing each citizen equality before the law, protection of life, property, and honor, safeguards from arbitrary arrest, and freedom to publish newspapers and to organize associations. The second section, while accepting the separation of powers in principle, concentrated power in the legislative branch at the expense of the executive. The legislature now obtained, in addition to the powers given to it earlier, the authority to appoint, investigate, and dismiss premiers, ministers, and cabinets, to judge ministers for "delinquencies," and to approve annually all military expenditures.

The executive, on the other hand, was declared to "appertain" to the shah but to be carried out by the ministers. The shah was to take his oath of office before the deputies. His court budgets had to be approved by the National Assembly. His sons, brothers, and uncles were barred from the cabinet. His person was vested with the nominal command of the armed forces. His sovereignty was described to be derived not from God but the people: "The sovereignty is a trust confided (as a Divine gift) by the People to the person of the King." His ministers were responsible to parliament only, and could not "divest themselves of their responsibility by pleading verbal or written orders from the monarch." "If the National Assembly shall, by an absolute majority, declare itself dissatisfied with the cabinet or with one particular minister, that cabinet or minister shall resign their or his ministerial functions." The shah, in fact, retained only one important source of power: the prerogative to appoint half of the Senate. But even this turned out to be a hollow privilege: no Senate was convened for another forty-three years.

The deputies, in adopting the Belgian constitution, made two major adaptions to suit local conditions. They recognized the existence of the provincial councils by endowing them with the authority to "exercise free supervision over all reforms connected with the public interest provided that they observe the limitations prescribe by the law." And they acknowledged in a number of clauses the importance of religion in general and of the religious leaders in particular. The judicial branch was divided into civil tribunals and ecclesiastical courts with extensive jurisdiction over religious laws. The Twelver doctrine of Shi'ism was declared to be the official religion of Iran. Only Muslims could be appointed as cabinet ministers. The executive undertook the duty of banning "heretical" organizations and publications. And a "supreme committee" of mujtaheds was to scrutinize all bills introduced into parliament to ensure that no law contradicted the shari'a. This committee, comprising at least five members, was to be elected by the deputies from a list of twenty submitted by the 'ulama. The committee would sit until "the appearance of the Mahdi (May God Hasten His Glad Advent)." The traditional gospel of Shi'ism had been incorporated into a modern structure of government derived from Montesquieu. The spirit of society, to paraphrase Montesquieu, had helped formulate the laws of the constitution.

The shah, seeing the demise of all royal authority, refused to ratify the Supplementary Fundamental Laws. Instead he denounced four outspoken leaders of the opposition—Malek al-Motakallemin, Jamal al-Din, Mirza Jahanger Khan of the paper *Sur-i Israfil*, and Muhammad Reza Shirazi of *Mosavat*—as "heretical Babis" and "republican subversives." He proclaimed that as a good Muslim he could accept the Islamic term *mashru'* (lawful) but not the alien concept *mashrut* (constitutional).[80] In the same breath, he waxed enthusiastic for the German constitution and proposed that the head of state should appoint all ministers, including the war minister, enjoy real as well as nominal command of the armed forces, and retain personal control over 10,000 bodyguards.

The counterproposals initiated public protests in the main cities, especially in Tehran, Tabriz, Isfahan, Shiraz, Mashad, Enzeli, Kermanshah, Kerman, and Rasht. At Kermanshah, for example, the British consul reported that "the whole of the trades and employment of the bazaar, down to the porters, went into *bast* in the telegraph office."[81] At Tabriz, a crowd of 20,000 vowed to remain on strike and even threatened to "separate Azerbaijan from the rest of the country unless the constitution was immediately ratified." Some of the telegrams from Tabriz to the shah were signed threateningly "mellat-i Azerbaijan."[82] At Tehran, the various associations and clubs formed a Central Society (Anjuman-i Markazi), organized a general strike in the bazaar and in the government bureaucracy, held a mass meeting of over 50,000, and mobilized 3,000 armed volunteers (mostly from the Society of Azerbaijanis) for the defense of the National Assembly. Meanwhile, a moneylender from Tabriz, probably with connections to Haydar Khan's cell of Social Democrats, assassinated premier Amin al-Sultan and promptly committed suicide outside the parliament building. Some 100,000 mourners, according to a British eyewitness, assembled to pay homage to the dead assassin and demonstrate support for the revolution.[83]

The shah, shaken by the assassination and the mass demonstration, retreated. As the same eyewitness reported: "The Shah with his unarmed, unpaid, ragged, starving soldiers, what else can he do in face of the menace of a general strike and public riots?"[84] He sent his princes to parliament to take the oath of allegiance to the constitution. He appointed Naser al-Mulk, an Oxford-educated and liberal-minded nobleman, as prime minister. The shah himself appeared meekly before the National Assembly, vowing to respect the constitution, and placing the royal seal upon the Supplementary Fundamental Laws. To prove his sincerity, he sought and obtained admission into the Society of Humanity for himself and an entourage of courtiers. By

---

[80] For a discussion of these two terms, see Taqizadeh, "The First National Assembly," *Ittila'at-i Mahaneh*, 5 (July-August 1954), 3-6.

[81] Great Britain, *Correspondence*, vol. 1, no. 1, p. 27.

[82] Kasravi, *Tarikh-i Mashruteh-i Iran*, pp. 305, 519.

[83] Browne, *The Persian Revolution*, p. 153.

[84] Ibid., p. 137.

early 1908, courtiers, princes, and senior civil servants formed over half of the society's 314 members.[85] The shah, who had intended to perpetuate the Qajar system of despotism, had sworn to accept Auguste Comte's concepts of equality, fraternity, legality, and modernity. For the time being, the constitution had been secured.

THE CIVIL WAR (JUNE 1908-JULY 1909)

The ancien régime had collapsed without a voice being raised on its behalf. Wealthy merchants and street peddlers, wholesale dealers and small shopkeepers, seminary students and Dar al-Fonun graduates, clergymen and civil servants, rising commercial companies and declining craft guilds, Muslims and non-Muslims, Persians and non-Persians, Haydaris and Ni'matis, Shaykhis and Mutashar'is, Sunnis and Shi'is, bazaaris in the capital and bazaaris in the provinces, all had joined together to batter down the traditional power structure. The Moderate group in parliament, by electing a committee of Western-educated intellectuals to adapt the Belgian constitution, acknowledged the debt of the traditional middle class to the modern intelligentsia. Malekzadeh of the Revolutionary Committee, in turn, recognized the debt of the modern intelligentsia to the traditional middle class when he admitted in his history of the revolution that without the participation of the bazaars the destruction of the old order would have been unthinkable. And a Marxist writer, commenting years later on the anarchist theory of insurrection, observed that the Iranian revolution, with its successful use of peaceful processions, mass meetings, and general strikes, was unique in the annals of bourgeois revolutions. If there was any section of the population that supported the court, it expressed itself neither in word nor in deed. Even the aged and conservative khans of the Qajar tribe accepted the hopeless situation and advised the shah in October 1907 to ratify the constitution.[86]

The royalist position gradually improved, however, as the Liberals, dizzy with success, pressed ahead for additional reforms—especially for a balanced budget and a more representative electoral system. Their budget proposals, which gained the support of the Moderates and thus the approval of the National Assembly, cut court expenses, reduced royal pensions and salaries, eliminated many tuyuls (tax farms), and abolished tasirs (conversions) that permitted landlords to pay their

---

[85] Ra'in, *Faramushkhaneh*, I, 677-91.

[86] Malekzadeh, *Tarikh*, II, 28; H. Arsanjani, "Anarchism in Iran," *Darya*, 17 (July 1944); British Minister to the Foreign Office, "Annual Report for 1908," *F.O. 371/ Persia 1910/956-2836*.

assessments in cash rather than in kind—but at conversion rates pre-dating the sharp rise in prices.[87] Their bill for electoral reform, which antagonized the Moderates and thus did not pass into law, proposed to lower the property qualification, redistribute seats in favor of the provincial cities, and establish representation for the religious mi-norities.[88] One deputy warned that universal adult male suffrage would be dangerous in a society in which the vast majority was both poor and illiterate. Another protested that special representation to the religious minorities would violate the fundamentals of the shari'a. Yet another denounced the bill as the heretical scheme of foreign agitators: "Since we have treated our minorities so well for over one thousand years, I don't understand who else can be behind such an outrageous demand."

The radicals outside parliament, meanwhile, initiated a campaign for secular reforms. The paper *Sur-i Israfil* instigated a major scandal by suggesting that the 'ulama should keep their hands out of politics and by satirizing the mullas as "money grabbers" who concealed their slimy interests with sublime sermons.[89] This was the first anticlerical article to be published in Iran, but it was not to be the last. *Habl al-Matin* ridiculed the authors of the constitution for having instituted a supreme committee to judge the religious legitimacy of all bills introduced into the National Assembly: "This makes as little sense as having a supreme committee of five merchants to scrutinize the com-mercial validity of all laws deliberated by the people's representatives." The same paper started another uproar when it placed the whole blame for the decline of the Middle East on clerical ignorance, su-perstitions, petty-mindedness, obscurantism, dogmatism, and insist-ent meddling in politics.[90] The Iskandari family, at the same time, created a scandal by founding a school for girls and a Society for Women. Conservative deputies, including some Moderates, took turns to denounce such organizations as atheistic, heretical, and anti-Is-lamic.[91] Cautious Liberals pleaded that women's organizations could not be considered anti-Islamic since they had existed throughout Is-lamic history. More daring Liberals argued that the secular laws (*qan-*

[87] A. Navai'i, "The Budget in the First National Assembly," *Ittila'at-i Mahaneh*, 1 (October-November 1948), 8-19.

[88] For the debates on electoral reform, see *Parliamentary Proceedings*, 1st Majles, pp. 188-204, 500-502.

[89] "Charivari," *Sur-i Israfil*, 13 February 1907.

[90] "The Senate of the 'Ulama," *Habl al-Matin*, 18 June 1907; "Defence," *Habl al-Matin*, 1 August 1907.

[91] For a debate on the women's question, see *Parliamentary Proceedings*, 1st Majles, pp. 483-85, 530-32.

uns) of the state should be separate from the religious laws (shari'a) of the country.

The intelligentsia, moreover, alienated a large number of court employees by drafting an austerity budget. They threatened not only the luxury of a few courtiers, but also the livelihood of the thousands employed in the royal palace with its extensive gardens, stables, kitchens, storehouses, armories, and workshops. A day after the budget was passed, the Household Treasury, which unlike the State Treasury enjoyed the reputation of scrupulously honoring all its commitments, informed the palace employees that it could no longer pay their regular salaries and wages.[92]

What was worse, these measures occurred at a time of continuing bad harvest and increasing food prices.[93] Unwilling to lower taxes because of their determination to balance the budget, and at the same time reluctant to control prices because of their inclination toward laissez-faire economics, the deputies became obvious targets for lower-class discontent. As the British minister reported in October 1907, "the majlis is being attacked on several sides. The whole Court is hostile, and the population of the town is discontented because bread is as dear as ever." A month later, the same minister noted that the "reactionaries" were quietly recruiting followers from the "city's lower classes."[94] The court had finally broken through its political isolation.

The royalists appeared in the streets in late December, as soon as they had won over Shaykh Fazallah Nouri, the highly respected but ultraconservative mujtahed who had joined Behbehani and Tabatabai during the protests of 1906. Now frightened off by the secular radicals, Shaykh Fazallah helped the royalist imam jom'eh of Tehran to form a conservative organization named the Society of Muhammad, and he called upon all devout Muslims to gather in the large Cannon Square to defend the shari'a from the "heathen" constitutionalists. So many heeded the call that, in the words of one hostile eyewitness, "the reactionaries packed the expansive square to full capacity."[95] The crowd was formed of diverse groups: mullas and theology students, especially from Shaykh Fazallah's seminary; courtiers and retainers, particularly armed lutis; peasants from the royal estates in Veramin near Tehran; unskilled workers and the poorest of the poor from the Tehran bazaar; and thousands of craftsmen, muleteers, servants, and

[92] Kasravi, *Tarikh-i Mashruteh-i Iran*, pp. 487-88.
[93] Nazem al-Islam Kermani, *Tarikh-i Bidari*, I, 234.
[94] Great Britain, *Correspondence*, vol. I, no. 1, pp. 27, 14.
[95] Qodsi, *Kitib-i Khatirat-i Man*, I, 157.

footmen employed in the "miniature economy" of the royal palace.[96] These pampered court lackeys, Malekzadeh wrote, were such fanatical reactionaries that the terms "groom mentality" and "footman's intelligence" became expressions of common abuse.[97] At the meeting, Shaykh Fazlallah denounced the concept of equality as an alien heresy, traced the contemporary problems of instability, immorality, and ideological insecurity to the subversive influence of that "atheist Armenian Malkum," and declared that the Majles Liberals, like the French Jacobins, were paving the way for socialism, anarchism, and nihilism.[98] Aroused by these words, the crowd attacked any passerby who happened to be wearing the short European-styled hat as an "atheistic constitutionalist," and prepared to march on the National Assembly.[99]

The march had to be called off in face of massive public support for the National Assembly, however. When the Society of Guilds organized a general strike in the bazaar in support of the constitution, over 100,000 citizens, including some 7,000 armed volunteers from the Society of Azerbaijanis and the Society of College Graduates, rushed to defend the National Assembly. A British visitor described the scene for Edward Browne:

It is typical of the movement that the rallying-point of the people should be the House of Parliament and the Mosque, standing side by side. In and around these two buildings gathered the strongest throng which has ever been seen fighting the old, old battle against the powers of tyranny and darkness. Europeanized young men with white collars, white-turbaned *mullas*, Sayyids with the green and blue insignia of their holy descent, the *kulah-namadis* (felt-capped peasants and workmen), the brown *'abas* (cloaks) of the humble tradesfolk;—all in whose hearts glowed the sacred fire gathered there to do battle in the cause of freedom. Who does not instinctively remember Carlyle's fiery chapter on the Bastille day?[100]

The shah promptly retreated. He asked his adherents to disperse, agreed to transfer the Cossack Brigade to the War Ministry, promised to banish the lutis and courtiers involved in the demonstration, and again took an oath of allegiance to the constitution. He had failed to undo the revolution; but he had succeeded in rallying some support against it.

A number of factors further improved the royalist position during

[96] Great Britain, *Correspondence*, vol. I, no. 1, p. 109; Heravi-Khurasani, *Tarikh-i Paydayesh*, p. 126.

[97] Malekzadeh, *Tarikh*, IV, 59.

[98] Shaykh Fazlallah, "A Proclamation to the Devout," reprinted by Nazem al-Islam Kermani, *Tarikh-i Bidari*, I, 324.

[99] "Charivari," *Sur-i Israfil*, 30 December 1907.

[100] Browne, *The Persian Revolution*, p. 164.

the first half of 1908. The Anglo-Russian Agreement of 1907, with its implicit partition of Iran into zones of influence, inevitably de-moralized many constitutionalists. One of the magnates who was threatened by the budget advanced the monarch a sum of £10,000; much of the loan was immediately distributed as a special bonus to the Cossacks. Rahim Khan, the chief of the Shahsaven tribes in Azerbaijan, declared his allegiance to the shah. And Amir Mofakham, the head of the Hajji Ilkhani Bakhtiyaris and the husband of a Qajar princess, also declared for the shah and arrived in Tehran with a contingent of his own tribesmen. The monarch now enjoyed armed strength as well as some public support.

The shah struck in June. The Cossack Brigade, commanded by its Russian colonel named Liakhoff, bombarded the lightly armed vol-unteers, and, after considerable bloodshed, broke their resistance; according to British estimates, over 250 were killed in the fighting.[101] The tribal contingents, meanwhile, occupied the central telegraph office, and a large mob, similar to that of the Cannon Square dem-onstration, looted the National Assembly, the headquarters of various societies, and the homes of prominent constitutionalists. Nazem al-Islam Kermani noted in his journal that the "common people" at the time of the coup tended to sympathize with the court. Malekzadeh admitted grudgingly that Shaykh Fazlallah had had considerable effect on the uneducated masses. And Malek al-Shua'ra Bahar, a leading poet and a participant in the revolution, wrote years later: "During the upheavals, the upper class and the lower classes supported des-potism. Only the middle class remained true to constitutionalism."[102]

The shah, having carried through a successful coup d'état, declared martial law, appointed Colonel Liakhoff military governor of Tehran, banned all societies and public meetings, including passion plays, dis-solved the National Assembly, and seized thirty-nine of his opponents who had failed to escape or take sanctuary in the Ottoman embassy. These prisoners, who included some of the leading figures in the constitutional movement, were dealt with in diverse ways: Malek al-Motakallemin and Jahanger Khan, the editor of *Sur-i Israfil*, were strangled; Qazi Qazvini, a liberal high court judge, and Sultan al-'Ulama, the editor of *Ruh al-Qods*, were poisoned; Sayyid Hajji Ibra-him Aqa, a Liberal deputy from Tabriz, was killed while trying to escape; Yahya Mirza Iskandari was tortured and subsequently died;

---

[101] British Minister to the Foreign Office, "Annual Report for 1908," *F.O. 371*/Persia 1909/956-2836.

[102] Nazem al-Islam Kermani, *Tarikh-i Bidari*, I, 363; Malekzadeh, *Tarikh*, III, 55; Malek al-Shua'ra Bahar, *Tarikh-i Ahzab-i Siyasi-yi Iran* (History of Political Parties in Iran) (Tehran, 1944), p. 2.

Jamal al-Din Isfahani was banished to Hamadan, where he died under suspicious circumstances; and Behbehani as well as Tabatabai were placed under house arrest. Meanwhile, nineteen others were given prison sentences. These included four merchants, one tobacconist, one tailor, two former army officers, one prince, two journalists, six civil servants, and two household servants belonging to one of the princely prisoners.[103]

The royalists had seized Tehran; but Tehran was not the whole of Iran. In the past such a seizure could have been decisive; now it proved to be merely deceptive. Three of the five main mujtaheds in Karbala and Najaf promptly supported the constitution and bluntly denounced the shah: "Allah has cursed tyrants. You may be victorious for the moment, but you will not remain so for long."[104] Armed volunteers rose in defense of the revolution first in Tabriz, later in Isfahan and Rasht, and eventually in most other cities, including Tehran. In the past the capital had determined the course of events in the provinces. Now the provinces determined the course of events in the capital.

The drama of the civil war took place mostly in Tabriz. The Provincial Council, receiving news of the coup, promptly expelled its half-hearted members, and, in the absence of the National Assembly, declared itself the Provisional Government of Azerbaijan. The Society of Guilds organized another general strike in the central bazaar. The shaykh al-islam, who, in accordance with local custom, was a Shaykhi, demanded an immediate reconvening of Parliament. The Secret Center, merging with a group of Armenian intellectuals, voted to build a "proletarian organization" separate from the "democratic movement," formalized its ties with the Social Democrats in Baku, and received from the Caucasus some one hundred armed volunteers.[105] And the city volunteers, who, as one eyewitness described, were mostly from the educated classes in the Shaykhi wards, rallied behind two local heroes—Sattar Khan and Baqer Khan.[106] Sattar Khan, a former luti and horse dealer, was the kadkhuda in the main Shaykhi ward

[103] For the treatment of the thirty-nine prisoners, see Malekzadeh, *Tarikh*, IV, 101-63; Kasravi, *Tarikhi Mashruteh-i Iran*, pp. 662-65; S. Vahidniya, "Concerning the Constitutional Revolution," *Vahid*, 10 (June 1952), pp. 56-57.

[104] Malekzadeh, *Tarikh*, IV, 174-75.

[105] The Tabriz branch of the Social Democratic party began with thirty members. These members concentrated their activities in the Shaykhi wards, in the Armenian community, and in the local currier factory. See "Concerning the Social Democrats of Tabriz," *Donya*, 22 (Winter 1961), 74-79.

[106] I. Amir-Khizi, *Qiyam-i Azerbaijan va Sattar Khan* (The Uprising of Azerbaijan and Sattar Khan) (Tabriz, 1960), p. 410.

of Amir-Khizi.[107] Baqer Khan, a master bricklayer and also a luti, was a kadkhuda in the neighboring Shaykhi ward of Khiaban.

While the constitutionalists took over the middle-class Shaykhi and Armenian wards of Amir-Khizi, Khiaban, and Maralan, the royalists, headed by the local imam jom'eh and reinforced by Shahsaven tribesmen, barricaded themselves in the lower-class Mutashar'i wards of Sarkhab and Davachi. Isma'il Amir-Khizi, one of the armed fighters, wrote in his memoirs that the conservative mullas had duped the common people into hating the liberals as apostates, unbelievers, and dangerous atheists.[108] Kasravi, also an eyewitness of the civil war in Tabriz, commented:

In Tabriz during the constitutional revolution, as in Paris during the French Revolution, the sans-culottes and the propertyless poor reared their heads. The driving force of these men was toward anarchy. First to overthrow the despotic power of the court, then to turn against the rich and the propertied classes. It was with the backing of such men that Danton and Robespierre rose to power. In Tabriz no Dantons and Robespierres appeared, but if they had we would have had our own "reign of terror." Instead we lived through a period of chaos, instability, and fear.[109]

The British consul reported at the same time that the Provincial Council, unable to prevent inflation and reactionary oratory, feared a popular uprising. One member of the council warned his colleagues that the mob would be no respector of persons. The slums had turned into hotbeds of reaction; the middle-class districts had become the bastions of the revolution.[110]

During the subsequent struggle, the constitutionalists, using hand grenades imported from the Caucasus, broke through the enemy lines, blew up their strongholds, and, after heavy losses, routed their

[107] N. Hamadani, *Pedaram Sattar Khan* (My Father Sattar Khan) (Tehran, 1970).

[108] Amir-Khizi, *Qiyam*, p. 169.

[109] Kasravi, *Tarikh-i Mashruteh-i Iran*, p. 355.

[110] Great Britain, *Correspondence*, vol. I, no. 2, pp. 97-99. The revolutionary role of the middle class was reflected in the list of forty-four constitutionalists who were executed during 1911 by the Russians in Tabriz. Among the thirty-one whose occupations are known, there were five merchants, three religious leaders, including the shaykh al-islam, three civil servants, two shopkeepers, two gunmakers, two pharmacists, one carpenter, one tailor, one baker, one coffee-house keeper, one jeweler, one cobbler, one auctioneer, one musician, one journalist, one barber and his apprentice, one painter, one theology student, and one high-school principal. Another four were hanged for being related to prominent revolutionaries: two were nephews of Sattar Khan; another two were sons of "Monsieur" 'Ali Karbala-yi, the head of the local Social Democrats. For these executions see: Malekzadeh, *Tarikh*, V, 184-222; A. Kasravi, *Tarikh-i Hejdah Saleh-i Azerbaijan* (Eighteen-Year History of Azerbaijan) (Tehran, 1967), pp. 297-422; and Taherzadeh-Behzad, *Qiyam-i Azerbaijan*, pp. 351-69.

troops and leaders. But having "liberated" the whole city, they found themselves blockaded in by armed Shahsavens and hostile peasants. Amir-Khizi discovered that the villagers, like the urban poor, abhored his side as heretical. And Kasravi noted in his memoirs that the peasantry in his native village a few miles north of Tabriz sided with the reactionary clergy.[111]

In other areas, the civil war was less dramatic but more decisive. In Rasht, four Muslim intellectuals and three Armenian radicals, headed by a brick manufacturer named Yeprem Khan, formed a secret Star Committee and established contact with Social Democrats, Social Revolutionaries, and Armenian Dashnaks in the Caucusus.[112] (The Dashnaks, as socialists as well as nationalists, supported independence for Armenia and social revolution for the Middle East.) Reinforced by thirty-five Georgians and twenty Armenians from Baku, Yeprem Khan captured Rasht and then implanted his red flag on the town hall of Enzeli. Further reinforced by Muhammad Vali Sephadar, the main landed magnate of the Caspian provinces, Yeprem Khan marched his forces of Caucasian guerrillas and Mazandarani peasants toward Tehren. One British eyewitness described these guerrillas as "walking arsenals."[113]

Meanwhile in Isfahan, Samsam al-Saltaneh of the Ilkhani faction, which had recently lost the Bakhtiyari ilkhanship to the court-connected Amir Mofakham of the Hajji Ilkhani faction, rallied his tribal contingents, allied with Sardar As'ad Bakhtiyari of the Revolutionary Committee in Tehran, settled old land disputes between his family and the neighboring Arab tribes, and, capturing Isfahan, marched his tribesmen and Isfahani volunteers north toward Tehran.

These events inspired other revolts.[114] In Bushire and Bandar 'Abbas, regional councils took over local administration. In Kermanshah, constitutionalists expelled royalists and elected a new mayor. In Mashad, the city guilds organized a bazaar strike and seized the royalist governor, while a group of Azeri-speaking radicals formed a Jami'yat-i Mujahedin (Association of Fighters). Affiliating with the Social Dem-

[111] Amir-Khizi, *Qiyam*, p. 169. Kasravi, *Zendigani-yi Man* (My Life) (Tehran, 1946), pp. 32-33. Kasravi confessed that during the civil war he disappeared into his study in order to conceal his liberal sympathies from his Mutashar'i family and conservative community. Another observor of the civil war in Tabriz noted in his diaries that the local peasants believed the mullas who told them that the revolutionaries were all "heretical Babis." See M. Baqer-Vajieh, *Balva-yi Tabriz* (The Tabriz Turbulence) (Tehran, 1977), p. 77.

[112] Yeprem Khan, "Memoirs," *Ittila'at-i Mahaneh*, 2 (July 1948), 19-21.

[113] J. Hone, *Persia in Revolution* (London, 1910), p. 27.

[114] The shah succeeded in reviving communal conflicts in only six cities: Qazvin, Shiraz, Shustar, Ardabel, Zanjan, and Dezful. Kasravi, *Tarikh-i Mashruteh-i Iran*, pp. 80, 195-97. D. Fraser, *Persia and Turkey in Revolt* (London, 1911), p. 243.

ocrats in Baku, the association issued an extensive proclamation. This manifesto, which was the first socialist program to be published in Iran, called for the armed defense of the constitution; use of parliament for attaining "social justice" and "eventual equality"; extension of suffrage to all citizens irrespective of religion and class; redistribution of Majles seats according to the size of population in each region; guarantee of the right to publish, speak, organize, assemble, and strike; free schools for all children; free hospitals and clinics for the urban poor; sale of royal villages and "excess" estates to landless peasants; taxation of income and wealth, not of households; an eight-hour work day; and two years of compulsory military service for all adult males.[115]

As the provinces rose in revolt and the two rebel armies converged, the royalist position in Tehran rapidly deteriorated. Foreign banks refused further credits to pay the Cossacks and the tribal contingents.[116] Court magnates, having strained their own finances, failed to find new resources. Three hundred merchants, summoned to court to contribute, promptly fled to the Ottoman embassy. Guild elders organized a new strike in the bazaar. And opposition leaders who had evaded arrest now reorganized their followers. Consequently, when, on July 13, Yeprem Khan and Samsam al-Saltaneh reached Tehran, armed volunteers within the city ensured a swift victory by opening the main gates. As the royalists fled in disarray, the Shah took sanctuary in the Russian legation. The civil war was over.

Five hundred delegates, drawn from the dissolved parliament, from the Bakhtiyari and guerrilla forces, from the bazaar, and from the liberals in the court, met promptly in Tehran and declared themselves a Grand Assembly. Functioning as a constituent body, the assembly deposed Muhammad ʿAli Shah, nominated his twelve-year-old son, Ahmad, to be the new shah, and elected ʿAzud al-Mulk, the aged but liberal ilkhan of the Qajar tribe, to serve as royal regent. It distributed the cabinet posts among the notables that had supported the constitutional movement: Sepahdar received the premiership and the Ministry of War, Sardar Asʿad the Ministry of Interior. Next it instituted a special tribunal to try the leading royalists; five outspoken opponents of the constitution, including Shaykh Fazallah, were executed. Finally, the Grand Assembly ratified a new electoral law that implicitly rewarded the social forces that had helped the parliamentary cause

[115] "The Program of the Association of Fighters in Mashad," *Donya*, 3 (Winter 1964), pp. 89-97.

[116] Fraser claimed that the shah tried to sell the crown jewels, but the foreign banks, frightened of reprisals from the revolutionaries, declined the offer. See *Persia and Turkey in Revolt*, p. 60.

during the civil war. This law lowered the property qualification from 1,000 tomans to 250 tomans, abolished representation by class and occupation, reduced Tehran's allocation from 60 seats to 15, increased that of the provinces from 96 to 101, and created four seats for the recognized religious minorities—1 for the Jews, 1 for the Zoroastrians, and 2 for the Christian Assyrians and Armenians. On August 5, 1909, exactly four years after Muzzafar al-Din Shah consented to convene the Constituent Assembly, the cabinet decreed the calling of the Second National Assembly. The revolution had finally secured the constitution.

THREE

Reza Shah

A patriotic soldier who awoke his people from dreams of ancient glory and propelled them into the twentieth century.

—D. Wilber, *Riza Shah Pahlavi*, p. i.

Altogether he thoroughly milked the country, grinding down the peasants, tribesmen, and laborers, and taking a heavy toll from the landlords. While his activities enriched a new class of "capitalists"—merchants, monopolists, contractors, and politican-favorites—, inflation, heavy taxation, and other measures lowered the standard of living of the masses.

—A. Millspaugh, *Americans in Persia*, p. 34.

THE PERIOD OF DISINTEGRATION (1909-1921)

The new era began with great expectations. The Second National Assembly opened in November 1909 amid wide public acclaim. It immediately gave a resounding vote of confidence to the government of Sepahdar and Sardar As⁽ad, and proceeded to pension off the ex-shah to Europe, to express its thanks both to the internal and foreign volunteer fighters, and to appoint Yeprem Khan, now enjoying a reputation as the Garibaldi of Iran, as the police chief of Tehran. During the next few months, the government succeeded in negotiating the withdrawal of almost all the Russian troops that had entered the northern provinces in the civil war, and in obtaining a loan of £1,250,000 from the Imperial Bank to rebuild the administrative structure. Moreover, it recruited, with the enthusiastic endorsement of parliament, eleven Swedish officers to organize a rural police force known as the gendarmerie, and sixteen American financial experts—headed by Morgan Shuster—to reorganize the tax administration. The age of reform had dawned at last.

Or so it seemed. It was not long, however, before the high expectations were wilting under the heat of internal conflicts and external pressures. By the middle of 1910, the National Assembly was sharply divided into two rival parties whose armed supporters threatened to turn the streets of Tehran into bloody battlegrounds. By mid-1911, the provinces were embroiled in tribal warfare, and the central government was thereby further weakened. By the end of 1911, British and Russian troops were moving into the main northern and southern cities. By 1915, Ottoman contingents had invaded the western regions and German agents were smuggling arms to the southern tribes. "The central government," in the words of the British minister," had ceased to exist outside the capital.[1] The deterioration proceeded apace. By 1920, autonomous governments had installed themselves in Azerbaijan and Gilan; tribal chiefs were in control over much of Kurdistan, Arabistan, and Baluchistan; the British were moving to "salvage" some "healthy limbs" in the south; the shah had packed his crown jewels to flee to Isfahan; and the propertied families, seeing the specter of Bolshevism, placed their hopes not in Parliament but in a man on horseback.[2] In early 1921, such a savior appeared in the shape of Reza Khan, then a colonel in the Cossack Division and soon to be the shah of Iran. Whereas the revolution of 1905-1909 had replaced the Qajar despotism with a liberal constitution, the coup d'état of 1921 was to clear the way for the demolition of the parliamentary structures and the establishment of the Pahlevi autocracy.

The divisions in the Second National Assembly appeared as early as 1910. While twenty-seven reformers formed a Democrat party (Firqeh-i Demokrat), fifty-three conservatives coalesced into a Moderate party (Firqeh-i I'tedal).[3] The Democrats were led by survivors of the pre-1906 radical societies: Taqizadeh and Muhammad Tarbiyat of the Ganjeh-i Fonun in Tabriz; Sulayman Iskandari and Muhammad Reza Musavat of the Revolutionary Committee in Tehran; and Hussein Quli Khan Navab, a former colleague of Malkum Khan in London and probably a secret member of the Humanity Society in Tehran. Almost all the twenty-seven Democrats came from the north: thirteen from Azerbaijan, two from north Khurasan, and seven from Tehran. The group included eight civil servants, five journalists, five religious leaders, one landowner, and one doctor; of the five religious leaders, three were Shaykhis and one was a clandestine 'Azali.

Outside parliament, the Democrat party was organized mainly by Haydar Khan and Muhammad Amin Rasulzadeh. Haydar Khan, who later became first secretary of the Iranian Communist party, served as the organization's executive secretary, linked the Democrats in Tehran

[1] British Minister to the Foreign Office, "Annual Report for 1914," *F.O. 371*/Persia 1915/34-2059.

[2] British Financial Adviser in Tehran to the Foreign Office, *Documents on British Foreign Policy, 1919-39* (London), First Series, XIII, 720, 735.

[3] H. Taqizadeh, "List of Members in the Second Majles," *Kaveh*, 15 July 1918.

to the Social Democrats in Baku, headed a band of armed volunteers, and helped form printers' and telegraphers' trade unions. His difficulty in speaking formal Persian barred him from standing for parliament. Rasulzadeh, who after the Russian Revolution was to become a Menshevik leader in Baku, had come from the Caucasus to fight in the civil war. He founded a newspaper entitled *Iran-i Now* (New Iran), which served as the party organ and soon gained the largest circulation of all papers published in Tehran. *Iran-i Now*, written mostly by Rasulzadeh, not only contained discussions of social reform, but also summarized the history of European socialism, and sought to propagate in Iran—for the first time—the fundamentals of Marxism.[4]

The Democrats, in formulating their program, borrowed heavily from the earlier manifestos of the Social Democrats. Malekzadeh, a founding member of the new party, years later admitted that although the word "socialist" was dropped in deference to the "conservative public," the program itself was taken more or less intact from that of the old party.[5] It began with the declaration that Europe had completed its transition from feudalism to capitalism and now threatened both the political independence and the archaic social structures of Asia: "The twentieth century is for the East what the seventeenth century was for the West—the transitional stage from feudalism to capitalism."[6] It continued with the admonition that decaying "feudalism" in Iran, as in the rest of Asia, was incapable of protecting national independence and initiating social reform. It concluded with the proclamation that the progressive forces, such as the Democrats, must therefore lead the country "into the caravan of human progress" by combatting foreign capitalism and local feudalism. The program called for a strong lower house and a continued delay in convening the upper house; extension of the vote to all adult males; free, direct, and secret elections; equality for all citizens, irrespective of religion and birth; separation of religion and politics; state control of religious foundations for public use; free education for all, with particular emphasis on the education of women; two years of military service for all males; abolition of capitulations; industrialization; direct and progressive taxation; limitation of work to less than ten hours a day; an end to child labor; and the distribution of land to those who tilled it.

[4] ʿA. Agahi, "The Beginnings of Marxism in Iran," *Donya*, 3 (Winter 1962), 47-52.

[5] Malekzadeh, *Tarikh*, V, 133.

[6] Democrat Party, "Party Program," reprinted in H. Jowdat, *Tarikh-i Firqeh-i Demokrat* (History of the Democrat Party) (Tehran, 1969), pp. 16-22. F. Adamiyat, *Fekr-i Demokrasi-yi Ijtemaʿyi dar Nahzat-i Mashrutiyat-i Iran* (The Concept of Social Democracy in the Iranian Constitutional Movement) (Tehran, 1975).

The editorials of *Iran-i Now* elaborated on the main points of the party program. They focused on the importance of waging a struggle against the traditional autocracy and the contemporary aristocracy—the former was referred to as "oriental despotism" (*mostabdeh-i sharqi*) and the latter as the "feudal ruling class" (*moluk al-tava'ifi*). They also warned of the dangers posed by Western imperialism, especially by the Anglo-Russian Agreement of 1907, which had demarcated Isfahan and the northern provinces as a Russian zone of influence, Seistan and Baluchistan as a British sphere, and the southern regions as a neutral zone. The articles furthermore stressed the benefits of railway construction, military conscription, secularization, land distribution, and rapid industrialization—all the while assuring craftsmen that modern factories would create rather than eliminate jobs. They also advocated political centralization, communal integration, and national unification. As an editorial on "We Are One Nation" argued, nationalism was the only sure safeguard against the revival of communalism and royal despotism: "The constitutional movement united the many communities, and thus brought down the despotic regime. To insure that no such regime will appear again, Iran must treat all its citizens—Muslims and Jews, Christians and Zoroastrians, Persians and Turkic speakers—as equal, free, and full Iranians."[7]

This program soon won over the other radical elements. The Armenian Dashnak party, declaring that the Democrats were a progressive force, formed an alliance with them against "reactionary feudalism." And the Social Democrats of Baku instructed their members to dissolve their branches in Iran and to join the new organization. The Iranian Social Democrats in the Caucasus, however, continued to work with the Russian Social Democrats, particularly with the Bolsheviks.[8]

Whereas the Democrat party spoke for the modern intelligentsia, the Moderate party espoused the cause of the landed aristocracy and the traditional middle class. Its fifty-three deputies included thirteen members of the ʿulama, ten landlords, nine merchants, ten civil servants, and three tribal chiefs. The composition of its leadership was similar: Behbehani and Tabatabai, the two prominent mujtaheds;

[7] "Concerning the Aristocracy," *Iran-i Now*, 13 November 1909; "Feudalism," *Iran-i Now*, 31 September 1909; "International Relations," *Iran-i Now*, 5 September-10 October 1909; "Iran Needs an Army," *Iran-i Now*, 20 September 1909; "Welcome," *Iran-i Now*, 22 September 1909; "Railways," *Iran-i Now*, 3 April 1910; "Industrial Factories," *Iran-i Now*, 13 April 1910; "We Are One Nation," *Iran-i Now*, 16 February 1910.

[8] Dashnak Party, "Official Resolution," *Iran-i Now*, 1 February 1910; Social Democrat Party, "Letter to Our Members in Iran," *Iran-i Now*, 1 February 1910; A Veteran Bolshevik, "A Short History of the Justice Party," *Azhir*, 18 July-27 November 1943.

Sepahdar, the northern magnate; and Prince 'Abdul Hussein Mirza, the European-educated patriarch of the aristocratic Farmanfarma family and the son-in-law of Muzaffar al-Din Shah, who, as governor of Kerman in 1906-1907, had extended valuable assistance to the constitutional movement. The British minister observed that the strength of the party lay mainly among the clergy, merchants, and artisans: "These classes look on the presence of the Moderates, especially Sepahdar, in the cabinet as necessary for the preservation of law and order." Malekzadeh admitted that the few graduates of the modern schools supported the Democrats, but the many in the bazaar, who were influenced by the traditional 'ulama, rallied behind the Moderates: "The clergy, who had a vested reason for opposing reform, fooled the public, especially craftsmen and tradesmen, into believing that the Democrats were the sworn enemies of Islam."[9]

The program of the Moderate party called, predictably, for strengthening the constitutional monarchy; convening the upper house; safeguarding religion—"the best bulwark against oppression and injustice"; protecting family life, private property, and fundamental rights; instilling "a cooperative attitude" among the masses through religious education; granting financial assistance to the "middle class" (*tabaqeh-i mutavasateh*), especially the small capitalists of the bazaar; enforcing the shari'a; and defending society against the "terrorism" of the anarchists, the "atheism" of the Democrats, and the "materialism" of the Marxists.[10]

The inevitable clash between Moderates and Democrats began in the parliamentary debates on secular reforms, and intensified in the process of electing a prime minister. The Moderates continued to stand behind Sepahdar; the Democrats pushed hard for Mirza Hassan Mustawfi al-Mamalek, a wealthy but liberally inclined civil servant who favored secular reforms. It intensified further with the death of the regent and the nominations for a successor. The Moderates, with the help of the Bakhtiyaris, rejected Mustawfi al-Mamalek, and instead elected Naser al-Mulk, a former liberal who now advocated caution, expressed distrust of visionaries, and described himself as a "realistic conservative."[11] The conflict eventually exploded when four armed men from Haydar Khan's band of volunteers assassinated the highly esteemed Behbehani. The Moderates promptly accused the Democrats of inciting the murder. Their 'ulama denounced Taqizadeh as

[9] British Minister to the Foreign Office, "Monthly Report for June 1910," *F.O. 371/Persia* 1910/34-950; Malekzadeh, *Tarikh*, IV, 212.

[10] Moderate Party, *Maramnameh-i Firqeh* (Party Program) (Tehran, n.d.).

[11] British Minister to the Foreign Office, "Annual Report for 1911," *F.O. 371/Persia* 1912/34-1441.

a heretic, and thus forced him into exile. Their guilds in Tehran organized a strike in the bazaar, held a mass meeting in the central mosque, and demanded the immediate arrest of all associated with the assassins. Their armed volunteers, meanwhile, ambushed Haydar Khan, and killed Hamid Khan Tarbiyat, who was a hero of the Social Democrats in Tabriz, the younger brother of the well-known Tarbiyat, and the brother-in-law of Taqizadeh. The final reckoning now appeared inevitable.

Anticipating such a confrontation, the Democrats and the Bakhtiyaris, together with a group of southern deputies, replaced Sepahdar with Mustawfi al-Mamalek. The new prime minister, with the support of Yeprem Khan, immediately decreed that all private citizens should hand in their weapons to the local police. Almost all the pro-Democrats obliged, but three hundred pro-Moderates, led by Sattar Khan and Baqer Khan of Tabriz, refused and barricaded themselves in the central part of Tehran. A much larger force of Bakhtiyari tribesmen and Yeprem Khan's policemen promptly surrounded the park, attacked, and eventually disarmed their former colleagues. The Iranian revolution, unlike other revolutions, did not devour its children; but, like other revolutions, it did ultimately disarm many of them.

While the capital was in the throes of political upheaval, the provinces were being torn apart by tribal convulsions. Turkomans in north Khurasan, Shahsavens in Azerbaijan, and Kurds in Luristan took advantage of the situation in Tehran to withhold their taxes, loot local villages, disrupt communication lines, and support the ex-shah when he reappeared in Iran in July 1911 for a last bid to regain the throne. Meanwhile, Qashqayis, Boir Ahmedis, Arabs, Baluchis, Khamsehs, and Kuhigiluyehs formed an alliance to stem the rising power of the Bakhtiyaris. For by mid-1911 Bakhtiyari chiefs held an impressive array of positions: Samsam al-Saltaneh, the ilkhan, presided over the cabinet in Tehran; Sardar As'ad, his younger brother, continued to enjoy the confidence of the Democrats; another brother headed the palace guard; the patriarch of the Hajji Ilkhani family controlled the War Ministry; and other relatives governed the regions of Isfahan, Arabistan, Yazd, Kerman, Boroujerd, Behbehan, and Sultanabad. What is more, the six leading chiefs of the Ilkhani and Hajji Ilkhani families had agreed to protect the installations of the Anglo-Persian Oil Company in return of a lucrative 3 percent share in the profits of that company. Not surprisingly, many of the other tribes began to view the constitution as a camouflage for Bakhtiyari domination, and took steps to remedy the situation. As the British minister reported to London, the Arab Bani Ka'ab tribe, headed by Shaykh Khaz'el, prepared to advance on Mohammerah, the Baluchis on Kerman, Boir

Ahmedis on Bushire, and the Qashqayis, together with the Khamseh, on Shiraz.[12] This alliance was further strengthened in 1911 when Prince Zil al-Sultan, who, as governor of Isfahan under Naser al-Din Shah had murdered Samsam al-Saltaneh's father, placed his estates under Russian protection and allied with the local clergy against the Bakhtiyaris. According to the British consul, Zil al-Sultan and the 'ulama removed the Bakhtiyari governor by exploiting public resentment against a bad harvest and high food prices, inciting a riot against the local Zoroastrians, and arranging a miracle to enflame a "revivalist movement among the lower orders."[13]

Tribal rivalries among the rebels, however, saved the central government and the Bakhtiyaris. The Baluchi offensive broke down under clan vendettas. Shaykh Khaz'el's confederation lost it cohesion. The Boir Ahmedis and Kuhgiluyeh succeeded in disrupting the countryside, but failed in coordinating their attacks, and thus did not capture any towns. And, most important of all, the Khamsehs and Qashqayis turned on each other as they entered Shiraz: while the Khamsehs occupied one part of the city, the Qashqayis forced Qavam al-Mulk, the Khamseh ilkhan, to take sanctuary in the British consulate, killed his brother, pillaged his home, and devastated the Jewish quarter, which had been under his family's protection during the past century. These upheavals, according to the British minister, closed the central and southern highways, terrorized the merchant community of Shiraz, and thus necessitated the immediate presence of British troops.[14] In October 1911 British detachments landed in Bushire and proceeded in haste to Shiraz and Isfahan. Tribalism, besides saving the Bakhtiyaris, had also reopened southern Iran to the British.

These internal conflicts coincided with external threats from Russia. The Russians threatened Iran partly to secure their markets, partly to implement the 1907 Agreement, and partly to eliminate the Shuster mission. Shuster, who had been appointed treasurer-general by a large majority in the National Assembly, asserted his authority with reckless zeal. He investigated the Belgian customs officials who enjoyed Russian support; organized a special force to collect taxes throughout the country, even in the northern provinces; and confiscated the property of a prince whom the government declared a traitor but who claimed Russian citizenship. This confiscation, in the words of the British

---

[12] British Minister to the Foreign Office, "Monthly Report for March 1910," *F.O. 371*/Persia 1910/34-950.

[13] Great Britain, *Correspondence Respecting the Affairs of Persia*, (London, 1909), vol. II, no. 2, p. 115.

[14] British Minister to the Foreign Office, "Annual Report for 1911," *F.O. 371*/Persia 1912/34-1441.

minister, overfilled the tsar's "cup of indignation."[15] The Russians, occupying Enzeli and Rasht in November 1911, delivered a three-point ultimatum to Iran: the dismissal of the Shuster mission; the promise not to hire foreign advisers in future without the consent of Britain and Russia; and the payment of an indemnity for the expeditionary force in Enzeli and Rasht. They threatened to occupy Tehran without further ado unless these demands were met within forty-eight hours.

The ultimatum fell on Tehran like a bombshell, promptly disrupting the relationship between the deputies and the ministers, and eventually destroying the Second National Assembly. The Democrats and Moderates, encouraged by the Dashnaks, voted by a large majority to reject the ultimatum and to extend their two-year session until the termination of the current crisis. One lone voice reminded the House that Cromwell had dissolved the Long Parliament for overextending its term. Meanwhile, three hundred women marched into the public galleries with pistols hidden under their long veils, and threatened to shoot any deputy willing to submit to the Russian ultimatum. Angry demonstrators attacked the city trams that were partly owned by the Russians. And a huge crowd, described by one eyewitness as the "largest up to that point in Iranian history," gathered outside parliament shouting, "Independence or Death."[16] But Premier Samsam al-Saltaneh, the regent, the cabinet, and Yeprem Khan with his fighters from the Caucasus, decided to accept the ultimatum to avoid a Russian occupation of the capital. As the prime minister accepted the Russian demands and as the regent accused the deputies of acting unconstitutionally, Yeprem Khan barred shut the doors of parliament. Whereas internal reaction had closed down the First National Assembly, foreign pressures had led to the dissolution of the Second National Assembly.

The Anglo-Russian occupation sparked mass protests. The ʿulama in Najaf and Karbala called for a public boycott of Russian goods. Demonstrators in Tehran smashed shop windows displaying Russian products, vigilantes prevented the sale of Russian tea, and unknown assailants killed a prominent businessman identified with Russian interests. Traders in Shiraz, leading a run on the Imperial Bank, refused to sell food to the British troops. A skirmish in Tabriz between Russian soldiers and city policemen led to the suicide of the deputy governor and the public execution of forty-four veterans of the Constitutional Revolution. Seizures of food by Russian troops in Enzeli and Rasht precipitated bloody confrontations in which forty-three were killed

---

[15] Ibid.
[16] "Demonstrations and Mass Meetings in Iran," *Ittilaʿat-i Haftegi*, 26 April 1951.

and over fifty injured. And the Russians in Mashad reacted to the assassination of one of their officers by attacking a large crowd that had taken sanctuary within the holy shrine of Imam Reza. They bombarded the shrine, looted the mosque, and injured over fifty protestors. The bombardment of the shrine of Imam Reza was to leave a deep imprint in the national history of modern Iran.

These protests, however, gradually petered out. Resistance produced martyrs but not victories. Civilian demonstrators were no match for trained soldiers. Suicides and assassinations may have impressed foreign diplomats, but they did not change the decisions of foreign governments. Boycotts and strikes hurt local bazaars more than ministers in London and St. Petersburg. Besides, the occupying powers brought some benefits to commercial interests by buying local commodities, controlling rural banditry, limiting tribal anarchy, and opening up the main trade routes. National opposition to foreign intervention was transformed from overt resistance to covert resentment.

By 1914, the country had resigned itself to a bleak future of foreign occupation and internal stagnation. The British and Russian authorities dealt directly with the tribal chiefs, guarded the main roads, and garrisoned the northern and southern cities. The Belgians not only regained their control of the customs administration but also inherited Shuster's post of treasurer-general. The provincial magnates successfully limited the size of the gendarmerie to less than six thousand men. The British and Russian representatives vetoed each other's projects for a Trans-Iranian Railway. Sepahdar, working closely with the Russians, turned much of the Caspian region into his private fiefdom. The Bakhtiyaris, collaborating mainly with the British, treated the central ministries as tribal booty. In the words of the British minister: "The [Bakhtiyari] khans have imported their custom of sharing tribal property into the central government. Major decisions are made at family councils. Also, when a member of the Ilkhani family obtains a post, a member of the Hajji Ilkhani family is secretly associated with him, and vice versa, to share the spoils of office."[17]

The radicals, meanwhile, were demoralized and leaderless. Taqizadeh, Haydar Khan, and Rasulzadeh had been forced into exile. Sulayman Iskandari, Musavat, and many others had fled into the central provinces. Yeprem Khan had been killed fighting the remnants of the ex-shah's forces. Of the radical groups that had fought for the revolution, only the Dashnaks and the Armenian volunteers in the police force remained organized. It was thanks mainly to these sur-

[17] British Minister to the Foreign Office, "Report on the Bakhtiari Khans," *F.O. 371/ Persia 1914/34-2073.*

vivors that the constitutional movement remained alive; for, after the ultimatum crisis had subsided, they, together with some guilds, threatened to strike unless the government fulfilled its constitutional obligation to hold general elections for a new National Assembly.[18]

The Third Majles convened soon after the outbreak of World War I. The deputies, encouraged by the early Russian defeats, refused to declare war against the Central Powers, dismissed the Belgian customs officials, and elected the leaders of the Democrat and Moderate parties to a Committee of National Resistance. The committee was headed by four party leaders: Sulayman Iskandari; Musavat; Sayyid Hassan Mudarres, the leading spokesmen of the Moderates, who, as a charismatic preacher from Isfahan, represented the Najaf and Karbala ʿulama in the National Assembly; and Mirza Muhammad Sadeq Tabatabai, a son of the famous mujtahed, who, being a graduate of modern languages from Istanbul and an active member of the pre-revolutionary Secret Society, edited the parliamentary gazette on behalf of the Moderate majority. The committee first set itself up within the sanctuary of Qum; but, when the Russians invaded that town, it fled to Kermanshah, where pro-Ottoman Kurds were fighting the British. There it formed a Government of National Defence, established contact with pro-German Swedish officers in the gendarmerie, and formed an alliance with Qashqayi and Baluchi tribesmen who were receiving German arms. To counter these activities, the British supplied weapons to the Khamseh, the Bakhtiyaris, and the Arabs headed by Shaykh Khazʿel, and formed a native police force under British command known as the South Persia Rifles. By 1916, the British captured Kermanshah, destroyed the Government of National Defense, forced some of its members into exile, and deported others, such as Sulayman Iskandari, to prison in India.

Meanwhile, the Russians in Gilan were harassed by a guerrilla force named Committee of Islamic Unity and famed as the Jangalis (Men of the Jungle). This movement drew its initial members predominantly from the small landed farmers in Gilan. It was headed by Mirza Kuchek Khan, a dynamic preacher from Rasht, who had fought in the civil war and joined the Moderate party in the Second National Assembly. Finally, in Germany, Taqizadeh and a group of Iranian students published an influential periodical entitled *Kaveh*. Named after a legendary blacksmith who had overthrown an unjust shah, *Kaveh* printed articles on al-Afghani, on the history of the constitutional movement in Iran, and on the development of socialism in Europe, including the growth of Marxism and the Second Interna-

---

[18] Great Britain, *Correspondence*, vol. III, no. 1, p. 16.

tional. But its principal focus was on the need for national independence and internal reforms, especially secular and educational reforms.
As one typical editorial stressed, the only way Iran could leave behind
the "Dark Middle Ages" was to follow the Western experience of
separating religion from politics and introducing scientific rational
knowledge into public education.[19]

The nationalist movement received a major boost from the Russian
Revolution of March 1917. As the tsarist empire collapsed and its
army in Azerbaijan disintegrated, political organizations revived
throughout Iran. In Tehran, the Democrats, according to the British
minister, reestablished their presence. "The first effect of the revolution was to allow the extreme Democrat party in Tehran to reacquire
much of its old power. It was surmised that revolutionary Russia would
adopt a different attitude in the Persian question, and Great Britain
would be left alone to fend for herself."[20] In Gilan, the Jangalis gained
new volunteers headed by Khalu Qurban and Ehsanallah Khan. The
former led a small force of gum workers and fellow Kurds from
Kermanshah; the latter, an Azeri intellectual who had been influenced
by anarchism while studying in Paris, brought a contingent of Democrats from Tehran.[21] By the end of 1917, the Jangalis were a major
force in the north. They controlled much of Gilan; exchanged a British prisoner of war for Sulayman Iskandari; and, robbing the rich to
feed the poor, achieved fame, in the words of an English eyewitness,
as the "Robin Hoods of the Caspian Marches."[22] Their paper *Jangal*,
published by the religious-landed rather than the secular-radical wing
of the movement, called for economic assistance to small farmers,
administrative autonomy for Gilan, protection of Islam, cancelation
of all unequal treaties, and the evacuation of British troops from Iran.

Meanwhile, Shaykh Muhammad Khiabani, the leading Democrat
in Azerbaijan, convened in Tabriz a conference of the provincial branch
of the Democrat party. Khiabani, a popular preacher in the Shaykh
ward of Khiaban, had adopted radical ideas while studying in the
Caucasus, fought in the revolution as a militant member of the haberdashers' guild, and achieved national fame as an outspoken Democrat in the Second National Assembly.[23] The four hundred fifty
delegates at the conference, representing most towns in Azerbaijan,

[19] "Public Education," *Kaveh*, 10 April 1921.

[20] British Minister to the Foreign Office, "Annual Reports from 1914 to 1922," *F.O.*
371/Persia 1922/9051-2911.

[21] A. Kambakhsh, "The October Revolution and Liberation Movements in Iran,"
Donya, 8 (Summer 1967), 34-57.

[22] M. Donohoe, *With the Persian Expedition* (London, 1919), p. 127.

[23] Z. Qiyami, "Reminiscences of Khiabani," *Donya*, 11 (Winter 1970), 76-83.

established a bilingual Azeri-Persian paper *Tajadod* (Renewal), changed the title of the branch of the Democrat party in Azerbaijan to the Democrat Party of Azerbaijan (Firqeh-i Demokrat-i Azerbayjan), and sent four major demands to the central government: the initiation of such democratic reforms as land distribution; the appointment of a governor-general who would be trusted by the people of Azerbaijan; the immediate reconvening of the National Assembly in Tehran; and the assembling of the provincial councils, as had been provided for in the constitution but which had not met since the last days of the civil war. Khiabani, in his closing speech, complained that Azerbaijan, despite its sacrifices in the Constitutional Revolution, received neither fair parliamentary representation nor just budgetary allocations from the central governments.[24] A few days after the conference, the organization expelled from the Democrat party a minority faction, headed by the historian Kasravi, for opposing the provincial demands and the name change.[25] For the first time, the regional problem had created an open schism within the radical movement. Until then, the conservatives, especially the tribal chiefs, jealously guarded local autonomy, whereas the reformers championed the establishment of an effective central government. But from 1917 on, the advantages and disadvantages of both centralization and decentralization were to preoccupy many reformers.

While the Democrats were holding their provincial conference in Tabriz, veteran Social Democrats sympathetic to the Russian bolsheviks gathered in Baku and announced the formation of the Justice party (Firqeh-i 'Adalat). Establishing a bilingual Azeri-Persian paper named *Huriyat* (Freedom), the Justice party dispatched a delegate to the forthcoming Sixth Bolshevik Congress in Petrograd, and began to organize unions among Iranian laborers employed in the Baku oilfields. Almost all the leaders of the new party were intellectuals from Iranian Azerbaijan who had worked closely with the Russian bolsheviks since 1906. Assadallah Khan Ghafarzadeh, the First Secretary, was a native of Ardabel and a graduate of the famous Dar al-Fonun. A veteran revolutionary, he had fought in the civil war and had helped smuggle Lenin's paper *Iskra* from Europe through Iran into the Caucasus. Mir Ja'far Javadzadeh, the editor of *Huriyat*, had been born in the small town of Khalkhal in Iranian Azerbaijan, but had spent the previous years teaching in a Baku high school. And Ahmad Sultanzadeh (Avetis Mikaelian), the party's leading theoretician and a prominent figure in the Third International, came from

---

[24] 'A. Azeri, *Qiyam-i Khiabani* (The Revolt of Khiabani) (Tehran, 1950), pp. 141-45.
[25] A. Kasravi, *Zendigani-yi, Man* (My Life) (Tehran, 1946), pp. 86-96.

an Armenian family in Iranian Azerbaijan and had spent much of his adult life in the bolshevik underground in Russian Azerbaijan.

As the nationalist and communist parties regrouped, the opposition to the central government in Tehran reached a new peak with the publication of the controversial 1919 Anglo-Iranian Agreement. In the prospective treaty, Britain promised to loan Iran £2,000,000 and to assist in the construction of railroads, revision of tariffs, and collection of war compensation from third parties. In return, Iran promised Britain a monopoly over the supply of arms, military training, and administrative advisers. To Lord Curzon, the architect of the treaty, the agreement would salvage Iran—with its strategic location, vast oil assets, and prospective investments—from picturesque decay, financial chaos, and, worst of all, bolshevik intrigue.[26] Similarly, it seemed to the Iranian premier, Mirza Hassan Vossuq al-Dawleh, and his fellow-aristocratic advisers, particularly Sepahdar, Prince Farmanfarma, and the Bakhtiyari chiefs, the agreement would finance administrative reforms, avert social revolution, and recognize the postwar dominance of Britain throughout the Middle East. But to the opposition and most foreign observers, the agreement was a typical imperialist scheme designed to transform Iran into a vassal state of the British Empire. As one American correspondent reported from Versailles, "the Agreement has deceived nobody. The moment its terms were made public, everybody recognized that a virtual protectorate over Persia had been established and that the British Empire had in effect received another extension."[27]

The Soviet government immediately denounced the agreement, contrasting its own earlier cancellation of tsarist privileges in Iran with Britain's continued accumulation of monopolies in the Middle East. Nine months later, the Red Army landed small detachments in Enzeli, both to eliminate a British force that was sending arms to the Caucasus, and to strengthen the Jangalis against the Anglophile government in Tehran. The leading mujtaheds in Karbala published fatwas against the British. According to a police report filed with the India Office, two mujtaheds even pronounced in favor of the Bolsheviks.[28] The Democrats of Azerbaijan—supported by local merchants who were convinced that the agreement was a Machiavellian scheme for diverting the trade routes through Bagdad—accused Tehran of selling Iran, repeated the demand for the convening of parliament and pro-

[26] Lord Curzon, "Memorandum on the Agreement," in *Documents on British Foreign Policy, 1919-1939*, IV, 1119.

[27] W. MacDonald, "Persia and British Honor," *The Nation*, 13 September 1919.

[28] India Office to the Foreign Office, "Police Report from Mesopotamia," *F.O. 371/ Turkey* 1920/44-5074.

vincial councils, called for the establishment of a republic, and moved further toward secession by replacing the title Province of Azerbaijan with the term Mamlek-i Azadistan (Country of Freedom).[29] Fortunately for the central government, the Shahsavens of Azerbaijan disrupted the main roads; the Kurdish tribe of Shakkuk, headed by the notorious Semko, turned their attention from massacring Assyrians to harassing Democrats; and the Cossacks in Tabriz, who policed the city and who opposed the arming of party members, rebelled and in September 1920 killed Khiabani.

The Justice party, meanwhile, was active in extending branches among the Iranian community in Tashkent, recruiting volunteers for the Red Army, and forming an alliance with the Jangalis. In June 1920 it convened in Enzeli its first major congress. The meeting was attended by forty-eight delegates, representing some six hundred members in the Caucasus, Central Asia, Gilan, and Azerbaijan. Almost all the delegates, except for a few Armenians, were Azeris.[30] According to the party's estimates, most of the rank and file were of the working class: 60 percent were workers and apprentices, 30 percent office employees, 17 percent craftsmen-tradesmen, and 3 percent intellectuals and soldiers.[31] The congress adopted the title Communist Party of Iran (Firqeh-i Komunist-i Iran) and elected Sultanzadeh to be the party's First Secretary (Ghafarzadeh had been killed a few months earlier).[32]

The Congress also debated two conflicting theses that were presented as party programs. The first, drafted by Sultanzadeh, argued that Iran had completed its bourgeois revolution and was now ready for a worker-peasants' revolution. Convinced that the socialist revolution was at hand, the document called for the immediate redistribution of land, the formation of militant trade unions, and the armed overthrow of the bourgeoisie and their clerical spokesmen as well as

[29] British Consul in Tabriz, "Annual Report for the Province," *F.O. 371*/Persia 1921/34-6440; Azeri, *Qiyam-i Khiabani*, p. 361.

[30] M. Fateh, *Panjah Saleh-i Naft-i Iran* (Fifty Years of Iranian Oil) (Tehran, 1956), p. 381.

[31] A. Shamideh, "Haydar Khan," *Donya*, 14 (Spring 1970), 113-24.

[32] For the First Congress, see "Report on the First Congress of the Iranian Communist Party," *Donya*, 9 (Summer 1968), 99-104; "Haydar Khan's Thesis," *Donya*, 12 (Summer 1971), 101-10; A. Sultanzadeh, *Sovremennaya Persia* (Contemporary Persia) (Moscow, 1922); ʿA. Kambakhsh, "Fifty Years of the Proletarian Party in Iran," *Donya*, 11 (Summer 1970), 2-15; "The Regulations of the Iranian Communist Party (1921)," reprinted in *Asnad-i Tarikhi-yi Jonbesh-i Kargari, Sosiyal Demokrat va Komunisti-yi Iran* (Historical Documents from the Workers', Social Democratic, and Communist Movements in Iran), edited by Mazdak (Florence, 1972), III, 36-44. For general analysis of the programs of the Communist party, see S. Zabih, *The Communist Movement in Iran* (Berkeley and Los Angeles, 1966).

of the monarchy, the feudal aristocracy, and the British imperialists. The second thesis, formulated by Haydar Khan, the famous Social Democrat who had just joined the Communist party, counterargued that Iran was moving toward a national rather than a socialist revolution. The document argued that the economy remained precapitalist, the state continued to be controlled by feudalists, the proletariat was lumpen rather than industrial, the peasantry held onto their religious superstitions, the large tribal population was still willing to fight on behalf of its reactionary khans, and the petite bourgeoisie, including the clergy, felt threatened by the onward march of British imperialism. Hence, the second thesis concluded, the immediate task of the Communist party was to lead all the discontented classes, especially the peasantry, the petite bourgeoisie, and the lumpen proletariat, against foreign imperialism and its local stooges. After much debate, the Congress accepted Sultanzadeh's radical thesis and drafted a maximalist program that stressed thorough land reform, militant labor unions, convening of provincial assemblies, the right of self-determination for the national minorities, and recruitment of "wage earners, peasants, doctors, teachers, office clerks, craftsmen, apprentices, household servants, and all who worked by hand." The party explicitly barred from its ranks "clergymen, landowners, merchants, moneylenders, and others who exploited the laboring classes."

The Communist party, moreover, announced at the end of the Congress that it had formed with the Jangalis in Gilan a Soviet Socialist Republic of Iran. This tenuous alliance between northern communists and local clerical-landed guerrillas was somewhat strengthened in September 1920 by the Conference of the Eastern Peoples held in Baku. At this conference, the Communist International rejected Sultanzadeh's ultraleft proposals and instead adopted more moderate resolutions similar to those formulated by Haydar Khan. A month later, a plenary meeting of the Iranian Communist party replaced Sultanzadeh with Haydar Khan, and announced that the latter's thesis would cement the alliance of all progressive national forces since it recognized both the importance of the local bourgeoisie and the influence of the clergy among the peasantry.[33] By the end of 1920, the Soviet Socialist Republic in Rasht—reinforced by the Red Army—was preparing to march into Tehran with its guerrilla force of some 1,500 Jangalis, Kurds, Armenians, and Azerbaijanis.[34]

The imminent danger from Gilan, the upheavals in Azerbaijan, the constant wars between the tribes, the presence of the Red Army in

[33] M. Akhundzadeh, "The Life of Akhundzadeh," *Donya*, 9 (Spring 1969), 55-58.
[34] British Military Attaché in Tehran to the Foreign Office, "The Situation in Gilan," *F.O. 371*/Persia 1920/34-4907.

the north and the British Army in the south, the outbreak of mutinies in the gendarmerie and the Cossack Division, and the inability of the government to convene a parliament that would ratify the unpopular Anglo-Iranian Agreement, all contributed toward creating an acute political crisis in the capital. The British minister telegraphed to the Foreign Office that a succession of six cabinets during the nineteen months subsequent to the publication of the agreement had failed to persuade citizens to serve on electoral boards; the European community was fleeing Tehran for the security of the south; the few pro-British politicians who remained were publicly denouncing the agreement and privately pleading with the legation to cancel it; the shah was "so nervous for his own safety that he was no longer accessible to reason"; and the men of property, fearing that the "Bolshevik poison was rapidly working among the populace," sought protection in either flight or drastic remedies.[35] The deteriorating situation was summed up by the commander of the British forces in Iran:

It does not appear to be realized at home how intensely unpopular the agreement was in Persia and how hostile the public opinion had become to Vosuq's Cabinet before it fell. It was believed that the agreement really aimed at the destruction of national independence and that the Prime Minister had sold the country to Britain. The secrecy with which the agreement was concluded, the fact that the Majles was not summoned and attempts were made to pack it by the most dishonest methods . . . , all added to the conviction that Great Britain was in reality no better than the hereditary foe, Russia. The feeling grew that Great Britain must be rooted out of the country at any cost. The revolts in Azerbaijan and the Caspian provinces were due to this feeling, and to it was also the spread of Bolshevik propaganda, for it was thought that Bolshevism could not be worse and might, if their profession of securing justice for the down-trodden was sincere, be much better.[36]

In the midst of the crisis, Colonel Reza Khan, a forty-two-year-old officer who came from an obscure Turkish-speaking military family in Mazandaran but had risen through the ranks to head the Cossack Brigade in Qazvin, marched his force of some three thousand men to Tehran. Before setting out, he probably consulted the British officers in Qazvin and obtained from them ammunition, supplies, and pay for his troops. Reaching the outskirts of Tehran, he secretly met junior officers from the gendarmerie and a young journalist named Sayyid Ziya Tabatabai. Sayyid Ziya enjoyed, on the one hand, the confidence of the British military mission, since his paper Ra'ad

[35] British Minister to the Foreign Office, Documents on British Foreign Policy, 1919-39, XIII, 481, 522, 545, 609, 657, 735.
[36] The Commander of the British Military Mission to the British Minister, ibid., p. 585.

(Thunder) had supported Britain throughout the war, and, on the other hand, the reputation of an independent-minded reformer. During the revolution, he had broken with his royalist clerical father to edit a proconstitutional paper in Shiraz named *Islam*; and, during his subsequent career, he had consistently advocated the overthrow of the landed aristocracy.[37] Having won the support of the gendarmerie officers and the British military advisers, Reza Khan marched into Tehran on the night of February 21, arrested some sixty prominent politicians, assured the shah that the coup d'état was designed to save the monarchy from revolution, and requested the appointment of Sayyid Ziya as prime minister.

The shah promptly complied, creating for Reza Khan the post of Sardar Sepah (Army Commander) and offering to Sayyid Ziya an aristocratic title to befit his new office. Sayyid Ziya immediately accepted the office but not the title, thus becoming the first untitled prime minister of Iran. In announcing the formation of their government, Sayyid Ziya and Reza Khan proclaimed that they would initiate an age of national revival by ending internal disintegration, implementing social transformation, and saving the country from foreign occupation. They at once signed a treaty of friendship with the Soviet Union and abrogated the 1919 Agreement with Britain. This Soviet-Iranian Treaty cancelled the debt to the tsarist regime, annulled almost all the concessions granted to Russia in the previous century, and, by guaranteeing that Iranian territory would not be used again for attacks on the Soviet Union, paved the way for the evacuation of the Red Army from Gilan. In abrogating the Anglo-Iranian Agreement, they requested British advisers to remain behind to help reorganize the army and the civilian administration. Sayyid Ziya privately informed the British minister that the agreement had to be canceled to "throw dust in the eyes of Bolsheviks and native malcontents" and to permit the formation of a viable forward-looking central government.[38] The coup d'état appeared to have ended the period of disintegration and revived the earlier hopes for national salvation.

THE RISE OF REZA SHAH (1921-1925)

The transformation of Reza Khan into Reza Shah was slow but steady. In February 1921, he sat in the cabinet with the new title of

[37] H. Hakim-Ilaha'i, *Zendigi-yi Aqa-yi Sayyid Ziya* (The Life of Mr. Sayyid Ziya) (Tehran, 1944), pp. 34-45.

[38] British Minister to the Foreign Office, *Documents on British Foreign Policy, 1919-39*, XIII, 731.

Army Commander. In May 1921, he ousted Sayyid Ziya and gained control of the War Ministry. During the next nine months, he consolidated his power over the military, transferring the gendarmerie from the Interior Ministry to the War Ministry, replacing the Swedish and British officers with his colleagues from the Cossack Division, and putting down gendarmerie mutinies in Tabriz and Mashad. In Tabriz, Major Lahuti, the commander of the local gendarmerie and a participant of the communist-sponsored Conference of Eastern Peoples at Baku, had rallied his troops, together with survivors of Khiabani's revolt, to challenge the central government. But the better-armed Cossacks soon forced him to flee to the Soviet Union, where he pursued a long, illustrious career as a Persian-Tajik revolutionary poet.[39] In Mashad, Colonel Muhammad Taqi Khan Pesyan, the Tabriz-born commander of the local gendarmerie, formed a revolutionary committee with local Democrats—many of them fellow Azeris—and established the Provincial Government of Khurasan with its own separate National Army (Qava-yi Melli). But he was killed in a skirmish with Kurdish tribes in Astarabad, and the Cossacks reoccupied Mashad soon afterwards.[40]

Reza Khan also strengthened his military position by defeating the Jangali movement. He defeated the insurgents partly by retaining friendly relations with the Soviet Union and thus obtaining the evacuation of the Red Army; partly by mobilizing a major expeditionary force; and partly by establishing contact with the secular-radical wing of the rebel movement. The religious guerrillas reacted violently once they realized that the Soviets now favored the central government and heard rumors that the radicals were plotting to assassinate Kuchek Khan. They murdered Haydar Khan, outlawed the Communist party, forced Ehsanallah Khan to leave with the Red Army, and, trying to kill Khalu Qurban, encouraged the Kurdish fighters to make peace with the central government. By December 1921, Khalu Qurban's men were helping the Cossacks fight the Kurdish rebel Semko in Azerbaijan, Haydar Khan's supporters had escaped from Gilan, and Kuchek Khan's head was on display in Tehran to prove to all that the Jangali movement had ended once and for all.[41]

[39] ʿA. Lahuti, *Shareh-i Zendigani-yi Man* (The Story of My Life) (Tehran, n.d.). Although this book is a forgery—probably by the police—it provides interesting information on the revolt and the communist movement in exile.

[40] J. Mujiri, "The Khurasan Revolt," *Donya*, 7 (Winter 1966), 101-18; ʿA. Agahi, "The National Revolt of Khurasan," *Donya*, 6 (Spring 1965), 74-80; ʿA. Azeri, *Qiyam-i Kolonel Taqi Khan Pesyan dar Khurasan* (The Revolt of Colonel Taqi Khan Pesyan in Khurasan) (Tehran, 1950).

[41] Jowdat, *Tarikh-i Firqeh-i Demokrat*, pp. 88-100.

The next four years saw a continuous consolidation of Reza Khan's military and political positions. He merged the 7,000 Cossacks and 12,000 gendarmes into a new army of five divisions totaling 40,000 men. To pay for this expansion, he gained control of government revenues from state lands and indirect taxes. With his new army, he organized a series of successful campaigns against the rebellious tribes; in 1922, against the Kurds of western Azerbaijan, the Shahsavens of northern Azerbaijan, and the Kuhigiluyeh of Fars; in 1923, against the Sanjabi Kurds of Kermanshah; in 1924, against the Baluchis of the southeast and the Lurs of the southwest; in 1925, against the Turkomans of Mazandaran, the Kurds of north Khurasan, and the Arabs supporting Shaykh Khaz'el of Mohammerah. He was also active in Tehran, making and unmaking a succession of cabinets, until October 1923, when he took the office of prime minister. By early 1925, he was strong enough to obtain from parliament the constitutional title of the Commander-in-Chief of the Armed Forces. Finally, in December 1925, he convened a Constituent Assembly to depose the Qajar dynasty and offer him, Reza Khan, the imperial throne. In April of the following year, wearing a military uniform and the royal jewels, Reza Khan crowned himself—in the style of his hero Napoleon—the Shah-in-Shah of Iran.

Although Reza Khan based his power predominantly on the military, his rise to the throne would not have been so peaceful and constitutional without significant support from the civilian population. Without such civilian support, he might have been able to carry out another military coup d'état, but not a lawful change of dynasty; he might have seized the capital, but not the whole country with an army of a mere 40,000 men; and he might have rigged enough elections to provide himself an obedient party, but not enough to enjoy a genuine parliamentary majority. Reza Khan's path to the throne, in short, was paved not simply by violence, armed force, terror, and military conspiracies, but by open alliances with diverse groups inside and outside the Fourth and Fifth National Assemblies. These groups were formed of four political parties: the conservatives of the misnamed Reformers' party (Hizb-i Eslah Taleban); the reformers of the Revival party (Hizb-i Tajadod); the radicals of the Socialist party (Hizb-i Sosiyalist); and the revolutionaries of the Communist party.

The Reformers' party was the heir of the earlier Moderate party. Espousing similar conservative programs, it was led by prominent clerics, wealthy merchants, and landed aristocrates: Mudarres, the outspoken preacher, who frequently admitted that he could not di-

vorce his religious convictions from his political decisions;[42] Prince
Firuz Farmanfarma, who, on Sayyid Ziya's ouster, had moved directly
from jail to the newly opened National Assembly; Ahmad Qavam al-
Saltaneh, a younger brother of Vossuq al-Dawleh and a major plantation owner in Gilan, who, as a young graduate from Europe in
Muzaffar al-Din Shah's court, had sided with the demands of 1905—
indeed, the royal proclamation granting the constitution had been
transcribed in Qavam's masterful calligraphic handwriting; Morteza
Quli Khan Bayat Saham al-Sultaneh, a landed magnate from central
Iran; Sayyid Ahmad Behbehani, the son of the famous mujtahed who
had been assassinated in 1909; Sayyid Mehdi Fatemi al-Saltaneh, a
wealthy landowner in Isfahan and a son-in-law of the powerful Zil al-
Saltaneh; and 'Ali Kazeruni Sadr al-Islam, a prosperous merchant
from Bushire.

These conservatives were able to muster a majority in the Fourth
National Assembly, paradoxically, because of an electoral law passed
by the reformers in the chaotic days of the Third National Assembly.
The new law, by introducing universal adult male suffrage, extended
the vote to the rural masses, and thus, ironically, strengthened the
rural elites. As Bahar, the famous poet and veteran Democrat, years
later admitted in his classic work on the *History of Political Parties in
Iran,*

This electoral law, which continues to plague the country even today in 1944,
is one of the most harmful and least thought-out bills ever passed by us
Democrats. By introducing a democratic law from modern Europe into the
paternalistic environment of traditional Iran, it weakened the liberal candidates and instead strengthened the conservative rural magnates who can herd
their peasants, tribesmen, and other retainers into the voting polls. It is not
surprising that when the liberals in the Fourth Majles tried to rectify their
mistake, the conservatives staunchly and successfully rallied behind the existing "democratic" law.[43]

The Revival party, which, with the help of Reza Khan, held a majority in the Fifth National Assembly, was formed of young Western-
educated reformers who had previously supported the Democrats.
They avoided the label Democrat, however, for a number of reasons.
First, the conservative influence of popular religion had convinced
them to seek reform not through appeals to the masses but through

---

[42] H. Makki, *Tarikh-i Best Saleh-i Iran* (Twenty-Year History of Iran), II (Tehran,
1945), 215-16.

[43] Malek al-Shua'ra Bahar, *Tarikh-i Ahzab-i Siyasi-yi Iran* (History of Political Parties
in Iran) (Tehran, 1944), p. 306.

alliances with members of the power elite—preferably with a strong man such as Reza Khan. Second, the term Democrat, although previously associated with the struggle against the foreign occupation, was now adopted freely by many local conservative groups. For example, in Fars during 1919-1924, the Qashqayis formed a Real Democrat party, the Khamseh a True Democrat party, the merchants of Shiraz an Eastern Democrat party, the urban landlords a Western Democrat party, and the Baha'i community of Abadeh an Independent Democrat party.[44] Finally, the Anglo-Iranian Agreement and the provincial revolts of 1919-1921 had divided the Democrats into two rival factions: the "organizationalists," who, fearing national disintegration, had rallied behind the central government; and the "anti-organizationalists," who, opposing the Agreement, had sympathized with the provincial rebels. Bahar explained his reasons for joining the former faction: "Realizing that provincial decentralization can easily lead to national disintegration, I backed the central government, even Vossuq al-Dawleh, and criticized Kuchek Khan, Khiabani, and Taqi Khan, even though I admired them personally. For the same reasons, I continue to favor the formation of a strong central government and warn against the establishment of provincial autonomy."[45]

The Revival party was organized mainly by ʿAli Akbar Davar, ʿAbdul Hussein Timourtash, and Sayyid Muhammad Tadayon. Davar, a son of a minor official and a former employee in the Justice Ministry, had studied law in Geneva, and, after his return in 1921, had waged a campaign for legal reforms through his newspaper *Mard-i Azad* (Free Man). Timourtash, a son of a landowner in Khurasan, was a graduate of the military academy in St. Petersburg, and an experienced administrator in the ministries of Justice and Interior—he had been governor of Gilan during the last stages of the Jangali revolt. Tadayon, another Khurasani, was a former school teacher who had participated in the revolution and had risen to prominence within the Democrat party during the upheavals of the 1910s. Many other veterans of the constitutional movement were also associated with the Revival party: Taqizadeh; Bahar; Mustawfi al-Mamalek; Muhammad ʿAli Zuka al-Mulk (later known as Foroughi), a former court tutor and Justice minister, a colleague of Malkum Khan, a law lecturer at the Dar al-Fonun, a member of the Revolutionary Committee in 1905, and a founder of the first official Freemason Lodge at Tehran in 1909; Shahroukh Arbab Keykhosrow, the representative of the Zoroastrian community, a graduate of the American school in Tehran, the director

[44] British Consul in Shirz, "Report on Fars," *F.O. 371*/Persia 1922/34-7805; British Consul in Shiraz, "Report on Fars," *F.O. 371*/Persia 1924/34-9629.

[45] Bahar, *Tarikh-i Ahzab*, p. ix.

of the telephone company, and also a founding member of the same Freemason Lodge; and Ibrahim Hakim al-Mulk (later known as Hakimi), the son of a court official, one of the first Dar al-Fonun graduates to be sent to Europe by Naser al-Din Shah, the personal physician of Muzaffar al-Din Shah, an active supporter of the Constitutional Revolution, a prominent Democrat in the Second Majles, and since 1909 a secret Freemason.

The program of the Revival party called for separation of religion from politics, creation of a well-disciplined army and a well-administered bureaucracy, an end to economic capitulations, industrialization, replacement of foreign capital by native capital, transformation of nomads into farmers, a progressive income tax, expansion of educational facilities for all, including women, careers open to talent, and replacement of minority languages throughout Iran by Persian.

Three influential journals expressed the general aspirations of the reformers: *Iranshahr* (Country of Iran), published in Berlin from 1922 until 1927 by Hussein Kazemzadeh, previously a diplomat in the London legation, a protégé of Edward Browne, and a brother of a prominent Democrat who had been banished from Tabriz by Khiabani; *Farangistan* (Europe), edited in Germany from 1924 to 1926 by Mushfeq Kazemi, a young member of the diplomatic corps; and *Ayandeh* (The Future), founded in Tehran in 1925 by Dr. Mahmud Afshar, a European-educated political scientist.

Although published in Berlin, *Iranshahr* was distributed in some forty towns in Iran. Its orientation was evident in the balance of the subjects it discussed: of the total of 236 articles published in the journal, 73 stressed the importance of public and secular education, 45 emphasized the need to improve the status of women, 30 described—in favorable terms—pre-Islamic Iran, and 40 discussed aspects of modern technology and Western philosophy, especially Voltaire's anticlericalism, Gobineau's racism, and Gustave le Bon's works on "irrational mobs." One recurring theme in the journal was the harmful consequences of ethnicity. As an article on "Religion and Nationality" stated, "the problem of communalism is so serious that whenever an Iranian traveling abroad is asked his nationality, he will give his locality—not the proud name of his country. We must eliminate local sects, local dialects, local clothes, local customs, and local sentiments." Another recurring theme was the theory that Iran's contemporary backwardness originated in the Arab Muslim invasions of the seventh century. One article, quoting Marx's description of religion as "the opium of the masses," argued that the country could not progress until it had freed itself from the shackles of the superstitious and reactionary clergy. Another claimed that Iran had to learn from the

French Revolution and liberate the "common masses" from clerical domination. Yet another argued that the long-range remedy lay in the closing of religious maktab schools and the opening of secular public schools. And yet another argued that clerical dogmatism, political despotism, and foreign imperialism, especially Arab imperialism, had retarded the "creative abilities of Iran's talented Aryan population."[46] One such article was accompanied with a picture depicting the "savage" Muslim Arab tribes looting, abusing, and massacring the "civilized" Zoroastrian population of ancient Iran. It is not surprising that *Iranshahr*, despite its wide circulation among the intelligentsia within Iran, continued to be published outside the country.

The contents of *Farangistan* were similar. Of some seventy articles published in the journal, fifteen dealt with modern education, eight with the status of women, ten with industrial technology, nine with Western political philosophy, including Gobineau's racism, Anatole France's socialism, and Marx's anticolonialism, three with pre-Islamic Iran, three with Azerbaijan, two with the secular movement in Turkey, four with international relations, and sixteen with Persian literature. Its opening editorial proclaimed that Iran had freed itself from royal despotism but now needed a "revolutionary dictator" who would forceably liberate the ignorant masses from the clutches of the superstitious clergy: "In a country where 99 percent of the population is under the electoral sway of the reactionary mullas, our only hope is a Mussolini who can break the influence of the traditional authorities, and thus create a modern outlook, a modern people, and a modern nation." In a follow-up article, the editor argued that although the Iranian press was calling for all types of reforms, the most important reform would be the expulsion of the clergy from public life and the destruction of popular superstitions: "Only a dictator, however, can initiate such a regeneration."[47]

The contents of the monthly *Ayandeh* were similar, but they focused mainly on the need to form a centralized state and a unified national identity. The editor launched the journal with an article entitled "Our First Desire: The National Unity of Iran:"

Our ideal is to develop and strengthen national unity. The same ideal created the nation-states of Germany, Italy, Poland, and Rumania. The same ideal

[46] "Religion and Nationality," *Iranshahr*, 2 (December 1924), 41-42; "The Fate of Mankind," *Iranshahr*, 4 (June 1926), 193-201; "The French Revolution and the Promised Iranian Revolution," *Iranshahr*, 1 (April 1923), 282-93; H. Kazemzadeh, "Religion and Nationality," *Iranshahr*, 3 (December 1924), 1-45; R. Shafaq, "The Glories of the Iranian National Character," *Iranshahr*, 2 (May 1924), 497-99.

[47] M. Kazemi, "What Do We Want?" and "The Iranian Press," *Farangestan*, 1 (May, August 1924), 1-11, 154-60.

destroyed the multinational state of the Ottoman Empire. What do we mean by "national unity"? We mean the formation of cultural, social, and political solidarity among all the people who live within the present borders of Iran. How will we attain national unity? We will attain it by extending the Persian language throughout the provinces; eliminating regional costumes; destroying local and feudal authorities; and removing the traditional differences between Kurds, Lurs, Qashqayis, Arabs, Turks, Turkomans, and other communities that reside within Iran. Our nation will continue to live in danger as long as we have no schools to teach Persian and Iranian history to the masses; no railways to connect the various parts of the country; no books, journals, and newspapers to inform the people of their rich Iranian heritage; and no Persian equivalents to replace the many non-Persian place names in Iran. Unless we achieve national unity, nothing will remain of Iran.[48]

The editor elaborated on the same theme in later issues. Warning that the country was threatened by many dangers—the red (Soviet), blue (British), yellow (Turkish), green (Arab), and black (clerical) dangers—he stressed that the essential tasks were to create a strong centralized state, to spread the Persian language among the non-Persian communities, and to move the Arab and Turkic tribes from the border provinces into the interior regions.[49]

The historian Kasravi concentrated on the same topic of national unification in his frequent contributions to *Ayandeh* and in his prolific works on the languages, tribes, religions, and place names of Iran. He wrote his first major work, entitled *Azeri: Ya Zaban-i Bastan-i Azerbaijan* (Azeri: Or the Ancient Language of Azerbaijan), in the aftermath of the Khiabani revolt, to prove that Azeri, the original Aryan tongue of his native province, had been destroyed by the Turkic invasions. He concluded that the existing foreign-imposed Turkish dialect should be replaced now by Persian, the state language. His second major book, *Tarikh-i Pansad Saleh-i Khuzistan* (Five Hundred-Year History of Khuzistan), tried to show the harmful consequences of tribal and religious conflicts in the southwestern regions. He undertook his monumental *Tarikh-i Mashruteh-i Iran* (History of the Iranian Constitution) to illustrate three essential points: the detrimental result of linguistic differences; the vital role played by Azerbaijan in the development of Iran; and the tragic shipwreck of the constitutional movement on the rocks of tribal, linguistic, and sectarian divisions.[50] Kasravi was to hammer away at these themes until his assassination in 1946 by a group of Shi'i fundamentalists:

[48] M. Afshar, "Our First Desire: The National Unity of Iran," *Ayandeh*, 1 (June 1925), 5-6.

[49] M. Afshar, "The Problem of Nationality and the National Unity of Iran," *Ayandeh*, 2 (November 1926), 559-69, 761-74.

[50] A. Kasravi, "Again Concerning Azerbaijan," *Parcham*, 6 December 1942.

All Iranians with a grain of awareness are saddened by the backwardness of their country—especially by the decline of Iran from a major and powerful empire into a minor and weak state. What lies at the root of this drastic decline? At the beginning of this century, reformers could claim that the main culprits were the despots who had a vested interest in keeping their subjects ignorant and unenlightened. After twenty years of constitutional government, however, we cannot in good conscience give the same answer. We now know that the main blame rests not with the rulers, but with the ruled. Yes, the chief reason of underdevelopment in Iran, perhaps in most Eastern countries, is disunity among the masses.[51]

The worst calamity that can befall a nation is disunity. A people who share a common territory and live together within one state must not be divided into rival factions. Contemporary Iran is a clear example of a nation that has not heeded this warning. Consequently, it is now suffering the worst miseries of backwardness.[52]

The famous heroes of modern Iran—Amir Kabir, Sepahsalar, Malkum Khan, Tabatabai, Shaykh al-Islam . . . —all, without exception, failed to achieve lasting reforms because they were unable to grasp this fundamental fact: the population is torn apart by rival communities.[53]

Factionalism is one of the worst maladies afflicting Iran. Factionalism caused by religious sectarianism: I can count fourteen separate sects, each with its own separate goals, interests, and leaders. Each, in fact, a state within a state. Factionalism caused by tribal and linguistic differences: there are innumerable tribes and at least eight major linguistic groups. And factionalism caused by wide social differences—between the city and the country, the young and the old, the modern educated elite and the traditional-minded masses.[54]

If we desire to remedy the ills of Iran like true statesmen, we must focus our attention on the source of the malady—on the masses. We must save the people from corrupting superstitions, instill in them a love for their country, arouse in them the instinct for social progress, teach them to make personal sacrifices, and, most important of all, unite them into a nationally conscious people.[55]

Whereas the Revival party was led by former Democrats who had lost confidence in the masses, the Socialist party was organized by former Democrats who retained the hope of mobilizing the middle and lower classes. Bahar, in an indirect criticism of the Socialist party, commented, "socialist ideas can but fall on barren ground in a backward environment such as Iran where there are no industrial capi-

[51] A. Kasravi, "The Chief Cause of Backwardness," *Parcham*, 27 April 1942.
[52] A. Kasravi, "Islam and Iran," *Payman*, 1 (February 1933), 9-10.
[53] A. Kasravi, "Corruption among the Masses," *Parcham-i Haftegi*, 15 April 1944.
[54] A. Kasravi, "A Short History," *Parcham*, 29 February 1942.
[55] A. Kasravi, "Why We Are Not Politicians," *Payman*, 7 (May 1942), p. 581.

talists, no industrial enterprises, and thus no industrial workers."[56] An article in *Ayandeh* argued that socialist parties would fail to find roots in Iran, since the urban working class was nonexistent, the professional middle class was small, and the landed upper class continued to control the rural lower classes.[57] The author concluded that socialist parties would be premature until industrialization had transformed the "feudal" socioeconomic structure. A reformer, sympathetic to socialism, elaborated on the same theme in a pamphlet entitled *Iran and the Bolsheviks*.[58] Arguing that the rural population of contemporary Iran resembled the "potatoes" described in Marx's *Class Struggles in France*, the author stressed that socialism would remain out of place in Iran until the industrial working class had emerged as a viable social force. Until then, he advised his readers, especially members of the Socialist party, to drop unrealistic revolutionary slogans in favor or realistic reformist aims, and to ally with the more liberal elements of the upper class.

The Socialist party was led by Sulayman Iskandari, Musavat, and Qassem Khan Sur, the editor of the radical *Sur-i Israfil* and nephew of the famous Sur-i Israfil who had been killed in 1906. To forestall clerical attacks, the Socialist party recruited into its parliamentary delegation Muhammad Sadeq Tabatabai—the highly respected but liberal son of the mujtahed who had led the constitutional movement. Eager to develop from a parliamentary caucus into a nationwide party, the Socialists opened branches in a number of cities, especially in Tehran, Rasht, Qazvin, Enzeli, Tabriz, Mashad, Kerman, and Kermanshsah. A group of local intellectuals in Rasht, headed by a high-school teacher named Hussein Jowdat, formed the Cultural Society.[59] A similar group in Qazvin, also led by a teacher, formed the Educational Society.[60] Both societies published literary journals and helped establish literacy classes, modern theaters, and women's organizations.

The party, however, centered its activities on Tehran. There it not only published four newspapers, including the popular paper *Tofan* (Storm), but also founded a Tenants' Association, a Union of Employees in the Ministry of Post and Telegraph, and a Patriotic Women's Society. *Tofan* was edited by Muhammad Farokhi, an outspoken poet

[56] Bahar, *Tarikh-i Ahzab*, p. 319.

[57] M. Chireh, "Political Parties and the Constitutional System of Iran," *Ayandeh*, 1 (March 1926), 473-80.

[58] *Iran va Bolshevikha* (Iran and the Bolsheviks) (n.p., 192?), pp. 1-24.

[59] R. Rusta, "Reminiscences on the Cultural Society in Rasht," *Donya*, 6 (Autumn 1965), 82-84; ʿA. Kobari, "Reminiscences on the Cultural Society in Gilan," *Donya*, 12 (Winter 1971), 80-83.

[60] ʿA. Kambakhsh, "Reminiscences on the Educational Society in Qazvin," *Donya*, 6 (Autumn 1965), 85-88.

from Yazd whose lips had been literally sewn together by the Qashqayis.[61] The Patriotic Women's Society was chaired by Muhtaram Iskandari, the wife of Sulayman Iskandari and the headmistress of one of the country's few girl schools. This society campaigned for laws to protect women, held literacy courses, published a journal, and put on plays to raise public consciousness.[62] According to the British military attaché, the Socialist party in Tehran recruited nearly 2,500 members, most of whom were "educated persons."[63]

The program of the Socialist party called for the eventual establishment of an "egalitarian society"; nationalization of the means of production, including agriculture; irrigation projects to help farmers; strengthening of the central government and convening of provincial assemblies; equal justice for all citizens "irrespective of birth and nationality (*melliyat*)"; freedom of speech, thought, press, and assembly, and the right to organize unions and strikes; elections that would be free, universal, equal, secret, and direct; compulsory education for all children of primary school age; use of "mother tongues" (*zaban-i madari*) in such schools; education for women; a ban on child labor; an eight-hour work day; pay for Friday holidays; and government projects to eliminate rural and urban unemployment.[64]

Closely allied to the Socialists was the Communist party. Indeed, the two parties worked so closely together and so many members of the latter were also members of the former that the British military attaché constantly confused the two organizations.[65] After the destruction of the Soviet Socialist Republic in Gilan, the Communist party had gone through a major transformation. It had changed the focus of its activities from the north to the interior, especially Tehran. It had discouraged provincial revolts and instead encouraged the state to strengthen the central administration.[66] It had toned down the call for armed insurrection, and, adopting Haydar Khan's minimalist platform, tried to "democratize the bourgeoisie," unite the country against

---

[61] H. Javan, "Muhammad Farokhi," *Setareh-i Surkh*, 1 (October 1950), 75-77.

[62] M. Firuz, "A Short History of the Womens' Movement in Iran," *Razm Mahaneh*, 1 (August 1948), 45-46.

[63] British Military Attaché to the Foreign Office, "A Report on the Socialist Party," *F.O. 371*/Persia (1923/34-9027.

[64] "The Program of the Socialist Party," *Donya*, 4 (January 1978), 58-63.

[65] British Military Attaché to the Foreign Office, "A Report on the Socialist Party," *F.O. 371*/Persia 1923/34-9027.

[66] I. Fakhrayi, *Sardar-i Jangal* (The Commander of the Jangal) (Tehran, 1963), pp. 311-16. When Lahuti fled to Baku after his unsuccessful revolt in Tabriz, he was received not as a heroic revolutionary but as a romantic troublemaker. When the Jangalis tried to revive their rebellion, the Communists refused to participate.

British imperialism, consolidate the party organization, and create viable trade unions throughout Iran.[67] By 1925 the Communists had opened branches in Tehran, Tabriz, Mashad, Isfahan, Enzeli, and Kermanshah, and underground cells in many of the southern cities.[68] They published intermittently six newspapers: *Haqiqat* (Truth) in Tehran; *Paykar* (Battle) in Rasht; *Nasihat* (Exhortation) in Qazvin; *Sada-yi Sharq* (Voice of the East) in Mashad; *Faryad-i Kargaran-i Azerbaijan* (Cry of the Azerbaijan Workers) in Tabriz; and *Banvor* (Worker), an Armenian-language paper in Tehran. They organized special sections within the party for women, for Armenians, and for youth—especially students at the Dar al-Fonun. And most important of all, they created with the help of the Socialists the *Shawra-yi Mutahedeh-i Ittehadieh-i Kargaran* (Central Council of Federated Trade Unions, CCFTU).[69]

The CCFTU began in 1921 with only nine affiliates in Tehran: the unions of printers, pharmacists, shoemakers, bath attendants, bakery assistants, construction laborers, municipal employees, tailors, and textile workers in Tehran's sole modern mill. In the following three years, the CCFTU grew to a total of over 8,000 members throughout Iran.[70] It organized May Day parades, attracting over 2,000 participants in Tehran. It won over the union of teachers, as well as the union of post and telephone employees. It led strikes among printers against press censorship, and among teachers, postal clerks, bakery assistants, and textile workers for higher incomes. Moreover, it helped organize twenty-one new unions in different regions of the country. These consisted of the union of dockers in Enzeli; carpet weavers in Kerman; textile workers in Isfahan; oil workers in the southwest; teachers, porters, tobacco workers, and rice cleaners in Rasht; teachers, tailors, shoemakers, office employees, carpet weavers, confectioners, and telegraphers in Mashad; as well as cooks, domestic ser-

---

[67] British Military Attaché to the Foreign Office, "A Report on the Communist Party in Persia," *F.O. 371*/Persia 1922/34-7805. In 1925 the Soviets instructed their representatives in Iran to avoid all direct contacts with the local Communists. See British Minister to the Foreign Office, "Letter from Moscow to the Soviet Representative in Tehran," *F.O. 371*/Persia 1925/34-10848.

[68] British Military Attaché to the Foreign Office, "Communist Activity in Persia," *F.O. 371*/Persia 1923/34-9027.

[69] M. Nashehi, "Workers' Organizations in Iran," *Rahbar*, 10 April 1944; Sh. Mani, *Tarikhcheh-i Nahzat-i Kargar-i dar Iran* (Short History of the Labor Movement in Iran) (Tehran, 1946); R. Rusta, "The Central Council of Federated Trade Unions," *Razm Mahaneh*, 1 (June 1948), 62-64; M. Ivanov, *Rabochii Klass sovremennogo Irana* (The Working Class in Contemporary Iran) (Moscow, 1969), pp. 200-10.

[70] A. Ovanessian, "Reminiscences of the Iranian Communist Party," *Donya*, 3 (Spring 1962), 33-39.

vants, carpet weavers, carriage drivers, carpenters, and tobacco workers in Tehran. Thus the early labor movement reflected the backward nature of the economy. Of the thirty-two unions in existence by 1925, only six represented workers in modern industry.

The Communist party and its trade unions drew their rank and file predominantly from the Azeri and Armenian populations. For example, in Tehran, many printers, textile workers, tobacco cleaners, construction laborers, and bath attendants were migrants from Azerbaijan; many of the pharmacists, telegraphers, shoemakers, and confectioners were Armenians. In Mashad, almost all the tailors, telegraphers, carpet weavers, and confectioners were Azeris who had supported Taqi Khan's unsuccessful revolt. Significantly, the Communist party failed to make any inroads among the peasantry.[71] As one British consul observed, the party, despite some successes among the urban workers, failed completely with the rural masses because the latter continued to consider the local oppressors as their "natural superiors."[72]

Although the Communists made a concerted effort to build a working-class base throughout Iran, the party leadership, like that of the preceding Justice and Social Democratic parties, remained predominantly intellectual and non-Persian (see Table 2). For example, Karim Nikbin, who became first secretary after Haydar Khan's assassination, was a journalist educated in Moscow University. Born in 1893 into a small merchant family in Tabriz, Nikbin had been raised in the Caucasus and sent to Moscow to study business. Joining the Bolsheviks at the height of the Russian Revolution, he had returned to Iran to fight in Gilan and later led the party organization in Tehran. Hussein Sharqi, Nikbin's successor as first secretary, was born in 1903 in Central Asia, where his father, a native of Tabriz, had been making a living as a tailor. Graduating from local Persian and Russian schools, Sharqi attended the Moscow University for the Toilers of the East, which trained party cadres for Asia and the Middle East. Finally, Ardasher Ovanessian, the head of the party's youth organization, came from a rural Armenian family in Iranian Azerbaijan but grew up with close relatives in Rasht. Forced by financial problems to drop out of the Armenian missionary school in Rasht, he had worked as a pharmacist, joined the Jangali movement, and fled to the Soviet Union where he studied modern languages—especially French, German, English, and Russian—at Moscow University for the Toilers of the East.

[71] A. Ovanessian, "The Organization of the Iranian Communist Party in Khurasan," *Donya*, 6 (Autumn 1965), 80-81; Kobari, "Reminiscences," p. 83.
[72] British Consul in Kerman, "Intelligence Report," *F.O. 416*/Persia 1926-76.

Reza Khan began his rise to power by forming an alliance with the conservative Reformers' party in the Fourth National Assembly. This alliance was translated into concrete benefits for the conservatives. Reza Khan released the aristocrats who had been imprisoned by Sayyid Ziya; supported the election of Qavam al-Saltaneh to replace Sayyid Ziya as prime minister; restored Sepahdar to his former prominent position in the Caspian provinces; welcomed members of the Shiʿi ʿulama who had fled from Iraq after an unsuccessful revolt against the British; and used martial law to suspend three radical newspapers—*Haqiqat, Tofan*, and *Setareh-i Surkh* (Red Star). Reza Khan also moved with the conservatives in formulating foreign policy. Hastening the departure of the British troops from Iran, Reza Khan sought aid from United States by both offering a northern concession to the Standard Oil Company of New York and appointing Dr. Arthur Millspaugh of the State Department as treasurer-general of Iran. In 1922, some two hundred merchants expressed their gratitude to Reza Khan in an open letter: "Before our beloved commander saved us, the Islamic Empire of Iran was fast disintegrating. The army had collapsed, the tribes were looting, the country was the laughing stock of the world. Thanks to the army commander, we now travel without fear, admire our country, and enjoy the fruits of law and order."[73]

The conservative deputies reciprocated by retaining Reza Khan as war minister; increasing the military budget to stamp out tribal revolts; and permitting him to collect government revenues from state lands and indirect taxes. They also placed many tribal areas under martial law, approved funds to send sixty officers per year to study in French military academies, and rallied behind him when Ahmad Shah tried to reassert his royal authority as commander-in-chief.

This alliance, however, ended abruptly in the last days of the Fourth National Assembly, as soon as Reza Khan introduced a bill for compulsory military conscription. The bill proposed that every adult male should serve two full years in the armed forces. For Reza Khan, mass conscription would transform the professional army into a truly national army. For many landed magnates, such conscription would erode their patrimonial authority and draw essential labor from their villages. And for the ʿulama, especially Mudarres, two years of indoctrination in a secular institution administered by anticlerical officers would corrupt social morality and public religiosity. As a number of mujtaheds declared in separate fatwas, military service endangered the principles of Shiʿism and the fundamentals of Islam.[74]

[73] Makki, *Tarikh-i Best Saleh*, II, 36-37.

[74] M. Farrukh, *Khatirat-i Siyasi-yi Farrukh* (The Political Memoirs of Farrukh) (Tehran, 1969), pp. 222-25.

TABLE 2
Leading Personalities of the Early Communist Movement

Name	Occupation	Education	Place of Birth
Ghafarzadeh, Assadallah	journalist	Dar al-Fonun	Iranian Azerbaijan
Sultanzadeh, Ahmad	journalist	high school	Iranian Azerbaijan
Haydar Khan, Amir ʿUghli	engineer	engineering school	Iranian Azerbaijan
Pishevari, Jaʿfar	teacher	high school	Iranian Azerbaijan
Nikbin, Karim	journalist	Moscow University	Iranian Azerbaijan
Sharqi, Hussein	journalist	Moscow University	Central Asia
Ovanessian, Ardasher	pharmacist	Moscow University	Iranian Azerbaijan
Yusefzadeh, Aqa Baba	teacher	high school	Iranian Azerbaijan
Akhundzadeh, Muhammad	teacher	high school	Iranian Azerbaijan
Dehkan, Muhammad	writer-translator	high school	Kashan
Javid, Salamallah	doctor	medical school	Iranian Azerbaijan
Sartipzadeh ʿAli	journalist	high school	Iranian Azerbaijan
Hejazi, Muhammad	typesetter	high school	Tehran
ʿAlizadeh, Ibrahim	civil servant	Dar al-Fonun	Iranian Azerbaijan

Reza Khan therefore took advantage of the period between the Fourth and Fifth National Assemblies to forge an alliance with the secular reformers who had championed the concept of mass conscription since 1906. Using the military to manipulate the elections in many tribal constituencies, Reza Khan was able to produce in the new parliament a working majority of the Socialist and Revival parties. This majority promptly initiated extensive reforms. It chose Reza Khan as prime minister, Foroughi of the Revival party as foreign minister, Sulayman Iskandari as education minister. It approved the bill for compulsory conscription; cut the court budget; abolished such aristocratic titles as al-Dawleh, al-Saltaneh, and al-Mamalek; obliged all citizens to obtain birth certificates and family names—Reza Khan adopted for his family the ancient Iranian name of Pahlevi. It also ended the negotiations with the Standard Oil Company; levied taxes on tea, sugar, and income to raise revenue for the proposed Trans-Iranian Railway; instituted a uniform system of weights and measures for the country; replaced the Islamic calendar with the pre-Islamic Iranian calendar;[75] rewarded Reza Khan for the successful campaign against Shaykh Khazʿel by granting him the title of Commander-in-

---

[75] Although the new calendar continued to use the Muslim Hejira as its base, it Persianized the names of the months and replaced the Arabic lunar year with the old Iranian solar year.

Date of Birth	Class Origin	Ethnic Origin	Subsequent Career
1876	urban middle class	Azeri	killed in Gilan
1889	urban middle class	Armenian	killed in Stalin's purges
1880	urban middle class	Azeri	killed in Gilan
1893	urban middle class	Azeri	led Democrat Party of Azerbaijan
1893	urban middle class	Azeri	killed in Stalin's purges
1903	urban middle class	Azeri	killed in Stalin's purges
1905	rural middle class	Armenian	Tudeh leader
1886	urban middle class	Azeri	killed in Stalin's purges
1884	urban middle class	Azeri	remained in Russia
?	urban middle class	Persian	retired from politics in 1928
1902	urban middle class	Azeri	led Democrat Party of Azerbaijan
1897	urban middle class	Azeri	anti-Tudeh politician in 1942-1953
1902	urban middle class	Persian	killed in Tehran prison in 1930
?	urban middle class	Azeri	member of Democrat Party of Azerbaijan

Chief—a title that had been vested in the shah by the constitutional laws; and, most explosive of all, drafted a bill to eliminate the two-thousand-year-old monarchy. The journal *Iranshahr* summed up the views of the parliamentary majority in an editorial on "Republicanism and Social Revolution":

Today almost all of Europe, including Russia, has adopted the republican system of government. There is no doubt in our minds that in the modern age the republican form of government is the best system of government. But while we have no doubts on the merits of republicanism, we must admit that republicanism is not an end in itself but only a means to a higher end— that of destroying royal and clerical despotism in order to lead the masses toward a social revolution. You will understand the need for such a revolution if you look at the minority party in the Majles. These clerical deputies have been elected by exploiting public ignorance, fears, backwardness, and su-perstitions. It is high time we eliminated the power of the monarchy. Once we have done so, we can turn our attention onto the more reactionary power of the parasitical clergy.[76]

Fearing such an assault and seeing the elimination of the sultanate precede the abolition of the caliphate in contemporary Turkey, the conservative deputies took the issue to the public. While Mudarres

[76] H. Kazemzadeh, "Republicanism and the Social Revolution," *Iranshahr*, 2 (February 1924), 257-58.

declared that an attack on the monarchy was an attack on the holy shari'a, the guild elders organized a general strike in the Tehran bazaar and a mass procession from the central mosque to the parliament building. The protestors shouted one main slogan: "We want to keep the religion of our fathers, we don't want a republic. We are the people of the Koran, we don't want a republic."[77] Meanwhile, the Revival and Socialist parties, supported by the CCFTU, held a counterdemonstration on the other side of the parliament building. Hostile witnesses claimed that the republican rally attracted no more than three hundred, and that many of the participants were civil servants, telegraphers, and post office workers, who had been given a day's paid vacation.[78]

Observing the imbalance between the two demonstrations and the danger of public disturbances, Reza Khan promptly compromised. After negotiations behind closed doors, Reza Khan requested the majority to withdraw the bill, released some two hundred demonstrators who had been jailed, and announced that he was setting out on a pilgrimage to the holy shrine at Qum. The parliamentary minority, at the same time, promised not to champion the cause of Ahmad Shah and the Qajar dynasty. The implications of this compromise soon became apparent. On one hand, Reza Khan publicly admitted that the "ideology of republicanism had created social confusion," arrested nine Communist activists—all of them Armenians— and announced that the "institution of constitutional monarchy was the best bulwark against Bolshevism." On the other hand, the conservative deputies spread the rumor that the Qajar court had been negotiating secretly with Shaykh Khaz'el against the central government. The 'ulama circulated a photograph of Ahmad Shah in Paris wearing a European straw hat and accompanying a group of French women. And the guild elders in Tabriz, encouraged by the local army commander, organized a bazaar strike and dispatched a telegram to Tehran threatening the "secession" of Azerbaijan from Iran unless the Majles replaced Ahmad Shah with Reza Pahlevi.[79]

This new alliance between Reza Khan and the conservative deputies reached its culmination in the autumn of 1925. The Revival party,

[77] Makki, *Tarikh-i Best Saleh*, II, 342-43.

[78] Ibid., pp. 319-49; M. Hedayat, *Khatirat va Kheterat* (Memoirs and Dangers) (Tehran, 1965), pp. 363-64; 'A. Mustawfi, *Sharh-i Zendigani-yi Man* (My Life) (Tehran, 1943-1945), III, 410-19; Y. Dawlatabadi, *Hayat-i Yahya* (The Life of Yahya) (Tehran, 1951), IV, 345-61.

[79] D. Wilber, *Riza Shah Pahlavi: The Resurrection and Reconstruction of Iran* (New York, 1975), p. 79; British Minister to the Foreign Office, "Annual Report for 1925," *F.O. 371*/Persia 1926/34-11500.

supported by almost all of the deputies from the Reformists' party, introduced a bill to depose the Qajars and entrust the state to Reza Pahlevi until the convening of a Constituent Assembly. Eighty deputies voted for the proposal, thirty abstained, and five opposed. The main spokesman against the bill was Dr. Muhammad Mossadeq (formerly Mossadeq al-Saltaneh), a European-educated aristocrat who had served recently as minister of justice, finance and foreign affairs, as well as governor of Fars and Azerbaijan. Mossadeq explained in a long speech that Reza Pahlevi was an excellent prime minister and commander-in-chief, but any additional position would make him into a threat against the cherished constitution.[80] As soon as the deputies passed the bill, Reza Khan banned all sale of alcohol, reduced bread prices, outlawed gambling, exhorted women to uphold "national honor," and promised to enforce moral conduct. He also proclaimed that his two ambitions in life were to attain peace for his people and implement the true laws of sacred Islam.[81] The day after the vote, the crown prince left Tehran to join Ahmad Shah in Paris. The British minister commented that he saw "not a single sign of regret for the ending of the Qajar dynasty."[82]

Using the ministries of War and Interior, Reza Khan packed the Constituent Assembly with his supporters from the Revival and the Reformers' parties. Not surprisingly, an overwhelming majority of the assembly voted to bestow the throne upon the Pahlevi family. Of the 260 deputies, only Sulayman Iskandari and two other Socialists abstained from the decision. Iskandari declared that although his party enthusiastically supported the reforms that had been championed by Reza Khan, its socialist-republican principles prevented it from endorsing the establishment of a new monarchy.[83] The British minister remarked that the left had become disillusioned with Reza Khan, but the right had developed the illusion that Reza Khan was now attached to its own chariot wheels. On the contrary, the minister added, Reza Khan had bound the right to his own chariot wheels.[84]

THE REIGN OF REZA SHAH (1926-1941)

The reign of Reza Shah saw the founding of a New Order. Gaining the crown in 1926, he moved to consolidate his power by building

[80] Dawlatabadi, *Hayat-i Yahya*, IV, 385-86.

[81] British Minister to the Foreign Office, "Report for October 1925," *F.O. 371*/Persia 1925/34-10840.

[82] British Minister to the Foreign Office, "Annual Report for 1925," *F.O. 371*/Persia 1926/34-11500.

[83] *Iran*, 13 December 1925.

[84] British Minister to the Foreign Office, "Annual Report for 1925," *F.O. 371*/Persia 1926/34-11500.

and strengthening his support on three pillars—the new army, the government bureaucracy, and the court patronage. For the first time since the Safavids, the state was able to control society through extensive instruments of administration, regulation, and domination. And having consolidated his power, Reza Shah was able to embark upon an ambitious program of social, cultural, and economic reforms. He successfully implemented many of the innovations that had been unsuccessfully proposed during the previous century by such reformers as Prince ʿAbbas Mirza, Amir Kabir, Sepahsalar, Malkum Khan, and the Democrats of the Constitutional Revolution. By 1941 Reza Shah had established a New Order, only to have the Anglo-Soviet invasion pave the way for his forced abdication.

Reza Shah relied on the modern army to be the central pillar of his New Order. As the annual defense budget increased more than fivefold from 1926 to 1941, and as the conscription law extended its reach into the population—first into the villages, later into the towns, finally into the nomadic tribes—the armed forces grew from five divisions totaling 40,000 men to eighteen divisions totaling 127,000 men.[85] It was supplemented by a small air force, a mechanized brigade of 100 tanks, and a few gunboats in the Persian Gulf. Reza Shah, moreover, systematically linked the military elite to his régime. He wore military uniforms for all public occasions, gave career officers a standard of living above that of other salaried employees, sold them state lands at discount prices, built for them an impressive club in Tehran, and sent the top graduates of the military academies to St. Cyr in France. He promoted loyal colleagues from the old Cossack Division to head the new army divisions, dealt harshly with any sign of disloyalty, and built an efficient chain of command from his military office within the royal court through the chiefs of staff to the field commanders. Finally, he raised his sons, especially Crown Prince Muhammad Reza, to be first and foremost active officers in the armed forces. He educated the heir apparent predominantly in military institutions—except for a brief break at the exclusive La Rosey School in Switzerland—and in 1940 commissioned him as special inspector for the armed forces.

Reza Shah also reinforced the New Order with a modern state bureaucracy. He gradually transformed the haphazard collection of traditional mustawfis, hereditary mirzas, and central ministers without provincial ministries into some 90,000 full-time government personnel employed in the ten civilian ministries of Interior, Foreign Affairs,

[85] War Office to the Foreign Office, "Memorandum on the Persian Army," *F.O. 371/ Persia* 1941/34-27206.

Justice, Finance, Education, Trade, Post and Telegraph, Agriculture, Roads, and Industry.[86] The Interior Ministry, which supervised the police, internal administration, medical services, elections, and military conscription, was entirely reorganized. The old division of few large provinces (*ayalat*) and innumerable small districts (*vilayat*) was abolished. Instead, the ministry was structured into eleven provinces (*ostans*), forty-nine counties (*shahrestans*), and numerous municipalities (*bakhshs*) and rural districts (*dehestans*). Provinces were administered by governors-general, counties by governors, municipalities by mayors, and some rural districts by official councils appointed by the Interior Ministry. For the first time in the modern era, the hand of the state reached out from the capital into the provincial towns, counties, and even some large villages.

Court patronage served as the third pillar of the New Order. Reza Shah, the son of a small landowner, and the former colonel who had lived on a modest salary in 1921, accumulated enough wealth during his reign to become the richest man in Iran. A sympathetic biography, published recently in the West, admits that on his abdication Reza Shah left to his heir a bank account of some £3,000,000 and estates totaling over 3,000,000 acres.[87] These estates, which were concentrated in the fertile province of Mazandaran, were obtained partly by outright confiscations, partly by forced sales, and partly by dubious claims to royal domain that had been alienated during the previous century. The British legation reported that the shah, with his "unholy interest" in property, expropriated the land of one major landowner for plotting against the state, confiscated the villages of another for neglecting national resources, and ruined a number of peasants by diverting their irrigated water.[88] This property financed the establishment of royal hotels, casinos, palaces, companies, charities, foundations, and led to a proliferation of court positions, salaries, pensions, and sinecures. The court thus grew into a wealthy landed-military complex offering lucrative posts, favors, and futures to those willing to serve the Pahlevi dynasty.

Equipped with the military, bureaucracy, and court patronage, Reza Shah was able to wield absolute control over the political system. During the previous twenty years, from the First to the Fifth National Assemblies, independent politicians had campaigned in the cities and rural magnates had herded their retainers into the voting polls. But

[86] "The Number of Government Employees," *Khvandaniha,* 19 September 1947.
[87] Wilber, *Riza Shah,* pp. 243–44.
[88] British Minister to the Foreign Office, "Report on the Seizure of Lands," *F.O. 371/ Persia 1932/34-16077;* "The Shah's Acquisition of Lands," *F.O. 371/Persia 1935/34-18992.*

during the next sixteen years, from the Sixth to the Thirteenth National Assemblies, the shah was to determine the outcome of each election, and thus the complexion of each Majles. His practice was to draw up, with the help of the police chief, a list of parliamentary candidates for the interior minister. The interior minister then passed the same names onto the provincial governors-general. Finally, the governors-general handed down the list to the supervisory electoral councils that were packed by the Interior Ministry to oversee the ballots. Parliament ceased to be a meaningful institution, and instead became a decorative garb covering the nakedness of military rule. As one of Reza Shah's premiers admitted years later, "since the shah insisted that all executive actions should be approved by the legislative branch, the Majles was retained to carry out a ceremonial function."[89] The deputies carried out their tasks so well that the shah found it unnecessary either to convene the long-forgotten Senate or to modify the Fundamental Laws. The British minister reported as early as 1926 that "the Persian Majles cannot be taken seriously. The deputies are not free agents, any more than the elections to the Majles are free. When the Shah wants a measure, it is passed. When he is opposed, it is withdrawn. When he is indifferent, a great deal of aimless discussion takes place."[90]

With the reduction of Parliament to a rubber stamp, the shah was able to hand pick his cabinet ministers. Whereas previous monarchs had formed cabinets only after extensive consultations with leading politicians, Reza Shah developed the new procedure of first choosing the prime minister and all his ministers, and then sending them off to the Majles to obtain the necessary but routine vote of confidence. All the administrations of this period received parliamentary approval. And all remained in office until they lost the confidence not of the Majles, but of the shah.

To ensure his absolute power, Reza Shah closed down independent newspapers, stripped the deputies of their parliamentary immunity, and, even more important, destroyed the political parties. The Reformers' party was banned once Mudarres and his clerical colleagues lost their parliamentary seats. The Revival party, which had faithfully supported Reza Shah, was replaced first by the New Iran party (Hizb-i Iran-i Now) and later by the Progressive Party (Hizb-i Taraqqi)—an organization modeled after Mussolini's Fascist party and Mustafa Kemal's Republican party. Even this Progressive party, however, was soon outlawed on the suspicion that it harbored dangerous "repub-

[89] A. Matin-Daftari, "Memoirs of Previous Elections," *Khvandaniha*, 5 April 1956.

[90] British Minister to the Foreign Office, "Annual Report for 1927," *F.O. 371*/Persia 1928/34-13069.

lican sentiments."[91] Similarly, the Socialist party was dissolved when Sulayman Iskandari was forced into retirement and the party's clubs were burned down by organized mobs. In Enzeli, for example, the police encouraged a religious mob to attack the Socialist Theater on the grounds that in a performance of Molière's *Tartuffe* a woman actor had appeared on the stage. And in Tehran, the police watched as a fanatical crowd stoned the Patriotic Women's Society and burned the journals of the same society.

But it was the Communist party that received the brunt of police repression. Meeting in Urmiah in early 1927, the Second Congress of the Iranian Communist party began a sharp turn to the far left that was to be completed in Moscow ten months later by the Sixth Congress of the Third International. Describing the 1921 coup as a British plot, the Congress denounced Reza Shah as an imperialist stooge, compared him to Chiang Kai-chek, who had just carried out the Shanghai massacre of Chinese communists, and called for a revolution of "peasants, workers, and national capitalists" against the Pahlevi regime of "feudalists, semicolonialists, and comprador capitalists."[92] The Congress, labeling the reformers as "petit bourgeois," pronounced the Socialists dead and buried, and demanded the formation of a federal republic to protect the many "nationalities" (*mellal*) of Iran—nationalities such as Arabs, Turks, Turkomans, and Kurds. The Congress also elected to the Central Committee Sultanzadeh, who previously had been shunned as ultraleft, and expelled from the party two leaders who continued to view Reza Shah as a representative of the "national bourgeoisie" fighting against "local feudalists and foreign imperialists."

In response, the government banned all trade unions, especially the CCFTU, and between 1927 and 1932 arrested 150 labor organizers. It seized 40 in Abadan, 30 in Mashad, 10 in Isfahan, 20 in Tabriz, 32 in Tehran, and 24 from the Qazvin Educational Society. Many of these were exiled to towns away from their native provinces. Moreover, 5 of the party activists died as a result of harsh treatment received in jail, and others, notably Pishevari and Ovanessian, remained incarcerated until 1941. In fact, the only party leaders that escaped imprisonment were those already in exile in the Soviet Union. But many of them, such as Sultanzadeh, Nikbin, and Sharqi, disap-

[91] British Minister to the Foreign Office, "Annual Report for 1932," *F.O. 371*/Persia 1933/34-16967.

[92] "The Thesis of the Second Congress of the Iranian Communist Party," *Donya*, 1 (Winter 1960), 115-46.

peared during the Stalinist purges.[93] Thus Stalin indirectly helped Reza Shah dismantle the Iranian Communist party.

Having undisputed political power, Reza Shah initiated a number of social reforms. Although Reza Shah never formulated a systematic blueprint for modernization—writing no major thesis, delivering no grand speeches, and leaving behind no last testaments—he implemented reforms that, however unsystematic, indicated that he was striving for an Iran which, on one hand, would be free of clerical influence, foreign intrigue, nomadic uprisings, and ethnic differences; and, on the other hand, would contain European-styled educational institutions, Westernized women active outside the home, and modern economic structures with state factories, communication networks, investment banks, and department stores. His long-range goal was to rebuild Iran in the image of the West—or, at any rate, in his own image of the West. His means for attaining this final aim were secularism, antitribalism, nationalism, educational development, and state capitalism.

The secular war was waged on many fronts. Davar, the Swiss-educated jurist, was assigned the arduous task of completely reorganizing the Ministry of Justice. He replaced the traditionally trained judges with modern educated lawyers; introduced modified versions of the French Civil Code and the Italian Penal Code, even though some of these statutes contradicted the Koranic canons; and codified shariʿa regulations concerning such personal matters as marriage, divorce, and children's guardianship. Davar also transferred the lucrative prerogative of registering legal documents from the ʿulama to secular attorneys; created a hierarchy of state courts in the form of county courts, regional courts, provincial courts, and a Supreme Court; and, most sweeping of all, gave the state judges the power to decide which cases should be handled in the religious or secular courts. Meanwhile, Reza Shah drastically reduced the clerical presence in the National Assembly; their number fell from twenty-four in the Fifth Majles to six in the Tenth Majles.[94] He disregarded the age-old custom of sanctuary within the compounds of major shrines; outlawed public

[93] The following five died in prison, probably as a result of torture and maltreatment: Muhammad Enzabi, a high school teacher from Azerbaijan; Muhammad Hejazi, a typesetter from Tehran; Muhammad Tanha, a typesetter who had moved to Abadan to organize oil workers; ʿAli Sharqi, a laborer from Azerbaijan; and Muhammad Sadeqpour, another native of Azerbaijan and a refinery worker in Abadan. See R. Namvar, *Yadnameh-i Shahidan* (Martyrs' Memorial) (n.p., 1964), pp. 9-11; "Forty-fifth Anniversary of the Founding of the Iranian Communist Party," *Mahnameh-i Mardom*, 6 (May-June 1965), p. 3.

[94] Z. Shajiʿi, *Nemayandegan-i Majles . . .* (Members of the Majles) (Tehran, 1965), pp. 196-97.

demonstrations on the ancient Day of Sacrifice and flagellation processions in the holy month of Muharram; and restricted the performance of passion plays mourning the martyrdom of Imam Hussein. Moreover, he opened to foreign tourists the main mosques of Isfahan; denied exit visas to applicants wishing to make the pilgrimage to Mecca, Medina, Najaf, and Karbala; ordered the medical college to ignore the Muslim taboo against human dissections; erected statues of himself in the main urban squares; and, most dramatic of all, decreed in 1939 a state takeover of all religious lands and foundations (*vaqfs*). As a result, the ʿulama lost influence not only in politics but also in legal, social, and economic affairs. The British minister expressed considerable anxiety over the consequences of these secular reforms: "The Shah, in destroying the power of the Mullas, has forgotten Napoleon's adage that the chief purpose of religion is to prevent the poor from murdering the rich. There is now nothing to replace religion, save an artificial nationalism which might well die with the Shah, leaving behind anarchy."[95]

The tribal policy was a continuation of the previous military campaigns. Having defeated the tribes, Reza Shah sought to ensure their permanent subjection by extending army outposts into their regions, disarming their warriors, conscripting their youth, stirring up their internal conflicts, confiscating their lands, undermining their chiefs, restricting their annual migrations, and, at times, forcing them into "model villages." For Reza Shah, as for many urban Middle Easterners, the tribes are uncouth, unproductive, unruly, and uneducated savages who have been left behind in the primitive state of nature.

Reza Shah's tribal policy is illustrated by his treatment of the Bakhtiyaris. During 1924-1927, when the military needed the help of the Bakhtiyaris to fight the Arabs, Lurs, Baluchis, and Qashqayis, the central government gave the Ministry of War and the governorship of Khurasan to Jaʿfar Quli Khan Sardar Asʿad, a prominent member of the Ilkhani family and a son of the famous Sardar Asʿad of the Constitutional Revolution. The government also confirmed the office of ilbeg to Amir Jang, Sardar Asʿad's younger brother, and that of ilkhan to Sardar Mohtesham, the head of the rival Hajji Ilkhani family. During 1927-1929, once the military no longer needed Bakhtiyari contingents, Reza Shah turned against his former allies. He carefully enflamed the simmering feuds both between the Ilkhani and the Hajji Ilkhani families and between the Haft Lang and the Chahar Lang branches. He shifted the tax burden onto the Haft Lang, reregistered

---

[95] British Minister to the Foreign Office, "Report on the Situation in Iran," *F.O. 371/ Persia* 1935/34-18992.

pastural lands, and created a new administrative district with its own ilkhan for the Chahar Lang. Consequently, when the Haft Lang rebelled in 1929, the Chahar Lang supported the central government. After the rebellion, Reza Shah disarmed the Haft Lang, settled some of their sections, obliged their chiefs to sell lands to local merchants, confiscated their oil shares, and imprisoned seventeen of their khans, including Sardar As'ad, Amir Jang, and Sardar Mohtesham. Having dealt with the Haft Lang, Reza Shah now turned against the Chahar Lang. These he disarmed and placed under military administration. The district of Bakhtiyar was carved up into the adjacent provinces. Their offices of ilkhan and ilbeg were eliminated in 1931 with the general abolition of all tribal titles. The tribal organizations on the lower levels, however, were left intact; for, as the British consul in Isfahan noted, an organizational vacuum on the local level threatened the influx of "dangerous radicalism":

The ruling Bakhtiari khans who abandoned nomadic life some thirty to forty years ago have acquired interests and responsibilities apart from their tribes. The nomads, meanwhile, continue in the loosely knit confederation of tribes with their local khans as rulers. They still pay dues, attend the tribal councils for the settlement of affairs, and still have no direct dealings with the government. . . . A few of the landowning khans have had difficulties with their peasant tribesmen who have rebelled and claimed that the land and water belong to God and those working on the land, namely themselves. In one village, a committee composed of ex-servants, who had been dismissed by the khans and had visited Tehran and Isfahan, adopted a program of an unmistakably Bolshevik complexion. They propagated among the villagers new ideas of freedom and equality. The government, therefore, has authorized the military to use force if necessary to get the peasants to pay to the local khans. The government is also taking steps to supress these Bolshevik tendencies in case they spread, especially in view of the large number of Bakhtiaris employed in the oil fields.[96]

The policy toward the tribes was closely related to the long-range ambition of transforming the multiethnic empire into a unified state with one people, one nation, one language, one culture, and one political authority. Literacy in Persian increased as the central government expanded public schools, state bureaucracies, secular courts, and mass communications. Conversely, literacy in non-Persian languages—especially Azeri, Arabic, and Armenian—decreased as the few community schools and printing presses were closed down. Although the Iranian Academy inevitably failed in its task of "purifying" the language of all foreign words—Arabic and Turkic words consti-

[96] British Consul in Isfahan, "Report on the Bakhtiari Tribes," *F.O. 371*/Persia 1928/ 34-13069.

tute nearly 40 percent of contemporary Persian—it did succeed in coining numerous Persian terms. For example, new titles replaced the old Arabic and Turkic ranks in the military. And the phrase *rushanfekr* supplanted the Arabic *munver al-fekr* to describe the modern intelligentsia.

Similarly, in 1928 the Majles outlawed traditional ethnic clothes and obliged all adult males, with the exception of registered clergymen, to wear the Western-styled dress and the "Pahlevi cap." Eight years later this cap was superceded by the "international" headgear, the European felt hat. Reza Shah chose these brimmed hats not only to eradicate ethnic identities, but also to interfere with the Muslim rule of prayer, which requires the faithful to touch the ground with their foreheads. The regime also, in an attempt to weaken social distinctions, abolished the remaining honorific titles, such as mirza, khan, beg, amir, shaykh, and sardar. It set up a Society of Public Guidance, modeled after propaganda machines in Fascist Italy and Nazi Germany, to instil national consciousness into the population through journals, pamphlets, newspapers, textbooks, and radio broadcasts. It reorganized the urban administration so that town kalantars, kadkhudas, and other vestiges of the old mahalleh system disappeared. Moreover, it altered many placenames—for example, Arabistan was changed to Khuzistan, Enzeli to Pahlevi, Luristan to Kermanshah, Kurdistan to West Azerbaijan, Urmiah to Rezaieh, Astarabad to Gurgan, ʿAliabad to Shahi, Sultanieh to Arak, and Mohammerah to Khorramshahr. Furthermore, in 1934 the shah, prompted by his Berlin legation, decreed that henceforth the name "Iran" would replace "Persia." A government circular explained that while the latter name was associated with recent Qajar decadence and referred to the province of Fars only, the former invoked ancient glory and signified the birthplace of the Aryan race.[97]

The campaign against foreign influence was equally impressive. He annulled the nineteenth-century capitulations that had granted extraterritorial jurisdiction to the Europeans. He fired Millspaugh from his post of treasurer-general with the pronouncement that "there can't be two Shahs in this country, and I am going to be *the* Shah."[98] He transferred the right to print money from the British-owned Imperial Bank to his recently established National Bank of Iran (Bank-i Melli Iran). He also took over the administration of the telegraph system from the Indo-European Telegraph Company, and the collection of customs from the remaining Belgian officials. Moreover, he prohib-

---

[97] British Minister to the Foreign Office, "Annual Report for 1934," *F.O. 371*/Persia 1945/34-18995.

[98] A. Millspaugh, *Americans in Persia* (Washington, D.C., 1946), p. 26.

ited aliens, particularly missionaries, from administering schools, owning land, or traveling in the provinces without police permission. He failed, however, in one major area—that of reducing the formidable influence of the Anglo-Iranian Oil Company. Although in 1932 he abruptly cancelled the unfavorable D'Arcy concession, a year later he backed down and signed an equally unfavorable agreement in order to prevent a confiscation of Iran's foreign assets.[99] Under the new agreement, the oil company was to give up 400,000 square miles of land (much of it unwanted land), train Iranians for responsible administrative positions, and increase Iran's share of the annual profits from 16 percent to a modest 20 percent. In return, Iran was to extend the concession an additional thirty-two years, from 1961 to 1993. This agreement of 1933 was to plague Anglo-Iranian relations for the next two decades.

The drive to raise the status of women began in 1934, immediately after Reza Shah's visit to Turkey, where Mustafa Kemal was waging a similar campaign. Educational institutions, especially Tehran University, opened their doors to both sexes. Public places, such as cinemas, cafes, and hotels, were threatened with heavy fines if they discriminated against women. Cultural organizations, often replacing the earlier Patriotic Women's Society of the Socialist party, functioned again. Above all, Reza Shah outlawed the veil, especially the traditional chadour, which covered the wearer from head to foot. After 1935, high-ranking officials risked dismissal unless they brought their wives unveiled to office parties. And low-ranking government employees, such as road sweepers, risked fines unless they paraded their wives unveiled through the main streets. Not surprisingly, many considered this to be not women's emancipation but police repression. In any event, the law continued to regard men as superior in a number of important points. Men retained the Muslim privilege of having as many as four wives at a time, and divorcing at will. They were still recognized as the legal head of the family, and enjoyed more favorable inheritance rights. Furthermore, women remained deprived of the right to vote and stand for public elections.

The educational reforms were the most impressive of the civilian reforms. Between 1925 and 1941, the annual allocations for education increased in real terms by as much as twelvefold. In 1925, there had been no more than 55,960 children enrolled in 648 modern primary schools administered by state officials, private boards, religious com-

[99] The shah was also intimidated by the arrival of British naval reinforcements in the Persian Gulf.

munities, or foreign missionaries.[100] By 1941, there were more than 287,245 children in 2,336 modern primary schools, almost all administered by the Ministry of Education. Meanwhile, the enrollment in the traditional maktabs rose slightly from 28,949 to 37,287. In 1925, 14,488 studied in 74 modern secondary schools, 16 of which were missionary institutions. By 1941, 28,194 studied in 110 private and 241 state secondary schools modeled after the French lycée system. During the same period, the number of theology students in the traditional madrasehs declined sharply, from 5,984 to 785.

Higher education also grew. In 1925, there had been fewer than 600 students in the country's six institutions of higher secular learning: in the colleges of Medicine, Agriculture, Teachers' Training, Law, Literature, and Political Science. In 1934, these six were consolidated to form Tehran University. In the late 1930s, five new colleges were added: of Dentistry, Pharmacology, Veterinary Medicine, Fine Arts, and Science and Technology. By 1941, there were over 3,300 enrolled in the eleven colleges of Tehran University. The figures for graduates in foreign universities were equally impressive. Although private individuals and occasionally ministries had sent students abroad since the mid-nineteenth century, the numbers remained small until 1929, when the government decided to finance 100 new scholarships each year to Europe. By 1940, over 500 of these graduates had returned, and another 450 students were completing their studies. Moreover, by 1941 ministries were training almost 3,200 employees in technical schools, and the Education Ministry was teaching 173,907 adults in evening literacy classes. Despite these improvements, over 90 percent of the rural population remained illiterate.

The vast majority of college and secondary school graduates entered government service as office workers, skilled technicians, public administrators, school teachers, court lawyers, medical doctors, or university professors. The intelligentsia thus expanded as the state bureaucracy and educational facilities expanded. Before Reza Shah, the intelligentsia had been a small stratum that had drawn its members from diverse occupations, family positions, income brackets, educational backgrounds, and ways of life. During Reza Shah's reign, however, the same intelligentsia grew to total nearly 7 percent of the country's labor force, and developed into a significant modern middle class whose members not only held common attitudes toward social, economic, and political modernization, but also shared similar educational, occupational, and economic backgrounds. The intelligentsia

[100] The statistics are from: Ministry of Education, *Salnameh-i Ahsayeh* (Annual Statistics) (Tehran, 1925); idem, *Salnameh-i va Amar, 1319-22* (Annual Statements and Statistics, 1940-43) (Tehran, 1943).

was thus transformed from a stratum into a social class with similar relationships to the mode of production, the means of administration, and the process of modernization. This was to become apparent in the period of open conflict after the removal of Reza Shah.

Economic development began with improvements in communications. Having consolidated his power in 1925, Reza Shah promptly started the much-discussed project for the Trans-Iranian Railway. By 1929, the Caspian port of Bandar Shah was linked to Sari in central Mazandaran, and the Gulf port of Bandar Shahpour to Dezful in northern Khuzistan. By 1931, the first train traveled all the way from Bandar Shah via Tehran to Bandar Shahpour. And by 1941, Tehran was connected to both Semnan en route to Mashad and Zanjan en route to Tabriz. Cutting through 1,000 miles of some of the most difficult terrain in the world, these tracks were constructed by engineers from Germany, Britain, America, Scandinavia, Italy, Belgium, Switzerland, and Czechoslavakia. Foreign technicians also helped in the building of new roads. In 1925, the country had no more than 2,000 miles of highway, much of it in disrepair. In 1941, the recently established Ministry of Roads kept in comparatively good condition some 14,000 miles of highway. Although these roads were built primarily for military reasons, they laid the infrastructure for economic, especially industrial, development.

Industrial development began in earnest during the 1930s, when the Great Depression drastically reduced the price of capital goods. The state encouraged industrialization by raising high tariff walls, imposing government monopolies, financing modern plants through the Ministry of Industries, and extending low-interest loans to would-be factory owners through the National Bank. The number of modern industrial plants, not counting the oil installations, increased as much as seventeenfold during Reza Shah's reign. In 1925, there had been fewer than 20 modern industrial plants. Of these, only 5 were large, each employing more than fifty workers: an arsenal in Tehran, a sugar refinery outside Tehran, a match factory in Khoi, and two textile mills in Tabriz. The rest were small modern enterprises: printing presses, breweries, and electrical plants in Tehran, Tabriz, Rasht, and Mashad. By 1941, however, the number of modern plants had reached 346.[101] Of these, 200 were small installations—car repair shops, silos, distilleries, tanneries, and electrical power stations in all the urban centers. But the other 146 included such major installations as 37 textile mills, 8 sugar refineries, 11 match-making factories, 8 chemical enterprises,

[101] Ministry of Labor, *Amari-i Sana-yi Iran* (Industrial Statistics of Iran) (Tehran, 1948).

2 modern glassworks, as well as 1 tobacco and 5 tea processing plants. Consequently, the number of wage earners employed in large modern factories increased from fewer than 1,000 in 1925 to more than 50,000 in 1941.

During the same period the labor force in the oil industry grew from 20,000 to nearly 31,000. Moreover, during the 1930s many of the small workshops, especially for shoemaking, carpentry, and tailoring, merged to form larger workshops, each often employing more than 30 workers. Thus the wage earners in oil and large modern factories, together with some 10,000 in small modern factories, 2,500 in the Caspian fisheries, 9,000 in the railways, 4,000 in the coal fields, another 4,000 in the port docks, and a substantial but seasonal number in construction, jointly produced a total of over 170,000 workers. A modern working class had been born.

Although this modern working class formed less than 4 percent of the total labor force, it was heavily concentrated in a few major towns alongside the traditional working class. Over 75 percent of the large factories were located in Tehran, Tabriz, Isfahan, Gilan, and Mazandaran. Tehran employed 64,000 wage earners in its sixty-two modern manufacturing plants and numerous handicraft workshops.[102] Tabriz had eighteen medium-sized factories. Isfahan, the Manchester of Iran, employed 11,000 in its nine large textile mills alone. Moreover, the oil company employed 16,000 workers at the refinery in Abadan and another 4,800 at the drilling wells in Khuzistan.

This first generation of industrial workers was drawn from diverse rural regions. According to the first national census taken in 1956, 14% of the migrants in Tehran were from neighboring villages, 23% from Azerbaijan, 19% from Gilan, 10% from Mazandaran, 10% from Kermanshah, 9% from Isfahan, 6% from Khurasan, 4% from Khuzistan, and 2% from Fars.[103] In Shahi—the industrial center of Mazandaran—52% of the migrants came from the local countryside, 20% from Tehran, 16% from Azerbaijan, 6% from Gilan, and 2% from Khurasan. In Abadan, 36% of the migrants originated in Isfahan and Yazd, 23% in Khuzistan, 22% in Fars, 3% in Kerman, 2% in Gilan, and another 2% in Azerbaijan.

This rapid growth in industry and state administration transformed the urban centers. On the one hand, it eradicated what remained of the old communal wards. By 1941, in most towns the Ni'mati, Haydari, Karimkhani, Shaykhi, and Mutashar'i mahallehs had passed into history. On the other hand, it created new industrial, commercial,

---

[102] H. Yekretgian, Jughrafiya-yi Shahr-i Ray va Tehran (The Geography of Ray and Tehran) (Tehran, 1953).

[103] Ministry of Interior, Amar-i Umumi (General Statistics) (Tehran, 1956), II.

governmental, and residential districts. For example, Tehran, as it grew from 196,255 in 1922 to nearly 700,000 in 1941, developed five distinct districts: the traditional central bazaar; an administrative area north of the old Cannon Square; a modern middle-class suburb farther north; an industrial zone in the southwest; and a shanty town on the southeastern road to the city's cemeteries.

The ambitious projects, particularly the new army divisions, the central ministries, the industrial plants, and the modern educational institutions, increased the government budget by as much as eighteenfold, from less than 245 million rials in 1925 to more than 4.3 billion rials in 1941.[104] This dramatic increase was financed in a number of ways. First, oil production grew, raising royalties from £1 million to nearly £4 million. Much of the royalties were set aside in a special budget for modern arms and industrial machinery. Second, higher tariffs and the recovery of trade after the dislocations of World War I increased the customs revenue from 91 million rials to 421 million rials. Third, a modest income tax, which had been introduced in 1925 in lieu of the old local levies, grew as the arm of the central government reached further into the provinces. By 1941, this income tax brought in 280 million rials. Fourth, earnings from state monopolies expanded from almost nothing to over 1.2 billion rials annually as the government imposed monopolies on such consumer goods as sugar, tea, tobacco, and fuel. Finally, beginning in 1937, the regime resorted to deficit financing, and thereby increased the volume of notes in circulation from 0.16 billion rials in 1932 to over 1.74 billion rials in 1941. This, coinciding with two bad harvests, drove the cost-of-living index from a base of 100 in 1936 to 218 in the summer of 1941. As one historian has stated, with some exaggeration, Reza Shah's New Order was a "house built on inflation."[105]

Thus Reza Shah in many ways resembled his better-known contemporary Mustafa Kemal of Turkey. Both aimed at transforming their traditional multicommunal societies into modern nation-states. Both associated modernization with Westernization; the past with administrative inefficiency, tribal anarchy, clerical authority, and social heterogeneity; the future with cultural uniformity, political conformity, and ethnic homogeneity. Both hoped to build sovereign states free of foreign influence. Both tried to force women out of their homes into public life. Both tried to develop their countries, especially the urban sectors, by raising revenue from internal sources—particularly from the rural masses. Both rose to power mainly with the assistance

[104] D. Nowruzi, "The Development of the Budget in Iran," *Razm Mahaneh*, 1 (November 1948), 11-18.

[105] P. Avery, *Modern Iran* (London, 1965), p. 304.

of the military, and held the conviction that social, cultural, and economic reforms could not be achieved without political absolutism. The two differed, however, in one important aspect. Whereas Mustafa Kemal conscientiously channeled the enthusiastic backing of the intelligentsia into the Republican party, Reza Shah gradually lost his initial civilian support, and, failing to secure social foundations for his institutions, ruled without the assistance of an organized political party. Thus whereas Mustafa Kemal's authority rested firmly on Turkey's intelligentsia, Reza Shah's state hovered somewhat precariously, without class foundations, over Iran's society.

REZA SHAH'S STATE AND IRAN'S SOCIETY

The political structure built by Reza Shah was stable in contrast to the political structures of traditional Iran, especially that of the previous dynasty. For it rested not on the sands of tribal contingents and communal manipulations, but on the three stone pillars of a standing army, a modern bureaucracy, and extensive court patronage. But it was unstable in comparison with the political structures of the modern world, particularly those of the West. For the new regime, despite impressive institutions, had no viable class bases, no sound social props, and was thus without firm civilian foundations. The Pahlevi state, in short, was strong inasmuch as it had at its disposal powerful means of coercion. But it was weak in that it failed to cement its institutions of coercion into the class structure.

Reza Shah's policy was to divide the upper-class families, coopting some and pushing aside the others. He integrated himself into the upper class by accumulating wealth and taking a Qajar noblewoman as his third wife. He also married off his eldest daughter, Princess Ashraf, to the Qavam al-Mulk family, and the crown prince to Princess Fawzieh of Egypt. At the same time, he became the guardian of the landowning class, ending all talk of land reform, transferring the agricultural tax from the shoulders of the landowners to those of the peasant cultivators, and, through the Department of Land Registration, encouraging regional magnates to place communal property under their own names. Similarly, he decreed that in future village kadkhudas were to be appointed not by the local communities but by the landlords. Thus with one stroke of the pen he destroyed the main safeguard of the rural communities. Finally, he rewarded reliable aristocrats with high positions in the Majles, the cabinet, the diplomatic corps, and the newly established state enterprises. For example, the landowners, who had constituted 8 percent of the First Majles and

12 percent of the Fourth, made up 26 percent of the Twelfth Majles.[106] Together with senior civil servants and nonbazaar businessmen, they formed as much as 84 percent of all Reza Shah's deputies. What is more, of the fifty ministers who filled ninety-eight cabinet posts in ten administrations between January 1925 and August 1941, thirty-seven had been born into titled bureaucratic and aristocratic families.[107]

While coopting some of the aristocratic families, Reza Shah also supplanted them both from their positions as local magnates—positions that they had occupied throughout the nineteenth century—and from their function as the country's ruling class, a function they had performed since the end of the Constitutional Revolution. He dispossessed many, forcing some to sell land at nominal prices, and depriving others not only of their power and property, but also of their liberty, dignity, and even lives. Sepahdar, threatened with a tax audit, committed suicide. Ahmad Qavam, accused of plotting against the monarch, fled to Europe. Mossadeq withdrew to his estates near Tehran after a brief spell in prison. Shaykh Khaz'el, Semko, and the last Qashqayi ilkhan, all died in suspicious circumstances while under house imprisonment. Eight prominent tribal leaders were executed, and another fifteen given long prison sentences; two of them failed to survive their sentences. For members of the old upper class, life was certainly not poor, but it could easily turn nasty, brutish, and short.

The mortality rate was even higher among the members of the upper class who first won but then lost the shah's confidence. Timourtash, the young progressive landowner who had supported Reza Shah since 1923 and been his court minister since 1926, was suddenly in 1933 condemned to five years' imprisonment on charges of bribery, extortion, and embezzlement. Five months later, he died from a presumed "heart attack."[108] Firuz Farmanfarma, the Qajar prince who had served as Reza Shah's right-hand man since 1923, was dismissed from the government in 1930 for misappropriating state funds. While still under house arrest eight years later, he was strangled to death. Sardar As'ad, whose Bakhtiyari contingents had given invaluable sup-

---

[106] Shaji'i, *Nemayandegan-i Majles*, pp. 175-78.

[107] Of the thirteen ministers who had been born into untitled families, two came from clerical homes and four from wealthy landowning but nonaristocratic families. Thirty-six of the fifty had long careers in public administration—mostly in the prestigious Ministries of Finance and Foreign Affairs. The group was also well educated: forty had higher degrees—twenty-six of them from Europe. Almost all spoke one or more European languages—thirty-four knew French, twelve English, eleven Russian, and six German.

[108] For the trials of jailors and policemen accused of these murders, see *Parcham*, 28 July-21 September 1942.

port to the central government from 1923 until 1928, was ousted as war minister in 1929, jailed without trial, and soon after murdered in his cell. Similarly, ʿAbdul Hassan Diba (Siqat al-Dawleh), a wealthy landlord and uncle of the future Empress Farah Diba, was dismissed as assistant minister of finance and murdered while awaiting trial. Not since the early days of Naser al-Din Shah had fallen statesmen been treated in such arbitrary fashion.

Although Reza Shah succeeded in coopting a segment of the old upper class, he failed to retain any significant support from the traditional middle class. The establishment of state-financed enterprises and government monopolies did create a few favored import-exporters and court-connected industrialists; but they also produced widespread discontent in the old business communities. As British consuls often observed, state control of foreign trade hurt private traders and even caused bankruptcies; taxes on income and consumer goods prompted merchants to complain confidentially that the new army and the railway projects were too expensive; modern textile factories destroyed many handicraft workshops;[109] and economic centralization inevitably antagonized the provincial bazaars:

The completion of one organic body out of different and to some extent independent local economies, such as that of Azerbaijan, artificially links the fortunes of this district with those of other districts. This means that if disaster comes it will be general and not local—a prospect not balanced by any promise of greater general prosperity. Also, Azerbaijan argues that it can, if left alone, very well provide its own prosperity. The north feels that the south has been carried away by meretricious doctrines, and that it will drag the north with it to disaster. The Shah, of course, is responsible for linking the north to the south and he is hated accordingly; even more, perhaps, since he is detested because in all the upsets he has created, he has contrived to acquire a very large fortune for himself.[110]

Paradoxically, Reza Shah further antagonized the commercial middle class by abolishing taxes on 216 guilds; for the abolition took away from the guild elders the power of determining how much each guild member paid in taxes, and thus paved the way for the weakening of the bazaar organizations.[111] As a spokesman for the bazaar later admitted, the elimination of the guild tax was a kiss of death designed to sap the control of the craft and trade masters over their apprentices,

[109] British Consul in Shiraz, "Conditions in Fars," *F.O. 371*/Persia 1934/34-18994; idem, "Conditions in the Province of Fars," *F.O. 371*/Persia 1937/34-20834.

[110] British Consul in Tabriz, "Economic Situation in Azerbaijan," *F.O. 371*/Persia 1937/34-20830.

[111] President of the Majles, "Law for the Abolition of the Guild Taxes," *Parliamentary Proceedings*, 6th Majles, 11 December 1926.

artisans, journeymen, and wage earners.[112] Furthermore, the secular reforms, especially the overhaul of the judicial system, the introduction of the "international hat," and the forced unveiling of women, created deep resentment among the ʿulama, the ideological leaders of the traditional middle class.

This middle-class opposition to the regime burst into the open in 1926-1927 and again in 1935-1936. The protests of 1926-1927 were triggered by the enactment of Davar's secular laws and the conscription of urban youth into the military. While the ʿulama of Tehran took sanctuary in Qum, the guilds organized general strikes in Tehran, Qum, Qazvin, Isfahan, Shiraz, and Kerman. The government ended the protests by promising not to conscript urban youth, and by appointing members of the clergy to a judicial committee. But this committee was disbanded within two years and the promise to limit conscription was broken within six years. The upheavals of 1935-1936 were sparked by the unveiling of women and the introduction of the "international hat." On July 10, 1935, the anniversary of the Russian bombardment of the Mashad shrine in 1911, the main preacher at the shrine took advantage of the emotional occasion to denounce the "heretical innovations," the high consumer taxes, and the prevalence of corruption in high places. The following day, a massive crowd from the bazaar and the neighboring villages flocked to the mosque, shouting "Imam Hussein protect us from the evil shah." Finding that the city policemen and the Khurasan army contingents refused to violate the sanctity of the shrine, the local authorities were unable to act for two full days. The British consul reported that these officials rushed to and from the telegraph office with their European hats hidden under their jackets, ready to produce them only when they passed each other.[113] The situation changed drastically on the third day, however, as army reinforcements arrived from Azerbaijan and promptly moved to clear the shrine. In the subsequent confrontation, nearly two hundred suffered serious injuries, and over one hundred, including many women and children, lost their lives. In the following months, the shrine custodian was executed; Mudarres, who had been living in forced retirement since 1927, died under suspicious circumstances; and three conscripts who had refused to fire into the unarmed crowd were shot. The British consul commented that although the prompt display of military force certainly deterred the opposition, the bloodshed served to widen the gulf between shah and country.

[112] A. Haerzadeh, *Parliamentary Proceedings*, 15th Majles, 28 June 1948.
[113] British Consul in Mashad, "Report on the Events in Meshed," *F.O. 371*/Persia 1935/34-18997.

The massacre at Meshed is not likely to be forgotten rapidly and while all this discontent will no doubt be driven underground by severe repression, it might crop up again at some favorable moment, such as the demise of the Shah. In addition to these grievances which affect the masses, I have the suspicion that among the governing classes, both military and civilian, there is serious heart-searching as to whether the Shah's policy is not radically on wrong lines.[114]

Whereas Reza Shah created intense hatred among the traditional middle class, he aroused ambivalent sentiments among the modern middle class. On the one hand, he provoked passive opposition from the younger generation of the intelligentsia. On the other hand, he first gained but then lost enthusiastic support from the older generation of the intelligentsia. These veterans of the civil war, who had failed to mobilize the masses during the period of internal disintegration, initially supported the creation of the New Order—especially the pacification of the tribes, the secularization of the society, and the centralization of the state. Their enthusiasm cooled, however, during the early 1930s as the shah signed an unfavorable oil agreement, intensified his quest for dynastic wealth, caused widespread inflation with his military expenditures, and concentrated power in his own hands by banning all political parties, including the reformist parties. By 1937, few of the early reformers remained in public life. Davar, the minister of justice, committed suicide, probably in anticipation of being either disgraced or murdered. Taqizadeh lost his ambassadorship in Paris, and made excuses for not returning to Iran. Sulayman Iskandari went into retirement in 1927 after serving briefly as governor of Kerman. Farokhi, the outspoken poet from the Socialist party, died in a prison hospital. Tadayon, who had played an important role in the Revival party and the republican campaign, was thrown out of the cabinet into jail when he complained that the budget allocated too little to his Education Ministry and too much to the War Ministry. 'Ali Dashti, a prominent writer whose paper *Shafaq Surkh* (Red Twilight) had helped Reza Shah since 1922, found himself deprived of parliamentary immunity and detained in a state sanitorium. And Kasravi lost his provincial judgeship soon after ruling in favor of a group of small landowners who had been dispossessed by the shah.

In a series of articles published in 1942, Kasravi summed up the ambivalent attitude of his generation toward Reza Shah. He gave the fallen monarch high marks for centralizing the state, pacifying the tribes, disciplining the clergy, unveiling women, eliminating aristo-

[114] Ibid.

cratic titles, introducing mass conscription, undermining "feudal" authorities, trying to unify the population, and establishing modern schools, cities, and industries. At the same time, he gave the fallen shah low marks for trampling over the constitution, favoring the military over the civilian administration, accumulating a private fortune, stealing other people's property, murdering progressive intellectuals, and widening the gap between the haves and the have-nots.[115]

The younger generation, however, found little to admire in Reza Shah. They tended to view him as not a patriot but a Cossack trained by the Tsarists and brought to power by the British; not a nation-builder but a self-seeking founder of a new dynasty; and not a genuine reformer challenging the traditional forces but an autocrat strengthening the conservative landed classes. As Kasravi stated in 1942, when he accepted the unpleasant responsibility of acting as defense attorney for a group of police officers accused of murdering political prisoners: "Our younger intellectuals cannot possibly understand, and thus cannot possibly judge the reign of Reza Shah. They cannot because they were too young to remember the chaotic and desperate conditions out of which arose the autocrat named Reza Shah."[116]

The opposition from the younger intelligentsia emerged gradually during the 1930s. In 1930, dissident students in Europe, convening a special congress in Cologne, demanded the release of all political prisoners, called for the establishment of a republic, and denounced Reza Shah as a "tool of British imperialism."[117] In the following year, a group of university students in Munich worked closely with remnants of the Iranian Communist party to publish a new periodical named *Paykar* (Battle).

To counter these activities, Reza Shah induced the German government to close down *Paykar* and ordered the Majles to pass a law for safeguarding national security.[118] This law threatened prison terms lasting as long as ten years for members of organizations that either endangered the "constitutional monarchy" or propagated a "collectivist ideology." The document used the vague and archaic Arabic term *ishtiraki* (collectivism) in order to include socialism as well as communism and anarchism. Legislation failed to deter the opposition, however. Student protests continued in Europe. Small groups of rad-

[115] A. Kasravi, "Concerning Reza Shah Pahlevi," *Parcham*, 23-25 June 1942.
[116] A. Kasravi, "The Case for the Defense of the Accused," *Parcham*, 16 August 1942.
[117] British Minister to the Foreign Office, "Student Protests in Europe," *F.O. 371/ Persia 1931/34-15352.*
[118] "The Closing of *Paykar*," *Donya*, 5 (Winter 1968), 104-107; Judiciary Committee, "Law for Safeguarding National Security," *Parliamentary Proceedings*, 8th Majles, 31 June 1931.

ical intellectuals were discovered and rounded up every so often in Tehran, Tabriz, Rasht, Isfahan, and Qazvin. The College of Medicine organized a successful strike in 1934 to remove its government-appointed dean. Three hundred students on state scholarships at the Teachers' College led an equally successful strike in 1936 against a government proposal that would have obliged them to work after graduation in public schools at salary scales fixed in the days before the recent inflation. The students in the College of Law closed down their campus in 1937 to protest the lavish sums spent to prepare the university for the visit of the crown prince. They complained that while the vast majority of villages still lacked educational facilities, over 120,000 rials had been wasted to scent the university corridors with eau de cologne.[119] And in the same year, twenty college graduates—many of them army conscripts—were arrested for advocating "fascism" and plotting against the shah's life. The leader of the group, a twenty-six-year-old lawer with the rank of second lieutenant, was secretly executed.[120]

The most important arrests came in May 1937, when the police detained fifty-three men and accused them of forming a secret ishtiraki organization, publishing a May Day manifesto, organizing strikes in the Technical College and in a textile factory in Isfahan, and translating such "atheistic tracts" as Marx's *Das Kapital* and the *Communist Manifesto*. Although five of the detainees were soon released, the group became famous as "the Fifty-three," and a few years later formed the nucleus of the Tudeh party. Of the forty-eight who were tried in November 1938, a large majority came from the ranks of the young generation of Persian-speaking intelligentsia residing in Tehran.[121]

[119] British Minister to the Foreign Office, "Strike at the College of Law," *F.O. 371/Persia* 1937/34-20835.

[120] A. Kasravi, "Mohsen Jahansouz," *Parcham*, 13 March 1942; British Minister to the Foreign Office, "New Arrests," *F.O. 371/Persia* 1937/34-20835.

[121] Information on the "Fifty-three" has been obtained from interviews, miscellaneous newspapers, and proceedings of the trials published in *Ittila'at*, 2-17 November 1938. For a first-hand account of the trial see B. 'Alavi, *Pajah-u-Seh Nafar* (The Fifty-three) (Tehran, 1944). In terms of occupation, the forty-eight included thirteen university students, twelve civil servants, four professors, three medical doctors, three high school teachers, two lawyers, two mechanics, two factory workers, one businessman, one writer, one tailor, one cobbler, one typesetter, one railwayman, and one peasant.

In terms of class origins, thirty-four came from the urban middle class, five from titled or wealthy families, and eight from peasant and urban poor households. In terms of ethnic origins, the group included thirty-six Persians, seven Azeris, two Qajars, and one Turkoman. Of the total, thirty-eight lived in Tehran, and thirty-four had been born in the predominantly Persian-speaking areas of Tehran, Qazvin, Alamut, and the central plateau. Finally, in terms of generational structure, only two were over forty years old, and the average age of the group was thirty.

Only nine came from the lower classes and only five had been born in Azerbaijan (see Table 3). For the first time in Iran, a Marxist group drew its membership from the non-Azeri and the non-Armenian intelligentsia.

At the trial, the defense attorneys admitted that their clients had formed an informal group to discuss socialism, denied that the group had any international connections, and argued that well-educated intellectuals and the offspring of "respectable" clergymen, merchants, and civil servants could not possibly harbor atheistic ideas. At the conclusion of the trial, three were acquitted but banished to the provinces; ten were given sentences varying from two to four years; seventeen were given five years; eight drew from six to eight years; and ten received the maximum possible sentence, ten years' imprisonment. The British minister reported that such sentences, unduly harsh for belonging to "what was nothing more than a student debating society," reflected the "general unpopularity of the regime" and aimed at "broadcasting a plain warning to all others with similar leftist tendencies."[122]

The central figure among "the Fifty-three" was a thirty-six-year-old professor of physics named Taqi Arani. The son of a minor official in the Finance Ministry, Arani was born in Tabriz but grew up in Tehran. Graduating with first-prize honors from the Dar al-Fonun and the Medical College, he won a state scholarship in 1922 to Germany. While studying for a doctorate in chemistry at Berlin University, Arani taught Arabic at the same institution, wrote three pamphlets on Persian culture—on Omar Khayyam, Saʿdi, and Naser Khusraw—formed a discussion group with fellow students from Tehran, and gradually turned his political interests from Iranian nationalism to modern socialism. As one communist biographer has admitted, "Arani had been carried away by chauvinism while studying in Tehran during the nationalist campaign against the Anglo-Iranian Agreement. He, like many of his contemporaries, believed that the country would be saved from backwardness and imperialism by cleansing the language of foreign words, by reviving the ancient religion of Zoroaster, and by rebuilding the centralized state of the Sassanids."[123]

Arani had continued to express such views during his early years in Germany. In an article on "The Great Heroes of Iran" published

---

[122] British Consul to the Foreign Office, "The Trial of the Fifty-three," *F.O. 371/Persia* 1938/34-21890.

[123] "Dr. Taqi Arani," *Mahnameh-i Mardom*, 5 (June 1960), 1. For biographies of Arani see R. Radmanesh, "Dr. Taqi Arani," *Nameh-i Mardom*, 3 (January 1949), 1-8; N. Kianouri, "Dr. Taqi Arani," *Donya*, 4 (Autumn 1963), 39-46; and A. Masʿoud, "Arani: An Eternal Light," *Mahnameh-i Mardom*, 6 (January-February 1970).

in *Iranshahr*, he listed Zoroaster, Ibn Sina, Khayyam, Ferdowsi, Darius, and Cyrus the Great, overlooking the nineteenth-century reformers and Mazdak, the famous fifth-century revolutionary. In another article on "Azerbaijan: A Deadly and Vital Problem for Iran" published in *Farangistan*, he advocated the elimination of Azeri from his native province and argued that the Mongol invaders had imposed their Turkic dialect on the local Aryan population: "All patriotic Iranians, especially the officials in the Ministry of Education, must do their very best to replace Turkish with Persian. We must send Persian journals, Persian newspapers, Persian textbooks, and Persian teachers to Azerbaijan—that ancient homeland of Zoroaster and of the Aryans."[124]

During his later years in Germany, however, Arani immersed himself in the works of Marx, Engels, Kautsky, and Lenin, took a keen interest in the European left-wing movements, and helped in the publication of the paper *Paykar*. By the time he returned to Iran in 1930, he was a well-read Marxist and a convinced socialist, although probably not a member of the Communist party. Teaching at Tehran University, he formed student discussion groups, and, with former colleagues from Europe, founded a highly theoretical journal named *Donya* (The World). Although *Donya* published numerous articles on historical materialism, and took its name from *Le Monde* edited by the French communist writer Henri Barbusse, its apolitical format and academic content convinced the censors that it was too dull and esoteric to be dangerous.[125] In a series of articles entitled "Historical Materialism," "Knowledge and the Elements of Matter," "The Materialist Concept of Humanity," "Women and Materialism," and "The Material Basis of Life and Thought," Arani explained for the first time to a Persian-reading audience the academic Marxist approach to contemporary problems in the social sciences. He also applied Marxism to the physical sciences in a collection of pamphlets on *The Fundamentals of Chemistry*, *The Fundamentals of Biology*, *The Fundamentals of Physics*, and *The Fundamentals of Matter*. In "The Materialist Concept of Humanity," his most explicitly political work, Arani summarized Engels' *Origin of the Family, Private Property and the State*, and stressed that society's economic structure determined its institutional, ideological, cultural, and political superstructure. He concluded the article

[124] T. Arani, "The Great Heroes of Iran," *Iranshahr*, 2 (September 1923), 63-64; idem, "Azerbaijan: A Vital and Deadly Problem for Iran," *Farangestan*, 1 (September 1924), 247-54.

[125] I. Iskandari, "Reminiscences of Dr. Arani and the Journal *Donya*," *Donya*, 10 (Winter 1969), 9-13. This issue also reprinted Arani's main articles on "Historical Materialism," "The Materialist Concept of Humanity," and "Knowledge and the Elements of Matter."

TABLE 3
Social and Political Background of the "Fifty-three"

Name	Occupation	Higher Education	Residence
Arani, Taqi	professor	Univ. of Berlin	Tehran
Kambakhsh, ʿAbdul Samad	aeroengineer & military academy instructor	Moscow University	Tehran
Bahrami, Muhammad	physician	Univ. of Berlin	Tehran
Shurshiyan, Muhammad	mechanic	none	Tehran
Sadeqpour, ʿAli	mechanic	none	Tehran
Boqrati, Mahmud	high-school headmaster	Dar al-Fonun	Tehran
Pazhuh, Muhammad	engineering student	Tehran University	Tehran
Alamuti, Ziya	civil servant	none	Tehran
Iskandari, Iraj	lawyer	Univ. of Grenoble	Tehran
Khameh, Anvar	student at teachers' college	Tehran University	Tehran
ʿAlavi, Bozorg	author	Univ. of Berlin	Tehran
Yazdi, Morteza	professor & physician	Univ. of Berlin	Tehran
Farjami, Muhammad	civil servant	none	Tehran
Jahanshalou, Nosratallah	medical student	Tehran University	Tehran
Azeri, ʿAbbas	cobbler turned railwayman	none	Tehran
Eʿzazi, Nosratallah	civil servant	none	Tehran
Fatouli, Akbar Afshar	typesetter	none	Tehran
Maleki, Khalel	high-school teacher	Univ. of Berlin	Tehran
Makinezhad, Taqi	engineering student	Tehran University	Tehran
Shandarmini, ʿAli	tailor	none	Abadan
Qodreh, Muhammad	student at teachers' college	Tehran University	Tehran
Radmanesh, Reza	professor & physician	Univ. of Paris	Tehran
Sajadi, Morteza	physician	Tehran University	Tehran
Razai, Mehdi	civil servant	?	Tehran
Naʿini, Jalal	civil servant	?	Qazvin
Razavi, Morteza	civil servant	none	Gurgan
Siyah, Saifallah	textile worker	none	Isfahan

Place and Date of Birth	Class Origin	Ethnic Origin	Previous Politics	Subsequent Politics
Tabriz, 1902	urban middle	Azeri	none	"died" in prison in 1940
Qazvin, 1904	Qajar nobility	Qajar	Communist & Socialist parties	Tudeh leader
Tafresh, 1898	urban middle	Persian	none	Tudeh leader
Gilan, 1885	lower	Persian	Communist & Socialist parties	Tudeh organizer
Qazvin, 1904	urban middle	Persian	Communist party	none
Rasht, 1904	urban middle	Persian	Communist & Socialist parties	Tudeh leader
Qazvin, 1906	urban middle	Persian	Communist party	Tudeh organizer
Alamut, 1914	urban middle	Persian	Socialist party	Tudeh leader
Tehran, 1908	Qajar nobility	Qajar	none	Tudeh leader
Tehran, 1917	urban middle	Persian	none	Tudeh organizer
Tehran, 1904	urban middle	Persian	none	Tudeh leader
Yazd, 1907	urban middle	Persian	Jangali revolt	Tudeh leader
Enzeli, 1905	urban middle	Persian (Baha'i)	none	Tudeh organizer
Tehran, 1912	urban middle	Azeri	none	Tudeh organizer
Tehran, 1900	lower	Azeri	none	Tudeh organizer
Tehran, 1901	urban middle	Persian	none	Tudeh organizer
Tehran, 1909	lower	?	none	none
Tabriz, 1910	urban middle	Azeri	none	Tudeh leader
Arak, 1915	urban middle	Persian	none	Tudeh organizer
Enzeli, 1917	lower	Persian	none	Tudeh organizer
Arak, 1912	urban middle	Persian	none	Tudeh organizer
Lahijan, 1906	landed upper	Persian	Jangali revolt	Tudeh leader
Arak, 1912	urban middle	Persian	none	none
Qazvin, 1898	urban middle	Persian	none	Tudeh organizer
Qazvin, ?	urban middle	Persian	none	none
Qazvin, 1915	urban middle	Persian	none	Tudeh organizer
Isfahan, 1902	lower	Persian	none	none

TABLE 3 (*cont.*)
Social and Political Background of the "Fifty-three"

Name	Occupation	Higher Education	Residence
Hakmi ʿAlinqali	law student	Tehran University	Tehran
Ashtari, ʿAbul Qassem	civil servant	none	Tehran
Tabari, Ehsan	law student	Tehran University	Tehran
Garkani, Fazallah	student at teachers' college	Tehran University	Tehran
Khajavi, Vali	peasant	none; illiterate	Alamut
Taqfi, Yusef	civil servant	none	Tehran
ʿEteqichi, Ezatallah	engineering student	Tehran University	Tehran
Alamuti, Rahim	civil servant	none	Tehran
Zamani, Shaʿyban	cobbler	none	Tehran
Tarbiyat, Hussein	high-school headmaster	Tehran University	Abadan
Nasemi, Raʿb ʿAli	civil servant	none	Tehran
Shomali, Bahman	mechanic & factory worker	none	Qazvin
Laleh, Mehdi	businessman	Tehran University	Tehran
Alamuti, Mirʿemad	civil servant	none	Qazvin
Sajadi, Hassan	physician	Tehran University	Isfahan
Sajadi, Mojtabi	college student	Tehran University	Tehran
Shahin, Taqi	civil servant	none	Tehran
Naraqi, ʿAbbas	law student	Tehran University	Tehran
Daneshvar, Mehdi	college student	Tehran University	Tehran
Habibi, Hassan	college student	Tehran University	Tehran
Turkoman, Ana	lawyer	?	Gurgan

with three major criticisms of contemporary racial theorists: first, their explanation for the contrast between East and West ignored the economic stages of historical development; second, their fundamental premise had been undermined by the biological evidence that most societies were formed of different but equal races; third, their idealization of the state and the nation concealed the harsh reality that the former was the "executive committee of the ruling class" and the latter was divided into contending classes with conflicting interests, ide-

Place and Date of Birth	Class Origin	Ethnic Origin	Previous Politics	Subsequent Politics
Tehran, 1912	urban middle	Persian	none	none
Tehran, 1915	urban middle	Persian	none	none
Sari, 1917	landed upper	Persian	none	Tudeh leader
Tehran, 1918	landed upper	Persian	none	Tudeh supporter
Alamut, 1893	lower	Persian	none	Tudeh organizer
Qazvin, 1913	urban middle	Persian	none	none
Tehran, 1917	urban middle	Persian	none	Tudeh organizer
Alamut, 1899	urban middle	Persian	none	none
Babul, 1916	lower	?	none	none
Abadan, 1908	urban middle	Persian	none	Tudeh organizer
Tabriz, 1917	urban middle	Azeri	none	none
Khalkhal, 1903	lower	Azeri	none	none
Tehran, 1901	urban middle	Persian	none	none
Alamut, 1911	urban middle	Persian	none	none
Arak, 1910	urban middle	Persian	none	none
Arak, 1913	urban middle	Persian	none	Tudeh supporter
Tabriz, 1905	urban middle	Azeri	Communist party	Tudeh organizer
Kashan, 1904	urban middle	Persian	none	Comrades' party leader
Shiraz, 1904	urban middle	Persian	none	none
Kermanshah, 1906	urban middle	Persian	none	none
Gurgan, 1898	?	Turkoman	none	none

NOTE: The "Fifty-three" are listed in order of those receiving the longest prison sentences.

ologies, associations, and political parties. Kasravi, who was by no means a racist, retorted in his famous work *Aiyin* (The Creed) that the Western concept of historical materialism was highly dangerous, since it would introduce the theory of class struggle into a country already fragmented by many social divisions.[126]

[126] A. Kasravi, *Aiyin* (The Creed) (Tehran, n.d.).

These intellectual discussions were ended abruptly by the police in 1937, as soon as Arani's group distributed a May Day manifesto on the university campus and established links with a few veteran trade unionists. At the trial, Arani compared the tribunal to Nazi kangeroo courts, denounced the police for using torture, declared that the 1931 law violated the constitutional right of free expression, and argued that no legislation could possibly prevent the inevitable introduction of such Western theories as socialism and communism: "If you wish to adopt Western clothes, Western styles, Western institutions, Western technology, and Western way of life, you must also adopt Western political philosophies."[127] Arani received the maximum sentence of ten years' solitary confinement, but died in a prison hospital sixteen months later. His colleagues suspected that the police had murdered him. The police claimed that he had succumbed to an incurable attack of typhus. The British legation reported later that he had probably succumbed to the cumulative effects of ill treatment.[128] Whatever the reasons, Arani became the spiritual founder of the Tudeh party.

The reign of Reza Shah also saw the emergence of a discontented industrial working class. Low wages, long hours, high consumer taxes, forced transfer of workers to the malaria-infested region of Mazandaran, and labor conditions that, in the words of a European visitor, "practically resembled slavery,"[129] all caused widespread industrial discontent. Since trade unions had been banned in 1926, the discontent took the form of underground cells and wildcat strikes. On May Day 1929, eleven thousand workers in the oil refinery struck for higher wages, an eight-hour day, paid annual vacations, company housing, and union recognition. Although the oil company granted the wage demands, the British navy dispatched a gunboat to Basra, and the Iranian authorities arrested over five hundred workers. The British foreign minister formally congratulated the shah for his "speedy and effective handling of the incident."[130] Five of the strike leaders remained in prison until 1941. In 1931, five hundred employees in the Vatan textile mill in Isfahan stopped work for better wages, an eight-hour day, and one day a week paid vacation. Although the strike organizers were jailed, the workers won a 20 percent wage increase

[127] T. Arani, "Defence at the Trial of the Fifty-three," *Donya*, 4 (Spring-Summer 1963), 107-20.

[128] British Minister to the Foreign Office, "Report on Political Murders," *F.O. 371/ Persia* 1944/2118-40228.

[129] British Minister to the Foreign Office, "Annual Report for 1934," *F.O. 371/Persia* 1935/34-18995.

[130] British Minister to the Foreign Office, "The Strike in Abadan," *F.O. 371/Persia* 1929/34-13783.

and a cut in the work day from ten to nine hours.[131] In late 1931, only two years after the completion of the first stretch of the Trans-Iranian Railway, eight hundred railway workers in Mazandaran went on a successful eight-day strike for higher wages. Their strike organizers were still in jail in 1941.[132] The British consul in Tabriz summed up the general labor situation in these words: "We are in a transitional stage between old and new. The employee is losing his personal association with his employer and much of his pride in the finished product. There is not, as yet, adequate provisions for injury or for unemployment to replace the moral responsibility of the old type employer. The government has broken down a structure without rebuilding in its place. . . . Reza Shah has, rather dangerously perhaps, dismissed Allah from the economic sphere and set himself instead in the moral ethics of industry."[133]

Meanwhile, Reza Shah's drive for national unification created further resentment among the religious and linguistic minorities. Baha'i schools, with over 1,500 pupils in Tehran alone, lost their license to teach in 1934 on the pretext that they had observed the anniversary of the Bab's martyrdom. The Jewish deputy in the Majles, Samuel Haim, was suddenly executed in 1931 for unexplained reasons. The Zoroastrian deputy, Shahroukh Arbab Keykhosrow, who had faithfully supported Reza Shah since 1921, was gunned down in the street by the police in 1940 because his son in Germany, against his father's wishes, had broadcast a series of pro-Nazi speeches. The Armenian community schools lost first their European language classes, and then, in 1938, their license to teach. In the same year, *Ittila'at* (Information), the semiofficial government daily, waged a front-page campaign against the Christian minority by running a series of articles on "dangerous criminals," all with obviously Armenian and Assyrian names. The British legation reported that such attacks echoed Nazi radicalism and were designed to appeal to the bigoted chauvinists and the most reactionary mullas.[134] The policy of closing down minority schools and printing presses, however, hit especially hard at the Azeris; being more urbanized than the Kurds, Arabs, Baluchis, and Turkomans, the Azeris had already developed their own indigeneous intelligentsia. As a result, cultural resentment increased as Persian schools,

[131] "A Short History of the Trade Unions in Isfahan," *Rahbar*, 18 June 1944.
[132] "A Short History of the Trade Unions in the Railways," *Zafar*, 9 August 1946.
[133] British Consul in Tabriz, "The Economic Situation in Azerbaijan," *F.O. 371*/Persia 1937/34-20830.
[134] *Ittila'at*, 28 November-4 December 1948; British Minister to the Foreign Office, "Annual Report for 1933," *F.O. 371*/Persia 1934/34-17909; British Minister to the Foreign Office, "Annual Report for 1936," *F.O. 371*/Persia 1937/34-20836.

papers, and printing presses supplanted Turkish-language schools, papers, and printing presses in Azerbaijan. Modernization had stimulated a new form of communalism—one based not on local villages, tribes, and urban wards, but on substate linguistic and cultural minorities.

The state increasingly resorted to violence to control class and ethnic opposition, so much so that by 1941 many Europeans, as well as Iranians, were speculating whether repression would work indefinitely, whether junior officers would overthrow the regime, or whether social tensions would sooner or later bring about a bloody revolution. But these speculations ended abruptly with the Anglo-Soviet invasion of August 1941. The Allies invaded not only for the obvious reasons of opening a new corridor to Russia, eliminating German agents, and safeguarding oil installations, but also for the less obvious reason of preempting any pro-Axis officers who might have been tempted to oust the unpopular shah and install a pro-German regime.[135] As the British minister warned the Foreign Office in May 1941, "the general discontent in Persia provides Germany with a good field for intrigue. The Shah is the object of almost universal execration and cannot count upon full support of his army. Movement for the removal of the Shah or even of his dynasty would be popular. Most people in Iran would welcome a revolution, however caused." Similarly, the British press attaché in Tehran reported, "the vast majority of the people hate the Shah and would welcome any change. . . . To such people, even the spread of war to Iran seems preferable to the continuation of the present regime. The general attitude is that, apart from the fact the Iran is obviously too weak to stand up to either the Germans or the Russians, there is no reason for them to fight: they hate the Shah and so why, they ask, should they fight to perpetuate his rule."[136]

The invasion promptly sealed Reza Shah's fate. Within three days of the invasion, the army, pounded by British and Soviet planes, was retreating faster than anticipated even by the Allied high command. Within four days, Foroughi, the independent-minded jurist who had been forced into retirement, was named premier to negotiate with the Allies.[137] Within one week, the new prime minister was suing for peace and secretly encouraging the Allies to remove Reza Shah. Within

[135] Foreign Office, "The Situation in Iran," *F.O. 371*/Persia 1941/34-27153.

[136] British Minister to the Foreign Office, "The Situation in Persia," *F.O. 371*/Persia 1941/34-27149; British Press Attaché in Tehran, "The Situation in Persia," *India Office*/L/P&S/12-3405.

[137] The British minister described Foroughi as a liberal statesman who "hardly expects any son of Reza Shah to be a civilized man." British Minister to the Foreign Office, 10 April 1942, *F.O. 371*/Persia 1943/34-31385.

ten days, the British, eager to obtain public support, were broadcasting blunt attacks on Reza Shah's mismanagement, greed, and cruelty.[138] Within two weeks, the hand-picked deputies were openly denouncing the shah for accumulating a vast fortune, murdering innocent citizens, and abusing his titles of Army Commander and Commander-in-Chief.[139] And within three weeks, the shah, without consulting the Allies, abdicated in favor of the crown prince and hurriedly left the country in the hope of salvaging his dynasty. The British minister wrote that the invasion had aroused not so much public resentment against the invaders as hopes of social improvement and thus feeling of friendship toward the Allies. The American minister arrived at a similar conclusion: "A brutal, avaricious, and inscrutable despot in his later years, his fall from power and his death later in exile were regretted by no one."[140] The fall of Reza Shah had ended the politics of state control; it had also begun the politics of social conflict.

[138] The British minister summed up the events leading up to Reza Shah's abdication: "Whereas the Persians expected that we should at least save them from the Shah's tyranny as compensation for invading their country, they found that they now had to bear both the foreign occupation and the Shah. The new Prime Minister, Mr. Foroughi, though he realized that it would be impossible to find a successor to Reza Shah who would wield the same authority, eventually came to the conclusion that the reforms that were essential could not be secured under Reza Shah. . . . His Majesty's Government thereupon agreed that the B.B.C. might now begin to give various broadcasts in Persian which had been prepared beforehand, starting with talks on constitutional government and increasing in strength and colour until all Reza Shah's mismanagement, greed and cruelty were displayed to the public gaze. It is probable that no broadcasts have been received with more excitement and approval than these. If the Persian public approved them, to the Shah they gave a violent shock, and he made an unsuccessful appeal to His Majesty's Minister that these broadcasts should cease. Encouraged by the lead given by the B.B.C., the Deputies in the Majles, who had been subservient for so many years, passed a resolution to the Shah, asking for reforms. A deputation of them was to wait upon the Shah on the 16th September, resolved it was alleged, to ask him to abdicate; but it is quite possible that in view of the fear in which they held him they would have withdrawn their request or been put off with promises. Early that morning, however, the Shah received news that the Russian forces were advancing from Qazvin, and he signed a deed of abdication, drafted by Mr. Foroughi, in favour of the Crown Prince." British Minister to the Foreign Office, "Annual Report for 1941," *India Office/* L/P&S/ 12-3472A.

[139] Deputies' speeches, *Parliamentary Proceedings*, 12th Majles, August-September 1941.

[140] British Minister to the Foreign Office, "The Effects of the Abdication," *F.O. 371/* Persia 1941/34-27153; American Minister to the State Department *Foreign Relations of the United States* (Washington, D.C., 1945), III, 385.

PART II

Politics of Social Conflict

FOUR

The Evolving Political System: From Military to Embattled Monarchy

No two Persians can ever work together for any length of time, even if it is jointly to extract money from the third party.
—British Consul in Isfahan, 15 April 1945, *F.O. 371*/Persia 1945/34-45476.

Our deputies—especially in the 14th and 15th Majleses that I attended—behaved as if they were the sworn enemies of the ministers. They acted as if the legislative was the antithesis of the executive. . . . I thoroughly agree with Western observers who describe Iran as a nation of anarchistic individuals. In our country, everyone considers himself a leader, sets his own goals, goes his own way, and without compunction tramples over others. It is because of this psychology of individualism that hundreds of fragmented and fragmenting parties clutter our political arena. Since 1941, political parties inside and outside parliament have appeared as easily and frequently as they have disappeared.
—R. Shafaq, *Khatirat-i Majles va Demokrasi Chist?* pp. 3-4.

NEW BEGINNINGS

In rupturing the autocracy, the Anglo-Soviet invasion of August 1941 unleashed the pent-up social grievances of the previous sixteen years. As officers fled to the capital and conscripts absconded to their villages, tribal chiefs, many of whom had given up hope of better days, escaped from police surveillance in Tehran and rushed home to their tribal warriors. Veteran politicians who had been nursing their wounds in forced retirement hurried back into public life. Religious leaders, emerging from seminary libraries, resumed the exhortative stance of pulpit preachers. Intellectuals, many of them too young to remember the difficulties of 1907-1925, plunged enthusiastically into politics, editing newspapers, publishing pamphlets, and forming political parties with the goal of building a new

Iran. Even the obsequious deputies and sycophantic bureaucrats suddenly found the courage to declare their political independence and denounce their former master. The reign of silence was superceded by the clamor of flamboyant deputies, lively journalists, outspoken party leaders, and discontented demonstrators.

During the preceding sixteen years, power had been centered firmly round one man. But during the next thirteen years, from the fall of Reza Shah's military monarchy in August 1941 until the rise of Muhammad Reza Shah's military monarchy in August 1953, power was to shift back and forth between five separate poles: the court, the Majles, the cabinet, the foreign embassies, and the general public. Moreover, each of these power centers had its own internal struggles. The court included civilian advisors seeking a genuine constitutional democracy as well as army officers anxious to reestablish a strong autocracy. The Majles was divided into conservative, liberal, and radical factions, as well as pro-British, pro-American, and pro-Russian factions. The cabinet contained ministers who owed their positions either to the court, or to one of the many parliamentary factions, or to the foreign powers. The foreign powers themselves turned hostile to one another as the Allies of the World War became the antagonists of the Cold War. Finally, the general public quickly divided into rival social forces once political parties had a chance to inspire, mobilize, and represent various interest groups.

These power centers fought many of their battles within the cabinet, causing permanent instability on the ministerial level. In the preceding sixteen years there had been only 8 premiers, 10 cabinets, and 50 ministers filling 198 cabinet posts. In the next thirteen years, however, there were to be as many as 12 premiers, 31 cabinets, and 148 ministers filling 400 cabinet posts. On the average, premiers lasted eight months and cabinets less than five months. This rapid turnover, however, did not mean that social mobility had come to Iran and the middle classes had entered the corridors of power. On the contrary, of the 12 premiers, 9 came from the nineteenth-century titled families, 2 from Reza Shah's bureaucracy, and 1 from his military elite. Similarly, of the 148 cabinet ministers, 81 were sons of titled and wealthy families, 13 were technocrats representing the court, 11 were army officers, and 8 were prosperous entrepreneurs outside the bazaar.[1]

Political instability was not confined to the cabinet. Over the pre-

[1] Of the 148 ministers, only fifteen were salaried personnel and modern educated professionals with roots in the middle classes and without links to the palace. What is more, of the fifty ministers who held three or more cabinet posts, thirty-nine came from titled and landed families, seven from the upper echelons of the bureaucracy, two from prominent military households, and only two from the salaried middle class.

vious sixteen years, the political arena—especially the streets—had been quiet. Some saw that this stability permitted the establishment of orderly parliaments, responsible newspapers, disciplined publics, and even punctual railways. But to many, it resembled the quiet of the dungeon. Over the next thirteen years, however, the country was to pass from one social upheaval to another, from one political crisis to another, from one diplomatic storm to another. For some, this instability was the progenitor of social anarchy and national disintegration. For others, it was the natural but painful product of political democracy and public participation. In the previous reign, the state had controlled interest groups, concealed internal conflicts, remolded society, and, in short, dominated the social structure. In the next thirteen years, the social structure would reveal deep-seated conflicts, transform these conflicts in the political arena, and thereby remold the political system. These thirteen years, therefore, provide a rare and valuable opening through which the social scientist can observe the deep-rooted internal conflicts that are usually hidden in developing countries by one-party systems, police censors, heavy-handed bureaucrats, and authoritarian generals.

The emergence of a multitude of parties, parliamentary groups, and professional associations in the years after August 1941 convinced many observers and participants, Iranians as well as non-Iranians, that the Iranian "national character" was marred by personal insecurity, distrust, jealousy, paranoia, anarchistic disobedience, intense cynicism, conspicuous individualism, and compulsive factionalism.[2] As one British representative exclaimed after failing to put together in the Majles a viable anti-Soviet bloc, "the Persians take a childish delight in any such 'grown up' disease as a political crisis. Being individualists without loyalty, discipline, or cohesion, they are loath to sink their differences, fix upon a common policy, and elect leaders to carry out that policy."[3] Likewise, an American social scientist has argued that factionalism in Iran was rooted in the "politics of distrust": "The precarious, ever-shifting balance of individuals and tiny factions that have denied men the power to act effectively as government also have denied them the power to act effectively as opposition."[4]

The fact is, however, that the complex maze of political parties and parliamentary groups reflected not psychological difficulties but political differences, not traits of megalomania—although, no doubt,

[2] H. Vreeland, ed., *Human Relations File on Iran* (New Haven), 1957.

[3] British Military Attaché to the Foreign Office, 20 November 1944, *F.O. 371*/Persia 1944/34-40206.

[4] A. Westwood, "Politics of Distrust in Iran," *Annals of the American Academy of Political and Social Sciences*, no. 358 (March 1956), pp. 122-23.

such traits did exist among some—but political issues between conflicting social forces, and not personal insecurities and irrational animosities but rational, although equally intense, disagreements over complex national and international problems.

The break in the political structure in August 1941 at once revealed the existence of two major forms of conflict in the social structure: class antagonisms, especially in the towns; and ethnic rivalries, particularly between neighboring tribes, religious sects, and linguistic groups, in the countryside. In the immediate years after the abdication, the British and American representatives were constantly warning that the disparity between the haves and the have-nots endangered national security and created an explosive situation in the cities; that intense distress among the masses, combined with the steady enrichment of merchants and landowners, threatened the whole fabric of society; and that the discontent of the lower classes, caused by the appalling lack of food, clothing, medicine, and education, could lead to a "violent revolution against the present ruling class." They also warned that "an early withdrawal of Allied forces could open the way to general disturbances in the nature of a revolution, expressing the widespread dissatisfaction of the people with the present government and social system." One British consul even compared the situation to early nineteenth-century England: "The situation resembles England before 1832, with the landowning classes in control of all local administration and virtually in charge of Parliament and of the Cabinet, with two classes in the country—one bloated with wealth, and the other abjectly poverty-stricken and powerless."[5]

The Iranian press was also preoccupied with class conflicts. Of the thirty-six newspapers that appeared regularly in Tehran during the four years after the abdication, almost all, including those owned by wealthy landlords, saw Iran as divided into antagonistic classes. Some argued that the general masses were suppressed politically by a small ruling class of feudal landowners, influential courtiers, army officers, and high-ranking government officials.[6] Others claimed that the toil-

---

[5] British Consul in Mashad, "Six Monthly Report for July-December 1943," *F.O. 371/ Persia 1944/34-40184*; idem, "Six Monthly Report for July-December 1942," *F.O. 371/ Persia 1943/34-35061*; British Minister to the Foreign Office, 15 October 1941, *F.O. 371/Persia 1941/34-27155*; British Military Attaché to the Foreign Office, 6 April 1943, *F.O. 371/Persia 1943/34-35110*; American Chargé d'Affaires to the State Department, 29 December 1943, *Foreign Relations of the United States* (Washington, D.C., 1943), IV, 427; British Consul in Kermanshah, "Monthly Report for October 1942," *F.O. 371/ Persia 1942/34-31402*.

[6] "The Social Classes of Iran," *Jeb'eh*, 3 March 1946; "The Present Crisis," *Umid*, 17 November 1946; "The Class Struggle Endangers Iran," *Umid*, 30 January 1944; 'A. Samdi, "The Class Struggle," *Mard-i Emruz*, 31 August 1946; "Social Conflicts Threaten the

ing masses were exploited economically by an upper class formed of large landlords, comprador capitalists, wealthy civil servants, and nouveaux riches industrialists.[7] Yet others saw a small hard-working middle class wedged between a rapacious upper class and a backward illiterate lower class.[8] Some saw their society polarized into, on one side, the old and new aristocracy, the industrial and comprador bourgeoisie, and, on the other side, the intelligentsia, the bazaar bourgeoisie, the urban working class, the nomadic tribesmen, and the landless peasantry.[9] Even *Ittila'at*, which on orders from Reza Shah had diligently avoided the divisive word "class" for years, now warned that class conflicts jeopardized the whole existence of Iran.[10]

Whereas Tehran newspapers focused on class antagonisms, British consuls in the provinces concentrated on ethnic rivalries, particularly between the tribes, between the Muslims and the non-Muslims, and between the major linguistic minorities and the Persian-dominated state. The British consul in Shiraz, in describing the Qashqayis, Boir Ahmedis, and Lurs, summed up the tribal situation throughout much of the country.

With the fall of Reza Shah his much-prided infantry and armies lost morale and were overthrown by the tribes. The nomads rejoiced in the reaccession of freedom, and buried arms saw light again and were carefully cleansed. New rifles were bought and acquired, some sold by the army or arms traffickers, others seized in daring raids on outposts of the army. Added to these were the many rifles of the deserters, some of whom had been conscripted from the tribes and were quick to return to their tents. The rearmament race had begun.

Those of the former Khans who had survived long exile or imprisonment slunk back to their tribes and set to reestablish their lost hold and recoup their confiscated lands. The latter awaits full accomplishment and has occasioned more than one bloody battle with the Government; whilst the former was not always easy because, although they were welcomed by the majority of their old subjects and weaker relatives who had been allowed to remain with the tribes, as fellow-sufferers from Reza Shah, there were not a few among the latter, who, thanks to the difficult accessibility of pastures, or to

---

State," *Kushesh*, 27 December 1944; "The Bayat Clique," *Ra'ad-i Emruz*, 8 December 1944.

[7] H. Arsanjani, "Class Struggles in Iran," *Darya*, 18-22 June 1944; "Class Relations," *Mehan*, 23 April 1946; "Our Program," *Sham'*, 9 April 1944.

[8] "The Division of Labor," *Parcham*, 2-6 April 1942; "It Originates from the People," *Parcham*, 9 February 1942; A. Kasravi, "Corruption among the People," *Parcham-i Haftegi*, 15 April 1944; "Why I Am a Satirist," *Qiyam-i Iran*, 21 November 1943.

[9] "The Class War," *Mardom*, 23 April 1943; A. Ovanessian, "Class Cleavages," *Rahbar*, 30 October 1946.

[10] 'A. Mas'oudi, "The Bells of Danger," *Ittila'at*, 31 July 1943.

lending themselves as tools to the Government, had escaped the worst oppression and had profited from the sufferings of their neighbours and now found irkesome a return to the absolute rule against which there is no appeal but mutiny or secession from the tribe.[11]

The British minister in Tehran commented that the central government could retain its influence in the tribal regions only through the old "policy of deliberately inciting one tribe against another and of keeping open tribal quarrels": "It is quite true that a policy of inciting one tribe against another will never lead to a permanent peace. But the preservation of a balance of power in certain areas may be the only way open to the Government at the present moment of keeping a temporary peace."[12]

The religious animosities appeared mostly in provincial towns. For example, in Tabriz, Muslim-Christian animosities reached such proportions that the British consul warned that blood would flow as soon as the Allies withdrew from Iran. In Urmiah, Assyrian church leaders expressed similar concern and sought British protection in case the war ended in the near future. In Mashad, Soviet troops had to intervene during the Muharram processions of 1944 to protect the Jewish quarter. In Ahwaz, a crowd of eight hundred angry Muslims, incited by the rumor that Jews had kidnapped a Muslim child, tried to burn down the local synagogue. In Kerman, an emotional mob led by a fanatical mulla attacked the Zoroastrian district, killing two men and plundering numerous houses. And in Shahrud, a similar mob attacked the Baha'i temple, lynching three men and sacking fifty shops.[13] Significantly, the Haydari-Ni'mati and the Shaykhi-Karimkhani-Mutashar'i rivalries of the nineteenth century failed to reappear with any meaningful force. In fact, the term "Haydari-Ni'mati" was used in this period to describe meaningless and archaic squabbles.

The language issue was most apparent in the Arab, Kurdish, and Azeri regions. Shaykh Chassib, the eldest son of the deceased Shaykh Khaz'el, returned to Iran in 1942 and promptly convened a meeting of Arab chiefs. Arguing that the "Emirate of Arabistan" had been "energetically independent until the twentieth century," the meeting

[11] British Consul in Shiraz, "Report on Tribal Areas," *F.O. 371*/Persia 1944/34-40180.
[12] British Minister to Provincial Consuls, "Note on Tribal Policy," *F.O. 371*/Persia 1944/34-40178.
[13] British Consul in Tabriz, "The Christian Minority in Azerbaijan," *F.O. 371*/Persia 1942/34-31430; British Minister to the Foreign Office, 9 January 1942, *F.O. 371*/Persia 1942/34-31430; British Consul in Ahwaz, 15 October 1943, *F.O. 371*/Persia 1943/34-35090; British Consul in Mashad, 8 September 1944, *F.O. 371*/Persia 1944/34-40184; *Rahbar*, 23 October 1946; H. Kuhi-Kermani, *Az Shahrivar 1320 ta Faj'eh-i Azerbaijan* (From August 1941 to the Disaster of Azerbaijan) (Tehran, 1946), II, 630.

accused the central government of robbing the Arab people of their freedom and of planning to destroy their national language. The meeting also sent a message to the British and American governments announcing that "we Arabs of Arabistan . . . , totaling one million people, believe that our day of liberation from the Iranian aggressors is fast approaching."[14] This movement lost impetus, however, partly because the British discouraged the dissidents, and partly because the largest Arab tribe, the Bani Turuf, refused to join Shaykh Chassib. The situation in the Kurdish areas was similar. As British visitors to the western provinces frequently observed, the Iranian authorities had to make long detours to avoid the numerous small independent republics that had appeared since August 1941.[15] Ann Lambton, touring Kurdistan on behalf of the British legation, reported in 1944: "From Tabriz to Mahabad, the towns and villages were full of heavily armed Kurds. I saw no Persian police or gendarmerie. The few Kurds I spoke to all talked of Kurdish independence with enthusiasm."[16] In these early years, however, the Allies, including the Soviets, declined to give material help to the Kurdish nationalists.

The language issue was even more explosive in Azerbaijan. The Soviet invasion and the subsequent flight of the Iranian authorities created a power vacuum in Tabriz. This vacuum was promptly filled by a local commission of notables who refused to recognize the central government, demanded the right to use Azeri in state schools, and raised a volunteer militia from the Muhajirin (Immigrants)—some 5,000 Turkish-speaking Iranians who had returned from the Soviet Union during the 1930s but had faced difficulties in finding jobs and integrating themselves into their new environment.[17] An American diplomat sent to observe the situation in Tabriz reported to Washington that the Soviet forces, after a brief flirtation with the local dissidents, had dampened down the genuine sentiment of the widespread popular movement for an autonomous Azerbaijan.[18] Although the central government, with the help of the Soviets, reestablished its authority in Tabriz, local organizations and newspapers continued to harbor and espouse Azerbaijani resentments against Tehran. As one American visitor reported, the Russians could, if they wished, take

[14] Minister of State in Cairo to the Foreign Office, "Petition of Arab Tribes in Persia," *F.O. 371*/Persia 1943/34-35074.

[15] British Consul in Kermanshah, 21 January 1943, *F.O. 371*/Persia 1943/34-35092.

[16] A. Lambton, "Report on Kurdistan," *F.O. 371*/Persia 1944/34-40173.

[17] British Consul in Tabriz, "Report on the Recent Occupation of Tabriz," *F.O. 371*/Persia 1941/34-27153. Reza Shah had distrusted the Muhajarin so much that he had forbidden them to reside in the cities.

[18] J. Moose, "Memorandum on Azerbaijan," (unpublished dispatch in the files of the U.S. State Department, Washington, D.C., sent 10 November 1941), pp. 1-22.

advantage of popular discontent to "set up a Soviet overnight in Azerbaijan."[19] And as *Azerbaijan*, the main newspaper in Tabriz, often stressed in its editorials,

What is the cause of Azerbaijan's misfortune? The main cause is the lack of unity within the nation (*mellat*) of Azerbaijan. Others have been able to manipulate and exploit us because of our internal disunity, especially between Sunnis and Shi'is, Muslims and Christians, peasants and nomads, Kurds and Azeris. We will gain our rights only when we put aside these differences and unite against our exploiters in Tehran.

What is our main aim? They have banned our paper in Tehran, claiming that we advocate the separation of Azerbaijan from Iran. Our main aim, however, is to protect the democratic right of the people to use their mother language. It is high time the government admitted that Azerbaijans are not and have never been Persian-speakers. Our official and mother language is Azerbaijani. We will do all we can to nurture our mother language in our schools and government offices. Those who have tried to destroy our language must change their attitudes.[20]

THE THIRTEENTH MAJLES (NOVEMBER 1941–NOVEMBER 1943)

Whereas class and ethnic conflicts provided the underlying theme of politics during the next thirteen years, the immediate issue confronting the country in 1941 was the survival of the monarchy. On his accession, the new shah tried to secure his position by making as many friends as possible. To win the confidence of the Allies, he promised full cooperation, even offering volunteers to fight in Europe and remaining silent at the arrest of some fifty pro-German army officers.[21] In return, Britain and the Soviet Union signed a treaty of alliance with Iran, implicitly guaranteeing the dynasty and explicitly promising to evacuate the country within six months after the war. To assure the public that the dictatorship would not be reimposed, the new shah granted amnesty to all political prisoners, and released over 1,250 dissidents during the next few months;[22] refused to protect two of his father's henchmen who were accused of murdering political prisoners; and decreed the return of ecclesiastical lands to the reli-

[19] American Ambassador to the State Department, 8 January 1943, *Foreign Relations of the United States* (1943), IV, 329.

[20] "What Is the Cause of Azerbaijan's Misfortune?" *Azerbaijan*, 8 December 1941; "What Is Our Aim?" *Azerbaijan*, 2 February 1942.

[21] War Office to the Foreign Office, "Memorandum on the Reorganization of the Persian Army," *F.O. 371*/Persia 1941/34-27251.

[22] British Minister to the Foreign Office, 11 October 1941, *F.O. 371*/Persia 1941/34-27154.

gious foundations. He also opened a theology college at Tehran University; transferred much of his landed inheritance to the state for eventual redistribution among the previous owners; and carefully portrayed himself in public as an apolitical youth who, having been educated in democratic Switzerland, had always been uncomfortable in his father's autocratic court. Moreover, to allay the concern of the upper class, the shah took his oath of office before the deputies, reintroduced parliamentary immunity for the deputies, encouraged the use of old aristocratic titles in court ceremonies, transferred the gendarmerie to the Ministry of Interior, and, above all, invited Parliament to participate again in the process of forming cabinets. Reza Shah had been in the habit of sending his chosen premier, with the royal farman (decree), to Parliament to obtain the vote of confidence for the cabinet. But now, the deputies first elected the premier, sent him to the shah to collect the farman, and then gave him a vote of confidence both for his program and cabinet.

In striving to preserve the dynasty, the shah was helped by one piece of good fortune. For the invasion had occurred just as Reza Shah had been putting the finishing touches to the elections for the thirteenth Majles. The new shah therefore inherited a Parliament that was willing to reach a compromise in which he did not dictate political matters, but did keep control of military matters. Consequently, the old chain of army command remained intact. Orders continued to go from the Military Office in the palace, through the chief of general staff directly to the field commanders, bypassing the war ministers. To ensure smooth communications between the shah and the field commanders, royalists were packed into the War Ministry. The ministry was reduced to a mere office of army supplies; the minister to a glorified regimental quartermaster.

Retaining the military as a royal preserve, the shah worked aggressively but quietly to keep the loyalty of the officer corps. He retained his personal interest in the military, organizing army maneuvers, taking inspection tours, scrutinizing promotions above the rank of major, especially in the tank brigade, and attending graduation ceremonies at the military colleges. At these ceremonies, he took the opportunity to remind his audiences that the army owed its existence to the Pahlevi dynasty. As one young officer admitted half apologetically to an anticourt intellectual: "It may be true that the old man dealt unfairly with you civilians, but you must remember that he did transform a rabble into a modern army. Without him we would have no real military."[23] The new shah, moreover, protected from

---

[23] R. Mustawfi, *Tehran Demokrat* (Democratic Tehran) (Tehran, 1942), p. 21.

public hearings the field commanders who had deserted their posts in August 1941; showered officers with promotions, creating twice as many colonels and generals in twenty months as his father had done in twenty years; and signed an agreement with United States for reorganizing, retraining, and reequipping the armed forces. Furthermore, the shah successfully lobbied to preserve the defense budget, increase officers' salaries, and even expand the size of the armed forces. The army, whose ranks had fallen sharply from 124,000 on the eve of the invasion to less than 65,000 after the mass desertions, gradually grew to reach 80,000 by mid-1943.[24] Sir Reader Bullard, the British minister, reported that the shah, being "doubtful of popular enthusiasm for his dynasty," cultivated his ties to the officers, "jealously guarded his own control over the military," and, thereby, "assumed both the title and the real authority of the Commander-in-Chief of the Armed Forces." He added that the shah planned eventually to create an army of half a million men: "What worries the Shah is the moral state of his people. He says that they have no ideal and he wants to give them an ideal through a large army."[25] Historians later argued that the dynasty survived because of the Iranian "mystique" for kingship. If any such sentiment existed in 1941-1943, the shah was unaware of it. On the contrary, he was much more aware of the immediate need to retain active control over the military.

The invasion thus washed away two of the three pillars that had supported Reza Shah's regime: the bureaucracy and the court patronage. The civil administration was taken over by ministers responsible to Parliament. And the royal estates were handed over to the government. Out of the wreckage, however, Muhammad Reza Shah managed to salvage the remnants of the central pillar, the military. It was true that the army was diminished in size, disillusioned in spirit, and shaken in discipline. But it was equally true that the same army was the country's largest institution, the main instrument of legitimate violence, and the best structured organization in the state. This pillar could continue to support the monarchy as long as Parliament was willing to keep its compromise with the shah.

The modus vivendi, however, weakened during the course of the Thirteenth Majles as the amorphous collection of deputies gradually coalesced into the following four fluid, fluctuating, but identifiable groups: the National Union Caucus (Fraksiun-i Ittihad-i Melli); the Patriotic Caucus (Fraksiun-i Mehan); the Azerbaijani Caucus (Frak-

[24] British Military Attaché to the Foreign Office, "General Ridley's Recommendations for the Reorganization of the Persian Army," *F.O. 371*/Persia 1943/3435129.

[25] British Minister to the Foreign Office, "Annual Report for 1942," *F.O. 371*/Persia 1943/34-35117; idem, "Conversations with the Shah," *F.O. 371*/Persia 1942/34-31385.

siun-i Azerbaijan); and the Justice Caucus (Fraksiun-i ʿAdalat) (the word *fraksiun* was borrowed from the German term "fraction" for parliamentary caucus).[26] These four groups disagreed not only over internal issues, especially the constitutional problem of who should control the military; but also over external issues, particularly the vital question of how to retain national independence during foreign occupation.

The National Unionists, who mustered the largest but not the majority bloc, represented the segment of the aristocracy that had been successfully coopted into Reza Shah's regime. Moreover, many of its members came from constituencies outside the Allied occupation but inside the tribally disturbed regions of the central and western provinces under Iranian martial law. In constitutional matters, they hoped to preserve the compromise with the shah. In foreign relations, they—like the shah—feared both Britain and the Soviet Union, and consequently sought to draw in United States to counterbalance the two traditional enemies. Their leader was Morteza Quli Khan Bayat (Saham al-Saltaneh), a large landowner who, with the help of the National Bank, had recently opened a coal field on his family estates in western Iran. A former member of the old Moderate party, Bayat had represented the district of Arak in the last nine National Assemblies. Hassan Esfandiari (Muhtashim al-Saltaneh), as the elder statesman of the caucus with forty years' uninterrupted experience in public service, was president of the Thirteenth Majles. In recent years, Hassan Isfandiari had invested considerable capital in the silk industry in Gilan and held a government concession for the export of cocoons. Finally, Sayyid Ahmad Behbehani, the son of the famous mujtahed of the Constitutional Revolution, tried to act as the group's spokesman in the bazaar. Although his father, as a true spiritual leader, had refused all financial and institutional ties to the state, Ahmad Behbehani had accepted from Reza Shah a government sinecure and a secure seat in six consecutive parliaments.

If the National Unionists were comparable to the Tories of seventeenth-century England, the Patriots can be described as the Whigs. Dissatisfied with the constitutional arrangement, the Patriotic Caucus was formed of landowners and merchants from southern and southwestern regions under British occupation. Hashem Malek Madani, the group's main spokesman, was a wealthy landowner-businessman who had represented his home town of Malayer in eight consecutive

[26] In the period between 1941 and 1953, most fraksiuns did not publish the names of their members. Moreover, foreign diplomats rarely understood Majles politics. This analysis of the fraksiuns has been obtained from memoirs, Majles speeches, voting records, and newspaper editorials.

parliaments. Madani was to lead the pro-British politicians in the next four parliaments. Mehdi Namazi, the group's wealthiest member, was the country's leading importer of British goods. He had been elected to four National Assemblies from his native town of Shiraz. Dr. Hadi Taheri, another prominent member of the caucus, was a millionaire silk trader from Yazd who had represented his home town since 1926. Taheri's family, like many provincial magnates, dominated local politics. For example, in 1945, one brother chaired both a dried fruit company and the main religious foundation in Yazd; another brother managed the local cotton-spinning factory; a nephew held the concession for the sale of skins and sat on the board of the city's cultural society; another nephew administered the state secondary school; another relative presided over the regional Department of Health; and yet another relative presided over the provincial Department of Land Registration.[27]

Although the Patriots had until only recently served as the shah's obedient servants, their objective now was to bring to power the Anglophile Sayyid Ziya Tabatabai, the premier of 1921 who had been ousted by his colleague Reza Shah. Having lived in exile for twenty years, mostly in British Palestine, Sayyid Ziya returned home in September 1943, and, in the words of the British legation, caused hysterical fear among the royalists and deep suspicions among the Soviet authorities. The American minister reported that the British had to work hard to persuade the shah to permit the return of Sayyid Ziya. The minister also reported that Sayyid Ziya would be an unsuitable candidate for the premiership because he was notorious as a "British tool," a vehement Sovietphobe, and an "unscrupulous schemer" in the coup d'état of 1921.[28]

Whereas the Patriots allied with Britain, the Azerbaijan Caucus was led by Qajar aristocrats who, out of opposition to both the shah and the British, were prepared to work closely with the Soviet Union as long as the latter did not advocate social revolution in Iran. The group, which mustered no more than a handful of deputies, was led by Muhammad Vali Farmanfarma, the brother of the famous Prince Firuz who had been murdered by Reza Shah. Ending his forced retirement in 1941, Farmanfarma won a delayed election in Soviet-occupied Sarab, where his family owned a number of villages. Amir Nasrat Iskandari, another prominent member of the group, was a direct descendant of Fath ʿAli Shah and an heir of the richest landlord

[27] "Dr. Taheri's Clique in Yazd," *Rahbar*, 26 January 1945.
[28] British Minister to the Foreign Office, 20 January 1944, *F.O. 371*/Persia 1944/34-40186; American Minister to the State Department, *Foreign Relations of the United States* (1943), IV, 329, 374, 389.

in the whole of Azerbaijan. These deputies from Azerbaijan hoped to bring to power Ahmad Qavam (Qavam al-Saltaneh), the veteran statesman who had headed four cabinets before Reza Shah forced him into exile, first to Paris and later to his tea plantation in Gilan. Bullard commented that although Qavam was neither straightforward nor an Anglophile, he was the most energetic, shrewd, skillful, courageous, ambitious, and authoritative of the old anticourt statesmen.[29] One Iranian observer wrote that Qavam reentered politics in 1941 "openly baring his teeth at the royal family and threatening to cut their ties to the military." Another observer claimed that Qavam planned to set up a republic with himself as its first president. The shah, in a conversation with the British minister, depicted Qavam as a dangerous schemer, who, having surrounded himself with a "gang of cut-throats," was waiting for the Russians to implement some desperate design.[30]

Whereas these three groups included the diverse segments of the landed upper class, the Justice Caucus represented the older generation of the intelligentsia. Formed of senior civil servants, technocrats, and older intellectuals, its members had originally supported Reza Shah but had gradually grown fearful of his dictatorial methods. In internal affairs, therefore, they intended to place the military under civilian control. In external affairs, they hoped to draw in United States as a third force to counterbalance the two major powers. Thus they converged with the National Unionists on the foreign issue, but diverged on the constitutional problem. The main spokesman for the Justice Caucus was ʿAli Dashti, a well-known writer, who, after years of supporting Reza Shah, suddenly found himself "detained" in a sanatorium. Pardoned and sent back to the Majles, Dashti became the main parliamentary critic of the court after the invasion, continually warning the young shah that "if he meddled in politics he would lose his throne."[31] The group's leading candidate for the premiership was ʿAli Soheily, a Western-educated civil servant from a nonaristocratic background. Having held a number of high posts in Tehran, Soheily had been disgraced in 1938 for unknown reasons and had been packed off to head the embassy in Kabul.

The weak position of the royalist National Union fraksiun became apparent in March 1942 when the nonroyalist Patriotic, Azerbaijani,

[29] British Minister to the Foreign Office, "Monthly Report for February 1943," *F.O. 371*/Persia 1943/34-35070; British Minister to the Foreign Office, 31 August 1943, *F.O. 371*/Persia 1943/34-35073.

[30] A. Sepehr, "Qavam al-Saltaneh after August 1941," *Salnameh-i Donya*, 15 (1959), 55-56; N. Shabstari, "Qavam al-Saltaneh," *Vazifeh*, 25 February 1946; British Minister to the Foreign Office, 31 August 1943, *F.O. 371*/Persia 1943/34-35073.

[31] ʿA. Dashti, *Parliamentary Proceedings*, 12th Majles, 6 September 1941.

and Justice fraksiuns united to bring down Foroughi, who had headed three procourt cabinets since August 1941. In the subsequent maneuvering to elect a new prime minister, the Patriotic Caucus, backed by the British legation, lobbied for Sayyid Ziya. Meanwhile, the Azerbaijani Caucus, helped by the Soviet legation, proposed Qavam. But since each group, helped by the American legation, vetoed the other's favorite, the Justice Caucus was able to muster enough votes for its own candidate, Soheily. Choosing his ministers with the advice of the fraksiuns, and even appointing an army general to head the War Ministry, Soheily obtained a large parliamentary majority for his administration. This majority melted away, however, in the course of the next five months as Soheily tried to satisfy the many contradictory interests. To retain the support of the deputies who feared that if the Allies poured large sums into the country the economy would drown in rising inflation, he delayed a bill to permit the National Bank to print 300 million rials for the occupying powers. This inevitably angered the Allies, who urgently needed the bank notes to pay their local employees. To protect some one hundred fellow technocrats whom the British discovered were communicating with the Germans, he made excuses for postponing their arrests. This eventually taxed the patience of the British. To please the Allies who argued that their lines of communications could not be secured unless the central government reached a compromise with the rebellious tribes, he announced that the government would permit annual migrations, punish unjust administrators, rectify past neglect, appoint a permanent commission for tribal affairs, and return the lands that had been expropriated by Reza Shah. This antagonized not only the new owners but also the military commanders. As a result, the army high command refused to intervene when food riots erupted in a number of provincial towns. Bullard observed that these popular disorders and the passive attitude of the army created "great fear among the wealthy."[32] Having lost his parliamentary majority, Soheily handed in his resignation by July.

Qavam, who was willing both to print the necessary bank notes and arrest the pro-German officials, now appeared to be the best candidate. Forming a government with the consent of the Azerbaijan, Patriotic, and Justice fraksiuns, Qavam kept the portfolio of the war minister for himself, and informed the deputies that in future the chief of staff would be subordinate to the war minister.[33] For the first time since 1921, civilians threatened to control the military. During the next four months, Qavam strengthened his ties with the Allies

[32] British Minister to the Foreign Office, "Annual Report for 1942," *F.O. 371*/Persia 1943/34-35117.

[33] "Qavam's Secret Session with the Majles," *Mardom*, 6 August 1943.

and tried to further weaken the shah. He arrested over 150 pro-German officials, including the military governor of Fars. He created an emergency currency commission to print as many bank notes as the occupying authorities needed. Moreover, he guided through parliament a special bill giving the administration of the country's finances to Dr. Millspaugh, the American economic expert who had served in Iran during the early 1920s. Furthermore, Qavam purged royalists from the War Ministry and instructed the cabinet members to communicate with the shah only through the office of the prime minister.

The conflict between Qavam and the shah spilled over into the streets of Tehran. The upheaval began as a peaceful demonstration on December 8 outside Parliament, organized by the bazaar guilds protesting the high food prices, the new issue of bank notes, and the recent income tax bill drafted by Millspaugh. The peaceful demonstration turned, however, into a violent assault on the Parliament building as hired thugs (*chaqukeshan*), and army officers announced that the shah would never permit the troops to fire upon "his beloved people."[34] While the army prevented the city police from intervening, the demonstrators beat up two deputies, broke into bakeries, looted luxury stores, pillaged Qavam's home, and threatened the wealthy residential district of the city. Order was not restored until the British rushed in their own troops. Although the Allies came in to bail out Qavam, the intervention convinced Britain and United States that the rivalry between the premier and the shah threatened to divert their meager military resources from the vital responsibility of transporting war materials to the thankless task of preserving law and order. Faced with choosing between Qavam or the shah, they opted for the latter. As the British military attaché stressed, "the army was the only effective force in the country." And as Vail Motter, the U.S. Army historian of the American involvement in Iran, has shown, the War Department in Washington overruled the American military advisors in Tehran and swung U.S. support behind the shah and against the prime minister.[35] In any case, the riots had jolted the deputies, es-

---

[34] The chaqukeshan and their varzeshgahan (athletic clubs) were heirs to the nineteenth-century lutis and their zurkhanehs. The social transformations of the century, however, had reached down into the underworld, dissolving the old ward ties and stressing the cash nexus between patrons and clients. Despite this, almost all the chaqukeshan retained their religious sentiments and refused to be hired by secular radical organizations. American Minister to the State Department, "Rioting in Tehran," *Foreign Relations of the United States* (Washington, D.C., 1942), IV, 219; British Minister to the Foreign Office, 9 December 1942, *F.O. 371*/Persia 1942/34-31886.

[35] British Military Attaché to the Foreign Office, "Memorandum on the Persian Army," *F.O. 371*/Persia 1942/34-35129; T. Vail Motter, *U.S. Army in World War II—The Middle East Theatre: The Persian Corridor and Aid to Russia* (Washington, D.C., 1952), pp. 162, 436, 471.

pecially the Patriotic and the Justice fraksiuns, into realizing that the breakdown of the military order could be an open invitation for social disorder. When Parliament reconvened in February 1943, Qavam had no choice but to hand in his resignation. The young shah had survived the first of many challenges to his military position. Bullard commented unfairly that the deputies had deserted Qavam because "they were a volatile race with no principle to guide them."[36]

After Qavam's departure, the Justice and Patriotic fraksiuns allied with the National Unionists to bring back Soheily. Obtaining a large majority, Soheily strengthened his position by wooing the religious establishment. He appointed a former shari'a judge as minister of justice; formally recognized the fact that the police no longer enforced the ban on the veil; relaxed government supervision of maktabs and madrasehs; promised to end coeducational classes in state schools; and introduced divinity classes into the state school curriculum. Soheily also strengthened his position by building new bridges to United States. He offered to visit Washington to negotiate a commercial treaty; secretly proposed a concession covering much of southwest Iran to the Standard Vacuum Oil Company; and granted Millspaugh additional powers to fine food hoarders and to control the prices, distribution, and import of a number of nonfood commodities. At the same time, to assure Bullard that his enthusiastic pro-American policy would not damage British interests, Soheily quietly offered to negotiate a concession with the British Royal Dutch Shell Company. Although the Cold War later overshadowed all other international rivalries, during 1941-1942 Anglo-American competition for economic advantages often caused intense suspicion in Iran. As the American legation frequently complained, the British authorities in Iran supported the "reactionary upper class," unnecessarily interfered in local affairs, and even blackmailed prime ministers by threatening to withhold essential food supplies. A personal emissary of President Roosevelt added that the British were so unpopular by 1943 that if Iranians had to choose between them and the Russians they would "unquestionably" prefer the latter.[37]

Although Soheily retained his parliamentary majority through 1943, his relations with the shah suffered three acute crises. The first was caused by his refusal to suppress newspapers that had revealed em-

[36] British Minister to the Foreign Office, 9 February 1943, *F.O. 371*/Persia 1943/34-35068.

[37] American Minister to the State Department, *Foreign Relations of United States* (1943), IV, 319, 330, 333, 363-369, 370, 534; Personal Representative of President Roosevelt to the President, *Foreign Relations of the United States* (1943), IV, 370.

barrassing personal information about members of the royal family.[38] The second erupted over the annual budget. Soheily, encouraged by Millspaugh, proposed to balance the budget by drastically reducing the army from 65,000 men to 30,000. The shah countered with the demand that the army should be increased to 108,000. Eventually, the head of the American military mission, General Ridley, set the figure at 86,000. The American minister commented, "the shah is averse to Millspaugh's curtailment of the military budget because this threatens his control of the army on which he hopes to maintain himself in power."[39]

The third crisis revolved around the Interior Ministry as the elections for the Fourteenth Majles drew nearer. Since the Interior Ministry appointed not only the provincial governors-general and the regional governors, but also, through them, the local Supervisory Electoral Councils, Soheily, the shah, and the Patriotic fraksiun fought a tug-of-war for the important ministry. In nine months, they produced three different interior ministers and ten new governors-general. At one point, Soheily quietly informed the American minister that "he would dissolve the Majlis and call for new elections were it not for fear that the shah and his army clique might in the interim seize the opportunity to institute a military dictatorship."[40] For his part, the shah, growing concerned about the election results, suggested to the Allies that the life of the existing Majles should be extended until the end of the war. The Allies, however, replied that the elections would be a valuable safety-valve, and that the people looked forward to the new Majles as a "safeguard for their liberties." The shah then proposed to convene the Senate as stipulated in the constitutional laws. But Bullard vetoed the idea on the grounds that another assembly would merely add to parliamentary "obstructionism." Finding himself in a precarious position, the shah eventually transferred $500,000 from New York to invest into the "political intrigue" of the unavoidable elections. Bullard commented, "Definitely scared about the composition of the new Majlis, the Shah wishes to take all possible precautions."[41]

[38] British Minister to the Foreign Office, 29 July 1943, *F.O. 371*/Persia 1943/34-35072.

[39] British Military Attaché to the Foreign Office, "General Ridley's Recommendation for the Reorganization of the Persian Army," *F.O. 371*/Persia 1943/34-35129; American Minister to the State Department, 14 April 1943, *Foreign Relations of the United States* (1943), IV, 520.

[40] American Minister to the State Department, 14 June 1943, *Foreign Relations of the United States* (1943), IV, 531.

[41] British Minister to the Foreign Office, 14 February and 13 March 1943, *F.O. 371*/Persia 1943/34-35068; idem, 27 May 1943, *F.O. 371*/Persia 1943/34-35070; idem, 11 April 1944, *F.O. 371*/Persia 1944/34-40187.

THE FOURTEENTH MAJLES ELECTIONS (NOVEMBER 1943-FEBRUARY 1944)

The elections for the Fourteenth Parliament were the most prolonged, the most competitive, and hence the most meaningful of all elections in modern Iran. Beginning as early as June 1943, six months before the closure of the Thirteenth Majles, the electoral campaign continued in some constituencies until as late as April 1944, three months after the opening of the Fourteenth Majles. Over 800 candidates competed for 136 seats. Moreover, the results were determined not by the state, but by the relative strengths, on one hand, of competing social forces, and, on the other hand, of organized groups, especially political parties, parliamentary fraksiuns, and their foreign protectors, within the government bureaucracy. Gone were the days when the shah could arrange the return of his faithful deputies. Instead, the country was galvanized by lively but highly complex elections between rival candidates attached to diverse interests, espousing different views, and appealing to antagonistic social forces.

The situation in the government bureaucracy varied greatly from region to region. Some governors worked closely with the Allies; some retained close ties with the shah; some obeyed the prime minister; and some depended on local magnates, regional interest groups, and national political parties. To further complicate the situation, the newly created Ministry of Provisions was able to influence the elections, since no one could vote without showing his ration cards. As a result, the prime minister, together with the ministers of interior and provisions, wielded most influence in Tehran and Mazandaran, the two main provinces outside both martial law and foreign occupation. The shah, on the other hand, carried most weight in constituencies under martial law, especially the disturbed regions of Isfahan, Fars, Kerman, and Kurdistan. The Allies, of course, had the upper hand in their respective zones of occupation: the British in Khuzistan, Kermanshah, and parts of Tehran Province; the Soviets in Azerbaijan, Gilan, and northern Khurasan.

None of these forces, however, monopolized the elections. Lacking definitive control over the votes going into the ballot boxes, they merely possessed the power to distort the votes coming out of the ballot boxes. Unable to dictate the results, they invariably restricted themselves to helping the candidates who already enjoyed a significant following in their locality. Although at the beginning of the elections the British legation instructed its provincial consuls to "encourage the best elements,"[42] the results showed that few candidates owed their

---

[42] British Minister to the Provincial Consuls, 18 March 1943, *F.O. 371*/Persia 1943/ 34-35068.

seats purely to foreign intervention. As the British Foreign Office remarked toward the end of the elections, "it is interesting that, in spite of all forebodings and the Cassandra-like prophecies of the Americans, the Anglo-Iranian Oil Company, and a host of others, the Russians have exerted little influence in the voting in their zone."[43]

The relative strength of the various social forces depended on the social structure of the constituencies. In rural regions, tribal chiefs and large landowners dominated the results by retaining control over their tribesmen and peasants. As one British consul correctly antici-pated, "the landlords are justifiably confident that, in spite of radi-calism in the towns, the majority of the peasants will continue to follow their lead on election day."[44] In small towns, however, the religious leaders and wealthy merchants again resorted to the bazaar guilds and local mosques to rally the traditional middle class. In the more modern cities, on the other hand, the religious leaders and wealthy merchants formed political organizations to hold their own against the radical intelligentsia with its own professional associations, revo-lutionary newspapers, and, most important of all, political parties. In trying to make sense out of the complicated and confusing picture, the British legation described sixteen political parties that entered the elections: "While Persian xenophobia has its reflections in the electoral situation, as does a bias here and there for or against a particular Ally, the broad division that appears to emerge is between interests com-monly styled reactionary and those tending to the Left, or, between those who have and those who have not." The same source reported at the end of the elections that the sixteen political parties had mul-tiplied to forty-two.[45] As one Iranian intellectual commented, "whereas under Reza Shah anyone who uttered the word 'party' risked im-prisonment, now every politician with grandiose ambitions gathers together his personal clique and announces to the world the formation of a new political party. We should name these few years the 'age of party-playing' (*partibazi*)."[46]

Many of these political parties either disappeared in the next two years or intentionally limited their activities to specific regions. The following six, however, remained active in the forthcoming years and tried to create statewide organizations: the Tudeh, which, headed by the "Fifty-three" Marxists who had been jailed by Reza Shah, appealed

[43] Foreign Office in London, 3 December 1943, *F.O. 371*/Persia 1943/34-35117.

[44] British Consul in Tabriz, 9 July 1943, *F.O. 371*/Persia 1943/34-35093.

[45] British Minister to the Foreign Office, "Memorandum on Parties Active in the General Elections," *F.O. 371*/Persia 1943/34-35074; idem, "A Note on Political Parties in Persia," *F.O. 371*/Persia 1945/34-45512.

[46] Mustawfi, *Tehran Demokrat*, p. 32.

mostly to the intelligentsia and the urban working class; the Comrades' party (Hizb-i Hamraham); the Iran party (Hizb-i Iran); the Justice party (Hizb-i ʿAdalat); the National Union party (Hizbi-i Ittihad-i Melli); and the Fatherland party (Hizb-i Vatan).

The Comrades' party was formed in November 1942 by a small circle of radical intellectuals who had worked closely with the Tudeh but had grown concerned by the latter's firm support for the Soviet Union. Mustawfa Fateh, the party's leading figure, was a British-educated economist and one of the highest-ranking Iranians in the Anglo-Iranian Oil Company. Having coedited the paper *Mardom* (The People) with the Tudeh leaders in a short-lived united front named the Anti-Fascist Society, Fateh left and founded his own newspaper, *Emruz va Farda* (Today and Tomorrow). In later years, he wrote an excellent Marxist study of the oil company entitled *Panjah Saleh-i Naft-i Iran* (Fifty Years of Iranian Oil). ʿAbbas Naraqi, another founding leader of the party, was a young lawyer who had been given a light sentence for being a "youthful and misguided" member of the "Fifty-three." Naraqi's family was well known in Kashan, where his father, a proconstitutional preacher, had been martyred during the civil war. The Comrades' party espoused two broad objectives: "the granting of political equality to all citizens"; and the nationalizations of the main means of production to provide 'each according to his work.' "[47] During the elections, the party focused its energies in the British-occupied zone and sponsored ten candidates, all of whom were Western-educated professionals and civil servants.[48]

The Iran party, which soon became the country's main secular nationalist organization, had developed out of an Engineer's Association created in October 1941. Mehdi Bazargan, a founding member of both the association and the party, later reminisced, "while studying in Europe during the 1930s, we marveled at the sight of free student associations, free religious fraternities, and free political parties. In Iran, the regime had destroyed all independent organizations. Consequently, as soon as the opportunity presented itself in 1941, we formed the Engineer's Association."[49] The association, however, split into two on the eve of the Fourteenth Majles elections. While the more radical members joined the pro-Tudeh labor movement, the more moderate ones formed the Iran party and joined other like-minded professionals—especially lawyers, doctors, and professors—to cam-

[47] Comrades' Party, "Party Program," *Emruz va Farda*, 28 April 1943.
[48] The ten candidates included five civil servants, two physicians, one journalist, one bank manager, and a legal adviser to the Anglo-Iranian Oil Company.
[49] M. Bazargan, *Dafaʿat dar Dadgah* (Defence at the Court) (n.p., 1964), p. 35.

paign on behalf of the highly respected Dr. Mossadeq as well as their own party leaders.

Mossadeq, whose views often coincided with those of the Iran party, had reentered politics in 1941 but had avoided party affiliations, since he took pride in being fully independent. Receiving support from guild leaders in Tehran as well as from professional associations, Mossadeq ran his electoral campaign on three major issues. First, he argued that Iran would preserve national independence only if it gave up the misguided foreign policy of the past, which he termed "positive equilibrium," and adopted a forward-looking neutralist policy, which he called "negative equilibrium."[50] According to Mossadeq, traditional leaders had at times played off Russia, the "northern neighbor," against Britain, the "southern neighbor"; at times granted concessions to the latter at the expense of the former; and at times looked for a "third force," such as Germany, France, or United States, to counterbalance the two major "neighbors." In pursuing this "open" policy, the traditional leaders had handed out concessions left and right, whetted the appetites of the foreign powers, and thereby turned Iran into a free-for-all. Mossadeq concluded that the only way to end this dangerous situation was to cease granting major concessions, and to assure the main powers, especially Britain and Russia, that Iran would pursue a strictly nonaligned course.

Mossadeq's second campaign issue involved the shah. Arguing that Reza Shah's dictatorship had been built on military foundations, he stressed that the newly inaugurated democracy would not last long unless the armed forces were taken out of royalist hands and placed under civilian/parliamentary control. His third issue focused on the need to change the electoral system. Insisting that social reforms were impossible so long as the landed families packed Parliament, he proposed to double Tehran's representation, disqualify illiterates—thus disenfranchizing the easily manipulated rural masses—and replace the Supervisory Electoral Councils with independent civilian committees headed by professors, teachers, and other "educated citizens."[51] Although Mossadeq soon obtained in the West the image of an old-fashioned and narrow-minded "xenophobic" aristocrat, his external policy was grounded on the premise that a mere moratorium on concessions would satisfy the foreign powers and would persuade them to leave Iran alone. Similarly, his internal policies, especially the stress on antimilitarism, constitutionalism, and political liberalism, appealed more to the middle classes than to the old landed families.

[50] H. Key-Ostovan, *Siyasat-i Muvazaneh-i Manfi dar Majles-i Chahardahum* (The Politics of Negative Equilibrium in the 14th Majles) (Tehran, 1950), 2 vols.

[51] M. Mossadeq, "Bill for Electoral Reform," *Ayandeh*, 3:2 (1944), 61-63.

TABLE 4
Early Leaders of the Iran Party

Name	Occupation	Higher Education	Residence	Date of Birth
Farivar, Ghulam 'Ali	engineer	Univ. of Paris	Tehran	1906
Shafaq, Rezazadeh	professor of literature	Univ. of Berlin	Tehran	1897
Zanganeh, 'Abdul Hamid	lawyer	Univ. of Paris	Tehran	1904
Mu'aven, Hussein	physician	Univ. of Paris	Tehran	1906
Mu'azemi, 'Abdallah	professor of law	Univ. of Paris	Tehran	1907
Sanjabi, Karim	professor of law	Univ. of Paris	Tehran	1904
Bazargan, Mehdi	professor of engineering	Univ. of Paris	Tehran	1907
Zirakzadeh, Ahmad	engineer	Univ. of Geneva	Tehran	1908
Saleh, Allahyar	civil servant	mission school	Tehran	1896
Amir 'Alai, Shams al-Din	lawyer	Univ. of Paris	Tehran	1895
Haqshenas, Jahanger	engineer	Tehran University	Tehran	1907
Hasebi, Kazem	engineer	Univ. of Paris	Tehran	1907
Parsa, Asghar	civil servant	Tehran University	Tehran	1915
Rejbi, Davar	professor of engineering	Univ. of Berlin	Tehran	1913
Ghaffari, Zaka	professor of politics	Univ. of Berlin	Tehran	1886

The Iran party helped bring about the election of not only Mossadeq, but also of five of its leaders: Dr. Rezazadeh Shafaq, Dr. Ghulam 'Ali Farivar, Dr. Abdul Hamid Zanganeh, Dr. Hussein Mu'aven, and Dr. Abdallah Mu'azemi. Like most other leaders of the Iran party, these five came from the ranks of the young generation of the Western-educated intelligentsia residing in Tehran (see Table 4). But unlike most other leaders of the party, these five were able to win Majles seats mainly because their families enjoyed substantial influence within their constituencies. For example, Zanganeh, although a radical lawyer who had spent most of his life in Tehran and Paris, won a seat from Kermanshah mainly because his father was the chief of a large Kurdish tribe based outside that city.

In addition to supporting Mossadeq's general policies, the Iran party advocated a diluted form of French socialism. It called for a national revolution against the feudal landlords to complete the re-

Place of Birth	Class Origin	Ethnic Origin	Previous Politics	Subsequent Politics
Enzeli	middle class	Persian	none	Mossadeq's National Front
Tehran	middle class	Azeri	Democrat party	left Iran party in 1945
Kermanshah	tribal nobility	Kurdish	none	Mossadeq's National Front
Kermanshah	upper class	Persian	prison in 1940	Mossadeq's National Front
Gulpayegan	upper class	Persian	none	Mossadeq's National Front
Kermanshah	tribal nobility	Kurdish	none	Mossadeq's National Front
Tehran	middle class	Azeri	none	left Iran party in 1946
Isfahan	middle class	Persian	none	Mossadeq's National Front
Kashan	middle class	Persian	none	Mossadeq's National Front
Tehran	Qajar nobility	Qajar-Persian	none	left Iran party in 1945
Tehran	middle class	Persian	none	Mossadeq's National Front
Tehran	middle class	Persian	none	Mossadeq's National Front
Khoi	middle class	Azeri	none	Mossadeq's National Front
?	middle class	Persian	none	Mossadeq's National Front
Tehran	middle class	Persian	prison in 1940	left Iran party in 1945

forms initiated by the constitutional movement. It argued that main social conflict in Iran was between the "exploited people" and the "exploiting rulers," not between the middle and the lower classes. It encouraged the state to implement a program for rapid industrialization, and claimed that agricultural countries, being "dumping grounds" for developed countries, could not be truly independent. It added that the state should own all the major industries, since laissez-faire capitalism concentrated economic and political power "in the hands of a few illiterate robber-barons who not only exploit the masses but also have little respect for skilled professionals and technicians."[52] Moreover, it waged a propaganda campaign against both

[52] "The Need for a National Revolution," *Jeb'eh*, 28 May 1946; Z. Zirakzadeh, "Contemporary Iran," *Jeb'eh*, 9 July 1946; M. Kuzudehpour, "The State Must Build Industry," *Jeb'eh*, 22 April 1946; 'A. Raski, "Our Party's Economic Plan," *Jeb'eh*, 11 May 1946.

the old and the new wealthy families. As one party pamphlet on the Iranian aristocracy declared, "the main obstacle to national progress is the privileged class":

In the days before Reza Shah, Iran was ruled by an intransigent aristocracy that opposed all reforms because its privileges were intricately tied to the status quo. . . . The reign of Reza Shah, however, broke this aristocracy into two segments. Those unwilling to accept the new order were forced into either exile or silence. Those willing to serve the new monarch were coopted into the regime. In comparing these two segments, we must remember that whatever the shortcomings of the former, they were minor in contrast to the crimes of the latter. If the first segment exploited in thousands of tomans and acted like feudalists, the second segment accumulated in hundreds of thousands of tomans and behaved like nouveaux riches capitalists as well as narrow-minded feudalists. Thus the reign did not solve the problem of class exploitation. It merely added a heavier burden to the existing problem. . . . The problem has grown so explosive that we are now on the brink of a violent revolution which could bring to the fore dangerous elements. Our only hope is to transfer power, through electoral reform, to the intelligentsia class (*ta-baqeh-i rushanfekr*).[53]

Whereas the Iran and Comrades' parties were headed by the young intelligentsia who had grown up in the 1930s, the Justice party was formed by the older intelligentsia who had participated in the political upheavals of the early 1920s. An offshoot of the Justice Caucus in parliament, the Justice party was headed by ʿAli Dashti, the outspoken deputy; Dadgar, an old Democrat who had helped the 1921 coup d'état and had served as Reza Shah's president of the Majles before escaping into exile in Europe; and Ibrahim Khajeh-Nouri, a journalist and previous director of press and propaganda. The papers close to the party—*Bahram* (Mars), *Nida-yi ʿAdalat* (Call of Justice), *Mehr-i Iran* (Sun of Iran), and *Qiyam-i Iran* (Rising of Iran)—called for reductions in the military budget, reforms in the government bureaucracy, expansion in educational facilities, recruitment of American advisers, and vigilance against both the evils of capitalism and the dangers of communism. But as Dadgar admitted years later, "we formed the Justice party in the chaotic days of the war to counter the 'Fifty-three' communists who had founded the dangerous Tudeh party."[54]

The National Union party was also an offshoot of a parliamentary caucus. Formed by the royalist deputies, the party and its main organ, the *Nida-yi Mellat* (Call of the Nation), advocated the same policies as

---

[53] A. Khalʿatbari, *Aristukrasi-yi Iran* (The Iranian Aristocracy) (Tehran, 1944), pp. 11-29.

[54] ʿA. Dadgar, "How I Reentered Politics," *Khvandaniha*, 2 March 1956.

the National Union fraksiun. In foreign affairs, they sought American aid, especially military aid, as a counterbalance to the influence of Britain and the Soviet Union. In home affairs, they intended to preserve the compromise with the shah and to pursue conservative social programs. In August 1944, in a bid to gain wider public support and challenge the Tudeh, they changed the organization's name to the People's party (Hizb-i Mardom), published a more radical-sounding paper entitled *Seda-yi Mardom* (Voice of the People), and even talked in generalities of the advantages of "socialism." Their day-to-day activities, however, continued to reflect their conservative-royalist backgrounds.

The Fatherland party was formed by Sayyid Ziya in September 1943, immediately after his return from exile. Reviving his old paper *Ra'ad* (Thunder) with the new title of *Ra'ad-i Emruz* (Today's Thunder), Sayyid Ziya tried to mobilize the bazaars, the 'ulama, and the tribes against the "dangerous vestiges of the military dictatorship," the "atheistic communism" of the Tudeh party, and the "corrupt oligarchy" of the titled landowning families. Five months later, Sayyid Ziya renamed the organization the National Will party (Hizb-i Eradeh Melli), and restructured it into a rigid centralized hierarchy. Although the party was closely identified with Britain, its structure reminded many Western observers, such as Millspaugh, of Italian fascism.[55] The party program called for the repeal of all laws that contradicted the spirit of the constitution; convening of provincial assemblies as promised in the fundamental laws; establishment of tribal committees in the Interior Ministry; protection of handicraft industries; strengthening of religion and patriotism through public schools, local clubs, and mass newspapers; ban of antireligious publications; distribution of state lands among the peasantry; formation of a volunteer army; encouragement of internal commerce; and destruction of both "the vestiges of personal autocracy and the foundations of class oligarchy."[56]

The party paper, *Ra'ad-i Emruz*, elaborated on the central themes of the program. It denounced Reza Shah, to whom it always referred as Reza Khan—for plundering the country, undermining religion, trampling over the constitution, intensifying class hatreds, squeezing the people with taxation, starting a cancerous bureaucracy, and diverting scarce resources from essential civilian needs to an overgrown

---

[55] A. Millspaugh, *Americans in Persia* (Washington, D.C., 1946), p. 78.
[56] National Will Party, *Maramnameh-i Hizb* (Party Program) (Tehran, 1945), pp. 1-25.

war machine.[57] To prevent the reestablishment of a military dicta-torship, it demanded the reduction of the army to 50,000 men, elim-ination of royal influence among the officer corps, public condem-nation of Reza Shah's henchmen, and state confiscation of all court assets as well as all royal estates. Moreover, *Ra'ad-i Emruz* continually argued that "the right to private property was a fundamental principle both of Islam and of the Iranian constitution"; that state monopolies and income tax placed a "heavy burden on the impoverished guilds"; that Reza Shah's "shameful practice" of inflicting corporal punishment on price-control violators should be stopped; and that the country would remain backward as long as power was concentrated in the "hands of the *Al-Saltanehs, al-Dawlehs,* and *al-Mamaleks.*" Furthermore, *Ra'ad-i Emruz* directed sharp attacks at the intelligentsia, accusing it of intellectual snobbism, of collaborating with Reza Shah's autocracy, of being atheistic, of wasting national resources on foreign degrees, and of mindlessly imitating everything that was Western.[58] As symbols of his sympathies, Sayyid Ziya insisted on using his religious title *sayyid* and wearing the old Persian-style fur hat.

Not surprisingly, Sayyid Ziya's programs appealed to the bazaar retailers, especially the shopkeepers' guilds, and to the conservative religious authorities, particularly a prominent preacher named Kha-lezadeh, who, in 1925, had helped organize the antirepublican move-ment. As the British military attaché reported, many merchants, guild leaders, and mullas, "fearing the Tudeh," flocked to Sayyid Ziya.[59] Despite this success, the Fatherland party refrained from sponsoring its own candidates in the Majles elections. Instead, it campaigned for the reelection of the deputies from the pro-British Patriotic Caucus. Sayyid Ziya, however, won a seat in Yazd, partly with the help of his party and partly with the influence of the wealthy Taheri family.

The complex interaction between the many candidates—whether party-sponsored or independent—the various social forces, and the

---

[57] "The Army Must Be Reformed," *Ra'ad-i Emruz,* 11 January 1944; "Reza Khan and the Army," ibid., 22 May 1945; "Reza Khan—The Enemy of Religion," ibid., 5 April 1945; "The Danger of Revolution," ibid., 9 August 1944; "The Cancerous Sit-uation," ibid., 15 June 1944.

[58] "The Military Budget," ibid., 8 June 1944; "The Court and Politics," ibid., 1 June 1944; "Iran Needs a True National Army," ibid., 30 January 1945; "Whatever Hap-pened to the Other 270 Million Tomans," ibid., 26 May 1944; "The Right of Private Property," ibid., 28 May 1944; "State Monopolies," ibid., 23 June 1944; "No More Corporal Punishment against Muslims," ibid., 17 May 1944; "The Intelligentsia: Iran's Misfortune," ibid., 11 May 1944.

[59] British Military Attaché to the Foreign Office, 12 April 1945, *F.O. 371*/Persia 1945/ 34-45446.

diverse pressures in the local bureaucracies can be seen best in the Isfahan, Shiraz, and Tabriz elections. The election in Isfahan began with five serious and more than twenty less serious candidates competing for the city's three seats. The strongest candidate was a young lawyer from the Tudeh party named Taqi Fedakar. He drew his support mainly from the recently unionized mill workers and partly from the bazaar wage earners. Describing the local situation as a classic example of class conflict between capital and labor, the British consul explained Fedakar's strength:

Under Reza Shah, the land and mill owners—who are mostly ignorant, believing that money can do everything, reactionary to a degree, and solely interested in making as much money as possible—reigned supreme in Isfahan with the help of the central Government. But with the change of regime in 1941 and removal of the ban on communist propaganda, the Russian-backed Tudeh, led locally by Fedakar, began to develop by taking advantage of this struggle between labour and capital. At present Isfahan is the center of this struggle because of the existence of an easily organized body of uneducated opinion among the millhands.[60]

The main opposition to the Tudeh party was headed by a local politician named Sayyid Hashem al-Din Dawlatabadi. The son of a prominent religious leader, Dawlatabadi drew considerable support from the guild elders and the bazaar merchants—especially merchants who had acquired through Reza Shah lands confiscated from the Bakhtiyari khans. In the words of the British consul, these merchants now feared, on one hand, Bakhtiyari "vengeance," and, on the other hand, "the workers' delegates who were flocking to their villages to agitate among the peasants."[61] Dawlatabadi also received support from the National Union party. Thus the traditional middle class in Isfahan, fearing both tribal reaction and peasant-workers' revolution, was willing to forget Reza Shah's antireligious policies in order to work together with the royalist National Union party.

The third major candidate was a wealthy merchant turned industrialist named Haydar 'Ali Emami. His main backing came from fellow millowners; from the old landed families; from Akbar Mas'oud, the heir of Zil al-Sultan, the famous Qajar prince who had governed Isfahan for three decades; from the police officers, who, according to the British consul, were receiving generous bribes;[62] and from the

[60] British Consul in Isfahan, "Report on Isfahan," *F.O. 371*/Persia 1945/34-45476.
[61] Idem, 3 May 1943, *F.O. 371*/Persia 1943/34-35120.
[62] Idem, 21 August 1943, *F.O. 371*/Persia 1943/34-31412.

Fatherland party, which was trying to organize conservative trade unions to counter the Tudeh labor movement.

The next important candidate was Saifpour Fatemi (Mosbeh al-Sultan). A major landowner as well as legal advisor to the Bakhtiyari chiefs, Fatemi's strength lay outside Isfahan, especially in Na'in and Chahar Mahal. Although the public considered Fatemi a British candidate and his family paper, *Bakhtar* (The West), reinforced this image, the British consul gave him little support, and even shunned him as "highly opportunistic."[63] The final candidate was Ahmad Quli Khan Bakhtiyari, the eldest son of Morteza Quli Khan Bakhtiyari. The patriarch of the Ilkhani family, Morteza Quli Khan had returned to politics in 1941 to reclaim his expropriated lands, reassert his authority over the Hajji Ilkhani family, and free the Bakhtiyaris of military control. By 1943, he had accomplished his main goals. He held the governorship of the entire Bakhtiyari area, from Dezful in the west to Chahar Mahal in the east, from Ram Hormuz in the south to Fereydun in the north. He had regained much of his family lands, and had forced the Hajji Ilkhani chiefs to accept his authority. What is more, he had persuaded the military, including the gendarmerie, to withdraw from the Bakhtiyari regions. As the British consul in Isfahan reported, the government withdrew from the Bakhtiyari regions as soon as it discovered that the troops were more eager to "shoot their officers than the armed tribesmen."[64]

As the electoral campaign progressed, the last two withdrew their candidacies to neighboring constituencies. Fatemi won the seat of Najafabad with the help of the Bakhtiyaris. Ahmad Quli Khan Bakhtiyari took Shahr-i Kurd, the market town of his tribes. Moreover, Muhammad Taqi Khan As'ad, his cousin who had spent ten years in jail, won the Dezful elections. With the last two out of the running, the top three, encouraged by the British consul and Akbar Mas'oud, who now chaired the Supervisory Electoral Council, formed a pact to invite their supporters to cast their three votes for each other. In the final count, Fedakar won with 30,499 votes; Dawlatabadi came second with 29,470; and Emami obtained the third seat with 27,870 votes. As the British consul admitted, the Tudeh candidate was placed first to provide a necessary "safety valve" for working-class discontent.[65]

The Shiraz election, on the other hand, was a latter-day version of the traditional policy of tribal manipulations. On one side was Naser Khan, the eldest son of the Qashqayi ilkhan who had been murdered by Reza Shah. After his release in 1941, Naser Khan established con-

---

[63] Idem, 10 March 1944, *F.O. 371*/Persia 1944/34-40163.
[64] Idem, 15 April 1943, *F.O. 371*/Persia 1943/34-31412.
[65] Idem, 16 August 1943, *F.O. 371*/Persia 1943/34-35121.

tact with German agents, formed an alliance with the Boir Ahmedis, and, at the battle of Semirum in July 1943, eliminated from his tribal regions the last remnants of military presence. Before the elections began, he offered to end his German connections if the central government revived the title of *ilkhan* and helped the election of six Qashqayi candidates. On the other side was Ibrahim Qavam (Qavam al-Mulk), the heir of the former Khamseh ilkhan, the uncle by marriage of the shah, and the close friend of the British. In the precarious days after the battle of Semirum, the central government appointed Ibrahim Qavam governor-general of Fars, and gave him 1,000 rifles to distribute among the Khamseh and the Mamasani Lurs, who also felt threatened by the Qashqayis. As the electoral campaign started, Ibrahim Qavam packed his supporters into the Supervisory Electoral Council, forced a Tudeh party candidate out of the city, and removed the ballot boxes from the Qashqayis and Boir Ahmedi districts. As a result, three of the five successful candidates—Mehdi Qavam, Imam Jom'eh, and 'Ali Dehqan—fully supported Ibrahim Qavam. The fourth, Sardar Fakher Hekmat (Heshmat al-Mamalek), staunchly opposed the Qashqayis because they were encouraging his peasants in the district of Khish to refuse handing over any part of the annual harvest. The fifth successful candidate, Mehdi Namazi, was a millionaire merchant from the Patriotic Caucus who managed to negotiate the Mamasani vote. Having lost in Shiraz, Naser Khan salvaged only the seat of Abadeh, in the midst of the Qashqayi territory, for his younger brother Sawlat Qashqayi.

The Tabriz election, and its subsequent debate in parliament, frequently made the headlines. Before the campaign started, the main industrialists in the city approached the British consulate for assistance on the grounds that the Tudeh party threatened private property, religion, representation of gentlemen in the Majles, and economic productivity, since "employees would not work without the constant supervision of their employers."[66] The British consul commented, "among the conservatives, the industrialists are the most nervous. They fear that the relatively compact groups of factory workers will support the communists. The landlords, however, are less nervous, being fairly confident that the majority of the peasants will continue to follow their lead."[67]

Rebuffed by the British, the industrialists left the city's nine seats to the following twelve candidates: Amir Nasrat Iskandari, the wealthy Qajar landlord of the Azerbaijan Caucus; Dr. Abdul Hussein Sadeqi,

---

[66] British Consul in Tabriz, 3 August 1943, *F.O. 371*/Persia 1943/34-35073.

[67] Idem, 8 July 1943, *F.O. 371*/Persia 1943/34-35092.

a European-educated medical doctor associated closely with the Iran party; Shaykh al-Islam, the son of the famous Shaykhi leader who had participated in the Constitutional Revolution and had been executed by the Russians in 1911; Dr. Yousef Mujtahedi, a large land-owner, the candidate of the Justice party, and a relative of prominent mujtaheds who had headed the conservative Mutashar'i community at the turn of the century; Ipekchian, a local merchant with commercial ties to the Soviet Union; Asghar Panahi, a wealthy business-man and landowner near Tabriz; ʿAli Sartipzadeh, an ally of the Shaykh al-Islam, and a veteran revolutionary who had fought in the Constitutional Revolution and had chaired the local branch of the Communist party until 1927, when he had been expelled from the organization for continuing to support Reza Shah; and, finally, three candidates sponsored jointly by the Tudeh party and its local trade union affiliates. These labor unions not only demanded economic reforms, but also called for the use of Azeri in state schools and law courts, protection for local industries, distribution of Reza Shah's estates among the landless peasantry, and safeguards for the religious minorities.[68] This slate of three was headed by Pishevari, the communist leader who had spent eleven years in prison.

As the elections started, the governor-general of Azerbaijan, Major-General Moqadam, packed fellow landowners into the Supervisory Electoral Council, placed all the ballot boxes outside the poor neighborhoods, and instructed the police to close the voting polls at six o'clock in the evening—the same hours as factories ended their day's work. The Soviet authorities reacted belatedly by forcing Moqadam to resign and using their own lorries to get workers to the polls. The British Foreign Office commented, "in Mashad, the Russian consul was too late in interfering and no Tudeh candidates got elected. The Russians now appear to be trying to make up lost ground in Azerbaijan. Since our own consuls have vetoed candidates in their own zones, we are in no position to be indignant. Nor does the present total of five Tudeh candidates seem unduly alarming."[69] In the final count, Pishevari and another Tudeh candidate headed the list of nine winners. The Supervisory Electoral Council, however, refused to endorse their credentials as qualified deputies. The council, instead, gave the seats to Amir Nasrat Iskandari, Sadeqi, Shaykh al-Islam, Sartipza-deh, Mujtahedi, Panahi, and Ipekchian. The repercussions of this act became apparent two years later with the revolt in Azerbaijan.

[68] Idem, "The Programme of the Azerbaijan Worker's Committee," *F.O. 371*/Persia 1942/34-31390.
[69] British Foreign Office, 20 December 1943, *F.O. 371*/Persia 1943/34-35092.

CONVENING THE FOURTEENTH MAJLES (FEBRUARY-MARCH 1944)

The arrival of the successful candidates in Tehran during the early weeks of 1944 intensified the forebodings of the shah. For, although few considered the forthcoming Majles infested with revolutionaries, many realized that the royalist deputies were in danger of being overwhelmed by antiroyalist landowners, tribal chiefs, intellectuals, civil servants, and religious leaders. As the British military attaché commented five weeks before the opening of the Majles, "the Army is likely to be a first class issue in the new Parliament, both in regards the share it consumes of the national budget with little benefit to the country, and in regards the Shah's pretensions to make it the instrument of his personal policy." A week later, the same source reported, "for some days it had become evident that the Majles would not be opened if the Shah could prevent it. He had disquieting reports about the temper of a strong constitutional group in Parliament that threatens to obstruct his aspirations to autocracy."[70] In a last bid to avoid the dangerous situation, the shah offered the premiership to Mossadeq, Tehran's leading deputy, if the latter declared the elections null and void on grounds of corruption and undue interference. Mossadeq, however, replied that he would accept only on condition the electoral system was reformed promptly and the new voting started without any delay.[71] The shah refused, calculating that it was safer to face the existing danger rather than be confronted a few weeks later with a larger danger produced by electoral reform.

With the convening of Parliament in February, the earlier fears of the shah seemed to be actualized. For although the new Majles resembled the previous ones in social composition, the presence of 60 freshmen in a House of 126 deputies drastically changed its political composition.[72] The royalist National Union Caucus (Fraksiun-i Ittihad-i Melli) had not only lost its dominant position but was now surrounded by six hostile groups: the Patriotic Caucus (Fraksiun-i Mehan); the Democratic Caucus (Fraksiun-i Demokrat); the Liberal Caucus (Fraksiun-i Azadi); the Independent Caucus (Fraksiun-i Mustaqel); the Tudeh Caucus (Fraksiun-i Tudeh); and the Individuals' Caucus (Fraksiun-i Munfaradin).

[70] British Military Attaché to the Foreign Office, 17 and 24 January 1944, *F.O. 371/Persia 1944/34-40205.*

[71] British Minister to the Foreign Office, 20 and 22 January 1944, *F.O. 371/Persia 1944/34-40186.*

[72] The Fourteenth Majles had 136 seats, but of the elected deputies, five had their credentials rejected, two died soon after the opening of the session, another two resigned, and one was imprisoned by the British for his pro-German activities.

The constantly shifting alliances between these seven fraksiuns transformed the Fourteenth Majles into a complex maze of political bargaining, and produced in the course of the next two years as many as 7 premiers, 9 cabinets, and 110 cabinet ministers. In fact, governmental instability became so acute and parliamentary debates often became so heated that many outside observers, particularly Western diplomats, gave up trying to understand the Majles and concluded that Iranian politics was nothing more than the sound and fury of underdeveloped minds. However, a close examination of the fraksiuns proves that the behavior of the deputies was invariably consistent with their regional interests, ideological outlooks, foreign associations, and, most important of all, social backgrounds.

The National Union Caucus mustered at most thirty deputies. Although it had lost considerable ground since the previous Majles, it had gained the support of the following four prominent deputies: ʿEzatallah Bayat, the representative of the Bayat household in Arak; Naser Quli Ardalan, the patriarch of a titled landowning family in Kurdistan; Dawlatabadi, the conservative delegate from Isfahan; and Sayyid Muhammad Sadeq Tabatabai, the head of the Moderate party in the 1910s and the son of the famous proconstitutional mujtahed. The Caucus was formed of twenty landlords, four civil servants, three religious leaders, two businessmen, and one lawyer. All had done well under Reza Shah: thirteen regularly sat in his parliament; fourteen held high positions in his bureaucracy; and three made large fortunes through his economic projects. Moreover, many of the group represented constituencies whose elections had been influenced mainly by the military commanders.

The Patriotic Caucus, on the other hand, included twenty-six deputies, many of whom represented constituencies in the British zone. Headed by Madani, Namazi, and Taheri—the same leaders as in the previous parliament—the Patriots now enjoyed the support of three important newcomers: Sayyid Ziya, the pro-British politician from Yazd; Emami, the industrialist from Isfahan; and Fatemi, the deputy from Najafabad. Their group was composed of thirteen landlords, five businessmen—who traded mostly with Britain—three journalists, three civil servants, one lawyer, and one religious notable. The views of the fraksiun were publicized outside the Majles not only by the Fatherland party and its successor, the National Will party, but also by a number of newspapers—the most important being *Kushesh* (Effort), edited by a pro-British deputy from Bushire.

The Patriots worked closely with the eleven deputies of the Democratic Caucus. Known by their opponents as the "tribal group" (fraksiun-i ʿashayir), the Democrats were led by the two Bakhtiyari deputies; by Sawlat Qashqayi; by ʿAbbas Qubadyan, the chief of the Kurdish Kalhur tribe in Khuzistan, who had spent fifteen years in prison and had lost much of his family lands; and by Muhammad Farrukh (Muʿtasim al-Saltaneh), a former minister who had been dismissed by Reza Shah, and had been elected to the Fourteenth Majles with the help of the tribes in Sistan. These Democrats naturally worked for their common interests: for the preservation of the advantages gained by the tribes since 1941; for the return of lost lands; for the right to bear arms and migrate annually as in the good old days; for the advancement of their supporters in the provincial administration; and for compensation to cover hardships caused by Reza Shah's policy of forcing them to give up their nomadic way of life.

Whereas many Patriots and Democrats came from the British zone, almost all Liberals represented constituencies in the Soviet zone. Successors to the Azerbaijan Caucus, the Liberals were led by the same northern aristocrats: Farmanfarma, Amir Nasrat Iskandari, and, outside parliament, Ahmad Qavam. Abul Qassem Amini, a new addition to the fraksiun, was a close relative of the last Qajar monarch. Forced out of public life by Reza Shah, Amini made a fortune in private business, and returned to politics in 1941 by publishing a newspaper named *Umid* (Hope). During the Fourteenth Majles, *Umid* functioned as the unofficial organ of the Liberal Caucus. Of the twenty deputies in the Caucus, twelve were aristocratic landowners, two were religious leaders who had been persecuted by Reza Shah, and four were northern merchants who hoped to strengthen commercial ties with the Soviet Union. As one of them stated, "since our farmers and businessmen desperately need a foreign market, and since such a market exists in the north, we must do all we can to improve our relations with the Soviet Union."[73]

The Liberals were supported on foreign and constitutional issues by the Tudeh party Caucus. Of the eight representatives in the Tudeh Caucus, all came from the ranks of the young intelligentsia, although two were from aristocratic families.[74] Five of the eight, including the two from the aristocratic families, had been imprisoned by Reza Shah for advocating Marxism. All except Fedakar of Isfahan were elected from the northern provinces. But they owed their seats not so much to the Soviet authorities as to the trade union voters and the pro-Russian landlords, such as Ahmad Qavam and Abul Qassem Amini. Although the Tudeh fraksiun, like the Tudeh party, refused to be

[73] Q. Rahimian, *Parliamentary Proceedings*, 14th Majles, 12 June 1945.

[74] Of the eight, two were lawyers, one a physician, one a university teacher, two were high school teachers, one an engineer, and one had spent much of his adult life in the trade union underground.

sidetracked from mass politics into the parliamentary cul-de-sac, nevertheless it made full use of the Majles both as a means of obtaining social legislation and as a propaganda forum. The three main party newspapers, *Mardom* (The People), *Rahbar* (The Leader), and *Razm* (Battle)—all edited by members of the fraksiun—closely followed the day-to-day events in the complicated maze of the Fourteenth Majles. Moreover, the Tudeh party had taken the initiative in July 1942 to bring together thirteen editors into a Freedom Front (*Jeb'eh-i Azadi*) directed at "class reaction" and "royal dictatorship."[75] The Freedom Front grew by February 1944 to include over twenty-seven national and provincial newspaper editors.

Very different from the Tudeh delegation was the Independent Caucus. Heirs to the Justice fraksiun of the Thirteenth Majles, the fifteen members of the Independent Caucus changed their parliamentary label for two major reasons. Headed by Dashti, the non-aristocratic civil servants in the group wanted to stress their independence from both the shah and the landed upper class. Moreover, since they owed their seats to the pro-American Soheily, they considered themselves independent of both Britain and the Soviet Union. The fraksiun was strengthened by the addition of 'Abbas Mas'oudi, the editor of the influential *Ittila'at*. Outside the Majles, the Independent Caucus was helped by the Justice party and its impressive array of well-financed newspapers.

Finally, the Individuals' Caucus was a loose coalition of some sixteen deputies who usually followed the lead of Mossadeq, especially on foreign and constitutional issues. Closest to Mossadeq were the five representatives of the Iran party and the two leaders of the Comrades' party. The others were nonparty deputies elected mainly from the northern constituencies. Outside the Majles, the Individuals' Caucus often received help from the following independent newspapers: *Muzaffar* (Victorious), edited by Hussein Key-Ostovan, a theorist for the policy of "negative equilibrium"; *Mard-i Emruz* (Man of Today), published by Muhammad Mas'oud, who was eventually assassinated because of his gadfly articles; and *Kayhan* (The World), the main competitor of *Ittila'at* as the country's leading nonparty newspaper.

Thus the seven parliamentary fraksiuns and their extraparliamentary allies differed on important foreign, social, and constitutional issues. On foreign issues, especially as the Cold War started, the Patriots and Democrats aligned with Britain, the Tudeh and Liberals with the Soviet Union, the Independents and National Unionists with United States, and the Individuals with none of the great powers. On

[75] The Freedom Front, "National Proclamation," *Rahbar*, 12 July 1944.

social issues, particularly on the need for fundamental reforms, the Tudeh, the Individuals, and, at times, the Independents pressed for drastic changes; but the Patriots, Liberals, and National Unionists worked to preserve the status quo. And on constitutional issues, especially on the immediate question of who should control the armed forces, the National Unionists stood isolated against the Patriots, Democrats, Liberals, Tudeh, Independents, and Individuals.

THE FOURTEENTH MAJLES (MARCH 1944-MARCH 1946)

The routine opening of the Majles turned into a sharp attack on the shah. The Liberals, Patriots, Democrats, Independents, and Individuals, together with the Tudeh deputies, easily isolated the National Unionists, and promptly drafted a new oath of office that stressed the duty of each deputy to defend the constitutional rights of the Majles. They also elected As'ad Bakhtiyari of the Democrats and Madani of the Patriots to be, respectively, the president and deputy president of the Majles. Moreover, they took the most important positions on the crucial parliamentary committees, where all vital legislation was hammered out. On the other hand, the National Unionists salvaged only five of the eighteen seats on the Finance Committee, two of the sixteen on the Foreign Affairs Committee, and two of the thirteen on the Military Committee. The last, which was essential for the shah if he was to retain control of the army, contained five tribal chiefs who had borne the brunt of the military campaigns in the previous decade. The army's enemies were to decide its fate.

Once the routine business was completed, the antiroyalist bloc pursued the offensive by forcing Soheily's resignation. Although Soheily was by no means a court favorite, he had antagonized many of the antiroyalists by including six royalists in his latest cabinet, by blatantly interfering in the elections, and by corrupt handling of the food distribution.[76] Even some of the Independents had lost confidence in him.

Directly after Soheily's fall, representatives from the main anticourt groups—Farmanfarma from the Liberals, Farrukh from the Democrats, Taheri from the Patriots, and Mossadeq from the Individuals—met for long hours in the caucus rooms and eventually compromised on Muhammad Sa'id (Sa'id al-Vizareh) as their future prime minister. As a career diplomat who had served abroad during the past

[76] British Minister to the Foreign Office, 14 February 1943, *F.O. 371*/Persia 1943/34-35069.

twelve years, Sa'id was considered independent of Reza Shah's establishment. Moreover, being a close friend of Madani and a native of Azerbaijan who had studied in Baku and headed the embassy in Moscow, he was acceptable both to the pro-British politicians and the pro-Soviet aristocrats. The British Foreign Office commented that Sa'id was honest, reliable, and friendly to the Allies, but lacked the strength of character to stand up against the deputies.[77] Having received a parliamentary majority and the royal farman, Sa'id proceeded to choose his ministers in close consultation with the fraksiuns. He insisted on keeping the Foreign Ministry for himself, but handed over three posts to the northern Liberals, one to the Independents, and four to the southern Patriots and Democrats. Years later, he complained that the fraksiuns interfered so much in the formation of the cabinet that he ended up with colleagues he had never seen before. At the same time, the royalist papers protested that the deputies, by participating so directly in the selection of ministers, violated the separation of powers between the legislative and executive branches of government.[78] This was the first of many constitutional criticisms directed at the Fourteenth Majles.

Presenting the ministers and a government program to the deputies, Sa'id obtained a large vote of confidence. The program promised two significant changes. First, it divided the annual budget for the armed forces into monthly installments, and thus required the army to live from day to day. Second, it stated that the first aim of the new government would be to reform the military and place it on a correct constitutional footing.[79] The subsequent discussion turned into a full-scale attack on the army.[80] A spokesman for the Liberals argued that the military had to be drastically cut and reorganized in order to safeguard civil liberties. Another Liberal proposed to shift a significant proportion of the army budget to the city police and the rural gendarmerie, administered by the Ministry of Interior. Yet another Liberal demanded public investigations into the financial dealings and the "treacherous activities" of all army officers who had willingly collaborated with Reza Shah. A spokesman for the Independents stressed the urgency of placing the military under civilian supervision. Farrukh, speaking for the Democrats, took the floor to expose the political

[77] British Foreign Office, 21 March 1944, *F.O. 371*/Persia 1944/34-40189.

[78] M. Sa'id, "My First Experience as Premier," *Salnameh-i Donya*, 15 (1959), 159-62; "Concerning the Role of the Majles in the Formation of Cabinets," *Ayandeh*, 3 (September 1944), 48-50.

[79] M. Sa'id, *Parliamentary Proceedings*, 14th Majles, 15 April 1944.

[80] For the debate on Sa'id's government, see *Parliamentary Proceedings*, 14th Majles, 6-16 April 1944.

activities undertaken by the chiefs of staff, especially the creation of a secret society for conservative officers. An Individual criticized the War Ministry for using racist propaganda against the linguistic minorities, particularly against the "Arabic-speaking Iranians of Khuzistan." Another Individual claimed that the senior officers had placed numerous loopholes in the cumbersome system of national conscription in order to fleece high-school graduates who wished to buy draft exemptions. The debate ended with Sayyid Ziya making a direct attack on the shah: "For twenty years we have wasted scarce resources on an inefficient, corrupt, and despotic army. This army has terrorized the public, persecuted innocent citizens, and betrayed the nation. It is high time we reduced the defense budget, placed the military under parliamentary supervision, and, most important of all, cut the ties between the field commanders and the shah."

The British military attaché reported that the Tudeh had approached Sayyid Ziya with an offer to work together against the court, and that the Majles was eager to confine the shah "within strictly constitutional bounds."[81] A legal expert at the Foreign Office, assigned the task of analyzing these "constitutional bounds," summed up the ominous truth: "The Shah is Commander-in-Chief but what this involves is in dispute. Since the interpretation of the Laws, according to the Supplementary Fundamental Laws, is the business of the Majlis, it is for the Majlis to say to what extent the Shah should command the armed forces."[82] Moreover, Bullard—now an ambassador, since the Allies had raised their legations in Tehran to embassies—reported that the shah, during a private interview, had bitterly complained of lack of authority in the constitution and had expressed the immediate fear that he would very soon be at the "mercy of the deputies."[83]

Outside the Majles, the antiroyalist deputies received valuable support from the Freedom Front and the American financial mission headed by Millspaugh. The Freedom Front, which had grown to thirty-one editors, now included such diverse newspapers as *Mardom* of the Tudeh party, *Bakhtar* of the Fatemi family in Isfahan, *Nidayi 'Adalat* of the Justice party, and *Umid* of the Amini in the Liberal fraksiun. Millspaugh, who persisted with his plan to balance the budget, proposed to increase state revenues by taking over the whole of Reza Shah's wealth, and decrease expenditures by ending armed campaigns against the tribes and reducing the period of military service from

[81] British Military Attaché, 3 April and 17 July 1944, *F.O. 371*/Persia 1944/34-40205.

[82] British Embassy, "Memorandum on Royal Prerogatives in the Constitution," *F.O. 371*/Persia 1944/34-40187.

[83] British Ambassador to the Foreign Office, 2 May 1944, *F.O. 371*/Persia 1944/34-40187.

twenty-four months to twelve months. The British military attaché later commented, "this reduction in national service would render the army a farce. Between one quarter and one third of the conscripts speak only Turki. Consequently, they take from six months to as many as twelve months to learn enough Persian to be able to understand orders."[84]

The battle was now joined, and a resolution of the constitutional crisis seemed unavoidable. Most expected the deputies to assert themselves over the shah and establish a genuine parliamentary democracy. A few thought that the shah would mount a preemptive coup to reestablish the military monarchy. But events took another turn. For only a few weeks after the opening of the Majles, foreign and social issues thrust themselves onto the political arena, dividing the opposition, and thereby giving a new lease on life to royal authority.

The social issue exploded in the form of a workers' upheaval in Isfahan. The crisis began when the local millowners, who had been retreating in face of the demands of the radical labor movement, initiated a counteroffensive. They first encouraged the Fatherland, the Comrades', and the Justice parties to organize less radical unions; then bribed the military commanders to declare martial law; and finally, in disgust, locked out their workers and absconded from the city. "The millowners," in Bullard's words, "were outraged that such important persons as themselves should be treated disrespectfully by mere workmen. . . . They were also outraged that their workmen were using such foreign slogans as 'equality.' "[85] The lockout endangered not only the workers' wages but also their daily bread, for they obtained their food rations from the factory granaries. In desperation, the workers broke through the army barricades into the factory granaries. It was estimated that over fifty suffered serious injuries. The other pro-Tudeh unions in Isfahan promptly showed their sympathy for the injured by organizing a general strike throughout the city.

The Isfahan upheaval, described by some as a "workers' revolt,"[86] produced major reactions in local, national, and parliamentary politics. In local politics, Naser Qashqayi, who had been fighting the army and the pro-British Khamseh since 1941, now sent contingents to help put down the "revolt," and signed a secret pact of friendship with Ibrahim Qavam of the Khamseh, Morteza Quli Khan of the Bakhtiyaris, and the governors-general of Fars and Isfahan. Moreover, Na-

[84] British Military Attaché to the Foreign Office, 14 March 1945, *F.O. 371*/Persia 1945/34-45458.

[85] British Ambassador to the Foreign Office, "A Note on Isfahan," *F.O. 371*/Persia 1944/34-40222.

[86] N. Fatemi, *Oil Diplomacy: Powderkeg of Iran* (New York, 1954), p. 216.

ser Qashqayi informed the shah that although his tribesmen had been persecuted by the previous regime, they bore no grudge against the crown and remained true "bulwarks of the monarchy." He also told the British consul that he would do everything possible to maintain order, since he feared the Russians both because of their maltreatment of the Turkomans and because of their increasing popularity among the urban poor in Iran. The British military attaché commented that this pact of friendship, directed against "Tudeh subversion," received enthusiastic support from "southern property owners." The British embassy added that former rivals were willing to put aside their past differences and work together because they, like "all men of property," hoped to prevent social revolution by creating some semblance of stability in their "feudal south."[87]

The repercussions on national politics were equally profound. Six anticourt editors, including Fatemi, resigned from the Freedom Front, and, encouraged by Sayyid Ziya, formed an anti-Tudeh newspaper coalition known as the Independence Front (Jebʿeh-i Isteqlal). Within a few months, the Independence Front grew to twenty-nine papers and journals, including *Bakhtar, Keshvar, Kushesh, Mard-i Emruz, Vazifeh,* and *Raʿad-i Emruz.*[88] In an editorial on "The Revolt in Isfahan," *Raʿad-i Emruz* summed up the fears of many conservative editors: "The Tudeh party, with its satanical doctrine of class struggles, has incited ignorant workers to violate the sacred right of private property and inflict social anarchy upon the industrial center of the country. The uprising proves that the Tudeh is an enemy of private property, of Iran, and of Islam. If the government does not stamp out the Tudeh, the local revolt will inevitably spread into a general revolution.[89] In other editorials, *Raʿad-i Emruz* praised Naser Qashqayi, Ibrahim Qavam, and Morteza Quli Bakhtiyari as national heroes, and changed its focus from attacking the shah to denouncing the Tudeh party.

The upheaval also split the Comrades' party. One faction, led by the party's two deputies, vehemently opposed the Tudeh, supported the southern tribal chiefs, and published a new paper named *Shamʿ* (Candle). Another faction, headed by the editors of *Emruz va Farda,* helped the Tudeh, criticized the tribal chiefs, and established a new

[87] British Military Attaché to the Foreign Office, 9 May and 7 August 1944, *F.O. 371*/Persia 1944/34-40187; British Consul in Shiraz, "Memorandum on Naser Khan," *F.O. 371*/Persia 1944/34-40180; British Ambassador to the Foreign Office, 18 July 1944, *F.O. 371*/Persia 1944/34-40187.

[88] Independence Front, "Our Program," *Kushesh,* 7 December 1944.

[89] "The Revolt in Isfahan," *Raʿad-i Emruz,* 15-25 May 1944.

organization named the Socialist party (Hizb-i Sosiyalist). Not for the last time, the "communist danger" had splintered a socialist party.

These local and national reactions inevitably appeared in parliamentary politics. As the British military attaché observed, the events of Isfahan, rumored in Tehran to have produced over six hundred casualties, immediately overshadowed the constitutional issue, and thereby split the Patriots and Democrats, the two southern conservative groups, from the Liberals, the northern pro-Soviet and anti-court aristocrats.[90] Forming a new majority bloc with the court National Unionists, the Patriots and Democrats soft-pedaled their anticourt activities, and, instead, intensified their anti-Tudeh policies. They drafted a so-called Labor Law that permitted governors to impose martial law on industrial plants. According to the bill, such a drastic remedy was necessary because two years of constant fighting between management and labor had brought the country to the verge of social anarchy.[91] They also sent a staunchly anticommunist royalist to Isfahan as governor-general with instructions to reestablish law and order at any cost, even if it meant distributing arms among potentially dangerous tribesmen. Moreover, they changed Sa'id's cabinet, replacing the Liberals with court nominees. They voted together in the biennial elections for parliamentary officers, winning a significant majority on the vital committees, especially on the Military Committee, and placing Muhammad Sadeq Tabatabai of the National Unionists as president of the Majles. The shah had made an unexpected parliamentary comeback.

The Patriots, Democrats, and National Unionists cemented their alliance during the next few months. When the government introduced the annual budget, the Liberals, left out of the Finance Committee, discovered that the allocations for Tehran were twenty times more than for the whole of western Azerbaijan, even though the population of the latter was estimated to be triple that of the former. One deputy from Tabriz complained, "every time the topic of public education comes up, you people insist that Turkish speakers must learn Persian. But, in actual fact, you are unwilling to spend even the revenue collected in Azerbaijan for the building of schools in the same province."[92] And when Sa'id proposed an emergency bill to give an additional 15 million tomans to the War Ministry, against the recommendations of Millspaugh, he received support not only from the

[90] British Military Attaché to the Foreign Office, 8 May 1944, *F.O. 371*/Persia 1944/34-40205.

[91] Minister of Industries, "The Labor Law," *Parliamentary Proceedings*, 14th Majles, 3 May 1944.

[92] Shaykh al-Islam, *Parliamentary Proceedings*, 14th Majles, 23 January 1945.

National Unionists but also from the Patriots and the Democrats.[93] Fatemi of the Patriots, who a few months earlier had demanded a drastic cut in the army, now declared, "unless we immediately finance an effective army, such uprisings as occurred in Isfahan will spread and destroy the whole foundation of private property." Similarly, a Democrat, whose spokesman had been vocal in denouncing the chiefs of staff, exclaimed, "now that our house is on fire, all citizens should be in favor of a strong military. Without a strong military, the fire will consume Iran."

Unable to prevent the passage of the emergency bill, the opposition turned the debate into a public denunciation of the military establishment. Proposing an unsuccessful motion to investigate corruption in the army, a Tudeh representative asked the rhetorical question, "although I am a medical doctor with ten years' experience, I can not afford to rent a decent house. Maybe my fellow deputies will explain to me how army officers with a few years' service can afford to buy not just houses but also whole streets?" Another Tudeh representative introduced a motion to set up a committee of inquiry to cashier the senior officers who had deserted the front in August 1941. A member of the Individuals' Caucus unsuccessfully reintroduced Millspaugh's earlier plan for reducing national service from two years to one year. Another Individual argued that according to the constitution all important matters, including military matters, should be under civilian supervision. The assistant war minister, who was present to speak on behalf of the emergency bill, replied that although the former speaker was correct on the whole, nevertheless the fundamental laws vested the supreme command of the armed forces in the person of the shah. At this point, Mossadeq took the rostrum to deliver a short history of the constitutional movement and direct a veiled threat at the court: "The shah has no right to interfere in national politics because, according to the Fundamental Laws, the ministers, not he, are responsible to the parliament. If he interferes, he can be held responsible. If he is responsible, then many of us deputies will conclude that shahs can be dismissed in the same way as ministers can be replaced." Mossadeq also criticized the prime minister for behaving as "if Iran was limited to Yazd, Kerman, and other parts of the south."

In spite of the lengthy debate, Sa'id carried the emergency bill, thanks to the support of the Democrats, Patriots, and National Unionists. The southern anticourt deputies, frightened by the Isfahan upheaval, had decided to call off their offensive against the shah. Their

---

[93] For the debate on the emergency bill for the War Ministry, see *Parliamentary Proceedings*, 14th Majles, 3-22 October 1944.

main aim no longer was to destroy the military foundations of royal autocracy, but to strengthen all institutional barriers against the social danger. To rephrase the old formula: no army, no king; no king, no private property. Thus the industrial workers, the newest class of modern Iran, had inadvertently given a new lease on life to the shah, the oldest institution of traditional Iran.

The alliance between the royalists and the southern conservatives was further reinforced in October 1944 by the emergence of a foreign issue in the form of an oil crisis. In early August, a member of the Individuals' Caucus leaked to the public the explosive information that Sa'id was secretly offering a southern oil concession to American and British companies.[94] It was also rumored that a northern concession would be given to Standard Vacuum as soon as the country was rid of the Soviet troops.[95] The Soviets reacted two months later, slowly but not unexpectedly, by demanding the northern concession for themselves. Sir Claremont Skrine, the British consul in Mashad, explained later in his memoirs: "It was the vigorous American intervention, the financial, military, and gendarmerie missions, the apparent drive by U.S. to capture the Persian market, and, above all, the efforts of Standard Vacuum and Shell to secure oil-prospecting rights that changed the Russians in Persia from hot-war allies into cold-war rivals."[96] Similarly, George Kennan, the American chargé d'affaires in Moscow, reckoned, "the basic motive of recent Soviet action in northern Iran is probably not need for oil itself but apprehension of potential foreign penetration in that area coupled with the concern for prestige. The oil in northern Iran is important, not as something Russia needs, but as something that might be dangerous for anyone else to exploit."[97]

Shaken by the Soviet demand, Sa'id replied that all oil negotiations would be postponed until the end of the war. At the same time, he informed Bullard that he had given this "evasive" answer because a straight "yes" would invite the Soviets to penetrate further into Iran, whereas a straight "no" would prompt them to encourage secessionist movements in Kurdistan and Azerbaijan.[98] He also told the oil companies that their bids would be taken up once the occupation was

[94] D. Tusi, *Parliamentary Proceedings*, 14th Majles, 10 August 1944.

[95] American Chargé d'Affaires to the State Department, 3 April 1944, *Foreign Relations of the United States* (Washington, D.C., 1944), V, 446.

[96] C. Skrine, *World War in Iran* (London, 1962), p. 227.

[97] American Chargé d'Affaires in Moscow to the State Department, 7 November 1944, *Foreign Relations of the United States* (1944), V, 470.

[98] British Ambassador to the Foreign Office, "Memorandum on the Present Political Situation in Persia," *F.O. 371*/Persia 1944/34-40187.

over. The Soviets, however, refused to accept the evasive answer, persisted in demanding an immediate agreement, and, failing to obtain such an agreement, began an intensive propaganda campaign against the "crypto-fascist Saʿid."

This oil crisis—which initiated the Cold War in Iran long before it had started in Europe—consolidated the position of the shah by sharpening the foreign-policy differences among his parliamentary opponents. Whereas the pro-Soviet groups—Liberals and Tudeh delegates—denounced Saʿid as a "British stooge," the pro-Western groups—Patriots, Democrats, and Independents—allied with the court National Unionists to support Saʿid's "heroic stand." The Individuals, however, retained their neutral position, opposing Soviet demands, criticizing the pro-Western Saʿid, and insisting that the whole crisis illustrated the theory that "concessions to one side invited the other side to demand equivalent concessions."[99] Outside the Majles, the Independence Front, calling for the rejection of the Soviet demands, obtained the support of twenty-nine newspaper editors. The Freedom Front, on the other hand, demanding the immediate resignation of Saʿid, received the help of twenty-seven editors. Meanwhile, the Tudeh party organized outside the parliament building an "orderly" rally of 35,000 demonstrators who requested the grant of an oil concession to the Soviets and the prompt termination of Saʿid's "reactionary administration."[100]

Confronted by public demonstrations and a Soviet offer to drop the oil demands if a "more trustworthy person" headed the government, the deputies—the National Unionists in particular—withdrew their support of Saʿid. Bullard, who continued to back Saʿid to the very end, commented that the deputies feared Soviet flirtations with northern separatists, and consequently lacked the courage to pursue the propaganda war. The British military attaché typically explained the behavior of the Majles in terms not of rational fears but of irrational, childish, undisciplined, unprincipled, and erratic national characteristics.[101]

The downfall of Saʿid began two weeks of intense searching, mostly in closed parliamentary sessions, for a suitable successor. It was clear that no pro-Western candidate would be acceptable to the Soviets. And it was equally clear that no pro-Soviet candidate would be ac-

[99] Mossadeq, *Parliamentary Proceedings*, 14th Majles, 11 October 1944.

[100] American Chargé d'Affaires to the State Department, 1 November 1944, *Foreign Relations of the United States* (1944), V, 461.

[101] British Ambassador to the Foreign Office, 9 November 1944, *F.O. 371*/Persia 1944/34-40188; British Military Attaché to the Foreign Office, 20 November 1944, *F.O. 371*/Persia 1944/34-40206.

ceptable to the West. As a result, the advantage lay with either the neutral Individuals or the court National Unionists. The Individuals, gaining the support of the Tudeh and the Liberals, and the lukewarm support of the National Unionists, mustered a majority for their candidate, Mossadeq. But Mossadeq, conscious of the precarious nature of his majority and anxious to retake his parliamentary seat if he lost the premiership, requested a special dispensation from the constitutional stipulation that required members of the executive to resign from all positions in the legislature. The deputies, led by the National Unionists, rejected his request, arguing that it would violate the principle of separation of powers.

The National Unionists now judged the time appropriate to approach the Patriots and Democrats with the court favorite, Morteza Bayat. A staunch conservative and a large landowner in British-occupied Kermanshah, Bayat was considered acceptable to the pro-British southern conservatives. Winning a small majority, Bayat gave seven ministries to fellow royalists and four to pro-British politicians. Bullard described the new administration as "a good cabinet."[102] Bayat then tried to alleviate the fears of the Liberals and Individuals. He admitted that previous premiers had made gross blunders by participating in secret oil negotiations. And he helped Mossadeq pass a stringent law against any public official who secretly discussed oil concessions with either a foreign company or a foreign government.

Bayat's base of support in parliament was to shift drastically during the course of the next six months. He took office in November 1944 with the backing of the Patriots, Democrats, and National Unionists. He left office in April 1945 with the Patriots, Democrats, and majority of National Unionists undermining him, but the Liberals, Tudeh, and minority of National Unionists supporting him. This shift was precipitated by the problem of what to do with Millspaugh. Forming the new administration, Bayat discovered that this foreign "adviser" not only controlled all major economic decisions, but also persisted in his design to cut the military budget, and even used his special powers to freeze the emergency 15 million tomans that had been obtained for the War Ministry by the previous administration.[103] Faced with the choice of a frustrated officer corps or an early exodus for Millspaugh, Bayat introduced a bill to limit the extensive powers granted two years earlier to the American financial mission. This immediately antagonized the staunch pro-Western groups, who argued that Iran needed all its foreign links to remain free of the Soviet Union. But it

[102] British Ambassador to the Foreign Office, "Three Monthly Report for October-December 1944," *F.O. 371*/Persia 1945/34-45446.
[103] "Government Actions against Millspaugh," *Iran-i Ma*, 5 January 1945.

automatically attracted the neutralists and the pro-Soviets, who saw Millspaugh as an albatross dragging Iran into dangerous foreign alliances. Although Western commentators have invariably blamed neutralists and communists for the ouster of Millspaugh, the decisive blow came from royalists fighting to safeguard the armed forces. The shift in Bayat's support was also reflected in the attitudes of the major powers. The Soviet embassy, which had undermined the previous premier, now pursued a policy of strict nonintervention. On the other hand, the British ambassador, who had earlier described Bayat's cabinet as "a collection of decent men," now reported that he had lost confidence in the same cabinet. A year later, he was to depict Bayat as "one of the most stupid men in Persia."[104]

Having antagonized his original friends, Bayat moved rapidly to win over his new friends. He helped them set up a parliamentary committee to investigate business associates to Sayyid Ziya who were implicated in a scandal involving the illegal sale of import licenses. He replaced the militant anticommunist governor-general of Isfahan with a moderate who stopped the distribution of arms among the tribes and relaxed the stringent restrictions placed upon the trade unions. The pro-British partisans declared that this change threatened to bring anarchy back to the city.[105] He was more generous than the previous premier in permitting the Tudeh to hold frequent mass rallies in Tehran. Instead, he used martial law against the anticommunists, restricting the activities of Sayyid Ziya's National Will party, and banning ten dailies affiliated with the Independence Front. The pro-British denounced this as an unlawful use of martial law to stifle the constitutional right of free expression.[106] Moreover, he introduced an electoral bill proposing to increase the representation of Isfahan from three to six deputies, Tehran from twelve to fifteen, and Azerbaijan from fifteen to twenty. Furthermore, he drafted the country's first comprehensive labor law, which limited work hours, regulated factory conditions, stipulated paid vacations, banned child labor, and guaranteed union rights, including the right to strike. The conservative *Ra'ad-i Emruz*, which had welcomed Bayat's election, now discovered that he had packed the cabinet with his "feudal relatives."[107] Meanwhile, the radical *Rahbar*, which had originally denounced Bayat as a "typical feudalist," now argued that with enemies such as the

[104] British Ambassador to the Foreign Office, 26 November 1944, *F.O. 371*/Persia 1944/34-40189; idem, 22 November 1945, *F.O. 371*/Persia 1945/34-45436.

[105] S. Bakhtiyari, *Parliamentary Proceedings* 14th Majles, 14 February 1945.

[106] Sh. Fatemi, *Parliamentary Proceedings*, 14th Majles, 8 February 1945.

[107] "The Bayat Clique," *Ra'ad-i Emruz*, 8 December 1944.

"reactionary" Sayyid Ziya, he needed and deserved the friendship of all progressive forces.[108]

Although Bayat correctly estimated that the pro-Soviet and neutralist votes would almost equal the pro-British votes, he grossly underestimated the fears of his fellow royalists. In initiating his innovative strategy, with the advice of the shah, he did not realize that many conservative royalists would view his policies as not expedient but highly inexpedient, not daring but extremely dangerous, not pragmatic but "flirtatious of fanatical communists."[109] These fears, which started in January with the replacement of the governor-general in Isfahan and grew rapidly in February with the new labor bill, broke into the open in March after a violent student demonstration outside parliament against "corrupt politicians." Blaming government permissiveness for the demonstration, conservative newspapers argued that the students were "rebels without a genuine cause" who wanted to establish a "dictatorship of the intelligentsia."[110] Moreover, they insisted that such a dictatorship would be set up unless Bayat ended the flirtations with the Tudeh.

The crisis split Bayat's own caucus, the National Union, into two. One, led by ʿEzatallah Bayat and formed of thirteen deputies, almost all from the western provinces, remained loyal to the prime minister. But the other, headed by Dawlatabadi and made up of sixteen deputies, all from the central and southern provinces, left and formed their own National Caucus (Fraksiun-i Melli). In doing so, they both brought down the government against the advice of the shah, and proved that they were not merely court placemen but independent-minded aristocrats whose views usually, although not always, coincided with those of their monarchy.

Bayat's fall initiated a six-week crisis during which the main fraksiuns lobbied on behalf of their own favorites. But unable to muster a majority for any of their favorites, they settled on a compromise candidate, Ibrahim Hakimi (Hakim al-Mulk). A former court doctor who had participated in the constitutional revolution and in the Democrat party, Hakimi received support, albeit lukewarm support, of royalists as well as antiroyalists. A native of Azerbaijan with old political ties to Fars, he was acceptable to both northerners and southerners. A respectable statesman without close foreign associations, he was backed half-heartedly by all groups. Even Bullard was willing to

[108] "Why We Voted for Bayat," *Rahbar*, 20 April 1945.
[109] Fatemi, *Oil Diplomacy*, p. 260.
[110] "The Dictatorship of the Intelligentsia," *Raʿad-i Emruz*, 10 March 1945.

accept him, even though he considered him a deaf, inexperienced, harmless nonentity.[111]

Receiving a tepid majority, Hakimi tried to form a "national government above factional politics." By choosing ministers without close affiliations to the parliamentary fraksiuns, Hakimi intended to continue half satisfying all groups. Instead he ended up dissatisfying most groups. As Bullard reported, the prime minister found himself confronted by general disapproval when he returned to the Majles to obtain the necessary vote of confidence for his administration.[112] The Liberals opposed him, pointing out that the north was not represented in the cabinet. The Individuals withdrew their support, arguing that an "impartial" statesman should have been invited to prepare the Interior Ministry for the forthcoming Fifteenth Majles elections.[113] Moreover, the Patriots and Democrats refused to participate in the vote, protesting that none of their spokesmen had been given ministries.[114] Thus the Hakimi government ended before it had even officially started. The American ambassador reported that the shah, in a confidential conversation immediately after Hakimi's fall, complained that Iranians would need another forty years before they could get used to democracy, and regretted that he did not have the constitutional powers to dissolve disruptive parliaments. The ambassador commented, "the shah was endeavoring to elicit from me some words that might encourage him to resort to personal rule without the benefits of parliamentary restraints."[115]

Hakimi's failure enticed the loyal royalists to throw all caution to the winds. Rejoining the disloyal royalists, the National Unionists allied with the Patriots and Democrats to support Mohsen Sadr (Sadr al-Ashraf), an eighty-year-old arch conservative judge who had served as Reza Shah's watchdog over the Qum clergy and had presided over the execution of liberal intellectuals during the Constitutional Revolution. Bullard now encouraged Sadr's candidacy, although two months earlier he had described him as a "stiff reactionary ex-mulla."[116] In the vote for Sadr, only three royalists heeded the shah's warning that such an extreme choice could "trigger desperate reactions from the

[111] British Ambassador to the Foreign Office, "Three Monthly Report for June-August 1945," *F.O. 371*/Persia 1945/34-45450.

[112] Ibid.

[113] Ipekchian, *Parliamentary Proceedings*, 14th Majles, 19 May 1945; Mossadeq, ibid., 20 May 1945.

[114] See Mossadeq's description of Hakimi's fall, ibid., 2 June 1945.

[115] American Ambassador to the State Department, 26 June 1945, *Foreign Relations of the United States* (Washington, D.C., 1945), VIII, 385-86.

[116] British Ambassador to the Foreign Office, 3 December 1945, *F.O. 371*/Persia 1945/34-351117.

opposition." As soon as he was elected, Sadr kept the Interior Ministry for himself, gave four ministeries to the royalists and five others—including the Foreign Ministry—to the pro-British. The American ambassador complained that the new foreign minister was far too pro-British.[117]

This choice of ministers so outraged Liberals, Individuals, Tudeh, and dissident Independents that they boycotted parliament for three full months, from mid-June until mid-September. Every time Sadr presented his cabinet to the Majles to obtain the necessary vote for approval, the opposition filed out of the chamber, reducing attendance below the required quorum, and thus terminating parliamentary transactions. In this constitutional crisis, the opposition championed the rights of the Majles by arguing that cabinets lacked legitimacy until they received parliamentary approval. The government supporters, however, resorted to royal prerogatives by claiming that cabinets obtained legitimacy from the moment the royal farman reached the prime minister.[118] For the former, the vote was fundamental, the farman ceremonial; for the latter, the farman was essential, the vote subsequential. One member of the cabinet, who, as a colleague of Sayyid Ziya, had recently demanded the curtailment of all court influence, now reinterpreted the constitutional laws to conclude that the shah retained the unlimited prerogative of appointing and dismissing all government ministers.[119] Finding themselves on shaky legal grounds, the government supporters shifted the debate to the moral wrongs of a minority obstructing a majority. The opposition, however, retorted that a minority was obliged to obstruct an undemocratic and unconstitutional majority from leading the country into external and internal disasters. Of course, Bullard saw the parliamentary crisis and the subsequent constitutional storm as one more proof of psychological immaturity among Iranians.[120]

The fears of the opposition were intensified as Sadr implemented his hard-line policies. He withdrew Bayat's reform bills, relaxed the restrictions placed on members of the Independence Front, and dissolved the parliamentary committee set up to investigate corruption in the sale of import licenses. He appointed a conservative Anglophile,

[117] British Ambassador to the Foreign Office, "Three Monthly Report for June-August 1945," *F.O. 371*/Persia 1945/34-45450; ibid., 3 November 1945.

[118] Parliamentary Minority, "An Open Letter," *Rahbar*, 18 June 1945; Parliamentary Majority, "An Open Letter," *Parliamentary Proceedings*, 14th Majles, 16 June 1945.

[119] K. Hedayat, *Parliamentary Proceedings*, 14th Majles, 27 September 1945.

[120] Parliamentary Minority, "A Message on Obstructionism," *Parliamentary Proceedings*, 14th Majles, 14 June 1945; *Rahbar*, 14 June 1945; British Ambassador to the Foreign Office, 15 August 1945, *F.O. 371*/Persia 1945/34-45436.

General Arfa`, as chief of general staff and instructed him to arm anti-Tudeh tribes and purge "leftist" officers from the armed forces. Moreover, he placed Iran solidly within the sterling area by signing a new financial agreement with the British-owned Imperial Bank of Persia.[121] In return, and in order to pressure the Soviets out of Iran before the forthcoming elections, the British announced that their troops would evacuate the country earlier than the scheduled deadline of six months after the war. Furthermore, Sadr used martial law in Tehran to curtail mass meetings, ban some forty-eight papers and journals affiliated with the Freedom Front, occupy the headquarters of the Tudeh, and arrest over one hundred of the party's cadres. He later expressed regret that parliamentary immunity had deterred him from detaining the eight Tudeh deputies. The American ambassador formed the distinct impression that the Iranian government was out to abolish the Tudeh party.[122] In such circumstances, the opposition felt that it had no choice but to persist in its parliamentary boycott.

The parliamentary storm continued into late summer, when it was finally overshadowed by a more heated storm in the society outside. In early September, Pishevari, whose credentials had been rejected by the Majles, returned to Tabriz, and, together with fellow veterans from the old Communist party and survivors from the Khiabani revolt of 1919-1920, announced the formation of a new organization named the Democratic Party of Azerbaijan (Firqeh-i Demokrat-i Azerbaijan). Intentionally adopting the same name as Khiabani's organization, the party leaders expressed the desire to remain within Iran, but demanded three major reforms for Azerbaijan: the use of the Azerbaijani language in state schools and government offices; the retention of tax revenues for the development of the region; and the establishment of the provincial assemblies promised in the constitutional laws. More ominously, they denounced the politicians in Tehran for disregarding genuine provincial grievances, and proclaimed their language, history, and culture had endowed the people of Azerbaijan with a "distinct national identity." Joined promptly by the provincial branch of the Tudeh party, the Democratic Party of Azerbaijan prepared for an armed uprising, while Soviet troops prevented Iranian military reinforcements from entering the province. Meanwhile in

[121] Iran agreed not to buy on credit outside the sterling area except for goods essential for its economy and unobtainable inside the sterling area. For U.S. complaints about this, see U.S. Chargé d'Affaires to the State Department, 9 December 1947, *Foreign Relations of the United States* (Washington, D.C., 1947), V, 993-94.

[122] M. Sadr, "The Story of My Administration," *Salnameh-i Donya*, 15 (1959), 40-44; American Ambassador to the State Department, *Foreign Relations of United States* (1945), VII, 417.

Mahabad, Kurdish nationalists, encouraged by the Soviets, formed the Democratic Party of Kurdistan and demanded similar rights for their region. The fears that had lurked during the past four years were now being realized. The American consul in Tabriz predicted that these dissident movements would probably collapse without Soviet protection, but nevertheless stressed that the same movements enjoyed substantial popular support and expressed genuine grievances against the central government.[123] Similarly, the British consul in Tabriz reported after an extensive tour of the northwest:

While it is of course inconceivable that the movement could have succeeded without Russian support, and while the Russians no doubt gave their support for their own ends, I cannot help observing that there is among the workers and peasants of this province what has always seemed to me genuine exasperation with the incompetence and corruption of the Iranian government, and that there exist real miseries and injustices which in any other country would be enough to produce a spontaneous revolt. I do not believe that the Russians have prefabricated the whole movement: it seems to me rather that they are exploiting a genuine revolutionary situation: they have stiffened the peasants with the Muhajirs, but the peasants themselves have gone to work with a will. . . . If a part of Iran must inevitably be governed by knaves and fools, the people of Azerbaijan have made up their minds that their native candidates can fill these roles as well as those from Tehran.[124]

The events of Azerbaijan and Kurdistan roused a furor in Tehran. Kasravi, who for a decade had stressed the importance of national solidarity, denounced the rebels for considering Azerbaijan a distinct nation and presenting demands that endangered the survival of Iran: "If similar claims are advanced by the other linguistic minorities—especially Armenians, Assyrians, Arabs, Gilanis, and Mazandaranis—nothing will be left of Iran." Afshar, the editor of *Ayandeh*, whose twenty-five-year-old articles on the national question were now under sharp attack from the paper *Azerbaijan*, repeated his previous arguments for eradicating minority languages, and added that the essence of nationality was not only language. "The essence of Iranian nationality must be based in its history, in its racial composition, and, above all, in the sentiments of its people." The newspaper *Ittila'at*, in an editorial on "Azerbaijan is the Center of Iranian Patriotism," exclaimed that Turkish was not the native language of Azerbaijan but a foreign tongue imposed on the region by the Mongol and Tartar invaders. "Whereas we are ashamed of Turkish as a disgraceful stigma of the humiliations Iran suffered under the barbarian invaders, we

---

[123] American Consul to the State Department, 28 November 1945, *Foreign Relations of United States* (1945), VIII, 456.

[124] British Consul in Tabriz, "Report of Visit to Mianeh," *India Office*/L/P&S/12-3417.

are proud of Persian as our rich literary language that has contributed generously to world civilization." The same paper, in a series of articles on "The Turkish Language in Azerbaijan" written by a well-known literary figure, argued that common history, common religion, common racial origin, and common culture had made Azerbaijan an integral part of Iran. The series ended with the rhetorical question, "who would exchange the cultured and world famous literature of Ferdowsi, Sa'adi, Mowlavi, and Hafez for the uncouth and unknown babble of the Turkic plunderers?" Finally, the paper *Kushesh*, which was affiliated to Sayyid Ziya's National Will party, insisted that Persian must continue as the sole language of instruction throughout the public schools because Turkish was only an "unfortunate deposit" left by the "savage Mongols" as they crossed Iran, plundering, destroying, and devastating the Middle East.[125]

Meanwhile, the upheaval in Tabriz had four immediate repercussions in the Majles. First, one deputy after another rose to argue that Iran constituted one nation, not many distinct nations, because its population shared a common history, culture, religion, and racial origin.[126] Some went so far as to cite the example of Switzerland, with its four official languages, as showing that language by itself did not necessarily create a separate national identity. But very few were willing to follow the example of Switzerland in giving official recognition to the minority languages. Second, the National Unionists came round to the shah's view that Sadr's administration threatened dire reactions from the opposition. Third, many northern anticourt deputies, who had previously criticized the shah and the army, now dropped their criticisms and instead advocated the expansion of the armed forces. As one prominent Liberal who had consistently denounced the military now exclaimed, "who but our soldiers can save the nation from these secessionists."[127] The crisis in the north was for many Liberals what the earlier uprising in Isfahan had been for the Patriots and Democrats. Fourth, a number of northern deputies who had formerly supported the Soviets because the latter did not encourage revolutionary secessionists in Iran, began to reconsider their own foreign policies. Resigning from the Liberal Caucus, six deputies joined the southern bloc in denouncing the Democratic Party of Azerbaijan for

[125] A. Kasravi, "Concerning Azerbaijan," *Parcham*, October 1945; M. Afshar, "A Reply," *Darya*, 28 October 1945; "Azerbaijan is the Center of Iranian Patriotism," *Ittila'at*, 24 September 1945; 'A. Eqbal, "The Turkish Language in Azerbaijan," *Ittila'at*, 12-20 November 1945; "Azerbaijan is Iran; Iran is Azerbaijan," *Kushesh*, 26 September 1945.

[126] For the debates see *Parliamentary Proceedings*, 14th Majles, September-November 1945.

[127] A. Sadeqi, *Parliamentary Proceedings*, 14th Majles, 24 October 1945.

"undermining the security of Iran."[128] One such Liberal declared, "this so-called Democratic Party of Azerbaijan is striking terror among peace-loving citizens and is spreading the false notion that Persian is not the mother language of all Iranians. It is high time we ended our parliamentary stalemate and began to build a stable government that will put a stop to further national disintegration."[129]

Influenced by these changes, the supporters and opponents of Sadr's administration reached a compromise. The former, especially the National Unionists, promised to give Hakimi another chance. The latter, particularly the Liberals and Individuals, agreed to permit the smooth passage of two major bills. The first postponed the elections for the forthcoming Majles until the occupying powers had evacuated all their troops. Mossadeq, however, unsuccessfully spoke against the bill, arguing that the postponement would not guarantee free elections but could result in a long intersession during which the country would be left without a parliament. "For twenty-five years we had no foreign troops on our soil, yet we did not have free elections. What we need is not electoral delay but electoral reform."[130] The second bill sharply increased the military budget, expanding the army from 90,000 to 102,000 men to create two northern divisions, and raising the allocations for personnel to improve officers' salaries and such fringe benefits as free housing, annual increments, child allowances, and cooperative societies. Only the Tudeh deputies refused to accept the war minister's argument that the military was the "sole organization capable of saving Iran from total anarchy."[131] The military logic had been accepted not only by the southern pro-British conservatives, but also by the pro-American civil servants and the northern anticourt pro-Soviet aristocrats.

With the successful passage of the two bills in October, Sadr stepped down in favor of Hakimi. The new premier came into office with a complex plan combining Bayat's "soft" attitude toward the Soviet Union with Sadr's "hard" treatment of the Tudeh party. The first part of the plan aimed at winning over the Liberals and Individuals, while persuading the Soviets to evacuate Iran and withdraw their protection of the dissident movements. The second part intended to calm the fears of the conservative deputies, especially the Patriots, Democrats, and National Unionists.

In implementing the first part, Hakimi gave three ministries to the

---

[128] The Group of 29 Deputies, "A Proclamation on Azerbaijan," *Kushesh*, 27 September 1945.

[129] S. Hekmat, *Parliamentary Proceedings*, 14th Majles, 27 September 1945.

[130] Mossadeq, *Parliamentary Proceedings*, 14th Majles, 11 October 1945.

[131] War Minister, *Parliamentary Proceedings*, 14th Majles, 2 October 1945.

northern pro-Soviets, one to a neutralist, six to the royalists, but none
to the southern pro-British. Moreover, he appointed Morteza Bayat
governor-general of Azerbaijan; nominated Qavam to a newly formed
council of senior advisers to the prime minister; and, taking Mossadeq's advice, invited himself to Moscow to negotiate directly with
Stalin. Not surprisingly, the Liberals, Individuals, Independents, and
National Unionists supported the new administration; but the Patriots
and Democrats abstained from the vote, proclaiming that the only
reason they had not voted against the government was their concern
for the "critical situation."[132]

In implementing the second part of the plan, Hakimi banned street
demonstrations, continued the military occupation of the Tudeh
headquarters, and spoke of outlawing the party entirely. Moreover,
he refused to negotiate with the "anarchists" leading the Democratic
Party of Azerbaijan, claimed that Kurds had no genuine grievances
because they were members of the Iranian race, and repeated the
argument that Turkish was a foreign tongue imposed on Azerbaijan
by the "barbarian Mongols."[133]

Although Hakimi's plan succeeded in gaining a parliamentary majority, it failed to allay Soviet hostility. On the contrary, the Soviets
announced that "they would prefer to greet in Moscow a Premier
Qavam rather than a Premier Hakimi."[134] They also demanded an
end to the restrictions placed on the Tudeh; refused to set an exact
date for their complete evacuation; stopped the transport of agricultural goods from Azerbaijan into southern Iran; and, most serious of
all, continued to prevent the entry of government troops into the
northern provinces. As a result, the Democratic Party of Azerbaijan
proceeded with its armed uprising, capturing the main towns in the
province, convening a "National Congress," and, in December, announcing the formation of the Autonomous Government of Azerbaijan. Meanwhile, the Democratic Party of Kurdistan went further,
to proclaim the establishment of the independent Republic of Kurdistan; and armed rebels in the Caspian provinces created a Jungle
party (Hizb-i Jangali) to revive the uprising of 1921 that had formed
in Gilan the Soviet Socialist Republic of Iran.

Hakimi not only failed with the Soviets but also antagonized the
British. Bullard, who distrusted this policy of "appeasement" right
from the beginning, now argued that "over-centralization was the real
cause of present disintegration," and began to safeguard British in-

[132] Patriotic Caucus, "A Proclamation to the People," *Parliamentary Proceedings* 14th
Majles, 5 November 1945.
[133] "Hakimi's Secret Speech to the Majles," *Kushesh*, 19 December 1945.
[134] Key-Ostovan, *Siyasat-i Muvazaneh*, II, 214.

terests by proposing that all provinces, especially southern ones, should gain administrative autonomy.[135] Moreover, the British Broadcasting Company announced in early January that Britain, the United States, and the Soviet Union would hold a tripartite commission to solve the internal problem of Iran. In the words of the American ambassador, the BBC announcement created panic in Tehran because nationalists had only one fear greater than seeing the Great Powers fight in Iran: the dread of the Great Powers sitting down, as they had done in the Anglo-Russian Agreement of 1907, in order not to fight, and in the process carving up Iran into spheres of foreign influence.[136] One possible escape route remained: Qavam could negotiate directly with the Soviets before the convening of the tripartite commission. As Mossadeq declared in Parliament, "if we do not talk directly with our northern neighbor, we are finished. For if the tripartite commission meets, Iran will be carved up as in 1907. We have no choice but replace Hakimi with a premier who will be welcome in Moscow."[137] This solution was supported not only by the Individuals, Tudeh deputies, and Liberals, but also by dissident Liberals who rejoined their caucus and even by prominent defectors from the other fraksiuns, such as Madani from the Patriots and Muhammad Sadeq Tabatabai from the National Unionists. Of course, the popularity of this solution was explained by the British military attaché in terms not of legitimate fears but of "national characteristics":

The Persian, though capable of spasmodic feats of bravery, is not renowned for that dogged brand of courage which sustains prolonged resistance in adverse circumstances. He was dismayed that recent approaches made to the Soviet Union did not immediately elicit favourable replies. So Persian courage is beginning to ooze away. Some forty-five deputies have signed a document pledging support to Qavam. Like most Persians he is obsessed with the idea of his own cleverness and believes that he can handle the Russians. This is a belief which few outside the ranks of his own countrymen would share.[138]

By the end of January, enough deputies had defected from the royalist and pro-Western fraksiuns to give Qavam a majority of one single determining vote. It was a thin majority, but it was the only majority attained by a pro-Soviet anticourt prime minister in the Fourteenth Majles. Unsure of his parliamentary position but sure of the

[135] British Ambassador to the Foreign Office, 27 November 1945, *F.O. 371*/Persia 1945/34-45436.

[136] American Ambassador to the State Department, *Foreign Relations of United States* (1945), VIII, 475.

[137] Mossadeq, *Parliamentary Proceedings*, 14th Majles, 9 January 1946.

[138] British Military Attaché to the Foreign Office, 21 December 1945, *F.O. 371*/Persia 1945/34-45458.

parliamentary calendar, which set March 11 as the end of the Fourteenth Majles, Qavam followed a policy of systematic procrastination. He spent three full weeks bargaining with the shah over the composition of the new administration. At the conclusion of the haggling, he kept the crucial ministries of Interior and Foreign Affairs for himself; gave five cabinet posts to his close supporters; yielded two others to court favorites; and handed the War Ministry to General Amir Ahmedi, a veteran of the Cossack Brigade and of Reza Shah's tribal campaigns, whose ambitions and independent mind had often disturbed the young shah.

Qavam presented this cabinet to Parliament only twenty hours before his scheduled flight to Moscow, and, with the help of the president of the Majles, persuaded Parliament to postpone debate for the vote of approval until the completion of his urgent mission. In Moscow, he extended the pressing visit into long drawn-out negotiations, offering an oil concession in the north and a peaceful settlement of the Azerbaijan question if, in return, the Soviets withdrew their troops by early May. At one point, he even interrupted the discussions to go on a leisurely sightseeing tour of Kiev. Meanwhile, his supporters back home boycotted the Majles to prevent a quorum from convening, and the Tudeh party organized mass demonstrations at the entrance of Parliament to deter the others from entering the chamber. Unable to hold official meetings, the opposition deputies spent the last days criticizing one another. The pro-British blamed the royalists for the fateful decision to postpone the elections for the next Majles. The royalists held the pro-British chiefly responsible for starting the dangerous situation by bringing Sadr to power. At long last, Qavam returned to Tehran a day before the final session, and presented himself to the deputies the following day, only one hour before the ending of the final session. With sardonic humor, he expressed regret that "the lack of time and quorum prevented the deputies from holding a meaningful debate on his administration and foreign negotiations."[139]

The Fourteenth Majles thus ended having revealed the country's main social divisions but without having resolved the three major political problems. The constitutional problem, although fast ebbing in importance for many southern conservatives, remained on the agenda for the northern aristocrats headed by Premier Qavam, for the middle classes led by Mossadeq, and for the labor movement mobilized by the Tudeh party. In the struggle to retain the military, the shah had won a series of skirmishes only to find his bête noire, Qavam, pre-

---

[139] A. Qavam, *Parliamentary Proceedings*, 14th Majles, 11 March 1946.

siding over the government and planning yet another campaign against the palace. Similarly, the foreign problem, especially the struggle to preserve national independence, could not lose its urgency as long as the Great Powers occupied the country, the Soviets demanded economic concessions, and the British-owned oil company controlled the country's main source of revenue. On the contrary, the foreign problem gained urgency as the Great Powers entered the Cold War, dividing the world into rival blocs, and, in the process, threatening to divide Iran into spheres of influence. Finally, the social problem, especially the need for internal reform, remained as potent as ever, pitting some ethnic groups against the Persian-dominated state, the middle and lower classes against the landed upper class. These three problems continued to dominate Iranian politics for the next seven years.

FIVE

The Evolving Political System: From Embattled to Military Monarchy

A constitutional system without a disciplined party is like a building without a roof.

> —Ahmad Qavam in "Notes from Qavam's Diaries," *Khvandaniha*, 28 September-2 November 1955

Iran, with its many conflicting groups, does not need a disciplined party with a precise program. On the contrary, Iran needs a loose coalition of organizations in a national front with a general and broad program. This is why I refuse to establish yet another political party.

> —Muhammad Mossadeq, cited by A. Maleki, "How the National Front Was Formed," *Khvandaniha*, 3 February-2 March 1956

QAVAM AS PRIME MINISTER (MARCH 1946-DECEMBER 1946)

Of all the old-time politicians, Ahmad Qavam was the most enigmatic. The public image he sought to project was that of a decisive leader in full command of the situation, but all the while he was under constant challenge from both the right—the shah, the army, and the tribal chiefs—and the left—the Tudeh, the Democratic Party of Azerbaijan, and the Democratic Party of Kurdistan. He portrayed himself as a world statesman fully the match of Stalin, Churchill, and Truman, even though in reality he represented a weak and underdeveloped country whose very existence could be erased overnight by any one of the Great Powers. He sought to assure his followers that he pursued a secret blueprint for national survival; but he was rarely in command of events, being left to muddle through one crisis after another by improvising from day to day, juggling political pieces, and exploiting rather than creating opportunities. He professed confidence that all would end well; but he was nonetheless a cold realist who recognized politics as the art of the possible, and was aware that the precarious political situation could produce the worst possible result both for himself and his country. These discrepancies in his image and reality, his hopes and fears, his aspirations and capabilities, led Qavam to disguise his true aims. He entered crises without committing himself to any particular course of action. He lived through them by playing one side against another and telling his listeners what they wished to hear rather than what he had to say. And he came out of crises with claims to have predicted the outcome in advance, with unverifiable accounts of secret discussions, and with doors left open for outwitted opponents—for he had learned that today's adversaries could well become tomorrow's allies.

Qavam was thus different things to different men at different times. His shifting alliances illustrate this clearly. The shah opposed him in 1941-1946 as the implacable enemy of Pahlevi rule; helped him in 1946-1947 as a bulwark against communism; forced him out of the country in 1947-1948 again as an enemy of the dynasty; and called upon him once again in 1952 as an ally against Mossadeq. Conversely, the Tudeh trusted him in 1941-1946 as a constitutionalist challenging the militarist; turned against him in 1946-1948 as a representative of the landed aristocracy; rallied around him in 1948-1949 to stem the rising power of the monarchy; and attacked him in 1952 as the lackey of the shah, of the British, and of the ruling class. The British helped him in 1942 as a strong-willed and pro-Ally premier; opposed him in 1943-1946 as a Soviet sympathizer; admired him in 1946-1947 for negotiating the Soviet evacuation; opposed him again in 1947-1948 for threatening British interests in Khuzistan and Bahrein; and favored him in 1952 as an alternative to Mossadeq. Similarly, Mossadeq criticized him in 1941-1945 for his foreign policy of "positive equilibrium," voted for him in 1945 as the only statesman capable of negotiating with the Russians, denounced him in 1946-1947 for weakening the Majles, supported him in 1947-1948 against the shah, and denounced him in 1952 as a tool of British imperialism.

But behind the enigmas, the lack of candor, and the apparent inconsistencies, lay a man committed to three major goals. As a veteran politician who had supported the Constitutional Revolution, headed five ministries—including the War Ministry—and presided over four cabinets before Reza Shah had exiled him, Qavam was intent on weakening the monarchy and establishing civilian control over the military. As a wealthy landowner, grandson of a court minister, son of a Qajar noblewoman, and husband of a rich aristocrat, Qavam naturally preferred to keep the status quo rather than run the risk of a social revolution. Nevertheless, he was willing to make use of revolutionaries against the shah as long as it did not weaken his own position. Finally, as a graduate from the traditional school of foreign policy that stressed the doctrine of "positive equilibrium," Qavam intended to counterbalance Russia against Britain, and, if possible, to call in the United States to achieve that balance.

Qavam began his tenure as prime minister in March 1946 with four major advantages. First, parliament, before electing him as premier, had passed a law postponing the elections for the next parliament until all foreign troops had evacuated. In the interim, the shah could not remove him without setting off a constitutional storm. Second, the Soviets expressed full confidence in him and insisted that they would negotiate troop withdrawals with no one else. Paradoxically, he also found favor in the U.S. State Department, which viewed him as the best-equipped politician in Iran to handle the Russians. Third, he enjoyed the backing of both his fellow aristocrats in the north and the Tudeh party and the two autonomous governments in Tabriz and Mahabad.

Fourth, Qavam and his supporters headed many of the important ministries. Qavam had kept for himself the Foreign and Interior ministries. His closest adviser, Muzaffar Firuz, held the title of Deputy Prime Minister. The son of the famous Prince Farmanfarma who had been murdered by Reza Shah, Muzaffar Firuz had worked with Sayyid Ziya in 1942-1944 until the latter had decided that the "red menace" overshadowed the Pahlevi danger. The British military attaché commented that Muzaffar Firuz was "clever and could write well but would probably sacrifice anything to bring about the downfall of the shah": "All his political activities are directed to one end—opposition to the present Shah, whom he wishes to remove as vengeance for the death of his father."[1] The communications minister, General Firuz Farmanfarma, was the uncle of Muzaffar Firuz and the brother of Muhammad Vali Farmanfarma, who had headed the Liberal Caucus in the Fourteenth Majles. A graduate of French and tsarist military academies, General Farmanfarma had held a number of important positions until Reza Shah had forced him into early retirement. The British embassy claimed that his extensive family estates in Azerbaijan led him to the conclusion that "appeal to Russia was the only practical policy."[2] The education minister, Malek al-Shua'ra Bahar, was a nationally known poet and veteran of the old Democrat party. As a committed constitutionalist, he had been banished from Tehran by Reza Shah. The agriculture minister, Shams al-Din Amir 'Alai, was

[1] British Military Attaché to the Foreign Office, 18 February 1946, *India Office*/L/ P&S/12-3505.
[2] Ibid.

a young French-educated lawyer from the Qajar nobility. Amir ʿAlai had joined his classmates from Paris in forming the Iran party, but had left the organization in 1945 to enter Qavam's political circle. Moreover, the war minister, General Amir Ahmedi, although by no means a Qavam man, was no court puppet either. In the words of the British ambassador, the shah distrusted and suspected Amir Ahmedi of harboring "his own political ambitions."[3]

Armed with these advantages, Qavam chose to tackle the foreign issue first and to postpone the constitutional confrontation for a more appropriate time. He continued negotiations with the Soviets after his return from Moscow in March, and reached an overall understanding with them in April. This understanding contained four parts: the Soviets would take out all their troops by mid-May; the Iranians would withdraw from the United Nations the complaints lodged by the previous premier; the central government would settle its differences with the provincial government of Azerbaijan in a "peaceful manner" and with regard for both needed reforms and the constitutional laws; and Qavam would propose to the Fifteenth Majles the formation of an Iranian-Soviet oil company holding a fifty-year lease in the northern provinces and dividing its profits equally between the two partners. Qavam's achievement was considerable. It permitted the Russians to leave without losing face. It had been reached without open intervention from the West.[4] It counterbalanced a Soviet concession in the north against the British company in the south. And it implicitly tied what Qavam wanted, the Soviet withdrawal, with what the Soviets seemed to want most, the oil agreement. For without troop withdrawal, there could be no elections; without elections, no Majles; and without Majles, no oil agreement. As the last Soviet contingents left in early May, the shah felt obliged to confer on Qavam the title of Jenab-i Ashraf (Noble Excellency).

While offering the Soviets an oil concession, Qavam tried to reassure the Americans by proposing to them an equivalent concession in the southeast and by renewing the U.S. military mission. The American ambassador reported that Qavam told him privately the northern concession was "inevitable and long overdue" because Iran in the past had "discriminated against Russia": "He interrupted his thoughts to stress that if any arrangements were signed with Russia over northern

---

[3] British Ambassador to the Foreign Office, 19 December 1943, *F.O. 371*/Persia 1943/34-35077.

[4] Although President Truman claimed that he sent "an ultimatum" to Stalin, no such ultimatum has been found. See J. Thorpe, "Truman's Ultimatum to Stalin in 1946: Fact or Fantasy?" *The Newsletter of the Society for Iranian Studies*, 4, (October 1972), 8-10.

oil he would see that Americans were given rights in Baluchistan. When I mentioned that Britain had sought a concession in Baluchistan, he said that Britain had received all the oil rights it would get in Iran. This bears out his long record of favoring American enterprise."[5]

At the same time, Qavam stretched a friendly hand to the left. Relaxing the restrictions placed on the Tudeh by previous administrations, he ordered the army to evacuate the party headquarters, released cadres from prison, ended martial law in Tehran, permitted mass meetings, and encouraged the party to reopen the clubs that had been burned down in the southern cities during Sadr's right-wing reaction. He arrested Sayyid Ziya; Taheri, the pro-British politician; Qubadian, the chief of the Kurdish Kalhur tribe in Khuzistan; Dawlatabadi, the royalist deputy from Isfahan; Dashti, the leader of the Justice party; and three merchants who had financed the National Will party. The British embassy reported that the more prudent Anglophile businessmen were leaving Tehran for vacations in the south, pilgrimages in Iraq, and prolonged medical cures in Palestine.[6] Qavam also closed down ten rightist newspapers; broadcast a "veiled" but "firm" warning to the shah not to interfere in politics;[7] and easily dismantled the Justice and National Will parties by confiscating their financial assets. Moreover, he arrested General Arfaʿ, the Chief of General Staff, for arming the anti-Tabriz Shahsaven tribes, and appointed General ʿAli Razmara as the new Chief of General Staff. Arfaʿ and Razmara were not only sworn personal enemies but also exact political opposites. The former, according to the British military attaché, was a conservative aristocrat who whole-heartedly supported Britain, suffered from a "spy-hunting mania," and, as a result, daily discovered leftist plots against the shah.[8] The latter came from a lower-middle-class home, intensely distrusted Britain, and thus sympathized with Russia and leftist junior officers. The war minister, General Amir Ahmedi, tried to prevent Razmara's appointment on the grounds that he was too friendly with Muzaffar Firuz and discontented noncommissioned officers.[9] The shah, for his part, informed the British em-

[5] U.S. Ambassador to the State Department, 22 March 1946, *Foreign Relations of United States* (Washington, D.C., 1946), VII, 369-73.

[6] British Military Attaché to the Foreign Office, 25 March 1946, *India Office*/L/P&S/12-3505.

[7] British Military Attaché to the Foreign Office, 22 May 1946, *F.O. 371*/Persia 1946/34-52710.

[8] British Military Attaché to the Foreign Office, 18 February 1946, *India Office*/L/P&S/12-3505.

[9] A. Amir Ahmedi, "My Role in Qavam al-Saltaneh's Cabinet," *Salnameh-i Donya*, 13 (1957), 80-84.

bassy that Razmara was a "viper that must be crushed": "he is disloyal, dishonest, and little better than a Russian agent."[10]

Furthermore, in June Qavam reached a tentative agreement with the Democratic Party of Azerbaijan. According to the agreement, the central government recognized the "National Government of Azerbaijan" as the Provincial Council of Azerbaijan; the "National Assembly" as the Provincial Assembly; and the armed volunteers (*feda'is*) that had carried out the rebellion as the local security forces.[11] The central government also agreed to choose future governors-general from a list drawn up by the Provincial Assembly; permit the Provincial Council to appoint heads of local government departments; spend in the region 75 percent of the taxes collected in Azerbaijan; use Azeri in primary schools, and both Azeri and Persian in law courts and government offices; officially endorse the Provincial Council's distribution of state lands among the peasantry; extend, as soon as possible, the Trans-Iranian Railway to Tabriz; submit to the Fifteenth Majles a new electoral bill enfranchizing women and increasing Azerbaijan's representation to correspond to its population; and help finance the construction of the University of Tabriz "in recognition of the sacrifices the people of Azerbaijan made during the Constitutional Revolution." The agreement deferred decisions on two sensitive issues, however. It promised a commission to hear the grievances of landlords who, because of their active opposition to the Democratic party, had lost their estates. And it set up a joint commission to resolve military difficulties, especially jurisdiction over conscription, role of the central army in the province, and status of Iranian officers who had deserted to Azerbaijan.

The agreement was well received in Tehran not only by the Tudeh but also by many of the independent papers. *Umid*, owned by the aristocrat Abul Qassem Amini, congratulated both sides for their willingness to compromise. *Muzaffar*, edited by Mossadeq's colleague Key-Ostovan, welcomed all the clauses except those permitting the use of the Azeri language: "A common language is the best cement for building national unity. This is why we must do all we can to spread Persian— the language of Ferdowsi, Sa'di, Nezami, and Mowlavi—into all parts of Iran, especially Azerbaijan."[12] And *Jeb'eh*, the organ of the Iran party, priased the Democratic party for "implementing extensive re-

---

[10] British Military Attaché to the Foreign Office, 9 July 1946, *India Office*/L/P&S/12-3505.

[11] "The Agreement between Tehran and Tabriz," *Azerbaijan-i Demokrat* (Democratic Azerbaijan), edited by A. 'Amidi-Nouri (Tehran, 1946), pp. 90-93.

[12] "The Government's Relations with Azerbaijan," *Umid*, 3 December 1946; "An Open Letter to Mr. Pishevari," *Muzaffar*, 10 September 1946.

forms in Azerbaijan and strengthening progressive forces throughout Iran."

When the movement in Azerbaijan started, many short-sighted people panicked, crying that the existence of Iran was threatened. We, however, made a realistic evaluation of the situation. We knew that Azerbaijan had no intention of separating from Iran and that the movement in Azerbaijan was an integral part of the progressive movement in Iran. Our optimism has been realized. The Azerbaijan government has not only accepted a just compromise, but has also built schools, roads, clinics, a university, lowered consumer taxes, distributed land among the peasantry, and done much to raise the standard of living.[13]

While helping the left and hindering the right, Qavam in mid-June took the precaution of forming his own organization named the Democrat party (Hizb-i Demokrat). He had two implicit, and paradoxical, reasons for establishing the new organization. On one hand, he intended to use it, together with the Interior Ministry, to defeat royalist and pro-British candidates in the forthcoming election, and thereby pack the Fifteenth Majles. He was using the machinery of modern politics to pursue his old struggle against the dynasty. Some suspected that he planned to create a one-party state. On the other hand, he hoped to use it to mobilize noncommunist reformers, steal the thunder from the left, and hence build a counterbalance to the Tudeh. The party label tried to give the organization the appearance of being both the heir of the old Democrat party and the rival of the Democratic Party of Azerbaijan. As one of Qavam's advisers admitted later, "the situation forced us to adopt a radical image to compete with the revolutionaries."[14] The Democrat party was thus a double-edged sword directed at the left as well as the right.

The party's Central Committee consisted of northern anti-British aristocrats and radical non-Tudeh intellectuals (see Table 5). The first group included Qavam, the party chairman; Muzaffar Firuz; Muhammad Vali Farmanfarma; Abul Qassem Amini; and Sardar Fakher Hekmat, the former deputy from Shiraz. Although he was a large landowner in Fars, Hekmat had worked closely with the northern anticourt aristocrats in the Fourteenth Majles, partly because he had been victimized by Reza Shah and partly because his family had traditionally opposed the pro-British Khamseh tribes. The second group included Bahar, the education minister; Mahmud Mahmud, another veteran of the old Democrat party and author of a popular exposé

---

[13] "The Azerbaijan Movement is Patriotic and Progressive," *Jeb'eh*, 30 September 1946.

[14] D. Farhang, "Revelations on the Democrat Party," *Khvandaniha*, 24 March 1948.

TABLE 5
Leaders of the Democrat Party

Name	Occupation	Place of Higher Education	Place & Date of Birth	Class Origin	Ethnic Origin	Previous Politics
Qavam, Ahmad	landowner	France	Tehran, 1878	Qajar nobility	Qajar-Persian	exiled by Reza Shah
Firuz, Muzaffar	landowner	England	Tehran, 1906	Qajar nobility	Qajar-Persian	collaborated with Sayyid Ziya
Farmanfarma, Muhammad	landowner	none	Tabriz, 1890	Qajar nobility	Qajar-Persian	leader of Liberal Caucus
Amini, Abdul Qassem	landowner	France	Rasht, 1906	Qajar nobility	Qajar-Persian	leader of Liberal Caucus
Hekmat, Sardar Fakher	landowner	France	Shiraz, 1890	landed upper class	Persian	leader of Liberal Caucus
Bahar, Malek al-Shua'ra	poet	none	Mashad, 1886	father a court poet	Persian	Democrat party
Mahmud, Mahmud	writer & civil servant	Iran	Tabriz, 1882	urban middle class	Persian	Democrat & Socialist parties
Arsanjani, Hassan	lawyer & journalist	Iran	Arsanjan, 1921	rural middle class	Persian	worked with Qavan, 1943-1946
Sadeqi, Abul Hussein	physician	France	Tabriz, 1900	landed upper class	Azeri	Iran party
'Amidi-Nouri, Abul Hassan	journalist & lawyer	Iran	Babul, 1903	urban middle class	Persian	worked with Qavan, 1942-1946
Vakil, Hashem	lawyer	Iran	Qum, 1876	urban middle class	Persian	none
Furuzesh, Za'in	lawyer	Iran	Tehran, 1920	urban middle class	Persian	Comrades' party
Naraqi, 'Abbas	lawyer	Iran	Kashan, 1904	urban middle class	Persian	leader of Comrades' party

of British intrigues in Iran; and Hassan Arsanjani, a young lawyer who in the 1960s became famous as the architect of land reform. The son of a low-ranking mulla who had supported the Constitutional Revolution, Arsanjani had studied in Tehran University, translated Montesquieu, and in 1944 founded an independent left-wing paper called *Darya*, which was denounced by the royalists as dangerously republican, by the British as "scurrilously" Marxist, and by the Russians as "crypto-fascist."[15]

[15] The royalists took strong objection to Arsanjani's call for a constituent assembly to reform the constitutional laws. See N. Shahstari, "Danger!" *Vazifeh*, 25 February

The program of the Democrat party called for extensive economic, social, and administrative reforms.[16] It promised "a drastic revision of the country's security forces—i.e. the army, police, and gendarmerie." It also promised distribution of state lands; women's suffrage; provincial assemblies as stipulated in the constitutional laws; elimination of unemployment; reintroduction of elections for village kadkhudas; and construction of rural clinics, schools, and irrigation projects. To convey its views to the public, the party established four major newspapers: *Demokrat-i Iran* (Democratic Iran), the party's daily; *Farman* (Decree), the party's evening paper; *Deplomat* (Diplomat), the Central Committee's organ focusing on international issues; and *Bahram* (Mars), designed to appeal to students. Moreover, the party planned to establish provincial, district, and local branches; youth, women's, and paramilitary organizations; biennial congresses to elect the Central Committee, chairman, and parliamentary candidates; and a disciplined parliamentary caucus whose members would "vow to remain under party instructions and follow the policies of the party chairman."[17] The Democrat party, however, intentionally kept away from the labor movement so as not to antagonize the Tudeh. As Qavam told the press, "since we have no desire to sow friction among workers, we will abstain from union activities." Similarly, Muzaffar Firuz announced that "the Democrat party will leave the working class to the Tudeh so long as the Tudeh leaves the peasantry to the Democrat party."[18]

Having formed the Democrat party, Qavam continued to move to the left. In mid-June, he set up a Supreme Economic Council and instructed it to draft plans to distribute crown lands, help peasants, end opium cultivation, set a minimum wage, implement a Five Year Program, and protect national industries.[19] In late June, he closed down the religious paper *Parcham-i Islam* (Flag of Islam) for inciting

---

1946. The British ambassador tried to suppress *Darya* when Arsanjani published Marx's *British Rule in India*. See British Chargé d'Affaires to the Foreign Office, 28 July 1944, *F.O. 371*/Persia 1944/34-40187. The Soviet objection was probably based on the fact that *Darya* ran a series of articles on the religious minorities, accusing Jews, Armenians, and Assyrians of being spies, traitors, smugglers, and bourgeois exploiters. See "The Problem of Religious Minorities in Iran," *Darya*, 1-16 January 1946.

[16] Democrat Party, "Party Program," *Demokrat-i Iran*, 24 October 1946.

[17] Democrat Party, "Party Handbook," *Demokrat-i Iran*, 25 October 1946.

[18] *Zafar*, 8 and 10 August 1946.

[19] The British embassy reported that although the talk of dividing crown lands was probably "window-dressing to secure further support from the Tudeh," it frightened some landlords into "gloomily predicting" more drastic forms of land reform. See British Military Attaché, "Monthly Report for June 1946," *F.O. 371*/Persia 1946/34-52710.

demonstrations against unveiled women, and arrested Ayatallah Abul Qassem Kashani, the leading political mujtahed, for organizing bazaar protests against the government.[20] In July, he ordered the army to stop supplying weapons to anti-Tudeh elements in Gilan and Mazandaran; named ʿAbbas Iskandari, a pro-Soviet politician, as mayor of Tehran; appointed another pro-Tudeh politician to be governor-general of Isfahan; placed a radical judge at the head of a special court that tried public officials accused of political corruption; and sent Muzaffar Firuz to Khuzistan to pressure the oil company into settling a massive general strike that had broken out among its 60,000 employees. By the end of July, the British authorities were reporting that the Tudeh had secured control not only over the city of Isfahan, but also over much of Gilan, Mazandaran, and Khuzistan.[21]

The swing to the left accelerated in August when Qavam—without consulting the shah—formed a coalition cabinet with the Democrat, Tudeh, and Iran parties. Again keeping the Ministries of Interior and Foreign Affairs in his own hand, Qavam created a Ministry of Labor and Information for Muzaffar Firuz, left the ministries of War, Transport, and Agriculture in the hands of Amir Ahmedi, Firuz Farmanfarma, and Amir ʿAlai, respectively; gave the ministries of Finance and Communications to two royalists; the Ministry to Justice to Allayar Saleh, a young judge from the Iran party; the ministries of Health, Education, and Trade and Industry to representatives of the Tudeh party; and offered the post of minister without portfolio to the Democratic Party of Azerbaijan. Sir John Helier Le Rougetel, the new British ambassador, claimed that eight of the eleven ministers were either communists or "fellow-travelling" communists.[22] Backed by a majority of the cabinet, Qavam decreed a comprehensive labor law; encouraged the Tudeh ministers to carry out major reorganization of their ministries; promised to recognize the Tudeh unions

[20] Kashani, who was later to become the main cleric to campaign for the nationalization of the oil company, already had a long career of political activity. In World War I, he had taken up arms against the British. In the 1921 Iraqi revolt, his father, a highly respected mujtahed, had been killed fighting the British. In 1923-1925, he had supported the Moderate party against the Socialists, and had spoken out against the republican movement. In 1925, he had opposed Reza Shah and had been forced into exile. In 1941, he had returned and with the help of the Tehran guilds won a Majles seat, but had been promptly arrested by the British for having links with the pro-German grand mufti of Jerusalem. And in 1946, he had regained his freedom and made his way to Tehran to work against Qavam.

[21] British Consul in Isfahan, "Monthly Report for June 1946," *F.O. 371*/Persia 1946/ 34-52736; British Military Attaché to the Foreign Office, Weekly Summaries for June and July 1946, *India Office*/L/P&S/12-3505.

[22] British Ambassador to the Foreign Office, 2 August 1946, *F.O. 371*/Persia 1946/ 34-52709.

officially as the sole representatives of the working class; and appointed a Supreme Labor Council to introduce unemployment insurance, wage scales, and negotiating committees between management and labor. The swing to the left reached its furthest point in September when Qavam, speaking to an enthusiastic audience in the Tudeh headquarters, announced that the Democrats would form an electoral alliance for the forthcoming parliament not only with the Tudeh and Iran parties, but also with the Azerbaijan and Kurdish Democratic parties. Most observers expected such an alliance to secure a large majority in the Fifteenth Majles and then raise the explosive constitutional issue against the shah.[23]

Qavam's plans, however, were shattered in October by an onslaught from the right: tribal insurrections, spearheaded by the southern chiefs; unrest in the army, led by the shah; and pressure from the Western powers, particularly Great Britain. The tribal intervention took the shape of a rapidly spreading insurrection. It began with Naser Qashqayi, who was fearful of Tudeh strength and mobilized his tribesmen, proclaiming that communism, atheism, and anarchism endangered democracy, Iran, and Islam.[24] Supported promptly by the Bakhtiyaris, the Qashqayis demanded for Fars and Isfahan concessions similar to those given to Azerbaijan: provincial assemblies, local officials appointed by the same assemblies, 66 percent of the taxes collected in the region to be spent within the two provinces, and extension of the Trans-Iranian Railway to Isfahan, Shiraz, and Bushire.[25] Joined by the Khamseh, Boir Ahmedis, Davoudis, and Mamsamis of Fars, as well as the Tangestanis of the Gulf coast, the tribal rebels captured Bushire and Kazerun, massacring the garrisons in both towns. Some fifteen thousand armed warriors converged on Shiraz. Encouraged further by the Arabs of Khuzistan, Shahsavens of Ardabel, Afshars of Ardalan, and Kalhur Kurds of Kermanshah, the rebels escalated their demands to include the dissolution of the coalition cabinet, exclusion of the Tudeh from future governments, ban of Tudeh organizations in the south, and appointment of two ministers without portfolio to represent the "southern movement."[26]

Opposition from the officer corps was nothing new. When Qavam had been negotiating the Soviet withdrawal, the war minister, suspicious of secret deals, told the press that Russians were reinforcing

[23] British Military Attaché, 16 October 1946, *F.O. 371*/Persia 1946/34-52711.

[24] British Military Attaché to the Foreign Office, "Document of the Resistance Movement in the South," *F.O. 371*/Persia 1946/34-52711.

[25] N. Qashqayi, "Open Letter to the Premier," *Dad*, 23 September 1946.

[26] "Negotiations between the Government and Naser Qashqayi," *Khvandaniha*, 1 October 1946.

rather than thinning out their contingents in Azerbaijan.[27] When Qavam had nearly reached a full settlement with Tabriz, field commanders instigated border incidents, and military representatives on the joint commission categorically refused to recognize the feda'is and army defectors as legitimate members of the armed forces.[28] When Qavam had sided with the Tudeh against the oil company during the general strike of Khuzistan, the military commander of Abadan had arrested the union leaders, distributed arms to Arab tribesmen, encouraged them to attack the Tudeh headquarters, and, after a heated argument with Muzaffar Firuz, pulled out a pistol to shoot him. Similarly, when Qavam had tried to arrest the military commander of Abadan, the chief of general staff had successfully intervened and threatened to resign if an army officer was humiliated in a public court.[29] Now when the tribal revolt broke out, "military circles and right-wing elements in Tehran" consulted the British embassy on the advisability of a coup d'état, while the military commander of Fars played down the army's capabilities, gave an exaggerated picture of rebel strength, and urged the government to give in to their demands.[30] The British consul in Shiraz suspected that the military commander had secretly worked to unite the chiefs against the left.[31] Meanwhile, the Tudeh ministers urged Qavam to ignore the military's recommendations and to arm the trade unions against the tribes.

The opposition of the Western powers intensified as Qavam drew closer to the Tudeh and the Soviet Union. In March Bullard expressed reservations on the wisdom of Qavam's mission to Moscow: "It is regrettable, but a fact, that the Persians are ideal Stalin-fodder. They are untruthful, backbiters, undisciplined, incapable of unity, and without a plan. The Soviet system is equipped with a complete theoretical scheme for everything from God to galoshes." In April the British

[27] M. Davoudi, *Qavam al-Saltaneh*, Tehran, 1947, pp. 115-16.

[28] British Military Attaché to the Foreign Office, 29 May 1946, *F.O. 371*/Persia 1946/34-52710. The shah later wrote: "Qavam even wanted to take back into our army the traitor officers who had deserted. . . . Qavam begged on his knees that I should accept this request, but I replied that I would rather have my hand cut off first." (See Muhammad Reza Shah Pahlevi, *Mission for My Country*, London, 1961, p. 117.) The American embassy reported that Qavam had told the U.S. chargé d'affaires "in the utmost confidence that his difficulties were not so much with Tabriz as with the Shah." (See U.S. Chargé d'Affaires to the State Department, 6-8 May 1946, *Foreign Relations of the United States*, 1946, VII, 449-54.)

[29] British Military Attaché to the Foreign Office, 18 September and 9 October 1946, *F.O. 371*/Persia 1946/34-52711.

[30] "Why the Coalition Cabinet Fell," *Khvandaniha*, 22 October 1946; British Military Attaché to the Foreign Office, 9 October 1946, *F.O. 371*/Persia 1946/34-52711.

[31] British Consul in Shiraz, "Conversations with the Military Commander," *F.O. 371*/Persia 1946/34-52737.

Foreign Office drew up contingency plans in case Qavam continued to "drift into the position of a Russian puppet." These plans called for pressure through the oil company, support for autonomous movements in the south, and, as a last resort, armed occupation of Khuzistan. In May the British military attaché commented, "whether Qavam has or has not sold his country to the Russians is a matter of opinion incapable, as yet, of proof. That his cabinet is susceptible to Tudeh pressure is a fact." By June Le Rougetel, Bullard's successor, was warning in alarm: "Qavam's reluctance to take action against the Tudeh is due to the increasing power of that organization. If he were to take strong line against them, they would almost certainly retaliate by forcing him from office and replacing him with an out and out communist." In July the British reinforced their base in Basra, anchored two warships off Abadan, and prepared to dispatch troops into Khuzistan.[32] In August the British consul in Isfahan was accused by the government of inciting the Bakhtiyaris to rebel. The British embassy commented: "It now seems evident to all patriotic Persians that Qavam has definitely sold his country to the Russians." And in September, when Qavam sought American help against Britain and the shah, the U.S. ambassador advised him to dismiss Muzaffar Firuz and the Tudeh ministers, reopen the Azerbaijan issue, stop denouncing his opponents as "fascist reactionaries," and tone down his "warm expressions of friendship towards the Soviet Union."[33]

By October, therefore, Qavam found himself in the midst of a dangerous dilemma. He could continue on his leftward course, arm the trade unions, and seek military assistance from the Russians; but this might spark a social revolution, if not a bloody civil war. Or he could take a sharp turn to the right, end the alliance with the Tudeh, compromise with the tribes and the officers; but this would postpone the constitutional struggle against the shah. He chose the latter course. He sent Muzaffar Firuz to be ambassador in Moscow; dismissed the ministers representing the Tudeh and Iran parties; shelved the ambitious decrees that had promised land reform and labor legislation; released former opponents such as Sayyid Ziya, Arfaʿ, Taheri, and Kashani; purged leftists from government positions and the Supreme

[32] British Ambassador to the Foreign Office, 29 March 2946, *F.O. 371*/Persia 1946/ 34-52670; British Foreign Office, "Memorandum on Persia," 13-16 April 1946, *F.O. 371*/Persia 1946/34-52673; British Military Attaché to the Foreign Office, 22 May 1946, *F.O. 371*/Persia 1946/34-52710; British Ambassador to the Foreign Office, 13 June 1946, *F.O. 371*/Persia 1946/34-52678; British Cabinet, 4 July 1946, *F.O. 371*/Persia 1946/34-52706.

[33] British Military Attaché to the Foreign Office, 16 October 1946, *F.O. 371*/Persia 1946/34-52711; U.S. Ambassador to the State Department, *Foreign Relations of United States* (1946), VII, 496, 522-29, 541-44.

Supervisory Council that was to oversee the forthcoming elections; and appointed hard-line anticommunists to be governors-general of Isfahan, Khuzistan, Gilan, and Mazandaran. Using martial law, these governors banned twelve leftist papers, occupied Tudeh offices, and arrested over 340 party militants. The organ of the Iran party commented, "for the first time since Reza Shah, the army is an important power center and openly interferes in political matters."[34]

Qavam also moved the Democrat party to the right. He recruited into its leadership Bakhtiyari and Qashqayi chiefs; Qubadian of the Kalhur tribe; Naser Zolfaqari, a magnate in Zanjan whose estates had been expropriated by the Tabriz government; Mas'oudi, the editor of *Ittila'at*; Emami, the industrialist and former deputy from Isfahan; Namazi, the millionaire businessman who had represented Shiraz in the previous Majles; 'Ali Vakili, president of the Tehran Chamber of Commerce; 'Aziz Nikpay, a wealthy landowner from Isfahan; and Muhammad Herati, a textile manufacturer from Yazd. One of Qavam's colleagues commented, "the Democrat party became the refuge for all who feared the Tudeh. It appeared to be the last bulwark against communism."[35]

Qavam's next step was to form a Central Syndicate of Iranian Craftsmen, Farmers, and Workers (ESKI). As a leader of the new organization admitted later, "the Democrat party created ESKI to undermine the inordinate power accumulated by the trade unions affiliated with the Tudeh."[36] The task of forming ESKI was assigned to Khosrow Hedayat, the director of railways, and Habib Nafisi, the director of state factories. The former, a Belgian-educated engineer, was the brother of a prominent royalist general, the son of a titled aristocrat, and the nephew of a premier under Reza Shah. The latter, a German-educated engineer, was the son of a tutor in Reza Shah's court and the grandson of a physician in the Qajar court. Helped by state-employed engineers and financed by the Ministry of Labor and Information, ESKI started a newspaper, *Kargaran-i Iran* (Workers of Iran), and opened branches in government enterprises—especially in tobacco factories, munition works, and railway plants.[37] The formation of ESKI drew sharp criticisms from the Tudeh. Denouncing the new organization as a "yellow union," it accused government bureau-

---

[34] "Who Has Power?" *Jeb'eh*, 21 November 1946.

[35] "Notes from Qavam's Memoirs," *Khvandaniha*, 15 October 1955.

[36] "Notes Concerning the Trade Unions," *Khvandaniha*, 7 October 1954.

[37] Despite the attempt to recruit workers, ESKI remained in the hands of managers and engineers. For example, at its first national congress twenty-one of the thirty-six delegates were engineers, and only two were workers. See "The First Congress of ESKI," *Kargaran-i Iran*, 6 November 1949.

crats of using bribery, coercion, and the threat of unemployment to divide the working class.[38] It held mass rallies to defend its clubs from the paramilitary organization of the Democrat party. And on November 12, it declared a twenty-four-hour general strike to protest the murder of a railway worker by street thugs allegedly hired by ESKI.

Furthermore, Qavam cooled his relations with Tabriz and Mahabad, and eventually, in December, permitted the military to invade Azerbaijan and Kurdistan. The events preceding the invasion remain shrouded in a fog of half-truths and misleading innuendoes. Afterwards Qavam claimed full credit for the whole enterprise, saying that he had worked for that conclusion from the very beginning.[39] Before the invasion, however, he moved with the utmost caution and gave Tabriz the impression that he was defending it against the unreasonable demands of the shah.[40] His caution arose partly from the fear of Soviet intervention; partly from the lack of confidence in the fighting capabilities of the army; partly from his knowledge that in the forthcoming parliament he could use against the shah the twenty-five deputies elected by the Azerbaijan and Kurdish Democrats; and partly from the suspicion that the military authorities, once in control of the region, would elect royalist deputies and thereby undermine his position in the Fifteenth Majles.

Despite these fears, Qavam found himself pressured into taking action. In early November, the military resumed arming opponents of the Tabriz government—especially Zolfaqari retainers, as well as Afshar and Shahsaven tribesmen. In late November, the army occupied Zanjan, an Azeri-speaking town on the border of Gilan. The British military attaché reported that Qavam had "for several months consistently refused to agree to the war minister's request for permission to occupy Zanjan."[41] The day after the capture of Zanjan, the military governor-general of Tehran used his emergency powers under martial law to ban *Bahram*, the youth organ of the Democrat party, for praising the prime minister for the successful operations.[42] Finally, on December 10, Qavam signed the order instructing the military to enter Azerbaijan and Kurdistan to "maintain law and security during the parliamentary elections." After two days of fighting, the autonomous governments—probably under Russian pressure—sued for

---

[38] Tudeh Party, "An Open Letter to Qavam," *Rahbar*, 26 November 1946.

[39] *Demokrat-i Iran*, 3 January 1947.

[40] British Consul in Tabriz, "Three Monthly Report for January-June 1946," *F.O. 371*/Persia 1946/34-52679.

[41] British Military Attaché to the Foreign Office, 27 November 1946, *F.O. 371*/Persia 1946/34-52711.

[42] *Bahram*, 26 November 1946.

peace, while their armed volunteers, equipped only with light weapons, surrendered or fled across the border into the Soviet Union. The shah, in an interview with the British minister, refused to concede to Qavam any "degree of responsibility for the favorable course of events." Qavam, on the other hand, privately argued that his credibility in Moscow had persuaded the Soviets not to intervene, and publicly claimed that he would have ordered the invasion much earlier if the army had been prepared for such a venture.[43] The autonomous governments had ended; the battle between the shah and the prime minister had only just started.

THE FIFTEENTH MAJLES ELECTIONS (DECEMBER 1946-JUNE 1947)

The reoccupation of Azerbaijan and Kurdistan provided the backdrop for the parliamentary elections. The parliamentary elections themselves thrust into the open the power struggle between Qavam and the shah. The struggle took place in a very different situation from that planned by Qavam, however, for of the four advantages he had enjoyed in March, Qavam had now largely lost three. His coalition with the Tudeh had been shattered, and his allies in Tabriz and Mahabad had been swept away. His main foreign supporter, Russia, no longer occupied northern Iran, and with the attack on Azerbaijan had cooled its support and awaited the fate of the tentative oil agreement. Finally, his control over the electoral machinery was challenged in many districts by army officers, independent local magnates, or pro-British provincial governors. The election thus turned into a three-way struggle between Qavam, the shah, and the pro-British conservative politicians.

Qavam's strength lay in Tehran, Khurasan, Isfahan, and Mazandaran. He so thoroughly controlled the Supervisory Electoral Council in Tehran that twenty-three prominent candidates with very different political views united to stage a public protest in the sanctuary of the royal gardens. The protest was headed by Mossadeq, whose distrust of the military was now overshadowed by his dislike of Qavam's policy on oil concessions and his fear that Qavam intended to establish a one-party state. The other protestors included Muhammad Sadeq Tabatabai, the president of the Fourteenth Majles; Farrukh, the spokesman of the tribal group in the previous Majles; Ardalan, the royalist landowner from Kurdistan who had joined the National Union

---

[43] British Military Attaché to the Foreign Office, 18 December 1946, *F.O. 371*/Persia 1946/34-52689; Qavam, *Parliamentary Proceedings*, 15th Majles, 12 December 1947.

Caucus; Dr. Hassan Emami, the imam jom'eh of Tehran and custodian of the largest ecclesiastical foundation, who, despite his family's long tradition of religious conservatism, obediently supported Reza Shah's secular reforms; and Dr. Ahmad Matin-Daftari, a German-educated lawyer from a titled family reaching back to the Zand dynasty, who had been premier in 1938-1949 and had been imprisoned by the Allies because of his German connections. While these politicians camped on the palace grounds, two hundred shopkeepers and six hundred university students took to the streets. The shopkeepers were protesting not only the unfair elections, but also the government's policy of favoring wealthy export-importers in the Chamber of Commerce at the expense of bazaar tradesmen.[44] The students, meanwhile, complained that "progressive intellectuals" in the Democrat party had been silenced by feudalists, reactionaries, and street thugs.[45] To end the protests, Qavam promised to permit free elections. Even so, the elections were rigged and the Democrats won all of Tehran's twelve seats, with only 30 percent of the city's electorate bothering to vote.[46]

The royalist strength, on the other hand, was dominant in regions under martial law, especially Azerbaijan, Kurdistan, and the tribally disturbed constituencies outside Kermanshah. For example, the commander of the expeditionary forces in Azerbaijan refused to accept the governor-general sent by the prime minister; pressured the cabinet into appointing a staunch royalist as the new governor-general; and forbade Qavam's Democrats to open a party branch in Tabriz. It is not surprising that Qavam had been reluctant to order the army into the northern provinces.

British influence, meanwhile, predominated in Khuzistan, where local administrators could not accomplish their daily tasks unless they worked closely with the Anglo-Iranian Oil Company. The governor-general, Mosbeh Fatemi ('Emad al-Saltaneh), had been appointed to his position with the full backing of the British embassy. A large landowner in Isfahan and son-in-law of the famous Prince Zil al-Sultan, Mosbeh Fatemi had served in Reza Shah's cabinets before losing royal favor but gaining British support. Helped by the oil company, he succeeded in placing his brother, Mehdi Fatemi, as governor-general of Fars, and giving many of the Khuzistan seats to pro-British landlords and tribal chiefs.

[44] *Aras*, 13-17 January 1947.

[45] B. Mobarez (pseudonym), *Hizb-i Demokrat-i Iran Beshenasid* (Get To Know the Democrat Party) (Tehran, 1947).

[46] Tehran, with a total population of 800,000 in 1947, had 230,000 potential voters. Of these, only 70,000 voted. *Mardom*, 22 January 1947.

In other constituencies, local magnates played a determining role. For example, Bakhtiyaris decided the outcome in Shahr-i Kurd, Qashqayis in Firuzabad, Khamseh chiefs in Fasa, Bayats in Arak, Zolfaqaris in Zanjan, Aminis in Rasht, and Hekmats in Shiraz, where the family owned large estates, in Bushire where a member of the household held the governorship, and, most important of all, in Kerman province where Sardar Fakher Hekmat ruled in theory as Qavam's governor-general but in practice as an independent magnate.

THE FIFTEENTH MAJLES (JUNE 1947-JUNE 1949)

As soon as the Fifteenth Majles convened it predictably divided into three major fraksiuns. The Democrat party, having taken eighty seats in Tehran, Gilan, Mazandaran, Khurasan, and Kerman, held a majority. The bloc was led by Hekmat, the spokesman of the party's landed conservative wing, and by the poet Bahar, the head of the party's intellectual radical wing. The bloc included such prominent Democrats as Arsanjani, Mahmud Mahmud, Sadeqi, Mas'oudi, Namazi, Abul Qassem Amini and his younger brother 'Ali Amini, and the two leading Qashqayi Khans. Over one-third of the eighty had been imprisoned at one time or another by Reza Shah.

The royalists, continuing to use the label National Unionists, formed the second largest bloc, and could muster thirty-five votes. They were led by 'Ezatallah Bayat from Arak, Ardalan from Kurdistan, and Matin-Daftari from a small Azerbaijani town he admitted he had never seen. Many of the fraksiun's backbenchers were landlords from Azerbaijan who had been kept out of the Fourteenth Majles by the Soviet authorities and whose estates had been expropriated by the Tabriz government. Matin-Daftari later wrote that he felt uncomfortable in the caucus meetings because almost all the other members spoke Azeri.[47]

The pro-British group, numbering twenty-five deputies, was the third largest fraksiun. Naming itself the National Caucus (Fraksiun-i Melli), the group was led by two prominent politicians from the previous Majles: Madani and Taheri. Many of the group's members represented constituencies in Khuzistan, Fars, and the Gulf coast. In crucial votes and closed debates, they candidly favored Britain. In public statement and open debates, however, they tended to stress the "communist expansionism" of the Soviet Union and the past isolationism of the United States rather than any inherent ties of friendship between Iran and Britain.

The Fifteenth Majles thus began with Qavam holding a substantial,

---

[47] A. Matin-Daftari, "Memoirs," *Salnameh-i Donya*, 19 (1963), 3-16.

if not a stable, majority. He shuffled the cabinet, bringing in two additional Democrats as ministers without portfolio. He helped Hekmat win the presidency of the Majles. He increased the allocations to all the ministries but the War Ministry, and held up a bill for negotiating $10 million worth of arms from the United States. And he vetoed the royal family's request to bring back Reza Shah's body for an elaborate state funeral. The cabinet meeting discussing the request ended in a fist fight when Amir Ahmedi denounced Amir ʿAlai as a traitor. Matin-Daftari complained that the situation was nearly hopeless: "We are powerless. This man Qavam will run the show for two years. And at the end of the two years he will be in a position to rig the next elections. Our one and only hope is to split the Democrat party."[48]

This hope materialized sooner than the most optimistic royalist could have expected. For Qavam, in his haste to undermine both the Tudeh and the shah, had recruited many contradictory elements into his party: aristocratic landlords, such as Hekmat, Amini, and Farmanfarma, as well as radical intellectuals, such as Bahar, Arsanjani, and Mahmud Mahmud; wealthy industrialists, like Nikpay, Namazi, and Herati, and trade unionists eager to woo away the rank and file of the Tudeh party; tribal magnates, particularly Aqa Khan Bakhtiyari and Khosrow Qashqayi, as well as urban administrators who had enthusiastically supported Reza Shah's campaigns against the tribes. These differences were vividly described by *Qiyam-i Iran*, a paper allied to the National Caucus: "The Democrat party includes wolves as well as sheep: millionaires, industrialists, and powerful merchants who coerce and terrorize the masses; as well as workers and peasants who are bribed and herded into the voting polls. The party press claims that ʿAziz Nikpay is a 'workers' representative'; in fact, he is a 'robber baron' who exploits his workers. What is more, Herati, the millionaire industrialist from Yazd, has the audacity to argue that he will protect workers better if he travels to the Majles in a Cadillac."[49]

These contradictions soon split apart the Democrat party. When the party caucus convened for the first time, the majority of the members, overriding Qavam's recommendation, decided to vote on the credentials of each deputy not as a bloc but according to their individual conscience.[50] As a result, conservative Democrats joined royalists and pro-British deputies to reject Arsanjani's credentials. Zolfaqari summed up the opposition to Arsanjani: "How on earth did he obtain enough votes to win a parliamentary seat? Before the elec-

[48] ʿA. Faramarzi, "Memoirs," *Salnameh-i Donya*, 19 (1963), 30-35.
[49] "The Democrat Party," *Qiyam-i Iran*, 3 July 1947.
[50] *Demokrat-i Iran*, 27 July 1947.

tion, he was neither a deputy, nor a minister, nor a governor, nor even a district administrator. He was a mere journalist. And what is worse, a journalist with dubious political connections."[51] When workers in a brick factory outside Tehran struck for higher wages, ESKI supported their demands, but the government sent troops to break the strike and occupy the ESKI printing house. When Qavam refused to call a biennial congress to remove the clause on women's rights, the three deputies with bazaar connections resigned from the party. When *Demokrat-i Iran* persisted in denouncing the wide gap between rich and poor, the wealthy deputies such as Aqa Khan Bakhtiyari protested that the "party was spreading insidious propaganda, and thereby inciting one class against another."[52] Meanwhile, the royalists catered to these views by arguing that the Democrats endangered Iran by using terrorist methods, inflaming social hatreds, and undermining the landed class.[53]

The defections inevitably eroded Qavam's majority. In late June, five more Democrats refused to honor their pledge to observe party discipline, and declared that they had been elected on their own merits without any help from the government. In early July, another five opposed Qavam's suggestion that internal differences should be resolved in the party caucus and not on the Majles floor. One member admitted that he had "little respect for some of the so-called party leaders." Another declared that "he, a hardworking professional, could hardly be expected to support corrupt idle millionaires."[54] And in October, when Qavam after much delay eventually submitted the Soviet-Iranian oil proposals to the Majles, the vast majority of the Democrats joined the opposition in rejecting the agreement. Qavam, however, skillfully used two tactics to defuse the issue. First, he refused to commit himself outright to the agreement, and thus avoided the danger that rejection of the agreement would be taken as a vote of no confidence in the government. Second, he followed up the rejection by mustering an attack on Britain, thereby salvaging the policy of "positive equilibrium." He obtained parliamentary permission to renegotiate the "unjust" 1933 agreement with the Anglo-Iranian Oil Company. He encouraged the press to demand the return of Bahrein on the grounds that "gun-boat imperialism" had seized the island from Iran. And he went on the radio to assure the country

[51] N. Zolfaqari, *Parliamentary Proceedings*, 15th Majles, 9 September 1947.
[52] *Demokrat-i Iran*, 29 December 1946 and 8 April 1947; A. Bakhtiyari, *Parliamentary Proceedings*, 15th Majles, 1 December 1947.
[53] Matin-Daftari, *Parliamentary Proceedings*, 15th Majles, 22 September 1947.
[54] *Khvandaniha*, 29 June and 7 July 1947.

and the Soviet Union that he would persevere in his course of "positive equilibrium."

Although Qavam survived the oil issue, he fell two weeks later when Hekmat resigned from the Democrat party. The reasons behind the resignation remain obscure. Whereas Qavam's followers claimed that Hekmat had been bribed by the opposition, Hekmat's supporters argued that Qavam had "betrayed the principles of the party by refusing to convene a biennial congress and implement social reforms." Hekmat himself wrote later that his followers had pressured him to break with his old colleague Qavam.[55] Whatever the reasons, Hekmat, in resigning, released from the party some twenty deputies he had helped elect from constituencies in Kerman and Fars. The opposition promptly went on the offensive by gathering in Parliament and demanding that the government seek a vote of confidence. Of the 112 deputies at the meeting, 36 voted against the government; 45—fewer than half of those present—voted for; and 31—almost all former Democrats—abstained. Just as Qavam handed in his resignation and flew to Paris for "medical treatment," the shah stripped him of the title Jenab-i Ashraf and the royalists introduced a bill to impeach him on the grounds that he had sold import licenses to fill the coffers of the Democrat party.

With Qavam gone, further splits appeared among the Democrats. When the youth organization declared its independence from the "conservative landlords" in the Central Committee, the Central Committee expelled the youth organization for "ultraleftist deviations" and denounced its paper, *Bahram*, for publishing a "scandalous" article entitled "The Plundering Rich." Similarly, the Central Committee expelled ESKI, at which ESKI members broke into the Central Committee's headquarters to gain control of the party assets. Democrats still loyal to Qavam protested in vain: "It is a well-known fact throughout the world that when a trade union interferes in politics it ceases to be a genuine trade union. The working class, the most troublesome class before Qavam's prudent policies calmed it down, has been again instigated into disruptive action. Regretably, the present instigators are former members of our own party."[56] Thus ended Qavam's ambitious plan to forge a disciplined political organization and perhaps even a one-party state.

The two years following Qavam's exit saw the entry of the shah onto the center of the political arena. Until 1947 the shah had projected the image of a constitutional monarch who reigned but did not

[55] A. Razavi, *Parliamentary Proceedings*, 15th Majles, 11 December 1947; S. Hekmat, "My Role in the Majles," *Salnameh-i Donya*, 21 (1965), pp. 250-54.

[56] M. Ashtianizadeh, *Parliamentary Proceedings*, 15th Majles, 18 January 1948.

rule, even though behind the scenes he controlled the military, and frequently intervened to weaken or strengthen individual ministers. But by 1948 he was openly involved in public policy, making and unmaking not only ministers but also prime ministers. And by 1949 he was powerful enough to convene a constituent assembly to enhance considerably his constitutional prerogatives at the expense of the Majles. The young monarch, who had begun his reign fighting a life-and-death struggle with the opposition, had not only survived the political turmoil but had also emerged as the country's central institution.[57]

Two factors explain the emergence of the shah: the continued expansion of the armed forces, and the balance of forces in the Majles. The armed forces, which had grown from 65,000 men in 1941 to 102,000 in 1946, continued to expand—with American assistance— to number 120,000 in 1949. Military morale also improved, mainly because of the "courageous victories" over the Kurdish and Azerbaijani rebels. By 1948, one of the few deputies who still dared to criticize the court warned, "it is a universal law that whoever controls the nation's guns also controls the nation's politics. This is why His Royal Highness, the Commander in Chief, by rebuilding the armed forces, poses an increasing threat to the country's constitutional liberties." At the same time, the Chief of Staff felt it necessary to assure the country publicly that a "patriotic army" of a mere 120,000 could not possibly endanger fifteen million "freedom-loving citizens."[58]

The shah was also helped, as in the previous parliament, by the balance of forces in the Fifteenth Majles. On one side were forty-five Democrats. Still loyal to Qavam, they pressed for the renegotiation of the 1933 oil agreement, and now sought American help against Britain. Their former enthusiasm for the Soviet Union had diminished, partly because of the failure of Qavam's oil negotiations, and partly because after 1947 Stalin ceased to take an active interest in Iran. On the other side were the twenty-five pro-British conservatives of the National Caucus. Although not openly supporting the 1933 oil agreement, they opposed any policy that would jeopardize Iran's ties with Britain. In between these two blocs were the thirty-five royalists and some thirty independent backbenchers. The royalists, organized into the National Union Caucus, followed the shah's lead in both foreign affairs and domestic policies. The independents, unattached

---

[57] The increasing power of the shah is reflected in *Khvandaniha*, the weekly digest of the national press. His picture appeared there only once in 1942-1943; once again in 1943-1944; twice in 1944-1945; twelve times in 1945-1946; and eighteen times, seventeen of them in military uniform, in 1947-1948.

[58] Razavi, *Parliamentary Proceedings*, 16th Majles, 28 February 1949; Razmara, "Speech to the Nation," *Ittila'at*, 29 September 1948.

to any one fraksiun, included four supporters of Mossadeq, two pro-Soviet politicians, and over twenty former Democrats who had left the party with Hekmat. Thus the royalists were in a position to play a decisive role by throwing their weight behind either the National Caucus or the Democrat party. Their only fear was that these two blocs might unite with each other and with the independents.

After Qavam's fall, the National Unionists joined the National Caucus and a few of the independents to elect Hakimi, Qavam's predecessor in 1946, as prime minister. Meanwhile, the Democrats and many of the independents sponsored Mossadeq, mustering for him only one vote less than obtained by Hakimi. The new premier gave four ministries to the pro-British, five to the royalists, and one to Soheily—the pro-American premier of 1943—to reassure the United States. In the next six months, Hakimi's administration implemented procourt and pro-British policies. It undermined all efforts to renegotiate the 1933 oil agreement. It introduced into the Majles a bill for creating the Senate promised by the constitutional laws of 1906. It helped draft impeachment charges against Qavam for misappropriating government funds. It sought credits for $20 million worth of arms. And it intensified the campaign against the left by closing down more Tudeh clubs, imprisoning 1,200 pro-Tudeh workers, and arresting the last governor-general of the autonomous regime in Azerbaijan, whom Qavam had effectively protected.

Hakimi's coalition, however, gradually fell apart. The National Caucus cooled its support partly because the army pressed ahead to disarm the southern tribes; and partly because the police procrastinated over investigating the mysterious assassination of Muhammad Mas'oud, the editor of the controversial paper *Mard-i Emruz*, who had been revealing embarrassing information about members of the royal family.[59] After the assassination, the pro-British deputies voted with the Democrats to cut the arms bill from $20 million to $10 million. And the pro-British newspapers joined the Democrats and the Tudeh party in forming a Press Front against Dictatorship. Meanwhile, the royalists concluded that a more determined pro-American, rather than pro-British, administration would obtain the $250 million needed to finance the ambitious Seven Year Plan. Hakimi resigned in early June when the fraksiun leaders went to the palace to inform the shah that the cabinet no longer enjoyed the confidence of the Majles.

The National Unionists now joined their former enemies, the Democrats, to elect 'Abdul Hussein Hezhir. The new premier was one of

---

[59] The correspondent of the London *Times* was summarily expelled from Iran for implying that members of the royal family had arranged Mas'oud's murder.

the few senior civil servants who remained on good terms with both Qavam and the shah. He enjoyed Qavam's support because he openly advocated closer ties with America and because he had served conscientiously in all his recent administrations. He also enjoyed court favor because he refused to criticize the military establishment and had worked in the government bureaucracy during Reza Shah's reign. The son of an armed volunteer in the Constitutional Revolution, Hezhir had risen from the lower eschelons of the bureaucracy to the post of inspector of the National Bank. Although he had become wealthy in the course of his career, he was the first premier since Soheily not to have been born into a titled family.

In forming a cabinet, Hezhir gave five ministries to the royalists and four to Qavam's associates. Moreover, he promised to withdraw the impeachment charges against Qavam, and began secret negotiations to "completely revise" the oil agreement of 1933.[60] In return, the Democrats supported the government in increasing the arms procurement bill from $10 million to $16 million, and in signing contracts with American companies to build military airports in Ahwaz and Firuzabad. The opposition reacted sharply. The religious opposition, headed by Kashani, organized a one-day general strike in the bazaar and a mass demonstration outside the Majles to protest the election of a "man who had been a willing tool of the military dictatorship for twenty years."[61] One demonstrator was killed and over seventy were wounded. Meanwhile, the pro-British National Caucus and a few of the independents filibustered the government, criticized the military allocations, sabotaged the efforts to dismiss the impeachment charges, and most effective of all, refused to vote on the annual budget.[62] Parliament bogged down in a morass of charges and countercharges, answers and questions, walk-ins and walk-outs. After four months of obstruction, Hezhir gave up and resigned.

The fraksiuns spent the next two weeks deadlocked over a successor. Exasperated by the delay, the shah took the initiative and called upon Sa'id, the premier of 1944, to form a new government. This promptly

[60] M. Fateh, *Panjah Saleh-i Naft-i Iran* (Fifty Years of Iranian Oil) (Tehran, 1956), p. 387.

[61] F. Keshavarz, "Hezhir's Government," *Razm Mahaneh*, 1 (July 1948), 16-19.

[62] Sayyid Ziya, in a press interview, declared that if he ever became premier he would cancel the arms agreement because "the country needed agricultural machinery and medical facilities, not guns and tanks." He added that he would remove the restrictions placed on the Tudeh because he believed in free competition between all political parties. *Khvandaniha*, 27 February 1948. The Oriental chancellor at the British embassy spent two hours trying to persuade Sayyid Ziya not to enter an alliance with the Tudeh. British Ambassador to the Foreign Office, 10 November 1948, *F.O. 371*/Persia 1948/ 34-68709.

set off a constitutional storm. Whereas the royalists argued that the shah had the constitutional prerogative to nominate ministers so long as these ministers received parliamentary approval, the Democrats counterargued that the Majles had the sole right to choose the cabinet, and that violation of this right threatened to throw Iran back to the dark days of "Qajar despotism."[63] Winning over enough independent deputies, Qavam's Democrats initiated an effective filibuster against the premier and declared that they were resorting to such drastic methods to show the nation how "reactionary courtiers" had misled the "young shah" into mocking the fundamental laws of Iran. It was clear that Qavam, although ousted, retained enough power to obstruct the shah. By January 1949, the American State Department heard rumors that the shah was seeking an opportunity to raise the question of constitutional reform and thereby strengthen his position vis-à-vis the Majles.[64]

The opportunity presented itself in early February, when the shah, visiting Tehran University, was shot and wounded by a young photographer. Although the assailant was killed on the spot without revealing his political connections, if any, his identification papers showed that he worked for the religious paper *Parcham-i Islam* and paid dues to the journalists' union affiliated with the pro-Tudeh labor movement.[65] Taking advantage of public sympathy and claiming that the would-be assassin belonged to a communist-religious conspiracy, the shah acted quickly to crush all opposition. He declared martial law

[63] For the constitutional crisis of 1948 see "The Shah and the Constitution," *Zendigi*, 8 November 1948; M. Tamadon, "Saʿid's Government," *Razm-i Mahaneh*, 1 (December 1948), pp. 73-80; and Democrat Party, *Aya Shah Metavanad dar Omur-i Mamlekat Modakheleh Kunad?* (Does the Shah Have the Right to Interfere in Politics?) (Tehran, 1948).

[64] State Department to the U.S. Embassy in Tehran, 1 February 1949, *Foreign Relations of United States* (Washington, D.C., 1949), 6, 476. The British embassy, as well as the American embassy, opposed any tampering with the Iranian constitution both because it did not fully trust the shah and because it wanted some form of parliamentary representation. As the Foreign Office noted, "the Majlis, though tiresome in internal matters, is a genuine form of national sentiment and in cases such as the Soviet-Persian agreement performs a very valuable function. Its effectiveness would be impaired if it were liable to dissolution. The Shah may even one day be pressured to dissolve it and install one more to the likings of the Russians." 9 March 1948, *F.O. 371*/Persia 1948/34-68711.

[65] At the time, it was rumored that a few Tudeh leaders, especially in the party's military branch, had plotted the assassination without consulting their colleagues. One Tudeh leader who left the party in 1957 subscribes to this theory: F. Keshavarz, *Man Mottaham Mikunam* (I Accuse) (Tehran, 1979), pp. 104-105. The theory can be doubted, however, for two major reasons. First, none of the Tudeh leaders took precautions to evade the ensuing police roundup. Second, neither the police nor defecting Tudeh leaders ever produced any substantial evidence linking the would-be assassin to the Tudeh.

throughout the country, closed down all the main newspapers critical of the court, outlawed the Tudeh, deported Kashani to Beirut, confined Mossadeq to his estates, and tried to implicate even Qavam in the conspiracy. What is more, the shah promptly convened a Constituent Assembly. Elected under martial law, the assembly unanimously voted to create a Senate, half of whose members would be nominated by the monarch, and granted the shah the right to dissolve Parliament whenever he wished, provided that he simultaneously decreed new elections and convened the new Parliament within three months.

The shah continued to obtain advantages in the last few months of the Fifteenth Majles. The Saʿid government, supported by a majority of the deputies, promised to strengthen the armed forces, raise military salaries, and ban all forms of propaganda that "undermined public law-and-order."[66] The press law was made more stringent against anyone criticizing the government and members of the royal family. Reza Shah was honored with the title of Kabir (The Great), and his body was returned to Tehran for a state funeral. The royal estates that had been given to the state in 1941 were transferred back to the shah. In speaking on behalf of the transfer, one royalist deputy argued,"His Royal Highness should own all these lands because our monarchy, being one of the oldest in the world, deserves to live in a style comparable to the wealthiest courts in Europe."[67] Finally, Dr. Manoucher Eqbal, a staunch royalist from a titled landowning family, became minister of interior to prepare the electoral machinery for the forthcoming Sixteenth Majles. As Qavam, Mossadeq, and other opponents complained, the shah had turned the assassination attempt into a royalist coup d'état.

THE SIXTEENTH MAJLES ELECTIONS (JULY 1949-FEBRUARY 1950)

The first part of the Fifteenth Majles had been dominated by the power struggle between Qavam and the shah, and the issue of the Soviet oil concession; the opening of the Sixteenth Majles was to be dominated by the constitutional struggle between Mossadeq and the shah, and the crisis over the Anglo-Iranian Oil Company. The monarch had survived the Machiavellian aristocrat only to find himself threatened by an incorruptible populist determined to establish both a genuine constitutional form of government and national control

---

[66] M. Saʿid, "The Government Program," *Parliamentary Proceedings*, 15th Majles, 28 February 1949.

[67] Gh. Sahab-Devani, *Parliamentary Proceedings*, 15th Majles, 11 July 1949.

over the country's natural resources. The old constitutional conflicts were to be fought again, but in new forms and with different weapons.

As the elections for the Sixteenth Majles and First Senate began, the shah's position appeared impregnable. The constitution had been modified to enhance the head of state. The armed forces remained under the personal direction of the commander in chief. The landed estates had been returned to the court. And the bureaucracy, especially the electoral machinery, was secure in royalist hands. The monarchy appeared to have almost as much power as in the era before August 1941.

These appearances were deceptive, however, for the shah suffered from two serious weaknesses. First, he gradually lost public support during late 1949 and early 1950, partly because he refused to challenge Britain on the oil issue, and partly because his emergence as a political force increasingly reminded the country of his dictatorial father. Second, he depended on America not only for military advisers and hardware, but also for economic aid to begin the much-discussed Seven Year Plan. But America, its fingers still burning from the Koumintang debacle, was not an eager giver. Congress, as the *New York Times* reported, had learned not to "pour money down a rat hole," and, consequently, demanded social reforms and elimination of corruption before considering further aid to Iran.[68] Meanwhile, the State Department felt that the shah ignored the military advisers, hastily changed the constitution, was obsessed with tanks, and unrealistically dreamed of $500 million in economic aid and $200 million in military aid to finance an eventual army of 300,000. The American ambassador even offered to give the shah "gentle harpoon therapy."[69]

These weaknesses became apparent in October 1949 as the shah prepared to visit America in search of aid, and the interior minister began to pack the Sixteenth Majles. A few days before the departure, Mossadeq led a crowd of politicians, university students, and bazaar traders into the palace grounds to protest the lack of free elections. It was a repeat performance of the 1947 protest, except this time the shah was the target. Once inside the gardens, the demonstrators elected a committee of twenty, headed by Mossadeq, to negotiate with Hezhir, the court minister. This committee, which soon became the nucleus

---

[68] The *New York Times*, 14 February 1950.

[69] American Chargé d'Affaires to the State Department, 14 February 1949; Assistant to the Secretary of Defense, "Memorandum on Military Assistance to Iran (1949)"; American Ambassador to the State Department, 18 November 1949, *Foreign Relations of United States* (1949), VI, 57-80, 479-80, 583; American Ambassador to the State Department, 3 September 1948, *Foreign Relations of United States* (Washington, D.C., 1948), V, 176-77.

of Mossadeq's National Front, contained three elements (see Table 6). The first included such prominent anticourt politicians as Amir ʿAlai, the aristocratic lawyer who had served in Qavam's administration; Mahmud Nariman, an independent-minded senior civil servant who had also served under Qavam; and Mushar Aʿzam, an old friend of Mossadeq and a veteran politician whom Reza Shah had forced out of the national arena. The second element contained such bazaar-connected politicians as Sayyid Abul Hussein Haerzadeh, a close ally of Kashani from the 1925 antirepublican campaign; Muzaffar Baqai, a European-educated lawyer whose political base lay in the conservative bazaar of Kerman; and Hussein Makki, a young government employee from a bazaar family in Yazd and the author of a popular proclerical and anti-Pahlevi book entitled *Tarikh-i Bist Saleh-i Iran* (Twenty-Year History of Iran). Makki, as well as Baqai and Haerzadeh, had entered the Fifteenth Majles as Qavam supporters but had soon deserted the Democrat party to organize bazaar protests against the government.

The third and most important element in the committee included a number of young and Western-educated radicals from the predominantly Persian-speaking intelligentsia. Among them were Dr. Karim Sanjabi and Ahmad Zirakzadeh, two leaders of the Iran party; Dr. ʿAli Shayegan, the dean of the law faculty and Qavam's minister of education in 1946; Hussein Fatemi, a French-educated journalist from the Fatemi family in Isfahan, who later became the main martyr of the National Front; and Ahmad Razavi, a French-educated engineer who despite his wealthy background—his father headed the Shaykhi community in Kerman—had supported both the Tudeh and the radical wing of the Democrat party.

The demonstration inside the royal gardens caused so much embarrassment that the court promised to end electoral irregularities. Obtaining the promise, the Committee of Twenty dispersed their followers, retired to Mossadeq's home, and, after lengthy discussions, made the fateful decision to form a broad coalition named the National Front (Jebʿeh-i Melli). In its first public declaration, the National Front put forward three specific demands: honest elections, lifting of martial law, and freedom of the press.[70] As one participant later wrote, the oil issue was not raised at the founding meeting because the leaders at the time were absorbed with the election, not with the Anglo-Iranian Oil Company.[71] The meeting also elected Mossadeq as the Front's chairman and appointed an organizational committee to draft both a

[70] National Front, "Declaration to the Public," *Shahed*, 24 October 1949.
[71] A. Maleki, *Tarikhcheh-i Jebʿeh-i Melli* (A Short History of the National Front) (Tehran, 1954), pp. 1-4.

program and a charter. The program, published a few months later, called for the establishment of social justice and implementation of the constitutional laws; free elections and free expression of political opinion; and the improvement of economic conditions.[72] The charter set up a central council and invited organizations, such as newspaper boards, student unions, professional associations, and political parties, but not individuals, to join the National Front. Mossadeq, both before and after the formation of the front, insisted that Iran was suited more for a loose coalition of organizations with a general goal than for a structured political party with disciplined members and elaborate programs. He also insisted that he wanted to speak not for any one party but for the nation as a whole.[73] In the months ahead, the following four organizations joined the National Front and formed the main structured support behind Mossadeq: the Iran party; the Toilers' party (Hizb-i Zahmatkeshan); the National Party of Iran (Hizb-i Mellat-i Iran); and the Society of Muslim Warriors (Jam'eh-i Mujahedin-i Islam).

The Iran party, although it had swung from a pro-Tudeh to a pro-Mossadeq position during 1947-1949, retained its original leadership, its socialistic ideology, and its professional middle-class base—especially among engineers, the party's founders; among university graduates employed in the government bureaucracy, particularly in the Ministry of Economics and the Department of Registration; among modern-educated women, for whom the party formed a women's organization; and among college students, for whom the party created a youth organization with a weekly paper called *Javanan-i Sosiyalist* (Young Socialists). Party members came exclusively from Muslim backgrounds, since the application forms barred non-Muslims from joining the organization.[74]

The party newspaper, renamed *Jeb'eh-i Azadi* (Freedom Front), called for the strengthening of the constitutional monarchy, establishment of national independence, ouster of the landed aristocracy, and creation of a socialist society. By strengthening of the constitutional monarchy, it meant breaking the ties between the court and the officer corps, revoking the amendments of the Constituent Assembly, and transforming the shah into a ceremonial head of state. In an article on "The Nation Must Rule, the Shah Must Reign," it quoted Montesquieu's *Spirit of the Laws* to argue that concentration of power in kings created a weak society and a corrupt populace. By

[72] National Front, "The Program and Charter of the National Front," *Bakhtar-i Emruz*, 1 July 1950.
[73] A. Ghaffari, "The Life of Dr. Mossadeq," *Khvandaniha*, 11 May 1948.
[74] Iran Party, "Conditions for Joining," *Jeb'eh*, 12 April 1946.

TABLE 6
Founding Members of the National Front

Name	Occupation	Country of Higher Education	Residence	Place & Date of Birth	Class Origin
Mossadeq, Muhammad	landowner	Switzerland & France	Tehran	Tehran, 1879	landed upper class
Fatemi, Hussein	journalist	France	Tehran	Na'in, 1917	landed upper class
Sanjabi, Karim	professor of law	France	Tehran	Kermanshah, 1904	tribal nobility
Zirakzadeh, Ahmad	engineer	Switzerland	Tehran	Isfahan, 1908	urban middle class
Shayegan, 'Ali	professor of law	France	Tehran	Shiraz, 1903	urban middle class
Razavi, Ahmad	engineer	France	Tehran	Kerman, 1906	landed upper class
Amir 'Alai, Shams al-Din	lawyer	France	Tehran	Tehran, 1895	Qajar nobility
Nariman, Mahmud	civil servant	Switzerland	Tehran	Tehran, 1893	urban middle class
A'zam, Mushar	civil servant	Iran	Tehran	Tehran, 1888	urban middle class
Kavyani, Muhammad	lawyer	France	Tehran	Tehran, 1915	urban middle class
Makki, Husssein	civil servant	Iran	Tehran	Yazd, 1912	urban middle class
Baqai, Muzaffar	lawyer	France	Tehran	Kerman, 1912	urban middle class
Haerzadeh, Abul Hussein	cleric	Iran	Tehran	Yazd, 1889	urban middle class
Ghorui, Ayatallah	cleric	Iraq (Najaf)	Tehran	Lahijan, ?	urban middle class
'Amidi-Nouri, Abul Hassan	lawyer	Iran	Tehran	Babul, 1903	urban middle class
Maleki, Ahmad	journalist	Iran	Tehran	Tehran, 1905	urban middle class
Na'ini, Jalali	lawyer	Iran	Tehran	Na'in, 1914	urban middle class
Azad, Abdul Qader	civil servant	none	Tehran	Sabzvar, 1893	urban middle class
Khaleli, 'Abbas	journalist & author	none	Tehran	Tehran, 1895	urban middle class
Khal'atbari, Arsalan	lawyer	France	Tehran	Babul, 1904	landed upper class

NOTE: Members listed in order of prominence within the National Front in subsequent years.

Ethnic Origin	Organizational Affiliation	Previous Politics	Subsequent Politics
Persian	none	opposed Reza Shah	heads the National Front (N.F.)
Persian	editor of Bakhtari-Emruz (Today's West)	supported Tudeh, 1941-1943	Mossadeq's administration
Kurdish	Iran party	Iran party	Mossadeq's administration
Persian	Iran party	Iran party	Mossadeq's administration
Persian	Lawyer's Association	Qavam's Democrat party	Mossadeq's administration
Persian	none	Qavam's Democrat party	Mossadeq's administration
Qajar-Persian	Lawyer's Association	Iran party, 1944-1945	Mossadeq's administration
Persian	none	Iran party, 1944-1945	Mossadeq's administration
Persian	none	opposed Reza Shah	Mossadeq's administration
Persian	Lawyer's Association	none	Mossadeq's administration
Persian	Tehran & Yazd bazaars	Qavam's Democrat party	leaves N.F. in 1952
Persian	Tehran & Kerman bazaars	Qavam's Democrat party	leaves N.F. in 1952
Persian	Tehran & Yazd bazaars	Qavam's Democrat party	leaves N.F. in 1952
Persian	Tehran & Gilan bazaars	none	leaves N.F. in 1952
Persian	editor of Dad (Justice)	Qavam's Democrat party	leaves N.F. in 1951
Persian	editor of Setareh (Star)	Qavam's Democrat party	leaves N.F. in 1951
Persian	editor of Keshvar (Country)	supported Sayyid Ziya, 1941-1945	leaves N.F. in 1950
Persian	editor of Azad (Freedom)	opposed Reza Shah	leaves N.F. in 1950
Persian	editor of Iqdam (Endeavor)	supported Sayyid Ziya, 1941-1945	leaves N.F. in 1950
Persian	none	Iran party, 1944-1945	leaves N.F. in 1950

establishment of national independence, it meant pursuing a strictly neutral course in foreign affairs: opposing imperialism, ending the American military mission, nationalizing both the British-owned oil company and the Soviet-run fishing industry, and waging an ideological struggle against the Tudeh party's "uncritical admiration for foreign communism." By ouster of the aristocracy, it meant using peaceful means, such as land reform, laws against corruption, and penalties against favoritism in the military, in order to erode the power of the "feudal families." And by a socialist society, it meant full equality between all citizens, including women, and social ownership of the main means of production. The party argued that only socialism could carry out rapid industrialization, establish true democracy—"majority rule with guarantees for minority views"—eliminate class war between the "exploiting rich" and the "exploited poor," and, unlike "atheistic international communism," recognize the legitimate rights of religion and national identity.[75]

The Toilers' party was formed by Baqai, the former Democrat, and Khalel Maleki, a Marxist intellectual who had left the Tudeh because of political differences with the party's leadership. The main clauses in the program of the Toilers' party called for the establishment of a genuine constitutional monarchy, elimination of upper-class privileges, encouragement of small industries, national independence from "all forms of imperialism, including Russian imperialism," and "alleviation of class tensions between employers and employees."[76] The party expounded its views through the paper *Shahed* (Witness), and, whenever that was banned, through a substitute named *'Atar* (Grocer). The party's membership, estimated at 5,000, came largely from three sources: Tehran University, where the party's youth paper *Niru-yi Sevum* (The Third Force) and intellectual journal *'Ilm va Zendigi* (Science and Life) enjoyed wide circulation; Kerman, Baqai's home town; and Kermani shopkeepers, especially grocers, in the Tehran bazaar. The first proclamation of the party pledged support not only to Mossadeq, but also to Kashani and Makki—the two favorites of the bazaar.[77] Moreover, the party obtained the support of an important street organizer named Sha'yban "the Brainless." A varzeshkar (athlete) in the red-light district of Tehran, Sha'yban "the Brainless" was feared by his opponents as a racketeering chaqukesh (cut-throat), but

[75] "The Nation Must Rule, the King Must Reign," *Jeb'eh-i Azadi*, 9 March 1953; "Foreign Policy," *Jeb'eh-i Azadi*, 23 February 1953; "Socialism and the Iran Party," *Jeb'eh-i Azadi*, 26 February-8 March 1953.

[76] Toilers' Party, "Our Party Program," *Shahed*, 16 May 1951.

[77] Toilers' Party, *Tashkil-i Hizb-i Zahmatkesh-i Iran* (The Formation of the Toilers' Party of Iran) (Tehran, 1951).

was admired by his supporters as a folk religious hero in the true luti tradition.

Whereas the central organ *Shahed* directed its appeal predominantly to the bazaar, the intellectual paper *Niru-yi Sevum* and journal *'Ilm va Zendigi* advocated neutralism and socialism as well as constitutionalism. In a series of articles on "What is the Third Force?" Khalel Maleki explained: "We are independent of both Western imperialism and the Soviet Union, of both the Tudeh party and the ruling class, of both internal militarism and international communism. We identify with the peoples of Africa, Asia, and Latin America, with the social democratic movements in Europe, and with the rank and file of the Tudeh that is dissatisfied with their pro-Russian and undemocratic leadership. We stand at the left wing of the National Front. The national bourgeoisie stands at its right wing."[78] He also explained that the Toilers' party accepted many of Marx's conclusions on economics, politics, history, and society, but rejected his materialist analyses of religion: "We respect Islam because it is the religion of our people and of our state. Moreover, it is the last of the great religions that have come into existence in order to raise mankind's social consciousness."[79] *'Ilm va Zendigi* concentrated on Western political philosophy, especially democratic socialism. It published articles on the Chartist movement, British Labour party, French socialist organizations, Second International, Yugoslav "Worker's Control," and the importance of Marx's *Communist Manifesto*. It also translated extracts from Mendès France's *Modern Socialism*, Richard Wright's *I Was a Communist*, André Gide's *God That Failed*, Bertrand Russell's *Bolshevism*, and Howard Fast's account of his disillusionment with communism. The Toilers' party was thus a strange combination of small shopkeepers from the traditional bazaar and socialist intellectuals from Tehran University. In later years this contradiction split the party.

The National party was founded by a young law student, Dariush Foruhar, who continued to play a role in the National Front until the Islamic Revolution of 1977-1979. The son of an army officer, Foruhar was born in 1929 in Isfahan but raised in Urmiah and Tehran. He began his political activities in 1943, soon after his father was arrested by the British on suspicion of having German contacts. An early admirer of Mossadeq, Dariush Foruhar had organized high-school demonstrations in support of Mossadeq as early as 1944, and had been detained during the 1949 mass arrests because of his activities in Tehran University. While in the university, he, together with a fellow

---

[78] Kh. Maleki, "What Is the Third Force?" *Niru-yi Sevum*, 22 August-29 September 1952.

[79] Kh. Maleki, "Religion and Communism," *Niru-yi Sevum*, 23 October 1952.

student named Mohsen Pezeshkpour, had formed an ultranational-istic organization called the Pan-Iranist party (Hizb-i Pan-Iranist-i Iran). But doubting his colleague's admiration for Mossadeq, Foruhar soon left the Pan-Iranist party and founded his own National party. Tracing its origins to Lieutenant Jahansouz, who had been executed in 1937 for organizing a "fascist conspiracy" against Reza Shah, the National party was vehemently anticourt, anticommunist, anticapitalist, anti-Semitic, and even anticlerical. It proposed to rebuild Iran by regaining the "lost territories" of Bahrein, Afghanistan, and the Caucasus. It claimed that the "pure Iranian race" was threatened not only by Soviet communism and British capitalism, but also by Arab and Turkish expansionism. Moreover, it argued that Iran's backwardness was due to the "reactionary mullas," "exploiting landlords," foreign powers, and religious minorities, especially the Jews and the Baha'is. Having only a few hundred members, most of them high-school students in Tehran, the National party did not carry much weight in the leadership of the National Front.

The Society of Muslim Warriors was led by Ayatallah Kashani, his family, three wealthy bazaar merchants, and a preacher named Shams al-Din Qonatabadi. A loosely structured group, the society drew its support mainly from the bazaar, especially from guild elders, seminary students, and small shopkeepers. Although highly religious, it was not dogmatically fundamentalist. The main purpose of the society was to strengthen Kashani's political position, and its barrage of public proclamations appealed to the bazaar by name, and called for the implementation of the shari'a, repeal of Reza Shah's secular laws, reimposition of the veil, protection of national industries, and Muslim unity against the West.

Closely associated with Kashani but not formally a member of the National Front was a small terrorist organization known as the Feda'iyan-i Islam (Devotees of Islam). It had been formed in 1946 by a twenty-two-year-old theology student in Tehran who had adopted the name Sayyid Navab Safavi to identify with the founders of the Shi'i state in Iran. Established to fight "all forms of irreligion," the Feda'iyan's first act was to assassinate Kasravi, the famous secular essayist and iconoclastic historian.[80] The assassins were acquitted by a military court partly because religious leaders lobbied on their behalf and partly because the authorities hoped to use them against the Tudeh.[81] But instead of cooperating with the authorities, the Feda'iyan

[80] "How Kasravi, Hezhir, and Razmara Were Murdered," *Khvandaniha*, 23 September-1 November 1955.

[81] Special Correspondent, "Revival of Iran's Fedayan Islam," *Jerusalem Post*, 18 March 1965.

worked with Kashani, helping him organize bazaar strikes against Qavam, public meetings in support of Palestinian Arabs, and the violent demonstration of 1948 against Premier Hezhir. By 1949 outsiders often mistook Kashani to be the leader of the Feda'iyan.

The Feda'iyan and Kashani's group, however, differed both in social composition and in ideological commitment. Whereas the latter attracted considerable support from the upper echelons of the traditional middle class throughout the country, the former drew its limited membership predominantly from the youth employed in the lower echelons of the Tehran bazaar.[82] Moreover, whereas Kashani was politically pragmatic, the Feda'iyan was dogmatically committed to fundamentalist Islam. Its program went beyond generalities on the virtues of the shari'a and spelled out such specific demands as prohibition of alcohol, tobacco, opium, films, and gambling; cutting off the hands of criminals and execution of incorrigible offenders; a ban on all foreign clothes; penalties for giving or accepting bribes; punishments for members of the 'ulama who abused their religious positions; elimination of non-Muslim subjects, such as music, from the school curriculum; and the veiling of women so that "they would return to their traditional and virtuous role within the home."[83]

The National Front, therefore, represented two divergent forces: the traditional middle class—the bazaar—formed of small merchants, clerics, and guild elders; and the modern middle class—the intelligentsia—composed of professionals, salaried personnel, and secular-educated intellectuals. The former, inspired by maktab teachers and mosque preachers, esteemed Islam as a way of life, the shari'a as the principal component of legitimate law, and the 'ulama as the true guardians of the Shi'i community. The latter, graduates of secular state schools, considered religion to be a private matter, the Napoleonic Code to be the suitable basis of civil law, and the Western-educated intelligentsia to be the best qualified organizers and modernizers of society. The former, tied to the bazaar trades, depended on business profits, favored free enterprise, and opposed state inter-

---

[82] For example, among eight Feda'iyan brought to trial in 1955 for murders committed in 1950, the average age of the leaders was only twenty-six. The group consisted of three theology students, two shopkeeper's assistants, one carpenter, one tailor, and one shirt maker. (See *Ittila'at*, 26 December 1955-16 January 1956.) Similarly, among twenty-nine Feda'iyan militants imprisoned in 1952, the average age was twenty-five. Of the fourteen in the group who were employed, four were peddlers, two were shirt makers, one was a preacher, one a student, one a bicycle repairer, one a weaver, one a builder, one an engraver, one a carpenter, and one a clothes cleaner. See *Ittila'at*, 17 July 1952.

[83] Feda'iyan-i Islam, *E'lamieh-i Feda'iyan-i Islam* (The Proclamation of the Feda'iyan-i Islam) (Tehran, 1950), pp. 1-96.

vention in the market economy. The latter, living on salaried incomes, distrusted business speculation, feared inflation—which had been rampant since 1937—and extolled the state as the vanguard of rapid modernization. The two differed even in their tastes for food, entertainment, clothes, and language. The traditional middle class frequented bazaar teahouses, rarely wore Western ties, and coloquially used Arabic terms learned from the scriptures, whereas the modern middle class ate in European-styled restaurants, dressed meticulously in Western clothes, and sprinkled their Persian with French expressions picked up from secular education and avant-garde publications. In short, one was conservative, religious, theocratic, and mercantile; the other was modernistic, secular, technocratic, and socialistic.

These divergent forces came together within the National Front because of three common bonds: the joint struggle against the court-military complex; the struggle against the British-owned oil company; and the political principles and charismatic personality of Mossadeq. As a former finance minister and governor-general who refused to favor family friends and line his own pocket, Mossadeq was famous for his incorruptibility—a scarce quality in an environment notorious for government corruption. As an outspoken parliamentarian who opposed the coup d'état of 1921, the military dictatorship of Reza Shah, and the persisting influence of the royal family, he embodied the high principles and the unfulfilled aspirations of the Constitutional Revolution. As a veteran statesman who consistently opposed foreign concessions, he enjoyed the reputation of a true patriot free of all outside connections. And as a rare aristocrat who lived in his own village, treated his peasants well, disdained conspicuous consumption, worked briefly in commerce, denounced the Fourteenth Majles as "a den of thieves," and criticized consumer and guild taxes, he came from the upper class but spoke with and for the middle classes.

Having put together the coalition, the National Front vigorously entered the Majles elections. It sponsored candidates in the main cities, especially Tehran, Isfahan, Yazd, Shiraz, Kashan, and Kerman. It denounced the Constituent Assembly as illegitimate, and hammered away at the need for honest elections. It helped the guilds organize strikes against the government's proposal to increase taxes on tradesmen and craftsmen. It also helped bakers mobilize protest meetings against the government's inefficiency in delivering wheat. It held a series of public meetings in the university and the bazaars, culminating in a rally of 12,000 outside the Majles. And it accused the court of persisting in its schemes to rig the results. The campaign reached a climax when a member of the Feda'iyan-i Islam—the same man who had murdered Kasravi in 1946—now assassinated Hezhir. Premier Sa'id promptly stopped the elections and ordered the Tehran voting to begin anew. In the ensuing elections, Mossadeq, Haerzadeh, Makki, Nariman, and Shayegan won in Tehran, Azad in Sabzevar, Baqai in Kerman, and Saleh in Kashan.[84] A delegation of only eight seemed insignificant in an assembly of over one hundred thirty deputies. But, as the forthcoming months proved, the eight, supported by the middle classes, could shake not only Parliament but also the shah and the whole country. In the words of Richard Cottam, the author of *Nationalism in Iran*, the shah "may well regard his decision to permit free elections in Tehran as the greatest mistake of his career."[85]

THE SIXTEENTH MAJLES (FEBRUARY 1950– MAY 1951)

Socially, the Sixteenth Majles was no different from the previous ones, in that it was chiefly composed of members of the upper class. Of the 131 deputies, 85 percent were landlords, wealthy merchants, or senior civil servants.[86] Politically it was divided into four groups: the small delegation from the National Front; a pro-British fraksiun of southern conservative magnates; some forty independent notables, such as Abul Qasem Amini, Khosrow Qashqayi, and Naser Zolfaqari; and a large majority of royalist deputies. This majority, moreover, could rely on the Senate, which had been packed with veteran royalists such as Esfandiari and Matin-Daftari, and prominent politicians who, despite earlier differences with the shah, now supported him, such as Taqizadeh, Hakimi, Malekzadeh, Farrukh, and 'Abbas Mas'oudi.

When the new session began in February 1950, the royalist majority deposed Sa'id, whose cabinet had included three pro-British ministers, and gave the premiership to 'Ali Mansur (Mansur al-Malek), who had been a prime minister under Reza Shah and had served as governor-general of Azerbaijan after the reoccupation of Tabriz. As expected, Mansur stacked his administration with staunch royalists. For the first time since 1941, the court had managed to exclude all other groups from the government.

Undaunted, the National Front continued to press the court, and declared that "although its delegation was small its voice would be

[84] Saleh, who had been minister of justice in Qavam's coalition cabinet in 1946, had joined the National Front soon after the incident in the royal gardens.

[85] R. Cottam, *Nationalism in Iran* (Pittsburgh, 1964), p. 261.

[86] Z. Shaji'i, *Nemayandegan-i Majles-i Shawra-yi Melli* (Members of the National Consultative Assembly) (Tehran, 1965), p. 176.

clear and loud since it represented the whole nation."[87] Mossadeq
charged that the new administration was proof that royal power had
grown excessively. He argued that since the country was not threatened by any foreign power the military budget should be cut sharply.[88]
And in another onslaught, he summed up the basic themes underlying
his political philosophy:

The Constituent Assembly was fake and illegitimate. Fake because it did not
represent the people. Illegitimate because it altered the constitutional laws.
In saying this I do not claim that the constitution is sacred and beyond any
improvements. But I do claim that changes can be made only by the true
representatives of the people. . . . I would like to take this opportunity to
reveal to the public the advice I gave the young shah in August 1941, when
I was freed from political confinement. I advised him not to identify too
closely with his father, since his father had made many enemies. I also advised
him to follow the example of the British monarchy. The king of England is
highly respected because he stands outside politics and avoids the dirty business of appointing and dismissing ministers, deputies, and governors. Moreover, Britain owes its greatness to its political system which nourishes capable
statesmen as well as patriotic, self-sacrificing, and conscientious citizens. A
country that lacks capable statesmen and patriotic citizens lacks everything.
This is my main reason for opposing personal dictatorships. The country
belongs to the people and the people have the inalienable right to choose
their representatives. If they do not exercise that right, a small minority can
gain control and work not for the interests of the majority but for its own
selfish profit. The shah must stand above politics but remain in touch with
the needs and feeling of the people. If the people wish to change the constitution, they have the right to do so—after all, the constitution belongs to
them. But the recent changes in the constitution are illegitimate since they
contradict the true wishes of the people.[89]

Meanwhile, Azad denounced the government for censoring the organ
of the Tehran guilds. Saleh spoke on behalf of government employees
striking for higher salaries. Haerzadeh argued that "the failure to
implement true justice, social equality, and Islamic laws instigated one
class against another—workers against industrialists, peasants against
landlords, intellectuals against religious leaders." He also argued that
the government created additional difficulties by bureaucratic interference in all aspects of the economy, especially in the bazaar.[90] Makki
proposed a parliamentary committee to investigate Mas'oud's assassination; accused the police of meddling in guild elections; blamed

[87] Baqai, *Parliamentary Proceedings*, 16th Majles, 2 July 1950.
[88] Mossadeq, *Parliamentary Proceedings*, 16th Majles, 20 June 1950.
[89] Ibid., 23 May 1950.
[90] Haerzadeh, *Parliamentary Proceedings*, 16th Majles, 31 August 1951 and 25 September 1950.

the rich for "encouraging communism" by wasting money on European tours; recommended import restrictions on cheap textiles; and complained that the government whipped small traders who infringed price controls but left alone big businessmen who speculated with millions.[91] And Kashani sent a message to the Majles protesting his continued banishment in Beirut, and warning that "a nation that has willingly spilled its own blood to obtain the constitution will never again fall victim to dictators and despots."[92]

The National Front, however, shifted from domestic to external affairs in June 1950, after the government, following years of secret discussions with the Anglo-Iranian Oil Company, finally submitted to the Majles proposals for revising the 1933 Agreement. Denouncing the proposals as a sell-out, the National Front—echoed by the now semiclandestine Tudeh—demanded nationalization of the oil company. It accused the company of paying inadequate royalties, by-passing local taxes, refusing to train Iranian personnel, using the threat of force to obtain the 1933 Agreement, interfering in national politics, and thereby depriving the country of its full sovereignty. Shaken by the outpouring of public support for nationalization, Mansur hesitated to submit the proposals to a vote, and, after a pro-British politician was assassinated, instead submitted his own resignation.

Anxious to settle the oil issue, the shah nominated Razmara, the Chief of General Staff, to be the new prime minister. Although little love was lost between the two men, the choice was in many ways astute. An ambitious no-nonsense general, Razmara was willing to push the oil proposals through parliament even at the risk of his own life. A high-handed but independent-minded officer, he was expected to deflect public hostility from the court to himself and his cabinet. A former critic of the court, he had drawn closer to the shah in recent years as they had cooperated to protect the military from Qavam and obtain modern equipment from America. A self-made man married to the sister of a prominent left-wing author, he was prepared to criticize the rich openly, woo the radical intellectuals, and thus widen the gap between the Tudeh and the National Front. And an advocate of social and administrative reforms, it was hoped that he could gain the confidence of the United States, and thereby obtain the economic aid needed for the Seven Year Plan. As the *New York Times* reported,

[91] Makki, *Parliamentary Proceedings*, 16th Majles, 20 June 1950 and 27 September 1951.
[92] Kashani, "Letter to the Majles," *Parliamentary Proceedings*, 16th Majles, 18 June 1950.

Razmara was the only man capable of saving Iran from political instability and financial bankruptcy.[93]

Razmara acted much as expected. He brought twelve new faces into the cabinet, recommended tax increases for the rich, and set up a special committee to investigate corruption in high places. He personally sponsored the proposals for the new oil agreement. He also introduced two major reform bills: one for distributing state lands among the peasantry; and the other to establish the provincial assemblies promised by the constitutional laws. To further woo the left, he refused to send troops to the Korean War, signed a trade treaty with the Soviet Union, and slightly eased the restrictions on the Tudeh party. When ten Tudeh leaders escaped from prison, it was generally rumored that Razmara had intentionally helped by appointing a leftist officer as their jailor.[94]

These schemes, however, proved to be too clever. The improvement of relations with Moscow cooled the friendship with Washington, and consequently jeopardized the search for economic assistance. The recommendations for reform and the reemergence of the Tudeh frightened the conservative deputies. As one deputy claimed, "talk of land distribution incites class hatred against our noble one thousand families—the families that are the main bulwarks of Iran and the recognized protectors of Islam." Another protested that "a small group of foreign-trained agitators were creating widespread distrust of landowners—a class that was always willing to sacrifice its own interests for the common good." Yet another proclaimed that discussions of land reform not only enflamed class rivalries but also raised "irrelevant issues:"

Proposals for land reform may have been suitable for medieval Europe, but are in no ways applicable to Islamic Iran. For Iran, unlike Europe, never experienced feudalism. Our peasants remained free men sharing in the process of production. And our landlords acted as responsible and peaceful citizens, treating the peasants as their own children. Consequently, the relationship between landlords and peasants has been one of love and respect. Those who today clamor for land reform plan tomorrow to bring in the dictatorship of the proletariat. The undermining of any law, especially the sanctity of private property, will endanger the whole of our fundamental laws. . . . Our enemies, as well as our friends, acknowledge that in Iran landlords and peasants have always been on good terms. The vast majority of landowners have respected Islam, spent the bare minimum on themselves, and given generously to their villagers. At the root of present discontent lies

[93] *New York Times*, 28 June 1950.
[94] "The Support Sought by Razmara," *Ittila'at-i Haftegi*, 27 February-3 April 1952; *Shahed*, 26 December 1950.

not the system of land ownership, but the heavy consumer taxes levied by the central government. If the government is serious about relaxing class tensions, it should lower these taxes and increase the agricultural budget.[95]

The bill for provincial assemblies was equally controversial. Baqai charged that "decentralization was a British plot to dismantle Iran." Shayegan argued that Qavam had accepted provincial assemblies only because he wanted to "save" Azerbaijan. (A royalist deputy protested that Azerbaijan had been saved by the shah, not by that "traitor" Qavam.) Makki warned that administrative decentralization was unwise in a country with so much linguistic diversity: "There is always the danger that one of the regional organizations will declare its independence from the center." Kashani sent a telegram to the Majles proclaiming that "no true Muslim would want to dismantle the thousand-year-old state." And Mossadeq stressed that provincial assemblies may have been useful during the Constitutional Revolution but were highly dangerous in the context of the Cold War: "Those who favor regional organization should keep in mind our recent experience in Azerbaijan and the present war in Korea."[96] It is not surprising that in the months ahead the National Front drew smaller crowds in Azerbaijan than in the rest of Iran.[97]

The oil proposals, however, proved to be the most controversial of Razmara's policies. The National Front declared that Razmara wanted to establish a military dictatorship to ram the proposals down the nation's throat. Makki argued that internal reforms should wait until the external issue was resolved: "The question of whether we should have land reform is insignificant compared to the danger posed by the British oil company." Saleh submitted a resolution from the faculty of Tehran University calling for "the assertion of national sovereignty over the oil industry." Mossadeq, addressing a rally of 12,000 in Tehran, criticized the government for not demanding more of Britain, and emphasized that the "conflict would not be resolved until the entire oil industry was nationalized." Kashani encouraged all "sincere Muslims and patriotic citizens to fight against the enemies of Islam

[95] For debates on the bill to distribute state lands, see *Parliamentary Proceedings*, 16th Majles, 6 March 1950, 22 June 1950, 20 March 1951. Quotes are from M. Shustari, ibid., 6 March 1950; A. Nazerzadeh-Kermani, ibid., 9 April 1950; B. Kahbod, ibid., 20 March 1951.

[96] For debates on the bill for provincial assemblies, see *Parliamentary Proceedings*, 16th Majles, 6 July-10 August 1950. Quotes are from Baqai, ibid., 6 July 1950; Shayegan, ibid., 12 July 1950; Makki, ibid., 30 July 1950; Kashani, ibid., 30 July 1950; Mossadeq, ibid., 10 August 1950.

[97] ʿA. Mujtahedi, *Parliamentary Proceedings*, 16th Majles, 11 June 1951.

and Iran by joining the nationalization struggle."[98] Finally, the Feda'iyan-i Islam assigned one of its members, a twenty-six-year-old carpenter, the "sacred mission" of assassinating that "British stooge" Razmara. The mission was successfully carried out in early March 1951 in Tehran's central mosque.[99]

The public rejoicing following Razmara's death scared the deputies into reasserting their parliamentary rights. Rejecting the shah's choice for successor, they reiterated the constitutional laws, and, after three weeks of closed meetings, voted for Hussein 'Ala. Two factors explain the choice of 'Ala: a titled aristocrat and court minister, he was trusted by the conservative landowners; a former diplomat with the reputation of being anti-British, he was acceptable to the National Front. Selecting his ministers with the advice of Mossadeq, 'Ala brought Amir 'Alai of the National Front into the cabinet and permitted Kashani to return to Tehran. 'Ala, moreover, refused to act when a nationalization bill introduced by Mossadeq obtained a majority first in a special parliamentary committee, then in the Majles, and finally on March 20 in the Senate. A small parliamentary minority, supported enthusiastically by the general public, had frightened the royalist and pro-British deputies into voting against their better judgment.

These fears turned into panic in early April when the Tudeh revealed its true strength. Protesting bad housing and low wages in the oil industry, the party led a general strike in Khuzistan and mobilized mass meetings against the government's procrastination in implementing the nationalization law. When the police in Abadan fired on demonstrators, killing six, and the British sent gunboats to the Gulf to "protect British lives and property," the Tudeh intensified its campaign by organizing sympathy strikes and street demonstrations in Tehran, Isfahan, and the northern cities. 'Ala declared martial law on the grounds that strikes and demonstrations, by fomenting class differences, helped the external enemy. Shafaq, now a senator, argued that class tensions had reached such a dangerous point that they threatened to break the whole fabric of society: "Foreign propaganda aims at instigating class warfare and thereby pushing the country into anarchy. Unfortunately, sweet-sounding slogans have deceived many of our citizens from the uninformed and illiterate classes. The only

---

[98] National Front, "A Proclamation to the Nation," *Parliamentary Proceedings*, 16th Majles, 27 June 1950; Makki, ibid., 26 March 1951; Saleh, ibid., 18 February 1951; Mossadeq, "Speech to the Nation," *Shahed*, 30 December 1950; Kashani, "Proclamation," *Shahed*, 21 December 1950.

[99] After the 1953 coup, the government made an unsuccessful attempt to link the assassin with Mossadeq, Kashani, Makki, Baqai, Shayegan, Nariman, and other National Front leaders. See *Ittila'at*, 26 December 1955-11 February 1956.

way to save Iran is to unite all the classes against the foreign enemy."
The shah, speaking over national radio, proclaimed class antagonisms
to be Iran's greatest misfortune: "These antagonisms poison our social
attitudes and political life. The best way to alleviate them is to apply
the laws of Islam. If we live as true Muslims class conflict will give
way to class harmony and national unity." And Jamal Emami, a veteran deputy, speaking on behalf of the majority in the Majles, offered
the premiership to Mossadeq so that he could implement the nationalization law: "Dr. Mossadeq has our confidence because he—unlike
many other politicians—comes from one of the oldest and most distinguished families of Iran." To many observers' surprise, Mossadeq
accepted the offer. *The Times* assessed the situation in these words:
"The inner tension of Persian society—caused by the stupidity, greed,
and lack of judgement by the ruling class—has now become such that
it can be met only by an acceleration of the drive against the external
scapegoat—Britain."[100]

PREMIER MOSSADEQ (MAY 1951-AUGUST 1953)

The election of Mossadeq in May 1951 shifted the focus of attention
away from the Majles to the prime minister and the streets, which
remained the main source of strength for the National Front. As the
royalist *Ittila'at* complained, Mossadeq constantly resorted to street
demonstrations to pressure the opposition and thereby "bring parliament under his influence."[101] Similarly, Jamal Emami protested from
the Majles floor:

Statecraft has degenerated into street politics. It appears that this country has
nothing better to do than hold street meetings. We now have meetings here,
there, and everywhere. Meetings for this, that, and every occasion. Meetings
for university students, high-school students, seven-year-olds, even six-year-
olds. I am sick and tired of street meetings.[102]

Is our premier a statesman or a mob leader? What type of premier says "I
will speak to the people" every time he is faced with a political question? I
always considered this man to be unsuitable for high office. But I never
imagined, even in my worst nightmares, that an old man of seventy would

---

[100] *The Times*, 14 April 1951; 'Ala, *Parliamentary Proceedings*, 16th Majles, 12 April
1951; Shafaq, *Parliamentary Proceedings*, 1st Senate, 13 April 1951; the Shah, "Message
to the Nation," *Tehran Mosavar*, 10 May 1951; J. Emami, *Parliamentary Proceedings*, 16th
Majles, 11 May 1951; Special Correspondent, "Internal Issues behind the Persian Oil
Demands," *The Times*, 22 March 1951.

[101] *Ittila'at-i Haftegi*, 20 June 1951.

[102] J. Emami, *Parliamentary Proceedings*, 16th Majles, 3 November 1951.

turn into a rabble rouser. A man who constantly surrounds the Majles with thugs is nothing less than a public menace.[103]

Although Mossadeq frequently appealed to the public, the composition of his first administration was noticeably conservative. He gave eight posts, including the important Ministries of Interior and Foreign Affairs, to senior civil servants sympathetic to the National Front, but left four others, including the War Ministry, in the hands of court favorites. This promptly antagonized the Fida'iyan-i Islam, who denounced the government for ignoring the shari'a and refusing to release Razmara's assassin, and who tried to kill Hussein Fatemi, the premier's special assistant. Kashani, on the other hand, told the Fida'iyan leaders that the "oil issue" should take priority over all other issues, and announced to the public that he would fully support Mossadeq as long as the National Front continued to wage "the sacred and national struggle against the British."[104]

As expected, Mossadeq addressed the oil issue first. A few days after taking office, he persuaded the Majles to elect four National Front deputies to a committee of five who were assigned the task of helping the government implement the nationalization law. In June, he sent the committee to Khuzistan to take over the oil installations. In July, he broke off negotiations with the oil company when the latter threatened to pull out its employees, warned tanker owners that receipts from the Iranian government would not be accepted on the world market, and revealed that the government would accept the principle of nationalization even if the principle were not actually implemented. In September, the company evacuated its technicians and closed down the oil installations, while the British government reinforced its naval force in the Gulf and lodged complaints against Iran before the United Nations Security Council. In October, Mossadeq went to New York to present the Iranian case before the Security Council, unsuccessfully sought financial assistance from the World Bank, and, accusing Britain of interfering in internal politics, closed down all British consulates. Thus by the end of 1951, Mossadeq was embroiled in a major diplomatic upheaval.

Preparations for the Seventeenth Majles, however, forced Mossadeq to turn his attention to internal politics. Eager to weaken the royalists and the pro-British conservatives, Mossadeq introduced a modified version of his 1944 bill for electoral reform. The new version no longer disqualified illiterates, but placed literates and illiterates in different

---

[103] Quoted by Fateh, *Panjah Saleh-i Naft-i Iran*, p. 580.

[104] "How Kasravi, Hezhir, and Razmara Were Murdered," *Khvandaniha*, 23 September-1 November 1955; Kashani, "Message to the Nation," *Bakhtar-i Emruz*, 7 July 1951.

constituencies, and considerably increased the representation of the urban population, especially of Tehran. The opposition rallied to defeat the bill, arguing that it would "unjustly discriminate patriots who had been voting for the last forty years."[105] Unable to pass the bill, the National Front entered the elections competing not only against the royalists and the military but also against the conservative land-owners and the tribal chiefs. In major cities, the National Front won many of the seats. In Tehran, where the turnout was double that of previous elections, the National Front took all twelve seats. But in most provincial constituencies, especially rural districts, the opposition gained the upper hand. For example, Taheri, the prominent pro-British politician, won in Yazd; Malek Madani, his colleague, in Mal-ayer; Naser and Muhammad Zolfaqari in their home town, Zanjan; and the royalist imam jom'eh of Tehran in Aher in northern Azer-baijan. Realizing that the opposition would take the vast majority of the provincial seats, Mossadeq stopped the voting as soon as seventy-nine deputies—just enough to form a parliamentary quorum—had been elected.

The Seventeenth Majles convened in February 1952. Of the seventy-nine deputies, thirty either belonged to or closely identified with the National Front. They included Sanjabi and Zirakzadeh of the Iran party; Baqai of the Toilers' party; Kashani and Qonatabadi from the Society of Muslim Warriors; nonparty supporters of Mossadeq, such as Shayegan, Razavi, Nariman, Makki, and Haerzadeh; and Khosrow and Naser Qashqayi, who joined the caucus after their elections from Fars. Many of the thirty were members of the modern and the traditional middle classes. The group included four lawyers, four engineers, three journalists, three university professors, one historian, and ten members of the 'ulama. The other forty-nine deputies, many of them landowners, divided into a royalist and a pro-British fraksiun.

Not daring to confront public opinion directly, the royalists and pro-British conservatives tried to weaken the government with side skirmishes. They elected the imam jom'eh of Tehran to be the president of the Majles. They refused to grant Mossadeq special powers to deal with the economic crisis caused by the rapidly dwindling oil revenues. And they began to voice regional grievances against the capital. Malek Madani, echoing a slogan coined by the Tudeh in the early 1940s, declared, "Iran is not just Tehran; the provinces are also a part of Iran." A deputy from Gilan alleged that the Caspian fisheries hired Armenians, Assyrians, Azeris, and Tehranis, but few Gilanis. A representative from Baluchistan claimed that "the provinces had

[105] A. Nabu'i, *Parliamentary Proceedings*, 16th Majles, 9 June 1951.

decayed because the bureaucracy was interested solely in Tehran."[106] A royalist estimated that the city of Tehran had 29 hospitals, 280 pharmacies, 468 doctors, and 87 dentists, whereas all the provinces together had no more than 79 hospitals, 386 pharmacies, 452 doctors, and 28 dentists. Another royalist accused the government of neglecting its national duty of building schools in the countryside: "Although Iran is formed of one nation, it contains many local dialects. Consequently, someone from Semnan cannot easily understand someone from Mazandaran, Luristan, Azerbaijan, or Baluchistan. The government should use schools, radios, and literacy courses to spread Persian throughout Iran."[107]

The National Front retaliated with a propaganda war against the landed upper class. Nariman argued that "the people must take power away from the privileged into their own hands to achieve social progress and full national independence." Zirakzadeh claimed that "the higher echelons of the administration were infested with corrupt bureaucrats but the lower ranks were staffed with honest and hardworking civil servants." Sayyid Javed Khalkhali, one of Kashani's colleagues, declared: "Although there has been much talk of social reform ever since the Constitutional Revolution, little has been accomplished. At last, the people have found a true spokesman, Dr. Mossadeq, who is capable of implementing reforms, eliminating corruption, and narrowing the wide gap between the rich and the poor."[108] And ʿAli Mudarres, a protégé of Shayegan, warned that class conflicts endangered the nation:

The fundamental cause of our country's misery is the existence of two distinct classes. One is a social burden, living in lust, corruption, and waste. The other has been ground down by hunger, oppression, and exploitation. If we do not remedy this dismal situation, history will inevitably catch up with us and destroy our country. History teaches us that oppression, exploitation, and injustice destroys states, nations, and empires.[109]

After five months of parliamentary skirmishes, on July 16, 1952, Mossadeq escalated the conflict into a major national upheaval by suddenly exercising the premier's constitutional right to nominate the war minister. When the shah refused to accept his nomination, Mossadeq resigned and appealed over the heads of the deputies directly to the public:

[106] Malek Madani, *Parliamentary Proceedings*, 17th Majles, 22 February 1953; M. Rigi, ibid., 10 January 1952; A. Damavandi, ibid., 30 December 1952.

[107] H. Vakilpour, ibid., 19 February 1953; A. Faramarzi, ibid., 21 December 1952.

[108] Nariman, ibid., 20 August 1952; Zirakzadeh, ibid., 29 July 1952; J. Khalkhali, ibid., 4 January 1953.

[109] ʿA. Mudarres, *Parliamentary Proceedings*, 17th Majles, 26 November 1952.

In the course of recent events, I have come to the realization that I need a trustworthy war minister to continue my national mission. Since His Majesty has refused my request, I will resign and permit someone who enjoys royal confidence to form a new government and implement His Majesty's policies. In the present situation, the struggle started by the Iranian people cannot be brought to a victorious conclusion.[110]

For the first time, a prime minister had publicly criticized the shah for violating the constitution, accused the court of standing in the way of the national struggle and had dared to take the constitutional issue directly to the country.

The appeal received an enthusiastic response. The royalist and pro-British deputies elected Qavam as premier in the vain hope that he would attract his former supporters away from Mossadeq, while the National Front—supported by the Tudeh—called for protest strikes and mass demonstrations in favor of Mossadeq. Using even stronger language than before, Kashani denounced Qavam as "the enemy of religion, freedom, and national independence."[111] The shah at first tried to deal with the crisis by calling in the military; but after five days of mass demonstrations, bloodshed, and signs of dissension in the army, he gave up and asked Mossadeq to form a new government. Mossadeq had won hands down. The victory went into Iranian history as Siyeh-i Tir (July 21st).

During the July upheaval major strikes broke out in all the main towns, and over 250 demonstrators died or suffered serious injuries in Tehran, Hamadan, Ahwaz, Isfahan, and Kermanshah. The most violent confrontations took place in Tehran.[112] The crisis in the capital began on July 16, as soon as the news of Mossadeq's resignation reached the bazaar. Closing down their stores and workshops, the guild elders gathered in the central square of the bazaar and encouraged the public to demonstrate next day outside the Majles. The following morning as a large crowd proceeded from the bazaar to the Majles; government employees, railway workers, and bus drivers stopped work; and the National Front called upon the whole country to strike on July 21. A few hours later, the Tudeh also called for a general strike and mass rallies on July 21. The assigned day began with ominous quiet, while the whole city—even the wealthy northern

[110] Mossadeq, "Public Letter of Resignation," *Ittila'at*, 17 July 1952.

[111] Kashani, "Proclamation to the Nation," *Shahed*, 19 July 1952.

[112] For detailed description of the July uprising, see H. Arsanjani, *Yaddashtha-yi Siyasi* (Political Memoirs) (Tehran, 1956), pp. 1-80; "Siyeh-i Tir," *Salnameh-i Donya*, 9 (1953), 176-81; 'A. Shayegan, "The Uprising of *Siyeh-i Tir*," *Yaghma*, 5 (September 1952), 303-10; Qodsi, *Kitab-i Khatirat-i Man*, II, 733-36; *Ittila'at*, 17-24 July 1952; *Bakhtar-i Emruz*, 17-24 July 1952.

district—stood still. The storm broke as demonstrators proceeding to the Majles were intercepted by army tanks. For the next five hours, the city was in turmoil. One of the shah's brothers was nearly killed after his chauffeur took a wrong turn into an angry crowd. A deputy sympathetic to Mossadeq was pelted with stones when he tried to assure the shaken protestors that the issue could be solved peacefully. And six hundred detainees from the demonstrations of the previous four days broke out of jail when the city police took off their uniforms and went into hiding. After five hours of shooting, the military commanders, fearful of overstraining the loyalty of their troops, ordered them back to barracks, leaving the city in the hands of the protestors. A parliamentary committee appointed to investigate Siyeh-i Tir showed that the bloodiest confrontations had occurred in four separate places: in the bazaar, especially in the drapers', grocers', and metal workers' markets, where demonstrators shouting "Imam Hussein" clashed with the army; in the working-class districts on the eastern side of the city, particularly near the railway workshops and the industrial plants; en route from the university to the Majles; and in Parliament Square, the traditional rallying point for demonstrators. Of the twenty-nine killed in Tehran, the occupations of nineteen were later published. They included four workers, three car drivers, two craftsmen, two shoopkeepers' assistants, one peddler, one tailor, one student, and one barber.[113]

Mossadeq followed up his victory with a rapid succession of blows struck not only at the shah and the military but also at the landed aristocracy and the two Houses of Parliament. He excluded royalists from the cabinet and named himself acting minister of war. He declared Siyeh-i Tir to be a national uprising (*qiyam-i melli*) and the casualties to be national martyrs. He transferred Reza Shah's lands back to the state; cut the palace budget, and allocated the savings to the Health Ministry; placed the royal charities under government supervision; appointed Abul Qassem Amini to be minister of court; forbade the shah to communicate directly with foreign diplomats; forced Princess Ashraf, the politically active twin sister of the shah, to leave the country; and refused to act against Tudeh papers that denounced the court as "the center of corruption, treason, and espionage."[114] Indeed, he himself eventually accused the court of continuing to meddle in politics, and secured a special parliamentary committee to investigate the constitutional issues between the cabinet and the shah. The committee reported that the constitutional laws

[113] *Tehran Mosavar*, 15 July 1953.
[114] *Besu-yi Ayandeh*, 2 March 1953.

placed the armed services under the jurisdiction of the government and not of the shah. By May 1953, the shah had been stripped of all the powers he had fought for and recovered since August 1941.

Mossadeq also struck hard at the officer corps. He renamed the War Ministry as the Defense Ministry, cut the military budget by 15 percent and announced that the country would in future buy only defensive equipment. Moreover, he nominated General Vossuq, his own relative and a nephew of Qavam, to be assistant minister of defense; transferred 15,000 men from the army to the gendarmerie; and drastically reduced the budget of the secret service. He also set up two investigatory commissions: one under the finance minister to hear charges of corruption in the process of arms procurement; another under the cabinet to examine past procedures for military promotions. Furthermore, he spoke of ending the American military mission; purged the army of 136 officers, including 15 generals; and, placing the few officers he trusted in top positions, used martial law against his political opponents. One former war minister, taking sanctuary in the Senate, declared martial law to be "unconstitutional" and accused the government of "inciting class warfare."[115]

The blows against the civilian opposition were equally drastic. Mossadeq exacted from Parliament emergency powers for six months to decree any law he felt necessary for obtaining not only financial solvency, but also electoral, judicial, and educational reforms. At the end of six months, he successfully pressed Parliament to extend the emergency powers for another twelve months. With these powers, he decreed a land reform law that established village councils and increased the peasant's share of the annual produce by 15 percent. He drafted a new tax bill that shifted the burden of taxation away from low-income consumers. He also instructed the ministers of justice, interior, and education to reform thoroughly the judicial, electoral, and educational structures. When the Senate objected to these reforms, the National Front denounced it as "an aristocratic club" that violated "the egalitarian spirit of the Constitutional Revolution,"[116] and disbanded it by pushing through the Lower House a law that reduced the term of the Upper House from six years to two. Similarly, when the opposition in the Lower House plucked up enough courage to resist, the National Front deputies resigned en masse, reducing the assembly below its quorum, and, in effect, dissolving the Seventeenth Majles. To legitimize the dissolution, Mossadeq—supported by the Tudeh—called for a national referendum in July 1953:

[115] F. Zahedi, *Parliamentary Proceedings*, 1st Senate, 15 October 1952.
[116] Sanjabi, *Parliamentary Proceedings*, 1st Senate, 23 October 1952.

The people of Iran—and no one else—has the right to judge on this issue. For it was the people of Iran who brought into existence our fundamental laws, our constitution, our parliament, and our cabinet system. We must remember that the laws were created for the people; not the people for the laws. The nation has the right to express its views, and, if it wishes, to change its laws. In a democratic and constitutional country, the nation rules supreme.[117]

Mossadeq, the constitutional lawyer who had meticulously quoted the fundamental laws against the shah, was now bypassing the same laws and resorting to the theory of the general will. The liberal aristocrat who had in the past appealed predominantly to the middle class was mobilizing the lower classes. The moderate reformer who had proposed to disenfranchise illiterates was seeking the acclaim of the national masses. To ensure victory at the polls, positive and negative ballot boxes were placed in different places. As expected, Mossadeq received an overwhelming vote of confidence, winning over 2,043,300 of the 2,044,600 ballots cast throughout the country and 101,396 of the 101,463 ballots cast in the capital.[118]

By mid-August 1953, therefore, Mossadeq appeared to be in full control. He had packed his supporters into the cabinet and the bureaucracy. He had stripped the court of military, financial, and political influence, reduced the monarch to a ceremonial figure head, and thereby won the constitutional struggle against the shah that Qavam had lost. Moreover, he had routed the aristocratic opposition, dissolving Parliament, decreeing land reform, and appealing directly to the electorate. Furthermore, he had nationalized the Anglo-Iranian Oil Company, taken over the Soviet-administered Caspian fisheries, and thus implemented his policy of "negative equilibrium." Iran, like many other Asian countries, appeared to be taking the road of republicanism, neutralism, and middle-class radicalism. Not since 1925 had so much power been concentrated in the office of the prime minister and so little in the hands of the shah.

Mossadeq's strength, however, proved to be illusory. For while winning new victories, Mossadeq was losing old allies. While promising extensive social reforms, he was caught between dwindling oil revenues, increasing unemployment, and escalating consumer prices. And while celebrating the referendum, he was already endangered—unbeknownst to him—by a group of army officers who a week later abruptly overthrew him and reestablished royal power. The easy success of this coup can be explained by two factors: the widening gap

---

[117] Mossadeq, "Speech to the Nation," *Bakhtar-i Emruz*, 27 July 1953.
[118] *New York Times*, 4-14 August 1953.

between the traditional and middle classes within the National Front; and the increasing alienation of the whole officer corps from the civilian administration.

The National Front, despite internal differences, remained outwardly united so long as Britain and the shah seemed menacingly dangerous. Moreover, until Siyeh-i Tir Mossadeq did his very best to please the traditional as well as the modern wing of the nationalist movement. In his first cabinet, he chose Baqer Kazemi (Mohzab al-Dawleh), a highly religious elder statesman trusted by the ʿulama, to be foreign minister, and Mehdi Bazargan, the founder of the Islamic Society, to be assistant minister of education. He outlawed the sale of alcoholic beverages; raised tariffs to encourage handicraft industries; and restricted the activities of Kasravi's disciples. He also drafted an electoral bill that ignored women and retained the ʿulama in the supervisory councils; and, after the brief clash with the Fedaʾiyan-i Islam, freed twenty-eight of their members, including Razmara's assassin.

The traditional wing, however, gradually broke off in the months after Siyeh-i Tir as Mossadeq, confident that he had defeated the shah and thrown out the British, pressed ahead for fundamental social changes. When he gave the Ministries of Interior, Agriculture, and Transport to leaders of the secular Iran party, the Ministry of Justice to Abu al-ʿAli Lufti, an anticlerical judge who had helped Reza Shah reorganize the judicial system, and the Ministry of Education to Dr. Mehdi Azar, a university professor from Azerbaijan sympathetic to the Tudeh party, Qonatabadi and other clerical leaders of the National Front expressed guarded fears for the future.[119] When the minister of transport proposed to nationalize the bus companies of Tehran, Makki warned that such an act would open the way for the state to take over all small businesses, even groceries: "We would end up like the Soviet Union where the state owns everything and citizens nothing. Anyway, we all know that our bureaucrats are incompetent businessmen."[120] When the minister of economics tried to reduce food prices by opening new bakeries, the bazaar guilds—encouraged by Kashani—protested that the government had no right to interfere with the free market.[121] When the minister of communications recommended that the country's telephone companies be nationalized, Kashani solicited petitions from shareholders, and Haerzadeh proclaimed that "Islam protects private property and prohibits

[119] Qonatabadi, *Parliamentary Proceedings*, 17th Majles, 31 July 1952.
[120] Makki, ibid., 1 February 1953.
[121] *Ittilaʿat*, 3 September 1952; Qonatabadi, *Parliamentary Proceedings*, 17th Majles, 4 January 1953.

expropriations."[122] When Fatemi complained that the prohibition against the sale of alcohol reduced government tax revenues and increased the consumption of pure alcohol, Qonatabadi exclaimed, "I cannot believe my ears. Here is an assistant minister who considers himself a Muslim and represents a Muslim country proposing to legalize what the shari'a has clearly made illegal."[123] When Mossadeq's advisers proposed to enfranchize women on the grounds that the spirit of the constitution treated all citizens as equals, the 'ulama, supported by theology students and guild elders, protested that "the religious laws undoubtedly limited the vote to men."[124] Kashani stressed that "the government should prevent women from voting so that they would stay home and perform their true function—rearing children."[125] One clerical deputy argued that the existing laws adequately protected women and warned that any change would "encourage political instability, religious decay, and social anarchy."[126] One demonstrator was killed and ten were seriously wounded as theology students in Qum took to the streets to protest the proposal of extending the vote to women.

The conflict between the traditional and modern wings of the National Front reached a climax when Mossadeq asked Parliament for a twelve-month extension to his emergency powers. Opposing the request, many of the clerical deputies left the National Front and formed their own Islamic Caucus (Fraksiun-i Islam). Kashani denounced the emergency powers as "dictatorial"; informed foreign journalists that "true democracy in Iran needs a faithful implementation of the shari'a; and told Behbehani, the royalist ayatallah, that Mossadeq's "leftist advisers were endangering national security."[127] Qonatabadi claimed that the ministers of justice and education were replacing good Muslim employees with "Kremlin-controlled atheists"; that he had always suspected the Iran party because of that party's alliance with the Tudeh in 1946; and that the "government's dictatorial methods were transforming Iran into a vast prison."[128] Another clerical deputy suddenly discovered that Mossadeq's doctoral dissertation, written thirty-five years earlier in Switzerland, contained strong

[122] *Ittila'at*, 10-13 November 1952.

[123] Qonatabadi, *Parliamentary Proceedings*, 17th Majles, 5 February 1953.

[124] Nariman, ibid., 30 December 1952; Qonatabadi, ibid., 1 January 1953.

[125] Kashani, "A Message," *Tehran Mosaver*, 4 April 1952.

[126] B. Jalali, *Parliamentary Proceedings*, 17th Majles, 4 January 1953.

[127] *Ittila'at*, 29 July 1953 and 12 October 1952; "The Conflict between Mossadeq and Kashani," *Khvandaniha*, 22 February 1957.

[128] Qonatabadi, *Parliamentary Proceedings*, 17th Majles, 4 November 1952, 19 January and 25 May 1953.

secular and anticlerical views.[129] Haerzadeh denounced Mossadeq as a "typical aristocrat who had obtained the Fars governorship in 1920 because of his British connections": "When we first created the National Front no one imagined that we would be helping a man who would destroy our country with class warfare." Likewise, Baqai compared Mossadeq to Hitler; praised the army as "a bulwark against communism; and claimed that he supported a national "uprising" (*qiyam*) but not a social "revolution" (*inqilab*).[130] In breaking with Mossadeq, Baqai also expelled Khalel Maleki from his Toilers' party, on the grounds that the latter propagated Marxism and supported the "dictatorial government."[131]

Expelled from the Toilers' party, Khalel Maleki formed a new organization, naming it after his newspaper *Niru-yi Sevum* (Third Force), and promptly obtained the support of the youth and women's sections of the Toilers' party. Fully supporting Mossadeq, the Third Force accused Baqai of collaborating with "antipatriotic elements"; denounced the clergy of mixing politics with religion; and warned that the Tudeh continued to "blindly follow the Kremlin."[132] The Third Force also praised Marxism as a useful tool for analyzing society; advised members to separate sociology from theology and not confuse Marxism with moral philosophy; and called for a "social democratic revolution" that would bring extensive reforms, including land distribution and women's suffrage.[133]

The Iran party was equally supportive of Mossadeq. It continued to stress the need for neutralism, nationalism, and socialism. It argued that Islam was too "sacred a religion to mix with the bread-and-butter issues of daily politics." It accused Baqai of seeking help from the military to form armed gangs and "racketeer unions." It also described Kashani as a "political mulla" and the other defectors, especially Qonatabadi, Makki, and Haerzadeh, as "self-seekers" who had schemed to fill the ministries with their friends and relatives.[134]

[129] Quoted by Atesh (pseudonym), *Qiyam dar Rah-i Saltanat* (The Uprising for the Monarchy) (Tehran, 1954), pp. 50-56.

[130] Haerzadeh, *Parliamentary Proceedings*, 17th Majles, 19 May 1953; Baqai, ibid., 15 and 19 January 1953; M. Baqai, *Cheh Kesi Munharef Shud: Doktor Mossadeq ya Doktor Baqai?* (Who Deviated: Doctor Mossadeq or Doctor Baqai?) (Tehran, 1960), pp. 1-360.

[131] *Ittila'at*, 12 October 1952.

[132] "The Nation Supports Mossadeq," *Niru-yi Sevum*, 9 January 1953; Kh. Maleki, "The 'Ulama and Politics," *Niru-yi Sevum*, 28 November 1952; "Our Party Program," *Niru-yi Sevum*, 12 June 1953.

[133] Kh. Maleki, "Religion and Marxism," *Niru-yi Sevum*, 23 October 1952; "Cultural Revolution," *Jahani-i Now* (New World), 19 October 1952.

[134] "Demagogy," *Jeb'eh-i Azadi*, 10 April 1953; "Recent Events," *Jeb'eh-i Azadi*, 23 February 1953; "Kashani's Press Conference," *Jeb'eh-i Azadi*, 22 June 1953.

Thus by August 1953, the underlying contradictions between the traditional and the modern middle class were out in the open. Mossadeq, by siding with the latter, had lost the support of the three groups representing the bazaar—the Society of Muslim Warriors, the Toilers' party, and the Feda'iyan-i Islam—but retained the allegiance of the three organizations representing the intelligentsia—the Iran party, the National party, and the Third Force—as well as radical advisors such as Fatemi, Shayegan, and Razavi. In short, the National Front had been transformed from the movement of the two middle classes into that of the modern middle class only. Mossadeq, the man who saw himself as the living tradition of the constitutional movement, had been forced by history to repeat the experience of the Constitutional Revolution.

While Mossadeq was losing his traditional supporters, disgruntled royalist officers were secretly planning a military coup d'état. Meeting regularly at the Officers' Club in Tehran, a group of military commanders retired by Mossadeq after Siyeh-i Tir decided to form a secret Committee To Save the Fatherland (Komiteh-i Najat-i Vatan). The committee's charter declared that it was the patriotic duty of the officers to fight for the monarchy and the armed forces, combat extremism, and save the country from social dissolution.[135] The committee's leading figure was General Fazallah Zahedi—the same general who had been arrested by the British in 1943 for his pro-German activities, and who had been instrumental in 1946 in undermining Qavam's coalition government. A former Cossack lieutenant who had fought against the Jangalis and reached the rank of colonel under Reza Shah, Zahedi had such a distaste for that "upstart" Razmara that he had flirted with the National Front before concluding that the monarchy and the military would stand or fall together. Siding with the shah, he had openly denounced Mossadeq but remained on good terms with Baqai, Makki, and Kashani.

The secret committee included many other prominent military figures: General Moqadam, a member of a wealthy Azerbaijani family and the head of the gendarmerie during Siyeh-i Tir; General Arfa', the leader of the pro-British clique in the army and the archconservative chief of general staff in 1945-1946; General Hejazi, a close friend of Arfa' since their days in the Cossack Brigade; and General Hedayat, the aristocratic staff officer who had worked closely with the shah since 1941. Moreover, the secret committee established contact with the British secret service, which, after the breaking of diplomatic relations with London, had left behind in Tehran a working group

---

[135] "The Secret Events of the Uprising," *Ittila'at-i Haftegi*, 4 September 1953.

under the supervision of Rashidian, a wealthy businessman who had supported Sayyid Ziya in the 1940s and continued to finance thugs in the Tehran bazaar.

The secret committee further widened its network once Mossadeq initiated his campaign against the officer corps, and the new administration in Washington, headed by General Eisenhower, reversed previous policy, decided to support Britain against Iran, and sent Kermit Roosevelt of the Central Intelligence Agency to Tehran to finance a military coup.[136] Helped by Roosevelt, Zahedi and his secret committee won over officers holding crucial positions: Colonel Nasiri, the commander of the Imperial Guards; General Gilanshah, the chief of the air force; General Timour Bakhtiyar, a cousin of Queen Soraya and commander of the armored division in Kermanshah; Colonel Ardubadi, the chief of the gendarmerie; Captain M'utazed, the head of the secret police; Major Qahrani, the commander of the motorized division in Rasht; and, most important, such crucial tank commanders in the Tehran garrison as Colonels Ghulam Reza Oveissi and Muhammad Khajeh-Nouri.[137]

Having extended the secret network, the royalist officers worked to destabilize the government. They supplied weapons to rebellious tribes, especially the Shahsavens, Bakhtiyaris, Afshars, and Turkomans. They established contact not only with prominent conservative clerics such as Ayatallah Behbehani and Ayatallah Boroujerdi, but also with dissidents from the National Front, particularly Kashani, Qonatabadi, Makki, Baqai, and Sha'yban "the Brainless." They hired other thugs to carry Tudeh banners and to desecrate mosques. They also assassinated General Afshartous, the main officer supporting Mossadeq, and left his badly mutilated body outside Tehran as a warning to other pro-Mossadeq officers.

Next the royalist officers moved to overthrow Mossadeq. On August 16, three days after the shah left for the Caspian to take a "rest cure," Colonel Nasiri of the Imperial Guards arrived at the premier's doorstep with a royal decree replacing Mossadeq with Zahedi as premier. The attempt, however, was a complete fiasco, for the pro-Mossadeq chief of the army, tipped off by the Tudeh military network, surrounded Nasiri and his Imperial Guards as they approached the premier's residence. The following day the shah fled to Bagdad, the

[136] This description of the 1953 coup has been pieced together from interviews with a former CIA operative who participated in the events and from the following published sources: Cottam, *Nationalism in Iran*, pp. 227-29; G. de Villiers, *The Imperial Shah* (Boston, 1977), pp. 177-206; and K. Roosevelt, *Countercoup: The Struggle for the Control of Iran* (New York, 1979).

[137] I. Davrupanha, "The 1953 Coup," *Ittila'at*, 19 August 1979.

National Front set up a committee to decide the fate of the monarchy, and the Tudeh crowds poured into the streets, destroying royalist statues. In some provincial towns, such as Rasht and Enzeli, the Tudeh took over the municipal buildings. The next morning, Mossadeq, after a fateful interview with the American ambassador, who promised aid if law and order was reestablished, instructed the army to clear the streets of all demonstrators. Ironically, Mossadeq was trying to use the military, his past enemy, to crush the crowd, his main bulwark.[138]

Not surprisingly, the military used this opportunity to strike against Mossadeq. On August 19, while the Tudeh was taken aback by Mossadeq's blow against them, Zahedi, commanding thirty-five Sherman tanks, surrounded the premier's residence, and after a nine-hour battle captured Mossadeq. Acoustical effects for the event were provided both by Sha'yban "the Brainless," who led a noisy demonstration from the red-light district to the bazaar, and by the gendarmerie, who transported some eight hundred farm hands from the royal stables in Veramin to central Tehran.[139]

As the shah returned home, the armed forces proceeded to dismantle the National Front as well as the Tudeh. They arrested Mossadeq, Razavi, Shayegan, and, after a three-month search, Fatemi, who had taken shelter in the Tudeh underground. They also arrested eight high-ranking officers who had supported Mossadeq; the main cabinet ministers, including Abul Qassem Amini; and the leaders of the Iran party, the National party, and the Third Force. With the exceptions of Fatemi, who was executed, and Lufti, the justice minister, who was murdered, the other National Front leaders received lenient treatment—often prison terms no longer than five years. The treatment meted out to the Tudeh, however, was much harsher. As the Tudeh underground was gradually unearthed in the next four years, the security forces executed forty party officials, tortured to death another fourteen, sentenced some two hundred to life imprisonment, and arrested over three thousand rank-and-file members. The regime could feel confident that it had eliminated the organization, if not the appeal, of both the Tudeh and the National Front. Muhammad Reza Shah, like his father Reza Shah, could now rule without an organized opposition. History had come full circle.

[138] Cottam, *Nationalism in Iran*, p. 226; S. Margold, "The Streets of Tehran," *Reporter*, 10 November 1953; *Time*, 31 August 1953.

[139] "The Uprising of August 19th," *Ittila'at-i Haftegi*, 28 August 1953. According to a pro-Mossadeq officer, 164 soldiers and demonstrators were killed in the coup. See C. Fersharki, "The 1953 Coup," *Ittila'at*, 20 August 1979.

SIX

The Tudeh Party

The aim of the Tudeh party is to unite the masses—the workers, the peasants, the traders, the craftsmen, and the progressive intellectuals. Of course, these classes have economic differences. For example, while workers possess nothing but their own labor power, craftsmen control their tools of production, and peasants either own some land or aspire to own it. In contemporary Iran, however, these differences are overshadowed by the common struggle against imperialism, against absentee landlords, against exploiting capitalists, and against industrial robber barons. Our duty is to unite the exploited classes and forge a party of the masses.

—Iraj Iskandari, "Address to the First Party Congress," *Rahbar*, 4 September 1944

FORMATION (SEPTEMBER 1941-OCTOBER 1942)

The Tudeh party emerged immediately after the abdication of Reza Shah and the release of the "less dangerous" political prisoners. Meeting in Tehran on September 29—thirteen days after the abdication—twenty-seven younger members of the famous "Fifty-three" Marxists imprisoned in 1937 announced the formation of a political organization with the ambitious label of Hizb-i Tudeh-i Iran (The Party of the Iranian Masses).[1] In launching the organization, the founders gave the party chairmanship to Sulayman Iskandari, the highly respected radical prince who had fought in the Constitutional Revolution, helped establish the Democrat party in the Second Majles, led the Committee of National Resistance during World War I, and presided over the Socialist party from 1921 until its dissolution in 1926.[2]

The group set itself four immediate goals: release of the rest of the "Fifty-three"; recognition of the Tudeh as a legitimate organization; the publication of a daily newspaper; and the formulation of a broad

---

[1] I. Iskandari, "Concerning My Life," *Iran-i Ma*, 5 August 1946.

[2] Sulayman Iskandar had lost his civil service positions after 1926, and, unlike most Qajar aristocrats, having no private income, had been forced to earn a living working as a retail merchant.

program that would not antagonize the ʿulama, as previous secular programs had done, but would attract veteran Democrats, Socialists, and Communists, as well as young Marxists and even non-Marxist radicals.

These goals were attained during the following six months. The rest of the "Fifty-three" gained their freedom in mid-October, when the government extended amnesty to all dissidents imprisoned by Reza Shah. The official recognition came in early February, when the police issued the party a permit to hold a public service to commemorate the first anniversary of Arani's death. The group also obtained a daily organ in mid-February when ʿAbbas Iskandari, a member of the Tudeh and a second cousin of Sulayman Iskandari, revived his pre-Reza Shah newspaper named *Siyasat* (Politics). At the same time, the group helped start an Anti-Fascist Society with a paper named *Mardom* (The People) and a Freedom Front formed of editors whose newspapers had been banned by Reza Shah.

Moreover, the Tudeh published its provisional program in late February. This program stressed the need to eliminate "the vestiges of Reza Shah's dictatorship"; to protect constitutional laws, civil liberties, and human rights; to safeguard the rights of all citizens, especially of the masses; and to participate in the world wide struggle of democracy against barbarism and fascism.[3] As one of the party leaders later indicated, the main intention of the provisional program was to unite all citizens against both "internal fascism" encouraged by Reza Shah's gang and international fascism led by Hitler and Mussolini.[4] To avoid attacks from the ʿulama, the Tudeh kept Marxist demands out of its program, commemorated Arani's death with a religious service, and organized a mass meeting in memory of Arani, of Mudarres, the leading religious opponent of Reza Shah, and of Farokhi, the radical but highly devout poet who had been murdered in 1939.

Although the founding members of the Tudeh were Marxists (and, as later events showed, staunch supporters of the Soviet Union) they did not call themselves communists. In addition to their fear of the ʿulama, the leaders gave a number of reasons for being cautious: the

[3] Tudeh Party, "Provisional Party Program," *Siyasat*, 22 February 1942. For later discussions of this program, see ʿA. Kambakhsh, "Reflections on the History of the Tudeh Party," *Donya*, 7 (Spring 1966), 48-68; ʿA. Kambakhsh, "The Formation of the Tudeh Party," *Donya*, 7 (Autumn 1966), 24-36; ʿA. Iskandari, *Tarikh-i Mashrutiyat-i Iran* (History of the Iranian Constitution) (Tehran, 1943), I, 13-15.

[4] I. Iskandari, "A Few Remarks on the Formation of the Tudeh Party," *Donya*, 1 (September 1974), 2-7; I. Iskandari, "The Tudeh Party's First Year of Struggle," *Donya*, 1 (December 1974), 13-18.

1931 law banning all "collectivist ideologies"; twenty-five years of government propaganda that had "instilled in segments of the population a hostile attitude toward socialism, communism, and the Soviet Union"; a desire to attract "reformers and progressives as well as radicals and revolutionaries"; and a realization that the industrial working class still constituted a small fraction of the total population.[5] As one of the "Fifty-three" put it,

A true communist must always adapt Marxism to the local environment. If an Iranian communist adopts wholesale the program of the German Communist party, or of any communist party in the industrialized countries, he will undoubtedly fail to appeal to the broad masses. Such a person will be violating the elementary rules of dialectical logic and Marxist philosophy. Consequently, he cannot be considered a true communist. On the contrary, he should be described as a political provocateur.[6]

There was, however, an unstated and more complex reason for avoiding the communist label. Whereas the founders of the Tudeh sought to attract the younger activists and the rank and file of the old Communist party, they had no intention of subordinating themselves to the veteran leaders of the same organization.[7] Whereas the founders of the Tudeh were predominantly young, residents of Tehran, and Persian-speaking, the surviving Communist leaders were middle-aged, natives of Azerbaijan, and Azeri-speaking. Whereas the Tudeh founders were university-educated intellectuals who had reached Marxism through the left-wing movements of Western Europe, the Communist leaders were activists and self-taught intellectuals who had reached the same destination through the Leninism of the Russian Bolshevik party. Whereas the Tudeh founders, as European-educated Marxists, saw politics through the class perspective only, the Communist leaders, having experienced the ethnic pogroms of the Caucasus and the re-

---

[5] Iskandari, "The Tudeh Party's First Year of Struggle," pp. 13-18; S. Iskandari, "Address to the First Tehran Conference," *Rahbar*, 30 January 1943.

[6] B. ʿAlavi, *Panjah-u-Seh Nafar* (The Fifty-three) (Tehran, 1944), p. 189.

[7] Mistaking the Tudeh leaders for mere "front men" for the veteran Communists, Western specialists arrived at the false conclusion that the Tudeh was nothing more than the open section of the old clandestine Communist party. For example, G. Lenczowski claims that the Tudeh was really led by Pishevari, and that Pishevari was no other than the veteran communist Sultanzadeh. See G. Lenczowski, *Russia and the West in Iran, 1918-48* (Ithaca, 1949), pp. 223-25. Similarly, the CIA in 1954 suspected that the Tudeh was controlled by the veteran communist Kamran. See the U.S. Embassy to the State Department, "Anti-Tudeh Campaign," *The Declassified Documents Retrospective Collection*, Microfiche 1952-54 (75), 309A. These specialists not only overlook the wide differences between the Tudeh founders and the old Communists, but also ignore the fact that the revolutionaries such as Sultanzadeh and Kamran had been "eliminated" during Stalin's purges in the 1930s.

gional revolts of Khiabani and Kuchek Khan, tended to see society through communal as well as class perspectives. These differences were not obvious in 1941-1943, but came into the open in later years.

Having formulated its provisional program, the Tudeh turned its attention to organizing itself, beginning with Tehran. By October 1942, it was ready to convene its First Provisional Conference. This meeting brought together thirty-three observers from the provinces and eighty-seven delegates from Tehran.[8] Each delegate represented ten members. According to one party leader, the Tudeh had six thousand members spread throughout the country.[9] The same source stated that a quarter of the members were intellectuals (*rushanfekran*), and most of the rest were "workers, artisans, and craftsmen." Meeting over a week, the conference hammered out a detailed program to replace the provisional program; designed an elaborate structure on the basis of "democratic centralism"; and elected a Provisional Central Committee to serve as the leadership of the whole organization pending the convening of the First Party Congress.

The new program went beyond the general appeal to all citizens to unite against fascism. Instead, it spelled out specific proposals to attract the masses—especially "workers, peasants, women, and such members of the middle class (*tabaqeh-i mutavasateh*) as intellectuals (*rushanfekran*), small landowners (*khordeh-i malekin*), craftsmen-traders (*pishevaran*), and low-ranking government employees (*karmandan-i pay'in*)."[10] To workers, the program promised labor legislation, an eight-hour day, paid vacations, pay for Fridays, overtime scales, disability insurance, government-subsidized housing, pensions, and a ban on child labor. To peasants, it offered the redistribution of state and crown lands; buying of large private estates by the government and their resale to the landless at low interest rates; retention of a larger portion of the harvest for the sharecroppers; election of kadkhudas by the village community; elimination of feudal levies and obligations; formation of an agricultural bank and village cooperatives; and construction of rural clinics, village schools, and irrigation projects. To women, it pledged political rights, welfare assistance for indigent mothers, and equal pay for equal work. To traders and craftsmen, it offered viable guilds, state-subsidized workshops, and protection from foreign competition. And to the salaried middle class, it promised job security, higher incomes, lower consumer taxes, state controls on rents and food prices, and government projects to employ university and

[8] Tudeh Party, "Proceedings of the First Provisional Conference of Tehran," *Rahbar*, 30 January-10 February 1943.

[9] R. Radmanesh, "Address to the First Tehran Conference," *Rahbar*, 30 January 1943.

[10] Tudeh Party, "Party Program," *Rahbar*, 12 February 1943.

high-school graduates. The program also called for "national independence from all forms of colonialism and imperialism"; protection of civil liberties and human rights; observance of the constitutional laws, especially the separation of powers between the judiciary and the executive; and "a special supreme court to judge public officials who have in recent years violated the fundamental laws."

In discussing the new program, the conference passed a number of significant resolutions. It created special organizations for women and youth. It instructed the leadership to concentrate on building an extensive trade union movement. It expelled ʿAbbas Iskandari for working too closely with Qavam, disowned the paper *Siyasat*, and adopted the daily *Rahbar* (Leader) as the party's central organ. It also encouraged participation in the forthcoming parliamentary elections, and discussed the possibilities as well as the limitations of using the constitution for bringing about major social changes. An editorial in *Rahbar* summed up the party attitude toward the constitution in these terms:

Is the Tudeh party communist? Our enemies, especially Sayyid Ziya, smear us with the label to frighten the capitalists and the traders. The Tudeh party is fully committed to the fundamental laws. Why? Because we believe that communism is an ideology suitable for social conditions that do not exist in Iran. A communist party will not find mass roots in our environment. We know that our immediate task is to unite the majority against the exploiting oligarchy and to strengthen the forces of democracy. We support, therefore, the constitution.[11]

Similarly, a party intellectual, in an article on "How to Change the System: Through Revolution or Parliament?" argued that the experience of Spain had shown to Iran the dangers of a premature revolution. He elaborated that Iran was not ready for revolution partly because of the international situation, particularly the danger of fascism, and partly because of the internal situation, especially the lack of mass organizations. Concluding that talk of revolution was irresponsible, he argued that the party should try to weaken the ruling class by "uniting all progressive forces" and "working inside and outside parliament."[12]

The party rules and regulations approved by the conference stressed the need for both a "strong center" and "democratic behavior."[13] It structured the organization into local branches at places of work;

[11] "The Tudeh Party and Partisanship in Foreign Policy," *Rahbar*, 17 May 1944.

[12] H. Mutasavi, "How to Change the System: Through Revolution or Parliament?" *Mardom*, 21 December 1943.

[13] Tudeh Party, "The Party Constitution," *Rahbar*, 12 February 1943.

provincial conferences, at which each delegate would represent ten members, to meet once a year to discuss any subject pertinent to the party and elect a provincial central committee as well as representatives to the national party congress; and the party congress itself, which would have one delegate for every 150 members and would meet annually to evaluate the party's progress, formulate future strategy, and elect a national central committee with the needed special commissions. The Tudeh handbook, *Fundamentals of Party Organization*, explained that the concept of "democratic centralism" gave rights and duties to all party members.[14] Each member had the right to debate issues freely, elect officials, and participate in the formulation of party policies. Each member also had the duty to obey the elected officials and carry out party policies—even if he or she had voted against the official or opposed the policy in question. Thus the implementation of decisions would be centralized, but the formulation of decisions would be democratic.

The Provisional Central Committee elected by the Tehran Conference consisted of fifteen founders and future leaders of the Tudeh party. In addition to Sulayman Iskandari, who was reelected chairman, the committee included Dr. Muhammad Bahrami, Dr. Morteza Yazdi, Iraj Iskandari, Nuraldin Alamuti, ʿAbdul Hussein Noshin, ʿAli Kobari, Nosratallah Eʿzazi, Ibrahim Mahazari, Reza Rusta, Dr. Fereydoun Keshavarz, Ardasher Ovanessian, Dr. Reza Radmanesh, ʿAli Amir-Khizi, and Ziya Alamuti.[15]

Bahrami, a medical doctor, had been sentenced to ten years' imprisonment for being a senior member of the "Fifty-three." The son of a prominent physician, Bahrami was born in Tehran province, raised in the capital, and educated in Berlin where he had met Arani. Yazdi, another senior member of the "Fifty-three," was a professor at Tehran University and one of the country's best-known surgeons. The son of an outspoken preacher from Yazd who had been imprisoned in 1908 for supporting the constitution, Yazdi was born in Tehran, educated in the Dar al-Fonun, jailed briefly in 1921 for distributing Jangali pamphlets, and sent to Berlin in 1925 on a government scholarship. Iraj Iskandari, yet another member of the "Fifty-three," was a nephew of Sulayman Iskandari and the son of the famous Yahya Mirza Iskandari, the radical prince murdered by the shah during the Constitutional Revolution. Raised in Tehran by his uncles, Iraj Iskandari had completed the Dar al-Fonun, won a government schol-

[14] A. Ovanessian, *Osul-i Tashkilati-yi Hizb* (Fundamentals of Party Organization) (Tehran, 1943).

[15] Biographical information has been obtained from interviews, newspaper memoirs printed from 1941 to 1953, and obituaries published from 1953 until 1978.

arship to study law in France, and, on his return to Iran, coedited the journal *Donya* with Arani. At the time of his election to the committee, he edited the party organ *Rahbar*. Nuraldin Alamuti, a senior judge, was one of the few members of the committee over the age of forty-five. A native of the rural district of Alamut in the northern tip of Tehran province, he had joined the Democrat party in 1919, gone to jail briefly in 1923 for agitating among the local peasantry, and entered the Justice Ministry during Reza Shah's secular reforms. Nuraldin Alamuti had been arrested with Arani, but had been tried separately from the "Fifty-three."

Noshin, a friend of Arani's colleagues, was the country's leading theater director. Born into a middle-class family in Mashad, he had as a teenager participated in Colonel Taqi Khan's short-lived rebellion, moved to Tehran to enroll in the Dar al-Fonun, and won a government scholarship to study modern theater in France. Although closely associated with the "Fifty-three," Noshin escaped imprisonment because at the time of the arrests he had been representing Iran at a world congress of dramatists. Kobari, a survivor of the early labor movement, was a middle-level official in the Ministry of Communications. Raised in Rasht, he had graduated from the city's sole modern school, contributed to the Jangali paper, and after the revolt helped form the local cultural society as well as unions for local teachers, rice cleaners, and tobacco workers. E'zazi, another middle-ranking government employee, had participated in the early labor movement in Tehran before his arrest as a member of the "Fifty-three." Mahazari, also a survivor of the early trade unions, was a lathe worker in the army munitions factory outside Tehran. The son of an Azerbaijani freedom-fighter who had been killed in the Constitutional Revolution, Mahazari had migrated to Gilan in search of work and been imprisoned a number of times during the 1930s for his illegal union activities.

Rusta, the most important figure in the history of the Iranian labor movement, was the son of a Gilani peasant and a graduate of an agricultural school in Rasht. He had taught literacy classes in the local cultural society; helped establish the first teachers' union; joined first the Socialist party, then the youth section of the Communist party; spent two years in Moscow; and returned to Iran in 1929 to organize factory unions in Tehran, Isfahan, and Bandar 'Abbas. Captured in 1931, he had spent the following ten years in prison, where he befriended the "Fifty-three."

Keshavarz, the only member of the committee without a political past, was a medical doctor teaching in Tehran University. The son of a Gilani merchant who had taken part in the Constitutional Revolution, Keshavarz had first studied in Rasht, later in the Dar al-Fonun, and finally in Paris on a government scholarship. He had been recruited into the Tudeh by his friend Sulayman Iskandari only three months after the formation of the party. Ovanessian, the sole non-Muslim in the committee, was the same activist who in the early 1930s headed the youth section of the Communist party. Born in an Armenian village in Azerbaijan, he had moved with his family to Gilan, studied pharmacy at the American missionary school in Rasht, helped organize unions in Tehran, and, having joined the Communist party, spent two years studying in Moscow. Imprisoned after his return to Iran, he served eleven years in prison, where he met the "Fifty-three." Although only thirty-seven years old, Ovanessian had already published a series of pamphlets on Marxism and political organization, and thus had established himself as a leading party theorist. An informant to the British claimed that Ovanessian was "the main brains of the Tudeh" and "one of the two dominating personalities" in the early party conferences.[16]

Radmanesh, the other "dominating personality," was a French-educated physicist teaching at Tehran University. Although from a land-owning family in Gilan, he had helped the local Jangalis as a teenager; joined the Socialist party while at the Dar al-Fonun; met Arani while studying in Europe; and, on his return, found himself sentenced to five years' imprisonment as a junior member of the "Fifty-three." The informant reported that Radmanesh played an important role partly because of his competent editing of *Mardom*, but mainly because he was respected—even by his worst enemies—as "sincere and not actuated by personal gain."[17] Amir-Khizi, the second oldest member of the committee, had a long history of political activity. His brother had edited Khiabani's newspaper during the upheavals of 1917-1919 in Tabriz. He himself had fought in the Jangali movement; joined first the Socialist party and then the Communist party; participated in the formation of the first teachers' union in Tehran; and, after a brief spell in prison during the mid-1930s, worked in the provinces as the manager of a small cardboard-making factory. Finally, Ziya Alamuti, the younger brother of Nuraldin Alamuti, was a middle-level official in the Ministry of Roads in Mazandaran. A veteran of the Socialist party, he had been sentenced to ten years' imprisonment as a senior member of the "Fifty-three."

The early leadership thus came largely from the young generation of Persian-speaking intelligentsia residing in Tehran. If one excludes

[16] British Chargé d'Affaires to the Foreign Office, "Memorandum on the Tudeh Congress," *F.O. 371*/Persia 1944/34-40187.
[17] Ibid.

Sulayman Iskandari, the average age of the committee members was only thirty-seven. The fifteen included one retired high-ranking civil servant, one judge, three professors, one doctor, one lawyer, one theater director, two former teachers, three middle-level civil servants, one ex-pharmacist, and one factory worker. Only four came from the upper tier of titled aristocrats, wealthy landowners, and rich merchants.[18] Six had received higher education in Western Europe, two in Tehran, and two in the Soviet Union. Eight were born in Tehran province, three in Gilan, three in Azerbaijan, and one in Khurasan. Of the fifteen, eight were members or close associates of the "Fifty-three"; three had been active mostly in the old Democrat and Socialist parties; and three had been prominent in the youth section of the banned Communist party.

Although younger members of the Communist party were active in the Tudeh, the surviving older leaders were conspicuous with their absence. Pishevari, the most prominent survivor of the early years, had been incarcerated in the same prison as the "Fifty-three," but had refused to associate with these "young inexperienced intellectuals." On his release, he first tried to revive the Democrat party and then gathered some old colleagues to establish an independent newspaper named *Azhir* (Alarm).[19] This paper was not only independent of the Tudeh, but also at times highly critical of the party leadership. When Reza Shah died, it printed a favorable obituary and sent condolences to the royal family.[20] When the Tudeh was trying to heal old wounds between reformers and radicals, *Azhir* published the memoirs of an unnamed "veteran communist" denouncing the Democrats of 1917-1921 as right wing, reactionary, and petty bourgeois. When the Tudeh announced that it would concentrate on building a labor movement, Pishevari, in a series of articles on "What Is a Genuine Party?" argued that all the existing organizations lacked substance, and claimed that

[18] Although eleven of the early leaders came from the middle and lower classes, opponents of the Tudeh focused on the other four to argue that the party had been created by "disgruntled members of the upper class." For example, the editor of *Ittila'at* insisted that the Tudeh was misnamed because it was headed by "Qajar princes." See 'A. Mas'oudi, "The Bells of Danger," *Ittila'at*, 31 July 1943. Arsanjani, Qavam's advisor, claimed that "old landed aristocrats" of the Tudeh were misleading the "young radical intellectuals" of Iran. See Dr. Darya, "Iranian Communism," *Iran-i Ma*, 4 July 1943. Similarly, Qavam's Democrat Party argued that the Tudeh could not represent "workers, toilers, and intellectuals" because it was created and led by "wealthy landlords." See 'A. Mahmudi, *Iran Demokrat* (Democratic Iran) (Tehran, 1945), p. 76.

[19] "Storm in Azerbaijan," *Ittila'at-i Mahaneh*, 4 (November 1951), pp. 7-10; H. Jowdat, *Tarikh-i Firqeh-i Demokrat* (History of the Democrat Party) (Tehran, 1969), pp. 111-45.

[20] For details of this incident, see H. Arsanjani, *Parliamentary Proceedings*, 15th Majles, 16 September 1947.

any party trying to represent the working class was bound to fail because "our workers are not real proletarians but mere craftsmen, apprentices, journeymen, and artisans."[21] And when Bozorg ʿAlavi, a disciple of Arani and a leading literary figure, published his classic work entitled *Panjah-u-Seh Nafar* (The Fifty-three), an anonymous reviewer in *Azhir* took the opportunity to write a personal diatribe against the Tudeh leaders:

This book claims to be history. In fact, it is simply the personal experiences of the author who is a typical member of the "Fifty three." . . . Dr. Arani, even though not a member of the Communist party, was an enlightened Marxist. The same cannot be said of his colleagues. These men had no political experience. All they had done was to read some books, publish a journal, and accidently get involved in a strike. . . . ʿAlavi confesses that he craved a cigarette when he was arrested. From this the reader may get the wrong impression that all political prisoners react in the same weak manner. Although there were among us old prisoners some who showed signs of weakness, we were on the whole far superior to these "Fifty-three." I prefer, however, to forget the shortcomings of these young prisoners. . . . But I do not understand why the author exaggerates the importance of his colleagues. These intellectuals may be honorable men, but they obviously lack the experience and ability to lead a political movement.[22]

Ovanessian, using a pseudonym, promptly came to the defense of the "Fifty-three."[23] Describing his prison experiences, Ovanessian clearly identified himself with Arani's group, and bluntly denounced "an older prisoner who should remain unnamed" for treating the young Marxists arrogantly, sabotaging their hunger strike against the prison authorities, and now slandering them through malicious newspaper articles. Ovanessian added that former radicals who criticized the Tudeh were behaving like irresponsible provocateurs, one day shouting ultraleft slogans, another day ultraright ones. Thus the Tudeh party was not—as some claimed—the direct descendant of the old Communist party.

EXPANSION NORTH (NOVEMBER 1942-AUGUST 1944)

In the months after the First Tehran Conference, the Tudeh pushed to expand into the provinces, especially the northern towns and the textile manufacturing center of Isfahan. In some areas, it absorbed

[21] "A Short History of the Justice Party," *Azhir*, 18 August-2 November 1943; J. Pishevari, "What Is a Genuine Party?" *Azhir*, 13-22 June 1944.

[22] "Concerning the Book *The Fifty-three*," *Azhir*, 22-29 October 1944.

[23] A. Ahʾin, *Yaddashtha-yi Zindan* (Prison Memoirs) (Tehran, 1943), pp. 1-80.

existing organizations. In other areas, it created new organizations. In Mashad, for example, it formed a branch by merging two existing groups: one composed of Persian-speaking intellectuals who had been publishing their own newspaper; the other composed of Turkish-speaking workers from the local Muhajarin community—the community of Iranians who had been repatriated from the Soviet Union during the 1930s. In Rasht, the party opened a branch as soon as a veteran of the cultural society who had been in prison with the "Fifty-three" revived the local teachers', rice cleaners', and tobacco workers' unions. In Isfahan, the Tudeh obtained a ready-made organization when it was joined by a group of radical intellectuals and militant trade unionists who in 1942 had led a series of successful strikes in the textile mills.

By mid-1943, when the elections for the Fourteenth Majles began, the Tudeh, according to British officials, was the only party with a determined policy, a well-designed structure, and a nationwide organization.[24] In the provinces north of Tehran, it had branches in all the twenty-one cities with a population of over twenty thousand, and in nine of the seventeen towns with a population of between ten thousand and twenty thousand. In the provinces south of Tehran, it had open branches and secret cells in six of the twenty-three cities with populations of over twenty thousand: Isfahan, Arak, Qum, Hamadan, Ahwaz, and Kermanshah. Moreover, the Tudeh published six major newspapers: *Rahbar, Mardom*, and *Razm* (Battle) in Tehran; *Rasti* (The Truth) in Mashad; *Azerbaijan* in Tabriz; and *Jowdat* (Bounty) in Ardabel. The party's strong showing in the north can be explained by the radical history of Gilan and Azerbaijan, the new factories located in Tehran and Mazandaran, and the support given by the Soviets. Its relative weakness in the south was due to the British, and, more important, the reluctance of the Tudeh to move into the vital oil industry while the war in Europe continued.

In the elections for the Fourteenth Majles, the Tudeh sponsored twenty-three candidates, including ten members of the Provisional Central Committee. Eight ran in Tehran province, five in Azerbaijan, two in Mazandaran, two in Gilan, two in Khurasan, two in Isfahan, and two for the two seats reserved for the Christian minority. Of the candidates, eight were from the old Democrat and Socialist parties, six from the "Fifty-three," four from the Communist party, and five had no previous political affiliation. Three of the candidates were not Tudeh members: two veteran Democrats who ran in Azerbaijan; and

[24] British Minister to the Foreign Office, "Memorandum on Parties Active in the General Elections," *F.O. 371*/Persia 1943/34-35074.

Pishevari, who at the very last minute formed an electoral alliance with the Tudeh in Tabriz. Of the list, eight won: two in Gilan, two in Khurasan, one in Tehran province, one in Mazandaran, one in Isfahan, and one in the northern Christian constituency. Receiving nearly 200,000 votes, the twenty-three candidates obtained over 70 percent of the votes cast in their constituencies, over thirteen percent of those cast in the whole country, and over twice as many as any other political party.[25] For the first time in Iranian history, a secular radical organization had found popular support. According to the British authorities, the electoral campaign had shown that the Tudeh with its "serious" organization could effectively fan the discontent of the lower classes and place the urgency of social reform at the center of the stage.[26]

The growth of the Tudeh continued unabated after the elections. When Sulayman Iskandari died, his funeral procession in Isfahan drew more than twenty-five thousand mourners—the largest street demonstration in the city's history. When the Tudeh celebrated its second anniversary, its rally in Tehran attracted over thirty thousand. According to *Mardom*, this was the largest public meeting in the country's history, surpassing even the proconstitutional crowds of 1906-1909 and the anti-Russian demonstrations of 1911.[27] When *Rahbar* celebrated its own anniversary, it sold over sixty thousand copies and thus almost outdid *Ittila'at*, the country's main mass circulation newspaper.

The Tudeh's most notable success, however, was in organizing labor. On May Day 1944, a group of veteran labor organizers closely associated with the Tudeh announced the merger of four union federations into a Central Council of Federated Trade Unions of Iranian Workers and Toilers (Shawra-yi Mutahedeh-i Markaz-i Ittehadieh-i Kargaran va Zahmatkeshan-i Iran). Using a title similar to the pre-1925 unions, the CCFTU began with sixty affiliates, some hundred thousand members, a newspaper named *Zafar* (Victory), and the determination to organize as soon as possible all urban wage earners, except those employed in the sectors of the economy vital to the war effort. Its success was soon apparent. For example, the British consul in Mashad reported that the local unions had enrolled over two thousand members—including five hundred women carpet weavers—taught

---

[25] R. Radmanesh, "Report on the Election Results," *Rahbar*, 4 August 1944.

[26] British Minister to the Foreign Office, 17 March 1943, *F.O. 371*/Persia 1943/34-35109; British Military Attaché to the Foreign Office, 22 April 1943, *F.O. 371*/Persia 1943/34-35109.

[27] *Mardom*, 22 October 1943.

workers how to stand up for better conditions, and thereby instilled into the wealthy the fear of a popular uprising. The consul in Tabriz wrote in alarm that the Tudeh with its labor unions had completely paralyzed the local government and threatened to take over the city administration. And the consul in Isfahan described how the Tudeh defeated the company unions by successfully organizing a seven-day strike throughout the textile mills. In a memorandum to the Foreign Office, the British ambassador summed up the labor situation: "One of the features of the political life of Persia in recent months has been the rise of several unions throughout the country, especially in the north, in Isfahan, and in Tehran. . . . The Tudeh, backed in many ways by the Russians, remains the one strong party in the country."[28]

It was in the midst of these labor successes that the Tudeh convened its First Party Congress. Meeting in Tehran during August 1944, the congress included 168 delegates representing over 25,800 members.[29] Of the delegates, 44 came from Tehran province, 44 from Azerbaijan, 38 from Mazandaran, 11 from Gilan, 10 from Khurasan, 8 from Kurdistan, and 13 from the cities of Isfahan, Arak, and Ahwaz. The occupations of 107 delegates are known. These included 29 wage earners, 1 coal dealer, and 77 members of the intelligentsia—27 writers, journalists, and translators, 13 engineers, 9 professors, 9 middle-ranking civil servants, 7 doctors, 6 high-school headmasters, 3 teachers, and 3 lawyers. Since many of the working-class delegates from Azerbaijan could not speak Persian, the Congress decided at its initial session to conduct all meetings in both Persian and Azeri. For the first time in Iranian history, a political organization had reached down below the middle classes and discovered the stark reality that many citizens could not communicate in the official language.

Acting as the party's highest authority, the Congress began by scrutinizing the activities of the Provisional Central Committee. A delegate from Gilan complained that the party had ignored the rural masses. The leadership later admitted that at the time of the Congress only 2 percent of the members were peasants, while over 23 percent were intellectuals and office employees.[30] A party intellectual argued that the Tudeh had done little to recruit university and high-school stu-

[28] British Consul in Mashad, 7 May-23 June 1943, *F.O. 371*/Persia 1943/34-35061; British Consul in Tabriz, 5 June-13 July 1944, *F.O. 371*/Persia 1944/34-40178; British Consul in Isfahan, 7 April-13 July 1944, *F.O. 371*/Persia 1944/34-40163; British Ambassador to the Foreign Office, 18 July 1944, *F.O. 371*/Persia 1944/34-40187.

[29] Tudeh Party, "Proceedings of the First Party Congress," *Rahbar*, 2 August-7 September 1944.

[30] 'A. Kambakhsh, "The Tudeh Party in the Struggle to Create a Democratic United Front," *Donya*, 5 (Autumn 1964), 6-19.

dents, and that over 80 percent of the organization's militants had already been active politically in the years before 1941. Another intellectual denounced some of the leaders for lacking ideological commitment, collaborating with the devil to win Majles seats, showing signs of parliamentary opportunism, and permitting the entry of undesirable characters into the organization. A labor organizer protested that the policy of keeping out of the war-related industries not only held back the labor movement, but threatened to help in future rival organizations. He concluded with the declaration, "it is high time we moved south." A delegate from Gurgan complained that the leaders had focused on the capital at the expense of the provinces. Another from Sarab in Azerbaijan—speaking in Azeri—argued that the Central Committee had often underestimated and misunderstood the needs of the provinces. The last point was illustrated by a delegate from Gilan who testified that he, a Persian intellectual unable to speak a word of Azeri, had been sent to organize workers and peasants in Zanjan, an Azeri-speaking district.

The Congress tried to rectify some of these shortcomings. It created a Peasants' Union as a sister organization to the CCFTU, and instructed the future leadership to give more attention to the rural masses. It placed the party's Youth Organization under the direction of Radmanesh, the university professor who had been considered one of the dominating personalities of the earlier conference. It also created a weekly journal named *Mardom Bara-yi Javanan* (*Mardom* for the Young) and advised the paper *Razm* to focus more on intellectual and university issues. It established an Inspection Commission to purge "undesirable elements" and tightened the rules of entry into the party: future applicants had to be recommended by five rather than two members, and the recommendations had to be approved by the local branch. It resolved—in a secret session—that since the war against fascism was drawing to a close the party could push southward into the oil industry. And it decided that the center should take more interest in the provinces and that the party should pursue provincial grievances more aggressively. An informant to the British Embassy reported that the Congress in a secret session approved of "reasonable" regional demands, but "utterly disapproved of any separatist tendencies likely to impair the integrity of Iran and of any propaganda likely to sow discord between Persian-speakers and Turki-speakers."[31]

Having passed these resolutions, the Congress debated and approved a new party program drafted predominantly by Radmanesh,

[31] British Chargé d'Affaires to the Foreign Office, "Memorandum on the Tudeh Congress," *F.O. 371*/Persia 1944/34-40187.

Ovanessian, and Iraj Iskandari. The new program kept the previous program, but added two significant, though vague, clauses, and made one important change of emphasis.[32] The old program had mentioned neither the linguistic nor the religious minorities. The new program, as a modest concession to the delegates from Azerbaijan, demanded "complete freedom for the minorities in matters relating to religion and culture (*farhangi*)," and "complete social equality between all citizens of the Iranian nation (*mellat*) irrespective of the citizen's religion and birth (*nezhad*)." The old program had emphasized the need to unite the "masses" against fascism, despotism, and the supporters of Reza Shah's dictatorship. The new program stressed the importance of mobilizing the "exploited classes" against the exploiting feudal and capitalist classes. This subtle change of emphasis was explained in the party handbook published immediately after the Congress:

The primary aim of the Tudeh is to mobilize within the party the workers, peasants, progressive intelligentsia, traders, and craftsmen of Iran. In our contemporary society, there are two major classes: those who own the main means of production; and those who do not own significant amounts of property. The latter include workers, peasants, progressive intellectuals, traders, and craftsmen. They work but do not receive the fruits of their labor. They are oppressed by the oligarchy. Moreover, they have little to lose but much to gain if the social structure were radically transformed and the main means of production were owned jointly by the people. . . . When we say that our intention is to fight despotism and dictatorship we are not referring to specific personalities but to class structures that produce despots and dictators. In August 1941 many thought that Reza Shah's abdication had ended overnight the dictatorial system. We now know better; for we can see with our own eyes that the class structure that created Reza Shah remains. What is worse, this class structure continues to create petty Reza Shahs—oligarchs in the form of feudal landlords and exploiting capitalists who, through their ownership of the means of production, control the state.[33]

The program thus became socialist in content while remaining constitutionalist in form.

After endorsing the program, the Congress elected a nine-man Central Committee and an eleven-man Inspection Commission. Of the twenty-one elected, eleven had been in the Provisional Central Committee: Nuraldin Alamuti, Bahrami, Ovanessian, Iraj Iskandari, Amir-Khizi, Radmanesh, Keshavarz, Yazdi, Noshin, Rusta, and Ziya Alamuti. The newcomers were Parvin Gonabadi, Ehsan Tabari, Mah-

[32] Tudeh Party, "Party Program," *Rahbar*, 5-7 September 1944.

[33] A. Qassemi, *Hizb-i Tudeh-i Iran Cheh Miguyad va Cheh Mikhuahad?* (What Does the Tudeh Party of Iran Say and Want?) (Tehran, 1944), pp. 2-5.

mud Boqrati, ʿAbdul Samad Kambakhsh, Dr. Hussein Jowdat, Khalel Maleki, ʿAli Olovi, Ahmad Qassemi, and Dr. Nuraldin Kianouri.

The social and political backgrounds of the new members were similar to those of the former members. Gonabadi, a respected scholar of Persian literature, was headmaster of the state girls' school in Mashad. Born into a clerical family in the small town of Gonabad in Khurasan, he had studied in Mashad, where he had joined the Democrat party, helped form a teachers' union, and taught literacy courses for workers. His political connections had earned him brief prison sentences in 1926 and 1929. Tabari, a leading party theoretician, was an employee of the Anglo-Iranian Oil Company. From a prominent landed family in Mazandaran, he had studied in Britain and in Tehran University, where he had met Arani. As a junior member of the "Fifty-three," Tabari had been sentenced to three years' imprisonment. Boqrati, a senior member of the "Fifty-three," had been headmaster of a state secondary school in Mashad. Born into a medical family in Gilan, he had studied at the Dar al-Fonun, joined the youth section of the Communist party, and helped form the first teachers' union in Tehran. Bograti was one of the few "Fifty-three" with a Communist background.

Kambakhsh, who was to be a prominent Tudeh leader in future years, was also one of the few "Fifty-three" with experience in the youth section of the Communist party. The son of a Qajar prince, he was born and raised in Qazvin, and sent in 1915 to study in Russia. Deeply impressed by the Bolshevik Revolution, he had, on his return to Qazvin, joined the Socialist and Communist parties, and helped organize the local educational society. Despite his political affiliations, the government sent him to Russia in 1927 to study mechanical engineering. At the time of his arrest in 1937, Kabakhsh was an instructor of engineering at the military academy and the manager of the army mechanics school outside Tehran. The contacts he developed in these years proved highly useful later when the Tudeh decided to form cells within the military.

Jowdat, a young physics professor, was one of the party's leading activists in the labor movement. Born into a middle-class family in Tabriz, he was raised in Azerbaijan, educated at the Science College in Tehran, and sent to France by the government to study physics. On his return to Iran in 1938, he joined the faculty of Tehran University. Khalel Maleki, a future thorn in the Tudeh's side, was a German-educated intellectual and a junior member of the "Fifty-three." From an Azeri-speaking family, he grew up in Arak and Tehran, won a state scholarship to Berlin, where he met Arani, and taught science at a secondary school in Tehran until his arrest in 1937. At the party congress, Khalel Maleki was the most vocal critic of the previous leadership, arguing that it had cooperated with the devil to gain Majles seats, recruited members from unreliable class backgrounds, ignored the importance of ideological clarity, failed to enforce party discipline on the labor movement, and, most serious of all, sought to find the nonexistent parliamentary road to socialism. In later years, however, he argued that since his student days in Berlin he had identified more with Kautsky, democratic socialism, and the German Social Democrats, than with Lenin, autocratic communism, and the Russian Bolsheviks.

Olovi, a future Tudeh martyr, was a former civil engineer now working as a full-time party organizer in the provinces. From an Azeri-speaking family that had migrated from the Caucasus, he was born and raised in Tehran. Qassemi, the author of the handbook, *What Does the Tudeh Party of Iran Want and Say?*, was a leading party theoretician who had been sent to work among the Turkomans in Gurgan. From a clerical family in Isfahan, Qassemi grew up in Isfahan and Tehran, and, after graduating from the Law College, headed the departments of the Education Ministry in Yazd and Kermanshah. Joining the Tudeh in early 1942, he had given up a high administrative position in Tehran University to organize the party branch in eastern Mazandaran. Finally, Kianouri, another party theoretician and future First Secretary of the Tudeh, was a professor of architecture at Tehran University. The grandson of the famous Shaykh Fazallah Nouri of the constitutional revolution and the son of a nonwealthy aristocrat, Kianouri was born in Tehran, studied in Tehran University, where he met Arani, and left for Germany on a state scholarship just before the arrest of the "Fifty-three."

The First Party Congress, after electing the Central Committee and the Inspection Commission, approved the new Central Committee's nominations for general secretaries and for the Finance, Publicity, and Organization commissions. The post of general secretary was shared by Iraj Iskandari, Bahrami, and Nuraldin Alamuti. The commissions were filled by five members of the new Central Committee, two members of the Provisional Central Committee—Kobari and E'zazi—and nine newcomers to the leadership—Taqi Fedakar, Taqi Makinezhad, Mohammad Farjami, Anvar Khameh, Dr. Ghulam Hussein Forutan, Dr. 'Ali 'Aqili, Khair Khuah, Sulayman Muhammadzadeh, and Hussein Jahani.

Fedakar, the most prominent newcomer, was the leader of the labor movement in Isfahan. The son of a lowly mulla in Isfahan, Fedakar practiced law in his native city, and had given legal advice to workers accused of sedition by Reza Shah's police. He had organized the local unions after 1941, and won an impressive victory in the 1943 parliamentary elections. Makinezhad, a childhood friend of Khalel Maleki from Arak, was an engineer who had been sentenced to five years' imprisonment as a junior member of the "Fifty-three." Khameh, another junior member of the "Fifty-three," was a writer-translator and high-school teacher from a middle-class clerical family in Tehran. He had been arrested in 1937 while studying at Tehran University. Farjami, a senior member of the "Fifty-three" who had been sentenced to ten years, was an intellectual working in the state-owned tobacco industry. From a Baha'i family in Gilan, he had studied briefly in Russia, and worked with Rusta and the other labor organizers before being arrested.

Forutan, an intellectual active in the CCFTU, was a European-educated professor of biology at Tehran University. Born into a middle-class family in Tehran, he had joined the Tudeh soon after its formation and moved to Kermanshah to organize the local trade unions. 'Aqili, another university professor, was a French-educated lawyer. From a modest clerical family in Tehran, he too had enrolled in the Tudeh soon after its formation. Khair Khuah, the son of a small merchant in Tehran, was the country's leading stage actor. He had been arrested in 1937 for writing "anti-state poetry," and, although tried separately from the "Fifty-three," had been imprisoned with them. Muhammadzadeh, an engineer, had been born in Mashad but worked in the state railways in the Caspian region. Although he had no political past, he had joined the Tudeh soon after its formation. Finally, Jahani, a prominent leader of the CCFTU, was a carpenter born and raised in Tehran. The son of a carpenter, as a youth he had joined the first carpenters' union and the Socialist party.

Thus the leadership of the Tudeh party was still drawn predominantly from Tehran's young generation of Persian-speaking intelligentsia. The thirty-one on the Central Committee and the four Commissions consisted of seven professors and former professors, four engineers, four middle-ranking civil servants, four teachers and ex-teachers, two writer-translators, two lawyers, two high-school headmasters, one judge, one medical doctor, one theater director, one actor, one former pharmacist, and one carpenter. Twenty-five had received higher education: eight inside Iran, six in Germany, another six in France, and five in the Soviet Union. The average age of the thirty-one was less than thirty-six. All but two came from Muslim households. In terms of class background, twenty-one had been born in middle- and lower-class families; ten in prominent clerical, mercantile, and titled families. Only one, however, enjoyed any substantial independent income in 1944. In terms of regional background, fifteen were born in Tehran province, five in Gilan, three in Azerbaijan, three in Khurasan, two in Isfahan, one in Mazandaran, and two in the town of Arak. In 1944, however, twenty-five resided predominantly in Tehran city, one in Isfahan, one in Mashad, one in Rasht, one in Gurgan, one in Sari, and one in Kermanshah. In terms of linguistic background, twenty-two were raised in Persian-speaking homes, six in Azeri homes, one in an Armenian home, and two in Qajar households using both Persian and Turkish. Of course, all thirty-one were fluent in Persian. And in terms of political background, sixteen were members or close associates of the "Fifty-three"—including two former youth members of the Communist party, three who had been active in the youth section of the Communist party, three who were veterans of the Democrat and Socialist parties, and nine who had entered politics after Reza Shah's abdication.

EXPANSION SOUTH (AUGUST 1944-OCTOBER 1946)

In the months after the First Party Congress, the Tudeh continued its rapid expansion—now mostly into the southern provinces. It opened branches in all the forty-four cities with populations over 20,000, and in thirty-two of the thirty-six towns with populations over 10,000. It started recruitment in the south not only in large urban centers such as Yazd, Bushire, Dezful, and Zahedan, but also in smaller industrial centers such as Agha Jari, Ram-i Hormuz, Bandar Mashʿur, and Dasht-i Meshan. It also started six provincial newspapers: *Surat* (The Face) in Rasht; *Safa* (Purity) in Sari; *Gurgan* in east Mazandaran; *Besitun* (Mt. Besitun) in Kermanshah; *Rahnama* (The Guide) in Hamadan; *Ahangar* (The Blacksmith) in Isfahan; *Surush* (The Herald) in Shiraz; and *Rahbar-i Yazd* (The Leader of Yazd) in Yazd. *Rahbar*, the central organ, felt able to declare in 1945, "we can now say that we are a truly nationwide party with organized and open branches in the southern as well as the northern provinces."[34]

Moreover, the Tudeh continued to hold larger and larger street demonstrations. To protest the government's refusal to grant an oil agreement to the Soviet Union, in late October 1944 the Tudeh organized mass meetings in twenty-two cities. According to the U.S. embassy, the meeting outside the Majles drew over 35,000 orderly demonstrators. The *New York Times* reported that this meeting was largely responsible for the fall of the government a few days later. To observe Constitution Day on August 6, 1945, the Tudeh held public rallies in over twenty cities. According to a non-Tudeh paper,

[34] *Rahbar*, 8 January 1945.

the rally in Tehran attracted nearly 40,000 people. To celebrate May Day in 1946, the Tudeh and the CCFTU organized street parades in every significant population center, including conservative southern towns such as Kerman, Na'in, and Rafsanjan. A non-Tudeh paper wrote that the Tehran parade mustered over 60,000.[35] The Tudeh had become the party of the masses in fact as well as in name.

Impressed by these crowds, the reporter for the *New York Times* estimated that the Tudeh and its allies could win as much as 40 percent of the vote in a fair election. He also commented that the Tudeh was "stimulating the masses to think and act politically for the first time." The British ambassador stressed in June 1946 that the "Tudeh was the only coherent political force in the country and is strong enough to nip in the bud any serious opposition since it has almost complete control of the press and of labour throughout the country." Similarly, the American ambassador reported in May 1946, "the Tudeh is the only large, well organized, and functioning political machine in Iran. This is why Premier Qavam wishes to conciliate the Tudeh before the forthcoming elections."[36]

While expanding its mass organizations, the Tudeh also strengthened its political alliances. It recruited new editors into the Freedom Front, so that by early 1946 the Front consisted of over fifty anti-British journalists, including such independent papers as *Dad, Darya*, and *Farman*. The northern branches of the Tudeh absorbed the local offices of a small organization of intellectuals named the Patriotic party (Hizb-i Mehan) when the central leadership of that organization voted to merge with the Iran party. Similarly, the youth section of the Tudeh assimilated the youth section of the small Freedom party (Hizb-i Azadi) as soon as the latter's leadership, headed by Arsanjani, decided to fuse with Qavam's Democrat party. And most important of all, the Tudeh in June 1946 allied with the Iran party to form a United Front of Progressive Parties (Jeb eh-i Mo talef-i Ahzab-i Azadikhah). In announcing the formation of the United Front, the two parties invited others to join them in their combined struggle for national independence, social progress, and recognition of the CCFTU as the only legitimate organization of the Iranian working class."[37] The Iran party

[35] American Ambassador to the State Department, 27 October 1944, *Foreign Relations of United States* (Washington, D.C., 1944), V, 461; *New York Times*, 17 March 1945; *Tofeq*, 7 August 1945; *Farman*, 4 May 1946.

[36] *New York Times*, 15 June 1946, 17 March 1945; British Ambassador to the Foreign Office, 13 June 1946, *F.O. 371*/Persia 1946/34-52664; American Ambassador to the State Department, 31 May 1946, *Foreign Relations of United States* (Washington, D.C., 1946), VII, 490.

[37] Tudeh and Iran Parties, "Joint Declaration," *Jeb'eh*, 30 June 1946.

added that "it had full confidence in the militant and patriotic leaders of the Tudeh party."[38] This United Front was soon joined by the small Socialist party in Tehran, the recently revived Jangali party in Gilan, and the Democratic Parties of Azerbaijan and Kurdistan that had taken over in the northwestern provinces. Finally, Qavam, in preparation for the forthcoming Majles, announced that his Democrat party intended to form an electoral alliance with the United Front.

The rapid expansion of the Tudeh during 1945 and 1946 can be illustrated further by the striking growth of the party's regional organizations in Tehran, in the traditionally conservative cities of Shiraz and Yazd, and in the oil province of Khuzistan. In Tehran, the party increased the number of district clubs from five to thirteen; doubled the readership of *Rahbar* so that on the fifth anniversary of the paper its circulation reached an all-time high of 120,000; and convened the Second Tehran Provincial Conference with 192 delegates—105 more than at the First Provincial Conference. It celebrated its fifth anniversary by holding a mammoth rally of some 100,000. *Rahbar* claimed that this was the largest rally held by a nongovernment organization in the history of the Middle East, and the same source estimated that 75 percent of the demonstrators were wage earners and 20 percent were peasants from nearby villages.[39] The Tehran organization also helped the Peasants' Union by sending cadres into the countryside, especially to the villages near Ray, Karaj, and Veramin. By the summer of 1946, the British ambassador was writing in alarm that the Tudeh endangered Tehran's grain supply by persuading local peasants to refuse to share any part of the harvest with the landlords and the government.[40]

In Shiraz the Tudeh opened its first branch in April 1944, when the editorial board of the city's main intellectual paper, *Oqiyanus* (The Ocean), voted to join the party. The branch was soon joined by a number of young intellectuals: Fereydoun Tavalloli, one of the country's leading poets; Khanum Pirghaibi, a prominent Shirazi poetess; Iraj Zandpour, the headmaster of the main secondary school; and ʿAbdullah ʿAfifi, the editor of *Surush*, which soon served as the party's provincial organ.

Having found a base in the intellectual community, the Tudeh went ahead to organize the local population. It established a youth section and a women's organization. It led a series of successful strikes, especially in the city's two textile factories and in the large sugar mill

[38] M. Poursartip, "Long Live the Tudeh Party," *Jebʿeh*, 2 October 1946.

[39] *Rahbar*, 6 October 1946.

[40] British Ambassador to the Foreign Office, 25 June 1946, *F.O. 371*/Persia 1946/34-52678.

located at Mervdasht on the road to Persepolis. It created a number of trade unions, particularly among cab drivers, electricians, textile employees, and sugar mill workers. And in mid-1946 it began to send militants into the neighboring countryside to organize peasant unions and persuade sharecroppers not to hand over the harvest to landlords. To stem the Tudeh tide, Shirazi notables distributed free food, clothing, and fuel; opened a new orphanage and medical clinic; financed a local organization known as the Party of Hussein (Hizb-i Husseini); hired mullas to preach that the Tudeh intended to abolish polygamy; and sent soldiers in mufti to burn down the Tudeh clubhouse in Mervdasht. The British consul reported that these efforts failed partly because the Tudeh effectively directed its attacks on the "reactionary and mean spirited feudal baron Ibrahim Qavam"; and partly because the local magnates, especially Qavam, Naser Qashqayi, and the governor-general, were still at each other's throats.[41]

The Tudeh developed along similar lines in Yazd. It established its first branch in late 1944, after a strike in one of the city's four textile mills. The branch was led by ʿAbbas Ustadan, a young lawyer educated in Tehran but with family ties in Yazd. The organization grew rapidly as it attracted young intellectuals both from the Muslim population and from the local Zoroastrian community, and led a series of successful strikes in the textile mills. By mid-1945, the Tudeh had organized almost all the mill workers, many of the municipal employees, and initiated a campaign into the neighboring villages. The mill owners retaliated by hiring thugs to intimidate union members, assault Ustadan, and burn down the Tudeh headquarters. The British consul at Kerman reported that in Yazd, "as a result of organized activity at least 70% of the population who represent the working class have been affected. The remainder, who are mill owners, land owners, and merchants, have shown signs of marked nervousness and some of these—notably the Zoroastarian—have frequently asked if it would be possible for them to adopt British nationality." He also reported that Tudeh's activities in Yazd were having "a contageous effect on the normally passive minds of the Kermanis,"[42] encouraging truck drivers, city sweepers, and intellectuals to organize a Tudeh branch. In Kerman over one thousand workers paraded on May Day in 1946.

It was Khuzistan, however, that provided the Tudeh with its most dramatic success. After four years of restrained underground activity among the oil workers, the Tudeh emerged in Abadan in 1946 with

[41] British Consul in Shiraz, "Two-Weekly Reports for 1945," *F.O. 371*/Persia 1945/34-45457.

[42] British Consul in Kerman, 15 August and 15 February 1945, *F.O. 371*/Persia 1945/34-45455.

a massive May Day parade of some eighty thousand. A Labour Member of the British Parliament, after an official tour of Khuzistan, stressed that communist literature had influenced the semi-literate workers and that "81,000 people who are intent on serious business is an industrial force to be reckoned with."[43] Leading a series of oil strikes in May and June, the Tudeh revealed its full strength in July when it organized a general strike of over sixty-five thousand workers throughout Khuzistan. This was the largest industrial strike in Middle East history. After three days of street clashes in which nineteen were killed and over three hundred wounded, Premier Qavam sent a mediation committee to press the oil company to meet some of the strikers' demands. The committee, which included Tudeh leaders, successfully completed its task. A British delegation investigating the crisis reported that "the trade union movement is a genuine one and we recommend winning over Tudeh trade unionists to British ideas." A member of the British cabinet noted in London that "I cannot get it out of my mind that the Tudeh Party, though admittedly a revolutionary party, may be the party of the future which is going to look after the interests of the working man in Persia."[44]

The Tudeh reached its zenith in August 1946, when Qavam gave three cabinet ministries to Keshavarz, Yazdi, and Iraj Iskandari. In the words of Western observers, the Tudeh now contained a core of some 50,000 members and a total of 100,000 active members; controlled by far the largest political organization in the country; and acted with vitality, efficiency, determination, and resourcefulness.[45] Its ministers were able to place party members in crucial positions in the three ministries of Health, Education, and Trade and Industry. Its ally, the Iran party, was able to do the same within the Ministry of Justice. Its other allies, the Democratic Party of Kurdistan and Azerbaijan, were entrenched in the northwestern provinces. Its CCFTU claimed 355,000 members, and, to use the words of an American report, exercised "effective control over labor in general."[46] Its peasant union was making headway, especially in the villages near the

[43] J. H. Jones, "My Visit to the Persian Oilfields," *Journal of the Royal Central Asian Society*, 34 (January 1947), 56-68.

[44] British Foreign Office, "Report of the Parliamentary Delegation to Persia," *F.O. 371/Persia 1946/34-52718*; British Cabinet, Notes on the Report of the Parliamentary Delegation to Persia, *F.O. 371/Persia 1946/34-52616*.

[45] U.S. Congress, Committee on Foreign Affairs, *The Strategy and Tactics of World Communism* (Washington, D.C., 1949), pp. 7-9; British Labour Attaché to the Foreign Office, "The Tudeh Party and Iranian Trade Unions," *F.O. 371/Persia 1947/34-61993*; U.S. Congress, *The Strategy and Tactics of World Communism*, pp. 7-9; British Ambassador to the Foreign Office, 8 October 1946, *F.O. 371/Persia 1946/34-52684*.

[46] U.S. Congress, *The Strategy and Tactics of World Communism*, p. 7.

main towns. Its Freedom Front, according to the British press attaché, influenced many of the 172 papers, journals, and periodicals appearing in 1946. And above all, the party's local branches, at times with armed militias, had virtually taken over the administration of industrial towns such as Abadan, Ahwaz, Isfahan, Sari, Rasht, and Enzeli. The British military attaché reported:

In the Caspian provinces all Persian officials from the Governor downward are under Tudeh supervision. No government official is allowed to send telegraphic messages in code. No movement of gendarmerie can take place without prior permission of the Tudeh. The railway administration is completely under Tudeh control. In fact, the Tudeh can take over whenever it wished to do so.[47]

Expecting a Tudeh takeover in Tehran, the British government began to put into force its contingency plans. These plans involved not only reinforcement of troops in Iraq, anchoring of warships off Abadan, and encouragement of tribal rebels to set up pro-Western autonomous governments in the southern provinces, but also instructions to the Tehran embassy to weaken the Tudeh by digging up embarrassing evidence of Soviet connections and by instigating a split within the party organization. The British ambassador replied, however, that the evidence was hard to find, and that any attempt to cause a split could well boomerang:

Unfortunately, I have not yet succeeded in obtaining any evidence which I consider conclusive regarding relations between the Russians and the hard core of the Tudeh Party—apart from the fact that they are demonstrably close and that the Tudeh line of talk and publicity is identical with the line of the [Russian] Communist Party.[48]

[47] British Military Attaché to the Foreign Office, 25 January 1946, *F.O. 371*/Persia 1946/34-52710.

[48] British Ambassador to the Foreign Office, 27 December 1946, *F.O. 371*/Persia 1946/34-52686. A decade later, the Iranian government tried and failed to find direct links between the Tudeh and the Soviet Union. In recanting and giving evidence for the police, Bahrami in 1957 admitted that he had seen no such links during the fifteen years he had sat on the Central Committee and during the years he had served as general secretary: "The issue of links between the Tudeh and the Soviet Union remains dark and confusing. Invariably, one's guess is prejudiced by one's political views. Even members of the Central Committee, not to mention the rank and file, are in the dark about the issue. In the years I was in the leadership, I often met Alioff, the Secretary of the Soviet Embassy, in both social parties and outside social occasions. But we limited our conversations to subjects of general nature, such as the world situation, the policies of the Soviet Union, and, at times, theoretical problems we had encountered. We never discussed issues concerning the organization of the Tudeh party." Military Governor of Tehran, *Seyr-i Komunism dar Iran* (The Evolution of Communism in Iran) (Tehran, 1957), pp. 215-16.

The organization and methods of the Tudeh are such that it would be impossible to split the Tudeh. The Tudeh Party was originally composed of progressive Left-wing elements without any definite ideological affiliations, but it is now closely associated with the Communist Party. A direct attack on it would be immediately detected, denounced, and nipped in the bud. In fact, it might prove a boomerang to those who had launched it. The attack on Tudeh integrity should therefore be indirect and aimed at detaching individual members as opportunity offers.[49]

REPRESSION (OCTOBER 1946-FEBRUARY 1950)

The tribal revolts in the south, Qavam's sharp turn to the right, and the reoccupation of the northern provinces began four years of intermittent repression for the Tudeh. In Kerman, Fars, and Sistan, armed tribesmen looted party headquarters, destroyed newspaper presses, and forced labor organizers to flee north. In Isfahan, military contingents occupied the party's main offices and drafted union militants into the army. In Khuzistan, the military governor-general deported party leaders while the oil company discharged over 1,000 "troublesome" workers. In Kermanshah, the police shot dead 12 Tudeh demonstrators. In Tehran, the government, using martial law, banned all outdoor meetings, broke a general strike called by the CCFTU, and issued warrants for the arrest of Ovanessian, Kambakhsh, Amir-Khizi, and Iraj Iskandari on the grounds that they had encouraged the Azerbaijan revolt. In the Caspian provinces, military tribunals hanged 3 party activists for planning an armed uprising, sentenced 4 to life imprisonment, and arrested over 140 for possession of weapons. Not surprisingly, the bloodiest reprisals occurred in Azerbaijan and Kurdistan. According to British estimates, over 500 rebels died fighting, 1,200 Azerbaijanis and 10,000 Kurds fled to the Soviet Union, and some 300 insurgent leaders were arrested.[50] In the subsequent months, 45 of them, including 20 army deserters, were executed.

Although the government hit hard at the Tudeh, especially at its provincial branches and union affiliates, and at the armed rebels, it stopped short of banning the party completely. On the contrary, it permitted the central organization to continue holding indoor meetings, publishing newspapers, and working among students, women, and intellectuals. This restraint can be attributed to a variety of factors.

---

[49] British Ambassador to the Foreign Office, "Memorandum on the Present Situation in Persia," *India Office*/L/P&S/12-3491A.

[50] British Military Attaché to the Foreign Office, 1 January 1947, *India Office*/L/P&S/ 12-3505.

The Western embassies argued that it would be wise to allow public discontent a visible outlet.[51] Qavam probably hoped that one day he could again use the Tudeh against the shah. He may also have been reluctant to antagonize the Russians by outlawing the Tudeh. Moreover, he may have calculated that free discussion would encourage dissidents within the Tudeh to challenge the party leaders and openly blame them for the recent disasters. Such a challenge would weaken the Tudeh and indirectly strengthen the government-sponsored Democrat party.[52]

As Qavam expected, the setbacks did trigger a major crisis in the party. Immediately after the fall of Tabriz, the second-tier leaders, headed by Khalel Maleki, forced the top leadership to convene an emergency plenum of the Central Committee, the Inspection Commission, and the Central Committee of Tehran province. The plenum eliminated the post of General Secretary and replaced the Central Committee and the Inspection Commission with a seven-man Provisional Executive Committee. The new leadership consisted predominantly of junior members of the "Fifty-three" and former leaders who had not been closely associated with the policy of supporting either Qavam or the Azerbaijan Democrats. The seven were: Radmanesh, a university professor and head of the youth organization; Keshavarz, a militant young doctor and university teacher who had entered politics in 1941; Yazdi, a well-known surgeon and close colleague of Arani; Forutan, a biology professor who had given up his university position to join the labor movement; Khalel Maleki, a vocal critic at the congress, and leader of party dissidents in Tehran; Tabari, a Marxist theorist and one of the youngest of the "Fifty-three"; and Noshin, a famous theater director and probably the best-known figure in Tehran's intellectual circles. Of the previous Central Committee, Gonabadi and Nuraldin Alamuti, the two former Democrats, were excluded because they were not full-fledged Marxists. Ovanessian, Kambakhsh, Amir-Khizi, Iraj Iskandari, Bahrami, and Boqrati were excluded because the first four had been forced to leave the country, and all six were blamed for the recent disasters.

The Provisional Executive Committee replaced *Rahbar*, which had been edited by Iraj Iskandari, with *Mardom*, which was to be coedited by Radmanesh and Khalel Maleki. It dissolved the whole party organization in Mazandaran for ultraleftism, and expelled twelve of the

---

[51] Ibid.

[52] Hoping to get new recruits, a leading Democrat stated that the government did not hold the "one million adherents" of the Tudeh responsible for the "treasonable acts committed by their leaders." See British Ambassador to the Foreign Office, 29 December 1946, *F.O. 371*/Persia 1946/34-52689.

local leaders for advocating an armed struggle. It quietly disbanded the informal groups that had been formed in the army since 1944 on the grounds that such groups invited police repression. It publicly reaffirmed the party's support for democracy, constitutionalism, and "the legal parliamentary road to social change." It announced that the party did not intend to establish a workers' state, but, on the contrary, favored such economic and political systems as existed in Sweden, Switzerland, Britain, America, and France. It also announced that the party would boycott the forthcoming elections, since the government party and the military had already made plans to rig it.[53]

The election of a new leadership did not end the internal divisions. On the contrary, it began sixteen months of polemics, recriminations, and factional struggles. Some argued that the Tudeh had failed because it had "ignored the armed road to socialism," "underestimated the class struggle," "overestimated the possibility of the parliamentary road," and promoted intellectuals instead of workers to leadership positions. In short, the Tudeh had behaved more like a Menshevik than a Bolshevik organization.[54] Others argued that the Tudeh had failed because it had shouted extremist slogans, fallen victim to "infantile disorders," stifled free discussion, and stressed centralism at the expense of party democracy. In brief, the Tudeh had been both irresponsible and bureaucratic.[55] Still others argued that the Tudeh had failed not through any fault of its own but because of forces and circumstances outside its control: the mistakes made by the Azerbaijan Democrats; the devious policies pursued by Qavam; the reactionary role played by the military; and the Machiavellian plots hatched by the British. In short, the Tudeh had made the best of an impossible situation.[56]

Of the many pamphlets published during the debates, the most important were *Hizb-i Tudeh-i Iran Sar-i Dow Rah* (The Tudeh Party at the Crossroads) and *Cheh Bayad Kard?* (What Is To Be Done?). Both were written by a young economist of Assyrian background named Eprim Eshaq who had recently returned from England where he had studied with Keynes.[57] A close associate of Khalel Maleki, Eshaq argued in the first pamphlet that the Tudeh could blame no one but

[53] A. Qassemi, "Tribute to Rouzbeh," *Tudeh*, 1 (April 1966), 1-3; Provisional Executive Committee, "Proclamation," *Mardom*, 5 and 10 January 1947.

[54] "Marxist Circles," *Mardom*, 4 June-24 August 1947; *Tabaqeh-i Kargar Cheh Mikhuahad? Hizb-i Tudeh Cheh Miguyad?* (What Does the Working Class Want? What Does the Tudeh Party Say?) (Tehran, n.d.).

[55] *Haqayeq-i Goftani* (Truths That Must Be Said) (Tehran, 1947).

[56] B. Mobarez (pseudonym), *Aya Hizb-i Tudeh-i Iran Shekasht Khurd?* (Has the Tudeh Party of Iran Been Defeated?) (Tehran, 1947).

[57] In later years, Eshaq became Fellow of Wadham College in Oxford University.

itself for the recent setbacks, and that these setbacks had been caused by the failure of the party both to develop a coherent ideology and prevent the entry of undesirable elements into the higher echelons as well as into the rank and file of the organization.[58] The lack of a coherent theory, he claimed, had created within the party a contemptuous attitude toward intellectuals and a fatalistic mood toward the future, leading many members to feel that the party was a helpless victim of circumstance rather than an active agent of history. The failure to recruit selectively, he also argued, had permitted the party to be flooded by a horde of opportunists and half-hearted members. To overcome these shortcomings, he proposed two types of reform: increased use of theory, both in formulating policy and training cadres; and division of the Tudeh into a disciplined core formed exclusively of full-fledged militants and a broad front consisting of supporters and sympathizers.

Eprim further elaborated on this second theme in his work entitled *What Is To Be Done?*[59] After giving credit to the Tudeh for having mobilized thousands of intellectuals, workers, and peasants, "many of whom had not heard of democracy and socialism before 1941," he took the party to task for its organizational and ideological shortcomings. As far as organization was concerned, Eshaq argued, the party had stressed quantity of members rather than their quality, and consequently had found itself with many liberals and opportunists as well as radicals and sincere revolutionaries. As far as ideology was concerned, Eshaq added, the party had wavered between reformism and revolution, parliamentary politicking and street rabble-rousing, constitutionalism and armed struggle, trade union economism and clarion calls for radical socialism. To remedy the problem, Eshaq suggested that the Tudeh should be divided into a vanguard party and a people's front. The vanguard party would be composed of militant revolutionaries educated in Marxist theory, fully committed to the principles of democratic centralism, and ready for the armed struggle that would inevitably occur, since ruling classes were not in the habit of giving up power without a fight. The front, on the other hand, would be a broad alliance of progressive organizations such as trade unions, professional associations, and allied political parties. The pamphlet also argued that the Tudeh should strengthen its ties with the left in all countries, particularly in Britain and France.

The supporters of the old leadership retorted that the Tudeh may have made some mistakes, promoted a few unsuitable spokesmen,

[58] Alatur (pseudonym), *Hizb-i Tudeh-i Iran Sar-i Dow Rah* (Tehran, 1947), pp. 1-145.
[59] Eprim, *Cheh Bayard Kard?* (Tehran, 1947), pp. 1-24.

and underestimated theoretical training, but it did create the first mass movement in Iranian history.[60] They argued that the formation of a vanguard would bring charges of élitism and would alienate intellectuals from workers and peasants; that the party had already established organizations for liberals and sympathizers in the form of women's societies, trade unions, and professional associations; and that participation in the cabinet and Majles was justified both because the party had used these platforms to propagate socialism and because other revolutionary parties, such as the French Communist party, had done the same. They added that purists who wanted to keep the party's hands clean of politics were arm-chair revolutionaries incapable of understanding the importance of political participation. They also argued that "ultraleft" demands would scare people from socialism; that the Tudeh should not indiscriminately adopt slogans from other countries and other centuries—such slogans as "the dictatorship of the proletariat"—for, as Lenin had stated, "all parties need not imitate our experience"; and that the Tudeh, as a true Marxist organization, should formulate policies to suit the national environment and should put into practice Marx's maxim that "in a capitalist society the workers fight to overthrow the bourgeoisie, but in a feudal society they help the progressive bourgeoisie to overthrow the reactionary aristocracy." They warned that militants who did not take into account their national environment would be behaving like agents provocateurs.[61]

These open debates avoided, however, two highly sensitive issues. The first concerned the policy of giving unconditional support to the Soviet Union, even when the latter pursued goals that were embarrassing for the Tudeh. For example, when the Soviet Union first demanded an oil concession, forty-three unnamed but important party members privately told the prime minister that they backed his refusal to negotiate.[62] They also complained that the Russians had made their demands only two days after Radmanesh had advocated in parliament the cancellation of past oil agreements and the granting of no future agreements. The second issue concerned the ethnic problem in general and the Azerbaijan rebellion in particular. Some party intellec-

[60] E. Tabari, "A Study on the Conditions in Which the Tudeh Emerged, Developed, and Struggled," *Nameh-i Mardom*, 1 (April 1947), 1-13.

[61] *Tahlil az Avaz-i Hizb* (A Study on the Party's Condition) (Tehran, 1947), pp. 1-40, esp. pp. 6, 10-12, 15; *Rah-i Hizb-i Tudeh-i Iran* (The Road of the Tudeh Party of Iran) (Tehran, 1946), pp. 1-35, esp. pp. 7-8, 19; A. Qassemi, "On the Verge of the Split," *Nameh-i Mardom*, 2 (January 1948), 3-8.

[62] British Ambassador to the Foreign Office, 25 October 1944, *F.O. 371*/Persia 1944/ 34-40241.

tuals, especially those from Persian-speaking homes, were opposed to any demand that would strengthen the provinces at the expense of the central state, the minority languages at the expense of the official language, and the regional authorities at the expense of national sovereignty. They had been uneasy with the ethnic grievances raised at the First Party Congress, feared the armed revolts carried out in Tabriz and Mahabad, and quietly but persistently criticized the Tudeh alliance with the Democratic Parties of Kurdistan and Azerbaijan (see Chapter Eight). These two issues were kept hidden until 1951, when Khalel Maleki published a tract entitled *Hizb-i Tudeh Cheh Miguyad va Cheh Mikard* (What the Tudeh Party Says and What It Did).[63] In describing his reasons for leaving the Tudeh, Khalel Maleki accused the party leaders of blindly following the Russians and of allying with the Azerbaijan Democrats, who "threatened to dismantle Iran." In 1946-1947, however, Khalel Maleki and the other dissidents meticulously avoided these issues in order not to criticize the Russians on either the oil concession or the Azerbaijan rebellion.

When the debates began in late 1946, the dissidents, calling themselves the party reformers, held a large majority. In fact, at the Third Provincial Conference of Tehran convened in July 1947, they won eight of the eleven seats on the local Central Committee. But when the debates ended in late 1947, the dissidents had been reduced to an insignificant minority. A combination of factors caused their reversal. The previous leaders gained votes as the trade unions and the provincial branches recouped from Qavam's blows. The CCFTU opposed the dissidents largely because it continued to be directed by Rusta, one of the original Tudeh leaders who, in the words of the British labor attaché, continued to "retain his popularity with the working class."[64] At the same time, the provincial network as a whole distrusted the dissidents because some branches favored regional demands and some branches communicated with Tehran through Boqrati, another of the original leaders. What is more, many party members had greater personal respect for the previous leaders than for the dissidents, since most of the latter were newcomers to politics, whereas most of the former had risked long prison sentences during Reza Shah's dictatorship.

Furthermore, as the debates unfolded the party reformers themselves divided into leftists, centrists, and rightists. The leftists, led by a veteran communist who had spent ten years in jail, wanted to trans-

[63] Kh. Maleki, *Hizb-i Tudeh Cheh Miguyad va Cheh Mikard* (What the Tudeh Party Says and What It Did), Tehran, 1951.

[64] British Labour Attaché to the Foreign Office, 31 March 1948, *F.O. 371*/Persia 1948/34-68705.

form the Tudeh into an orthodox Leninist party espousing the dictatorship of the proletariat, denouncing the "petty bourgeois constitution," calling for a violent revolution, and officially representing the international communist movement. Labeled by the others as agents provocateurs, the leftists resigned and formed a Communist party (Hizb-i Komunist). This organization, however, dissolved itself a few months later when the Soviets denounced it as an agency of the secret police. Meanwhile, the centrists were led by the young theoreticians Tabari, Qassemi, Jowdat, Forutan, and Kianouri. At first they joined the rightists headed by Khalel Maleki to expel the non-Marxists from the leadership and to stress theoretical training for the party cadres. But as the issues, especially the two sensitive issues, crystalized, they found themselves on the same side as the previous Central Committee. They wanted the party to represent some moderate demands of the provincial branches and the linguistic minorities. And they had no intention of breaking with the Soviet Union, partly because they admired Russia as the first socialist country; partly because they believed in international solidarity; and partly because they suspected that if the Tudeh brazenly charted an independent course the Soviets would create their own organization to rival the Tudeh. Thus the centrists ended up accusing the rightists of failing to distinguish between constructive and destructive criticisms, of conspiring to organize factions within the party, and of refusing to abide by majority decisions and the principles of democratic centralism.[65] Tabari added that those who criticized for the sake of criticizing displayed negativism, cynicism, anarchism, intense individualism, and other character disorders prevalent in Iranian society.[66]

Anticipating expulsion, Khalel Maleki and the staunch dissenters resigned. These "separatists," as they were labeled, included nine prominent intellectuals, three of whom sat on the Central Committee of Tehran Province: Tavalloli and Parvizi, two famous writers from Shiraz; Eshaq, the economist; Makinezhad, a childhood friend of Khalel Maleki and a junior member of the "Fifty-three"; Jalal al-Ahmad, a young essayist who soon became one of the country's leading writers; Ibrahim Golestan, another talented writer who in the 1960s achieved fame as a film director; Nader Naderpour, a young poet and translator of French literature; Ahmad Aram, another translator and well-known

[65] "Criticisms on the Present Situation in Our Party," *Nameh-i Mardom*, 1 (June 1947), 23-33; E. Tabari, "What Is a Party?" *Nameh-i Mardom*, 1 (May 1947), 1-10.

[66] E. Tabari, "A Character Disorder," *Nameh-i Mardom*, 1 (July 1947), 1-3; E. Tabari, "Concerning Some Deviations," *Nameh-i Mardom*, 2 (February 1948), 1-8; E. Tabari, "The Struggle and Method of Reflection," *Nameh-i Mardom*, 1 (January 1947), pp. 80-86.

poet; and Dr. Rahim ʿAbedi, a French-educated professor of chemistry at Tehran University. On leaving the Tudeh, Khalel Maleki and some of his supporters announced the formation of the Socialist Tudeh Society (Jamʿiyat-i Sosiyalist-i Tudeh). This society, however, disbanded a few weeks later when it failed to draw members from the Tudeh and obtain recognition from the Soviet Union. In later years, Khalel Maleki returned to politics by helping form the Toilers' party.

Freed of the dissidents, the Tudeh in April 1948 convened the Second Party Congress. Meeting in semiclandestine conditions in Tehran, the congress included 118 delegates from all regions of the country except the northwestern provinces, where Tudeh members had joined the Azerbaijan and Kurdistan Democratic parties.[67] The congress was a thorough victory for the former leaders and their centrist allies. It endorsed the decision to participate in the cabinet and Majles. The debate, however, was heated enough to make the leaders wary of joining any future government. It also endorsed the decision to ally with the Democratic parties of Azerbaijan and Kurdistan on the grounds that these two parties had "respected the constitutional laws and had tried to strengthen the progressive forces in other parts of the country."[68] It adopted resolutions in support of provincial rights, especially the right to have provincial assemblies. It did not call for formal affiliation with the world communist movement, but did pass motions in support of the communist struggles in Greece, China, and Vietnam. It reaffirmed the party's allegiance to the constitution and stressed the need to wage a broad struggle against "the danger of a new dictatorship."[69] And it approved new party bylaws that strengthened the hand of future leaders. According to the new bylaws, the Congress would elect a Central Committee of nineteen and an Advisory Board of fourteen. The Central Committee, in turn, would elect an Executive Board, three special secretaries, and various committees, including the Inspection Commission, which previously had been chosen by the Congress delegates.

Having accepted the new bylaws, the Congress voted for the Central Committee and the Advisory Board. Of the nineteen elected to the Central Committee, sixteen came from the earlier Central Committees and their special commissions: Radmanesh, Tabari, Jowdat, Rusta, Keshavarz, Forutan, Kambakhsh, Bahrami, Yazdi, Qassemi, Boqrati,

---

[67] The proceedings of the Second Party Congress have not been published, but for brief summaries see: E. Tabari, "A Study on the Proceedings of the Second Party Congress," *Nameh-i Mardom*, 2 (May 1948); B. ʿAlavi, *Kampfendes Iran* (Berlin, 1955), pp. 101-104.

[68] M. Yazdi, "Evidence to the Military Court," *Ittilaʿat*, 16-21 May 1955.

[69] *Mardom*, 5 May 1948.

Kianouri, ʿOlavi, Amir-Khizi, Noshin, and Iraj Iskandari. Kamba-khsh, Amir-Khizi, and Iskandari were elected even though they lived in exile.[70] The three newcomers were Nader Sharmini, Samad Ha-kimi, and Ghulam ʿAli Babazadeh. Sharmini, the new head of the youth organization, was a civil engineer and translator of communist classics from Russian. Born in Tehran into an Azeri-speaking family that had immigrated from the Caucasus, Sharmini had grown up in Tehran and joined the Tudeh in 1942 while studying at the university. He was the bête noire of the Khalel Maleki faction, since he had played a crucial role in swinging the youth organization behind the former leadership. Hakimi, a prominent member of the CCFTU, was a fifty-year-old skilled railway worker. Born into a working-class fam-ily, he had joined the early labor movement and had been arrested in 1937 for organizing unions among railway workers in the Caspian provinces. Babazadeh, another prominent member of the CCFTU, was also a railway worker who had been active in the early labor movement. Born into a poor family in Azerbaijan, he had spent his adult life working in Tehran and the Caspian provinces. This new Central Committee chose Radmanesh as general secretary, Tabari as secretary of the Political Commission, and Keshavarz as secretary of the Inspection Commission.

Whereas the Central Committee contained many former leaders, the Advisory Board of fourteen brought into the upper echelons thirteen new faces: Mahazari, Bozorg ʿAlavi, ʿAli Shandarmini, Ismail Shabrang, Morteza Ravandi, Amanallah Qoreishi, ʿAli Motaqi, Mar-yam Firuz, Muhammad Hussein Tamadon, Akbar Ansari, Jahanger Afkari, Mirza Agha Sayyid Ashrafi, Abul Fazel Farahi, and Hassan Emamvardi. Mahazari, the only member from the earlier leadership, was the lathe worker who had been elected in 1942 to the Provisional Central Committee. Bozorg ʿAlavi, the most distinguished member of the board, was the author of *The Fifty-three* and one of the best-known writers in Iran. Born into a merchant family that had sup-ported the constitutional movement and had later migrated from Iran to Germany, Bozorg ʿAlavi had grown up in Tehran and Berlin, where he had met Arani and taken a keen interest in Freudian psy-chology as well as Marxian philosophy. His elder brother, Morteza ʿAlavi, had joined the Iranian Communist party and served as the main link between the Third International and the Iranian left-wing students in Germany. Returning to Tehran in the early 1930s, Bozorg ʿAlavi taught at the Technical College, published *Chamadan* (Suitcase),

[70] Of the exiled Tudeh leaders, only Ovanessian was absent from the new leadership. He had transferred his activities to the Communist party in Soviet Armenia.

a collection of short stories influenced more by Freud than by Stalinist social realism, helped Arani bring out the journal *Donya*, and eventually received a seven-year sentence as a leading member of the "Fifty-three." Although he had been a founding member of the Tudeh, his literary pursuits had permitted him little time to serve on the previous Central Committees.

Shandarmini, another survivor of the "Fifty-three," was a young tailor from Enzeli who now worked as *Mardom*'s resident reporter in Isfahan. Shabrang, a veteran of the Cultural Society in Rasht, was a former teacher who had joined the Tudeh in 1943 and now acted as the party's chief accountant. Ravandi, a young lawyer, was the editor of *Ahanger*, the Tudeh organ in Isfahan. In later years, he published a major Marxist study entitled *Tarikh-i Ijtima'i-yi Iran* (Social History of Iran). Qoreishi, a translator and party organizer in the southern provinces, was a former army lieutenant who had been imprisoned in 1937 for taking part in a "fascist conspiracy" against Reza Shah. Serving his sentence in the same prison as the "Fifty-three," he had become a Marxist and joined the Tudeh in early 1942. Motaqi, another ex-lieutenant imprisoned for "fascist activities," was a journalist and the party's main organizer in Shiraz. Maryam Firuz, the head of the women's organization, had been a militant party member since 1942. She was a relative of the famous Farmanfarma who had been murdered by Reza Shah, the sister of Muzaffar Firuz, who worked with Qavam, and the wife of Professor Kianouri, who was on the party's Central Committee.

Tamadon, a French-educated journalist, had been the foreign correspondent of *Rahbar* and was now the party's analyst of Majles politics. In later years, he was appointed editor of the party's main newspaper. Ansari, an engineer employed in the Ministry of Agriculture, had been active in the Tudeh since 1943 and was the party's main specialist on peasant problems. Afkari, a young journalist, was a writer and translator of French works on literature and philosophy. Ashrafi, a party militant since 1943, was an intellectual from Azerbaijan and the main liaison with the Democratic Party of Azerbaijan. Farahi, one of the few board members over fifty years old, was a veteran of the early labor movement. He had been active since 1942 in the party organization in northern Khurasan. Finally, Emamvardi, a textile engineer, had joined the youth organization while studying in Tehran University. In 1948 he was manager of the state silk factory in Chalous.

Thus the social composition of the Tudeh leadership remained much the same as before, even though sixteen new personalities entered the top echelons. Among the thirty-three elected to the Central Committee and the Advisory Board, there were eight writers, journalists, and translators, six professors and former professors, five engineers, four teachers and ex-teachers, two lawyers, two railway workers, one former headmaster, one medical doctor, one theater director, one tailor, one lathe worker, and one middle-ranking office employee. Twenty-three had received higher education: eleven in Western Europe, eight only in Iran, and four in the Soviet Union. The average age of the group was less than thirty-seven. All thirty-three came from Muslim families. Twenty-four had been born into middle- or lower-class households; the other nine came from prominent clerical, merchant, and aristocratic families. But only one of the nine was considered wealthy in 1948. Fifteen had been born in Tehran province, six in Gilan, four in Azerbaijan, two in Mazandaran, two in Isfahan, two in Fars, and two in Khurasan. But in 1948, nineteen resided in Tehran, three in exile, three in Gilan, two in Isfahan, two in Shiraz, one in Mazandaran, one in Azerbaijan, one in Khurasan, and one in Khuzistan. Nine were from the "Fifty-three," one had been a close associate of Arani, two were ex-fascists imprisoned with the "Fifty-three," three had been in the youth section of the Communist party, three were veterans of the early labor movement, and fifteen were young Marxist intellectuals who had entered politics after August 1941. The new leadership, however, differed from the previous one in one significant aspect. Of the thirty-one appointed to the top positions by the First Party Congress, six came from Azeri-speaking households and two from Qajar families. But of the thirty-three appointed by the Second Party Congress, as many as eleven came from Azeri households and three from Qajar families. Consequently, over 42 percent of the leadership was now Turkic-speaking.

In the months following the Second Congress, the Tudeh leaders forged a two-pronged strategy. On the one hand, they worked to form a broad alliance of antiroyalist forces and to regain the freedom to create mass organizations, especially trade unions. Thus they espoused support for liberal democracy in general and for the Iranian constitution in particular. They stressed that the CCFTU was a nonpolitical organization separate from the Tudeh. And they shunned street demonstrations, industrial strikes, and other direct confrontations with the state. On the other hand, they concentrated on strengthening the provincial branches and building cadres that would be well disciplined in the rules of "democratic centralism" and well educated in the principles of Marxism and Leninism. Speaking to an audience of Tudeh organizers, Tabari argued that a party could not create a new society unless it had disciplined cadres who had a thorough knowledge of Marxism, of the strategy and tactics of the party, and of the history and social problems of the country. Similarly, Qassemi announced that the Tudeh intended to produce cadres that would be fully committed to the party goals, thoroughly grounded in Marxism, and prepared to make personal sacrifices for the common good.[71] He cited Lenin as saying that a true revolutionary party was not just an organization appealing to wage earners and calling for higher wages, but a disciplined army recruiting only the most politically conscious members of society and the most eager fighters for the working-class revolution. Thus the Tudeh simultaneously tried to moderate its activities and radicalize its members.

The emphasis on radical ideology was reflected in the party's intellectual journal *Nameh-i Mardom* (The People's Letter). Before the Second Congress, the journal had published sympathetic articles on such diverse socialists as Saint Simon, Kautsky, Plekhanov, and Jean Paul Sartre. After the Congress, it narrowed its interests and concentrated on Lenin, Stalin, and "social realism." It printed articles on Lenin's *One Step Forward, Two Steps Back*; Zhadanov's *Social Realism in the Arts*; and Stalin's *Question of Nationalities, Marxism and Linguistics, Internal Contradictions of the Party*, and *Short History of the Bolshevik Party*. It also criticized Sartre's "Anti-Democratic Philosophy of Existentialism," praised Soviet research in genetics, and translated from Russian journals such articles as "Stalin: The Man with the Mind of a Philosopher, the Revolutionary Spirit of a Worker, and the Clothes of a Humble Soldier."

The two-pronged strategy made headway. By May 1948, the Tudeh headquarters in Tehran was holding regular classes for cadres and sending trained organizers to assist the provincial branches. By June, the party newspapers joined Qavam's Democrats, Sayyid Ziya's supporters, and other anticourt editors to form a Press Front against Dictatorship. Sayyid Ziya even announced that if he became premier he would free the Tudeh of police restrictions, since the "Tudeh is a law-abiding and patriotic organization."[72] By August, Yazdi and Keshavarz had a special audience with Premier Hezhir and presented him with a four-point reform program calling for a new labor law; an immediate 15 percent increase in the peasant's share of the harvest; a freeze on the military budget; and the lifting of martial law in Khuzistan, Mazandaran, Isfahan, Azerbaijan, and north Khurasan.[73] And by February 1949, the Tudeh obtained a police permit to hold a memorial service for Arani. This was the first public meeting sponsored by the party since December 1946. The turnout, estimated

[71] E. Tabari, "Lessons from Past Experiences," *Nameh-i Mardom*, 2 (July 1948), pp. 50-56; A. Qassemi, "The Training of Cadres," *Nameh-i Mardom*, 2 (June 1948), 59-71.
[72] Sayyid Ziya, "If I Became Prime Minister," *Khvandaniha*, 27 February 1948.
[73] Tudeh Party, "Proposals to Premier Hezhir," *Mardom*, 9 August 1948.

between 10,000 and 30,000, surprised the government. Western newspapers, which had earlier published the party's obituaries, now warned that the Tudeh was daily gaining new ground. *Le Monde* reported that the disintegration of Qavam's Democrats had left the Tudeh as the country's only effective party. The *New York Herald Tribune* and the *Christian Science Monitor* cited foreign diplomats' estimates that the Tudeh had the sympathy of over 33 percent of the country and over 80 percent of the urban population.[74] Similarly, the British embassy, in a confidential report for the Foreign Office, detailed the quiet revival of the Tudeh:

The policy of the Tudeh organization during the past twelve months has been to avoid public activities and to concentrate on consolidating its organization and recruiting reliable members. The veil has been so tightly drawn that many opponents of the Tudeh both in government and the trade union circles have convinced themselves that the organization is moribund and no longer dangerous. In point of fact, however, there is evidence to show that the Tudeh has not wasted its time and it may have the support, tacit or avowed, of some 35% of the industrial population. To have obtained, and retained, this sympathy whilst the movement has been under a certain amount of pressure from the government and could not arouse enthusiasm by demonstrations or positive action, is a considerable achievement.[75]

The Tudeh revival ended abruptly, however, with the mysterious attempt on the shah's life made on the day of Arani's memorial service. In the wake of the assassination attempt, the government declared martial law and detained not only Tudeh leaders but also prominent politicians such as Mossadeq and Kashani. In the following week, the premier accused the Tudeh of masterminding the plot to kill the shah, and presented evidence linking the would-be assassin to the religious paper *Parcham-i Islam* as well as to the journalists' union affiliated with the CCFTU. Although the government soon dropped the assassination charges for lack of hard evidence, it invoked the 1931 law to ban the Tudeh as a communist organization. It also charged the Tudeh with undermining the constitutional monarchy during 1944-1946 by inciting riots in Abadan, organizing strikes in Khuzistan, arming workers in Mazandaran, and encouraging secessionists in Azerbaijan and Kurdistan.[76]

In the crackdown that ensued, the police occupied the Tudeh of-

---

[74] ʿAlavi, *Kampfendes Iran*, p. 84. Military Governor of Iran, *Seyr-i Komunism*, pp. 107-108; *Le Monde*, 18 October 1948; *New York Herald Tribune*, 24 May 1950; *Christian Science Monitor*, 7 June 1950.

[75] British Ambassador to the Foreign Office, 31 March 1948, *F.O. 371*/Persia 1948/34-68705.

[76] *Ittilaʿat*, 2 March-22 April 1949.

fices, confiscated its assets, and arrested over two hundred of its leaders and organizers. During the following months, military tribunals tried many of the leaders. The four who had escaped in 1946—Ovanessian, Kambakhsh, Amir-Khizi, and Iraj Iskandari—were condemned to death in absentia. So were another five who had evaded arrest in February 1949—Radmanesh, Babazadeh, Rusta, Keshavarz, and Tabari. Seven others who had avoided arrest—Bahrami, Forutan, Babazadeh, Sharmini, Qoreishi, Bozorg 'Alavi, and Maryam Firuz—were tried and sentenced to long terms, even though they were absent. Finally, ten who had been captured—Kianouri, Qassemi, Yazdi, Jowdat, Mahazari, 'Olovi, Boqrati, Noshin, Hakimi, and Shandarmin—were sentenced to prison terms varying from ten months to ten years. Thus, by mid-1949, nine of the nineteen-man Central Committee were in prison and the other ten were either in exile or in hiding with heavy penalties hanging over their heads. The government, congratulating itself, pronounced the Tudeh dissolved.

REVIVAL (FEBRUARY 1950-AUGUST 1953)

The government declared the Tudeh dead and buried. In fact, the Tudeh may have been buried, but it was by no means dead. Taking over the leadership, the Advisory Board and the survivors of the Central Committee instructed the party branches to form underground cells of five to six members. They set up clandestine presses and continued to print *Mardom, Zafar*, and *Razm*. They encouraged sympathizers in the military to establish a secret network in the armed forces, since the party no longer risked the wrath of the government. Moreover, they waited patiently for better days, expecting an improvement in the political situation sooner or later.

The political situation improved sooner than the Tudeh could have expected. The controversial elections for the Sixteenth Majles and the government decision to allow relatively free balloting in Tehran gave the Tudeh the opportunity to circulate newspapers, publicize its views, and, although not sponsoring candidates, to hold public meetings. The appointment of Razmara as prime minister further helped the Tudeh, since the new premier, despite his military background, quietly relaxed police controls on the left in the dual hopes of placating the Soviet Union and undermining the National Front. After he named an officer with left-wing sympathies to be in charge of the main prison, not surprisingly nine Tudeh leaders—Yazdi, Jowdat, Kianouri, Noshin, 'Olovi, Qassemi, Hakimi, Boqrati, and Shandarmini—escaped and went underground. The election of Mossadeq helped the Tudeh even further, for the new prime minister accelerated the pace of liberalization. Although he neither repealed the 1931 law nor formally lifted the 1949 ban, he believed that police controls violated civil liberties and the constitutional laws. He argued that the royalists smeared social reformers as communists in much the same way as the Qajars had labeled their opponents "heretical Babis."[77] And he realized that he needed all the public support he could get in order to oust the British from the oil industry and expel the shah from politics.

As the government controls relaxed, the Tudeh and its sympathizers established an impressive array of newspapers and front organizations, each with a periodical. To have a legal paper, the party started the "independent daily" *Besu-yi Ayandeh* (Toward the Future), and appointed Tamadon of the Advisory Board as its editor in chief. To replace the outlawed youth and women's organizations, it created the Society of Democratic Youth and the Society of Democratic Women. To continue the work of the peasants' union and the CCFTU, it formed the Society to Help Peasants, the Society to Fight Illiteracy, the Society for Free Iran, and the Coalition of the Workers' Syndicates of Iran. To radicalize the nationalist campaign against the British, it established the National Society of Democratic Journalists, the Iranian Society of Peace Partisans, and the National Society against the Imperialist Oil Company. To appeal to the Azeri population, it founded the Society of Azerbaijan and demanded provincial assemblies, "equitable distribution of investments," and elimination of unemployment in the northern regions.[78] And to mobilize students and members of the modern middle class, it formed the Organization of High School Students, the Society of Democratic Lawyers, the Union of Tenants, and numerous occupational associations such as the Union of Teachers, Union of Engineers, and Union of Government Employees. Meanwhile, the underground network continued to publish the party organs and carry out its organizational functions. Ironically, circumstances had forced the Tudeh to separate open activities from covert activities, and thus adopt organizational methods that it had three years earlier denounced as élitist and vanguardist.

With the formation of these organizations, the Tudeh reemerged as a major political force. In the spring of 1951, at the height of the nationalization campaign, the Tudeh first organized a series of strikes in the oil fields and then repeated the major success of 1946 by organizing a general strike of 65,000 in Khuzistan and the oil industry. Fateh, the anticommunist leader of the defunct Comrades' party, wrote: "One must admit that the Tudeh was a major force partici-

---

[77] M. Mossadeq, *Parliamentary Proceedings*, 16th Majles, 4 July 1950.
[78] *Besu-yi Ayandeh*, 2 October 1951.

pating in the struggle to nationalize the oil company." In May 1951, when the government permitted May Day celebrations for the first time since 1946, the Tudeh held rallies in all the main cities, mobilizing as many as 35,000 demonstrators in Tehran.[79] In the summer of 1951, when Mossadeq was in the midst of negotiating with the United States, the Tudeh organized mass protests against the visit of Averell Harriman. The protests left 25 dead and over 250 injured.

The Tudeh continued to gain strength in 1952. In the dramatic events of the July uprising, the participation of the pro-Tudeh unions made the general strike a success throughout the country. Tudeh workers took the leading roles in industrial centers such as Isfahan, Abadan, and Agha Jari—and Tudeh demonstrators in Tehran helped bring victory to the National Front. Fateh commented, "although diverse elements participated in the July uprising, the impartial observer must confess that the Tudeh played an important part—perhaps even the most important part." Arsanjani, writing on behalf of Qavam, argued that the Tudeh was the chief force defeating the shah. And Kashani, the day after the riots, sent a public letter to the pro-Tudeh organizations thanking them for their invaluable contribution toward the national victory. In assessing Tudeh strength, a CIA memorandum dated October 1952 reported that the front organizations had a mass following, and estimated that the party had as many as 20,000 hard-core members, with 8,000 of them in Tehran.[80] The memorandum added that the party's rank and file were predominantly proletarian; that its thirty candidates for the Seventeenth Majles had been defeated not because of electoral weaknesses but because of ballot stuffing; that its propaganda "mentioned the northern neighbor from time to time, but softly, not to the blare of trumpets"; and that its organization was remarkably efficient in retaining secrets. The memorandum concluded by admitting that "practically nothing is known of the party's internal activities": "In a country notorious for lack of discipline, information which has been obtained regarding the clandestine Tudeh Party has revealed little beyond the lowest echelons."

The Tudeh gained even more strength in 1953. On May Day, it held rallies in all the major towns and in some, such as Abadan, it outdid even the massive parades of 1946. In late May, the Society of Democratic Youth organized a festival in Tehran that attracted over 50,000 students. And on the anniversary of the July uprising, the Tudeh called for a mass meeting outside parliament, and, according

[79] Fateh, *Panjah Saleh-i Naft-i Iran*, p. 491; *Time*, 14 May 1951.

[80] Fateh, *Panjah Saleh-i Naft-i Iran*, p. 608; H. Arsanjani, *Yaddashtha-yi Siyasi* (Political Memoirs) (Tehran, 1956), p. 4; *New York Times*, 23 July 1952; U.S. Embassy to the State Department, "The Tudeh Party Today," *The Declassified Documents*, 308D.

to reliable estimates, mobilized nearly 100,000, outnumbering the National Front ten to one. Fateh commented: "If in the rallies before March 1952 one-third of the demonstrators had been Tudeh and two-thirds had been National Front, after March 1952 the proportions were reversed."[81] By the last days of Mossadeq's administration, observers were reporting that the Tudeh had over 25,000 members, some 300,000 sympathizers, and, despite police restrictions, the most effective organization in the country. One foreign correspondent warned that the Tudeh was gaining so many adherents that it would "sooner or later take over the country without even the need to use violence."[82]

As the Tudeh gradually reemerged as a major force during 1951-1953, the party leadership was confronted with the inevitable question: whether or not to support the Mossadeq administration. Not surprisingly, the leaders were sharply divided. The more experienced members of the Central Committee, especially the former deputies who had often found themselves on the same side as Mossadeq in the complicated maze of the Fourteenth Majles, favored an alliance, even if the alliance was only tacit and indirect. They argued that the Tudeh should help the National Front because the latter represented the national bourgeoisie fighting British imperialism and working for a national democratic revolution, and because the former could gradually transform this national democratic revolution into a socialist working-class revolution through petitions, meetings, and other forms of mass action. As an editorial in the party organ stated, the Tudeh could work with Mossadeq since his National Front represented the "national bourgeoisie and the liberal aristocracy," genuinely opposed the British oil company, advocated the redistribution of land, even if too cautiously, and wanted to undermine the feudal class structure.[83]

The newer members of the Central Committee, however, not only opposed such an alliance but advocated direct confrontations with the National Front. They viewed Mossadeq not as the leader of the national bourgeoisie fighting British imperialism, but as the puppet of the comprador bourgeoisie attached to American imperialism; not as a great liberal constitutionalist but another Qavam who would inevitably doublecross the Left; and not as a determined reformer but a vacillating aristocrat who would eventually make his peace with the

[81] *Zafar*, 14 May 1953; *Javanan-i Demokrat*, 1 June 1953; *New York Times*, 23 July 1953; Fateh, *Panjah Saleh-i Naft-i Iran*, p. 653.
[82] Military Governor of Tehran, *Seyr-i Komunism*, p. 316; F. Curtois, "The Tudeh Party," *Indo-Iranica*, 7 (June 1954), 14-23; *Time*, 13 July 1953.
[83] "Concerning the Movement of the Liberal Bourgeoisie," *Razm*, 26 June 1950.

forces of reaction, even with the shah.[84] They concluded that the Tudeh should "expose" the National Front, undercut its social support, and, mobilizing the middle class, single-handedly carry out the national democratic revolution as well as the socialist working-class revolution.[85]

The debate was won by the hard-liners. They owed their victory to a combination of factors. First, many of the more experienced leaders lived in exile, and thus found themselves cut off from the day-to-day decisions of the underground organization. Second, the disastrous experience under Qavam had a chilling effect on the most warm-hearted advocates of a united front. Even the most secure members of the Central Committee remembered the heated debates and public recriminations of 1946-1948. Third, the provincial organizations largely opposed Mossadeq, since he adamantly refused to grant concessions to the provinces and the linguistic minorities. Fourth, the labor organizers were in constant confrontation with the administration not only over wages, strikes, and demonstrations, but also over legislation imposing rigid controls on trade unions. Finally, the Soviets most probably sided with the hard-liners, since Stalin in 1951-1953 saw the world sharply divided into socialist and imperialist countries, with no room left for neutrals like Mossadeq.

Having won the debate, the hard-liners put into effect their policy. The Coalition of Workers' Syndicates held mass meetings to demand higher wages, protest government restrictions, and complain that the police were helping the rival unions set up by the Toilers' party and its main thug Sha'yban "the Brainless." The Union of Railway Workers organized demonstrations to challenge Mossadeq's proposal to disenfranchise illiterates. The Society of Democratic Youth sponsored teach-ins to "expose the conspiracy between the shah and his prime minister."[86] The Society of Democratic Women celebrated the forty-fifth anniversary of the Constitutional Revolution by demanding the right to vote and criticizing the government for its reluctance to extend the franchise. The Tudeh press constantly portrayed Mossadeq as a feudal landlord, a devious old-time politician, and a stooge of the United States. And the National Society against the Imperialist Oil

---

[84] "The Iranian Ruling Class," *Besu-yi Ayandeh*, 29 November 1951; "Government Policies," *Besu-yi Ayandeh*, 27 November 1951; "The Anti-National Policies of Dr. Mossadeq," *Besu-yi Ayandeh*, 22 July 1952; "Is There a Deal between Mossadeq and the Shah?" *Besu-yi Ayandeh*, 3 December 1951.

[85] "Only the Working Class Can Head the Revolution against Imperialism and Feudalism," *Razm*, 1 May 1953.

[86] *Besu-yi Ayandeh*, 18 October 1951; *Ittila'at-i Haftegi*, 24 May 1951; "Is There a Deal between Mossadeq and the Shah?" *Besu-yi Ayandeh*, 3 December 1951.

Company brazenly defied a government ban on street parades and organized demonstrations that clashed violently with the police and the Toilers' party.[87] The administration retaliated by imposing martial law on Tehran and arresting eighty-six Tudeh activists. In 1951-1952 the Tudeh supported the National Front only during the July uprising, when the danger from the shah appeared imminent.

In later years, the more moderate leaders criticized the hard-liners for pursuing "ultraleft policies." One recent historian of the student movement has written that the party's youth organization during the Mossadeq era held unauthorized demonstrations, published inflammatory articles, manifested symptoms of romantic heroism, and considered itself rather than the working class as the vanguard of the socialist revolution. Kambakhsh wrote that inexperienced leaders had undermined Mossadeq by raising irresponsible demands, such as the immediate establishment of a democratic republic. Kianouri, speaking at a seminar on the national bourgeoisie, declared, "an incorrect assessment of the role of the national bourgeoisie sometimes leads to mistakes. . . . Such left-wing sectarian mistakes were made by our Tudeh party between 1949 and 1953 during the struggle for oil nationalization."[88] Iraj Iskandari explained,

During the struggle for the nationalization of the Iranian oil industry we did not support Mossadeq, who undoubtedly represented the interests of the national bourgeoisie. We thought along these lines: Mossadeq is fighting for the nationalization of Iranian oil, but the American imperialists are backing his movement, which means that they are guiding it. And so we drew the incorrect conclusion that the communists should not support the nationalist movement.[89]

Similarly, a plenary meeting of the leadership held after the 1953 coup admitted that the Tudeh had made a drastic mistake in not fully backing Mossadeq, in failing to appreciate the "anti-imperialistic content of the national bourgeoisie," and in pursuing "ultraleft sectarian policies."[90]

The discussions of 1951-1953 had nonetheless been somewhat ac-

[87] *Besu-yi Ayandeh*, 7 August 1951; "The Toilers' Party of America," ibid., 14 October 1952; *Bakhtar-i Emruz*, 16 July 1951.

[88] A. Heraz, "The Tudeh Party and the Youth of Iran," *Donya*, 3 (August 1976), 89-97; 'A. Kambakhsh, *Nazari Beh Jonbeshi Kargari va Komunist-i dar Iran* (Comments on the Workers' and Communist Movement in Iran) (Stockholm, 1975), II, 103-104; N. Kianouri, "The National Bourgeoisie," *World Marxist Review*, August 1959, pp. 61-65.

[89] I. Iskandari, "What Do We Mean by the National Bourgeoisie?" *World Marxist Review*, September 1959, pp. 10-15.

[90] Tudeh Party, *Darbareh-i Bist-u-Hashteh-i Mordad* (Concerning August 19th) (n.p., 1963), pp. 1-64.

ademic, since the final decision rested with Mossadeq, not with the Tudeh. And Mossadeq opposed the formation of a united front, for he realized that if he allied with the Tudeh he would antagonize the United States. If he antagonized the United States, he would lose economic, political, and, most important of all, diplomatic assistance. And if he lost these forms of assistance, he would face additional financial difficulties, increased military instability, and further diplomatic isolation in the conflict with Britain. Moreover, the other leaders of the National Front were divided in their approach toward the Tudeh. Whereas the Iran party and the more anticourt politicians, such as Fatemi and Razavi, favored a tacit alliance, the Pan-Iranist and Toilers' parties, not to mention the clerical leaders, vehemently opposed any form of cooperation. The day after the July uprising, the organ of the Toilers' party denounced the Tudeh as a foreign conspiracy hatched jointly by Russia and Britain. Using more sophisticated arguments, Khalel Maleki warned that the Tudeh was making impressive inroads into factories, schools, and government offices because the authorities complacently believed their own propaganda about the "dissolved party" and lacked the courage to restrict the activities of international communism. He added that an alliance with the Tudeh would prove disastrous for the National Front.[91]

As a result, Mossadeq followed an inconsistent policy toward the Tudeh. On the one hand, he refused to ban all demonstrations, to outlaw the front organizations, or to crack down on the not-so-secret underground network. At times he even "welcomed" its support, brought three of its sympathizers into the cabinet, and publicly announced that it was an integral part of the Iranian nation.[92] On the other hand, he retained the 1949 ban, continued to keep the exiled leaders out of the country, and refused to initiate formal negotiations for a broad alliance.

The mutual suspicions between The Tudeh and the National Front eventually helped to destroy Mossadeq. On August 16, 1953, as the shah fled from the country, Tudeh crowds poured into the streets, destroying royal statues, demanding a republic, and criticizing Mossadeq for not acting decisively enough. In some provincial towns, Tudeh demonstrators occupied municipal buildings and raised red flags. It appeared as if the royalist defeat had become a communist rather than a nationalist victory. The following day, Mossadeq, at the urging of the American ambassador, instructed the army to clear the

---

[91] "The Tudeh Conspiracy," *Shahed*, 23 July 1952; Kh. Maleki, "Notes of the Month," *'Ilm va Zendigi*, April-May 1953, pp. 100-105; "An Alliance with the Tudeh Will Weaken the National Front," *Niru-yi Sevum*, 27 July 1953.

[92] Kambakhsh, *Nazari*, II, 102.

streets of Tudeh demonstrators. Moreover, the organs of the National Front declared in their early-morning issue that the danger from the shah had ended but the danger from the communists loomed large and would destroy the nation unless promptly stamped out. As the army moved into the streets, the Tudeh leaders informed Mossadeq by phone that their military sympathizers had evidence to prove that the royalist officers had conspired to use the premier's instructions to reestablish law and order as a cover to overthrow the National Front. They also urged Mossadeq to form a broad alliance and to appeal to the nation over the radio to resist with arms the impending coup d'état.[93] Mossadeq, however, replied that such action would lead to mass bloodshed.

Rejected by Mossadeq, the Tudeh failed to act against the coup. A small minority in the leadership advocated armed resistance and the distribution of weapons through the party's military network. But the majority argued that such policies would be futile as long as the National Front refused to join in a broad alliance and the royalists continued to have an overwhelming military superiority.[94] Instead, they proposed that the party should patiently wait for better days, recruit new members, and continue with its underground but peaceful activities.

The shah, however, had no intention of allowing the Tudeh even a limited existence. Dismantling the Tudeh underground in a series of police roundups from 1953 to 1958, the regime arrested over three thousand party members. Although many rank-and-file members were soon released after signing public recantations, party leaders, militant activists, and military members were severely punished. Forty, including 'Olovi of the Central Committee, were executed. The others among the forty consisted of nine party organizers, three sailors, and twenty-seven military officers. Another fourteen, including Farahi of the Advisory Board, were tortured to death. And over two hundred, led by Yazdi, Bahrami, and Sharmini, had their death sentences commuted to life imprisonment. By 1959, little remained of the once impressive underground organization. But, as the American embassy warned, although the Tudeh had lost an effective organization, it had gained a valuable record of bravery and martyrdom.[95]

[93] Ibid., pp. 101-102; Captain Fesharki, "The 1953 Coup," *Ittila'at*, 20 August 1979.
[94] "Concerning National Resistance," *Mardom*, 12 January 1954.
[95] U.S. Embassy to the State Department, "Anti-Tudeh Campaign," *The Declassified Documents*, 309A.

SEVEN

Class Bases of
the Tudeh

After Reza Shah's abdication the Tudeh Party cleverly exploited the situation
to spread its communistic propaganda among the population, especially among
intellectuals and workers. Gradually the propaganda bore fruit: factory workers behaved disrespectfully towards their superiors, refusing to obey orders,
and began to join strikes. Simple minded and inexperienced workers were
easily misled by the barrage of Tudeh papers using such false slogans as
"reactionary," "ruling class," "the people," "the campaign against imperialism," and "the necessity of preventing the recurrence of another dictatorship."
—Military Governor of Tehran, *The Evolution of Communism in Iran*, pp. 8-9.

CLASS PROFILE

The Tudeh party began in 1941 with general appeals to
all citizens, irrespective of class, to unite in a mass movement against Reza Shah's dictatorship. During the following three
years, however, it gradually narrowed its appeal, so that by the end
of the First Congress it spoke less of the general rights of citizens than
of the specific grievances of workers, peasants, intellectuals, traders,
and craftsmen. And during the next four years, especially after the
Second Congress, it narrowed its appeal further, so that by 1953 it
was projecting itself as the "vanguard of the proletariat and landless
peasantry." The Tudeh's image of itself did not correspond fully to
reality, of course, for although wage earners helped to give the movement a broad mass base throughout the thirteen years between 1941
and 1953, it was the modern middle class that formed the major
portion of the party's top, middle, and lower echelons. The modern
middle class also made up an important portion of the party's general
rank and file and sympathizers.

Top Echelons. Of the fifteen delegates elected by the Tehran Provincial Conference to the Provisional Central Committee in October

1942, thirteen (87%) were professionals, intellectuals, salaried personnel, and other members of the modern middle class. Only one (7%) was a worker. Of the thirty-one appointed by the First Congress to the Central Committee and its commissions, thirty (97%) came from the modern middle class and only one (3%) from the urban working class. And of the thirty-three placed by the Second Congress on the Central Committee and the Advisory Board, twenty-nine (88%) were middle-class and four (12%) were wage earners.

Middle Echelons. Among the sixty-eight provincial leaders who in 1946 sat on the Central Committees of Tehran, Fars, Isfahan, Khurasan, Khuzistan, Gilan, and Mazandaran, fifty-two (76%) came from the modern middle class and fourteen (21%) from the working class. Among the 107 delegates at the First Congress whose occupations are known, seventy-seven (72%) were middle-class and twenty-nine (27%) were urban wage earners. And, according to the leader of the CCFTU, among the 192 delegates at the Second Provincial Conference of Tehran, almost half were workers and the other half were intellectuals, professionals, and office employees.[1]

Lower Echelons. The role of the modern middle class remained important, though less so, among the party's organizers, activists, and militants. Of the twenty-nine militants arrested in November 1946 for possession of arms in Mazandaran, twenty (69%) were workers and eight (28%) were middle-class.[2] They included six laborers, four foremen, three railway repairmen, three train inspectors, three terminal operators, two engine drivers, two office clerks, one truck driver, one railway shunter, one wagon car manager, one building inspector, one coffee-house owner, and one full-time party organizer.

Of the 183 party activists who were arrested with the party leaders in February 1949 in the wake of the assassination attempt, seventy-nine (43%) were middle-class and ninety-eight (54%) were urban wage earners.[3] They consisted of seventy-one factory workers, thirty-two office employees, sixteen high-school students, twelve mechanics, twelve engineers, seven university students, seven housewives, six booksellers and newspaper sellers, five writers, four peddlers, three teachers, three coffee-house keepers, two doctors, one lawyer, one photographer, one tailor, and one peasant.

Similarly, of the 168 party activists who were arrested for organizing

[1] R. Rusta, "Speech to the Conference," *Rahbar*, 21 August 1945.
[2] Iranian Government, *Iqdamat-i Ghayreh-i Qanuni* (Illegal Activities) (Tehran, 1947), pp. 62-63.
[3] Compiled from *Dad* and *Ittila'at*, February 1949-May 1950.

demonstrations during the summer of 1951 and whose occupations are known, 105 (62%) came from the modern middle class and sixty (36%) from the urban working class.[4] They included sixty-one students, fifty-eight workers, eighteen office employees, seventeen teachers, four journalists, three engineers, two agricultural workers, one doctor, one clergyman, one peddler, one craftsman, and one full-time party organizer.

Rank and File. The class composition of the rank and file was reflected in public recantations given by nearly 3,000 former members after the 1953 coup and published in *Ittila'at* from 1 September 1953 until 1 May 1957. Of the total, some did not describe their occupations and some had been former leaders, organizers, and party activists. But of the 2,419 who had been ordinary members and whose occupations were indicated, 1,276 came from the modern middle class, 860 from the urban working class, 169 from the traditional middle class, and 69 from the peasantry (see Table 7). Thus the intelligentsia, who formed less than 8% of the country's labor force, constituted more than 53% of the party's rank and file; and the urban wage earners and town peddlers, who together totaled as little as 15% of the labor force, made up as much as 36% of the rank and file. Conversely, the rural masses, who totaled over 54% of the labor force, contributed only 3% of the rank and file. The most represented occupations were civil servants, who formed over 15% of the membership but only 2% of the adult population; teachers, who contributed nearly 7% of the membership but less than 0.6% of the adult population; university students, who composed as much as 8% of the membership but as little as 0.07% of the adult population; and oil, railway, skilled, and large factory workers, who totaled more than 15% of the membership but less than 1.7% of the adult population.

SALARIED MIDDLE CLASS

If the modern middle class played an important role in the Tudeh party, the Tudeh party played a no less important role in the modern middle class. It recruited intellectuals and white-collar workers into the party apparatus. It directed its newspapers, journals, and periodicals toward the intelligentsia. It created professional associations, and by 1946 affiliated to the CCFTU twenty-four white-collar unions, including the Syndicate of Engineers and Technicians, Union of

---

[4] Listed in *Besu-yi Ayandeh*, 14 October 1951; 2 March 1952; 9 October 1951; 21 April 1952.

Teachers and Educational Employees, Association of Lawyers, Society of Doctors and Veterinarians, and Union of Oil Company Employees. The influence of the Tudeh was so pervasive that the meaning of "rushanfekr" changed again. In the 1910s and 1920s, "rushanfekr" had been a subjective term describing the intellectuals who wanted rapid change. In the 1930s, it had been an objective term characterizing the salaried occupations and modern educated professionals, especially teachers, doctors, engineers, lawyers, and civil servants. In the 1940s, however, it again became a subjective term describing the radical middle class that wanted thorough economic, social, and political changes. Vocal opponents of the Tudeh, such as Sayyid Ziya, used "rushanfekr" much in the same way that European rightists during the 1930s used the terms "communist sympathizer" and "fellow traveler."

Although the Tudeh had extensive influence throughout the salaried middle class, its strength can best be seen among engineers, university professors and students, intellectuals, especially writers, modern-educated women, and, most surprising of all, military officers. Tudeh influence among engineers appeared as early as April 1943, when technicians in the department of mines and factories within the Ministry of Trade and Industry struck for higher salaries, job security, and representation on the administrative board of the ministry. Although the strike was initially sponsored by the nonpolitical Association of Engineers, the Tudeh helped organize a series of strikes for similar demands and for "show of solidarity with fellow members of the rushanfekran."[5] Participating in these work stoppages were doctors and veterinarians in the Interior Ministry and science and law instructors in Tehran University, as well as engineers in the Tehran municipality, tobacco monopoly, and ministries of Roads, Interior, and Agriculture. After an impressive strike lasting three full weeks, the government gave in, raised salaries, and permitted skilled personnel to have representation on the administrative boards. And a few months after the victory, the engineers who sympathized with the Tudeh criticized the leaders of the Engineers' Association for working too closely with the Iran party, and, resigning from the association, formed their own Syndicate of Engineers and Technicians. At its first congress, the syndicate affiliated with the CCFTU and resolved to press the government to fight unemployment, invest in heavy industry, hire native technicians before foreigners, and carry out land reform.[6] By the end of 1946, the Syndicate of Engineers and

[5] *Mardom*, 28 and 29 April 1943.

[6] Syndicate of Engineers and Technicians, "Resolutions of the First Congress of the Syndicate," *Jeʿbeh*, 2 July 1946.

TABLE 7
Occupational and Regional Background of Tudeh Rank and File Members

	Tehran	Tehran Province	Azerbaijan[a]	Gilan	Mazandaran	Kurdistan	Kermanshah	Khuzistan	Isfahan[a]	Fars	Khurasan	Kerman	Sis.&Baluch.	Unspecified	Total
Salaried Middle Class															1276
Teachers	13	4	15	19	60	6	2	10	6	2	5	1		22	165
Doctors	7		1	4	8	1			2	1		1		4	29
Engineers	10	1		4	3	1	1		1					1	22
Pharmacists & dentists	4	2	3	1	2			1	1		2			1	17
Lawyers	3	2			2										7
Intellectuals[b]	19	1	7	2	3	1	2	3	1					2	41
Nurses	12	2	3	5	1	1	2	1	5	2	1				35
Govt. employees[c]	115	19	36	45	54	6	12	29	14	5	16	4	2	29	386
Oil company employees							2	20							22
Private company employees	16	4	4	4	3		2	4	2					3	42
Unspecified office employees	6	4	3	3	7				3					1	27
University students[d]	52	10	16	21	31	3	7	7	20	7	4	4	2	17	201
High-school students	63	11	13	37	65	8	8	29	6	2	2	1	1	15	261
High-school graduates	6	1	1	1	2	2					1			3	17
Unemployed	2				1					1					4
Working Class															860
Skilled workers[e]	43	6	8	18	15	3	3	7	10		2			10	125
Oil workers								37							37
Railway workers	6	3	3	4	3			3						6	28
Small factory	16	2	12	4	7				2		2			3	48
Large factory:															
Textiles	8	5	2	1	53				8					3	80
Silos	5	5													10
Cement	10														10
Munitions	12														12
Tobacco	15		2												17
Other large	20	4	11	2	4				3					1	45
Tailors	13	3	5	11	9			2	4		2			5	54
Shoemakers	12	1	17	8	2	1	2	2	9		1			5	60
Carpenters	10	1	7	3	5	1		1	7					4	39
Drivers[f]	14	3	12	3	6	1	1	6	9	2	2			7	66
Roadsweepers	1	2	2					1	1						7
Laborers[g]	5	2	5	1	2			1						7	23
Shop assistants[h]	5		4	2	7			1	1					7	27
Peddlers	2	1	14	2	3		1		1		2	1		5	32
Unspecified	29	5	36	11	16	2	1	1	9	1	2			8	121
Unemployed	7	2		4	2			1	1					2	19

TABLE 7 (*cont.*)

	Tehran	Tehran Province	Azerbaijan[a]	Gilan	Mazandaran	Kurdistan	Kermanshah	Khuzistan	Isfahan[a]	Fars	Khurasan	Kerman	Sis.&Baluch.	Unspecified	Total
Propertied															
Middle Class															169
Shopkeepers[i]	15	2	22	23	22		1	6	2					20	113
Merchants	2		1	11	2		1	2				2		4	25
Small landowners			1		3		1							1	6
'Ulama							1								1
Craftsmen-															
workshop-owners	7			3	5		1		2			4		2	24
Peasants		13	2	19	22		1	1	6					5	69
Other															
Housewives	9	4	5	7	8		1	1	3	1	1			5	45
Total for all occupations															2419

[a] The Azeri-speaking town of Zanjan in Gilan has been included in Azerbaijan. The Persian-speaking districts of Arak, Malayer, Kashan, and Mahallat have been included in Isfahan.

[b] The category of intellectuals includes writers, journalists, translators, painters, architects, sculptors, and musicians.

[c] Government employees include not only civil servants in the ministries, but also white-collar workers in the municipalities, Plan Organization, National Bank, railway network, tobacco monopoly, forestries, and National Customs.

[d] The students were at Tehran University. The location identifies their birthplace.

[e] Skilled workers includes modern craftsmen such as mechanics, electricians, railway drivers.

[f] Drivers includes truck drivers, cab drivers, and chauffeurs.

[g] Laborers includes porters and construction workers.

[h] Shop assistants includes menial office workers.

[i] Shopkeepers includes bakers, grocers, booksellers, barbers, butchers, and coffee-house keepers.

Technicians had far more members than the rival Association of Engineers.

Whereas the Tudeh had a competitor among engineers, it enjoyed an open field among university students. It began campus activities in April 1943, when the youth organization, which had been formed a month earlier, opened a club near the College of Medicine, and, attracting members, established a student union. By February 1945, the union won recognition from the university authorities as the official representative of students in the colleges of Medicine, Dentistry, and Pharmacology. And by December 1945, after a campuswide strike against a rival organization set up by the university administration, the union won recognition as the sole representative of students in the colleges of Law, Science and Technology, Literature, and Agriculture, as well. In early 1946, the chancellor of the university admitted to the British ambassador that many of his four thousand students were strongly influenced by the Tudeh.[7]

Despite the political setbacks of 1946-1947 and the internal splits of 1947-1948, the Tudeh retained its strength at Tehran University. In September 1947, the Tehran branch of the youth organization held a provincial conference and announced that it had grown 20 percent in the last two years, and that over 40 percent of the members were high-school and university students.[8] In November 1948, the pro-Tudeh union of students organized a successful strike throughout the university to protest a government ban on campus university activities. The Tudeh estimated that over half of the college students were either party members or party sympathizers.[9] Although the youth organization and the student union were outlawed in February 1949 together with the Tudeh, party members on the campus formed first the Society of Democratic Youth and later the Organization of Tehran University Students, which affiliated with the International Union of Students in Prague. In November 1949, these new organizations led a successful strike for improved living conditions and better student dormitories. In March 1950, they closed down the Medical College, demanded written contracts for interns, and after three weeks won their demands when the other colleges threatened to join the strike. And in early 1951, they organized a general strike throughout the colleges to demand the removal of police from the campus, to support the campaign against the British, and to protest the expulsion of eight communists from the university. Bazargan, a founding member of the Iran party, summed up the situation of 1950-1951 when he was dean of the College of Science and Technology:

In those days, the university administration's worst headache was the Tudeh party. This organization had successfully intensified its student activities after 1947 so that by 1951 we were besieged from all sides—by students, professors, clerical workers, and even campus cleaners. The communist students had taken over the university clubs, held their meetings in classrooms, incited employees to strike for higher wages, and, worst of all, continually interfered

---

[7] British Ambassador to the Foreign Office, 7 February 1946, *F.O. 371*/Persia 1946/34-52664.

[8] ʿA. Kambakhsh, *Nazari Beh Jonbesh-i Kargari va Komunisti dar Iran* (Comments on the Workers' and Communist Movement in Iran), (Stockholm, 1975), I, 119.

[9] E. Tabari, "Eight Years of Struggle," *Razm Mahaneh*, 1 (September 1948), 2-5. The British Embassy reported in late 1948 that Tudeh influence among university students was increasing daily. British Ambassador to the Foreign Office, 8 December 1948, *F.O. 371*/Persia 1948/34-68709.

with the curriculum. The communist influence was so pervasive that the university administration had no say on its own campus.[10]

Tudeh influence among college students continued through the Mossadeq years. In mid-1951, *Tehran Mosavar* (Tehran Illustrated), a popular weekly magazine, reported that 25 percent of the university students were secret Tudeh members and another 50 percent were party sympathizers; that the Organization of Tehran University Students had channeled funds to the striking oil workers in Khuzistan; that Tudeh militants held key positions in all the branches of the university, especially in the colleges of Medicine, Dentistry, Pharmacology, Literature, Science and Technology, and Law; and that the Iran and Toilers' parties, the only potential rivals of the Tudeh, had limited success exclusively in the colleges of Agriculture, Law, and Science and Technology.[11] By late 1951, the university administration was warning that 75 percent of the incoming freshmen were communists because of political indoctrination by their high-school teachers. And by 1953, Khalel Maleki was complaining that 80 percent of the university students were "misled" by the Tudeh because the government had failed to restrict communist propaganda.[12]

The recantations given after 1953 indicate not only the significance of Tehran University as a whole to the Tudeh Party, but also the relative importance of particular faculties. Of the 140 students who mentioned their field of specialization, 32% were studying medicine; 29% science and engineering; 13% dentistry, pharmacology, and veterinary medicine; 11% literature; 9% art; and 6% law. The recantations also indicate the importance of Tehran University to the leadership of the underground youth organization. Of the twenty-two on the Central Committee of the youth organization in late 1953, ten were students or recent graduates of the university. And of the six on the Central Committee of the organization's Tehran branch, three were from Tehran University.

Tudeh influence among intellectuals, especially writers, was even more impressive. In addition to prominent writers such as Bozorg ʿAlavi, Noshin, Tavalloli, Parvizi, al-Ahmad, Aram, and Golestan, who were active in the organization, numerous other well-known writers sympathized with the party, particularly in the period before 1947. They included Nima Yushej (ʿAli Esfandiyari), the father of modern Persian poetry; Bahar, the veteran Democrat and living symbol of

[10] M. Bazargan, *Dafaʿat dar Dadgah* (Defense at the Court) (n.p., 1964), p. 40.

[11] "The Activities of the Tudeh Party in Tehran University," *Tehran Mosavar*, 2 August 1951.

[12] J. Emami, *Parliamentary Proceedings*, 16th Majles, 31 October 1951; Kh. Maleki, "Notes of the Month," *ʿIlm va Zendigi*, April-June 1953, pp. 100-105.

classical poetry; and Sadeq Hedayat, generally considered the leading figure of modern Persian literature. Nima Yushej, who continued to support the Tudeh until his death in 1957, was born in 1895 in Mazandaran into a farming family, but grew up in Tehran among intellectual relatives. During the 1920s, his elder brother, an active communist, had fled to the Soviet Union, where, it was later revealed, he fell victim to the Stalinist purges. During the 1930s, Nima Yushej developed the new style of poetry, but much of his works remained unpublished, partly because their radical content antagonized the political authorities and partly because their modern form annoyed the classical authors. It was not until the 1940s that Nima Yushej became a popular poet with ready access to the public both through *Mahaneh-i Mardom*, the intellectual magazine of the Tudeh, and through *Payam-i Now* (New Message), the organ of the Soviet-Iranian Cultural Society.

Bahar, the main literary critic of Nima Yushej, was often a close supporter of the Tudeh, although never a party member. He sympathized with the Tudeh during the early 1940s, and, although he joined Qavam's Democrats, he consistently advocated an alliance with the left. In 1950 he became chairman of the Peace Partisans and remained at that post until his death in April 1951. Hedayat, one of the few pro-Tudeh writers from an aristocratic background, was the brother-in-law of Razmara and the relative of a royalist general. Educated in Europe, Hedayat was strongly influenced by Kafka and Chekhov, both of whom he translated, and, like his close colleague Bozorg ʿAlavi, combined psychological themes with social analyses. Although Western readers know him best for his psychological work *The Blind Owl* (*Buf-i Kur*), Iranian readers during the 1940s admired him most for his satirical piece *Hajji Agha*. Despite his ingrained pessimism, he wrote a number of political and optimistic works during his involvement with the Tudeh. After the debacle of late 1946, he left Iran and three years later committed suicide in Paris.

The Tudeh also won the sympathy of many talented younger authors as well as lesser-known older intellectuals. They included Sadeq Chubak, the author of a collection of short stories entitled *Khayma Shab Bazi* (The Puppet Show); Behazin (Mahmud Eʿtemadzadeh), a former naval officer, who had translated Shakespeare's *Othello* and combined Hemingway's realism with Balzac's social criticism in a collection of short stories titled *Besu-yi Mardom* (Toward the People); Saʿid Nafisi, a highly regarded professor of literature, translator of French, and historian of the Arab conquest of Iran; Muhammad Afrashteh, the editor of a popular satirical paper named *Chalangar* (Locksmith), and a talented poet who, despite retaining the classical form, dealt with everyday issues and revolutionary ideas; Ahmad

Shamlou (Bamdad), the leading disciple of Nima Yushej; Muhammad Muʿin, a professor of literature and prolific writer on Iranian history; and a host of new but gifted poets such as Fakhraldin Gurgani, Nader Naderpour, Naqi Melani, Mehdi Eʿtemad, Muhammad Javaheri, Muhammad Tafazouli, and Ahar Mʿuiri (Zaghcheh). Thus the list of pro-Tudeh writers reads like a Who's Who of modern Persian literature. As the London *Times* noted in 1947, the Tudeh at its height attracted the "most talented and best educated of the young generation of Persians." Similarly, the French journal *L'Observateur* commented in mid-1952: "Western diplomats agree that 30 percent of Iranian intellectuals are active in the Tudeh, and the rest, with the small exception of Anglophiles and Americanophiles, are party sympathizers."[13] In a culture that placed great value on literature, especially poetry, it is not surprising that these writers had considerable influence among the reading public.

Tudeh activity among women began in 1943 with the formation of the women's organization for party members and the women's society for party sympathizers. After 1949, these two were replaced by a unified Society of Democratic Women. The main personalities in these organizations were often relatives of party leaders—but relatives who had achieved prominence in their own professions or had been active in the early women's movement, especially in the Patriotic Women's Society created by the Socialist party. They included Zahra and Taj Iskandari of the famous radical family; Maryam Firuz of the Advisory Board; Dr. Khadijeh Keshavarz, a prominent lawyer, the author of a book on women's legal rights, and the wife of the Dr. Keshavarz on the Central Committee; Dr. Akhtar Kambakhsh, a well-known gynecologist and author of a book on child rearing, who was the sister of Nuraldin Kianouri and the wife of ʿAbdul Samad Kambakhsh of the Central Committee; Badrimoner ʿAlavi, the sister of Bozorg ʿAlavi; ʿAliyeh Sharmini, a veteran of the early movement and the mother of the Sharmini who headed the youth organization in 1947-1948; Loretta (Varto Tarian), the country's leading actress and a member of Noshin's theater company; Sadiyeq Amir-Khizi, another veteran of the early movement and the wife of the Amir-Khizi on the Central Committee; and Homa Houshmandar, a high-school teacher and editor of the party's feminist journal *Bidar-i Ma* (Our Awakening). As an exposé in *Tehran Mosavar* stated, the Women's Organization of the Tudeh party focused its activities on students, teachers, and other modern educated women.[14]

Although the party leaders often complained that the movement

[13] *The Times*, 24 October 1947; J. La Hervé, "L'Iran," *L'Observateur*, 5 June 1952.
[14] "The Communist Danger Threatens Women," *Tehran Mosavar*, 26 March 1952.

had not attracted enough women and although no more than 3.4 percent of the rank and file were women, the Tudeh was the only political organization that consistently mobilized women and vigorously championed women's rights.[15] Its Society of Women called for the extension of political and social rights to all citizens, irrespective of sex; literacy courses and educational clubs for women; equal pay for equal work; and more schools for girls despite a campaign by the religious authorities to close down the existing ones. Its press often argued that Reza Shah's reforms were inadequate since they had been modeled after fascism, which aimed not at true equality but at "placing women in the home as wives, mothers, housekeepers, and cooks." Its deputies in the Fourteenth Majles caused a minor uproar by introducing a new electoral bill that proposed to enfranchise adult women.[16] Moreover, the Tudeh repeatedly embarrassed the Mossadeq administration by convening women's congresses, by demanding full equality between the sexes, by collecting over 100,000 signatures for the extension of the suffrage, and by encouraging women to disregard the law and to participate in the 1953 referendum against the shah.

The Tudeh had considerable success even among the military officers. This was surprising, since military personnel received preferential treatment as the pillar of the monarchy, went through ideological indoctrination that stressed royalism and anticommunism, obtained special training and weapons from the West, and risked heavy penalties for associating with any political party. Moreover, as Samuel Huntington has emphasized in *The Soldier and the State*, the professional ethos of the officer corps tends to be hierarchical and highly conservative.[17] Although the Tudeh did not establish its Military Organization until after 1949, officers sympathetic to the party had formed their own informal groups as early as 1944.[18] These groups had not developed into formal organizations for a number of reasons. First, twenty left-wing officers stationed in north Khurasan had mutinied in August 1945, and, without party authorization, tried to organize an uprising among the Turkoman tribes. Failing to establish contact with the Turkomans, they had been routed by the

[15] Qassemi, "The Training of Cadres," *Nameh-i Mardom*, 2 (July 1948), p. 69; Of the 2,419 who recanted and gave their occupations, only 82 were women. Besides the 45 housewives, they included 11 university students, 10 nurses, 5 office workers, 4 tailors, 2 teachers, 3 high-school students, 1 doctor, and 1 writer.

[16] Society of Women, "Program of Our Society," *Rahbar*, 22 October 1943; "Women's Equality," *Rahbar*, 2 October 1946; Tudeh Party, "Proposals for a New Electoral Law," *Parliamentary Proceedings*, 14th Majles, 15 August 1944.

[17] S. Huntington, *The Soldier and the State* (Cambridge, 1959), p. 59.

[18] Lieutenant Vatandoust, "Information on Tudeh Activities in the Military," *Ittila'at*, 22 May-1 June 1956. These discussion groups in 1944 read Kasravi, Marx, and Engels.

gendarmerie. Although in later years the Tudeh lauded the rebels as "national heroes," at the time it refused to be associated with the rebellion.[19] Second, in the aftermath of the Khurasan mutiny, the government arrested forty-three other leftist officers and rushed through parliament an emergency loan of 35 million rials to improve living conditions in the army. Third, the revolts in Azerbaijan and Kurdistan encouraged some thirty officers to desert and join the rebels. Twenty of them were later executed. Finally, the Tudeh, anxious to preserve its legal status, had in late 1946 instructed sympathizers in the armed forces to disband their informal groups.[20]

It was not until after the 1949 ban that the Tudeh created its Military Organization. The organization was led by Colonel Siamak and ex-Captain Khosrow Rouzbeh.[21] Siamak, a native of Gilan, had been friends with some of the Tudeh leaders, especially Kambakhsh, since the early 1920s, when they were members of the Educational Society of Qazvin. Secretly retaining these contacts, Siamak joined the gendarmerie and won important commissions throughout Reza Shah's reign. Even his contacts with Arani remained undetected. Rouzbeh, the son of an army officer, had been born in Malayer and grew up in Hamadan and Kermanshah. Entering the army as a career, he excelled at the military academy and won a teaching post at the Officers' College, where he impressed not only his students but also his commanding officer, General Razmara. After Reza Shah's abdication, Rouzbeh joined the informal left-wing groups in the army, and as a result was arrested in the aftermath of the Khurasan mutiny. While waiting for his trial, he wrote three short books on chess, artillery warfare, and Marxism. At his trial in 1946, he denied membership in the Tudeh, and argued that whereas he was a full-fledged revolutionary, the Tudeh was merely a reformist party that wanted gradual change through parliamentary legislation.[22] Found guilty of spreading seditious ideas in the army, he was cashiered and sentenced to fifteen years' hard labor. Four years later, he, together with the nine Tudeh leaders, managed to escape from prison. In hiding, Rouzbeh continued to work among his army colleagues, first setting up secret cells independent of the party and then establishing the Military Organization of the Tudeh party.

---

[19] Central Committee of the Tudeh Party, "A Reply to False Accusations," *Farman*, 7 October 1945.

[20] Qassemi, "Tribute to Rouzbeh," *Tudeh*, 1 (April 1966), p. 2.

[21] 'A. Kambakhsh, "Notes on the History of the Iranian Army," *Donya*, 6 (Summer 1965), 27-47; H. Qayampanah, "The Tudeh Party and the Armed Forces," *Donya*, 15 (July 1976), 98-102; "Kambakhsh," *Donya*, 12 (Autumn 1971), p. 6.

[22] Kh. Rouzbeh, *Eta'at-i Kurkuraneh* (Blind Obedience) (Tehran, 1946), pp. 57-58.

Beginning with fewer than 100 members in 1950, the Military Organization had over 500 by 1954. A CIA report later observed that most of the Tudeh officers, who came from the lower middle class, for four years "forestalled detection by excelling at their work." Uncovered in 1954, 466 military personnel were brought to trial during the next three years. They included 22 colonels, 69 majors, 100 captains, 193 lieutenants, 19 sergeants, and 63 cadets. Rouzbeh, Siamak, and 25 others were executed; 144 were sentenced to life imprisonment; 119 to fifteen years; 79 to ten years; and the others to shorter terms ranging from eight years to eighteen months.[23] Western correspondents who observed the executions told the CIA that the officers had marched to their deaths defiantly shouting Tudeh slogans, and that the chief executioner had to administer the coup de grâce because the forty-man firing squad had missed, out of nervousness or because of their sympathy for the victims. The CIA reported that "large segments of the public are emotionally impressed by the display of defiance and bravado put on by the condemned men."[24]

The size and determination of the military network has raised the question of why the Tudeh did not try either to carry out its own coup or preempt the eventual royalist coup. That it did neither can be explained partly by the political divisions between the Tudeh and the National Front, but mainly by the location and specialization of the pro-Tudeh officers. Among the 466 brought to trial, none commanded a motorized division in or near Tehran.[25] The vast majority were from the military academies, gendarmerie, police, and inconsequential air force, as well as the medical, engineering, and communication corps. Of the colonels and majors, only five came from the cavalry and none from the tank divisions in Tehran. The personal screening carried out by the shah had prevented Tudeh influence from reaching the crucial sectors. With army doctors, air force cadets, and bridge-building engineers, the Tudeh could influence rank-and-file troops and even distribute weapons to party members, but could not possibly pull off a successful coup d'état.

Among the salaried middle class, the extent of Tudeh success was

[23] U.S. Embassy to the State Department, "Anti-Tudeh Campaign," *The Declassified Documents Retrospective Collection*, Microfiche 1952-54 (75), 309A; Military Governor of Tehran, *Ketab-i Siyah* (The Black Book) (Tehran, 1956). Among those given a life sentence was a young lieutenant named ʿAli Muhammad Afghani, who, six years later, impressed the literary circles by publishing a Tolstoy-length social novel entitled *Shohar-i Ahu Khanum* (Mrs. Ahu's Husband).

[24] U.S. Embassy to the State Department, "Anti-Tudeh Campaign," *The Declassified Documents*, 309A.

[25] One had been assigned the responsibility of supervising the personal safety of the shah in 1952-1953 and of organizing the visit of Vice President Nixon in 1953.

apparent, but the reasons for this success were not. They are particularly intriguing, since the Tudeh was, as a Marxist organization, associated with such radical concepts as the destruction of the bourgeoisie and the triumph of the proletariat, the elimination of classes and the introduction of social equality, the withering away of nationalism and the emergence of international communism. As one Western social scientist has argued, "no avowedly anti-nationalist movement has a chance in the modern Middle East: the only question is whether its founders would be jailed first or lynched."[26] To understand why this did not happen in Iran it is necessary to examine the economic, social, and ideological forces that drew the intelligentsia toward the Tudeh party.

The main economic problem besetting the salaried middle class was spiraling inflation. The cost of living in the urban centers had risen in the last years of Reza Shah from an index of 100 in 1936-1937 to 162 in 1940-1941; jumped rapidly during the war to an all-time high of 1,030 in 1944-1945; dipped slightly during the postwar recession to 832 in 1947-1948; and during the oil crisis again escalated rapidly to a new peak of 1,047 in late 1953.[27] Thus the intelligentsia had to raise their salaries by over ten times just to preserve their 1936 standard of living. Although white-collar employees of prospering private companies obtained significant pay raises, civil servants and government employees had to wage a continuous struggle to keep their heads above water. In this struggle, the Tudeh played a vital role organizing an impressive array of white-collar unions and actively helping them obtain salary increases. In August 1943, for example, when the clerical staff of the Justice Ministry struck for higher salaries, the Tudeh helped organize sympathy strikes in the ministries of Roads, Finance, and Trade and Industry. In March 1947, when elementary-school teachers stopped work for better salaries, the Tudeh encouraged secondary-school teachers to do the same. And in February 1952, when left-wing civil servants formed the Alliance of Government Employees as a successor to the banned Union of Government Employees, the Tudeh announced that it would help the affiliates of the alliance to bargain for "just salaries and improved working conditions."[28]

The Tudeh's attraction for the intelligentsia resulted chiefly from the country's class structure. In the eyes of the intelligentsia, especially

[26] D. Rustow, "The Politics of the Near East" in *The Politics of Developing Areas*, edited by G. Almond and J. Coleman (Princeton, 1960), p. 432.

[27] Bank Melli Iran, "Cost-of-Living Index," *Bulletin*, no. 142 (January 1954), pp. 19-20.

[28] *Razm*, 10 August 1943; *Rahbar*, March-April 1947; *Besu-yi Ayandeh*, 25 February 1953.

once the euphoria of August 1941 receded, the destruction of Reza Shah's autocracy had heralded not a true democracy but a corrupt oligarchy of feudal landlords, tribal magnates, robber barons, grasping courtiers, and dangerous army generals. Moreover, the snobbish attitudes of the traditional upper class constantly irritated the modern middle class. For example, the leader of the royalist caucus in the Fourteenth Majles contemptuously told one of the few deputies who came from the intelligentsia,

The whole trouble with this country is that amateurs like you are sticking their noses into politics. Electrical and civil engineers should spend their time building houses and bridges, instead of sitting here and shooting off their mouths on state issues and other matters they know nothing about. If everyone did what they were trained to do, the country would not presently be in such a sorry condition.[29]

The target of this attack responded that the French president was an electrical engineer, that deputies had no right to slander the country's educated class, and that the Majles should be purged of illiterates and those without modern education.[30] Furthermore, the names appearing and reappearing in the cabinet reinforced the middle-class view that politics was a game of musical chairs played exclusively by members of the so-called "one thousand families."

In the struggle to batter down the walls of class privilege, the Tudeh was at the forefront. In the words of one veteran Democrat who was by no means friendly to the Tudeh,

Those who know Iran well realize that communism has little appeal. Yet the Tudeh had much appeal. Why? Because the Tudeh was the only movement that posed a real challenge to the ruling class. For fifty years, ever since the Constitutional Revolution, the middle class has yearned to get rid of the oligarchy. But it was not until the Tudeh was formed that the middle class found a well-organized party. Ironically, the oligarchy should be considered the best friend of the Tudeh.[31]

During most of these years, Tudeh newspapers, parliamentary candidates, and mass demonstrations focused on the real and imaginary abuses of the upper class. The party program proposed to distribute the large estates, increase taxes on wealth, and decrease taxes on salaries, wages, and consumer goods. The extensive propaganda machine hammered away on the social injustices produced by the vast inequality between rich and poor. And the party intellectuals pub-

[29] M. Tabatabai, *Parliamentary Proceedings*, 14th Majles, 11 September 1944.
[30] H. Farivar, *Parliamentary Proceedings*, 14th Majles, 11 September 1944.
[31] H. Qodsi, *Kitab-i Khatirat-i Man ya Tarikh-i Sad Saleh* (Book of My Life or History of One Hundred Years) (Tehran, 1963), II, 641-42.

lished a series of works both on the concept of class struggle in Marxist theory and on the politics of class conflict in contemporary Iranian history. Ovanessian analyzed the word "class" in a dictionary of sociopolitical terms, and discussed the issue of social conflict in numerous articles on "Class Cleavages," "The Paris Commune," and "The Russian Revolution of 1905."[32] Kianouri wrote a popular handbook entitled *Class Struggle*.[33] Qassemi came out with books on *What Is Law?* and *Get To Know Society*, and articles on the Mazdak revolt, the oligarchical nature of the Senate, and "July 14th: The Day that Inaugurated a New Age for Mankind."[34] Tabari published studies on "The World Outlook of Marxism," "What Is Surplus Value?" "Historical Lessons," and "The Relationship between Society and Sociology."[35] Other party intellectuals produced pamphlets entitled *Lenin and Leninism, Communism, The 1905 Revolution, Property from the Perspective of Dialectical Materialism, The State from the Perspective of Dialectical Materialism*, and *Imperialism and Militarism in the Present Age*.[36] Still others wrote articles on "Income and the Standard of Living in Iran," "Landownership in Iran," "The Cost of Living in Iran," "The Laws of Iran and the Interests of the Toiling Classes," "Materialism and the History of Philosophy," and "The Centenary of the *Communist Manifesto*."[37] Thus the Tudeh and its Marxist doctrine were in tune with the intelligentsia and its dislike of the upper class.

The British consuls often noted that the Tudeh was highly successful in channeling into its own ranks middle-class antagonisms to-

[32] A. Ovanessian, *Farhang-i Loghat va Estelahat-i Siyasi va Ijtema'yi* (Dictionary of Social and Political Terms) (Tehran, 1946); "Class Cleavages," *Rahbar*, 30 October 1946; "The Paris Commune," *Nameh-i Mardom*, 1 (November 1946), 83-93; "The Russian Revolution of 1905," *Nameh-i Mardom*, 1 (March 1947), 66-77.

[33] N. Kianouri, *Mobarezat-i Tabaqati* (Class Struggle) (Tehran, 1948).

[34] A. Qassemi, *Qanun Chist?* (What Is Law?) (Tehran, 1947); *Jam'ehra Beshenasid* (Get to Know Society) (Tehran, 1946); "Mazdak," *Nameh-i Mardom*, 2 (September 1947), 51-66; "Concerning the Senate," *Razm Mahaneh*, 1 (June 1948), 7-13; "July 14: The Day That Inaugurated a New Age for Mankind," *Nameh-i Mardom*, 2 (July 1948), 75-81.

[35] *Nameh-i Mardom*, 1 (October 1946), 32-39; (November 1946), 17-23; (December 1946), 1-5; 2 (October 1947), 1-21.

[36] *Lenin va Leninism* (Tehran, 1947); *Komunism* (Tehran, 1947); *Inqilab-i 1905* (Tehran, 1946); *Malekiyat dar Nazar-i Materyalism-i Dialaktik* (Tehran, 1948); *Dowlat dar Nazar-i Materyalism-i Dialaktik* (Tehran, 1948); *Imperialism va Miylitarism dar Dowreh-i Hazer* (Tehran, 1948).

[37] E. Eshaq, "Income and the Standard of Living in Iran," *Nameh-i Mardom* 1 (September 1946), 30-36; A. Ansari, "Landownership in Iran," *Nameh-i Mardom*, 2 (May 1949), 91-98; D. Nava'in, "The Cost of Living in Iran," *Razm Mahaneh*, 1 (October 1948), 11-18; M. Farnai, "The Laws of Iran and the Interests of the Toiling Classes," *Nameh-i Mardom*, 1 (November 1946), 31-35; M. Kaveh, "Materialism and the History of Philosophy," *Nameh-i Mardom*, 2 (February 1948), 8-20; M. Babak, "The Centenary of the *Communist Manifesto*," *Nameh-i Mardom*, 2 (March 1948), pp. 6-9.

ward the upper class. For example, the consul in Mashad reported in 1945 that the forty-seven party members in the small nonindustrial town of Birijand included eleven teachers, ten tradesmen, eight government employees, six lawyers, three small landowners, three laborers, two bank clerks, two mullas, and two gendarmes. He commented that the local party consisted of the "discontented bourgeoisie" and that the unifying factor among the members was the dislike of the local magnates, especially the famous ʿAlam family, on whom the Tudeh had "declared war." The consul in Hamadan noted that the Tudeh attracted the local intellectuals, professionals, and civil servants because it posed the main threat to the well-known Qaragozlu family. Finally, the consul in Kermanshah observed that the Tudeh appealed to many intellectuals and government employees in his region because it mobilized the whole of its local machinery to challenge the unpopular Qubadian house.[38]

The political outlook of the intelligentsia also tended to correspond with the ideology of the Tudeh party. This outlook had three component parts: constitutionalism, socialism, and nationalism. The intelligentsia of the 1940s, like that of the 1890s but unlike that of the 1920s, believed that constitutional liberties were indispensable as well as desirable both for individual well-being and for social progress. In the eyes of the generation that had lived through the instability of the 1910s, the constitution had lost its mystique, whereas the concept of the Leviathan had grown attractive. But for the generation that had experienced Reza Shah's autocracy, the Leviathan had lost its appeal, whereas the constitution had regained its former mystique. The new generation, moreover, continued the previous generation's attachment to modernization, secularization, and industrialization. But although the old associated these reforms with liberalism and the French Revolution, the new tended to associate them with socialism and the Russian Revolution. To be sure, for the Iranian intelligentsia socialism meant not necessarily public ownership of the means of production, but instead energetic state planning for rapid industrialization and extensive social reforms, especially redistribution of land, extension of public education, and elimination of the landed upper class. The intelligentsia of the 1940s, furthermore, was as nationalistic as its predecessors. But whereas the latter viewed nationalism purely in political terms, the former had reached the conclusion that political

[38] British Consul in Mashad, 18 July and 3 November 1945, *F.O. 371*/Persia 1945/34-40184; British Consul in Hamadan, Monthly Reports, *F.O. 371*/Persia 1946/34-52759; British Consul in Kermanshah, Monthly Reports, *F.O. 371*/Persia 1946/34-52698.

independence could not be fully secured without economic independence.

The political views of the intelligentsia were reflected in *Sukhan* (The Word), a high-quality journal started in 1943 as the organ of the Society of Degree Holders from Teachers' College and published after 1946 as an independent monthly specializing in literary, educational, and social issues, and catering to intellectuals, professors, teachers, school administrators, and university students. Its editor was Dr. Parviz Natel Khanlari, a well-known writer, teacher, and literary critic. Between 1943 and 1954, *Sukhan* carried numerous articles on the importance of political as well as legal rights for women; of land reform to raise the standard of living and "destroy the political power of the feudal aristocracy"; and of mass education to create a modern society, a socially conscious public, and an economically useful citizenry.[39] It also published favorable pieces on Marx, Engels, Lenin, Laski, Bernard Russell, Louis Aragon, and Maurice Thorez, as well as commentaries on the socialist content of literary figures such as Walt Whitman, Anatole France, Bernard Shaw, H. G. Wells, Gorky, Chekhov, Aldous Huxley, Malraux, Ehrenburg, and Jack London. The attitude of *Sukhan* toward the Tudeh was summed up by Khanlari in an editorial on "Art and Society." Drawing parallels between contemporary Iran and other "revolutionary situations," he argued that the writer could not remain neutral, both because art was an act of social as well as individual expression and because neutrality in the class struggle helped the exploiters against the exploited. But in criticizing nonpartisanship, he argued that the writer should not be fully committed to a political party, both because the morass of day-to-day politics should be avoided and because the role of the intellectual should be separate from that of a journalist. He agreed with Anatole France's last testament exhorting intellectuals to help the "class struggle so as to destroy capitalism, establish socialism, and pave the way for human fulfillment."[40]

Of the three isms, the Tudeh was closely identified with the first two. It championed the radical social reforms associated with socialism. It also espoused constitutionalism, and viewed itself as the surviving heir of the Constitutional Revolution. It denounced Reza Shah for violating the fundamental laws; stressed that the constitutional laws would not be fully implemented until the army was brought

---

[39] F. Hoveida, "A Few Words on Land Reform," *Sukhan*, 3 (May 1946), 149-56; "Educational Disgrace," *Sukhan*, 4 (April 1953), 429-32; A. Birshak, "What Do We Want from Education?" *Sukhan*, 4 (September 1953), 509-15.

[40] "Art and Society," *Sukhan*, 2 (November 1945), 721-29; P. Khanlari, "Anatole France," *Sukhan*, 1 (July 1944), 557-64.

under civilian control; held annual rallies to commemorate the victory of 1906; and hailed as national heroes not only Haydar Khan, but also Sattar Khan, Baqer Khan, al-Motakallemin, Sayyid Behbehani, and Sayyid Muhammad Tabatabai. Moreover, it criticized ultraleft radicals who smeared the Constitutional Revolution as just another conspiracy hatched by the British.[41] Instead it praised the revolution as a people's movement that, despite "bourgeois leadership and eventual imperialist sabotage," had challenged the feudal rule of divine kingship and thereby had inaugurated a new age in Iran. The Tudeh denied any contradiction between working for a socialist future and, at the same time, espousing the ideals of the Constitutional Revolution. It argued that since the content of the revolution had been popular, even though its form had been bourgeois, certain outdated laws could be changed peacefully to conform with the true spirit of the constitutional movement. Even on the sensitive issue of the monarchy, the Tudeh remained silent until August 1953, when radicals in the National Front demanded the formation of a republic.[42]

Although the Tudeh attitudes toward socialism and constitutionalism were straightforward, its relationship with nationalism was much more complex. Many foreigners in 1941-1944 predicted that the intelligentsia would denounce the Tudeh as a Trojan horse introduced by Russia, Iran's traditional enemy. These predictions, however, turned out to be much exaggerated for a number of reasons. First, the vast majority of the intelligentsia considered Britain to be a far greater danger than Russia, since the British owned the country's main source of income, controlled military bases in Iraq and the Persian Gulf, and supported Sayyid Ziya, the self-appointed enemy of the rushanfekran. Second, nationalists in the past had not been averse to allying with one foreign power against another. During the tobacco crisis of 1891, the rebels had sought Russian help against the British. And during the revolution of 1905-1909, the constitutionalists had obtained British assistance against the Russians. The test of a true nationalist was not the rejection of all foreign assistance, but rather selectivity in whose assistance was sought and at what time. Third, the many intellectuals who accepted the Marxist analysis of imperialism argued

[41] "Heroes of the Constitutional Revolution," *Besu-yi Ayandeh*, 5 July 1952. For the Tudeh perspective on the constitutional movement, see E. Tabari, "Concerning the Constitutional Revolution," *Nameh-i Mardom*, 2 (August 1948), 1-8; M. Babak, "Concerning the Constitutional Revolution," *Nameh-i Mardom*, 2 (July 1948), 83-86; A. Qassemi, "Concerning the Constitutional Revolution," *Razm Mahaneh*, 1 (August 1948), 20-39; A. Qassemi, "The Stages of the Iranian Revolution," *Razm Mahaneh*, 1 (November 1948), pp. 55-60.

[42] M. Yazdi, "Evidence to the Military Court," *Ittila'at*, 16 August 1955.

that Britain, with its capitalist economy, needed to expand to find outlets for investments, whereas Russia, having established a socialist society, had ceased to be imperialistic. Fourth, reformers saw the Soviet Union as the main advocate of radical change and the British as the chief supporters of the landed upper class, especially of the southern tribal chiefs. An American general visiting Iran in 1943 on behalf of President Roosevelt reported, "if the Iranians had to decide today between the British and the Russians they would in my opinion unquestionably choose the Russians." The British Foreign Office warned that there was a real danger that the Russians would attract the "younger generation" while the British would be left with the "old reactionary gang."[43] Similarly, the British military attaché analyzed these issues in a frank report sent in April 1943:

There has been recently a very noticeable change in the sentiments of the Persian people towards Russia. Closer contact with Russia and experience in Russian methods have already done much to modify the conception, hitherto popular among the masses, of Russia as a bogey and of Russians as brutal savages. The generally admirable discipline of Russian troops in Persia, their good behavior towards the people, their professed sympathy with the lower classes, their advertised contentment with their own system, the good relations apparently existing between officers and men and the obviously magnificent morale of the Russian people have greatly affected preconceived ideas of the Soviet system. . . . The less frightful Russia is to the masses the more of a bogey does she become to the propertied classes. A situation seems to be developing where the masses may draw closer to Russia and the propertied classes come to be associated more closely than they are now with Great Britain. Indeed, Russia is already beginning to be regarded as the champion of the oppressed and is being looked to by the leaders of the discontented as a possible supporter of a revolution against the present ruling class.[44]

Soviet popularity suffered in 1944-1946, however, partly because of the demands for an oil concession in the northern provinces and partly because of the uprisings in Azerbaijan and Kurdistan. As the British embassy reported, even some of the Tudeh leaders had privately criticized the Soviet oil demands. And as Kasravi warned in a pamphlet on *What Will Happen to Iran?* the Soviet sponsorship of the Azerbaijan and Kurdistan rebellions could destroy the country, since it would encourage malcontents in other provinces to put forward similar demands for local autonomy and even "national" independ-

[43] General Hurley to President Roosevelt, 13 May 1943, *Foreign Relations of the United States* (Washington, D.C., 1943), IV, 363-70; Comment of the Foreign Office in London, 19 April 1943, *F.O. 371*/Persia 1943/34-35070.

[44] British Military Attaché to the Foreign Office, 22 April 1943, *F.O. 371*/Persia 1943/34-35109.

ence.[45] These crises were not as detrimental to the Tudeh as they would seem at first glance, however. The Soviet oil proposals held out the hope of jobs for thousands of workers and technicians, and, with the clause on equal profit sharing, offered much more favorable terms than the existing British concession.[46] Moreover, many Iranians, including Mossadeq, argued that the real culprit in the whole crisis was not the Soviet Union but the West, since it had been the American and British companies that initiated secret negotiations for new oil concessions.

We have always rendered homage to the generosity of the Soviet Union. . . . If our premier had not initiated secret negotiations with Western companies and if the United States had not been so anxious to obtain an agreement before the end of the war, the Soviet Union would not have made its own request. When companies from the other side of the world are asking for concessions, why should not our immediate neighbor seek similar concessions.[47]

Likewise, the Azerbaijan crisis proved less lethal to the Tudeh than expected. Once the rebels took over Tabriz, they demanded autonomy, not independence, placed their demands within the context of the constitutional laws, implemented extensive social reforms, and stressed that they were an integral part of the "progressive movement of Iran." In fact, the so-called "Republic of Azerbaijan" existed only in the minds of conservative politicians in Tehran and in the works of Western writers who tended to see Iranian history through the perspective of those politicians. By late 1946, Western visitors were again complaining that the Soviets were regaining popularity and that Britain was still identified in the public mind with the "corrupt and effete landowning aristocracy."[48]

After 1947, the Soviet actions of 1944-1946 receded into history, while the British presence moved into the foreground. Max Thornburg, a Harvard economist who helped draft the first Seven Year Plan, wrote that the British constantly used tricks to obstruct development: "I am disposed to agree with the prevailing opinion among serious Persians that the most dangerous influence in this country is

[45] British Ambassador to the Foreign Office, 25 October 1944, *F.O. 371*/Persia 1944/34-40241; A. Kasravi, *Sar Nevesht-i Iran Cheh Khvahad Bud?* (What Will Happen to Iran?) (Tehran, 1945), p. 51.

[46] The British Foreign Office expressed the concern that the "Soviets would spend lavishly on housing, schools, and wages to attract labour and technicians from the AIOC." Comment of the Foreign Office in London, 4 April 1946, *F.O. 371*/Persia 1946/34-52672.

[47] M. Mossadeq, *Parliamentary Proceedings*, 14th Majles, 8 October 1944.

[48] E. Edwards, "Persia Revisited," *International Affairs*, 23 (January 1947), 56.

not Russia but Britain."[49] By 1951, the vast majority of the intelligentsia felt that the most immediate threat to Iran came not from the north but from the "southern neighbor." In such an environment, it was not difficult for the Tudeh to regain its image as an indigenous movement fighting not only the upper class but also the British oil company.

The ideological appeal of the Tudeh among the salaried middle class can be seen in Rouzbeh's final testament. Speaking for six hours before the military tribunal, Rouzbeh narrated how he had grown up in an economically hard-pressed lower-middle-class home, had constantly suffered financial humiliation, and had sacrificed his ambition to study engineering in the university. Entering the less expensive military academy, he had graduated with honors, written thirty-five pamphlets, and obtained a teaching position in the Officers' College. But all these years he had retained his earlier dislike of the capitalist system.

I hate capitalism because it begets all the present sins of humanity and all the ills of Iranian society. I am an enemy of a system that concentrates all the riches of life in the hands of a thousand families but leaves nothing for the other eighteen million people. While children of peasants die of starvation, children of landlords are taken by plane to hospitals in Europe. . . . My hatred of the existing system does not mean that I am against the national independence of Iran. On the contrary, I am against capitalism precisely because it is destroying Iran, hindering its development, undermining its security, and disregarding the well-being of its citizens. Even the most staunch opponents of the Tudeh admit that the Tudeh is the most important, the most determined, and the most organized party that has appeared in our fifty years of constitutional history. It is also the most revolutionary and the most resolute movement for progress, liberty, and national independence. This is why I have chosen the road of the Tudeh party and I am now willing to sacrifice for its cause my skin, my bones, my blood, my life. I will not live to see socialism but I die convinced that socialism will inevitably triumph in Iran.[50]

URBAN WORKING CLASS

The Tudeh was like an iceberg, with the party organization corresponding to the visible tip, and the much larger labor movement to the hidden mass below. The labor movement came into being immediately after Reza Shah's downfall. In some areas, notably in the

[49] M. Thornburg, "Private Papers, 1946-51" (unpublished papers in the Collection of the Harvard Advisory Group to Iran), p. 12.

[50] Kh. Rouzbeh, *Akherin Dafa' dar Dadgah-i Nezami* (The Last Defense in the Military Court) (n.p., 1970), pp. 40-41.

coalfields of Shamshak near Tehran and in the textile mills of Chalus and Sari, workers spontaneously took advantage of the power vacuum to form their own unions and even occupy the local factories. In other areas, especially Tehran, Isfahan, and Tabriz, survivors of the early labor movement returned to the workshops and factories to rebuild the old unions. By the summer of 1942, many of the labor organizers in Tehran came together to form the Council of United Workers. And by the summer of 1943, the same organizers convened in Tehran the First Conference of the Council of United Workers. Coming predominantly from Tehran, northern Khurasan, and the Caspian provinces, the delegates represented over twenty-six industrial, craft, and white-collar unions.[51]

Most of the leading figures in the Council of United Workers were from the top echelons of the Tudeh party. They included Rusta, the experienced labor organizer from the late 1920s; Ovanessian, the Armenian pharmacist from the old Communist party; Kobari, the middle-ranking civil servant who had been elected in 1942 to the Provisional Central Committee; Mahazari, the lathe worker who had also been elected to the Provisional Central Committee; Jowdat, the young physics professor turned labor organizer; Farjami and Khameh, two young intellectuals from the "Fifty-three" who were appointed to the top commissions at the first party congress; Jahani, carpenter and veteran of the early labor movement who was also placed on one of the commissions by the first party congress; Hakimi and Babazadeh, two railway workers who were later elected to the Central Committee; and Shandarmini, a tailor from the "Fifty-three" who was designated to the Advisory Board by the second party congress.

The leadership of the council, moreover, included three others who were members but not prominent figures of the Tudeh. Qazar Simonian, the main organizer among clerical workers, was an Armenian intellectual from Arak employed as a medium-ranking civil servant in Tehran. A close colleague of Rusta from the days of the early labor movement, Simonian had spent much of the 1930s in prison, where he translated Tolstoy's *Anna Karenina*. In the elections for the Fourteenth Majles, he almost won for the Tudeh the seat allotted to the Christian minorities in the central and southern provinces. Reza Ibra-

[51] The twenty-six unions included service workers such as restaurant waiters, cinema attendants, and municipal roadsweepers; workshop employees—tailors, carpenters, cobblers, stonecutters, and bakery assistants; white collar employees, particularly clerks in the Ministry of Justice; as well as industrial wage earners such as miners, railwaymen, train mechanics, textile workers, glycerine workers, silo workers, match manufacturers, brewery workers, construction laborers, and cement workers.

himzadeh, the main delegate of the railway union, was himself a railway worker. A native of Tabriz, he fought in the Khiabani revolt and had migrated to Mazandaran, where he was arrested in 1931 for organizing the first railroad strike. In prison, he had befriended the "Fifty-three." Mehdi Kaymaram, the chief spokesman of the shoe-makers' union, was a cobbler who had helped form the first shoe-makers' union in Tehran during the early 1920s. He had been im-prisoned briefly in the 1930s and joined the Tudeh in early 1942.

Thus all the fourteen leaders of the Council of United Workers were members of the Tudeh party. Of the fourteen, seven were wage earners, and the other seven were intellectuals who had participated in the early labor movement or had joined the labor movement at the first opportunity after August 1941. Twelve had been imprisoned at one time or another during Reza Shah's reign: three as members of the "Fifty-three"; nine as labor organizers or as activists in the youth section of the Communist party. All came from lower-class and lower-middle-class families. Although others soon joined them as union organizations proliferated, these fourteen remained the nucleus of the pro-Tudeh labor movement.

Besides electing the leadership, the First Conference of the Council of United Workers passed a number of resolutions. It declared that the council was "an independent organization unaffiliated with any political group but was willing to accept help from all parties interested in furthering the cause of the working class." It resolved that the unions would concentrate on economic and social issues; would accept as members all workers irrespective of religion, language, and political views; would take as labor organizers those intellectuals who by their past sacrifices had proved their sincere desire to help the working class; but would exclude other intellectuals from organizational po-sitions so that reactionaries would not be able to claim that the unions were tools of the middle class.[52] The conference also approved a detailed program for the council. This program called for an eight-hour work day; the right to form unions, bargain collectively, and strike if necessary; free transport to place of work; pay for Fridays, the day of rest; double pay for overtime; two weeks' paid vacation per year; old-age pensions, sick pay, and unemployment insurance; equal pay for men and women performing the same tasks; safeguards against arbitrary dismissals; a ban on child labor; safety measures against industrial accidents; and "penalties against employers and managers who maltreat, abuse, and insult their workers."[53] These

[52] A. Khameh, "Statement for the Conference," *Rahbar*, 10 August 1943.
[53] Council of United Workers, "Our Program," *Rahbar*, 1 March 1943.

remained the main goals of the labor movement for the next full decade.

The conference, however, intentionally avoided discussion on the sensitive issue of whether or not to encourage strikes while the war in Europe continued. Whereas the rank and file, hard pressed by inflation, were increasingly demanding militant action, the union leaders, ideologically committed to the Soviet Union, were fearful of disrupting the war effort. To resolve these differences, the council reached a tacit agreement. It would discourage strikes and labor organizing in the sectors of the economy deeply involved in the war effort, but it would encourage such activity in service and light consumer industries. In line with this policy, the council in 1943 helped organize strikes among textile workers in Isfahan, Tehran, Tabriz, and Behshahr; road sweepers in Tehran and Bushire; telephone operators in Shiraz; tea and tobacco cleaners in Lahijan and Tehran; leather processors and match makers in Tabriz; and office attendants in the Ministry of Justice in Tehran. The council kept out of the vital oil industry, however, advised caution in the equally vital railway system, and even denounced as "pro-fascist sabotage" the wildcat strikes that broke out in 1943 at the AIOC installations in Kermanshah, at the coal mines in Shamshak, at the cement factory in Tehran, and at the state-owned ammunition plant near Tehran. As one member of the council later admitted, "our enemies took advantage of our reluctance to organize strikes and constantly accused us of being friendly with the factory owners." Similarly, Kambakhsh confessed years later that the unions would have made much greater progress in 1942-1943 had it not been for the "party's reluctance to disrupt the economy as long as the Allies were fighting a life-and-death struggle with fascism."[54]

This reluctance, however, gradually diminished in early 1944 with the turn of the tide on the Eastern Front. Initiating an aggressive policy, the council established new branches, expanded the existing ones, outbid smaller rivals, and, merging with three other groups in Azerbaijan, Tehran, and Kermanshah, announced on May Day 1944 the formation of the Central Council of the Federated Trade Unions of Iranian Workers and Toilers—the CCFTU.

During the next thirty months, the CCFTU enjoyed excellent conditions for organizing labor. First, the Tudeh leaders continued to encourage union militancy as they shed their inhibitions about the war effort. The oil industry, however, remained out of bounds until

[54] *Rahbar*, 21 November 1943; H. Nouri, "Speech at the First Party Congress," *Rahbar*, 21 August 1944; A. Kambakhsh, "History of the First Party Congress," *Donya*, 9 (Spring 1968), 25-41.

Japan surrendered in August 1945. Second, wage earners often had little choice but to join unions and strike for higher wages, since the cost-of-living index rose from 472 in 1942-1943 to 1,030 in 1944-1945. In fact, throughout the period between 1941 and 1953 the annual number of major strikes (involving fifty or more workers) corresponded closely with the rate of inflation (see figure). Third, the Allies continued to employ large numbers of Iranian workers. Not surprisingly, this created labor shortages and thereby strengthened labor's bargaining position. The British consul in Bushire reported that the city's road sweepers easily won their demand for higher wages because the local airport and lorry assembly plant had exhausted the labor market. And a delegate to a trade union conference stated: "I don't mind losing my present job in the cement factory because I

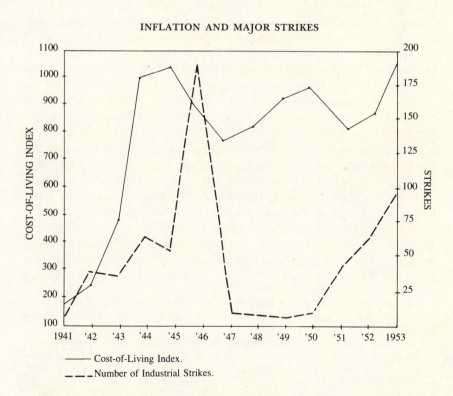

INFLATION AND MAJOR STRIKES

——— Cost-of-Living Index.

– – – Number of Industrial Strikes.

NOTE: The cost-of-living index has been compiled from the Bulletin of the National Bank. The number of industrial strikes has been compiled from newspapers, especially *Ittilaʿat, Mardom, Zafar, Kayhan, Besu-yi Ayandeh, Bakhtar-i Emruz,* and *Mard-i Emruz.*

know that I can always find work elsewhere, especially in the construction industry."[55] Fourth, the CCFTU had no viable competitors. Its main competitor, the Union of Workers, was created in 1942 by Yousef Eftekhari, a radical but vehemently anticommunist labor organizer who had spent eleven years in prison for his role in the 1929 oil strike. Although a genuine trade unionist, Eftekhari failed to recruit many workers, lost some of his early supporters to the Tudeh, and found himself relying more and more on Sayyid Ziya, who had no intention of encouraging labor militancy.

Finally, the CCFTU obtained valuable assistance from the Tudeh. Party organizations collected contributions for striking workers. Party intellectuals set up literacy courses, published *Zafar* for the CCFTU, and publicized labor grievances through the impressive array of left-wing newspapers. Party lawyers formed a legal aid society to defend trade unionists. Moreover, pro-Tudeh judges, engineers, and police officers at times used their influence to protect strikers and labor organizers. For example, engineers in the sugar mill in Tehran threatened to close down the whole plant when their manager tried to fire eight militant workers. The British consul reported that the authorities in Yazd during 1946 did not even bother to arrest demonstrating workers, for they knew that the local courts were controlled by the Tudeh. The consul in Bandar ʿAbbas wrote in 1946 that a strike in the town's textile mill had been successful mainly because the manager supported the Tudeh. The consul in Shiraz described how the police broke a strike in the city's electrical plant by arresting all the ringleaders, but the local courts promptly restarted it by releasing them. And the consul in Zahedan claimed that the Tudeh created a "semblance of unity among workers against the ʿAlam family because the party had sympathizers in the local courts, police, and gendarmerie."[56]

Making full use of these advantages, the CCFTU moved into action. In 1944, it led over forty major strikes, absorbed smaller unions in Isfahan, Fars, and Kerman, and thereby increased its membership from 100,000 to nearly 200,000.[57] Similarly, in 1945 it helped organize

[55] British Consul in Bushire, 15 May 1943, *F.O. 371*/Persia 1943/34-35087; M. Sultani, "Speech to the First Conference of the Council of United Workers," *Rahbar*, 1 August 1943.

[56] M. ʿAzimi, "Speech to the First Conference of the Council of United Workers," *Rahbar*, 1 August 1946; British Consul in Kerman, 30 December 1946, *F.O. 371*/Persia 1946/34-52749; British Consul in Bandar ʿAbbas, 30 June 1946, *F.O. 371*/Persia 1946/34-52699; British Consul in Shiraz, 30 April 1944, *F.O. 371*/Persia 1944/34-40162; British Consul in Zahidan, 30 June 1946, *F.O. 371*/Persia 1946/34-52756.

[57] The 1944 strikes included those among textile workers in Isfahan, Tehran, Yazd, Mashad, Chalus, Semnan, Behshahr, and Ahwaz; among telephone operators in Shiraz and Tehran; among electricians in Shiraz; among dock workers in Bandar Shahpour

another forty major strikes, and, establishing new branches, could boast of having thirty-three affiliated unions with a total membership of over 275,000.[58]

The CCFTU's peak came, however, in the following year. By mid-1946, it claimed 186 unions with a total membership of 335,000—90,000 in Khuzistan, 50,000 in Azerbaijan, 50,000 in Tehran, 45,000 in Gilan and Mazandaran, 40,000 in Isfahan, 25,000 in Fars, 20,000 in Khurasan, and 15,000 in Kerman.[59] Having unionized some 75 percent of the industrial labor force, it had branches in almost all of the country's 346 modern plants, and was recognized by the World Federation of Trade Unions as the "only genuine labor organization in Iran."[60] Moreover, the members of its 186 affiliates came from diverse walks of life. They included industrial wage earners such as the unions of oil workers, textile workers, railway workers, and tobacco processors; skilled modern wage earners, particularly the unions of printers, garage mechanics, and truck drivers; skilled traditional handicraftsmen, notably the union of carpet weavers; relatively unskilled wage earners—for example, the unions of construction workers, municipal road sweepers, and house painters; service employees, espe-

(Khomeini); among shoemakers, carpenters, and road sweepers, as well as silo, bakery, and brewery workers in Tehran; and among factory workers in sixteen of the eighteen industrial plants in Tabriz.

[58] The 1945 strikes included those among textile workers in Yazd, Mashad, Ahwaz, Chalus, and Semnan; road sweepers in Kerman; carpet weavers in Mashad; skilled oil workers in the Abadan refinery; unskilled workers in the AIOC installation in Kermanshah; and general strikes in Tabriz, in Mashad, and in the Isfahan cotton mills. The 275,000 included 20,000 railwaymen, 3,000 munitions workers, 45,000 construction laborers, 8,000 miners, 45,000 oil workers, 2,200 tobacco workers, 12,000 brewery workers and food processors, 40,000 textile workers, 20,000 carpet weavers, 2,000 printers, 600 electricians, 6,000 truck and taxi drivers, 3,000 cart drivers, 2,000 glass makers, 3,000 sugar workers, 3,500 silo workers, 1,200 cement mixers, 2,300 chemical workers, 3,000 slaughter house workers, 3,000 clerks in the Education Ministry, 1,500 municipal workers, 1,500 bath assistants, 2,700 hospital workers, 11,000 dockers, 9,000 craftsmen, 2,000 cotton cleaners, 2,000 silk workers, 5,000 fishery workers, 8,000 tobacco growers, 1,500 employees in the War Ministry, 1,000 technicians, and 150 newspaper sellers. See British Labour Attaché to the Foreign Office, "The Tudeh Party and the Iranian Trade Unions," F.O. 371/Persia 1947/34-61993.

[59] R. Rusta, "Speech to Railway Workers," Zafar, 15 August 1946.

[60] World Federation of Trade Unions, Report on the Activity of the W.F.T.U.: Report on Iran (October 1945-April 1949) (Milan, 1949), p. 167. Reluctant to antagonize the Iranian government, the International Labor Office refused to recognize the CCFTU as the "only genuine labor movement," but did describe it as the "only organization with a national network." International Labor Office, Provisional Record of the Twenty-Seventh Session (Paris, 1945). A few years later, however, an ILO report stated that "trade unionism may be said to owe its existence to the Tudeh Party." D. Jamalzadeh, "Social and Economic Structure of Iran," International Labour Review, 43 (February 1951), 178-91.

cially the unions of restaurant waiters, clothes cleaners, and cinema attendants; professional and white-collar associations, such as the Syndicate of Engineers and Technicians, Association of Lawyers, and union of teachers and educational employees; wage earners in the bazaar workshops, particularly the unions of tailors, carpenters, and shoemakers; and even some shopkeepers, notably the guilds of pharmacists, confectioners, and newspaper sellers.

Furthermore, the CCFTU during the first nine months of 1946 led over 160 successful strikes for higher wages. These strikes included textile workers in Bushire, Rasht, Kashan, Shiraz, and Bandar ʿAbbas; tailors in Rasht; dockers in Bushire, Bandar ʿAbbas, and Bandar Shahpour; railwaymen in Qazvin; miners in Shamshak; printers, tobacco processors, butchers' assistants, railway repairmen, bus drivers, clothes cleaners, electricians, and brewery workers in Tehran; and general strikes in Khuzistan, Isfahan, Nowshahr, and Chalus. For the first time since 1936, real wages among skilled factory workers caught up with and even surpassed food prices.[61] As one foreign visitor noted, "the Tudeh was successful in obtaining a momentous improvement in the conditions of factory workers. It was under Tudeh's pressure, and also with an eye to winning labor away from Tudeh's influence, that Ahmad Qavam in May 1946 decreed the most advanced labor legislation in the Middle East."[62] The new labor law promised to set minimum wages based on local food prices; to outlaw the employment of children; to limit the work day to eight hours; to enforce pay for Fridays and for six days' vacation per year, including May Day; and to permit unions to organize and bargain with management. On paper, at least, the Tudeh and the CCFTU had won many of their initial demands.

The reasons for the rapid development of the labor movement between 1941 and 1947 can best be seen in the textile mills of Isfahan and in the oil industry of Khuzistan. In Isfahan, the Tudeh obtained its first organization as early as March 1942, when Fedakar, the young lawyer who later won a Majles seat, opened a party branch. His right-hand man was ʿAbbas Azeri, a member of the "Fifty-three" and a cobbler from Azerbaijan who had been employed as a mill worker in Isfahan at the time of his arrest. Within five weeks of opening the first branch, the Tudeh had numerous cells in two of the nine large textile mills. These factories proved fertile ground for the Tudeh partly because prices in the previous five years had jumped from an index of 100 to 243 but daily wages had risen only from 4 to 8 rials;

[61] World Federation of Trade Unions, *Report (1945-49)*, p. 167.
[62] M. Hindus, *In Search of a Future* (New York, 1948), p. 88.

partly because the war had cut off foreign competition and thereby brought windfall profits to the owners; partly because the work day had been increased from nine to ten hours to meet the new demand; and partly because work conditions in the mills were even worse than those in most industrial plants. The British consul commented that the Isfahan mill owners had grown accustomed to phoning the local army barracks whenever they were faced with labor problems. The mill workers themselves complained bitterly that in 1939 the police had murdered one of their union organizers; that the managers used the contemptuous term *ajir* (hired hand) instead of the more acceptable word *kargar* (worker); and that the factory owners had for years handed over batches of Isfahan workers to Reza Shah as birthday presents to transport to his private mills in malaria-infested Mazandaran.[63]

The first sign of Tudeh success came in August 1942, when the workers in the two mills formed the Union of Isfahan Workers and demanded a 30 percent wage increase, the eight-hour day, and special rates for overtime work. At first the mill owners refused to negotiate, fired the ringleaders, and dismissed the union as a bunch of troublemakers who would prove incapable of working together for long. But confronted with a determined strike in both factories, and reluctant to lose markets to their rivals, the mill owners backed down and met all the major demands. Not unexpectedly, this encouraged the workers in the other seven mills to join the union and to put forward similar demands. Rebuffed again, the union organized a general strike among the 10,500 workers employed in the nine mills. To break the strike, the mill owners persuaded and perhaps bribed General Zahedi, the commander of the local garrison, to arrest the ringleaders and place troops around the factories.[64] This tactic failed, however; for the central government, fearful of street confrontations and Tudeh-led sympathy strikes elsewhere, stepped in to dismiss Zahedi and impose a settlement on the mill owners. The settlement not only met the wage demands, but also gave mill workers the eight-hour work day, monthly medical checkups, food subsidies, two suits per year, a ban on child labor, and one month's bonuses to share the windfall profits.[65] The government, moreover, promised to draft a labor law to cover all industrial workers. The British ambassador commented,

[63] British Consul in Isfahan, 10 July 1945, *F.O. 371*/Persia 1945/34-45476; "A Short History of the Trade Union Movement in Isfahan," *Rahbar*, 18-20 June 1944.

[64] British Consul in Isfahan, 31 August 1942, *F.O. 371*/Persia 1942/34-31412.

[65] British Ambassador to the Foreign Office, "Report on Industrial Developments in Isfahan," *F.O. 371*/Persia 1944/34-40222.

"because of considerable labour activity, the government is under pressure to regulate relations between management and labour."[66]

In the months after the big victory, the Union of Isfahan Workers consolidated its organization in the nine mills. A British officer stationed in Isfahan reported that by the end of 1942 the executive committee of the union was a significant force in the city.[67] It included representatives from all the mills, kept discipline on the shop floor, transmitted grievances to the managers, obtained recognition from the owners as the proper spokesman of the workers, and acted as "an arbitrator of any trouble between men and management because its negotiations were invariably successful." The British officer added that although in theory the Union was independent of all political parties, in practice most of its leaders came from the Tudeh party.

The union won another victory in July 1943, ironically as a result of an abortive attempt by the mill owners to undo their previous defeat. Complaining that high taxes and exorbitant wages were ruining private industry, the mill owners took the offensive. They threatened to end the food subsidies, invited Sayyid Ziya to extend his party into Isfahan, and encouraged the Bakhtiyari chiefs to prepare for an invasion of the city.[68] One mill owner who had villages nearby brought peasants into the city to physically attack Fedakar. The union reacted sharply, threatening not only demonstrations and strikes in the mills but also a general strike throughout Isfahan. This ultimatum worked; for the central government, again fearful of bloody repercussions, quickly intervened and forced the mill owners to back down. In the new agreement, signed before the governor-general, the factory owners agreed to continue the food subsidy, to negotiate only with the pro-Tudeh union, and to obtain union permission before laying off any workers. In return, the union promised to protect company property, enforce work discipline, and permit the firing of unneeded labor. The British consul reported that the industrialists had reluctantly signed the "humiliating agreement" but had not given up their intrigues: "The Governor General has made himself very unpopular among vested interests by his refusal to suppress the workers' party. . . . The rich hope to remove him and to use the army, by bribing the commander, to suppress all political activity among the workers."[69] Similarly, the British ambassador summarized the situation of early 1944 in a special report:

[66] British Ambassador to the Foreign Office, 26 May 1944, ibid.

[67] E. Sykes, "Isfahan," *Journal of the Royal Central Asian Society*, 33 (July-October 1946), 307-17.

[68] British Consul in Isfahan, 3 July 1943, *F.O. 371*/Persia 1943/34-35120.

[69] British Consul in Isfahan, 16 August 1943, *F.O. 371*/Persia 1943/34-34121.

Two years ago the exploitation of workers was almost complete. They were made to work ten hours a day for a wage as low as ten rials. No precautions were taken to safeguard their health and no compensation was given for injuries. Meanwhile, the owners amassed immense fortunes. When the first sign of resistance made their appearance, the owners and the government had no understanding of its importance. They feared Soviet Russia and worried that their mills would fall prey to the allegedly communist ideas now spreading among the workers. Moreover, they feel outraged that such important persons as themselves, literally cousus d'or, should be treated disrespectfully by mere workmen. They are motivated by fear and injured dignity. To these may be added greed—for their sole thought is money and more money and the thought of losing any of their enormous profits to the workers is unpalatable to them. They find the whole topic of labour disputes distasteful, and usually take the line that disputes are mere work of agitators and that workers are too ignorant to exercise responsibility. . . . In Persia we are clearly at the beginning of a new era and are seeing the rise of a new social movement. The advantages which the workers have won are considerable and they will certainly continue to make the employers feel their newly discovered power.[70]

Despite the opposition of the mill owners, the Tudeh continued during 1943 to expand in Isfahan—especially among the bazaar wage earners, the Armenian and Jewish communities, and the four small factories located in the city. In the elections for the Fourteenth Majles, Fedakar won with some 30,000 votes. In the memorial services for Sulayman Iskandari, the Tudeh procession drew over 25,000 mourners. And in the send-off given to Fedakar as he left for Parliament, all thirteen factories in the city closed down and nearly 30,000 admirers gathered at the airport. The British consul reported that the send-off was so enthusiastic that one workman "offered to sacrifice his son as a token of his gratitude for Fedakar's efforts on behalf of the mill operators."[71]

Meanwhile, the mill owners schemed to undermine the previous agreements. They helped Sayyid Ziya's Fatherland party to create a Union of Peasants and Workers, and to recruit the mill hands that had been laid off with the consent of the Tudeh union. They encouraged violent confrontations between the two rival unions. And they sparked a major crisis in April 1944 by suddenly locking out the workers from the factories and the factory granaries—their only source of bread. As expected, hungry workers battled the army to break into the granaries, and the Tudeh organized a general strike in Isfahan. Eyewitnesses estimated that fifty were injured in the week-long crisis.

---

[70] British Ambassador to the Foreign Office, "Report on Labour Conditions in Persia," *F.O. 371*/Persia 1944/34-4022.

[71] British Consul in Isfahan, 4 February 1944, *F.O. 371*/Persia 1944/34-40163.

Tehran newspapers, however, described the event as a workers' revolt, and claimed that over five hundred had been injured. In the subsequent agreement drafted by the central government and the Tudeh, the mill owners ended the lockout while the pro-Tudeh union opened the shop floors to the rival union. Shortly after the agreement, the Union of Isfahan Workers affiliated with the CCFTU.

The Tudeh suffered temporary setbacks in Isfahan during the first half of 1945. The Soviet demand for oil provided the opposition with a propaganda weapon. The affiliation with the CCFTU caused some defections from the union, since Isfahanis were traditionally resentful of any form of control from Tehran. The Bakhtiyari, Qashqayi, and Khamseh chiefs, shaken by the upheaval, formed an alliance against the Tudeh. The archconservative administration of Premier Sadr named a staunch anticommunist politician as governor-general of Isfahan. The new governor-general placed the large mills under martial law, arrested some of the labor leaders, and distributed arms to the local tribes. The takeover of the mills also frightened the bazaar community, especially since many of the merchants held shares in the textile companies. Sayyid Ziya's paper, *Ra'ad-i Emruz*, exclaimed, "the Tudeh threatens small as well as large capitalists since its aim is to abolish all forms of private property."[72] The two leading preachers in the city began a religious campaign against the Tudeh, denouncing it as an atheistic communist conspiracy. In the words of the British consul, "one important advantage enjoyed by the Tudeh opposition is the strong latent feeling of religiosity which can easily be stirred up."[73] Moreover, the large landlords drew closer to the mill owners once they saw the Tudeh mount a concerted drive into the countryside. For example, Akbar Mas'oud, the son of Zil al-Sultan and the city's elder statesman, threw his support behind the industrialists as soon as he discovered Tudeh agitators in his villages. Two years earlier, Mas'oud had rebuffed the same industrialists as social upstarts who lacked the finesse to handle their workmen. Furthermore, the mill owners continued to undermine the Union of Isfahan Workers, on the one hand firing 150 members of the union, and on the other hand contributing generously to the Fatherland party, and awarding 10 percent wage increases to members of the Union of Peasants and Workers.

The Tudeh reached its low point in April 1945, when Sayyid Ziya's party collected some 1,000 men—many of them from the neighboring villages—to attack and loot the offices of the Union of Isfahan Work-

---

[72] *Ra'ad-i Emruz*, 1 May 1944.
[73] British Consul in Isfahan, 3 March 1945, *F.O. 371*/Persia 1945/34-45476.

ers. The police refused to intervene. The British consul reported that the mill owners were confident that the Tudeh had been "scorched for good." He also predicted that the overconfident mill owners would soon revert to their old ways, lowering wages, opposing all unions, and scheming to make more and more money.[74]

In fact, the Tudeh began to recover as soon as Qavam was elected premier. Giving the governorship to a more impartial civil servant, the new government arrested Sayyid Ziya, expropriated his party funds, and warned industrialists to keep out of union politics. By March 1946, the Union of Isfahan Workers was strong enough to lead a general strike in the nine large mills. By April, it was sufficiently strong enough to defeat an attempt made by the mill owners to transport some 5,000 peasants into the factories. By May Day, it could once again bring out as many as 40,000 supporters into the streets. And by August, the British consul was reporting that the Tudeh had frightened the local authorities into submission; scared the mill owners so much that they did not dare enter their plants; and controlled much of the local administration as well as all of the textile factories. He also warned that the Tudeh was "ready to seize power in Isfahan as completely as the Democrats had done in Tabriz."[75] Contributing to this revival, according to the consul, were the political protection extended from the central government; the genuine support enjoyed by the Tudeh among many mill workers; the disillusionment of other mill workers with Sayyid Ziya's party; and, most important of all, the remarkable ability of the pro-Tudeh union to win favorable contracts.[76] According to the contract signed in May 1946, for example, the textile workers obtained the eight-hour work day, the highest wages in the country, pay for Fridays, two free suits per year, and no layoffs without union approval.

The Tudeh was equally successful among the oil workers of Khuzistan. The party first appeared in the oil installations in early 1943, but quickly withdrew after its organizers were arrested, and its leaders resolved to keep out of the vital industry. Instead they decided to form local unions among nonoil workers, such as road sweepers, irrigation cleaners, taxi drivers, cotton spinners, and bakery assistants. Disappointed by this decision, a group of radical intellectuals in Abadan organized some two hundred AIOC employees into a Union of Iranian Workers, and in May 1945 helped a wildcat strike of twelve

[74] Ibid., 19 June 1945.

[75] British Consul in Isfahan, 31 December 1946, *India Office*/L/P&S/12-3529; idem, 1 May and 1 June 1946, *F.O. 371*/Persia 1946/34-52736.

[76] British Consul in Isfahan, 1 April, 1 June, 1 December 1946, *F.O. 371*/Persia 1946/34-52736.

hundred laborers at the Kermanshah refinery. Although the party leaders condemned the strike and the CCFTU intervened to end it, the British ambassador felt that the whole incident had been engineered by the Tudeh, and advised the AIOC to improve their housing and medical facilities to deprive the Tudeh of legitimate grievances.[77] In a separate report on labor conditions in the oil fields, the British embassy warned that the shortage of housing and other amenities could provide the Tudeh with a splendid opening. The officials of AIOC, however, replied that such criticisms were unjustified and that the only true protection against subversion was armed might. "Although the (local) Arab villagers are well armed, they are inadequate. The only adequate safeguard against the likelihood of serious labour disorders which may follow the withdrawal of foreign troops is the introduction of a strong police force."[78]

The problems of the oil industry were compounded in 1944-1945 with labor unrest among the British employees. Finding their work hours raised and their home leaves canceled without consultation, British employees formed a Union of Shift Workers, threatened to strike, and denounced the consuls as "company clerks."[79] The British government promptly dispatched a parliamentary delegation led by a woman member of the Conservative party to investigate the situation. When the leader of the delegation lectured the British employees on how lucky they were not to be in a Japanese prison, angry members of the audience suggested taking her "on a tour of the Abadan graveyard" or "dealing with her in some dark corner in the proper Japanese fashion."[80] The Foreign Office commented that the British employees were unlikely to strike as long as the war continued since many of them were communists; but that their unconventional behavior was likely to "adversely influence the Persian workmen."[81]

The Tudeh moved into the oil industry as soon as the war ended. Opening party branches in the oil centers, the Tudeh set up the Union of Khuzistan Workers as the provincial section of the CCFTU, absorbed the independent Unions of Iranian Workers, and organized

[77] British Ambassador to the Foreign Office, 31 May 1945, *F.O. 371*/Persia 1945/34-45448; idem, "Discussions with the AIOC (September 1945)," *F.O. 371*/Persia 1945/34-45461.

[78] British Embassy to the Foreign Office, "Labour Conditions in the Oil Fields," *F.O. 371*/Persia 1946/34-52713; Anglo-Iranian Oil Company to the Foreign Office, "Memorandum on Security (June 1944)," *F.O. 371*/Persia 1944/34-40197.

[79] British Ambassador to the Foreign Office, 24 February 1944, *F.O. 371*/Persia 1944/34-40158.

[80] AIOC Employees to the Foreign Office, "The Situation in the Oil Industry," *F.O. 371*/Persia 1944/34-40158.

[81] British Foreign Office, 17 March 1944, *F.O. 371*/Persia 1944/34-40158.

the massive but orderly May Day parade of 1946. Speakers at the parade demanded higher wages, better housing, pay for Fridays, the eight-hour work day, and a comprehensive labor law. A woman orator described oil as the jewel of Iran, accused the British of spending more on dog food than on workers' wages, and urged the takeover of the AIOC.[82] This was probably the first time that a public audience in Abadan heard the cry for oil nationalization.

The Tudeh followed up the successful May Day rally with a series of well-organized strikes against the oil company. The very next day, in fact, some 250 artisans and laborers at the Abadan distillation plant stopped work, demanding higher wages and shorter work hours. The company met their demands a week later, when employees at the local asphalt factory and locomotive plant called for sympathy strikes. On May 10, the entire labor force of 2,500 at the Agha Jari oilfield stopped work, requesting benefits similar to those won recently by the Isfahan textile workers—especially higher wages, pay for Fridays, and better overtime rates. At first the company dismissed the requests as unreasonable and cut off the water supply to Agha Jari. But it reluctantly came to the negotiating table three weeks later when the Tudeh threatened a general strike in Abadan, collected contributions for Agha Jari, and persuaded Qavam to send a mediation committee to Khuzistan. In the eventual settlement, the company not only met many of the original demands, but also gave wages for the three-week strike and promised to implement any labor legislation drafted by the central government. The correspondent of the London *Times*, unfamiliar with labor conditions in Isfahan, commented that "it was unprecedented in Iranian history to give seven days pay for only six days work." The British embassy reported that the AIOC had no choice but to negotiate, since the Tudeh was in an extremely strong position, having enrolled in its union some 75 percent of the oil workers. Similarly, the British consul in Khorramshahr wrote that the company accepted the unfavorable settlement and treated the Tudeh as the proper representative of the workers because it was alarmed by the extent of communist influence and feared the spread of the strike to the Abadan refinery.[83]

By mid-June, the Tudeh organization in Khuzistan paralleled, rivaled, and, in many towns, overshadowed the provincial administration. In the words of the British consul in Ahwaz, "the effective gov-

---

[82] British Consul in Khorramshahr, "Report on Tudeh Activities in the Oil Industry (1946)," *F.O. 371*/Persia 1946/34-52714.

[83] *The Times*, 30 July 1946; British Ambassador to the Foreign Office, 20 May 1946, *F.O. 371*/Persia 1946/34-52713; British Consul in Khorramshahr, "Report on the General Strike," *India Office*/L/P&S/12-3490A.

ernment of the province has passed into the hands of the Tudeh."[84] Its branches determined food prices, enjoyed the support of the local fire brigades, and controlled communications, especially truck communications, between the main urban centers. Its unions represented workers' grievances before management, collected funds for future emergencies, organized an elaborate shop-steward system, and opened forty-five clubhouses in Abadan alone. Moreover, its militias patrolled the streets, guarded the oil installations, and impressed foreign observers by quickly transporting 2,500 volunteers from Abadan to Khorramshahr to build an emergency flood wall. The British authorities reported that during the flood warnings "the company admitted that they could not, nor could the Persian authorities, have commanded the Abadan workers in the numbers organized by the Tudeh. It was certainly an impressive illustration of Tudeh power over the worker." The British ambassador added, "it is indeed true to say that at the present time the security of the refinery and fields, and the safety of the British personnel, depends on the good will and pleasure of the Tudeh Party."[85] Similarly, the British military attaché reported in mid-June:

The present situation in Abadan and Agha Jari, though quiet on the surface, is extremely precarious. The Tudeh Party is in complete control of labour at the refinery and is gaining ground in the fields. The Anglo-Iranian Oil Company's management exists only on sufferance. At any moment, at any reason, a strike could be called which would bring production to a standstill. Hitherto the Tudeh leaders have used their power to maintain order. Although inciting to violence in theory, they have discouraged it in practice. The Tudeh has constituted itself the *de facto* representative of labour in Persia and the management is discussing with it, in that capacity, the organization of the trade unions contemplated under the new labour law. By doing so the company can maintain some sort of contact with the representatives of labour and production in the fields, but few will believe that such a course of action will result in anything more than a short respite.[86]

The expected confrontation came on July 10, but, as it turned out, it was instigated by the authorities rather than the Tudeh. On that day, the company rescinded its promise of Friday pay, the Anglophile governor-general declared martial law, and the military commander of Agha Jari arrested the local labor leaders, whom he had invited

---

[84] British Consul in Ahwaz, 30 June 1946, *F.O. 371*/Persia 1946/34-52700.

[85] M. Audsley, "Report on the Oil Fields," *F.O. 371*/Persia 1946/34-52723; British Ambassador to the Foreign Office, "The Tudeh Party in the Oil Industry," *F.O. 371*/Persia 1946/34-52714.

[86] British Military Attaché to the Foreign Office, 10 June 1946, *F.O. 371*/Persia 1946/34-52710.

for discussions. A spontaneous strike broke out at Agha Jari, and the Tudeh and the CCFTU quickly endorsed it. In addition, they called upon all employees throughout Khuzistan to stay away from work on July 13 and to remain absent until the central government removed the governor-general, lifted martial law, released the labor leaders, and guaranteed pay for Fridays. Their call for a general strike was heeded by over 65,000 workers, making it the largest industrial stoppage in Iran and one of the largest in the Middle East. It involved not only 50,000 manual workers and clerical employees of the oil company; but also 200 Indian artisans at the Abadan refinery; thousands of firemen, truck drivers, road sweepers, railwaymen, textile spinners, and high-school students throughout Khuzistan; hundreds of shopkeepers, craftsmen, and small traders located in the town bazaars; and even cooks, chauffeurs, and servants working for European households. The British consul in Ahwaz reported that the "strike was enforced with great efficiency." The Khorramshahr consul wrote that in Abadan the strike began with an orderly procession directed at the military authorities. Similarly, the British military attaché reported that the general strike started peacefully and "immediately gave the Tudeh complete control over the industrial regions of Khuzistan."[87]

Although the general strike began in a peaceful manner, it soon turned into violent confrontations between the oil workers, the military authorities, and the local Arab community. In entering an industry noted for its ethnic diversity, the Tudeh had made a special effort to recruit workers from different religious, regional, linguistic, and tribal backgrounds. It had been remarkably successful among migrant laborers from the Bakhtiyari, Luri, Khamseh, and Qashqayi tribes; unskilled workers from Isfahan, Shiraz, Kerman, and Bushire; and skilled workers, especially welders, artisans, and truck drivers, from the Azeri, Armenian, and Assyrian communities. It had failed, however, among the Arab population.

Three factors explain this failure. First, the Arabs, unlike the Qashqayis, Khamsehs, and Bakhtiyaris, resided within their own territories. Whereas the others had stepped out of the jurisdiction of their kadkhudas, kalantars, and khans, the Arabs continued to live under the watchful eyes of their tribal leaders. In short, the Arabs remained bound by kinship ties. Second, the Arabs employed in the oil industry were hired not as individual wage earners but as members

[87] British Consul in Ahwaz, 1 August 1946, *F.O. 371*/Persia 1946/34-52700; British Consul in Khorramshahr, "Report on the General Strike," *India Office*/L/P&S/12-3490A; British Military Attaché to the Foreign Office, 23 July 1946, *F.O. 371*/Persia 1946/34-52711.

of construction teams led by private contractors, many of whom were Arab chiefs. As contract workers, they remained dependent on their tribal shaykhs, received pay for piece work instead of daily work, and therefore did not share with the vast majority of oil workers the concern for higher wages, shorter hours, and pay for Fridays. Third, the leaders of the Arab community had political, economic, and social reasons for opposing the Tudeh. The British consuls reported that the Arab chiefs had traditionally looked upon Britain as their guardian protector; that the Arab landlords were worried the Tudeh would "irretrievably poison ignorant minds" and "undermine their slender autority over the peasantry";[88] and that the Arab business community, especially shopkeepers and corn merchants in Abadan, grew alarmed when it saw Tudeh "policemen and street guards wearing arm bands, ordering people in the streets, controlling the number of passengers in buses, and giving orders to bakers about prices."[89]

The Arab opposition to the Tudeh surfaced in early July, when the tribal chiefs, at the urging of the governor-general, formed a farmers' union. They soon changed the name to the Arab Union on the grounds that "they were a martial race not a lot of farmers."[90] The Iran party sarcastically commented that "the Arab Union is a union in the same way Reza Shah's government was a constitutional government." The Tudeh charged that the so-called Arab Union was scheming to separate Khuzistan from Iran and was receiving arms from the AIOC as well as from the governor-general.[91] The British consul wrote that the opening of the Arab Union's headquarters in Abadan created concern among the Tudeh rank and file since the urban population had been traditionally fearful of tribal attacks.[92]

These fears turned into panic on the second day of the general strike, when news reached Abadan that armed Arab tribesmen had surrounded Agha Jari and were preparing to invade Abadan. The British consul reported that he had advised the Arab leaders to keep their men out of Abadan, but "there were strong rumors the Governor had instructed the Arab sheikhs to bring in their tribesmen and to burn down the Tudeh offices." The consul added that the governor-general had probably "turned to the Arabs" because the Abadan gar-

[88] British Military Attaché, 10 July 1946, *F.O. 371*/Persia 1946/34-52742; British Consul in Khorramshahr, 1 June 1946, *F.O. 371*/Persia 1946/34-52742; British Consul in Ahwaz, 1 July, 1946, *F.O. 371*/Persia 1946/34-52700.

[89] British Consul in Khorramshahr, "Report on the General Strike," *India Office*/L/P&S/12-3490A.

[90] Ibid.

[91] *Jeb'eh*, 18 July 1946; *Zafar*, 5 September 1946.

[92] British Consul in Khorramshahr, "Report on the General Strike," *India Office*/L/P&S/12-3490A.

rison had only 250 troops.[93] As the rumors spread, angry crowds gathered outside the offices of the Arab Union. And as the police panicked and fired, the angry crowds attacked the offices and thus began a night-long riot that left 19 dead and 338 hospitalized. Among the dead were 12 Arabs, including their leading contractor and richest merchant. Contradicting the evidence sent by the British consuls in Ahwaz and Khorramshahr, the British military attaché in Tehran informed the Foreign Office and the Western press that the whole crisis had been instigated by "Tudeh hooligans."[94]

The riots lasted until the following morning, when an emergency delegation from Tehran landed at Abadan airport. The delegation included Muzaffar Firuz of the Democrat party, Radmanesh of the Tudeh, and Jowdat of the CCFTU. After six hours of discussions with the AIOC, the governor-general, and the Tudeh unions, the delegation imposed a settlement on the warring sides. By the accord, the Tudeh agreed to end the general strike, drop the demand for the removal of the governor-general, and cease making inflammatory denunciations of the AIOC and of the Arab Union. In return, the military authorities released the union leaders, and the company agreed both to pay for Fridays and to raise minimum wages to 35 rials per day. Thus the oil workers' union won its main economic demands. Once the employees started returning to work, Noel Baker, the British secretary of state, confidentially told his fellow cabinet ministers that the entire upheaval had been caused by the company's intransigeance on Friday pay. Similarly, an anonymous official of the AIOC wrote to the Foreign Office that the four-day general strike should be blamed on diehard company leaders who failed to appreciate the problems of workers and had no experience of dealing with organized labor, and whose "knowledge of trade unionism is limited to the repetition of worn-out jokes that went out with crinolines." Finally, the British consul in Ahwaz, concluding his reports on the general strike, warned that the economic gains had strengthened communist influence over labor and that the workers continued to insist that the Tudeh should represent them in their negotiations with the oil company.[95]

With the successful general strikes in Isfahan and Khuzistan in the summer of 1946, the CCFTU reached its peak. But with Qavam's sharp turn to the right in the fall of 1946, the CCFTU entered a

[93] Ibid.

[94] British Military Attaché, 31 July 1946, *F.O. 371*/Persia 1946/34-52711.

[95] Noel Baker, 17 July 1946, *F.O. 371*/Persia 1946/34-52719; Letter to the Foreign Office, 18 July 1946, *F.O. 371*/Persia 1946/34-52720; British Consul in Ahwaz, 1 September 1946, *F.O. 371*/Persia 1946/34-52700.

period of acute crisis. In Khuzistan, the provincial authorities deported 120 labor organizers, and the oil company fired 813 strike leaders and discharged, on the grounds of being absent without leave, over 1,000 workers who had been arrested earlier for their union activities. In Isfahan, the military occupied the Tudeh headquarters, arrested some 100 party militants, and, in the words of the British consul, conscripted into the army as many workers as possible.[96] In Fars and Kerman, the rebellious tribes forced the labor organizers to flee to Tehran. In the Caspian provinces, the authorities arrested 140 union activists, executed three, and, as the British consul in Rasht reported, "made every effort possible to break the Tudeh grip on workers going to the lengths of planning to move whole industries from one town to another."[97] And in the capital, the Tudeh and the government openly clashed when, on November 12, the CCFTU organized a one-day general strike in Tehran to protest the arrests in the provinces and the formation of the rival labor organization, ESKI. According to the Tudeh, the strike was 100 percent successful, with the vast majority of the CCFTU's 50,000 members in Tehran staying away from work. But according to the British military attaché, the strike was only 50 percent successful since the government arrested 150 union organizers, occupied the headquarters of the CCFTU, used army trucks to break through picket lines, hired unemployed workers to replace the strikers, and offered an extra day's pay to all employees who came to work.[98]

The general strike in Tehran ended a major chapter in the history of the CCFTU. After four years of spectacular growth, the CCFTU began four years of intermittent decline. There were three major reasons for this. First, government repression continued on and off during the next four years. In December 1946, the military authorities arrested the main labor leaders, including Rusta, on the grounds that they had encouraged the secessionist movement in Azerbaijan. In January 1947, Qavam confiscated the assets of the CCFTU, claiming that the organization's aims were political rather than economic. And in February 1949, the shah outlawed the CCFTU together with the Tudeh. Second, ESKI waged an aggressive war to undermine the CCFTU. Using government funds, it coopted the Arab Union in Khuzistan, absorbed the union of peasants and workers in Isfahan, set up new labor organizations, and promised to use its political connections to obtain substantial benefits for all wage earners. Third, the

[96] British Consul in Isfahan, 31 December 1946, *India Office*/L/P&S/12-3529.

[97] British Consul in Rasht, 31 November 1946, *F.O. 371*/Persia 1946/34-52796.

[98] *Rahbar*, 13 November 1946; British Military Attaché to the Foreign Office, 18 November 1946, *India Office*/L/P&S/12-3505.

economic trends of the previous four years reversed and grew more unfavorable for labor organizers. On the one hand, the cost-of-living index, which had jumped from 472 in 1942-1943 to 1,030 in 1944-1945, dropped to 780 in 1946-1947 and 832 in 1947-1948. Thus there was no longer spiraling inflation to drive apolitical workers into labor militancy. On the other hand, the demand for labor fell drastically as the Allied forces withdrew, as the oil industry contracted to adjust to the smaller postwar market, and as the native factory owners found themselves again challenged by European industrialists. With thousands outside the factory gates seeking work, those inside were hardly in a position to threaten strikes. Labor organizers, consequently, were caught between falling prices and rising unemployment. Not surprisingly, the number of major industrial strikes, which had shot up from 3 in 1941 to a record of 183 in 1946, dropped to 8 in 1947, 5 in 1948, and 4 in 1949.

Although the pro-Tudeh unions lost much of their organizational effectiveness after 1947, the party retained a great deal of its appeal among the urban working class. The British consul in Isfahan warned that the Tudeh nucleus remained intact in the textile mills; that "the authorities, having got rid of the Tudeh cereberus, are shy of substituting for it even the most docile-looking watch-dog of their own"; and that the Tudeh would continue to "have appeal as long as the E.S.K.I. leaders are puppets of the government and the employers display little interest in the workers' conditions."[99] The Ahwaz consul reported that Qavam's party took its time to move into Abadan because the oil industry remained a Tudeh stronghold. The British labor attaché, in a memorandum on "Labour Conditions in the A.I.O.C.," admitted that the vast majority of workers had supported the shop steward system set up by the Tudeh. He added that they "hope the Tudeh leaders would return to complete their work" and "await fulfillment of the promises made by the departed leaders." Similarly, a U.S. Congressional report in 1949 stated that "A.I.O.C. officials estimate that some 95 percent of its Iranian employees in Abadan are members of the [Tudeh] union, and as long as they are denied an increase in real wages and improvements in housing and transportation the possibility of a Tudeh come-back must be reckoned with."[100]

The expected comeback occurred in 1951-1953. Helped by the

[99] British Consul in Isfahan, 30 December 1946 and 1 January 1947, *India Office*/L/P&S/12-3529.

[100] British Consul in Ahwaz, 1 December 1946, *F.O. 371*/Persia 1946/34-52742; British Labor Attaché, "Labour Conditions in the A.I.O.C.," *India Office*/L/P&S/12-3490A; U.S. Congress, Committee on Foreign Affairs, *The Strategy and Tactics of World Communism*, (Washington, D.C., 1949), p. 9.

relaxation of political controls, the disintegration of ESKI, and the return of inflation, the CCFTU renamed itself the Coalition of Workers' Syndicates, reorganized the provincial affiliates, and quickly established itself as an important political force. Having organized strikes among silo workers and railwaymen in February 1951, the CCFTU burst into the political arena in the following month by leading a series of strikes in the oil industry. The new crisis began on March 20, the eve of the Iranian New Year, when the AIOC announced immediate cuts in wages, travel allowances, and housing subsidies on the grounds that rents and food prices had fallen. The following day, the workers at Bandar Mashʿur struck to protest this "New Year gift." And three days later, they were joined by the workers at the pipelines, at the machine repair shops in Masjid Sulayman, and at the oil fields in Agha Jari and Naft-i Sefid. By April 1, most of the company's 45,000 employees were on strike, the government had instituted martial law, and the British were strengthening their fleet in the Persian Gulf. Shaken by the strike and pressed by the central government, the oil company on April 10 rescinded all the recent cuts and invited its employees to return to work. This settlement, however, was short-lived, for the day after the employees returned the company announced that workers would not be paid for the three weeks they had been absent. Reacting quickly, the pro-Tudeh unions called a general strike throughout Khuzistan, and demanded not only the three weeks' backpay but also the nationalization of the oil industry. The economic demands of the unions had been joined to the political demands of both the Tudeh and the National Front.

The call for a general strike was heeded by over 65,000, including truck drivers, railwaymen, road sweepers, shopkeepers, bazaar craftsmen, and high-school students, as well as the 45,000 employees of the oil company. This time even the Arab contract workers joined in. Although the general strike began with peaceful processions, it quickly degenerated into violent riots once the police tried to arrest the strike leaders, and, in the tense situation, fired into the demonstrators, killing four men and two women. In the ensuing upheaval, angry mobs lynched three Europeans. This xenophobia did not last long, however, and the following morning European correspondents were able to mingle with the crowds. The strikers gradually drifted back to work in the course of the next two weeks, as their union funds dwindled, the government promised to investigate their grievances, the company agreed to compensate them for some of their wage losses, and the leaders of the National Front warned that their intransigence could invite a British invasion. By April 25, the general strike was over. The reporter for *Ittilaʿat-i Haftegi*, the conservative weekly, claimed that the workers had been too ignorant to understand the reasons for the strike, but confessed that he had been impressed by the workers' strong feelings of unity and solidarity.[101]

The crisis of spring 1951 was not limited to Khuzistan. As soon as the riots broke out there, the pro-Tudeh unions in Isfahan organized a sympathy strike in the nine large textile mills. Besides supporting the oil workers, the Isfahan unions demanded the nationalization of the AIOC and industrial projects to alleviate unemployment. The strike soon spread to the other factories in the city and even to the workshops in the bazaar. *Ittila'at-i Haftegi* reported that the strike involved over 30,000 workers, and was the largest and most impressive in the city's turbulent history.[102] To prevent the strike from developing into an uprising, the military placed machine guns, tanks, and armored vehicles around the textile mills and the city's southern section, which contained the working-class quarter. Despite the precautions, one worker and one policeman were killed when a demonstration of 10,000 tried to make its way from the factories to the city's central square.[103]

The CCFTU followed up the general strikes of Isfahan and Khuzistan with a conference of its Tehran affiliates. Convening 20 observers from the provinces and 350 delegates from all the major factories in the capital, the meeting elected new leaders to replace those who had fled abroad and enlarged its Executive Committee to bring in representatives from most sectors of industry.[104] After the conference, the pro-Tudeh unions throughout the country waged an aggressive campaign to raise wages and obtain government recognition. They held massive parades in July to commemorate the 1946 general strike in Khuzistan. They organized a large demonstration outside parliament in October to demand nationalization of the oil company, removal of military personnel from factories, and an end to government restrictions on labor unions. They held even larger rallies the following year to celebrate May Day. What is more, they sponsored a record number of successful strikes. There were thirty-two major industrial strikes during the last eight months of 1951; fifty-five in 1952—excluding the nation-wide general strike during the July uprising; and seventy-one, plus the national strike to commemorate the July uprising, during the first eight months of 1953. The CCFTU had managed to repeat its 1946 victories.

Not surprisingly, the revival of the CCFTU shook the establishment.

[101] "The Crisis in Khuzistan," *Ittila'at-i Haftegi*, 12-30 April 1951.
[102] "The Situation in Isfahan," *Ittila'at-i Haftegi*, 19 April 1951.
[103] M. Malekzadeh, *Parliamentary Proceedings*, 1st Senate, 20 April 1951.
[104] "Tudeh Influence among Workers," *Tehran Mosavar*, 4 October 1951.

Ittila'at-i Haftegi exclaimed that the Tudeh "fire" that had almost engulfed Iran in 1946 had suddenly reappeared in the factories and again threatened to burn down the whole country. *Tehran Mosavar*, the other major weekly, warned that the "subversive" labor organizers had returned to the factories and were displaying utter contempt for the authorities. A senator proclaimed, "foreign-paid agitators are misleading our workers. Everytime they exact concessions, they demand more. The result is demonstrations, street battles, strikes, and more strikes. They will not be satisfied until production comes to a halt and the country is dragged into an atheistic revolution." And a conservative deputy argued that the Tudeh was daily gaining ground among workers because it fought for higher wages and better conditions, because the other parties lacked interest in the labor movement, and because ESKI, with its "corrupt leaders," had proved to be ineffective.[105]

The National Front, meanwhile, tried to counter the pro-Tudeh unions. Kashani appealed to religious sentiments to draw workers away from the Tudeh.[106] Khalel Maleki argued that in times of national emergency economic strikes were as dangerous as political sabotage.[107] And Baqai's supporters tried to form unions to rival the CCFTU. These attempts failed, however, mainly because of the policies pursued by Mossadeq's administration. The inability of the government to cut the civil service payroll once the oil revenues dried up caused another burst of inflation. Prices rose from an index of 789 in 1950-1951 to 977 in August 1953. The government proposal to disenfranchise illiterates hardly appealed to the average worker. Moreover, the Law for Social Stability decreed by Mossadeq further alienated workers, since it restricted labor unions, tried to control wage increases, and threatened prison sentences for those found guilty of inciting others to strike.[108] Designed to weaken the Tudeh, this law served to strengthen it. By late 1952, Qonatabadi and many others admitted that the National Front had lost its war to win over the working class:

Our country is being torn apart by strikes, demonstrations, and labor disputes. What can we do about it? To answer that question we must examine the situation in the factories. In most factories, there are three distinct groups: first, the communists who hammer away with the propaganda argument that

[105] *Ittila'at-i Haftegi*, 20 April 1951; *Tehran Mosavar*, 6 September 1951; R. Shafaq, *Parliamentary Proceedings*, 1st Senate, 26 June 1951; 'A. Raji, *Parliamentary Proceedings*, 16th Majles, 23 May 1951.

[106] *Ittila'at*, 8 October 1952.

[107] Kh. Maleki, "Strikes," *Niru-yi Sevum*, 29 June 1952.

[108] *Ittila'at*, 23 October 1952.

the rich in our country are corrupt and own everything while the workers own nothing; second, the patriots who support the National Front; third, the neutrals who will follow the lead of any organization that will represent their interests vis-à-vis the factory owners. . . . We must admit that the initiative is now with the first group. The communists lead the neutrals, and, consequently, control the vast majority of the urban working class.[109]

PROPERTIED MIDDLE CLASS

The Tudeh began with the hope of mobilizing not only the proletariat and the intelligentsia, but also the petit bourgeoisie of the bazaars—small merchants, shopkeepers, traders, workshop owners, self-employed craftsmen, and middle- and low-ranking ʿulama. Its early rallies stressed that the bazaar population, like the rest of the "toiling masses," had been exploited and oppressed by Reza Shah's dictatorship. Its press hammered away on the theme that the national bourgeoisie was threatened by the foreign imperialists on the one hand, and by the comprador bourgeoisie, feudal landlords, wealthy industrialists, and royalist generals on the other hand. Moreover, its program promised independence for the craft and trade guilds, tariff protection for the handicraft industries, and state subsidies for the private workshops. The Tudeh attitude toward the propertied middle class was summed up by the handbook entitled *What Does the Tudeh Party of Iran Say and Want?*:

There are no fundamental contradictions between the small capitalists and the proletariat. It is true that the former do not work for wages, but they, like the latter, are dominated by the large owners of the means of production. Consequently, they are drawn to support the workers against the upper class.[110]

Despite these hopes and appeals, the Tudeh failed to attract many members of the propertied middle class. No bazaari faces appeared in the party's top echelons, very few in the middle echelons, and only a scattering in the lower echelons. Of the 2,419 rank-and-file members who recanted in 1953-1957, only 169 (7 percent) came from the traditional middle class. They included 113 small shopkeepers, 25 merchants, and 24 self-employed craftsmen. The CCFTU had tried to win over the bazaar organization with the creation of separate associations in 1942-1943 and the Society of Free Iran in 1951. In fact, the few trade and craft guilds that did support the Tudeh were limited to those with high proportion of Armenians and Assyrians—the guilds

[109] Sh. Qonatabadi, *Parliamentary Proceedings*, 17th Majles, 28 October 1952.
[110] A. Qassemi, *Hizb-i Tudeh-i Iran Cheh Miguyad va Cheh Mikhuahad?* (Tehran, 1944), p. 119.

of confections, pharmacists, newspaper sellers, and food and drink sellers. While few guilds rallied behind the Tudeh, the vast majority supported the anti-Tudeh politicians—first Sayyid Ziya, and later Mossadeq, Kashani, Qonatabadi, Makki, Baqai, and Haerzadeh.

The Tudeh failure among the propertied middle class can be explained partly by the economic conflicts between employees and employers; and partly by the ideological differences between Islam, as interpreted by the 'ulama, and the secular radicalism espoused by the Marxist Tudeh party.

The economic conflict evolved around wages. The Tudeh, viewing itself as the champion of the working class, started in early 1942 to form unions in the bazaar stores and workshops, especially among shopkeepers' assistants, leather cleaners, tailors, carpenters, and shoemakers. Moreover, as wages lagged behind escalating food prices, the Tudeh helped these unions organize a series of successful strikes—of which the most important was a general strike in 1944 in the ten large shoe workshops of Tehran, where some five thousand cobblers were employed. Similar work stoppages, including a general strike in the same workshops, recurred during the inflation of 1951-1953. Thus spiraling food prices divided bazaar employees from bazaar employers, and thereby forced the Tudeh to champion the interests of the former against the latter.

The gap between the Tudeh and the bazaar was widened by other economic pressures. Many money lenders, small merchants, and even shopkeepers, especially in Isfahan, Mashad, and Tabriz, held shares in the local consumer industries established during Reza Shah's reign. Inevitably, the strikes sponsored by the Tudeh against the private companies, such as the textile firms of Isfahan, alienated the small shareholders as well as the large industrialists. Moreover, the wholesale dealers, merchants, and shopkeepers were in constant conflict over prices and credits with the sizable underclass of the bazaar—the thousands of peddlers, street vendors, and itinerant sellers. By aggressively recruiting members of this underclass that had been systematically excluded from the established trade guilds, the Tudeh further alienated the propertied middle class.

The ideological conflict between the Tudeh and the bazaar was instigated by the 'ulama. Right from the beginning, the Tudeh tried to avoid such a conflict. It exempted ecclesiastical foundations from discussions of land reform. It praised Islam in general as "a great force for human freedom" and "a forerunner of socialist equality," and the clerical leaders in particular as the "main heroes of the Constitutional Revolution."[111] It even paid respects to Ayatallah Hajji Aqa Hussein Qumi, the highly conservative mujtahed who had resided in Karbala since his expulsion from Iran during the early 1930s.[112] It stressed that the majority of the party members were Muslims and descendants of Muslims; that some of the party leaders, notably Yazdi, came from prominent clerical families; and that any party member who "blasphemed" would be expelled, since Islam was the religion of the vast majority of the people.[113] Moreover, it occasionally organized religious meetings. For example, during the Muharram ceremonies of 1944, it led street processions in Mashad and held a memorial service in Tabriz for the proconstitutional Shaykh al-Islam who had been executed by the Russians in 1911. Furthermore, its mass circulation papers avoided discussions of Islam, while its theoretical journals tended to apply Marxism to other religions, particularly Christianity. The party policy towards Islam was so cautious that Kasravi, the famous iconoclast, complained that the Tudeh had turned reactionary in its eagerness to appease the conservative mullas.[114]

Despite the wooing of the ʿulama, the Tudeh won over only two prominent clerics: Shaykh Hussein Lankrani, who helped the party in Azerbaijan during the war years; and Ayatallah Sayyid ʿAli Akbar Borghaʾi of Qum, who openly campaigned for the Peace Partisans during the Mossadeq years. The vast majority of the ʿulama, however, distrusted the Tudeh not only because it advocated Marxism, but also because it attracted anticlerical intellectuals such as Hedayat, and espoused secularism, equal rights between Muslims and non-Muslims, women's suffrage, coeducational schools, and discarding of the veil. Meanwhile, the establishment politicians worked hard to placate the ʿulama and turn them against the Tudeh. They returned the ecclesiastical lands that had been confiscated by Reza Shah, opened a theology college in Tehran University, introduced scripture classes into the school curriculum, and helped establish a Society for the Propagation of Islam. As the British ambassador noted in 1943, "the official government policy is to foster religion to turn men's minds away from communism. . . . There is now an open alliance between the clergy

[111] "The Anniversary of Imam ʿAli's Martyrdom," *Rahbar-i Yazd*, 22 August 1944; "The Tudeh Party and Religion," *Mardom*, 6 January 1947; "The Heroes of the Constitutional Revolution," *Besu-yi Ayandeh*, 4 August 1952.

[112] "The Greatest Living Divine," *Rahbar*, 4 June 1943.

[113] "Religion and the Tudeh Party," *Rahbar*, 9 April 1944; Tudeh Party, "Our Majles Candidate: Dr. Yazdi," *Mardom*, 25 October 1943; "The Tudeh Party and Religion," *Mardom*, 6 January 1947.

[114] Kasravi, *Sar Nevesht-i Iran Cheh Khvahad Bud?*, pp. 14-15.

who are hoping to recover some of their lost influence and the merchants who wish to use religion to protect them from communism."[115]

By 1946, many members of the ʿulama had come out against the Tudeh. The British consul in Bushire reported that the leading mujtaheds at Karbala and Najaf expressed deep concern over the spread of communism, even though they refused to declare a jehad against the Tudeh. The Tabriz consul wrote, "in many parts of Azerbaijan the mullas are energetically preaching against the Tudeh, condemning it as atheistic. In Ardabel, the men of God are said to have flung not only texts but also brickbats at the Tudeh." The Kermanshah consul noted that the local conservative interests were working closely with the mullas to revive religion against the Tudeh. Similarly, the Ahwaz consul observed that in some districts the clergy refused Tudeh members entry into their mosques.[116]

The ʿulama made common cause with the propertied middle class, but their lack of influence over the bazaar wage earners can be seen in a secret government poll made on the eve of the 1949 elections.[117] Surveying the Tehran bazaar, the report showed that almost all the occupational groups were politically divided, with the guild elders, workshop owners, and shopkeepers supporting conservative politicians, religious leaders, or Mossadeq, but the guild members, wage earners, and shop assistants favoring the Tudeh party. For example, the shoe manufacturers endorsed Sayyid Ziya, whereas their 5,000 cobblers backed the Tudeh; the owners of barber shops supported Mossadeq, Kashani, Behbehani, or Masʿoudi, while many of their employees were members of the Tudeh; the 400 owners of bath houses leaned toward Mossadeq, Kashani, Behbehani, and the Imam Jomʿeh of Tehran, but the 4,000 bath attendants were members of the CCFTU; the 250 clothing manufacturers helped Baqai, Makki, and Haerzadeh, whereas their 8,000 tailors backed the Tudeh; the 1914 coffee-house keepers endorsed Kashani, Mossadeq, and the Imam Jomʿeh, but their 4,500 waiters and assistants favored the Tudeh. Thus class conflicts had entered the bazaar, dividing employees from employers, and shattering the guilds that had been so effective and united in the

[115] British Ambassador to the Foreign Office, 12 July 1943, *F.O. 371*/Persia 1943/34-35072.

[116] British Consul in Bushire, 3 February 1946, *F.O. 371*/Persia 1946/34-52727; British Consul in Tabriz, 3 April 1945, *F.O. 371*/Persia 1945/34-45478; British Consul in Kermanshah, 7 January 1945, *F.O. 371*/Persia 1945/34-45488; British Consul in Ahwaz, 16 February 1945, *F.O. 371*/Persia 1945/34-40176.

[117] Kh. ʿIraqi, "Secrets from Razmara's Administration: A Secret Survey of the Bazaar," *Khvandaniha*, 23 January 1956.

past, especially during the Constitutional Revolution and the 1925 antirepublican campaign.

RURAL MASSES

The Tudeh made persistent efforts to attract the rural masses. Party branches, journals, and newspapers frequently discussed agricultural programs. City cadres went into the countryside to recruit villagers and agitate against landlords. The Peasants' Union was created in the hope that it would eventually parallel the massive CCFTU. Moreover, the party program allocated as much space and promised as many benefits to the rural masses as to the urban working class. It vowed to distribute state and crown lands; sell private estates at low interest rates; increase the sharecroppers' portion of the harvest; eliminate feudal levies and obligations; finance an agricultural bank; set up village cooperatives; construct rural clinics, schools, and irrigation canals; and bring back the old system by which village and tribal communities had elected their kadkhudas. As party organizers often mentioned, the Tudeh could not be considered a people's movement in the full sense of the term until it had roots among the rural masses.

Despite these aspirations, the Tudeh failed to mobilize the countryside. On the eve of the 1943 elections, a British diplomat correctly predicted, "the landlords are justifiably confident that, in spite of radicalism in the towns, the majority of the peasantry will continue to follow their lead on election day.[118] At the time of the First Party Congress, according to Kambakhsh, only 2 percent of the members were peasants.[119] Of the 183 party activists arrested in the wake of the 1949 assassination attempt, one was a peasant. Of the 168 activists detained in 1951, two were agricultural workers. And of the 2,419 former members who recanted after 1953, only 69 came from the rural population. Moreover, the party's support in the countryside was limited to Gilan, Mazandaran, and the villages near major cities. As the list of recanters showed, 60 of the 69 peasant members came from the Caspian provinces and from the villages around Tehran and Isfahan.

Various explanations have been offered to explain why the Tudeh and other radicals have failed to mobilize the rural masses. One interpretation, favored by historians who believe that religion molds popular culture, argues that the Islamic "doctrine of passive obedience"

[118] British Consul in Tabriz, 9 July 1943, *F.O. 371*/Persia 1943/34-35093.
[119] Kambakhsh, "The Tudeh Party in the Struggle to Create a Democratic United Front," *Donya*, 5 (Autumn 1964), p. 6.

kept the peasantry unawakened, apathetic, and fatalistic.[120] Another interpretation, often offered by the Tudeh itself, claims that whole of the past, not just religion, weighed so heavy on the shoulders of the peasantry that they internalized oppression and accepted the status quo. As Iraj Iskandari stated, few peasants joined the Tudeh because the vast majority remained sceptical about the possibility of experiencing social change.[121] Yet another interpretation, formulated by Maoist and New Left critics of the Tudeh, argues that Iranian radicals, unlike those of China, Cuba, and Vietnam, failed to ignite rural revolutions because they overlooked the interests, grievances, and aspirations of the peasants. As one guerrilla group wrote in 1971, "the countryside has not risen in revolt because previous radical organizations, especially the Tudeh and the National Front, failed to articulate rural interests, develop a coherent agricultural policy, and mobilize the peasantry into a disciplined political movement."[122]

These explanations are not convincing, although each contains a grain of truth. The religious interpretation forgets that Islam, like Christianity and Judaism, expounds contradictory themes. On the one hand, it preaches passive obedience. But on the other hand, it exhorts active resistance against social injustice, political oppression, and economic exploitation. Since the radical theme was often sounded in urban upheavals such as the Constitutional Revolution, it could have been voiced just as well in the countryside, if conditions had been comparable. This explanation also forgets that most peasants and tribesmen hardly ever saw a mulla, and that organized Islam did not appear in most villages until the 1960s and the 1970s. The cultural interpretation naively takes the outward appearance of submission to be proof of the inward acceptance of oppression. But, as an Iranian anthropologist discovered in the 1960s, peasants often expressed intense hatred for the landlords in private, although in public they rushed to obey his orders "as if they were commands from the Almighty." Similarly, a French sociologist studying the Caspian region has drawn a sharp contrast between the peasant's internal thinking and his outward "humility, docility, and apparent acceptance of feudal authority."[123] Finally, the New Left interpretation underestimates

[120] S. Scheikh-ol-Islami, *Iran's First Experience of a Military Coup d'Etat* (Heidelberg, 1965), p. 75.

[121] I. Iskandari, "Histoire du Parti Toudeh," *Moyen Orient*, 2 (December 1949), 10.

[122] Organization of Freedom Fighters of Iran, *Rusta va Inqilab-i Safed: Berasi-yi Sharayit-i Inqilabi-yi Rustaha-yi Iran* (Villages and the White Revolution: An Investigation into the Revolutionary Situation in the Iranian Countryside) (n.p., 1971), p. x.

[123] J. Safinezhad, *Talebabad* (Tehran, 1966), pp. 136, 336; P. Vieille, *La Féodalité et l'etat en Iran* (Paris, 1975), pp. 51-56.

Tudeh's interest in the countryside, and overlooks the tradition of rural radicalism in the societies that have experienced peasant revolutions. The Tudeh failure came not from want of trying but from the lack of peasant response. On the other hand, the Chinese Communists succeeded not because they had developed a master formula for igniting rural revolutions, but because, as Mao Tse-Tung pointed out in 1927, the peasantry had articulated their own demands, established their own secret societies, and created their own liberated zones long before their existence was appreciated by urban radicals.[124] In China, the urban revolutionaries merged with the rural rebels to form a massive prairie fire. In Iran, the urban revolutionaries failed to ignite a prairie fire because the countryside was not dry enough for their spark to spread.

To understand why the Tudeh failed, one must examine not only the party's policy toward the peasantry, but, more important, the social structure of the rural population. In comparing Iran with the countries that experienced large-scale peasant rebellions, one major difference stands out. Whereas the Iranian countryside was inhabited predominantly by sharecroppers, landless laborers, and tribesmen, the village population of the countries with rural rebellions contained an important class of "middle" peasants who owned and farmed their own land. In the words of Eric Wolf, the author of *Peasant Wars in the Twentieth Century*, this middle peasant has not only the willingness but also the ability to revolt. On the one hand, he owns enough land to be economically and socially independent of the local magnates and the central government: "He enjoys the minimum tactical freedom required to challenge the status-quo." On the other hand, he does not own so much as to become a large-scale employer, and thereby a supporter of the status quo. Moreover, he is susceptible to market fluctuations, since he often has a surplus to sell. The rich peasant, in contrast, is an employer of labor, a money lender, a representative of the state, and consequently a bulwark of the established order. The poor peasant, in turn, is so completely dependent on others for food, wages, and land that he is incapable of challenging the established order: "He has no tactical power for he is completely within the power domain of his employer."[125] Not surprisingly, Wolf and others have found that it was the middle peasantry that initiated rural rebellions in such diverse countries as Russia, China, Vietnam, and Mexico. In the words of Hamza Alavi, another specialist on peasant revolts, "from the examination of the actual experience of the Russian and Chinese

[124] Mao Tse-Tung, "Report on the Peasant Movement," reprinted in *Revolutions: A Reader*, edited by B. Mazlish (New York, 1971).

[125] E. Wolf, *Peasant Wars in the Twentieth Century* (New York, 1969), pp. 290, 291.

Revolutions it was found that, contrary to expectations, the 'rural proletariat' and the 'poor peasants' were, initially, the least militant classes of the peasantry whereas the small-holding independent proprietors, the 'middle peasants,' were initially, the most militant."[126]

Although Iranian statistics on land ownership are imprecise, scholars agree that peasant holding played little, if any, part in the village economy before the 1960s. Ann Lambton, in her classic study on *Landlord and Peasant in Persia*, concludes that little land belonged to the peasants and the little that did was confined to inhospitable mountain areas or to the barren edge of the central plateau.[127] Two Iranian sociologists estimate that 50% of the cultivated land belonged to large proprietors, 25% to small absentee proprietors, 20% to religious foundations, and only 5% to peasant cultivators.[128] The Tudeh calculates that 37 families owned over 20,000 villages, whereas 60% of the peasantry remained completely landless.[129] The same source shows that 23% of the peasantry owned less than 1 hectare, 10% between 1 and 3 hectares, and only 7% more than 3 hectares—the minimum required for an adequate small holding. According to the Ministry of Agriculture, Iran in 1957 contained 39,409 villages, with each village traditionally divided into 6 parts (*dangs*).[130] Of these 39,409 villages, the crown owned 812 (2%); the state 1,444 (4%); the religious foundations 713 (2%); private landlords, each with at least one dang, held 4,330 (11%); large landlords, each with at least all six dangs of one village, owned 9,234 (23%); and small landlords, including merchants, civil servants, clergymen, army officers, and absentee landlords, together held 16,525 (40%). As one analyst of these figures has concluded, few of the small holdings belonged to resident farmers.[131]

In the virtual absence of a middle peasantry, the tenant sharecroppers (*nasaqdars*) and landless laborers (*khoshneshin*) formed the vast majority of the rural population. In larger villages, the landless laborers tended to outnumber the sharecroppers. In smaller villages, the reverse was true. But whether tenant sharecropper or landless laborer, the poor peasant was economically and socially dominated

[126] H. Alavi, "Peasant Classes and Primordial Loyalties," *Journal of Peasant Studies*, 1 (October 1973), 23-61.

[127] Lambton, *Landlord and Peasant in Persia* (London, 1953), pp. 280-81.

[128] Sh. Rasekh and J. Behnam, *Jam'eh Shinasi-yi Iran* (The Sociology of Iran) (Tehran, 1969), pp. 232, 282.

[129] 'A. 'Ayin, "The Pahlevi Dynasty, Agricultural Land, and the Peasantry," *Donya*, 16 (February 1976), 72-73.

[130] D. Homayoun, "Land Reform in Iran," *Tahqiqat-i Iqtesadi*, 2 (September 1963), 18-25.

[131] Kh. Khosravi, *Jam'eh Shinasi-yi Rusta-yi Iran* (The Sociology of Rural Iran) (Tehran, 1972), pp. 28-29.

by the landlord and his representatives—the village kadkhuda and bailiff (*mobasher*). The landless laborers could not reside in a village for any length of time without the permission of the local kadkhuda. They could not obtain employment on the landlord's estates without the goodwill of the mobasher. They could not gain access to communal pastures, wells, and woods without the special dispensation of the village elders. Moreover, they earned their main, if not only, source of income by working for the landlords, grazing cattle, weeding fields, threshing corn, picking cotton, digging ditches, and helping with the harvest. In short, the landlord totally controlled the economic existence of the landless laborers.

The landlord also exercised, in the words of a French sociologist, monopolistic control over the tenant sharecroppers.[132] He could circumvent and undermine the right of cultivation (*nasaq*), since these rights—unlike manorial contracts in Medieval Europe—were usually unwritten and therefore precarious. He could deny them seed, water, loans, and, through local oxen owners, plough animals. He could allocate them inferior land and even exclude them from the production teams (*boneh*s), for the team leaders were appointed by the mobasher. He could refuse to have the cultivation rights passed on to heirs or to accept the permanence of these rights unless the tenant built houses and gardens. He could weaken the tenant's bargaining position by resorting to the ever-increasing pool of unemployed laborers. He could order the kadkhuda to impose fines, inflict corporal punishment, and even conscript troublesome villagers into the army. He could use the state authorities, especially the gendarmerie and the courts, to trump up criminal charges. He could dry up whole villages by diverting water or refusing to repair the expensive irrigation canals. In some areas, he extracted labor services, demanding that tenants transport the crop, graze cattle, build houses, and repair roads, bridges, and irrigation canals. In other regions, he exacted dues in kind, requiring firewood, eggs, hens, butter, and other agricultural products. In still other regions, he levied such seasonal dues as for new year celebrations, weddings of tenants, and entertainment of visiting dignitaries.

Economic hegemony was reinforced by social dependency. In tribal areas, which formed as much as 25 percent of the settled rural population, kinship ties, myths, and ethos bound the cultivator to his kadkhuda, kalantar, and khan. In nontribal areas, the age-old need for protection against threatening nomads, rival villages, and greedy tax collectors helped tie the peasant to his landlord. The landlord

---

[132] Vieille, *La Féodalité*, p. 53.

took the shape not just of an economic exploiter, but also of a social protector and political patron. As the British consul in Tabriz reported in 1942, most peasants "stuck with their landlords as islands in a sea of instability."[133] In short, tribal and patrimonial ties helped to bridge the wide class division between landlords and peasants.

The landlords' economic and social power is reflected in a survey carried out by Tehran University on the eve of the 1963 land reform.[134] Asked why they endured the landlord's power, 64% of the 1,418 respondents cited fear, 19% respect, 8% attachment, and 8% respect for the law. Of the respondents who cited respect and attachment, 17% said that they had willingly supported their landlord because he had backed them against other sharecroppers in village disputes; 17% said he had given them emergency loans and free advice; and 10% said he had mediated village disputes. Of the respondents who cited fear, almost all mentioned the dread that the landlord would take away their right of cultivation, deny them irrigation water, fabricate criminal charges, or sow dissension between themselves and their neighbors. To borrow Wolf's words, the sharecropper in Iran, like the poor peasant in other countries, was "completely within the power domain of his employer," and thus lacked sufficient resources to assert even a minimum degree of political independence.

The landlords, moreover, did their very best to perpetuate their power by preserving the traditional insularity of the rural communities. They discouraged geographical mobility by denying rights of cultivation to absentee sharecroppers; in fact, nasaq rights were considered to be "residential privileges." They restricted peasant contact with the market by controlling the sharecroppers' sales in the local towns. One Iranian anthropologist found that even in the late 1960s some bonehs could not trade their surplus without the special permission of the mobasher.[135] They limited peasant dealings even with state officials by opposing such innovations as village schools. Another Iranian anthropologist writes that "some big landlords would not let government agents into their villages."[136] They also narrowed peasant relations with the outside world by making the kadkhuda the official intermediary between the village and neighboring communities. As a European anthropologist has argued, the landlords hindered horizontal mediation among peasants and instead channeled all relations

---

[133] British Consul in Tabriz, 28 January 1942, *F.O. 371*/Persia 1942/34-31426.

[134] Research Group of Tehran University, *Barresi-yi Natayej-i Eslahat-i Arzi* (A Study on the Effects of Land Reform) (Tehran, 1963), pp. 60-63.

[135] Safinezhad, *Boneh* (Production Teams) (Tehran, 1974), pp. 42-43, 87-88.

[136] I. Ajami, "Land Reform and Modernization of the Farming Structures in Iran," in *The Social Sciences and Problems of Development*, edited by K. Farmanfarmaian (Princeton, 1976), pp. 191-92.

vertically through themselves or their representatives. "In order to secure their control the landlord had to try and isolate the peasant from all contacts which could potentially give them influence or access to other forms of mediators."[137] Of course, in preserving rural insularity the landlords of the 1940s continued to be helped by the high rate of illiteracy; the persistence of tribal, linguistic, and religious divisions; the traditional peasant distrust of urban intruders; the prevalence of subsistence farming; and the lack of roads, radios, and other forms of communication.

In such an environment, rural discontent could be expressed only if an outside organization intervened, offered protection to the peasantry, and then challenged the landlords and their representatives. The Tudeh was unable to undertake such an ambitious task until 1945-1946. This was partly because the authorities restricted rural activities, partly because the party gave priority to the urban trade unions, and partly because it lacked members with roots and personal contacts in the countryside. As Kambakhsh admitted years later, the party was short of cadres who had first-hand knowledge of agricultural problems, could speak the rural dialects, and knew how to appeal to the peasants.[138] Despite these handicaps, the Tudeh in 1945-1946 initiated a major campaign of sending urban cadres into the neighboring countryside to organize the villagers and to set up peasant unions.

Although in some areas the landlords defeated the campaign, in others the Tudeh won notable, if only temporary, successes. These successes are reflected in the British consular reports. Outside Mashad, peasants heeded the call to keep the whole harvest. In Hamadan, Tudeh activity among the peasantry was so widespread that the landlords were suddenly inspired to make pilgrimages to Karbala. Outside Yazd, Ardekan, Bam, and Kerman, villagers who had been incited by the Tudeh clashed with the landlord's representatives and armed retainers. Finally, in Tehran province, especially in the villages of Veramin, Garmsar, Shahriyar, and Sanjbulagh, the Tudeh was so effective in inciting disorders and persuading peasants to keep the harvest that Premier Qavam had to declare martial law and promise land reform.[139] These successes, however, were short-lived, for once

[137] R. Loffler, "The Representative Mediator and the New Peasant," *American Anthropologist*, 73 (October 1971), 1084-85.

[138] ʿA. Kambakhsh, "Notes from the History of the Tudeh Party," *Donya*, 9 (Spring 1968), 32.

[139] British Consul in Mashad, 1 July 1946, *F.O. 371*/Persia 1946/34-52707; British Consul in Hamadan, 1 August 1946, *F.O. 371*/Persia 1946/34-52759; British Consul in Kerman, 1 July 1946, *F.O. 371*/Persia 1946/34-52749; British Military Attaché to the Foreign Office, 28 July 1946, *F.O. 371*/Persia 1946/34-52711.

the government clamped down on the Tudeh in late 1946 the rural campaign dried up, and most regions returned to normal. The Tudeh did not gain the opportunity to repeat the 1945-1946 campaign until 1952-1953, when it was again cut short by government repression.

The one major exception to the Tudeh's difficulties in the villages was the Caspian region, where it enjoyed relatively sustained success. This can be explained by a combination of historical, economic, and geographical factors. The Jangali tradition lived on, especially in Gilan and western Mazandaran. Reza Shah, in accumulating lands, had dispossessed many villagers, particularly Turkomans, outside Gurgan in eastern Mazandaran. The rural communities were less isolated than in other provinces since the population density was much higher, the peasantry was linguistically more homogeneous, the literacy rate was slightly better, local markets had existed from the medieval era, and modern communications, together with commercial farming, had been introduced in the second half of the nineteenth century. Moreover, the landlords did not exercise omnipotent power: their estates were relatively small; they lacked tribal ties with their peasants, since the vast majority of the population was nontribal; the semitropical climate diminished the importance of expensive wells and irrigation canals; the absence of nomadic tribes in Gilan lessened the need for patronage and protection; and, most important of all, many of the peasants were not insecure sharecroppers, but tenants free of labor services and armed with fixed rents and long leases.

The inability of the Tudeh to find rural roots elsewhere proved in the final analysis to be disastrous. Without rural support in a society in which villagers and tribesmen formed over half the population, the Tudeh, however successful in the cities, remained an oasis in a desert of peasant conservatism. As the Tudeh leaders admitted in analyzing the defeat of August 1953, the royalist officers could not have carried out their coup d'état if their peasant rank and file had mutinied or the rural masses had risen up in revolt.[140] Had the countryside rebelled or the army troops refused to obey orders, the Tudeh party, with its effective urban network, would undoubtedly have tried to lead a Bolshevik-style revolution. Without a peasant uprising, the Tudeh failure was sociologically pre-determined.

[140] Tudeh Party, *Darbareh-i Bist-u-Hasteh-i Mordad* (Concerning August 19th) (n.p., 1963), p. 33.

EIGHT

Ethnic Bases of
the Tudeh

Iran is a state formed of numerous nationalities (*melli*). These nationalities,
however, are brought together by many common bonds. They have shared
for long centuries a common destiny. They have worked together to create
a rich and flourishing culture. Moreover, they have fought shoulder to shoulder to preserve the freedom and independence of Iran. Despite these common bonds, some have been deprived of their national rights. This has weakened the unity of Iran, and retarded the political, economic, and cultural
development of the whole country. The Tudeh party favors the strengthening
of the bonds between the many nationalities. It believes that true and fundamental unity will be achieved only when equality is established between the
various peoples (*khalq*) of Iran and all forms of national oppression are eradicated. The Tudeh party, therefore, believes that a democratic government
must solve the national problem by:
a. recognizing the right of national self-determination
b. establishing full social, educational, and national rights for all the national
minorities living in Iran.

—Tudeh Party, *Barnameh va Asasnameh-i Hizb* (Program and Statutes
of the Party) (1960), pp. 7-8

ETHNIC PROFILE

The Tudeh perceived itself, and to a great extent it was, a
class movement. Its roots were in the intelligentsia and the
industrial working class through the length and breadth of Iran—in
Tabriz, Semnan, and Mashad, as well as Ahwaz, Shiraz, and Kerman.
It appealed to wage earners and salaried employees irrespective of
religion, language, and tribe. Its supporters included Azeri-, Gilaki-,
and Persian-speaking factory workers; Turkoman, Yazdi, and Shirazi
construction laborers; Armenian, Assyrian, and Jewish truck drivers,
carpenters, mechanics, and electricians; Luri, Qashqayi, and Bakhtiyari oil workers, along with Persian, Azeri, and Armenian oil company
clerks. It extended its organization wherever modern industry and

state bureaucracy were to be found—the textile mills of Isfahan, Shiraz, and Shahi; the sugar factories of Karaj, Mianduab, and Mervdasht; the tobacco plants of Lahijan, Rasht, and Tehran; and the government offices and public schools from Ardabel to Amul, from Mashad to Mahabad, from Behbehan to Bandar 'Abbas. In short, the Tudeh flourished wherever the two modern classes existed.

This regional distribution of the Tudeh membership is reflected in the list of 1953-1957 recanters. Of the 2,213 former members who stated both their occupations and their residences in the recantations, 1,713 (78 percent) lived in the more modernized provinces of Tehran, Gilan, Mazandaran, and Azerbaijan. Only 441 (19 percent) lived in the moderately modernized provinces of Isfahan, Khuzistan, and Kermanshah. And a mere 77 (3 percent) lived in the backward provinces of Kurdistan, Fars, Kerman, Sistan, and Baluchistan. Moreover, 1,967 (89 percent) resided in cities with a population of over 20,000, with the other 11 percent coming mostly from industrial and communication centers such as Chalus, Karaj, Lahijan, Langrud, Behshahr, Babulsar, Shahrud, Bandar Gaz, Bandar Langeh, and Bandar Ma'shur.

Although the Tudeh was predominantly a class-based party, two minorities played a particularly prominent role in the movement: the Azeri-speaking population, both inside Azerbaijan and outside, especially in Tehran, Gilan, and Mazandaran; and the Christian communities of Armenians and Assyrians concentrated in Tehran, Tabriz, Enzeli, Urmiah, Isfahan, Arak, and Hamadan. Of the fifteen members of the Provisional Central Committee in October 1942, eight were Persian speakers, four were Azeris—including three from Rasht—two were Qajars, and one was Armenian. Of the thirty-one elected to the Central Committee and its various commissions in August 1944, twenty-two had Persian as their mother tongue, six came from Azeri homes—four of them from outside Azerbaijan—two were Qajars, and one was Armenian. Of the thirty-three elected to the Central Committee and the Advisory Board in April 1948, nineteen were Persian-speaking, eleven were Azeris, and three were Qajars. Finally, of the twelve elected to the Executive Committee of the CCFTU in July 1946, six were Azeris, five were Persians, and one was Armenian. Thus the Azeri and other Turkic groups, which totaled less than 27 percent of the population, formed between 32 and 43 percent of the party leadership. Even more strikingly, the Christians, who totaled less than 0.7 percent of the population, formed as much as 3 to 8 percent of the leadership.

The Azeris and Christians were also well represented in the party's middle and lower ranks. Of the 168 delegates at the First Congress,

44 (26 percent) represented party branches in Azerbaijan. Among the others, there were at least 18 (10 percent) Azeris from outside Azerbaijan, 7 (4 percent) Armenians, and 4 (2 percent) Assyrians. Of 218 party activists arrested in the main cities in the summer of 1951, 28 (13 percent) resided in Tabriz. Among the 108 arrested in Tehran and Isfahan, there were 7 Christians. Of 24 civilian members of the party who were executed or died in prison between 1953 and 1960, 9 (37 percent) were Azeris and 6 (25 percent) were Armenians. Finally, of the 2,419 former members who recanted after 1953, 121 (5 percent) had Armenian and Assyrian names. While it is wrong to see the Tudeh as a party of disgruntled minorities, as some scholars have done,[1] the number of Christians and Azeris active in the movement was certainly disproportionate.

CHRISTIANS

Although the Tudeh promised equality, full citizenship, and secular reforms to all the religious minorities, it made noticeable inroads only among the Christians, and, despite individual recruits, failed on the whole among the Sunnis, Baha'is, Jews, and Zoroastrians. The Sunnis were confined predominantly to tribal groups, particularly Kurds, Baluchis, Arabs, and Turkomans, living in the more backward regions. Moreover, the Sunni Arabs and Baluchis had traditionally looked upon Britain as their protector against the central government. The Baha'is stood aloof from the Tudeh and other parties mainly because the violent persecution suffered by their predecessors, the Babis, had persuaded them to shun politics, especially radical politics. The Jews, after a brief interest in the Tudeh during the war years, turned more toward Zionism, and the migration of some 50,000 to Israel drained their intellectual and proletarian element, leaving behind a community made up predominantly of small traders. The Zoroastrian minority, with the exception of a few pro-Tudeh intellectuals and workers, tended to be conservative partly because it identified itself with Reza Shah's brand of secular nationalism; partly because it kept close contact with its coreligionists, the Parsis of India; and partly because it was concentrated in Yazd and Kerman, two cities with commercial ties to the British empire.

The Tudeh success among the Christians can be explained mainly by geographical and class factors. Whereas nearly 75 percent of the Muslims lived in villages and small towns, some 75 percent of the

---

[1] G. Lenczowski, "The Communist Movement in Iran," *Middle East Journal*, 1 (January 1947), 28-40.

Christians lived in cities with a population of over 20,000—notably Tehran, Tabriz, Urmiah, Hamadan, Kermanshah, Isfahan, Abadan, Ahwaz, and Masjid Sulayman. Whereas the vast majority of the Muslims were peasants, tribesmen, and bazaaris, a large proportion of the Christians were clerks, professionals, skilled craftsmen, and urban wage earners—especially shoemakers, carpenters, mechanics, electricians, and truck drivers. It was precisely these occupations that provided many of the Christian activists in the Tudeh party. For example, of the ten men elected in 1946 to the Executive Committee of the union of skilled workers, which included mechanics, electricians, and technicians, six were Christians. Of the twelve on the Executive Committee of the union of cinema attendants in 1944-1946, three were Christians. Of the twenty-four on the Executive Committees of the unions of carpenters, tailors, and shoemakers in 1944-1947, four were Christians. Finally, among the 121 Christians who recanted after 1953, there were 18 shoemakers, 15 high-school teachers, 13 skilled workers, 10 truck drivers, 9 university students, 9 office employees, 6 carpenters, 4 tailors, 3 oil workers, 3 doctors, 3 nurses, 2 dentists, 2 small factory workers, and 2 railway workers.

The Tudeh appeal among the Christians, however, extended beyond the intelligentsia and the urban working class into the peasantry and the commercial middle class. The Armenian Ramgavar party, led by merchants and shopkeepers, supported the Soviet Union and worked closely with the Tudeh. The Christian-dominated guilds of confectioners, pharmacists, and food and drink sellers were members of the CCFTU. Many Armenian villages near Arak and Isfahan emigrated en masse to Soviet Armenia in 1946-1950—the same villages had voted for the anti-Tudeh candidate in the 1943 elections because of the overwhelming influence of their landlords.

The radicalism of the Assyrian and Armenian villages near Urmiah was vividly described by the British consul in Tabriz in his periodic travel reports on western Azerbaijan. In the aftermath of the Allied invasion, these villages set up "independent councils," refused to pay taxes, formed partisan bands, and expelled not only the gendarmes but also the civilian authorities. By January 1942, gendarmes, government representatives, and landlords were too nervous to venture into the area. The consul commented, "these peasants had been so brow beaten by the Persian officials and gendarmes, and so fleeced and ground down by the landowners that when they now see the government incapable of keeping order and the landowner too frightened to visit them, they are ready to take matters into their own hands and to do without gendarmes, officials, and landlords." As the government gradually reestablished its authority in the region after 1944, the consul reported that the "Assyrian and Armenian peasants warmly supported the Tudeh," while the Kurdish tribesmen, following the lead of their chiefs, vehemently opposed the Tudeh and even prevented it from opening branches in their villages.[2] He added,

I ventured into the countryside to enable me to get a clearer picture of the tangled skein of races whose animosities form the permanent pattern of life in this district. As usual, it is the Assyrian community which is the most restless and lends itself most easily to leftist, pro-Russian movements, such as the Tudeh. Their priests told me of their difficulty in restraining their hotheads from participating in politics and are full of fears for the safety of the Assyrian element when the Moslems can again give full rein to their pent-up fanaticism.[3]

Not surprisingly, the Armenian and Assyrian peasant took an active part in the 1945 uprising against the central government, even though pro-Soviet Kurdish leaders distrusted the Christian villagers, silenced all talk of land reform, and prevented the Tudeh from entering the turf of the Kurdish Democratic party. In the heavy fighting between government tanks and rebel volunteers outside Urmiah in December 1945, forty-one of the fifty-five killed were local Assyrians and Armenians. At the same time, Assyrian clerical leaders confidentially asked the British consul whether their congregations could emigrate en masse to Iraq if the central government reoccupied the area.[4] After the collapse of the Azerbaijan rebellion, many of the Armenian villagers emigrated to the Soviet Union. Paradoxically, many of the Assyrian villagers emigrated to the United States.

Besides the protection given by the Soviet Union, a number of ethnic factors explain the Christian support for the Tudeh. The Tudeh was the only nationwide party that called for complete social and political equality between Muslims and non-Muslims. It was the only nationwide party that openly represented the interests of the Christian community, publishing Armenian and Assyrian papers, criticizing Reza Shah for closing down community schools, encouraging the reestablishment of Armenian schools in 1942, recommending state aid to establish Assyrian schools, and proposing the creation of a parliamentary seat for the Assyrians since the two seats reserved for the Christians were invariably taken by the Armenians.[5] Moreover, it was the only nationwide party that willingly recruited non-Muslims, in-

[2] British Consul in Tabriz, 3 and 28 January 1942, *F.O. 371*/Persia 1942/34-31426; British Ambassador to the Foreign Office, 25 September 1945, *F.O. 371*/Persia 1945/34-45451.

[3] British Consul in Tabriz, "Report on a Visit," *F.O. 371*/Persia 1944/34-40178.

[4] British Consul in Tabriz, "Situation in Rezai'eh," *F.O. 371*/Persia 1945/34-52661.

[5] "Proposals for Electoral Reform," *Besu-yi Ayandeh*, 24 December 1952.

tegrated them with Muslims in its cells, did not discriminate on religious grounds, and promoted Christians to high positions. Even the secular Iran party closed its doors to non-Muslims, while the radical Azadi party, led by Arsanjani, published inflammatory articles against the religious minorities. Meanwhile, the nationalist Dashnak party, the only real rival of the Tudeh within the Armenian community, had been drastically weakened, partly because of the mass arrests carried out by the Allies in 1941-1944, and partly because its policy of supporting the Pahlevi dynasty had been discredited by Reza Shah's sudden attack on the Christian minority in 1938-1939. For the Armenians who did not emigrate, one major political path remained open in the 1940s: participation in the Tudeh, the major secular movement that promised full citizenship and true equality with the Muslims.

AZERIS

The early leaders of the Tudeh, being Persian-speaking Marxists in Tehran, tended to overlook and even scorn the grievances of the linguistic minorities. Arani, the party's spiritual founder, was a good case in point. Born in Tabriz but raised in Tehran, he, like many intellectuals of his generation, was an outspoken advocate of centralization and Persianization. In an article on "Azerbaijan: A Vital and Deadly Problem for Iran," he had argued that Azerbaijan, "the cradle of Iran," had lost the Persian language because of the "barbaric Mongul invasions."[6] He warned that this loss created a dangerous situation because some natives of Azerbaijan falsely thought of themselves as Turks and even harbored separatist tendencies. To remedy the situation, Arani insisted that the state should do everything possible to eliminate Turkish and spread Persian.

Although Arani's disciples did not necessarily share his views on Azerbaijan, they were by no means overly concerned with linguistic and provincial grievances. The party's first manifesto spoke in general terms of the political grievances of all citizens against Reza Shah's autocracy. The program adopted by the First Provisional Conference ignored provincial and linguistic issues, but spelled out specific demands for workers, peasants, office employees, traders, craftsmen, intellectuals, and women. Similarly, the program presented to the Fourteenth Majles by the party's parliamentary delegation appealed not to the linguistic minorities, but to the proletariat, peasantry, intelligentsia, petit bourgeoisie, and women. What is more, the party newspapers in these early years focused on class injustices and rarely mentioned ethnic causes. Thus the Tudeh founders, living in Tehran,

---

[6] T. Arani in *Farangestan*, 1 (September 1924), 247-54.

tended to underestimate the regional conflicts between the capital and the provinces. Orthodox Marxists, they viewed society through a class perspective, ignoring the ethnic dimension. As Persian and Persian-ized intellectuals, they favored the rapid expansion of the state ed-ucational system. And as Western-educated intellectuals, they asso-ciated centralization with modernization, linguistic diversity with traditional inefficiency, and regional autonomy with administrative anarchy.

Nevertheless, the Tudeh quickly succeeded in attracting Azeris both inside and outside Azerbaijan. This can be explained by four major factors. First, a tradition of radicalism: Azerbaijan had been the center of revolutionary activity and of the Social Democratic party since the days of the Constitutional Revolution. Second, the degree of urban-ization: Azerbaijan, being one of the more advanced provinces, had few nomads but significant numbers of office employees, profession-als, and urban workers. There were as many as twelve towns with a population over 10,000 in Azerbaijan, but as few as five in Isfahan, four in Fars, three in Kerman, and two in Sistan and Baluchestan. Third, demographic changes: Azerbaijan was the first region to ex-perience significant population growth. Until 1917, the surplus pop-ulation of Azerbaijan tended to migrate north to Baku, Tiflis, and Astrakan. After 1917, it moved south to the industrial centers of Tehran, Rasht, Enzeli, Shahi, Behshahr, Mashad, Ahwaz, and Aba-dan. By the 1940s, Azeri laborers, peddlers, craftsmen, and factory workers could be found throughout Iran. Fourth, outside influence: the common language with Soviet Azerbaijan provided the Russians with a valuable propaganda weapon. During the war years, the Soviets disseminated their views not only through Baku radio, Azeri language publications, and cultural tours from the Caucasus, but also through Azeri-speaking officers and soldiers stationed in Iranian Azerbaijan.

The Tudeh created its first branch in Azerbaijan in early 1942 by merging three radical clubs in Tabriz.[7] One club was formed of local intellectuals, one of Armenians, and one of mujaherin—the Azeri emigres from the Soviet Union. Expanding rapidly, the Tudeh or-ganization in Azerbaijan soon claimed 12,000 members, established a regular newspaper called *Azerbaijan*, and opened branches in Ar-dabel, Maragheh, Astara, Sarab, and Mianeh. Speaking on behalf of the Central Committee in Tehran, Amir-Khizi in 1943 praised his colleagues in Azerbaijan for having built the party's largest provincial organization.[8]

The Tudeh in Azerbaijan was led by five local organizers: Sadeq

[7] "Information about Azerbaijan," *Iran-i Ma*, 8 December 1945.

[8] ʿA. Amir-Khizi, "Report on the Tudeh Party in Azerbaijan," *Rahbar*, 23 November 1943.

Padegan, Ghulam Yahya Daneshyan, ʿAli Shabistari, Mir Rahimi Valaʾi, and Muhammad Biriya. Padegan, the chairman of the provincial organization, was a veteran of the Khiabani revolt and the Communist party. Born into a middle-class family in Tabriz, he had spent most of his life in Azerbaijan and thus spoke Persian with some difficulty. Arrested in 1938, he had spent three years in prison in Tehran, where he had met the "Fifty-three" and studied ancient Iranian languages. Daneshyan, the party's main organizer in Sarab, Mianeh, and Zanjan, was a former file cutter who, according to the British embassy, "possessed exceptional courage and determination."[9] The son of a peasant, he had migrated to the Caucasus, studied in Baku—some claimed at the military school—and found himself imprisoned on his return to Iran in 1937. Shabistari, the editor of *Azerbaijan*, had been prominent in the Khiabani government, and was one of the few local Tudeh leaders who had reached middle age. A native of Tabriz, he had fled to Soviet Azerbaijan and had not returned until 1941. Valaʾi, the assistant editor of *Azerbaijan*, was a twenty-seven-year-old intellectual who had been arrested in 1937 for propagating subversive ideas. Born into a middle-class family in Tabriz, he had spent most of his life in Azerbaijan, except for his prison years in Tehran. Finally, Biriya, the head of the pro-Tudeh labor unions in Tabriz, was an effective organizer and a talented Azeri poet. Born in Tabriz in 1918, he had fled north in the 1930s, studied literature in Baku, and returned home with the Soviet army in August 1941.

The Tudeh in Azerbaijan found its main support among the factory workers of Tabriz, especially those in the city's five textile mills, four tanneries, two match manufacturing plants, three breweries, one silo, five soap factories, and numerous carpet weaving workshops. The program of the Tudeh in Tabriz and its Union of Workers was similar to that published by the Central Committee in Tehran. Both programs called for elimination of the vestiges of Reza Shah's dictatorship, the eight-hour day, Friday pay, collective bargaining, protection for local industries, free education, equality for women, and close ties between workers' organizations throughout Iran. They differed, however, in one significant way. Whereas the Tehran program overlooked ethnic issues, the Tabriz program demanded the establishment of the provincial assemblies promised in the constitutional laws, and the use of Azeri both in the local law courts and in the first four grades of public schools.[10]

[9] British Military Attaché to the Foreign Office, 12 November 1946, *India Office*/L/P&S/12-3505.

[10] British Consul in Tabriz, "Soviet Policy towards Tribes and the Azerbaijan Workers' Committee," *F.O. 371*/Persia 1942/34-31390.

The British consul in Tabriz reported in early 1943 that the Tudeh and its Union of Workers found eager listeners among the hungry workers, whose wages had lagged far behind the eightfold rise in bread prices since mid-1941. After a series of successful strikes during the winter of 1943, the unions forced the industrialists to raise wages and subsidize bread prices. The British consul quoted a Russian officer as saying that the speeches made in the Bolshevik Revolution were mild compared to those heard in the Tabriz factories. Similarly, after a burst of strikes during the summer of 1943, the unions compelled the central government to send a committee to mediate. This committee extracted from the local industrialists the eight-hour day, a minimum wage, a ban on child labor, one kilo of free bread a day, three free suits a year, free medical facilities, one month of paid vacation a year, and arbitration boards with union representation. The British consul predicted that this "generous agreement" would not last long, since the unions, "like Oliver Twist," would soon ask for more.[11]

This prediction was borne out the following year as prices continued to escalate. In July 1944, after the police fired on a workers' demonstration, killing six and wounding fifteen, the union at the largest match factory occupied the plant, demanded a share of the "enormous profits," and threatened to lynch the manager unless wages were promptly increased.[12] The British consul reported:

The factory owner, unable to rely on any protection from the police, gave way to these demands, although realizing that similar and even more extravagant demands are likely to follow. . . . The other factory owners are threatened with similar trouble, and one textile factory, under threats of violence, has promised to pay its workers a three month bonus at Now Rouz.[13]

The consul added that the Tudeh in Azerbaijan acted like a state within a state, and that its Union of Workers, having joined the CCFTU, was strong enough to "do very much as it liked without interference from the local government."[14]

The rapid expansion of the Tudeh into Azerbaijan did not resolve the ethnic problem. On the contrary, it brought the ethnic problem into the Tudeh party. The problem revolved around the question of nationality (*melliyat*) in general and the definition of nation (*mellat*) in particular. According to many of the Tudeh leaders in Tabriz, the

[11] British Consul in Tabriz, 5 January, 1 April, 10 October, and 16 October 1943, *F.O. 371*/Persia 1943/34-35092.

[12] British Consul in Tabriz, 13 July 1944, *F.O. 371*/Persia 1944/34-40178.

[13] Ibid., 10 August 1944.

[14] British Consul in Tabriz, 14 December 1944, *F.O. 371*/Persia 1944/34-45478.

Azeri language made Azerbaijan into a separate nation (*mellat*) with the inalienable right of electing its own provincial assemblies and using its own language in local schools, law courts, and government offices. A few of the Tabriz leaders went even further and argued that the distinct language entitled Azerbaijan to Lenin's unqualified right of national self-determination. But according to the Tudeh leaders in Tehran, Azeri was not a national (*melli*) language but a local (*mahalli*) dialect, Azerbaijanis constituted not a nationality (*melliyat*) but a people (*mardom*), and Azerbaijan was not a separate nation (*mellat*) but an integral part of the Iranian nation (*mellat*) sharing common economic, cultural, and historical features with the rest of the country. Many of the Tehran leaders also warned that provincial autonomy might help the Tudeh in Azerbaijan, but it would certainly weaken the party in regions dominated by tribal chiefs, military authorities, and pro-British landlords. For Tabriz, Iran contained diverse nationalities; for Tehran, Iran was one indivisible nation.

These differences reared their heads at the first party congress.[15] An Azeri delegate from Gilan complained that the party had underestimated the deep-seated grievances of the provinces. One delegate from Tabriz protested that the party leadership had given priority to Tehran and ignored the provinces, especially Azerbaijan. Another such delegate, speaking in Azeri, argued that the Central Committee had hindered his branch by being obsessed with the imaginary dangers of "ultraleftism." Another remarked that party publications were useless in his home town since they were all written in Persian. Yet another complained that the central organization had done nothing when the Tabriz police had recently shot down six workers. And Daneshyan, heading the Sarab delegation, expressed the general mood of the Azerbaijani delegates when he exclaimed: "The party should talk less and act more." This was later adopted as the main slogan of the Azerbaijani rebellion.

These circumstances were described more fully by Khalel Maleki twenty-two years later.[16] Sent by the Central Committee to investigate the situation in Azerbaijan on the eve of the first congress, Khalel Maleki reported that he had been shocked to discover that many party militants could not understand Persian, that his refusal to address meetings in Azeri antagonized the local leaders, and that his insistence on the use of Persian in schools caused a showdown with Biriya. Khalel Maleki returned to Tehran with the suspicion that some party leaders

---

[15] Tudeh Party, "Proceedings of the First Party Congress," *Rahbar*, 2 August-7 September 1944.

[16] The Society of Iranian Socialists, "Text of Khalel Maleki's Defence at His Trial," *Sosiyalism*, 2 (October 1966), 36-56.

in Azerbaijan, especially Biriya, were covering up their "true separatist aims" under the cloak of seeking provincial assemblies, Azeri schools, and a higher share of taxes.

The lobbying by the Azeri delegates at the first congress persuaded the Tudeh leaders to accept for the first time some of their more moderate requests. They agreed to take more interest in the outlying areas and to air provincial grievances more openly. They allowed local branches to hold rallies for the formation of the provincial and regional assemblies that had been promised in the constitutional laws. They permitted the organizations in Azerbaijan and Gurgan to translate party manifestos into Azeri and Turkoman. They started a newspaper campaign on the theme "Iran is not just Tehran; and Tehran is not just northern [residential] Tehran." They encouraged the Majles to allocate more funds for Azerbaijan on the grounds that although "all Azerbaijanis consider themselves Iranians" Reza Shah had treated them as second-class citizens.[17] Moreover, they took steps to stop ethnicity from dividing the labor organizations. For example, the pro-Tudeh union of silk weavers in Mazandaran issued a warning that Sayyid Ziya was trying to destroy the organization by manipulating Persians against Azeris. The union of tobacco workers in Tehran declared that right-wing parties were planning to sow dissension between Persian and Azeri employees. And the CCFTU intervened to force the coalfield at Shamshak to rehire some three hundred Azeri miners who had been fired as a result of violent confrontations between Persian and Azeri workers. In a letter to *Zafar* in Tehran and *Azerbaijan* in Tabriz, the Azeri miners protested: "Do you know why they evicted us? Because we are Azerbaijanis. Do you know what they call us? They call us Turks. Are we or are we not Iranians? Do we or do we not have rights in Iran? Is the law impartial or weighed against us?"[18]

Furthermore, the Tudeh leaders at the first congress also modified the party program in the hope of satisfying the Azerbaijani delegates. After stressing that the Tudeh was dedicated to democracy, the program now called for the protection of "all individual liberties—the freedom of *zaban* (expression/language), speech, press, belief, and assembly."[19] And after emphasizing that the Tudeh was a party of workers, peasants, craftsmen, traders, and progressive intellectuals, the program demanded complete social equality between all citizens

---

[17] A. Ovanessian, *Parliamentary Proceedings*, 14th Majles, 23 January 1945.

[18] Union of Silk Weavers in Mazandaran, "A Declaration," *Rahbar*, 27 June 1945; Union of Tobacco Workers in Tehran, "A Declaration," *Zafar*, 11 April 1946; Three Hundred Workers, "Letter to the Editor," *Azerbaijan*, 27 November 1945.

[19] Tudeh Party, "Party Program," *Rahbar*, 5-7 September 1944.

of the Iranian nation (*mellat*) irrespective of the citizen's religion and birth (*nezhad*); and complete freedom for the minorities (*aqaliyat*) in matters relating to religion and culture (*farhang*). These clauses were significant in that many of them had been absent in the previous programs. But they were vague in four major areas. By speaking of the Iranian nation, they implied that the people of Azerbaijan were not a nation. By failing to specify what languages should be taught in the educational system, they avoided the central linguistic problem. By refusing to define *aqaliyat* (minorities), they left the impression that the party was referring not to the linguistic minorities, but to the legally constituted religious minorities—Christians, Jews, and Zoroastrians. And by using vague terms such as *nezhad* (birth), *farhang* (culture), and *zaban* (expression/language), they implied that the party was concerned more with the civil and constitutional rights of individuals than with the educational and cultural rights of linguistic minorities.

This ambiguity continued after the first party congress. In an article on "Nation and Nationality," Ovanessian skirted around the question of whether Iran contained one or more nationalities, and took refuge in Stalin's formula that a nation is formed of a people with a common language, culture, economy, and territory. The same ambivalence appeared in a book on *The National Question* written by a party intellectual in Tehran who was an Azeri doctor educated in Russia.[20] The author began with a clear statement expressing the urgency of the problem:

The question of nationalities and their rights is a vital issue in countries such as Iran where diverse peoples live together. It is a subject that no progressive party can avoid, for it is closely related to many social and political issues: to the struggle for national independence; to the fight for the liberation of the peasantry; and to the war against the exploitation of the working class.

He underlined the urgency by reminding his readers that patriotic sentiments could easily be used by reactionaries against progressives: "Class-conscious workers are not tempted by bourgeois flags, but peasants are." He then set himself the question, "What Is a Nationality?" After describing, at considerable length, the debates between West European and Russian Marxists, he arrived at the conclusion that Stalin's definition was correct: "A nationality is formed of a people who are held together by a common language, culture, territory, and economy." From this point on, however, the book turned obscure. The author, instead of pursuing his line of argument and applying

---

[20] A. Ovanessian, "Nation and Nationality," *Rahbar*, 26 August 1946; R. Hashtrudiyan, *Masaleh-i Melliyat* (The National Question) (Tehran, 1945), pp. 1-75.

this definition to the various communities in Iran, injected the issue of imperialism and colonialism into the discussion: "The question of nationalities, which was formerly an internal problem, has now become an international issue closely tied to the danger of imperialism." The concluding chapter on "How To Solve the Problem" summarized Lenin's theory of imperialism and avoided dealing with the question of nationalities in Iran. Thus a book that had started by emphasizing the importance of the subject to Iran ended without mentioning Iran. Nowhere did the author deal with the immediate issues. Nowhere did he define which minorities in Iran qualified as nationalities. Nowhere did he specify their grievances and their national rights.

The vague program permitted the party to espouse different, if not contradictory, views. On the one hand, the Tehran leaders who had opposed the airing of provincial grievances continued to stress class injustices and to gloss over ethnic problems. For example, Keshavarz and Radmanesh, in separate three-hour speeches in parliament, detailed the party program for land distribution, industrialization, public health, free education, electoral reform, and many other reforms, but mentioned neither linguistic issues nor provincial assemblies. Similarly, the Tehran organization at its second provincial conference ignored the ethnic problem and instead instructed the local branches to start classes for teaching Persian to illiterate workers.[21] For the intelligentsia in Tehran, it seemed that these classes would educate the illiterates; for the intelligentsia in Tabriz, it seemed that they would further Persianize the Azeri migrants.

On the other hand, local leaders and regional organizations that harbored ethnic grievances began to press for their demands. For example, the party organizations in Gilan and Mazandaran, as well as Azerbaijan, held mass rallies for the convening of provincial and local assemblies. Likewise, Qassemi, the main organizer among the Turkomans of Gurgan, gave a broad interpretation to the party program when writing the second edition of his *What Does the Tudeh Party of Iran Say and Want?* Interpreting *zaban, aqaliyat,* and *nezhad* to mean language, linguistic minority, and cultural community, he sought educational and cultural safeguards for the non-Persians, especially the Azeris, Turkomans, Kurds, and Arabs:

States sometimes deprive minorities of their schools, literature, and history. This has two disastrous consequences: it destroys minority cultures, preventing them from contributing to world civilization; and it alienates the

[21] F. Keshavarz, *Parliamentary Proceedings*, 14th Majles, 25 May 1945; R. Radmanesh, *Parliamentary Proceedings*, 14th Majles, 26 May 1945; Tudeh Party, "Proceedings of the Second Provincial Conference of Tehran," *Rahbar*, 19-22 August 1945.

minority from the majority, eventually causing a civil war, as happened between Turks and Greeks in the Ottoman empire. Thus, a state should respect
its minorities not only for the sake of [world] culture, but also to safeguard
its own existence. Iran is a multilingual state, and although we all have a
common history, the rights of the linguistic minorities should be respected,
as the Tudeh party has stated in its program. Otherwise, our enemies will
take advantage of internal differences to destroy our state.[22]

In spite of the fact that the Central Committee and the First Congress rejected the more nationalistic demands sent from Tabriz, the
Tudeh continued to expand throughout Azerbaijan. The local party
opened new branches, doubled its membership, won over the Kurdish
Shakkak tribe near Lake Urmiah, and in January 1945 convened its
first provincial conference. Formed of 130 delegates, this conference
endorsed the demand for provincial assemblies; remained silent on
the linguistic issue; expelled Shabistari, the editor of *Azerbaijan*, for
publishing extreme nationalistic articles; started the paper *Khaver Now*
(The New East) to replace *Azerbaijan* as the local party organ; and
elected to the provincial central committee Amir-Khizi and Ovanessian, two members of the main central committee who were natives
of Azerbaijan and sympathized with the more moderate demands of
Azerbaijan. Ousted from the Tudeh, Shabistari kept on publishing
Azerbaijan and founded a Society of Azerbaijan dedicated to the preservation of the Azeri language and heritage.

The Union of Workers in Tabriz and other affiliates of the CCFTU
in Azerbaijan also continued to grow rapidly. They enrolled bazaar
workers, road sweepers, cart drivers, garage mechanics, tailors, office
clerks, and teachers, and by early 1945 claimed over 50,000 members.[23] They set up an effective shop steward system, held union
elections, and in late 1944 forced the Tabriz industrialists to raise
wages by an additional 25 percent. The British consul reported that
although Biriya and other party intellectuals were popular on the
shop floors, the workers preferred to elect representatives from their
own ranks to watch over their economic interests.[24] The unions also
organized unarmed militias, guarded the plants, and formed workers'
cooperatives to run factories that had gone bankrupt. In January
1945, the British consul in Tabriz reported:

There are signs that the Workers' Union is becoming more responsible and
better organized than it was a year ago. Politically, its activities are completely

[22] A. Qassemi, *Hizb-i Tudeh-i Iran Cheh Miguyad va Cheh Mikhuahad?* (What Does the
Tudeh Party Say and Want?) (Tehran, 1944), pp. 31-32.

[23] A. Amir-Khizi, "Address to the First Provincial Conference of the Tudeh Party in
Azerbaijan," *Rahbar*, 28 January 1945.

[24] British Consul in Tabriz, 2 November 1944, *F.O. 371*/Persia 1944/34-40178.

coordinated with those of the Tudeh party, and both its methods and functions often appear to be more those of some sort of local government rather than a trade union. It has, for example, at different times in the past six months, usurped the functions of both police and judiciary, settling disputes, from industrial grievances to street-fights, by its own laws. In its proper field it has done some good work, particularly in combatting the exploitation to which the workers in small private concerns—like bakeries, bath houses, and workshops—are exposed, and it has taken up the cause of the most depressed class of all, the bazaar porters. The threat of large-scale unemployment has been the union's chief preoccupation, and this has caused it to accept some compromises in the factories, and even sanction the dismissal of workers, which it had always previously rigidly opposed, not without some justification in a country where no unemployment insurance exists.[25]

Furthermore, in 1945 the peasants' union in Azerbaijan launched a campaign into the countryside. The campaign took the form of sending party cadres into the villages to advocate land reform, denounce the gendarmerie, form peasant unions, and persuade sharecroppers to give up no more than one-fifth of the harvest to the landlords. In fact, these cadres failed in most areas, but they succeeded in some. In the Bukan region, for example, they recruited over one thousand Kurdish villagers and forced the landlords to increase the peasants' share of the sugar beet harvest. In the Maragheh region, they frightened off the local landowners. In the Sarab region, they incited the peasants to kill one of the more notorious landlords and to withhold the whole harvest. In the villages near Tabriz, thirty landlords sent a telegram to the central government warning that they would have no wheat to sell to the state unless the gendarmerie used force to collect the harvest. And in the Ardabel area, gendarmerie officers decided not to interfere in landlord-peasant disputes.[26] By mid-1945, the British consul was writing that the Tudeh campaign had caught on in eastern Azerbaijan:

Farm bailiffs, despairing of receiving any assistance from the gendarmerie, are now appealing to the Tudeh party for assistance in collecting the landlords' due. It is the practice of the Tudeh secretaries to give them letters addressed to the peasants of their villages. But, even so, the peasants appear to be standing firm and refusing to give them no more than an eighth—putting this share aside and telling the bailiffs to take it or leave it. Some villages have objected to the sharing being done through bailiffs and have demanded that the landlords come in person. Few if any landlords have dared to do so this year.[27]

[25] British Consul in Tabriz, 12 January 1945, *F.O. 371*/Persia 1945/34-45478.
[26] Ibid., 16 May, 13 July, 28 July, 6 September 1945.
[27] Ibid., 6 September 1945.

With the rapid growth of the party organizations, the Tudeh became the de facto government of Azerbaijan. As the British consul reported, its leaders exercised more power than the governor-general, its militias rivaled the city police, its rural cadres had more authority than the gendarmerie, its unions ran the factories, and its program appealed to discontented merchants as well as to workers, peasants, and intellectuals:

The contempt in which the incompetent and corrupt local government is held by all classes, and a growing feeling of indifference of the Central Government to Azerbaijan, may lead even the right-wing to take the view that the measures urged by the Tudeh cannot make conditions any worse than they are at present. . . . The party leaders are conscious of their power locally. The exercise of their power is so obvious as to lead cynics to enquire why the Governor-General does not retire to Tehran and leave his prerogatives to Mohammad Biriya.[28]

The course of events in Azerbaijan took an unexpected turn in September 1945, however, when the Soviet authorities, reacting sharply to the archconservative administration of Premier Sadr, decided to sponsor armed rebellions in Azerbaijan and Kurdistan. A clear sign of this change in Soviet policy was the sudden appearance of Pishevari in Tabriz. A veteran communist who had remained aloof from the Tudeh, Pishevari had recently stepped up his criticisms of the Tudeh, arguing that it lacked determination, did not represent the true interests of Azerbaijan, and should be replaced by a more effective organization.[29] Pishevari arrived in Tabriz with two colleagues from the old Communist party: Dr. Salamallah Javid and Ja'far Kaviyan. Javid, born in the same village as Pishevari, had attended high school in Baku, where he had joined the early 'Adalat party. He moved to Tabriz in 1920, participated in the Lahuti revolt, and then fled back to Baku, where he studied medicine. Returning to Iran in 1920, he found himself in prison, where he pursued his hobby of Azerbaijani history. Kaviyan, also a veteran of the Lahuti revolt, had lived in Soviet Azerbaijan from 1921 to 1925. On his return to Iran, he had also been arrested and kept in prison until 1941. Both Javid and Kaviyan, like Pishevari, had refused to join the Tudeh.

Once in Tabriz, Pishevari, Javid, and Kaviyan announced on September 3 the formation of a new organization named the Democratic Party of Azerbaijan (Firqeh-i Demokrat-i Azerbaijan). In its first statement, written in both Azeri and Persian, the Firqeh declared Azer-

---

[28] Ibid., 14 December 1945.
[29] Bamshad (pseudonym), "Pishevari's Disappointment with the Tudeh," *Aras*, 1 January 1947.

baijan to be a distinct nation (*mellat*), expressed the desire to remain within Iran, praised Khiabani's "heroic struggle," and demanded provincial assemblies, use of Azeri in local schools and government offices, and retention of tax revenues for the development of the region. On September 5, Shabistari's Society of Azerbaijan joined the Firqeh, and his *Azerbaijan*, now published only in Azeri, became the official organ of the Firqeh. Meanwhile, leaflets distributed by the Firqeh promised to use peaceful means to resolve all issues, especially the agrarian issue, and criticized the Tudeh for having taken in "self-seekers, corrupt persons, and violent troublemakers."[30] And on September 7, the local Central Committees of the Tudeh and the CCFTU voted without even consulting Tehran to break with the Tudeh and to join the Firqeh. A year later, Keshavarz of the Central Committee in Tehran was to explain that the Azerbaijan organization had abruptly broken with the Tudeh because it felt that the central organization had not represented aggressively enough the interests of Azerbaijan.[31]

Having obtained a ready-made organization, the Firqeh spent the next four weeks consolidating its network, publicizing its program, and recruiting new members, especially small merchants and local landlords. Its policy was to minimize class differences within Azerbaijan and maximize the communal conflict with Tehran. As editorials of *Azerbaijan* declared: "Our aim is to unite all the people of Azerbaijan. The class struggle will not appear until we have safely secured our national rights. Our party is interested in the rights of all classes living in Azerbaijan." "All classes, especially industrialists and workers, must put aside their differences and work together for the national good of Azerbaijan. We must cooperate to bring prosperity to our land. Strikes and bankruptcies harm the worker as much as the factory owner."[32]

By the first week of October, the Firqeh was ready to convene its first party congress. Meeting in Tabriz, the congress repeated its demands, reaffirmed its desire to remain within Iran, and announced that "the various nationalities living in Iran have the right to determine their destinies and manage their affairs by means of provincial and regional assemblies."[33] The party congress also declared that Azerbaijan must elect its governor-general, that landlords could keep one-fifth of the harvest, and that the people of Azerbaijan, having learned one important lesson from Khiabani's defeat, would protect them-

[30] British Consul in Tabriz, 15 September 1945, *F.O. 371*/Persia 1945/34-45478.

[31] F. Keshavarz, "The Azerbaijan Crisis," *Aras*, 1 January 1947.

[32] "Unity Is the Basis of Our Certain Victory," *Azerbaijan*, 17 September 1945; "Workers and Industrialists," *Azerbaijan*, 5 September 1945.

[33] British Consul in Tabriz, 26 October 1945, *F.O. 371*/Persia 1945/34-45478.

selves with armed volunteers (*feda'is*). The delegates announced that the old Firqeh had lost because it had been unarmed, but the new Firqeh would win because it would be well armed.

With light weapons received from the Soviets, the Firqeh organized an almost bloodless revolt throughout Azerbaijan. The uprising began in mid-October with the seizure of Sarab, Ardabel, and Mishkinshahr. It continued in late October with the occupation of Maragheh, Miaaneh, and Mianduab. And it ended in early November with the entry of the victorious feda'is into Tabriz. Meanwhile, the Soviet army prevented Iranian troops from entering the northwestern provinces, and the newly created Democratic Party of Kurdistan, helped by local tribes, carried out a similar revolt in neighboring Kurdistan. The British consul reported that most of the feda'is in Azerbaijan were ordinary workers and peasants, and added that the uprising "sounded the death knell of the moribund Persian administration": "The administration did not fall because it had already reached bottom. All the rebels had to do was sweep up the pieces."[34] The only major confrontation occurred near Urmiah, where fifty-five volunteers were killed attacking eight government tanks. The British consul commented, "the Fedi'is force was very mixed. For the first time in Rezaieh's history of racial and religious butchery, Kurds, Azerbaijanis, Muslims, Assyrians, and Armenians fought side by side against a common enemy."[35]

Having negotiated the surrender of the army garrison at Tabriz, the Firqeh on November 21 convened a National Congress of Azerbaijan. The congress was made up of 325 delegates, including some from Zanjan in Gilan and from Urmiah in Kurdistan. Eleven of the delegates were Christian. The main function of the congress was to send a declaration of autonomy to the central government. The declaration summed up the Firqeh's main aspirations:

1. The People of Azerbaijan have been endowed by history with distinct national, linguistic, cultural, and traditional characteristics. These characteristics entitle Azerbaijan to freedom and autonomy, as promised to all nations by the Atlantic Charter.

2. The Nation (*Mellat*) of Azerbaijan has no desire to separate itself from Iran or to harm the territorial integrity of Iran, for it is aware of the close cultural, educational, and political ties that exist between itself and the other provinces, and is proud of the great sacrifices it has made for the creation of modern Iran.

[34] British Consul in Tabriz, 31 December 1945, *F.O. 371*/Persia 1945/34-52740.
[35] British Consul in Tabriz, "Situation in Rezaieh," *F.O. 371*/Persia 1945/34-52661.

3. The Nation of Azerbaijan supports, with all its might, democracy, which in Iran takes the form of a constitutional government.

4. The Nation of Azerbaijan, like all citizens of Iran, will participate in the functioning of the central government by electing deputies to the Majles and by paying taxes.

5. The Nation of Azerbaijan officially and openly declares that it has the right to form its own government, like other living nations, and to administer its internal and national affairs, observing the integrity of Iran.

6. The Nation of Azerbaijan, having made great sacrifices for freedom, is determined to base its autonomy on the firm foundation of democracy. It, therefore, calls for a National Congress that will elect the ministers for the Autonomous Government of Azerbaijan.

7. The Nation of Azerbaijan has a special attachment to its national and mother language. It realizes that the imposition of another language on the people of Azerbaijan has hindered their historical progress. This Congress therefore instructs its ministers to use the Azerbaijan language in schools and government offices as soon as possible.

8. This Congress, supported by 150,000 signatures, declares itself a Constituent Assembly and appoints a Committee to administer Azerbaijan and implement the above resolutions until the convening of a National Majles.[36]

The National Majles met in Tabriz on December 12. Formed of 180 representatives, almost all from the Firqeh, the Majles reaffirmed the Firqeh program. It declared the formation of the Autonomous Government of Azerbaijan and again expressed its desire to remain within Iran. It promised to use Azeri in schools and offices, encourage local industry, protect private property, reorganize provincial finances, eliminate unemployment, alleviate class differences, create a national army, and reform the administrative structure. The British consul reported that most minor civil servants stayed on, since almost all were Azerbaijanis.[37] The Majles also elected a national government. This cabinet included Pishevari as premier; Javid as interior minister; Kaviyan as defense minister; Biriya as education minister; Rabi'i Kabiri, a wealthy landlord in Maragheh and a veteran of the Khiabani revolt, as communications minister; Ghulam Reza Ilahami, a high-ranking civil servant, as finance minister; Yousef 'Azima, a young local lawyer, as justice minister; Dr. Orangi, an apolitical doctor from Tabriz, as health minister; and 'Ali Shams, a wealthy textile manufacturer, as commerce minister. The National Majles appointed no foreign minister in order to protect itself from accusations that it

[36] National Congress of Azerbaijan, "The Declaration of National Autonomy," *Azerbaijan*, 26 November 1945.

[37] British Consul in Tabriz, 30 January 1946, *F.O. 371*/Persia 1946/34-52663.

planned to separate Azerbaijan from Iran. Since only one (Biriya) of the nine ministers had been in the Tudeh, the Firqeh was not, as many scholars have described it to be, merely the Tudeh in disguise.[38]

Indeed, the initial reaction of the Tudeh leaders to these events was one of surprise, shock, and dismay. It was revealed years later that as soon as news reached Tehran that the Firqeh had been formed and the provincial Tudeh had been dissolved, the party secretaries called an emergency plenary meeting of the Central Committee and the Inspection Commission.[39] Some leaders felt that the proclamations coming from Tabriz were bad jokes if not police forgeries. Others argued that all conclusions should be deferred until the party obtained first-hand information. Yet others emphasized that these events, if true, endangered not only the Tudeh in Azerbaijan but also the whole socialist movement throughout Iran. After an all-night discussion, during which the news was confirmed, the vast majority endorsed a strong resolution largely drafted by Khalel Maleki. The resolution overruled the provincial organization's decision to disband, declared that the Tudeh, being a national party, would continue to have branches in all regions of the country, and by referring to the Firqeh-i De-mokrat-i Azerbaijan as simply the Firqeh-i Demokrat, refused to accept its ethnic identity. Only one member of the Central Committee, whose identity was not revealed, opposed the resolution, and even his opposition was based on the argument that it was too early to pass judgment. The resolution did not reach the public, however, for the Soviet embassy intervened the following morning and persuaded the Tudeh leaders that the statement would harm not only the Iranian left but also the international socialist movement. Not for the last time, the Soviets brought the Tudeh leaders into line by appealing to their sense of international solidarity.

Caught between Soviet needs and their own policies, the Tudeh leaders steered a difficult course, keeping a fair distance so as not to be too closely identified with the Firqeh, but at the same time not drifting so far as to openly antagonize the Soviets. In pursuing this policy, they neither praised the Firqeh nor denounced it. Instead they underemphasized its ethnic aims, and overemphasized its desire for social reform. For example, Radmanesh, in a major speech before

[38] G. Lenczowski, *Russia and the West in Iran, 1918-1948* (Ithaca, 1949), pp. 223-25, 287; F. Nollau and H. Wiehe, *Russia's Southern Flank* (New York, 1963), p. 28; D. Wilber, *Contemporary Iran* (New York, 1963), pp. 139-40; E. Groseclose, *Introduction to Iran* (New York, 1947), p. 233.

[39] Society of Iranian Socialists, "Text of Khalel Maleki's Defence at His Trial," *Sosi-yalism*, 2 (October 1966), 45-46. See also Kh. Maleki, "The Azerbaijan Crisis," *Niru-yi Sevum*, 12 December 1952.

parliament, ignored the linguistic issue, and argued instead that the whole crisis had been caused by the refusal of the central government to carry out social reforms, especially land distribution, the expansion of public education, and the implementation of a comprehensive labor law. He concluded his speech with the warning that economic grievances could cause similar rebellions elsewhere:

Do not imagine that this crisis is peculiar to Azerbaijan, for southerners have even less food, clothing, and necessities of life. . . . The government must solve the problem quickly and peacefully. Otherwise, tomorrow some other group elsewhere will form an organization and will say: "Yes, sir, we are Arabs, and we want our Arabistan." What will you reply?[40]

The party's main organ, *Rahbar*, also glossed over the ethnic issue and focused on Azerbaijan's economic problems. In implementing this editorial policy, *Rahbar* was helped, ironically, by the central government, which imposed a ban on all Tudeh papers in early September and did not lift the ban until mid-November. When *Rahbar* reappeared, it refrained from commenting on the Firqeh and limited its coverage of Azerbaijan to translations of West European accounts, especially BBC reports. It was not until November 27 that *Rahbar* published a full-length article on Azerbaijan. Written by Anvar Khameh, a teacher in Tehran and junior member of the "Fifty-three" who had been elected to the Inspection Commission, the article described the economic stagnation of Azerbaijan, placed the blame for the crisis on the shoulders of the ruling class, and, without mentioning the language problem, supported the demand for provincial assemblies.[41] In the same issue, it summarized without comment the resolutions passed by the congress meeting in Tabriz, and translated the famous Declaration of National Autonomy that had just been published in Azerbaijan. But in translating the declaration, it substituted the Persian word *mardom* (people) for the Arabic term *khalq*, even though the Firqeh's own Persian version of the text had used the controversial word *mellat* (nation).

Rahbar published no other major articles on Azerbaijan for four full months. On March 26, it broke its silence with an equivocal editorial arguing that the Azerbaijan crisis would not be solved until Iran convened a Constituent Assembly.[42] Three days later, it printed the very first article on the crisis by a member of the Central Committee. Written by Amir-Khizi, who had quietly but angrily left Azer

[40] R. Radmanesh, *Parliamentary Proceedings*, 14th Majles, 25 December 1946.
[41] A. Khameh, "Our Party and the Internal Situation of Iran," *Rahbar*, 27 November 1945.
[42] "The Need for a Constituent Assembly," *Rahbar*, 26 March 1946.

baijan as soon as the Firqeh had appeared, the article ignored the language question, arguing that, although the Tudeh had been effective in Tabriz, "force of circumstances," especially the danger of imperialism, had given the people of Azerbaijan no other choice but to take over the provincial administration.[43] Drawing parallels with the Constitutional Revolution, Amir-Khizi concluded that the revolt in Azerbaijan could help "all progressive, freedom-loving, and anti-colonial forces in Iran."

Similar arguments were presented by three articles that appeared in *Rahbar* during the course of the next two months. The first, written by Anvar Khameh, dismissed the linguistic issue as a secondary problem, and argued that the main cause of the crisis was the economic and political pressures exerted by the corrupt ruling class. He stressed that "these pressures are aimed not at the people of Azerbaijan exclusively, but at the whole nation (*mellat*) of Iran." The second, written by Khalel Maleki, emphasized Azerbaijan's contribution to Iranian history, and advised the Firqeh not to confuse the useful functions of the state with the exploitative role of the parasitical upper class. The third, signed by Ovanessian, who had returned to Tehran with Amir-Khizi, argued that the terror unleashed by Premier Sadr against the Tudeh in the central and southern provinces had forced the people of Azerbaijan to take matters into their own hands. He concluded the article by stressing that the revolt in Azerbaijan could help the radical movement throughout Iran.[44]

Of the many newspapers associated closely with the Tudeh, only *Zafar*, the organ of the CCFTU, gave unequivocal support to the Firqeh's ethnic demands. Edited by Rusta, the Azeri labor leader from Rasht, *Zafar* championed the right to have provincial assemblies, and published a series of congratulatory messages sent to the "democratic movement of Azerbaijan" by "Azeri-speaking workers in Tehran, Gilan, and Mazandaran."[45] Moreover, in a lengthy article on "Attachment to Language," *Zafar* emphasized that for centuries Azeri had been the mother tongue of Azerbaijan:

What disturbs most the so-called patriots of Iran is the desire of the Azerbaijan nation to speak in its own mother tongue and to use this mother tongue as the official language of the province. These so-called patriots refuse to rec-

[43] British Consul in Tabriz, 3 October 1945, *F.O. 371*/Persia 1945/34-45478; ʿAmir-Khizi, "The Role of Azerbaijan in the Struggle for the Creation of an Independent and Free Iran," *Rahbar*, 29 March 1946.

[44] A. Khameh, "Concerning Azerbaijan," *Rahbar*, 23 April 1946; Kh. Maleki, "The Experience of Azerbaijan," *Rahbar*, 26 April 1946; A. Ovanessian, "The Democratic Movement in Azerbaijan," *Rahbar*, 15 May 1946.

[45] *Zafar*, 22 April 1946.

ognize the reality of the last six hundred years, and do not even admit that Iran contains linguistic and cultural minorities. They persist in claiming that the people of Azerbaijan, who have spoken Azeri during the last six hundred years, are really Persian-speakers, just like the residents of Isfahan, Shiraz, and Yazd. . . . With due respect to these "patriots," the recognition of Azeri as an official language will not weaken the unity of Iran. The existence of three official languages in Switzerland has not weakened the unity of that state. But if we refuse to accept reality and recognize the existence of Azeri, we will alienate a large minority and thus undermine Iran. We all know what happened to the tsarist regime that tried to Russify its non-Russian population. We also know that the Union of Soviet Socialist Republics has nurtured its many languages and nations, and has, thereby, created a viable and strong society.[46]

Whereas *Zafar* supported the Firqeh, and *Rahbar* as the party organ published ambigious articles, most other newspapers closely associated with the Tudeh expressed concern over the Azerbaijan crisis, especially on the linguistic issue. *Shabaz* (The Falcon), edited by Rahim Namvar, an important party intellectual who later became chairman of the National Society against the Imperialist Oil Company, published a frank editorial entitled "The Persian Language Is the Best Means of Safeguarding Our National Unity:"

We realize that our brothers in Azerbaijan have a strong attachment to their local (*mahalli*) language. We also realize that imperialists have much maligned these local languages in order to create artificial divisions between Iranians. This is why we support the use of local languages and oppose the creation of internal divisions. While we understand that the people of Azerbaijan have genuine feelings for their language, we would like to point out that it would be highly dangerous if these feelings grew so exaggerated as to endanger Persian—the national and traditional language of Iran. We are certain that the Firqeh-i Demokrat has taken into account this important consideration. We are also certain that the Firqeh will pursue a course that will not lead to the cultural breakdown of Iran. . . . When we have true democracy and complete independence, all citizens will have the right to use any language they choose. But in the present era, all citizens, especially those who want democracy and independence, should view Persian as a cement of unity and should encourage its use in Azerbaijan. Although the people of Azerbaijan respect their local language, they must not disrespect the national and traditional language of Iran.[47]

Iran-i Ma (Our Iran), another daily allied to the Tudeh in 1945-1946, expressed similar concern in five separate editorials. The first

[46] Keramatallah, "Attachment to Language," *Zafar*, 14 December 1945.
[47] "The Persian Language Is the Best Means of Safeguarding Our National Unity," *Shabaz*, 20 January 1946. *Shabaz* was adopted briefly in 1948 as the central organ of the Tudeh party.

told its readers not to be misled by the false rumor that the Firqeh had "separatist aims," but at the same time advised the Firqeh not to exaggerate the linguistic issue at the expense of social and economic problems. The second praised the Firqeh for its "progressive policies," but criticized it for underestimating Azerbaijan's ties to Iran: "The people of Azerbaijan, like the people of the other provinces, are members of the Iranian nation (*mellat*). They share with the rest of the country a common history, a common culture, a common literature, and the other ingredients necessary to form a living nation." The third, entitled "Persian Is the National Language of Azerbaijan," argued that the local (*mahalli*) language of the province should not be considered its national (*melli*) language, since Azerbaijan was an integral part of the Iranian nation. The same editorial suggested that the Firqeh leaders could eliminate many misunderstandings between themselves and other progressives if they only replaced the slogan "the Azerbaijan nation (*mellat*)" with the more acceptable phrase "the Azerbaijan people (*mardom*)." The fourth, entitled "Persian Is the Most Valuable Symbol of Iran's Greatness," described Persian as "the world's richest language," and claimed that Iran had survived many barbarian invasions, including the Arab conquest, because of its invaluable language and literature. The same editorial warned, "today we hear of the 'national language' of Azerbaijan; tomorrow we may hear of the 'national language' of Khuzistan." The final editorial, published on the eve of Premier Qavam's negotiations with the autonomous government, advised the Firqeh to moderate its language demands in order to retain the support of the left in Tehran: "Dr. Keshavarz, the main Tudeh spokesman in the Majles, may be willing to accept the use of Azerbaijani in the first three grades of school, but I am sure that he will never accept the demand that all classes in Azerbaijan be conducted in the local language."[48]

Sukhan, the organ of the Society of Degree Holders from Teachers' College, best summed up the attitudes of the radical intellectuals inside and outside the Tudeh party. In a detailed article on the language problem, Khanlari, the chief editor, took a middle position between the Persian chauvinists, who wanted to eliminate the many regional dialects, and the Azerbaijani nationalists, who viewed Azeri as their one and only mother tongue.[49] He argued that a country could not

[48] "The Question of Azerbaijani Separatism," *Iran-i Ma*, 21 November 1945; "The Issue of Language and Nationality," *Iran-i Ma*, 1 December 1945; "Persian Is the National Language of Azerbaijan," *Iran-i Ma*, 9 December 1945; "Persian Is the Most Valuable Symbol of Iran's Greatness," *Iran-i Ma*, 10 December 1945; "Tehran Can and Must Retain Azerbaijan," *Iran-i Ma*, 20 March 1946.

[49] P. Khanlari, "Dialects and Languages," *Sukhan*, 3 (April 1946), 81-87.

experience social progress, especially educational growth, land reform, and industrial expansion, unless it had national unity. He further argued that a country was more likely to attain national unity if it had a common culture and a common language. Iran, he continued, possessed a common culture, since its inhabitants shared similar values, similar customs, and similar historical experiences. But Iran did not possess a common language, since many of its rural inhabitants spoke their own local dialects. He added that the situation had been further complicated by the recent expansion of the state educational system. On the one hand, state schools had strengthened Persian. On the other hand, they had endangered valuable dialects, deprived peasant children of reading books in their own languages, and inadvertently made it harder to spread literacy. To preserve local dialects, encourage literacy, and expand the national language, Khanlari concluded that dialects should be used in the first four grades, but Persian should be the only language of instruction in the rest of the educational system.

For its part, the Firqeh avoided a direct debate with the Tudeh, but did open a barrage of newspaper attacks on other intellectuals in Tehran who were using similar arguments. In an editorial attack on Bahar, Qavam's minister of education (who considered Persian to be a valuable tool for achieving national unity), the paper *Azerbaijan* exclaimed that it was high time intellectuals in Tehran realized that the people of Azerbaijan had their own national language.[50] In a polemic against Dr. Afshar, the editor of *Ayandeh* who favored the expansion of Persian into the provinces, Pishevari denounced all "chauvinists" who refused to tolerate cultural minorities, and insisted that Azerbaijan would never compromise on the language issue. "We are willing to compromise on political issues, for politics is not vital for us. But we cannot compromise on the language issue, for the right to use our language is vital for us."[51] Similarly, in a broadside on ʿAbbas Eqbal, the well-known Persian writer who had argued that Turkish was a foreign language imposed on northern Iran by the "barbaric Mongol invaders," Pishevari declared:

We have absorbed our mother language with our mothers' milk and with the invigorating air of our motherland. Those who insult our language by claiming that it was imposed on us are our sworn enemies. In past centuries, many enemies of Azerbaijan have tried to stifle and strangle our beautiful language. Fortunately, they have all failed and our language has survived. Intellectuals in Tehran must realize that Azeri is not a passing dialect. It is a genuine

[50] "Mr. Bahar," *Azerbaijan*, 22 October 1945.
[51] J. Pishevari, "A Speech to Persian Intellectuals," *Azerbaijan*, 5 September 1946.

language with deep popular roots. It contains not only popular stories, epics, and poems, but also major literary works created by talented poets and writers. Our duty is to nourish it, modernize it, reveal its charm, and clean off the dust of neglect. We will clean it, purify it, and return it to our people.[52]

Ultimately, the differences between the Firqeh and the Tudeh did not come out into the open. This can be explained by four major reasons. First, the Soviets acted behind the scenes to prevent an open clash. Since both parties identified themselves closely with the Soviet Union and neither was willing to embarrass their mutual ally, they agreed to avoid public polemics. Second, the Azeri speakers within the Tudeh, especially the Azeri labor organizers from outside Azerbaijan, used their influence to restrain the party leaders. Living outside their native province, they lacked the incentive to raise the provincial and the linguistic issues. But once these issues were raised by the Firqeh, they could not resist taking a stand in favor of their "compatriots." Third, the rebels moderated their demands once they entered negotiations with Tehran. They withdrew from the border city of Zanjan, and agreed to transform the feda'is into an organized force equivalent to the gendarmerie but without that hated label. They also agreed to limit the teaching of Azeri to primary schools, and to use both Azeri and Persian in law courts and government offices. Moreover, they dropped the terms National Majles, Autonomous Government, cabinet minister, and prime minister in favor of Provincial Assembly, Provincial Council, department head, and governor-general. In fact, the term Democratic Republic of Azerbaijan, adopted later by historians to refer to the autonomous government of Azerbaijan, was not used by the rebels themselves at any stage of the crisis.

Finally, the Firqeh, once secure in power, carried out extensive social reforms. It enacted the country's first land reform, distributing government estates to peasants, confiscating private estates of enemy landlords, and, on other estates, allocating to sharecroppers as much as six-sevenths of the harvest.[53] It extended the vote to women for the first time in Iranian history, abolished corporal punishment, and set up at the local level elected councils to supervise the work of district governors, mayors, and government departments. It decreed a com-

---

[52] J. Pishevari, "Our Language," *Azerbaijan*, 5 September 1945.

[53] The land law, enacted in April 1946, distributed state villages and private estates of enemy landlords in such a way that no peasant household was to obtain more than five hectares. It also increased the sharecropper's portion of the harvest by revaluating the relative importance of labor, land, water, seeds, and implements. For rain-fed crops, the shares were to be: 3 for labor, 2 for land, 1 for seeds, and 1 for implements. For irrigated crops, the shares were to be: 5 for labor, 2 for implements, 3 for water, 1 for land, and 1 for seeds.

prehensive labor law; tried to stabilize prices by opening government food stores; and shifted the tax burden from food and other necessities to business profits, landed wealth, professional incomes, and luxury goods. It also changed the face of Tabriz by asphalting the main roads; opening clinics and literacy classes; founding a university, a radio station, and a publishing house; and renaming streets after Sattar Khan, Baqer Khan, and other heroes of the Constitutional Revolution. Even opponents of the Firqeh had to admit that more was accomplished in one year than in the twenty years under Reza Shah.[54] The British consul in Tabriz reported that the land reform gained many friends, the work projects alleviated unemployment, the administrative reforms brought more efficiency, and the changes, on the whole, found considerable popular support.

The brief tour [through Azerbaijan] has enabled me to see for myself that the provincial administration has emerged as something smarter, more efficient and far stronger than the old Persian administration. The tour has also afforded me an opportunity to make the acquaintance of some of the Democrat officials. They are drawn chiefly, it seems, from the skilled stratum of the proletariat. . . . In general, the Democrat officials, while obviously lacking the graces of some of the old Persian officials, strike me as men of much shrewdness and practical experience. They are interested in their own local affairs and are, I have no doubt, far more capable municipal administrators than the officials formerly sent by Tehran. . . . Underneath the stock propaganda phraseology and slogans of their conversation, I feel a genuine strain of local patriotism and enthusiasm which is not likely, even without Russian encouragement, to acquiesce in any attempt to restore the old conditions.[55]

These reforms brought the Tudeh and the Firqeh closer together. By April 1946, the Tudeh was praising the Firqeh for its reforms and willingness to moderate its demands. By May, *Rahbar* was arguing that the two parties agreed on goals and differed merely on tactics. And by June, the Tudeh was openly inviting the Firqeh to join the Iran, Socialist, and Jangali parties in the recently formed United Front of Progressive Parties. Three months later, when the Firqeh leaders visited Tehran to complete negotiations with Qavam, they took the opportunity to begin discussion with the Tudeh on joining the united front, especially on the matter of the Front's main plank, which insisted that all member parties had to "recognize the CCFTU as the only legitimate organization of the Iranian working class." At a public gathering of the united front, leaders from the Tudeh and the Firqeh

[54] R. Cottam, *Nationalism in Iran* (Pittsburgh, 1964), p. 126.

[55] British Consul in Tabriz, "A Tour from Tabriz to Khoi, Julfa, and Maku," *F.O. 371*/Persia 1946/34-52679.

praised each other, stated their party policies, and in so doing revealed the differences that still existed between the two organizations. Radmanesh, speaking on behalf of the Tudeh, declared:

There is now in Iran a militant labor movement unprecedented in our country's history. Its creation was not easy, for it is not a task that anyone can undertake. One must first gain the confidence of the working class, and those who try to appeal to both employers and employees will inevitably fail. The CCFTU, as a result of its correct policies, heroic struggles, and numerous sacrifices, has won the confidence of all workers from the Araxes river in the north to the Persian Gulf in the south. The first duty of all patriots and progressives is to recognize the united organization of the Iranian working class and to work for the future of the labor movement.[56]

Javid, representing the Firqeh, without directly criticizing the previous speaker, gave a very different analysis of the situation:

The people of Azerbaijan have spent more time on action than on theoretical discussions. Their leaders have fortunately realized that they must have internal class unity, for their adversaries do not differentiate between workers, landowners, merchants, and peasants. When a town or a village lies in ruin, all suffer—including the wealthy merchant who is forced to send his son away to school. As a result of years of oppression, the people of Azerbaijan have correctly diagnosed their former disease of disunity, and have successfully built a national movement. Only when we have created a united front of progressive parties, only then can we discuss the need to have one worker's organization. . . . All classes in Iran—landowners, merchants, intellectuals, workers, and peasants—must unite to protect their state. After attaining this unity, we can sit down and solve any class differences that may still exist.[57]

Behind the scenes, however, the discussions were less restrained. When Javid accused the Education Ministry of neglecting Azerbaijan, Khalel Maleki, then the assistant to the minister of education, retorted that he had difficulty recruiting teachers for Azerbaijan since even Tudeh members who could not teach Azeri had been hounded out of the province.[58] Similarly, when Pishevari started to lecture the Tudeh on the need for an armed uprising throughout Iran, Bozorg 'Alavi interrupted him to point out that Soviet troops were not stationed in Tehran, Isfahan, and Abadan, and that the Tudeh in most areas had to contend with not only the army, but also the police, gendarmerie, and armed tribes.[59] The Firqeh leaders left Tehran without joining the united front.

[56] Radmanesh, "Address to the Meeting," *Rahbar*, 12 September 1946.

[57] S. Javid, "Address to the Meeting," ibid.

[58] The Society of Iranian Socialists, "Text of Khalel Maleki's Defence at His Trial," *Sosiyalism*, 2 (October 1966), 49-50.

[59] Bamshad (pseudonym), "The Tudeh and the Firqeh," *Aras*, 9 January 1947.

Although the Firqeh eventually reached a satisfactory settlement with both the central government and the left in Tehran, its position within Azerbaijan was gradually undermined by adverse political, social, and economic pressures. First, the shah tried to sabotage Qavam's settlement by refusing to accept the feda'is as part of the Iranian army, and by sending weapons to the opponents of the Tabriz government—especially the Zolfaqari clan in Zanjan, the Afshar tribes near Mianduab, and the Shahsavens outside Ardabel. By mid-1946, the provincial government was rushing troops from one district to another to stamp out tribal revolts. Second, the Firqeh was constantly embroiled in disputes with the neighboring Republic of Kurdistan over the ethnically mixed regions of Urmiah, Khoi, and Mianduab. In sharp contrast to the local Azeris and Christians, who favored the Tabriz government, the Kurds—especially their chiefs, who opposed land reform—preferred the more conservative administration of the Mahabad republic. The British Consul in Tabriz reported that an armed confrontation was narrowly averted in October 1946 only because the two governments at the last moment agreed to share jurisdiction over the disputed territories.[60] From outside, the Kurdish Republic and the Azerbaijan government both appeared to be artificial creations of the Soviet Union. From inside, however, it was quite apparent that deep-seated ethnic differences separated the two administrations.

Third, the Soviets, for reasons best known to themselves, gave the Firqeh little in the way of military equipment. Whereas the Americans refurnished the royalist army with trucks, tanks, and heavy artillery, the Russians provided the Tabriz government with no more than rifles, handguns, and light artillery. As the British consul observed, "the Russians have not left the Azerbaijan army much in the way of equipment."[61] Fourth, the Firqeh, despite periodic promises to respect private property, failed to attract capital into Azerbaijan. As the British consul noted, the Tabriz government failed not only in attracting new capital, but also in raising loans from local entrepreneurs and in preventing profits from leaving the province.[62]

Finally, the Firqeh gradually lost much of its former popularity. In coping with food shortages produced by a bad harvest in the summer of 1946, the Firqeh imposed price controls, extracted as much as 20 percent of the crop from peasants and 70 percent from landlords, and threatened death sentences for those caught smuggling grain out of Azerbaijan. Opponents of the regime blamed land reform and

[60] British Consul in Tabriz, 31 October 1946, *F.O. 371*/Persia 1946/34-52740.
[61] British Consul in Tabriz, 7 May 1946, *F.O. 371*/Persia 1946/34-52667.
[62] British Consul in Tabriz, 29 February 1946, *F.O. 371*/Persia 1946/34-52740.

price controls for the food shortages. In fact, the main reason for these shortages was bad weather, especially floods and late rains. In creating a standing army, the Firqeh decreed two-years' military service for all adult males, arrested draft dodgers as deserters, and threatened to execute the volunteer feda'is who refused to serve outside their home districts. In trying to raise revenues and reduce expenditures, the Firqeh cut military pay, tightened up on the collection of tax arrears, and imposed new levies on heating oil and slaughter houses. And in attempting to increase industrial profits and workers' productivity, it laid off redundant employees, cut fringe benefits, and stressed the need for more discipline on the shop floor. The British consul commented,

The Azerbaijan Government, faced with the problems of reducing the cost of living and running the factories they have taken over, are beginning by docking the factory workers' allowances. Whereas under the old regime every factory worker was provided with free bread and charcoal as well as with two suits of clothes and a pair of shoes in the year, now he is to receive his bare pay, with, perhaps in some cases, one suit of working clothes. The factory workers are not liking it, but, as it is their erstwhile champions who are now in power, there is little they can do about it.[63]

The problems confronting the Tabriz government were summed up in a report sent by the British consul in late September:

On all fronts, the Democrats are embarrassed. Their financial position is desperate, Kurdish activities in Urmieh are keeping them on tenterhooks, while forces of irregulars, equipped, say the Democrats, by the Persian authorities, have been in conflict with the Feda'is in Ardabel. The Provincial Government scheme, for the collection of grain for winter needs, is meeting with resistance from landowners and farmers alike, and tax defalcations keep the Government tills empty. . . . The scarcity of bread is becoming more acute and the Party has to contend with a populace of which 90 percent are either hostile or completely apathetic. Trade is stagnant, as people who have any money either hide it, or transfer it to Tehran for security.[64]

The Azerbaijan government was grappling with these difficulties when suddenly on December 10 the royalist army mounted a three-pronged attack into the province. In debating what to do, the Firqeh leadership divided into two camps. The first, led by Javid and Shabistari, argued that resistance would cause a senseless slaughter of the poorly armed Feda'is. The second camp, headed by Pishevari and Biriya, proposed a prolonged guerrilla campaign against the central government. After a twelve-hour debate, Javid and Shabistari, prob-

---

[63] Ibid., 31 May 1946.
[64] Ibid., 30 September 1946.

ably supported by the Soviet consul, won over the majority of the leaders and promptly ordered the provincial forces to cease fighting.[65] The Iranian army entered Tabriz on December 12, exactly a year after the establishment of the provincial government. In the subsequent weeks, over 300 rebels lost their lives fighting, another 30 faced the firing squads, and some 1,200 fled into the Soviet Union. Of the top leaders, Biriya disappeared; Javid and Shabistari were taken to Tehran, where Qavam protected them from the shah; and others, notably Pishevari, escaped to Soviet Azerbaijan. According to Soviet sources, Pishevari died two years later in a car accident outside Baku.[66]

In the years after the collapse of the Tabriz and Mahabad governments, the Tudeh party shifted and then reshifted its position on the language problem and the provincial issue. From the fall of Tabriz in December 1946 until the convening of the second party congress in April 1948, the Tudeh leaders, pressed by Khalel Maleki's group of Tehran intellectuals, returned to their ambiguous policy of the pre-1944 years. For example, the central committee, in a major policy statement issued in January 1947, reiterated the party's economic, social, and political demands, but mentioned neither provincial assemblies nor minority languages. Similarly, Radmanesh, in an important article entitled "Azerbaijan Today," skirted around the problem while detailing how the central government had undone many of the Firqeh's reforms, especially its land reform.[67]

This ambiguous policy was abandoned soon after the defeat of the Khalel Maleki faction. At the second party congress, the delegates voted for the formation of elected provincial assemblies and the extension of cultural rights to the linguistic minorities. They also elected eleven Azeris and three Qajars to a Central Committee, and an Advisory Board totaling thirty-three members. Thus nearly 42 percent of the leadership became Turkic-speaking. Moreover, the second congress called for closer ties with the Democratic Party of Kurdistan and treated the Firqeh as the branch of the Tudeh within Azerbaijan. This arrangement was formalized twelve years later when the Democratic

[65] The British Consul in Tabriz reported that the Soviet authorities in Azerbaijan advised Pishevari both to moderate his stance and not to resist the central government. See British Consul in Tabriz, 30 November 1946, *F.O. 371*/Persia 1947/34-61978.

[66] Keshavarz, a member of the Tudeh Central Committee until 1957, claims that Pishevari was murdered by the leaders of the Soviet Azerbaijan. See Keshavarz, *Man Mottaham Mekunam* (I Accuse) (Tehran, 1979), p. 65.

[67] Provisional Executive Committee, "Proclamation," *Mardom*, 5 January 1947; R. Radmanesh, "Azerbaijan Today," *Razm Mahaneh*, 1 (December 1947), 4-6.

Party of Azerbaijan became the provincial branch of the Tudeh in Azerbaijan.

Implementing the resolutions of the second party congress, the Tudeh intensified its publicity on the ethnic issue. Its street slogans grew to include "Long Live the Unity of the Iranian People (*Mardom*)," "Long Live the National (*Melli*) Movement of Azerbaijan and Kurdistan," "Down with All Forms of National Oppression," and "Support the Right of National Self-Determination for Kurdistan and Azerbaijan."[68] Its parliamentary candidates incorporated into their electoral platforms the demand for the establishment of provincial assemblies.[69] On the tenth anniversary of Arani's death, its main newspaper, in a special issue on "The Great Martyrs of Iran," not only listed famous figures from Azerbaijan, notably Haydar Khan, Sattar Khan, and Khiabani, but also praised the hundreds of Azeri and Kurdish fighters killed in the 1945-1946 uprisings.[70] On the seventh anniversary of the establishment of the autonomous government of Azerbaijan, the Tudeh Central Committee publicly complimented the rebels for overthrowing the "feudal landlords," revitalizing the "national culture of Azerbaijan," and strengthening the "forces of democracy and patriotism throughout Iran."[71] Moreover, the Tudeh party set up in Tehran an organization called the Society of Azerbaijan; published a bilingual newspaper named *Nameh-i Azerbaijanian* (Letter of Azerbaijanis); and recruited into its ranks many Azeris living outside Azerbaijan—especially government employees, intellectuals, shopkeepers, peddlers, and factory workers.

The crystallization of the Tudeh policy toward the linguistic minorities can be seen in a party pamphlet entitled *Nation and Nationality*.[72] Published under a pseudonym in September 1949, the pamphlet was prefaced by a member of the Central Committee, and was frequently reprinted by the party press in the years between 1949 and 1953. It began with Lenin's and Stalin's thesis that a nation is formed of a people with a common language, a common culture, a common economy, and a common territory. It continued with a description of the nationality problem in the Austro-Hungarian empire and a warning that if Marxists did not support the right of national self-determination they would alienate the oppressed minorities. It then con-

[68] Central Committee of the Tudeh Party, "The Slogans of the Tudeh Party," *Razm*, 29 December 1952.

[69] *Nameh-i Azerbaijanian*, 8 January 1952.

[70] *Mardom*, 3 February 1949.

[71] Central Committee of the Tudeh Party, "Glory to the Peoples of Azerbaijan and Kurdistan," *Razm*, 15 December 1952.

[72] Montezam (pseudonym), *Mellat va Melliyat* (Nation and Nationality) (Tehran, 1948).

cluded with an attempt to apply Lenin's and Stalin's thesis to Iran. In doing so, it argued that although Iran was formed of many different nationalities, each with its own language, yet these nationalities were brought together by virtue of their participation in the creation of a rich culture, and their joint struggles against feudalism, despotism, and imperialism. To strengthen the bonds between these nationalities, the pamphlet proposed that Iran should protect the linguistic minorities and recognize the right of national self-determination. The Tudeh party had finally succeeded, however tenuously, in combining the Marxist theory of class struggle with the Leninist thesis of national self-determination.

PART III

Contemporary Iran

NINE

The Politics of Uneven Development

The Shah's only fault is that he is really too good for his people—his ideas are too great for us to realize them.
　　—The court minister, quoted by M. Laing, *The Shah* (London, 1977), p. 231.

CONSOLIDATION OF POWER (1953-1963)

In the decade after the 1953 coup d'état, the shah worked to consolidate his power. He placed the coup leaders in key positions; for example, General Zahedi became prime minister, General Bakhtiyar military governor of Tehran, and General Hedayat chief of general staff. He obtained from the United States emergency financial aid totaling $145 million between 1953 and 1957 to ward off government bankruptcy, boost morale among royalists, and inject confidence into the business community. He received technical assistance from the Israeli intelligence service, as well as from the CIA and the FBI, to establish in 1957 a new secret police named Sazman-i Ittila'at va Amniyat-i Keshvar (National Security and Information Organization), soon to become notorious under its acronym SAVAK. He used martial law, military tribunals, and the 1931 decree against "collectivist ideology" to crush not only the Tudeh but also the National Front and all other opposition parties. For example, the Iran party—the main pillar of the National Front—was outlawed in 1957 on the grounds that ten years earlier it had formed an alliance with the communist movement.[1] The shah was also helped by the ending of the oil dispute with Britain. Putting aside Mossadeq's insistence on national control, the shah agreed to the principle of sharing the profits equally, and signed a contract with a consortium formed of British Petroleum, the former owners of AIOC, and eight other European and American oil companies. As a result of the new agreement, Iran's

---

[1] *Ittila'at*, 31 January 1957.

oil revenues increased from $34 million in 1954-1955 to $181 million in 1956-1957, $358 million in 1960-1961, and $437 million in 1962-1963.[2] With the substantial oil revenues, together with $500 million worth of military aid sent by the United States between 1953 and 1963, the shah was able to expand the armed forces from 120,000 men to over 200,000, and raise the annual military budget from $80 million in 1953 to nearly $183 in 1963 (at 1960 prices and exchange rates).[3]

By the late 1950s, the shah had consolidated his control over much of the country, especially over the intelligentsia and the urban working class. Provincial governors used the gendarmerie and the town police to tightly supervise parliamentary elections and thereby control both the Majles and the Senate. Veteran courtiers, notably Dr. Manoucher Eqbal and Assadallah ʿAlam, divided Parliament into two royalist parties. The former, who proudly described himself as the shah's "household servant" (*chaker*), headed the National party (Hizb-i Melliyun). The latter, a childhood friend of the shah and a major landlord in Sistan, led the People's party (Hizb-i Mardom). These two organizations were known as the "yes" and the "yes sir" parties. Moreover, constitutional amendments on the one hand weakened any future opposition in Parliament by lowering the size of the quorum required to pass legislation; and on the other hand strengthened the shah by giving him the power to veto financial bills. Other laws enlarged the Majles from 136 deputies to 200, and extended its sessions from two years to four. Furthermore, SAVAK gradually expanded its networks, created through the Labor Ministry an array of trade unions, and scrutinized anyone recruited into the university, the civil service, and the large industrial plants. As a result, the number of major industrial strikes fell from 79 in 1953 to 7 in 1954, and further to 3 in 1955-1957. On taking office as prime minister in April 1957, Eqbal declared, "I have a personal distaste for this word 'strike.' It is a term introduced into our language by the Tudeh party. As long as I am premier, I don't want to hear of any strikes."[4]

Although the shah acted decisively against the intelligentsia and the working class, he carefully tried to avoid policies that would alienate the large landed families and the bazaar middle class. Mossadeq's decree increasing the sharecropper's portion of the harvest was shelved. Aristocratic families, such as the ʿAlams, ʿAlas, Hekmats, Zolfaqaris,

[2] F. Fersharaki, *Development of the Iranian Oil Industry* (New York, 1976), p. 133.

[3] Stockholm International Peace Research Institute, *World Armaments and Disarmament: Year Book for 1972* (Cambridge, Mass., 1972), p. 86.

[4] Quoted by R. Namvar, *Rezhim-i Teror va Ekhtenaq* (Regime of Terror and Strangulation) (n.p., 1962), p. 13.

Qaragozlus, Ardalans, Bayats, Davalous, Bakhtiyaris, Hedayats, and Farmanfarmaians continued to enjoy power both in the provinces and in Tehran. The landed element in Parliament increased from 49 percent of the Seventeenth Majles (1952-1953) to 50 percent of the Eighteenth Majles (1953-1956), and to 51 percent of the Nineteenth Majles (1956-1960).[5] Moreover, in April 1955, when Premier Zahedi tried to bar the head of the Zolfaqari family from Parliament, the shah, to consolidate his own power, dismissed Zahedi and gave the premiership to ʿAla, the veteran courtier.

The shah displayed a similar degree of caution when dealing with the traditional middle class. He and his wife, Queen Soraya, made periodic pilgrimages to Mecca, Karbala, Qum, and Mashad. Prominent religious leaders, especially Ayatallah Boroujerdi, Ayatallah Behbehani, and the Imam Jomʿeh of Tehran, continued to enjoy easy access to the court. Ayatallah Kashani and his colleage, Qonatabadi, were briefly imprisoned in 1956, but were released as soon as they publicly disassociated themselves from the Fedaʾiyan-i Islam and agreed not to protest the execution of Razmara's assassins. The government vowed to uphold religion, and continually denounced the Tudeh as the "enemy of private property and Islam." The military general of Tehran in 1955 encouraged a religious mob to ransack the main Bahaʾi center in Tehran. What is more, the bazaars retained much of their independence. The shah imprisoned only two merchants for their role in the Mossadeq administration, avoided price controls, kept the army out of the market places, and permitted the guilds to elect their own elders even after 1957, when a High Council of Guilds was set up in Tehran. In the ten years between 1953 and 1963, only once did the shah violate his hands-off policy. In 1954, when the guild leaders organized a strike to protest the oil agreement with the consortium, he ordered the troops into the Tehran bazaar. The occupation lasted only two days, however.

This dual policy of wooing the traditional classes and tightening controls over the modern classes was suddenly disrupted in 1960-1963 by an acute economic crisis and by American pressures for land reform. The economic crisis had been brewing since 1954, when the government, discovering that the oil revenues could not pay for the ambitious Seven Year Plan as well as for the escalating military expenditures, resorted to deficit financing and heavy borrowing from abroad. Deficit financing, compounded by a bad harvest in 1959-1960, forced the cost-of-living index, which had been fairly stable in 1954-

[5] Z. Shajiʾi, *Nemayandegan-i Majles-i Shawra-yi Melli* (Members of the National Consultative Assembly) (Tehran, 1965), p. 176.

1957, to climb over 35 percent between 1957 and 1960.[6] Meanwhile, heavy borrowing completely depleted the country's foreign reserves and thus obliged Iran to seek emergency aid from both the International Monetary Fund and the U.S. government. The IMF promised $35 million if Iran trimmed its budget, froze salaries and wages, and shelved some development projects. The Kennedy administration, acting on the belief that liberal reforms were the best guarantees against communist revolutions, offered $85 million on condition that the shah brought liberals into the cabinet and took meaningful steps to implement land reform.

Inevitably, these economic difficulties and external pressures destablized the regime. The number of major strikes, which had totaled no more than three in 1955-1957, jumped to over twenty in 1957-1961. Some ended in bloody confrontations between the strikers and the armed forces. Meanwhile, the elections for the Twentieth Majles, which began in June 1960 as a controlled tournament between the two royalist parties, quickly developed into a heated contest once the shah, to please Washington, permitted independent candidates and the National Front to enter the race. Embarrassed by widespread accusations of election rigging, the shah stopped the voting and replaced Premier Eqbal, who also headed the National party, with Ja'far Sharif Emami who, although a veteran courtier, belonged to no party. Sharif Emami lasted only nine months, however, for he failed to obtain American aid, grew increasingly unpopular as the austerity measures took their toll, and found himself blamed for a violent confrontation that took place outside Parliament between the police and government employees, especially teachers, who were protesting the salary freezes.

With Sharif Emami's resignation, the shah offered the premiership to Dr. 'Ali Amini, the American favorite. The United States favored Amini for a number of reasons. As ambassador in Washington during the late 1950s, he had won the confidence of the State Department. As the chief Iranian negotiator with the oil companies in 1954, he had shown that he had the strength of character to take unpopular decisions. As finance minister in Mossadeq's administration, he had remained on speaking terms with many leaders of the National Front. And above all, as a maverick aristocrat, he had advocated land reform since the mid-1940s when he, together with his elder brother Abul Qassem Amini, had belonged to Qavam's inner circle. For his part, the shah intensely disliked Amini, distrusted his past associations with Qavam and Mossadeq, and suspected him of planning political changes as well as economic reforms. As the shah later admitted to an Amer-

---

[6] Central Bank of Iran, *Bulletin*, 8 (June 1970), 673-93.

ican correspondent, it was the Kennedy administration that had forced him to name Amini as prime minister.[7]

On taking office, Amini made a series of controversial decisions. He dissolved the newly elected Twentieth Majles, many of whose members were conservative landlords. He exiled the notorious General Bakhtiyar, who had headed SAVAK since 1957. He initiated discussions with the National Front. Moreover, he gave three ministries to middle-class reformers who had in the past criticized the political influence of the shah as well as the corrupt practices of the landed families. The Justice Ministry, with its powerful anticorruption division, went to Nuraldin Alamuti, a former Tudeh leader who had left the party in 1947 to join Qavam's circle. The Education Ministry went to Muhammad Derekhshesh, who, as the vocal representative of the teaching profession, drew support from both the Tudeh and the National Front. And above all, the Agricultural Ministry went to Hassan Arsanjani, the radical journalist who had worked closely with Qavam and had been advocating land reform since the early 1940s.

Within four months, Arsanjani launched Iran's first serious nationwide attempt to redistribute land. The 1962 Land Reform Act, later known as the first stage of land reform, contained three major provisions. First, landowners had to sell to the state all agricultural property in excess of one whole village or of six *dangs* (parts) in different villages. Exemptions were given to orchards, tea plantations, groves, and mechanized fields. Second, compensation offered to the landlords was to be based on previous tax assessments and was to be given in the course of the next ten years. Third, land bought by the state was to be promptly sold to the sharecroppers working on the same land. As Arsanjani often stressed, the aim of land reform was to create a class of independent farmers.[8] Freed of parliamentary obstacles, Arsanjani began to implement his land reform, beginning in Azerbaijan, where memories of the 1946 attempt at land redistribution lingered on.

Although the Amini administration carried out land reform and instituted stringent measures requested by the IMF, it lasted only fourteen months. Amini fell partly because the stringent measures intensified public discontent; partly because the National Front refused to help unless he dissolved SAVAK and held free elections;[9] and partly because he failed to obtain American support when he

[7] *U.S. News and World Report*, 27 January 1969.

[8] H. Arsanjani, "The Issue of Land Reform in Iran," *Majaleh-i Masa'el-i Iran* 1 (December 1962), 97-104.

[9] Executive Committee of the National Front, *'Elamieh* (Proclamation) (Tehran, 1962), pp. 1-2.

clashed with the shah over the need to cut the military budget. Not for the first time, the U.S. had sided with the monarch against a reforming prime minister.

With Amini gone, the shah asked ʿAlam, the head of the People's party, to form a government. In the following months, ʿAlam rigged the elections for the Twenty-first Majles, placed an army general in charge of the Agricultural Ministry, drastically cut the funds for rural cooperatives, and, even more significantly, watered down Arsanjani's plans for the second stage of land reform. In the watered-down version, landlords not effected by the first stage were allowed to keep as much as 150 hectares of nonmechanized land and were offered five choices as to what to do with the excess. They could rent the land to peasants on thirty-year leases; sell the land to peasants at mutually agreed prices; divide the land in proportion to the past division of the harvest; set up landlord-peasant stock companies; or buy outright the peasant's rights of cultivation. Moreover, religious foundations were permitted either to lease their lands for ninety-nine years or to rent them on five-year contracts. Thus the second stage allowed landowners to retain as much as half a village so long as they replaced sharecroppers with tenant farmers, wage laborers, or agricultural machinery. Arsanjani's intention had been to create as many independent farmers as possible; the shah's intention was to eliminate sharecroppers but retain as many commercial landlords as possible. In later years, this subtle difference was to have major repercussions.

Even though land reform originated in the Amini administration and its radical content soon disappeared, nevertheless the shah claimed it as his own and used it to launch with much fanfare a six-point program known as the White Revolution. Besides land distribution, the six points called for nationalization of forests, sale of state factories to private entrepreneurs, profit-sharing for industrial workers, extension of the vote to women, and establishment of a rural literacy corps. To legitimize the "revolution," the shah organized a nationwide referendum. According to the government, in January 1963 99.9 percent of the voters endorsed the six-point reform program.

The absurdity of these results became apparent in June 1963, when, during the mourning month of Muharram, thousands of shopkeepers, clergymen, office employees, teachers, students, wage earners, and unemployed workers poured into the streets to denounce the shah. The call for the denunciation came from the guild leaders, the bazaar merchants, the National Front, and, most significant of all, a new figure in the opposition—Ayatallah Ruhallah Khomeini. A sixty-four-year-old mujtahed, Khomeini came from a long line of traders, small landowners, and minor clerics. His great-grandfather, a small merchant, had migrated from Khurasan to Kashmir. His grandfather, who had been born in India, had returned to Iran and bought land in the village of Khomein near Arak. His father had lived off these small estates until 1901, when he had been dispossessed and murdered by the local governor. After his father's death, Khomeini had been raised by his mother's side of the family, many of whom were minor clerics. They had sent him first to the main maktab in Arak, and then to the famous Fayzieh madraseh in Qum to study with Ayatallah Abdul Karim Ha'iri, the leading Shi'i theologian of the time. After completing his education, Khomeini taught Sufi philosophy and Islamic jurisprudence at the Fayzieh, worked as a special assistant to Ayatallah Boroujerdi, married the daughter of a prominent mujtahed, and later married his own daughter to Boroujerdi's son. It is also rumored that he wrote Sufi poetry and had mystic experiences—taboo behavior among the orthodox mujtaheds.

Khomeini published his first major work in 1943. Entitled *Kashf-i Asrar* (Secrets Revealed), the book argued on behalf of establishing an Islamic system of government, and, without rejecting the whole principle of monarchy, took Reza Shah to task for maltreating the clergy. Despite his views, Khomeini remained aloof from the political struggles of the 1940s and the 1950s. Three pressures explain this aloofness: the fear of communism; the disdain shown by the nationalists, especially Mossadeq, for clerical causes; and the restraining hand of his patron, Boroujerdi, who continued throughout the 1950s to give valuable support to the shah. Freed of this restraint by Boroujerdi's death in 1961, Khomeini began to speak out in 1962-1963. Although many clerics opposed the regime because of land reform and women's rights, Khomeini, revealing a masterful grasp of mass politics, scrupulously avoided the former issue and instead hammered away on a host of other concerns that aroused greater indignation among the general population.[10] He denounced the regime for living off corruption, rigging elections, violating the constitutional laws, stifling the press and the political parties, destroying the independence of the university, neglecting the economic needs of merchants, workers, and peasants, undermining the country's Islamic beliefs, encouraging gharbzadegi—indiscriminate borrowing from the West—granting "capitulations" to foreigners, selling oil to Israel, and constantly expanding the size of the central bureaucracies.[11] Not for the last time, Khomeini had chosen issues with mass appeal.

[10] Only one proclamation published by Khomeini in 1961-1964 opposed women's suffrage.

[11] For Khomeini's speeches and declarations in 1963-1964, see Fayzieh Seminary, *Zendiginameh-i Imam Khomeini* (The Life of Imam Khomeini) (Tehran, 1979), II, 1-177.

The upheavals of June 1963 lasted three full days, left hundreds—maybe thousands—dead, and shook not only Tehran and Qum, but also Isfahan, Shiraz, Mashad, and Tabriz.[12] The regime weathered the storm, however. The riots did not spread to the other towns. The civil servants and the industrial workers, especially the oil workers, failed to organize a general strike. The armed forces, harassed for only three days, kept their discipline. Moreover, the opposition leaders sought not radical changes but moderate reforms. As Khomeini stated in one proclamation, "my generation remembers that in 1941 the Iranian people were actually happy that the invading foreigners threw out the shah. I do not want the present shah to meet the same fate as the old shah. This is why I beseech the shah: respect the religious authorities, don't help Israel, and learn from your father's mistakes."[13] It was not until the late 1960s that Khomeini raised the radical cry demanding the destruction of the monarchy and the creation of the Islamic Republic.

In the months following the 1963 riots, the shah arrested the National Front leaders and deported Khomeini into Turkey, from where he went to Iraq. Again the shah had routed the opposition. Although the shah managed to consolidate his power, the memories of the 1963 massacres remained a potent force ready to reappear at the opportune time. Just as the tobacco crisis of 1891-1892 had been a dress rehearsal for the Constitutional Revolution of 1905-1909, the Muharram upheavals of June 1963 were to be a dress rehearsal for the Islamic revolution of 1977-1979.

SOCIOECONOMIC DEVELOPMENT (1963-1977)

Two very different interpretations have been offered to explain the long-term causes of the Islamic revolution. One interpretation—accepted by supporters of the Pahlevi regime—claims that the revolution occurred because the shah modernized too much and too quickly for his traditional-minded and backward-looking people. The other—favored by opponents of the régime—argues that the revolution occurred because the shah did not modernize fast enough and thoroughly enough to overcome his initial handicap of being a CIA-installed monarch in an age of nationalism, neutralism, and republicanism. The contention of this chapter is that both interpretations are wrong—

[12] According to the *Washington Post* of 15 November 1978, over 1,000 died in Tehran alone. According to M. Zonis, an eyewitness in Tehran, "the number of dead and wounded certainly reached many thousands." See M. Zonis, *The Political Elite of Iran* (Princeton, 1971), p. 63.

[13] Quoted by Fayzieh Seminary, *Zendiginameh-i Imam Khomeini*, I, 40-41.

or, more correctly, both are half right and half wrong; that the revolution came because the shah modernized on the socioeconomic level and thus expanded the ranks of the modern middle class and the industrial working class, but failed to modernize on another level— the political level; and that this failure inevitably strained the links between the government and the social structure, blocked the channels of communication between the political system and the general population, widened the gap between the ruling circles and the new social forces, and, most serious of all, cut down the few bridges that had in the past connected the political establishment with the traditional social forces, especially with the bazaars and the religious authorities. Thus by 1977 the gulf between the developing socioeconomic system and the underdeveloped political system was so wide that an economic crisis was able to bring down the whole regime. In short, the revolution took place neither because of overdevelopment nor because of underdevelopment but because of uneven development.

The socioeconomic development was made possible largely by the increasing oil revenues. Hitting a new record of $555 million in 1963-1964, the oil income continued to climb reaching $958 million in 1968-1969, $1.2 billion in 1970-1971, $5 billion in 1973-1974, and, after the quadrupling of world petroleum prices, near $20 billion in 1975-1976.[14] Between 1964 and 1974, the cumulative oil revenue came to $13 billion. Between 1974 and 1977, it topped $38 billion. It was true, of course—as critics often pointed out—that substantial sums were squandered on palaces, royal extravagances, bureaucratic consumption, outright corruption, nuclear installations, and ultrasophisticated weapons too expensive even for many NATO countries. But it was also true that much greater sums were productively channeled into the economy, both indirectly through the government-subsidized Industrial and Mining Development Bank of Iran, which extended low-interest loans to private entrepreneurs, and directly through the annual state budget as well as the Third (1962-1968), Fourth (1968-1973), and Fifth (1973-) Development Plans. Spending over $9.5

[14] The statistics used in this section have mostly been compiled from: The Plan and Budget Organization of Iran, *Salnameh-i Amar-i Keshvar* (Annual Statistics for the State) (Tehran, 1977); A. Ashraf, *Shakhesha-yi Ijtima'i-yi Iran* (Social Indicators of Iran) (Tehran, 1976); Interior Ministry, *Amar-i Omumi* (National Census) (Tehran, 1957), II; Industrial and Mining Development Bank of Iran, *Fifteenth Annual Report* (Tehran, 1975); International Labor Office, "Employment and Income Policies for Iran" (unpublished report, Geneva, 1972), Appendices B-1; G. Lenczowski, ed., *Iran under the Pahlavis* (Stanford, 1978); J. Jacqz, ed., *Iran: Past, Present and Future* (New York, 1976); H. Amirsadeghi, ed., *Twentieth-Century Iran* (London, 1977); J. Amuzegar, *Iran: An Economic Profile* (Washington, D.C., 1977).

billion, the two completed plans helped the Gross National Product grow at the annual rate of 8 percent in 1962-1970, 14 percent in 1972-1973, and 30 percent in 1973-1974. The earlier plans concentrated on the country's infrastructure, notably the transport system, and on the agricultural sector, particularly land reform and large-scale irrigation works. The later plans focused on industry, mining, and human resources.

The Third and Fourth Plans spent over $3.9 billion on the infrastructure. Between 1963 and 1977, major dams were built at Dezful, Karaj, and Manjel. These dams helped increase the electrical output from 0.5 billion to 15.5 billion kilowatt hours. Port facilities were improved to handle a 400 percent rise in the volume of imports; Enzeli, Bandar Shahpour (Khomeini), Bushire, and Khorramshahr were modernized, and work began on the construction of a new harbor at Chah Bahar near the Pakistan border. Over 500 miles of rail track were laid, so that by the mid-1970s the Trans-Iranian Railway fulfilled Reza Shah's dream of linking Tehran with Isfahan, Tabriz, and Mashad as well as with the Caspian and the Persian Gulf. Similarly, over 13,000 miles of roadway were built, and by the mid-1970s asphalted roads connected the major cities and well-kept secondary roads linked larger villages with local market towns. These years also saw a dramatic growth in the mass media. The number of radios rose from 2 million to 4 million, televisions from 120,000 to 1,700,000, and the number of cinema tickets sold rose from 20 million to 110 million. These developments, together with the commercialization of agriculture and the settling of some tribes, produced two paradoxical results. In the central provinces, national identity took root in the countryside as the rural population lost its traditional insularity and forged links with both the towns and the central government. In the peripheral provinces, however, ethnicity grew as communal identity based on one's immediate village and tribe gave way to a broader identity based on one's language and culture. Villagers and tribesmen who had in the past viewed themselves as belonging to small local communities now saw themselves as Kurds, Turkomans, Arabs, Lurs, Baluchis, or Azeris. This had obvious implications for the future.

The Third and Fourth Plans also allocated some $1.2 billion to agriculture. The sum was spent in two ways. The first was through land reclamations and subsidies for the use of tractors, fertilizers, and pesticides. Between 1963 and 1977, irrigation projects brought under cultivation over 240,000 hectares. The number of tractors increased from 3,000 to 50,000. And the distribution of fertilizer rose from 47,000 tons to nearly 1,000,000 tons. The second way was through financing of the land reform program. Although Arsanjani's proposals were watered down, nevertheless the first two stages of land reform—together with the third stage decreed in 1973 to help the conversion of tenancy holdings into private holdings—undermined the old magnates, encouraged commercial farming, and thus radically transformed the rural class structure. By the early 1970s, there were three distinct classes in the countryside:

1. Absentee farmers, who included the royal family, religious foundations, agrobusinesses, including multinational corporations, and old-time landlords who had found loopholes left intentionally in the laws—loopholes that permitted owners to keep considerable amounts of land if they mechanized, cash rented, or cultivated tea, nuts, and fruits. According to a report issued in 1972 by the International Labor Office, 350 families had farms larger than 300 hectares; 1,000 families had farms between 300 and 200 hectares; and 4,000 families had farms between 100 and 200 hectares.[15] In addition to these large landlords, there were some 40,000 smaller landlords—many of them bureaucrats, army officers, and urban entrepreneurs—who owned farms ranging from 50 to 100 hectares. In short, 45,320 families owned as much as 3,900,000 hectares, nearly 20 percent of Iran's cultivated land.

2. Independent farmers, consisting of former peasant proprietors as well as some 1,638,000 families that benefited from land reform. The beneficiaries were mostly village headmen (*kadkhudas*), landlord's bailiffs (*mobashers*), and resident sharecroppers (*nasaqdars*). Before land reform, independent farmers had constituted less than 5 percent of the rural population. After land reform, they constituted as much as 76 percent of the rural population. Although land reform greatly increased the ranks of peasant proprietors, it failed to give most recipients enough to make them into viable, let alone prosperous, farmers. Of the 2,800,000 peasant households that owned land in 1972, 1,850,000 (65 percent) had holdings under five hectares—two hectares less than the minimum required in most regions to make an adequate living. Only 600,000 peasant households, totaling no more than 17 percent of the rural population, owned prosperous farms ranging from ten to fifty hectares. To alleviate the problem of small holdings, after 1967 the government encouraged poorer peasants to join state-run farm corporations and to exchange their plots for shares in these corporations. By 1976, over 33,000 families had joined eighty-nine such corporations. Thus the state was undoing Arsanjani's original goal of creating an independent peasantry.

[15] M. Garzuel and J. Skolka, *World Employment Research: Working Papers* (Geneva, 1976).

3. Rural wage earners formed mostly of khoshneshin (agricultural laborers) whom land reform had bypassed, and former nomads whose migratory routes had been closed off. Totaling over 1,100,000 families, this underclass survived working as farm hands, shepherds, village construction laborers, day commuters to nearby industrial towns, and wage earners employed in the many small plants that flourished in the countryside during the early 1970s—small plants manufacturing carpets, shoes, clothes, paper, sugar, tobacco, brass utensils, and household furniture.

The development plans had even greater impact on the urban population. Allocating more than $2.5 billion to industry, the Second and Third Plans set themselves two ambitious goals: to produce for the home market consumer goods such as clothes, canned foods, beverages, radios, telephones, televisions, and motor cars; and to encourage the growth of basic and intermediary industries, especially oil, gas, coal, copper, steel, petrochemicals, aluminum, and machine tools. Thanks to generous state investments, between 1963 and 1977 Iran experienced a minor industrial revolution. The share of manufacturing in the GNP rose from 11 to 17 percent. The annual industrial growth jumped from 5 to 20 percent. Moreover, the number of small factories (employing between 10 and 49 workers) increased from 1,502 to over 7,000; that of middle-sized factories (employing between 50 and 500 workers) increased from 295 to 830; and that of large factories (employing more than 500 workers) increased from 105 to 159. These large plants included not only the old cotton mills and oil installations of the 1930s, but also new textile factories in Isfahan, Kashan, Tehran, and Kermanshah; steel mills in Isfahan and Ahwaz; additional oil refineries in Shiraz, Tabriz, Qum, Tehran, and Kermanshah; petrochemical plants in Abadan, Bandar Shahpour, and Kharg Island; machine-tool factories in Tabriz, Arak, and Abadan; aluminium smelters in Saveh, Ahwaz, and Arak; fertilizer plants in Abadan and Mervdasht; and assembly plants for cars, tractors, and trucks in Saveh, Tehran, Arak, and Tabriz.

The manufacturing revolution is reflected in the rising output of some leading industries. In the decade between 1965 and 1975, the production of coal rose from 285,000 tons to over 900,000; iron ore from 2,000 tons to nearly 900,000; steel and aluminium sheets from 29,000 tons to 275,000; cement from 1,417,000 tons to 4,300,000; cotton and synthetic cloth from 350 million meters to 533 million meters; beer from 13 million liters to 42 million liters; paper from nil to 36,000 tons; gas ovens from 87,000 units to 220,000; telephones from nil to 186,000 units; televisions from 12,000 units to 31,000; tractors from 100 units to 7,700; and motor vehicles, including passenger cars, buses, and trucks, from 7,000 units to 109,000 units. Carried away by these statistics, the regime in 1976 began to boast that by the end of the decade Iran's standard of living would surpass that of Western Europe, and by the end of the century Iran would be one of the world's five industrial giants.[16]

The Third and Fourth Plans also spent some $1.9 billion on human resources. As a result of these expenditures, the number of hospital beds increased from 24,126 to 48,000; that of health clinics from 700 to 2,800; that of nurses from 1,969 to 4,105; and the number of doctors from 4,500 to 12,750. These improvements, together with the elimination of famines and major epidemics, lowered the infant mortality rate, swelled the ranks of children, and increased the population from 25,840,000 in 1966 to 33,491,000 in 1976. By the mid-1970s, half the population was under sixteen years of age and two-thirds was under thirty. This was to have far-reaching repercussions during the street politics of 1977-1979.

The allocations for human resources helped education even more. Between 1963 and 1977, the enrollment in kindergartens grew from 13,296 to 221,896; in elementary schools from 1,641,201 to 4,078,000; in the literacy corps from 10,500 to 691,000; in secondary schools from 369,069 to 741,000; and in technical, vocational, and teacher training schools from 14,240 to 227,497. Moreover, the number of students registered in foreign universities, especially in North America and Western Europe, increased from under 18,000 to over 80,000. Furthermore, the establishment of twelve new campuses—especially the Pahlevi University in Shiraz, Ferdowsi University in Mashad, Jundi Shahpour University in Ahwaz, and Melli, Teacher's, and Arya Mehr Industrial Universities in Tehran—expanded the college enrollment in Iran from 24,885 to 154,215. Thus during these fourteen years the educational system grew more than threefold.

Since new schools, health facilities, and industrial plants were located mostly in the towns, the period between 1963 and 1977 had a profound impact on the urban population. In general, the period saw the rapid expansion of the urban population. Whereas in 1966 only 38 percent of the country lived in towns with populations over 5,000, in 1976 nearly 48 percent lived in such towns. Whereas in 1966 only 21 percent resided in cities with populations over 100,000, in 1976 some 29 percent resided in such cities. For example, Tehran grew from 2,719,730 to 4,496,159; Isfahan from 424,045 to 671,825; Mashad from 409,616 to 670,180; Tabriz from 403,413 to 598,576; Shiraz from 269,865 to 416,405, and Abadan from 274,962 to 296,081. More

[16] E. Rouleau, "Iran: Myth and Reality," *The Guardian*, 24 October 1976.

precisely, the same period saw the rapid expansion of particular sectors of the urban population—especially the ranks of salaried employees, factory workers, and unskilled laborers. By the mid-1970s, urban Iran was formed of the following four classes:

1. *The Upper Class.* Totaling no more than one thousand individuals, the class consisted of six groups: a. the Pahlevi family with its 63 princes, princesses, and cousins; b. aristocratic families that had turned their interests to urban ventures long before the land reform of the 1960s—aristocratic families such as the Aminis, ʿAlams, Bayats, Qaragozlus, Davalus, Moqadams, and Jehanbanis; c. enterprising aristocrats, such as Khodadad Farmanfarmaian, Amir Timourtash, Mehdi Busheri, and Nouri Isfandiari, who survived land reform by setting up agrobusinesses, banks, trading companies, and industrial firms; d. some 200 elder politicians, senior civil servants, and high-ranking military officers who prospered by sitting on managerial boards and facilitating lucrative government contracts; e. old-time entrepreneurs who made their first million during the commercial boom of World War II and went on to make additional millions during the oil boom of the 1960s and 1970s—prominent among them were Mehdi Namazi, Habib Sabeti, Qassem Lajevardi, Habib Elqanian, Rasul Vahabzadeh, Hassan Herati, Assadallah Rashidian, Muhammad Khosrowshahi, Jaʿfar Akhavan, and Abul Fazel Lak; f. a half-dozen new entrepreneurs, notably Ahmad Khiami, Mahmud Rezai, Hojaber Yazdani, and Morad Arya, who built vast business empires during the late 1960s mainly because of their personal contacts with the royal family, the old entrepreneurs, and the multinational corporations.

These wealthy families owned not only many of the large commercial farms, but also some 85 percent of the major private firms involved in banking, manufacturing, foreign trade, insurance, and urban construction.[17] Although the vast majority of the upper class was Muslim, some senior officials had joined the court-connected Freemason Lodge in Tehran, and a few—notably Yazdani, Elqanian, and Arya—came from Bahaʾi and Jewish backgrounds. This provided fuel for rumors often heard in the bazaars that the whole upper class represented an international conspiracy hatched by Zionists, Bahaʾis centered in Haifa, and British imperialists through the Freemason Lodge in London.

2. *The Propertied Middle Class.* Numbering nearly one million families, this class contained three closely knit groups. The first, which

[17] F. Halliday, *Iran: Dictatorship and Development* (London, 1979), p. 151.

constituted the core of the class, was the bazaar community with almost half a million merchants, shopkeepers, traders, and workshop owners. The second was formed of fairly well-to-do urban entrepreneurs with investments outside the bazaars. These investments included thousands of neighborhood stores, 420,000 rural workshops, 44,000 middle-sized commercial farms, and 7,830 small and medium-sized urban factories employing between 10 and 500 workers. The third group was made up of an estimated 90,000 clergymen—some 50 Ayatallahs, 5,000 Hojjat al-Islams, 10,000 theology students, and an unknown number of low-ranking mullas, maktab teachers, madraseh lecturers, prayer leaders, and procession organizers. Although the second and third groups were not bazaaris in the literal sense of the term, strong family and financial ties linked them to the first group.

Despite the recent growth of modern industry, the propertied middle class, a predominantly traditional force, had succeeded in preserving much of its power. The bazaars continued to control as much as half of the country's handicraft production, two-thirds of its retail trade, and three-quarters of its wholesale trade. The bazaars retained their independent craft and trade guilds, whereas almost all other occupations had lost their unions and professional associations. Saved from the radical unions that had appeared in the 1940s, the guild elders were able to turn the clock back to the 1920s and reassert their power over the many thousand shop assistants, handicraftsmen, workshop employees, and small peddlers working in the urban bazaars.

Moreover, the clergy continued to control a large, though decentralized, establishment containing some 5,600 town mosques, numerous vaqfs (endowments), a few meeting halls known as Husseiniehs, and six major seminaries—in Qum, Mashad, Tabriz, Isfahan, Shiraz, and Yazd. In fact, the prosperous 1960s helped the religious establishment, for prosperity allowed well-to-do bazaaris to finance the expansion of the major seminaries. By the mid-1970s, the religious establishment was big enough to send preachers regularly into shanty towns and distant villages, probably for the first time in Iranian history. Paradoxically, prosperity had helped strengthen a traditional group. Furthermore, the influence of the bazaar reached far into the countryside. It did so partly through village shopkeepers and traveling peddlers, partly through the commercial farms established after land reform, and partly through the small industrial plants set up in the countryside during the late 1960s to meet the increasing demand for consumer goods such as shoes, paper, furniture, and carpets. Again economic development had stimulated the growth of the propertied middle class.

3. *The Salaried Middle Class.* The development plans of the 1960s doubled the ranks of the salaried middle class from under 310,000 in 1956 to over 630,000 in 1977. The 1977 total included 304,404 civil servants, 208,241 teachers and school administrators, and 61,066 engineers, managers, and white-collar workers. What is more, the 1977 total swells to over 1,800,000 if one includes the many aspiring to join the salaried middle class—the 233,000 college students, the 741,000 secondary school students, and the 227,497 enrolled in technical, vocational, and teachers' training schools.

The development projects created such an acute shortage of trained personnel that the government recruited more and more foreign technicians, and encouraged women to enter the civil service and the professions, especially the teaching and nursing professions. The number of foreign technicians, particularly Americans and Europeans, increased from fewer than 10,000 in 1966 to as many as 60,000 in 1977. Similarly, the number of women enrolled in higher education jumped from under 5,000 in 1966 to over 74,000 in 1977. By 1977, women constituted 28 percent of the civil service, 30 percent of the secondary school staff, 54 percent of the elementary school staff, and nearly 100 percent of the kindergarten staff. Women also constituted 36 percent of the incoming students into the Teacher's University, and 86 percent of the incoming students into the vocational and teachers' training schools. Thus the educational system prepared many women for middle-class professions, even though the professions assigned were the less prestigious ones.

4. *The Working Class.* There are no accurate statistics on wage earners employed in the various industrial sectors, but educated guesses indicate that the working class grew nearly fivefold in the period between 1963 and 1977. At the center of this class were some 880,000 modern industrial workers: over 30,000 oil workers; 20,000 electrical, gas, and power workers; 30,000 fishery and lumberyard workers; 50,000 miners; 150,000 railwaymen, dockers, truck drivers, and other modern transport workers; and 600,000 factory workers in plants with more than 10 employees. The total grows to 1,272,000 if one includes some 392,000 wage earners employed by urban services and small manufacturing plants: some 100,000 workshop employees; 140,000 shop assistants; and 152,000 wage earners in banks, offices and other agencies.

The total grows further to over 2,400,000 if one adds the rapidly increasing army of the urban poor. Impoverished immigrants from the countryside, this underclass squatted in the sprawling new shanty towns and scraped together a living either as construction workers, or, if there were no jobs on the construction sites, as peddlers, hawkers, menial laborers, and even beggars. The sans-culottes of the Islamic revolution, this underclass later became famous as the mostazafin (wretched).

The total grows even further to some 3,500,000 if one includes the rural wage earners—the agricultural laborers, village construction workers, and wage earners employed in the small rural factories. Thus the whole wage-earning class, which had formed only 16 percent of the entire labor force in the 1940s, constituted as much as 34 percent of the labor force by the mid-1970s. Reza Shah had brought the modern working class into existence; Muhammad Reza Shah had nourished it to become the largest single class in contemporary Iran.

POLITICAL UNDERDEVELOPMENT (1963-1977)

Although the shah helped modernize the socioeconomic structure, he did little to develop the political system—to permit the formation of pressure groups, open the political arena for various social forces, forge links between the regime and the new classes, preserve the existing links between the regime and the old classes, and broaden the social base of the monarchy that, after all, had survived mainly because of the 1953 military coup d'état. Instead of modernizing the political system, the shah, like his father, based his power on the three Pahlevi pillars: the armed forces, the court patronage network, and the vast state bureaucracy.

The shah continued to treat the military establishment as his central support. He increased its size from 200,000 men in 1963 to 410,000 in 1977: the army went from 180,000 to 200,000; the gendarmerie from 25,000 to 60,000; the air force from 7,500 to 100,000; the navy from 2,000 to 25,000; the elite commando unit from 2,000 to 17,000; and the Imperial Guard, which served as a praetorian force, from 2,000 to 8,000. He also increased the annual military budget from $293 million in 1963 to $1.8 billion in 1973, and, after the quadrupling of oil prices, to $7.3 billion in 1977 (at 1973 prices and exchange rates). Buying more than $12 billion worth of Western-manufactured arms between 1970 and 1977 alone, the shah built up a vast ultra-sophisticated arsenal that included, among other weapons, 20 F14 Tomcat fighter planes with long-range Phoenix missiles, 190 F4 Phantom fighter planes, 166 F5 fighter aircraft, 10 Boeing 707 transport planes, 800 helicopters, 28 hovercrafts, 760 Chieftain tanks, 250 Scorpion tanks, 400 M47 tanks, 460 M60 tanks, and 1 Spruance naval destroyer. By 1977, Iran had the largest navy in the Persian Gulf, the most up-to-date air force in the Middle East, and the fifth largest military force in the world. As if this were not enough, the shah placed orders for another $12 billion worth of arms to be delivered between 1978 and 1980.[18] These included 202 helicopter gunships, 326 troop carrying helicopters, 160 F16s, 209 F4s, 7 Boeing planes, 3 Spruance destroyers, and 10 nuclear submarines. Arms dealers began to jest that the shah read their manuals in much the same way as other men read *Playboy*.

The shah's military interests were not confined to arms purchases and annual budgets. He continued to take a keen interest in the wellbeing of his officers, supervising their training, participating in their military maneuvers, and giving them attractive salaries, generous pensions, and sundry fringe benefits, including frequent travel abroad, modern medical facilities, comfortable housing, and low-priced department stores. Moreover, he personally checked all promotions above the rank of major; performed most state functions wearing a military uniform; and often praised the officer corps for saving the nation in 1953. Furthermore, he assigned to senior officers the task of running the much-publicized literacy corps and the large state enterprises, particularly the major industrial installations. The destiny of the monarchy and the officer corps became so interwoven that the shah, in an interview with an American academic, described himself not as the state, like Louis XIV, but as the army, in the true tradition of Reza Shah.[19]

To bolster the military pillar, the shah also expanded the security organizations. SAVAK grew to a total of over 5,300 full-time agents and a large but unknown number of part-time informers.[20] Directed mostly by General Nasiri, one of the shah's old associates, SAVAK had the power to censor the media, screen applicants for government jobs, and, according to reliable Western sources, use all means necessary, including torture, to hunt down dissidents.[21] In the words of one British correspondent, SAVAK was the shah's "eyes and ears, and, where necessary, his iron fist."[22] In addition to SAVAK, the security organizations included the Imperial Inspectorate and the J2 Bureau. The former, established in 1958, was under the control of General Fardoust, a childhood friend of the shah. Its main function

[18] The Shah also earmarked $20 billion for a crash program to build twelve nuclear plants in the course of the next decade. This program had military implications, since it would have enabled Iran to produce enriched uranium—a vital element in the manufacture of nuclear weapons.

[19] B. Bayne, *Persian Kingship in Transition* (New York, 1968), p. 186.

[20] Revolutionary Prosecutor-General, "The Role of SAVAK," *Iran Times*, 31 August 1979.

[21] *New York Times*, 21 September 1972; *Newsweek*, 28 April 1972.

[22] R. Graham, *Iran: The Illusion of Power* (New York, 1979), p. 143.

was to watch SAVAK, guard against military conspiracies, and report on the financial dealings of the wealthy families. The latter organization, created in 1933, was modeled after the French Deuxième Bureau. A part of the armed services, it not only gathered military intelligence, but also kept a close watch on both SAVAK and the Imperial Inspectorate.

The second pillar, court patronage, strengthened the regime in that it enabled the shah to reward his followers with a vast array of lucrative salaries, pensions, and sinecures. The court never revealed the true extent of its wealth, of course, but Western estimates place the fortune accumulated by the royal family, both inside and outside Iran, at anywhere between five and twenty billion dollars.[23] This fortune was derived from four major sources. The original source was the farm lands amassed by Reza Shah. Although the royal family lost these estates during Mossadeq's administration, it regained them after the 1953 coup, and, having turned to mechanized agriculture before the land reform program was drafted, managed to retain a substantial portion of the best lands. As a result, the Pahlevis continued to be Iran's largest landowning family. The shah himself owned a large commercial farm near Gurgan. His brother, ʿAbul Reza, nicknamed "Iran's number one farmer," owned similar enterprises in Gilan. Other relatives had shares in agrobusinesses in Fars, Mazandaran, and Khuzistan.

The second source of wealth was the oil revenue. According to one reliable Western economist, in the last few years of the regime substantial sums—perhaps as much as $2 billion—were transferred directly from the oil revenue into the secret foreign bank accounts held by members of the royal family.[24] These transfers left no trace in the state treasury, but caused statistical discrepancies between the sum the oil companies paid to Iran and the sum the Iranian government received from the oil companies. The third source was business. Taking advantage of the economic boom, members of the royal family borrowed large funds from state banks, often at highly favorable terms, and invested the funds in a wide variety of commercial and industrial enterprises. By the early 1970s, the Pahlevis were the richest enterpreneurial family in Iran. The shah himself partly owned two machine-tool factories, two car plants, two brick-manufacturing companies, three mining firms, three textile mills, and four construction companies. His nephew, Prince Shahram, was a majority shareholder in eight large companies that specialized in construction, insurance,

[23] W. Branigin, "Pahlevi Fortune: A Staggering Sum," *Washington Post*, 17 January 1979.

[24] Quoted ibid.

cement, textiles, and transport. Other relatives had stock in some 150 companies whose activities ranged from banking and aluminum manufacturing to hotel catering and casino gambling.[25]

The final source of wealth was the well-known Pahlevi Foundation. According to Western bankers, this foundation received an annual subsidy of over $40 million, functioned as a tax haven for some of the Pahlevi holdings, and thereby "penetrated almost every corner of the nation's economy." By 1977, the foundation had shares in 207 companies, including 8 mining firms, 10 cement firms, 17 banks and insurance companies, 23 hotels, 25 metal companies, 25 agrobusinesses, and 45 construction companies. In the words of the *New York Times*, "behind the facade of charitable activities, the foundation is used in three ways: as a source of funds for the royal family; as a means of exerting influence on key sectors of the economy; and as a conduit for rewards to supporters of the regime."[26]

The state bureaucracy served as the regime's third pillar. In the course of these fourteen years, the state bureaucracy grew from 12 ministries with some 150,000 civil servants to 19 ministries with over 304,000 civil servants. The new ministries included that of Labor and Social Services, Art and Culture, Housing and Town Planning, Information and Tourism, Science and Higher Education, Health and Social Welfare, and Rural Cooperatives and Village Affairs. As the bureaucracies proliferated, the administrative map was redrawn to make the provincial districts more manageable. The number of provinces thus increased from 10 to 23. They consisted of Tehran, Gilan, Mazandaran, Zanjan, Semnan, West Azerbaijan, East Azerbaijan, Khurasan, Kurdistan, Kermanshah, Hamedan, Isfahan, Chahar Mahal and Bakhtiyari, Boir Ahmad, Kerman, Sistan and Baluchistan, Fars, Bushire, Yazd, Ilam, Hormozgan, Luristan, and Khuzistan.

The dramatic growth of the bureaucracy enabled the state to penetrate more deeply the everyday lives of ordinary citizens. In the towns, the state expanded to the point that it hired as many as one out of every two full-time employees. By the mid-1970s, the regime had the power to give to thousands of citizens—and, if necessary, to withhold from the same thousands—not only their salaries and wages, but also a widening range of social benefits, including medical insurance, unemployment insurance, student loans, pensions, and even low-income housing. This network, however, did not yet incorporate the bazaars. In the countryside, the state extended its reach into dis-

[25] For a detailed listing of Pahlevi holdings in Iran, see Shahab, "The Octopus with One Hundred Tentacles," *Chap,* 3 (November 1978), 1-5.

[26] A. Chittenden, "Bankers Say Shah's Fortune Is Well above a Billion," *New York Times,* 10 January 1979.

tant districts, and, for the first time in Iranian history, supplanted the local khans, kadkhudas, and landlords as the real ruler of the rural masses. For centuries, intermediaries such as local magnates had acted as buffers between the rural population and the state. Now nothing stood between the rural population and the gigantic government bureaucracy that not only regulated agricultural prices, water distribution, and the few remaining migratory routes, but also administered 89 state farms and closely supervised 8,500 state cooperatives with 1,700,000 members. In the words of one anthropologist who has studied the remote Boir Ahmadi tribe, the state finally fulfilled its ancient dream of gaining absolute control over the rural masses:

One is amazed at the high level of centralization achieved within the last decade. The government now interferes in practically all aspects of daily life. Land is contracted for cash by the government, fruits get sprayed, crops fertilized, animals fed, beehives set up, carpets woven, goods sold, babies born, populations controlled, women organized, religion taught, and diseases cured—all by the intervention of the government.[27]

The bureaucracy so thoroughly penetrated the rural population that in 1974 the government drew up plans to reorganize the whole countryside, depopulating some regions, repopulating others. A senior official told an American visitor, "there are too many villages in Iran. A lot of them are inaccessible. We can't get to them. We are planning to consolidate a number of them into what we call 'poles.' "[28] Another senior official explained that the country would be divided into, on the one hand, twenty "poles of development," and, on the other hand, the "marginal" underdeveloped zones.[29] The former would receive government assistance in the form of agricultural credits, irrigation works, roads, fertilizers, pesticides, tractors, schools, dispensaries, and cheap heating fuel. The latter would receive nothing, and thereby, it was hoped, would lose much of its population. For the state bureaucrats, this was social engineering on a grand scale. For the "marginal" peasants, it would have been social destruction on a massive scale.

Although the bureaucracy, military, and court patronage provided the regime with three large pillars, in 1975 the shah made the fateful decision to establish a fourth pillar—a one-party state. In the decade after the 1960-1963 crisis, the shah had remained content with his

[27] R. Loeffler, "From Tribal Order to Bureaucracy: The Political Transformation of the Boir Ahmad" (unpublished paper, Western Michigan University, 1975), p. 21.
[28] F. FitzGerald, "Giving the Shah What He Wants," *Harper's*, November 1974, p. 74.
[29] T. Brun and R. Dumont, "Iran: Imperial Pretensions and Agricultural Dependence," *Middle East Research and Information Project*, no. 71 (October 1978), p. 18.

two-party system. The only major change that had been made was the sudden replacement in December 1963 of the National party with the New Iran party (Hizb-i Iran Novin), and the appointment of Hassan Mansur, the latter's chairman, as prime minister. The son of ʿAli Mansur, who had been premier in 1940-1941 as well as in early 1950, Hassan Mansur was a full-fledged royalist with a long career both in the civil service and in the palace administration. But his tenure as premier was to be brief, for in January 1965 he was gunned down by a group of religious students who were outraged by his decision to sign additional concessions with foreign oil companies. Immediately after the assassination, the shah gave the premiership to Amir ʿAbbas Hoveida, Mansur's brother-in-law and the deputy chairman of the New Iran party. From a prominent bureaucratic family that originated in the seventeenth century and was rumored to have converted to Babism in the late nineteenth century, Hoveida was raised for government service and sent to Lebanon to study political science.[30] Returning home in the late 1940s, he had a successful career in the diplomatic corps, in the NIOC, and in the New Iran party. Appointed premier in January 1965, he lasted at the post until 1977—the longest tenure for any prime minister in modern Iran. During his twelve-year administration, Hoveida tightly controlled the New Iran party but at the same time permitted the People's party to function in the Majles. In fact, in these years the shah often reassured the royal opposition that he had no intention of creating a one-party system:

If I were a dictator rather than a constitutional monarch, then I might be tempted to sponsor a single dominant party such as Hitler organized or such as you find today in Communist countries. But as constitutional monarch I can afford to encourage large-scale party activity free from the strait-jacket of one-party rule or the one-party state.[31]

In March 1975, however, the shah did an about-turn. Dissolving the two parties, he created the Resurgence party (Hizb-i Rastakhiz), and announced that in future he would have a one-party state. In making the announcement, he argued that those reluctant to join the single party must be secret "Tudeh sympathizers."[32] These traitors, he continued, could either go to prison or else "leave the country tomorrow." When foreign journalists pointed out that such language differed sharply from the pronouncements in favor of the two-party system, the shah retorted: "Freedom of thought! Freedom of thought! Democracy, democracy! With five-year-olds going on strike and pa-

---

[30] A. Qassemi, *Alygarshi* (Oligarchy) (Tehran, 1979), pp. 5-25.
[31] M. R. Pahlevi, *Mission for My Country* (London, 1961), p. 173.
[32] *Kayhan International*, 8 March 1975.

rading in the streets! . . . Democracy? Freedom? What do these words mean? I don't want any part of them."[33]

The Resurgence party was designed by two groups of very divergent advisers. One group was formed of young political scientists with Ph.D.s from American universities. Versed in the works of Samuel Huntington, the distinguished political scientist at Harvard, these fresh returnees argued that the only way to achieve political stability in developing countries is to establish a disciplined government party. Such a party, they claimed, would become an organic link between the state and the society, would enable the former to mobilize the latter, and thus would eliminate the dangers posed by disruptive social elements. They ignored Huntington's observation that in the modern age monarchies are anachronistic.[34] They also underplayed his warning that the party should not be merely a government instrument controlling the masses, but should be a two-way conveyor belt that transmits pressures from society to the state as well as instructions from the state to society. The second group of advisers was formed of ex-communists from Shiraz who had left the Tudeh in the early 1950s—one had absconded with the party funds—and had reentered politics under the patronage of ʿAlam, the magnate from Sistan who was not only the minister of court but also the chairman of the People's party. This group argued that only a Leninist-style organization could mobilize the masses, break down the traditional barriers, and lead the way to a fully modern society. As the old saying goes, politics makes strange bedfellows.

However strange its origins, the main goal of the Resurgence party was quite clear. It was to transform the somewhat old-fashioned military dictatorship into a totalitarian-style one-party state. Absorbing the New Iran and the People's parties, the Resurgence party declared that it would observe the principles of "democratic centralism," synthesize the best aspects of socialism and capitalism, establish a dialectical relationship between the government and the people, and help the Great Leader (Farmandar) complete his White Revolution and lead his Iran toward a new Great Civilization (Tamadun-i Bozorg). In a handbook entitled the *Philosophy of Iran's Revolution*, the Resurgence party announced that the shah—the Light of the Aryan Race (Aryamehr)—had eradicated from Iran the concept of class and had resolved once for all the problems of class and social conflict.[35] The same handbook declared, "the Shah-in-Shah of Iran is not just the political leader of Iran. He is also in the first instance teacher and

[33] Quoted by FitzGerald, "Giving the Shah What He Wants," p. 82.
[34] S. Huntington, *Political Order in Changing Societies* (New Haven, 1968).
[35] Resurgence Party, *The Philosophy of Iran's Revolution* (Tehran, 1976).

spiritual leader, an individual who not only builds his nation roads, bridges, dams, and qanats, but also guides the spirit and thought and hearts of his people." Meanwhile, the shah told an English-language newspaper that the party's philosophy was "based on the dialectics of the principles of the White Revolution" and that nowhere in the world was there such a close relationship between ruler and people. "No other nation has given its *farmandar* such a *carte-blanche*."[36] The terminology, as well as the boast, revealed much about the shah at the height of his power.

The Resurgence party spent much of 1975 building a statewide organization. It formed a Central Committee, elected Hoveida as the secretary general of its Politbureau, and recruited almost all the Majles deputies. Moreover, it set up a women's organization, convened a labor congress for the state-controlled syndicates, held May Day parades, and founded five newspapers—the daily *Rastakhiz* (Resurgence), the *Rastakhiz-i Kargaran* (Workers' Resurgence), the *Rastakhiz-i Keshavarzan* (Farmers' Resurgence), the *Rastakhiz-i Javan* (Youth's Resurgence), and the theoretical *Andishiha-yi Rastakhiz* (Resurgent Concepts). Furthermore, it enrolled into its local branches some five million members, launched an intense campaign to register voters for the upcoming elections for the Twenty-fourth Majles—the Central Committee threatened "those who do not register are answerable to the party,"[37] and in June 1975 shepherded to the polls as many as seven million voters. After the election, the Resurgence party boasted, "our success is unprecedented in the history of political organizations."[38]

The growth of the Resurgence party had two major repercussions: the intensification of state control over the salaried middle class, the urban working class, and the rural masses; and, for the first time in Iranian history, the systematic penetration of the state into the propertied middle class, especially the bazaars and the religious establishment. Helped by SAVAK, the Resurgence party took over the ministries that controlled thousands of livelihoods—particularly the Ministries of Labor, Industry and Mines, Housing and Town Planning, Health and Social Welfare, and Rural Cooperatives and Village Affairs—and tightened state supervision over organizations dealing with communications and mass media—the Ministries of Information and Tourism, Art and Culture, Science and Higher Education, as well as the National Iranian Radio and Television Organization. The im-

[36] "Interview with the Shah-in-Shah," *Kayhan International*, 10 November 1976.

[37] *Kayhan International*, 31 May 1975.

[38] Quoted by P. Vieille and A. Bani Sadr, *L'Analyse des élections non concurrentielles* (Analysis of the Non-Competitive Elections) (Paris, 1976), p. 1.

pact on the realm of publishing was immediate. The number of titles published each year fell from over 4,200 to under 1,300.[39] One well-known writer was arrested, tortured for months, and finally placed before television cameras to "confess" that his works paid too much attention to social problems and not enough to the great achievements of the White Revolution. Another well-known writer was arrested for insisting that Azerbaijan had a "national language," and was tortured to declare publicly that Marxism threatened the Third World and that Marxism and Islam were inherently against each other. Yet another well-known writer decided to leave the country rather than compose odes for the Resurgence party. By the end of 1975, twenty-two prominent poets, novelists, professors, theater directors, and film makers were in jail for criticizing the regime. And many others had been physically attacked for refusing to cooperate with the authorities. A foreign correspondent was told by a professor who had been beaten up for failing to mention the White Revolution in his political science lectures: "There is nothing special about my case."[40] Similarly, a report published by the highly reputed International Commission of Jurists in Geneva concluded that the regime systematically used censorship and torture to intimidate the public.[41]

Even more significant was the impact of the Resurgence party on the propertied middle class. The party opened branches in the bazaars, forced donations from small businessmen, introduced a minimum wage for workers in small plants, and required shopkeepers and workshop owners to register their employees with the Labor Ministry and pay monthly contributions for their medical insurance. It also drafted a law to reform the guilds, dissolved the traditional ones, created new ones, and supplanted the easy-going High Councils of Guilds with tightly controlled Chambers of Guilds. In the provincial towns, the Chambers of Guilds were placed under the direct authority of the governors-general. In Tehran, the Chamber was directed by government functionaries and nonbazaar entrepreneurs. Moreover, the government directly threatened the economic basis of the bazaar by setting up state corporations to import and distribute basic foods, especially wheat, sugar, and meat. The government had rushed into a territory in which previous regimes had feared to tread. Not surprisingly, a petition circulated among Tehran shopkeepers protested that the government was using state corporations and large department stores to undermine the bazaars, "the pillars of Iranian soci-

[39] P.E.N., *Country Report*, no. 2 (March 1978), pp. 1-22.
[40] E. Rouleau, "Iran: Myth and Reality," *The Guardian*, 24 October 1976.
[41] International Commission of Jurists, *Human Rights and the Legal System in Iran* (Geneva, 1976), pp. 21-22.

ety."[42] Furthermore, the government-controlled press began to talk of the need to uproot the bazaars, build highways through the old city centers, eradicate "worm-ridden shops," replace inefficient butchers, grocers, and bakers with efficient supermarkets, and establish a state-run market modeled after London's Covent Gardens.[43] One shopkeeper later told a French journalist that the bazaar was convinced the shah and the "oil bourgeoisie" wanted to "throttle" the small businessman.[44] Another confided to an American journalist that "if we let him, the Shah will destroy us. The banks are taking over. The big stores are taking away our livelihoods. And the government will flatten our bazaars to make space for state offices."[45]

The regime carried out a simultaneous assault on the religious establishment. The Resurgence party claimed the shah to be a spiritual as well as a political leader; denounced the ʿulama as "medieval black reactionaries"; and, in declaring Iran to be on the road to the Great Civilization, replaced the Muslim calendar with a new royalist calendar allocating 2,500 years for the whole monarchy and 35 years for the present monarch. Thus, Iran jumped overnight from the Muslim year 1355 to the royalist year 2535. It should be noted that in the modern era few regimes anywhere have been foolhardy enough to scrap their country's religious calendar. The Resurgence party also discouraged women from wearing the chadour on university campuses; sent special investigators to scrutinize the accounts of the religious endowments; announced that only the state-controlled organization of vaqfs could publish theology books; and encouraged the College of Theology in Tehran University to expand the recently created religious corps (sepah-i din)—modeled on the literacy corps—and send more cadres into the countryside to teach peasants "true Islam." Moreover, the Majles, disregarding the shariʿa, raised the age of marriage for girls from fifteen to eighteen and for boys from eighteen to twenty. Furthermore, the justice minister instructed judges to be more diligent in enforcing the 1967 Family Protection Law. This law, again disregarding the shariʿa, gave secular courts jurisdiction over family disputes and restricted men's power over their wives. It stipulated that men could not divorce their wives without valid reasons and could not enter polygamous marriages without written permission from their other wives. It also stipulated that wives had the right to petition

---

[42] *Ittilaʿat*, 3 March 1978.

[43] For a survey of the government campaign against the bazaars, see P. Azr, "The Shah's Struggle against the Guilds," *Donya*, 2 (December 1975), 10-14.

[44] P. Balta, "Iran in Revolt," *Ittilaʿat*, 4 October 1979.

[45] J. Kendell, "Iran's Students and Merchants Form an Unlikely Alliance," *New York Times*, 7 November 1979.

for divorce and work outside the home without their husband's permission. In the words of an exiled newspaper closely associated with the ʿulama, the Resurgence party was trying to nationalize religion by taking over the vaqfs, recruiting mullas into SAVAK, offering sinecures to progovernment clerics, monopolizing the publication of theology books, and sending the religious corps into the countryside to turn the peasants against the country's spiritual authorities.[46]

The formation of the Resurgence party caused a sharp reaction among the ʿulama. Fayzieh, the main seminary in Qum, closed down in protest. In the ensuing street confrontations, some 250 theology students were detained and conscripted into the army. Ayatallah Hassan Ghaffari, a sixty-year-old cleric in Tehran, was arrested for writing against the regime. While in prison, he died mysteriously. Hojjat al-Islam Shamsabadi, a prominent cleric in Isfahan, was murdered a few days after preaching against the new calendar. Although the police arrested five students for the murder, the local ʿulama, disbelieving the authorities, organized a general strike in the Isfahan bazaar. Meanwhile, Ayatallah Rouhani, another prominent cleric, declared the Resurgence party to be against the constitutional laws, against the interests of Iran, and against the principles of Islam.[47] What is more, Ayatallah Khomeini, from his exile in Iraq, advised all true believers to stay away from the Resurgence party. This party, he argued, not only violated individual rights, constitutional liberties, and international laws, but also intended to destroy Islam, ruin agriculture, waste resources on useless weapons, and plunder the country on behalf of American imperialism.[48] A few days after this proclamation, the government arrested Khomeini's close associates in Iran, including many clerics who were to play prominent roles after the Islamic revolution, such as Ayatallah Beheshti, Ayatallah Montazeri, Ayatallah Hussein Qumi, Ayatallah Rabbani Shirazi, Ayatallah Zanjani, Ayatallah Anvari, Hojjat al-Islam Kani, Hojjat al-Islam Khamenehi, Hojjat al-Islam Lahuti, and Hojjat al-Islam Taheri. Never before had so many prominent clerics found themselves imprisoned at the same time.

Thus the aims of the Resurgence party and its actual achievements can be seen to be diametrically opposed. Its aim was to strengthen the regime, further institutionalize the monarchy, and firmly anchor the state into the wider society. The means it used were the mobilization of the public, monopolization of links between the government and the country, consolidation of control over office employees, factory workers, and the rural population, and, most important of all,

[46] "Nationalization of Religion," *Mujahed*, 3:29 (March 1975), pp. 6-10.
[47] A. Rouhani, "Proclamation," *Mujahed*, 4:30 (May 1975), 7.
[48] R. Khomeini, "Proclamation," *Mujahed*, 3:29 (March 1975), 1-11.

extension of state power into the traditional bazaars and the religious establishment. But instead of establishing stability, the Resurgence party weakened the whole regime, cut the monarchy further off from the country, and intensified resentment among diverse groups. For mass mobilization meant mass manipulation, which, in turn, produced mass dissatisfaction. The monopoly over organizations and communications deprived social forces of avenues through which they could channel their grievances and aspirations into the political arena. More and more individuals gave up hopes of reform and picked up incentives for revolution. The drive for public participation induced the government to discard its old premise, "those who are not actively against us are for us," and adopt the dangerous reasoning, "those who are not actively for us are against us." As a result, dissenters who for years had been left alone so long as they did not air their opposition now suddenly found themselves with no choice but to enroll in the party, sign petitions in favor of the regime, and even march in the streets singing praises for the 2,500-year-old monarchy. Finally, the drastic surge into the bazaars and the religious establishment destroyed the few bridges that had in the past connected the regime with the society. This surge not only threatened the clerical authorities, but also aroused the wrath of thousands of shopkeepers, workshop owners, small businessmen, and their bazaar retainers. Instead of forging new links, the party destroyed the few existing ones and in the process stirred up a host of dangerous enemies. Despite the banner of modernization, the Resurgence party had managed to further undo an already underdeveloped political system.

IRAN ON THE VERGE OF REVOLUTION

In the last three years of the regime, political tensions were heightened not only by the formation of the Resurgence party but also by the dramatic oil boom. The sudden fivefold increase in the oil revenues inflated people's expectations and thereby widened the gap between, on one hand, what the regime promised, claimed, and achieved, and, on the other hand, what the public expected, obtained, and considered feasible. It was true, as the government often boasted, that in the fourteen years of the White Revolution great strides were made in the areas of health and education—the number of medical personnel tripled, the infant mortality rate dropped from 20 percent to less than 12 percent, the literacy rate rose from 26 to 42 percent, the universities expanded fivefold, and the middle levels of education grew as much as threefold.[49] But it was equally true, as critics liked to point out, that after fourteen years of so-called White Revolution Iran still had one of the worst doctor-patient ratios, one of the highest child mortality rates, and one of the lowest hospital-bed-to-population ratios in the whole of the Middle East. Moreover, 68 percent of the adults remained illiterate, the number of illiterates actually rose from 13 million to nearly 15 million, fewer than 40 percent of the children completed primary school, the teacher-student ratio in public schools deteriorated, only 60,000 university places opened each year for as many as 290,000 applicants, and the percentage of the population with higher degrees remained one of the lowest in the Middle East.

It was true that the White Revolution helped the agricultural population, financing rural cooperatives, distributing land to 1,638,000 families, and increasing the number of tractors sixteen times and the volume of fertilizers used more than twenty times. It was also true, however, that farm cooperatives were inadequately funded; agricultural businesses rather than small farmers obtained credit; 96 percent of the villagers were left without electricity; and for every two families that received land one received nothing, and for every one that obtained adequate land (7 hectares) three obtained less than enough to become independent commercial farmers. Moreover, price ceilings on basic agricultural commodities such as grain favored the towns at the expense of the countryside. This lowered incentives to farm staple foods and helped stifle agricultural production. This, in turn, created a widening gap between the rising population and the stagnant agricultural production. As a result, Iran, which in the early 1960s had been a net exporter of food, by the mid 1970s was spending as much as $1 billion a year on imported agricultural products.

It was obvious that the standard of living for many families improved as they gained access to modern apartments, to state-financed social plans such as medical insurance, unemployment insurance, and industrial profit-sharing plans, and, of course, to consumer goods, especially refrigerators, televisions, motorcycles, and even private cars. But it was also obvious that the quality of life for many families deteriorated as the shanty towns proliferated, the air became more polluted, and the traffic turned the streets into nightmares. Between 1967 and 1977, the percentage of urban families living in only one room increased from 36 to 43. On the eve of the revolution, as much as 42 percent of Tehran had inadequate housing. And, despite the vast oil revenues, Tehran, a city of over 4 million, still had no proper

[49] The statistics in this section have been taken from Ashraf, *Shakhesha-yi Ijtima'i-yi Iran*, pp. 50-293.

sewage system, no subway system, and no proper public transport system. In a statement reminiscent of Maria Antionette, the shah's younger brother, who happened to own a helicopter plant, asked, "if people don't like traffic jams, why don't they buy helicopters?"[50] What is worse, the lower strata of the working class—especially laborers, peddlers, small factory employees, and temporary workers—did not benefit from the social welfare programs, since they were ruled ineligible for insurance plans and profit-sharing schemes. For these millions, most of whom had been forced out of the villages into the new shanty towns, the oil boom did not end poverty; it merely modernized it.

It was evident that in the period between 1963 and 1977, the GNP grew dramatically, drawing more and more people into the mainstream of society and integrating the outer provinces into the country's economy. But it was also evident that the growth did not benefit all equally. On the contrary, it benefited the rich more than the middle and the lower classes, and the central regions, particularly Tehran, more than the outer provinces. Iran has no reliable data on income distribution, but the Central Bank carried out extensive surveys in 1959-1960 and 1973-1974 on urban household expenditures. Expenditure data inevitably underestimate income inequality, of course, for the wealthy can afford to save more and tend to spend smaller portions of their income. The 1959-1960 survey shows that the richest 10 percent accounted for 35.5 percent of the total expenditures, and the richest 20 percent for 51.7 percent. At the other end of the social pyramid, the poorest 10 percent accounted for 1.7 percent of the total expenditures, and the poorest 21 percent for 4.7 percent. Meanwhile, the middle 40 percent accounted for 27.5 percent of total expenditures. According to an unpublished report written by the International Labor Office, this made Iran one of the most inegalitarian societies in the world.[51] What is more, this inequality became even worse during the 1960s. The 1973-1974 survey shows that the top 20 percent accounted for as much as 55.5 percent of the total expenditures; the bottom 20 percent for as little as 3.7 percent; and the middle 40 percent for no more than 26 percent (see Table 8). The oil boom brought to the middle classes decent housing, small cars, and an annual tour to Europe. But it brought to the rich business empires unimagined by earlier entrepreneurs, palaces worthy of ancient kings, and scandals that far overshadowed those of the previous

[50] Quoted by M. Tehranian, "Iran: Communication, Alienation, and Revolution," *Intermedia*, 7 (March 1979), 6-12.

[51] International Labor Office, "Employment and Income Policies for Iran" (unpublished report, Geneva, 1972), Appendix C, p. 6.

TABLE 8

Decile Distribution of Urban Household Expenditures
(percent)

Deciles (lowest to highest)	1959-1960	1973-1974	Deciles (lowest to highest)	1959-1960	1973-1974
1st	1.7	1.3	6th	7.3	6.8
2nd	2.9	2.4	7th	8.9	9.3
3rd	4	3.4	8th	11.8	11.1
4th	5	4.7	9th	16.4	17.5
5th	6.1	5	10th	35.3	37.9

generation. In the words of a journal associated with the Pentagon, "by 1977 the sheer scale of corruption had reached a boiling point. . . . Even conservative estimates indicate that such [bureaucratic] corruption involved at least a billion dollars between 1973 and 1976."[52]

Moreover, the regime's economic and social programs tended to increase regional inequalities. For example, Tehran obtained many of the new assembly plants and over 60 percent of the loans given by the Industrial and Mining Development Bank. Consequently, by 1975 Tehran produced over half of the country's manufactured goods and contained 22 percent of the country's industrial labor force. In Tehran, for every worker employed in manufacturing there were 0.7 in agriculture. But in East Azerbaijan the ratio was 1 : 2.6; in West Azerbaijan 1 : 13; and in Kurdistan 1 : 20. Similarly, the literacy rate was 62 percent in Tehran, but only 27 percent in East Azerbaijan, 26 percent in Baluchistan and Sistan, and as low as 25 percent in Kurdistan. The percentage of children in school was 74 in Tehran, but as low as 44 in West Azerbaijan, 40 in Baluchistan and Sistan, and 36 in Kurdistan. Tehran had one doctor per 974 people, one dentist per 5,626 people, and one nurse per 1,820 people. On the other hand, East Azerbaijan had one doctor per 5,589 people, one dentist per 66,156 people, and one nurse per 12,712 people. Kurdistan had one doctor per 6,477 people, one dentist per 57,294 people, and one nurse per 46,552. Finally, Baluchistan and Sistan had one doctor per 5,311 people, one dentist per 51,663 people, and one nurse per 27,064 people. The resentments built up by these ethnic and class inequalities remained hidden during the early 1970s. But once cracks appeared in the Pahlevi regime, they rushed forth in a torrent to engulf the whole society.

[52] A. Mansur (pseudonym), "The Crisis in Iran," *Armed Forces Journal International*, January 1979, pp. 33-34.

TEN

The Opposition

Interviewer: Your Majesty, on what do you base your prediction that within a generation Iran will be one of the five most advanced countries in the world?

The Shah: Energy, diligence of our people, our hegemony. Of course, a few demonstrate. Just imagine Iranians, if they are Iranians, demonstrating against their leader after what we have done for the country. It is true hegemony that we have in our country. Everybody is behind their monarch, with their souls, with their hearts.

—Interview with the shah, *The Guardian,* 19 January 1974

POLITICAL PARTIES (1953-1977)

The 1953 coup brought down an iron curtain on Iranian politics. It cut the opposition leaders from their followers, the militants from the general public, and the political parties from their social bases. For thirteen years, Iran had been shaken by the sound and fury of clashing political forces. But for the next twenty-four years—with the brief exception of 1960-1963—the country was to follow a quiet course, with the politics of social conflict giving way to those of social engineering. The shah interpreted the quiet to be a mandate for his regime. The opposition, on the other hand, saw it as an interlude before the inevitable storm. The coup d'état also constituted an iron curtain for the social scientists. The previous period had allowed them to see beyond the political surface into the inner depths of the country, especially its ethnic and class divisions. For the next quarter century, however, they were permitted to look only at what the authorities wanted to reveal. Not surprisingly, the focus of the few social scientists that studied Iran shifted away from the dynamics of social conflict to the politics of social engineering.

The iron curtain may have hidden the social tensions and the organized opposition, but it certainly did not succeed in eliminating them. On the contrary, the social tensions continued and intensified to explosion point, just as the opposition, despite the straight-jacket of police controls, survived to develop new ideas and new methods of translating these into concrete action. Students of the government-controlled media found nothing but intellectual stagnation, endless praise for the monarchy, and mindless imitation of the West. But an examination of the lively underground press shows a young generation of intellectuals thriving on new ideas, adopting them to their Shi'i culture, reconsidering the theories and tactics of their forerunners, and posing again and again the vital question, "What is to be done?" In fact, the twenty-five-year repression produced a new intelligentsia that formulated ideas far more radical than those of the Tudeh and the National Front. Moreover, the new generation helped shape the uncompromising character of the revolution that eventually destroyed the monarchy.

The Tudeh Party. Although the Tudeh survived to play a role, albeit a minor one, in the Islamic revolution, its strength declined drastically after the 1953 coup, and by the late 1950s the party was a mere shadow of its former self. Four major pressures account for this decline. First, the Tudeh bore the brunt of police repression. Immediately after the coup, the 1931 law against collectivism was stringently applied to round up Tudeh suspects. And immediately after the formation of SAVAK, the regime concentrated its police operations on destroying the Tudeh underground. Whereas rank and file members of other parties, notably the National Front, were reprimanded or kept in jail for a few months, ordinary members of the Tudeh lost their jobs or found themselves in prison for several years. Whereas most leaders of the National Front were given five-year sentences and were granted amnesty after three years—only Fatemi was executed—forty Tudeh militants were shot, fourteen were tortured to death, and another two hundred were sentenced to life imprisonment. Six of these remained in prison until the revolution. Moreover, SAVAK continued to bear down on Tudeh members mercilessly even after the party ceased to be a major danger. For instance, in 1973 a medical student who had formed a party cell in the university was kidnapped and murdered in prison. Similarly, in 1974 a former air force lieutenant who was an alternate member of the Central Committee was tortured to death after serving nine years of his life sentence. The regime wanted it known that the cost of associating with the Tudeh remained very high.

Second, the regime—helped by foreign propaganda experts—waged an intense psychological war against the Tudeh. It accused the Tudeh of being a "Trojan horse" and a spy network for the Russians; of supporting Stalin's demands in 1944-1947 for a northern oil concession; of not supporting the 1949-1950 campaign to nationalize the southern oil company; of creating an independent republic in 1946 in Azerbaijan; and of scheming to establish similar republics in future and to divide Iran into a number of small states annexed to the Soviet Union. It also hammered away on the theme that the Tudeh was controlled by Armenians, Jews, and Caucasian emigrés; and that the party preached atheism, smeared religion as the opiate of the masses, and attacked the holy Koran as well as the revered Shi'i 'ulama. In a word, the Tudeh was portrayed as the avowed enemy not only of monarchy and private property, but also of Iran and Islam. As if these charges were not damaging enough, SAVAK disseminated a variety of false and half false rumors. It implied that the Tudeh had helped the royalist officers carry out the coup against Mossadeq; that former members who were released from prison had agreed to collaborate with the police; and that the party apparatus in exile in Europe was thoroughly infiltrated with government agents. SAVAK also spread rumors that the Tudeh had murdered half-hearted members; that some party leaders were so disillusioned with the Soviet sale of arms to Iran that they had requested permission to return home; and that the Russians periodically handed such disillusioned members over to Iran to face the execution squads.[1]

Third, the social changes brought about by rapid modernization tended to weaken the Tudeh. Industrialization drew into the urban labor force some four million peasants who had been outside the political arena of the 1940s. Similarly, the rapid growth of the educational system drew into the intelligentsia the children of bazaar families—families that had in the past staunchly opposed the Tudeh. By the early 1960s, the only young workers and intellectuals that had favorable information about the Tudeh were the children of left-wing parents. Thus pro-Tudeh sympathies became more and more confined to families with left-wing traditions. This had obvious implication for the politics of the 1970s.

Fourth, the Tudeh leadership was weakened by deaths, infirmities of old age, and defections. Experienced leaders such as Rusta, Kambakhsh, and Noshin died in exile. Others, notably Ovanessian, Boqrati, and Amir-Khizi, were incapacitated by ill health. Yet others, especially Bozorg 'Alavi and Keshavarz, removed themselves from party politics. Moreover, the Tudeh was torn by three major splits. The first

---

[1] In 1964, the government announced the execution of Lieutenant Qobadi, a police officer who had helped the Tudeh leaders escape from prison in 1949 and who had lived in Russia from 1949 until 1964. At the time of the execution, it was rumored that the Russians had delivered him to Iran for execution. But after the revolution, it became clear through government documents that he had returned home after receiving a signed amnesty from the Iranian embassy in Moscow.

came in 1964 when a small circle of Kurdish intellectuals left the Tudeh and revived the Kurdish Democratic Party of Iran, which had lain dormant since the 1946 debacle.[2] Convening in Europe a second party congress, these Kurdish Democrats raised the slogan "Democracy for Iran, Autonomy for Kurdistan," and called for an armed struggle to establish a federal republic modeled after that of Yugoslavia on the grounds that Iran, like Yugoslavia, contained many diverse nations.[3] The Congress also denounced the former Kurdish Democratic party for refusing to distribute land among the peasantry, and implicitly criticized the Tudeh both for underestimating the nationality question and for refusing to initiate an armed struggle against the regime. Soon after the congress, the Kurdish Democrats tried to spark a peasant war in the Urmiah region; but, after three years of intermittent fighting, decided to give up the attempt and instead concentrate on recruiting members among the increasing numbers of Kurdish students enrolled in European universities. In the three years of fighting, fifty-three members of the Kurdish Democrats were killed. These included three shopkeepers, four intellectuals from Tehran, five workers, seven local mullas, and eighteen peasants, shepherds, and tribesmen.[4]

The second split came in 1965 when, in wake of the Sino-Soviet dispute, two senior members of the Central Committee—Qassemi and Forutan—left the Tudeh and formed a new group called the Tofan Marxist-Leninist Organization (Sazman-i Marksist-Leninist-i Tofan). The name Tofan (Storm) was borrowed from the radical newspaper of the 1920s edited by the revolutionary martyr Forokhi. In forming the new organization, Qassemi and Forutan announced that their former colleagues had become reformists and were trying to revise Marxism into an "opportunistic nonrevolutionary ideology."[5] They also accused the Tudeh leaders of blindly accepting the Soviet theory that capitalism and socialism could coexist peacefully; of denouncing Stalin on the question of personality cult without weighing all the evidence; and of refusing to learn from Mao's teachings on how to

[2] In 1967, the leadership of the Kurdish Democrat party passed on to ʿAbdul Rahman Qassemlou, an ex-army captain who had been arrested in 1956 for belonging to the Tudeh, and, having served his ten-year prison sentence, had emigrated to Europe.

[3] "The Second Congress of the Kurdish Democratic Party," *Tofan*, no. 15 (September 1965).

[4] "The Armed Struggle in Kurdistan," *Tudeh*, no. 19 (July 1971), pp. 1-31; Confederation of Iranian Students, *Dar Bareh SAVAK* (Concerning SAVAK) (n.p., 1969), pp. 165-68.

[5] A. Qassemi and Gh. Forutan, "Proclamation to Members of the Tudeh Party" (n.p., April 1965).

organize the peasantry for a mass armed struggle.[6] They further argued that the Soviet Union was not only betraying the revolution by selling weapons to the shah, but was also exploiting Iran through barter agreements on oil, gas, and steel.[7]

The final split came in 1966, when members of the Tudeh youth section left the party, and, repeating the charges made by the Tofan group, formed their own Revolutionary Organization of the Tudeh Party Abroad (Sazman-i Inqilab-i Hizb-i Tudeh dar Kharej).[8] Although both the Tofan group and the Revolutionary Organization viewed themselves as Maoist, they were kept apart by generational differences and doctrinal conflicts. The former, founded by old-time Tudeh leaders, argued that the Tudeh had originated as a genuine revolutionary movement, but had been led astray after 1963 by Soviet revisionists. The main task, they concluded, was to "revive" the revolutionary movement. The latter organization, founded by much younger members, argued that the Tudeh had been a reformist aberration from the start, and therefore the main task was not to revive it but to recreate the old Communist party of the 1930s.[9] Moreover, the former group, whose founders had participated in the urban upheavals of the 1940s, expected the revolution to start in the cities and then spread into the villages. For this group, the notion of starting the revolution in the countryside smacked of "Castroist deviations."[10] But the latter organization, rigidly applying Mao's theories, expected the revolution to begin in the villages, spread throughout the countryside, and then surround the cities.[11]

Despite these defections and setbacks, the Tudeh managed to survive and even regain some ground during the early 1970s. Its headquarters in exile received enough help from other communist parties, especially those of the Soviet Union, East Germany, Italy, and France, to keep some fifty full-time party workers in Europe. These workers ran a radio station called Paik-i Iran (Iran Courier), published two regular papers—the newspaper *Mardom* and the theoretical journal *Donya*—and in 1960 helped create in Europe a broad-based anti-shah organization called the Confederation of Iranian Students. The Tudeh also retained a fairly homogeneous group of leaders who had

[6] A. Qassemi, "What Really Happened," *Tofan*, no. 23 (March 1966), pp. 1-3.

[7] "New Documents on Treason," *Tofan*, no. 39 (September 1970), pp. 1-2.

[8] "A Revolutionary or a Reformist Program," *Tudeh*, 1 (April 1966), 1-3.

[9] "The Communist Movement in Iran," *Tudeh*, no. 21 (August 1971), pp. 1-92.

[10] "The Revisionists and the Revolutionary Organization," *Tofan*, no. 40 (December 1970), pp. 3-4; Tofan Marxist-Leninist Organization, *Nemuneh-i Manfi* (Negative Symbiosis) (n.p., 1970), pp. 1-78.

[11] Revolutionary Organization, *Mosabat-i Dovomin Konferans* (Regulation for the Second Conference) (n.p., 1965), pp. 1-15.

worked together since the early 1940s—leaders such as Iraj Iskandari, Kianouri, Radmanesh, Jowdat, Tabari, and Maryam Firuz. These elder leaders were helped in the late 1960s by a younger group of party activists, many of whom had been forced out of Tehran University in 1953 and had completed their higher degrees in Eastern Europe.

Moreover, the Tudeh managed to iron out its old-time differences with the Democratic Party of Azerbaijan. After a series of joint meetings between 1956 and 1960, the two merged to form a new organization named The Tudeh Party of Iran—The Party of the Iranian Working Class.[12] As a part of the final settlement, the Azerbaijan Democrats accepted the dominant position of the Tudeh; agreed that class issues were more important than the national question; and admitted that in 1946-1947 they had not done enough to coordinate their activities with the Tudeh. In return, the Tudeh brought Daneshyan, the chairman of the Azerbaijan Democrats, into its Politbureau; recognized the Democrats as the provincial branch of the Tudeh in Azerbaijan; agreed to the Democrats continuing to publish their Azeri-language paper named *Azerbaijan*; confessed that in 1941-1947 the party had underestimated the national problem; eulogized the late Pishevari as "the representative of the aspirations of the Azerbaijani people"; and formulated a new program acceptable to the Azerbaijan Democrats. The new program accepted the view that Iran was formed of diverse nationalities and that these nationalities had the right to advocate self-determination for themselves; but it also stressed that many cultural, historical, and political bonds brought together these same nationalities within the framework of the Iranian state. To strengthen these bonds, the party program declared that the central government should end discrimination against the non-Persians, establish provincial assemblies, and permit the use of national languages in schools, publishing houses, and local institutions.[13] The Tudeh thereby accepted the principle of national self-determination without actually advocating such self-determination.

Furthermore, the Tudeh managed to clarify many of the ambiguities left in the previous party programs. In a series of conferences held in Eastern Europe between 1956 and 1964, the Tudeh for the first time declared itself a Marxist-Leninist organization; voted to participate formally in international meetings of other communist parties;

[12] H. Farvardin, "Fifth Anniversary of Union," *Mahnameh-i Mardom* 6 (June-July 1965), 1-5; R. Radmanesh, "The December 12th Movement," *Donya*, 6 (Winter 1965), 9-18; "Concerning the December 12th Movement," *Donya*, 4 (September 1963), 156-69.

[13] Tudeh Party, *Barnameh va Asasnameh-i Hizb* (Program and Regulations of the Party) (Europe, 1960), pp. 7-8.

openly supported the Soviet Union on international issues and defended the Soviet sale of arms to Iran. It demanded—again for the first time—the establishment of a "democratic republic"; advocated that land should be given to the tiller but insisted that the shah's land reform would not benefit the peasantry; and, rejecting violence, argued that the regime could be brought down through peaceful methods: through formation of underground cells, infiltration of government unions, distribution of anti-shah literature, instigation of strikes in universities, offices and factories, organization of street demonstrations, and, if possible, even participation in parliamentary elections. The Tudeh also criticized itself for pursuing a "left sectarian" policy in 1951-1953 and giving only half-hearted support to Mossadeq; called for the formation of a patriotic united front against the shah and the United States; praised the National Front as a "national democratic movement"; applauded the "progressive clergy," especially Ayatallah Khomeini, for opposing the "capitulations" given to American military advisers; and, while admitting that the "final goal was the construction of a socialist society in Iran," stressed that the immediate goal was the establishment of a "national democratic republic."[14] In the words of the new party program,

In the present situation the main tasks confronting those who aspire for a revolutionary transformation of Iran is the overthrow of the anachronistic monarchy, the destruction of the reactionary state machinery, the abolition of big capitalists and landlords, and the transfer of power from these classes to the classes and strata that are patriotic and democratic—i.e. the workers, peasants, urban petit bourgeoisie (tradesmen, shopkeepers, and craftsmen), patriotic and progressive intelligentsia, and strata of national bourgeoisie. In short, the task is to establish a national democratic republic.[15]

Although the other parties rejected the offer of an alliance, the Tudeh succeeded in making modest gains during the early 1970s. For one thing, young militants who had left the party at the height of the Sino-Soviet dispute began to return to the fold. They returned partly because the two Maoist parties—the Revolutionary Organization and the Tofan group—failed to deliver their much promised "armed struggle"; partly because China, after Mao's death, lost its mystique as the world's revolutionary stronghold; but mainly because China during the 1970s openly supported the shah as a bulwark against Soviet "social imperialism," endorsed the vast arms expendi-

[14] Tudeh Party, "Our Tasks and the Country's Situation (The Thesis of the Eleventh Plenum of the Central Committee)," *Mahnameh-i Mardom*, 5 (February 1964), 1-4.

[15] Tudeh Party, *Barnameh-i Hizb-i Tudeh-i Iran* (The Program of the Tudeh Party of Iran) (n.p., 1964), p. 26.

tures, and even applauded Iran's military alliance with the West. By 1977, little remained of these two organizations except their newspapers *Tofan* and *Setareh-i Surkh* (Red Star). The Tudeh, on the other hand, had some five thousand members in Europe and Iran; published, in addition to *Mardom* and *Donya*, *Nuyid* (Harbinger) in Tehran and *Shu'leh-i Jenoub* (Southern Flame) in Khuzistan; and had small underground cells in Tehran University, in the oil regions, and in the major industrial centers. Moreover, by the early 1970s the Tudeh, together with the other opposition groups, was able to organize university strikes every year without fail on Azar 16 (December 7), the date designated as national student day by the Confederation of Iranian Students in honor of three demonstrators (two from the Tudeh and one from the National Front) who had been killed in Tehran University on December 7, 1953, while protesting the state visit of Vice President Nixon. In fact, Azar 16 became a useful gauge for measuring the regime's unpopularity and, conversely, the opposition's strength among the young intelligentsia.

The National Front. Most of the National Front leaders that had been arrested in August 1953 were released in the course of 1954. Although many of them emigrated or retired from politics, some maintained secret contact with Mossadeq (who remained under house arrest until his death in 1967) and in late 1954 reemerged under the new name of the National Resistance Movement (Nahzat-i Moqavemat-i Melli). Prominent in this organization were Sanjabi, the main spokesman of the Iran party and the former dean of the law faculty, who had served as minister of education in Mossadeq's last cabinet; Hasebi, Zirakzadeh, Zanganeh, and Asghar Parsa—four other old-time leaders of the Iran party who had held high positions in Mossadeq's administration; Shahpour Bakhtiyar, a younger member of the Iran party and a Paris-educated political scientist whose father, a Bakhtiyari khan, had been murdered by Reza Shah; Foruhar, the lawyer and founder of the pro-Mossadeq National party who had spent six months in prison after the 1953 coup d'état; and Khalel Maleki, the Marxist intellectual who after the coup changed the name of his Third Force to the Society of Iranian Socialists (Jam'eh-i Sosiyalist-ha-yi Iran).

Also prominent in the National Resistance Movement were Mehdi Bazargan and Hojjat al-Islam Mahmud Taleqani. Bazargan, who was to play a crucial role in 1978-1979, had been politically active since 1941. The son of a wealthy and highly pious bazaari merchant from Azerbaijan, Bazargan had been born in Tehran in 1906, raised in a distinctly devout milieu, and sent in 1931 to study civil engineering in Paris, where he had embarrassed his more secular compatriots by conscientiously performing his religious rituals and daily prayers. Returning home in 1936, he taught at the College of Science and Technology and, after Reza Shah's abdication, helped form not only the Engineer's Association and the Iran party, but also an Islamic Student Society at Tehran University. In his own words, the intention of this student society was to stem the Tudeh tide that threatened to engulf the whole university.[16] Indeed, his deep anticommunist convictions prompted him to resign from the Iran party in 1946 to protest that party's alliance with the Tudeh. From 1947 until 1951, he worked closely with Mossadeq, taught at the university, and eventually became the dean of the College of Science and Technology. With the election of Mossadeq as premier, Bazargan was sent to Abadan to settle labor disputes and serve as the first director of the National Iranian Oil Company. After the coup, he was allowed to sit on the board of the Tehran water authority, teach at the university, and continue encouraging the Islamic Student Society. As one of his closest colleagues later admitted, the society had little appeal before 1953 but gained some ground after the coup, since it was the only nongovernment organization permitted to function on the university campus.[17] Although deeply devout, Bazargan was critical of clerics such as Kashani who had betrayed Mossadeq, and was unwilling to follow the example of the religious establishment in giving tacit approval to the 1953 coup.

Taleqani, who became an Ayatallah later, was a maverick among the religious leaders. Born in 1910 in the village of Taleqan near Yazd, he received his early education from his father, a local mulla who had participated in the constitutional movement and who earned an income repairing watches, since he refused to live off public charity. In the early 1930s, the younger Taleqani went to Qum to study theology at the famous Fayzieh seminary. Completing his education in 1938, he moved to Tehran and taught scripture at a secondary school until 1940, when his antiregime lectures earned him a six-month jail sentence. This was to be only the first of many jail sentences. After Reza Shah's abdication, Taleqani remained in Tehran and became the main preacher at the Hedayat Mosque which, at the time, was a meeting center for a small group of radical clergymen. In the period between 1949 and 1953, he staunchly supported Mossadeq but was not prominent in national politics, partly because of his relative youth and partly because of Ayatallah Kashani's seniority. But when Kashani ceased to help Mossadeq, Taleqani became the main cleric in Teh-

[16] Bazargan, *Dafaʿat dar Dadgah* (Defense at the Court) (n.p., 1964), pp. 27-28.
[17] Narrated by E. Sahabi in N. Hariri, *Mosahebeh ba Tarikhsazan-i Iran* (Interviews with Makers of Iranian History) (Tehran, 1979), pp. 173-74.

ran—if not in the whole of Iran—openly supporting the National Front. Forced into retirement by the 1953 coup, he wrote two important works. One, a commentary on a constitutionalist treatise written in 1910, argued that Shi'ism was inherently against autocracy and for democracy. The other, entitled *Islam va Malekiyat* (Islam and Property), argued that socialism and religion were compatible because God had created the world for mankind and had no intention of dividing humanity into exploiting and exploited classes. Taleqani, like Bazargan, had two interrelated missions in life: to show that Islam had answers for modern problems and therefore was relevant to the contemporary world; and to bridge the deep gulf separating devout believers from secular reformers, traditional bazaaris from modern-educated professionals, conservative antiregime clerics from forward-looking radical intellectuals, and the religious establishment in Qum from the patriotic intelligentsia of the National Front. In short, they aimed at resolving the deep-seated issues that had helped wreck the constitutional movement as well as the 1949-1953 national struggle.

Although the National Resistence Movement began with high hopes, within four years it was in complete disarray. A number of factors accounted for the collapse. In 1956 the regime arrested almost all its leaders on the grounds that the organization was undermining the "constitutional monarchy." Moreover, the leadership divided: some—notably Bazargan and Taleqani—insisted on denouncing the shah by name and dismissing the whole regime as illegitimate, whereas others preferred to focus their attacks on specific issues and on particular ministers. The Iran party was convinced that if America restrained SAVAK, Mossadeq's supporters could win enough Majles seats to become a genuine parliamentary opposition. Khalel Maleki went even further and argued that the opposition could help destroy feudalism if it openly supported the liberal wing of the upper class against the more reactionary landlords. This gave the public the impression that secular radicals were wishy-washy reformers but religious radicals were uncompromising revolutionaries. Furthermore, the religious radicals, notably Bazargan, hoped to establish a working alliance with the 'ulama, whereas the secular radicals feared that such an alliance would tarnish their reputation as progressive reformers. Their fears were reinforced in late 1959 when Ayatallah Boroujerdi, in an open letter to Ayatallah Behbehani, tried to quash all talk of land reform by declaring that Islam protected the rights of private property.[18]

[18] Quoted by W. Floor, "The Revolutionary Character of the Iranian *'Ulama*: Wishful Thinking or Reality?" (unpublished paper, Netherlands, 1979), p. 8.

Thus internal conflicts and police repression combined to destroy the National Resistance Movement.

But the slight relaxation of police controls in 1960-1963 revitalized the opposition. Taking advantage of the new situation, Sanjabi, Foruhar, and Khalel Maleki recreated, respectively, the Iran party, National party, and Socialist Society, and then reestablished the National Front, naming it the Second National Front. Meanwhile, Taleqani, Bazargan, and a circle of like-minded reformers formed a group named the Liberation Movement of Iran (Nahzat-i Azad-i Iran), and joined it to the new National Front. In joining the Front, the Liberation Movement declared that its main goals were to strengthen the National Front and to "serve the people's religious, social, and national needs."[19] It also declared, "we are Muslims, Iranians, constitutionalists, and Mossadeqists: Muslims because we refuse to divorce our principles from our politics; Iranians because we respect our national heritage; constitutionalists because we demand freedom of thought, expression, and association; Mossadeqists because we want national independence."[20]

For three years the National Front was active again. It revived the newspaper *Bakhtar-i Emruz*; helped organize strikes both in the universities and in the major high schools; convened a Congress and elected a broad-based Central Committee; recruited a number of prominent guild leaders, bazaar merchants, and academics; and held a series of rallies, one of which drew as many as 100,000 people. Nevertheless, the National Front did not take long to collapse, for much the same reasons as before. After the bloody riots of June 1963, the shah clamped down hard, arresting many of the opposition leaders and again outlawing the affiliates of the National Front. Moreover, this time the internal divisions were even sharper than before, since they involved not just ideological issues but also tactical and organizational problems. Some, especially in the Liberation Movement and the Socialist Society, wanted to wage an ideological war against the regime and debate theoretical issues within the National Front. But others, especially in the Iran party, preferred to keep clear of ideological wrangles and attack the regime on concrete grievances such as the continued house imprisonment of Mossadeq, the lack of press freedom, and the proposed sale of state factories to wealthy busi-

[19] "The Liberation Movement and the National Front," *Nahzat-i Azad-i Iran*, 11 June 1961.

[20] "The Aims of the Liberation Movement," *Mujahed*, 5 (April 1977), 1-4; "Fifteenth Anniversary of the Liberation Movement," *Mujahed*, 4 (April 1976), 1-5; M. Mirzayi, "The Formation of the Liberation Movement," *Ittila'at*, 16 May 1979.

nessmen.[21] On one hand, the Liberation Movement favored a full alliance with the antiregime 'ulama, even with clergymen who openly opposed land reform and women's suffrage. On the other hand, the other organizations resisted such an alliance and formulated the slogan "Reform Yes, Dictatorship No."[22] Finally, the leaders of the Iran party, anxious to control radical elements within the movement, tried to transform the National Front from a loose coalition of independent organizations into a tightly knit party with one center, one official organ, and one political strategy. Not surprisingly, the Liberation Movement, the National party, and the Socialist Society resisted such attempts and insisted that the National Front should continue as a broad alliance of autonomous organizations.[23]

These frictions, especially over organizational issues, in 1965 broke the National Front into two rival blocs. One bloc, formed mostly of Iran party members, retained the title Second National Front, intensified its activities among the Confederation of Iranian Students in Europe, and continued to publish *Bakhtar-i Emruz* and to call for the establishment of a secular democratic state in Iran. The other bloc, formed of the Liberation Movement, the National party, and the Socialist Society, declared itself the Third National Front. Active among students in France and North America, the Third National Front published two newspapers—*Iran Azad* (Free Iran) and *Khabarnameh* (Newsletter)—and tried to establish a working relationship with exiled religious leaders, especially Khomeini in Iraq. As *Khabarnameh* stated in an article entitled "The Lessons of 1963,"

During Muharram 1963, it was the religious leaders and not the political parties that inspired and encouraged the masses. The major lesson to be drawn from 1963 is that the 'ulama have a crucial role to play in our anti-imperialist struggle—just as they did in the tobacco crisis of 1891-1892, in the constitutional revolution of 1905-1911, and in the nationalist movement of 1950-1953.[24]

Similarly, *Mujahed* (Freedom Fighter), the organ of the exiled Liberation Movement, declared in an editorial on "The Struggles of the Religious Leaders":

The Shi'i leaders have always helped Iran's struggle against despotism and imperialism. Since the days of the Constitutional Revolution, since the bleak years of Reza Shah's repression, and since the bloody demonstrations of 1963,

[21] National Front, *Qat'nameh* (Resolutions) (Tehran, 1963), pp. 1-2.

[22] National Front, *'Elam-i Khatar* (A Warning) (Tehran, 1963), pp. 1-2.

[23] M. Anusheh, "The Tudeh Party and the National Front," *Mahnameh-i Mardom*, 6 (September 1965), 1-5.

[24] "The Lessons of 1963," *Khabarnameh*, 7 (July 1969), 1-2.

the ʿulama have allied themselves with the masses. Ayatallah Khomeini, who has lived in exile since 1964, is now the main opponent of the regime. The shah, the so-called religious experts paid by the regime, and other national traitors do their very best to drive a wedge between us and the progressive religious leaders. . . . We will do all we can to create unity between the political opposition and the religious leaders, especially Ayatallah Khomeini. United we will destroy the hated regime.[25]

The Liberation Movement. Among the many groups affiliated with the National Front, the Liberation Movement was to play the most important role in the Islamic Revolution. The Liberation Movement owed its success mainly to the close links it established with Khomeini; and partly to Bazargan's and Taleqani's ability to attract a number of young professionals and radical technocrats, who, although modern-educated, sought to synthesize Islam and Western science. Even though the Liberation Movement was officially banned in 1963, it continued to hold secret meetings in Tehran, and to organize abroad, particularly in North America and France. After the Islamic revolution it obtained the key positions in Bazargan's Provisional Government.

In Tehran, the group's leadership included—besides Bazargan and Taleqani—Dr. Yadallah Sahabi, ʿEzatallah Sahabi, Hassan Nazeh, Dr. ʿAbbas Shaybani, and Sadeq Tabatabai. Yadallah Sahabi, a professor of geology at Tehran University, was an old friend of Bazargan. Together they had joined and left the Iran party, and then formed the Islamic Student Society, the National Resistance Movement, and finally the Liberation Movement. ʿEzatallah Sahabi, his son, had joined the Islamic Student Society while studying engineering in Tehran University. Sentenced to a four-year term in 1964, he was to spend much of the decade in and out of prison. Nazeh, who was to become the director of the National Iranian Oil Company after the revolution, was a young lawyer who had worked closely with Bazargan since the early 1950s. Born in Azerbaijan, Nazeh had been raised in Tehran and educated in Switzerland. Shaybani, a medical doctor, had entered politics through the Islamic Student Society and had been expelled from Tehran University in 1956 for organizing a demonstration in support of Nasser. Finally, Tabatabai, who was to become the first Minister of Information in the Islamic Republic, had studied in Lebanon and West Germany. He was also related by marriage both to Ayatallah Khomeini and to Imam Sadr, the leader of the Shiʿi community in Lebanon.

In North America, the Liberation Movement was led by four exiled

[25] "The Struggles of the Religious Leaders," *Mujahed*, 1 (September 1972), 1-2.

intellectuals: Muhammad Nakhshab, Dr. Ibrahim Yazdi, Mustowfa Chamran, and ʿAbbas Amir Entezam. Nakhshab, the oldest of the four, had entered politics in 1944 when, as a high school student in Rasht, he had joined the Iran party. Opposed to the Tudeh alliance, he soon left the party and formed first the Movement of God-Worshiping Socialists (Nahzat-i Khoda Parastan-i Sosiyalist) and later his Iranian People's party (Hizb-i Mardom-i Iran). Although neither organization succeeded in attracting many members, Nakhshab can be credited with being the first Iranian to attempt to synthesize Shiʿism with European socialism. After a spell in prison during 1953-1954, he moved to America, worked at United Nations, and, while completing a doctorate in public administration in New York University, represented the Third National Front within the U.S. division of the Iranian Student Confederation. Withdrawing from the confederation in the mid 1960s, he helped establish an Islamic Student Society (Anjuman-i Daneshjoyan-i Islami) in North America, and wrote articles for *Mujahed*, the exiled organ of the Liberation Movement. Having devoted much of his life to the radical cause, Nakhshab died in New York on the eve of the Islamic Revolution.

Yazdi, Nakhshab's main assistant in the Islamic Student Society, was an oncologist working in Texas. He had started his political activities as a student member of the National Resistance Movement. Sent to the U.S. in 1962 to study medicine, he remained there until 1979, helped organize the Islamic Student Society, and served as the group's main link with Khomeini. After the Islamic Revolution, Yazdi became minister for foreign affairs. Chamran, who in 1979 was named defense minister, had a doctorate in civil engineering from Berkeley. Active in the California branch of the Islamic Student Society, Chamran left for the Middle East in the mid 1960s, and received guerrilla training from both the Egyptian army and Amal, the Shiʿi militia in southern Lebanon. Entezam, another Berkeley graduate, was an early member of the Liberation Movement. Black-listed because of his student activities, Entezam had been sent by his father, a wealthy carpet manufacturer, to California to complete his engineering degree. While in America, he was active within the confederation as well as the Islamic Student Society. Permitted to return home in the early 1970s, he kept his ties with Yazdi, and set up a flourishing construction company. After the revolution, he became a deputy prime minister.

In France, the Liberation Movement and its Islamic Student Society were organized mostly by Sadeq Qotbzadeh and Abdul Hassan Bani Sadr. Qotbzadeh, a son of a bazaar merchant, had been an ardent supporter of Kashani during the early 1950s. Studying languages in Washington, D.C., in the 1960s, he had helped set up the local branch of the Student Confederation, but soon left that organization, claiming that it was dominated by Maoists. Moving to Paris, Qotbzadeh served as the main link between the Islamic Student Society in Europe and the radical Arab states, especially Algeria, Iraq, and Syria. Immediately after the Islamic Revolution, he obtained the vital post of director of National Iranian Radio and Television. Bani Sadr, the son of a highly respected ayatallah in Hamadan, was in Paris working toward a doctorate in economics. Initiated into politics during the 1951-1953 crisis while still in high school, Bani Sadr remained an active supporter of Mossadeq throughout the 1950s, although he scrupulously avoided joining any political party. Going into exile in the early 1960s, he continued to shun party affiliation, but helped the Liberation Movement and the Third National Front by joining the Islamic Student Society and writing numerous articles denouncing the state of the Iranian economy. In these articles, he argued that the multinational corporations had taken over; that the shah was systematically destroying agriculture to help foreign agrobusinesses; that the "state apparatus bourgeoisie" was wasting the country's precious resources on conspicuous consumption; and that the new industries, especially the assembly plants, were increasing Iran's dependence on the West.[26] To end this sorry situation, he argued, Iran had to end its dependence on the West, achieve self-sufficiency, particularly in food production, establish indigenous industries, and, on the intellectual level, formulate an "Islamic theory of economics." Any attempt he may have made to formulate such a theory must have been cut short by the Islamic Revolution.

But the outstanding intellectual of the Liberation Movement—if not of the whole of contemporary Iran—was a young Paris-educated sociologist named ʿAli Shariʿati. Born in 1933 in a village in north Khurasan, Shariʿati grew up partly in his home village and partly in Mashad, the nearest large town. As he later wrote, his approach to life was very much influenced by his father, a militant Muslim who, though not a trained mulla, taught Islamic history in local schools and came from a long line of competent scholars who had refused to leave their home province for the hustle and bustle of Tehran.[27] As a school boy, Shariʿati had attended political discussion groups organized by his father, and, together with him had joined the Movement of God-Worshiping Socialists. Following his father's footsteps, he decided to become an educator, entered the teachers' training college in Mashad, studied Arabic with his father, and, graduating from the college in

---

[26] P. Vieille and A. Bani Sadr, eds., *Petrole et Violence* (Oil and Violence) (Paris, 1974); A. Nobari, ed., *Iran Erupts* (Stanford, 1978).

[27] Cited in "The Life of Martyr ʿAli Shariʿati," *Mujahed*, 5 (July 1977), 1-9.

1953, worked for four years in elementary schools in north Khurasan. While teaching, he translated from Arabic and published in Mashad a book entitled *Abu Zarr: Khoda Parast-i Sosiyalist* (Abu Zarr: The God-Worshiping Socialist). Written by a radical Egyptian novelist, ʿAbdul Hamid Jowdat al-Sahar, the book traced the life of one of the Prophet's first followers, who, after Muhammad's death, denounced the caliph as corrupt, supported ʿAli, and on the latter's defeat, withdrew to the desert to lead a simple existence and keep alive the Islamic tradition of speaking out on behalf of the hungry poor against the greedy rich. For al-Sahar and Shariʿati, as for many other radicals in the Middle East, Abu Zarr was the first Muslim socialist. As the elder Shariʿati later wrote, his son considered Abu Zarr to be one of the greatest figures in Islamic history.[28]

In 1958 ʿAli Shariʿati entered Mashad University to study for a masters degree in foreign languages, specializing in Arabic and French. Upon completing his degree in 1960, he won a state scholarship to study for a doctorate in sociology and Islamic studies in Paris. In Paris at the height of the Algerian and Cuban revolutions, he immersed himself in student politics as well as in radical political philosophy. He joined the Liberation Movement and the Iranian Student Confederation; organized numerous demonstrations in support of Algeria—after one such demonstration he spent three days in hospital recovering from head wounds; and edited both *Iran Azad*, the organ of the Third National Front in Europe, and *Nameh-i Pars* (Pars Letter), the monthly journal of the Iranian Student Confederation in France. He also took courses with a number of famous Orientalists, attended lectures given by Marxist professors, and read the works of such contemporary radicals as Jean Paul Sartre, Che Guevera, Giap, and, of course, Fanon. In fact, he translated Guevera's *Guerrilla Warfare* and Sartre's *What Is Poetry?*, and started to translate Fanon's *Wretched of the Earth* and the *Fifth Year of the Algerian War*. While translating the last work, Shariʿati wrote three letters to Fanon challenging him on the question of religion and revolution. According to Fanon, the peoples of the Third World had to give up their own religions in order to fight against Western imperialism. But according to Shariʿati, the peoples of the Third World could not fight imperialism unless they first regained their cultural identity, which, in some countries, was interwoven with popular religious traditions.[29] They had to return to their religious roots before they could challenge the West.

Shariʿati returned to Iran in 1965. After spending six months in

[28] Cited in ʿA. Shariʿati, *Abu Zarr* (n.p., 1978), p. v.
[29] ʿA. Shariʿati, *Islam Shenasi* (Islamology) (n.p., 1972), Lesson 13, pp. 15-17.

jail, and on being denied a teaching position in Tehran University, he returned to Khurasan, where he taught first in a village school and later in Mashad University. But in 1967 he moved to Tehran to take up a lectureship at the Husseinieh-i Ershad, a religious meeting hall financed by veterans from the Liberation Movement. The next six years were to be the most productive in Shariʻati's life, for he regularly lectured at the Husseinieh, and these lectures were later transcribed into some fifty book-length volumes. Moreover, tapes of his lectures were circulated widely and received instant acclaim from college and high-school students, especially those with provincial but Shiʻi backgrounds. Growing fearful of Shariʻati's popularity and his more frequent references to contemporary problems, SAVAK in 1972 closed down the Husseinieh, arrested Shariʻati, and banned most of his works. He remained in prison until 1975, when a petition from the Algerian government secured his release. Kept under house detention for another two years, in May 1977 he was permitted to go to London where he died suddenly, a month later. His admirers argued that he had been murdered by SAVAK. The British coroner, however, reported that he had died of a massive heart attack. Even though Shariʻati did not live to see the shah's downfall, he is justly credited as the main intellectual, even the Fanon, of the Islamic Revolution.

To pacify the censors, Shariʻati spoke in allegories, used words with double meanings, and often avoided direct reference to immediate issues. Despite the sophistry, his works had one clear message: that Islam—particularly Shiʻism—is not a conservative, fatalistic creed, as charged by many secular intellectuals, nor an apolitical personal faith, as claimed by some reactionary clerics; but rather a revolutionary ideology that permeates all spheres of life, especially politics, and inspires true believers to fight against all forms of oppression, exploitation, and social injustice. The Prophet, Shariʻati stressed, had come to establish not just a community but a Muslim Ummat—a dynamic community in constant motion toward progress; and not just a monotheistic religion but a Nezam-i Towhid—a social order that would be completely united by virtue, striving toward justice, equity, human brotherhood, public ownership of wealth, and, most important of all, a classless society. Moreover, the Shiʻi Imams, especially Hussein, had raised the banner of revolt because their contemporary rulers—the corrupt caliphs and the court elites—had betrayed the Ummat and given up the goals of a Nezam-i Towhid. Thus, for Shariʻati, the Muharram passion plays depicting Hussein's martyrdom at Karbala contained one major lesson: that all Shiʻis, irrespective of time and place, had the duty to oppose, resist, and even rebel against overwhelming odds in order to eradicate their contemporary ills. As far as his own Iran was concerned, Shariʿati listed these ills as world imperialism, international Zionism, colonialism, exploitation, oppression, class inequality, cartels, multinational corporations, racism, cultural imperialism, and gharbzadegi (blindly following the West).[30]

While denouncing Western imperialism and class inequalities as the main long-range enemies, much of Shariʿati's works focus on two immediate targets: Marxism, especially the "Stalinist variety" that had been readily accepted by the previous generation of the Iranian intelligentsia; and misinterpretations of Islam, particularly the "conservative brand" of apolitical Islam that some members of the clergy fed to the Iranian masses. Because of these two targets, Shariʿati became highly controversial not only among the authorities but also within the opposition and the clerical establishment. Some, taking his religious slogans at their face value, concluded he was a devout believer and therefore a devoted follower of the traditional ʿulama. Others, surprised by his denunciations of the conservative clergy, suspected that he was a deep-seated anticlerical innovator who presented his secular alien ideas within an Islamic garb—that is, a modern Malkum Khan. Some, struck by his anti-imperialist and anticapitalist outlook, labeled him an Islamic Marxist. Others, impressed by his devotion to the Islamic world, praised him as the Muslim answer to Marx. Shariʿati, however, viewed himself as neither a Muslim Marxist nor an anti-Marxist Muslim, but rather a radical theorist who found his inspiration in Shiʿism and his tools of political analysis in Western social science—especially in Marxism. In short, Shariʿati saw himself as continuing and completing what the previous generation of radical believers, notably Bazargan, Taleqani, and Nakhshab, had started: formulating a secular religion that would appeal to the modern intelligentsia without alienating the traditional bazaaris and the religious masses.

Shariʿati had a love-hate relationship with Marxism. On the one hand, he admitted that one could not understand society and modern history without a knowledge of Marxism. He agreed with much of the paradigm that divided society into an economic base, a class structure, and a political-ideological superstructure. He even agreed that most religions should be placed within the last category, since rulers invariably tried to "drug" the masses with promises of rewards in the next world.[31] He accepted the view that much of human history is a history of class struggles. But in accepting this view, he added that

---

[30] ʿA. Shariʿati, *Shiʿi: Yek Hizb-i Tamam* (Shiʿis: A Complete Party) (n.p., 1976), pp. 27, 55; Shariʿati, *Islam Shenasi*, Lesson 2, p. 101; Shariʿati, *ʿAli Tanha Ast* (ʿAli Is Alone) (n.p., 1978), pp. 1-35.

[31] Shariʿati, *Bazgasht* (Return) (n.p., 1978), p. 81; Shariʿati, *Islam Shenasi*, Lesson 14, pp. 1-5; Shariʿati, *Mazhab ʿAliyeh Mazhab* (Religion against Religion) (n.p., 1978), p. 19.

the major struggles evolved around political power and not around material possessions. In his own words, since the days of Cain and Abel mankind had been divided into two antagonistic camps: on one side stands the oppressed—the people; on the other side, the oppressors—the rulers. He also tried to dispel the notion that Marx had been a crude materialist and an economic determinist who had viewed mankind as a cynical self-seeking herd and had refused to recognize the important role played by high ideals in the shaping of human history. In fact, Shari'ati praised Marx for being far less materialistic than most "self-styled idealists and religious believers."[32]

On the other hand, Shari'ati was highly critical of some aspects of Marxism—especially "institutionalized" Marxism of orthodox Communist parties.[33] He—like Fanon—argued that these parties, as well as other socialist movements in Europe, had fallen victim to the iron law of bureaucracy: that, having won mass support and government recognition, they had institutionalized themselves and thereby lost their revolutionary fervor.[34] He—again like Fanon—charged that these parties denied aid to national liberation movements, and refused to admit that in the modern age the main struggle was not between capitalists and workers but between imperialists and the Third World. Moreover, Shari'ati argued that much of Marxism was inapplicable to Iran because the latter, unlike Europe, had been molded by the "Asiatic Mode of Production," and had not experienced the Renaissance, the Reformation, the Enlightenment, the Industrial Revolution, and the dramatic transition of feudalism into capitalism. As a result, Iran remained backward, with a public that was still highly religious, a clergy that retained a great deal of social influence, and a bazaar bourgeoisie untouched by secularism, liberalism, and even the capitalist ethic.[35] In underlining the importance of Islam in Iranian culture, Shari'ati claimed that the Tudeh had alienated the masses by being indifferent to their religious sensibilities.

When I look at the early [Tudeh] publications what do I see but such titles as "Historical Materialism," "Knowledge and the Elements of Matter," "The Materialist Concept of Humanity," "The Material Basis of Life and Thought," "Marxism and Linguistics" [by Stalin]. . . . Not surprisingly, the people formed the impression that these gentlemen were atheists, enemies of God, country, religion, ethics, spirituality, morality, holiness, honor, truth, and tradition. In other words, the public came to the conclusion that these gentlemen had one aim: destroy our religion and import foreign atheism. Communism became

[32] Shari'ati, *Islam Shenasi*, Lesson 2, pp. 88-93; Lesson 15, pp. 1-26; Lesson 14, p. 7.
[33] Ibid., Lesson 14, p. 7.
[34] Shari'ati, *Cheh Bayad Kard?* (What Is To Be Done?) (n.p., 1973), pp. 70-71.
[35] Shari'ati, *Bazgasht*, pp. 161-66, 59-72, 61-64.

synonymous with atheism. The reader is probably smirking and saying "But these criticisms are cheap, vulgar, and common." Yes they are. But the common people are after all the main audience we are trying to reach. And most of our common people are peasants—not industrial workers as in Germany—and are highly religious—not secular as in capitalist Europe and post-revolutionary France. . . . Since our peasants and workers need to be educated in the realities of colonialism, the meaning of exploitation, and the philosophy of poverty, educators should avoid works that antagonize the devout and should concentrate on masterpieces that can raise social consciousness. When I look at the thousands of books published in Iran, I am shocked to find that no one has translated *Capital*.[36]

Significantly, Shari'ati avoided applying the stock argument the clergy used against the left: that Marxists are kafer (blasphemers), and blasphemers are by definition amoral, corrupt, sinful, and wicked. On the contrary, in discussing Marxism he argued that what defined a true believer was not possession of a subjective faith in God, the soul and the afterlife, but rather the willingness to take concrete action for the truth: "Examine carefully how the Koran uses the word *kafer*. The word is only used to describe those who refuse to take action. It is never used to describe those who reject metaphysics or refuse to accept the existence of God, the soul, and the resurrection."[37]

Shari'ati's main objection to Marxism, however, related directly to his attitude toward national culture and his earlier correspondence with Fanon. For classical Marxists, nationalism was a tool used by the ruling class to distract the masses from socialism and internationalism. But for Shari'ati, the nations of the Third World would not defeat imperialism, overcome social alienation, and mature to the point where they could borrow Western technology without losing self-esteem unless they first rediscovered their roots, their national heritage, and their popular culture.[38] In a series of lectures entitled *Bazgasht* (Return), Shari'ati declares,

Now I want to turn to a fundamental question raised by intellectuals in Africa, Latin America, and Asia: the question of "return to one's roots.". . . Since World War II, many intellectuals in the Third World, whether religious or nonreligious, have stressed that their societies must return to their roots and rediscover their history, their culture, and their popular language. I want to stress that nonreligious progressives as well as some religious intellectuals have reached this conclusion. In fact, the main advocates of "return to one's roots" have not been religious—Franz Fanon in Algeria, Julius Nyerere in Tanzania, Jomo Kenyatta in Kenya, Leopold Senghor in Senegal. . . . When

---

[36] Ibid., pp. 48-50.
[37] Shari'ati, *Islam Shenasi*, Lesson 13, pp. 7-8.
[38] Shari'ati, *Tamadon va Tajadod* (Civilization and Progress) (n.p., 1974), pp. 1-29.

we say "return to one's roots" we are really saying "return to one's cultural roots.". . . Some of you may conclude that we Iranians must return to our racial [Aryan] roots. I categorically reject this conclusion. I oppose racism, fascism, and reactionary returns. Moreover, Islamic civilization has worked like scissors and has cut us off completely from our pre-Islamic past. The experts, such as archaeologists and ancient historians, may know a great deal about the Sassanids, the Achaemedians, and even the earlier civilizations, but our people know nothing about such things. Our people do not find their roots in these civilizations. They are left unmoved by the heroes, geniuses, myths, and monuments of these ancient empires. Our people remember nothing from this distant past and do not care to learn about the pre-Islamic civilizations. . . . Consequently, for us return to our roots means not a rediscovery of preIslamic Iran, but a return to our Islamic, especially Shi'i, roots.[39]

Even while advocating a return to Islam, Shari'ati frequently criticized the traditional 'ulama in order to differentiate himself from conservative clerical Islam. As he declared,

It is not enough to say we must return to Islam. Such a statement has no meaning. We have to specify which Islam: that of Abu Zarr or that of Marwan the Ruler. Both are Islam, but there is a huge difference between the two. One is the Islam of the caliphate, of the palace, and of the rulers. The other is the Islam of the people, of the exploited, and of the poor. Which Islam do you advocate? Moreover, it is not enough to say that you advocate an Islam that is "concerned" with the poor. The caliphs said the same. True Islam is more than "concerned" with the poor. It struggles for justice, equality, and elimination of poverty.[40]

We have to clarify that we want the Islam of Abu Zarr, not that of the royal palace; of justice and true leadership, not that of the caliphs, class stratification, and aristocratic privileges; of freedom, progress, and awareness, not that of captivity, stagnation, and silence. We want the Islam of fighters, not that of *rouhani* [spiritual leaders]; the Islam of the 'Ali family, not that of the Safavi dynasty.[41]

Shari'ati made explicit and implicit criticisms of the conservative 'ulama. He accused them of becoming a part of the ruling class, of "institutionalizing" revolutionary Shi'ism, and thereby transforming it into a highly conservative religion. As he often stated, the mullas, together with the rulers and the wealthy, were an integral part of the oppressive class: "In the early stages of social development, the oppressors are represented by one individual—Cain. But as society develops, they form three dimensions: political—power; economic—

---

[39] Shari'ati, *Bazgasht*, pp. 11-30.
[40] Shari'ati, *Islam Shenasi*, Lesson 13, pp. 14-15.
[41] Ibid., Lesson 2, p. 98.

wealth; and religious—asceticism."[42] He also implicitly accused the conservative ʿulama of refusing to continue the work started by nineteenth-century reformers such as Jamal al-Din al-Afghani; of opposing progressive ideas imported from the West, particularly the constitutional laws of 1906-1909; and of demanding blind obedience from their congregations, preventing the public from gaining access to the basic texts, and trying to retain their monopolistic control over the scriptures.[43] Moreover, he argued that the conservative ʿulama refused to look ahead and instead looked back for some mythical "glorious age"; treated the scriptures as if they were fossilized scholastic sources rather than an inspiration for a dynamic revolutionary world outlook; and failed to grasp the true meaning of vital words such as Ummat, and thus forced Muslim intellectuals to turn to European Orientalists like Montgomery Watt.[44]

Furthermore, Shariʿati often stressed that the return to true Islam would be led not by the ʿulama but by the progressive rushanfekran (intelligentsia). In *Return*, he argued that the Islamic "renaissance" and "reformation" would be brought about more by the rushanfekran than by the traditional clergy. In a lecture entitled *Mahzab ʿAliyeh Mazhab* (Religion against Religion), he claimed that in the modern age the rushanfekran were the true interpreters of religion. In a work named *Cheh Bayad Kard?* (What Is To Be Done?), he insisted that the progressive intellectuals were the genuine exponents of dynamic revolutionary Islam.[45] Similarly, he declared in a pamphlet entitled *Entezar* (Expectation):

There are two different Islams. One is the revolutionary ideology for social development, progress, and enlightenment. The other is the scholastic education of philosophers, theologians, statesmen, and jurists (*faqih*). Islam as a revolutionary ideology belongs to Abu Zarr, the mujahedin (fighters), and now the intelligentsia. Islam as a scholastic education belongs to Abu ʿAli Sina, the mujtaheds, and the religious experts (ʿalem). The latter form of Islam can be understood by foreign specialists and even reactionary individuals. On the other hand, revolutionary Islam can be understood by the uneducated. In fact, sometimes the comprehension of the uneducated for genuine Islam surpasses that of the faqih, ʿalem, and prestigious theologian.[46]

[42] Shariʿati, *Cheh Bayad Kard?*, pp. 70-77; Shariʿati, *Islam Shenasi*, Lesson 2, p. 88, 93.

[43] Shariʿati, *Cheh Bayad Kard?*, pp. 31-33; Shariʿati, *Islam Shenasi*, Lesson 7, pp. 106-107.

[44] Shariʿati, *Entezar* (Expectation) (n.p., 1978), pp. 36-37; Shariʿati, *Islam Shenasi*, Lesson 1, pp. 13-32; Shariʿati, *Shiʿi*, p. 27.

[45] Shariʿati, *Bazgasht*, pp. 11-12; Shariʿati, *Mazhab ʿAliyeh Mazhab*, p. 44; Shariʿati, *Cheh Bayad Kard?*, p. 36.

[46] Shariʿati, *Entezar*, p. 21.

Shari'ati had immediate success among the young generation of the intelligentsia, especially among the thousands of graduates produced every year by the new provincial universities, high schools, and technical, vocational, and teachers' training schools. Like Shari'ati, many of his followers were born into the propertied middle class—into bazaar, clerical, and small landed families—grew up in devout households, and took advantage of the recent growth in the educational system to enter the new universities, colleges, and specialized schools. Like Shari'ati, his followers harbored a host of deep-seated grievances against the Pahlevi dynasty. They felt that the regime deprived them of access to political power; rode roughshod over their cultural sensibilities; and favored the rich at the expense of the middle and lower classes. Moreover, they argued that the regime spent vast sums on arms to help the American economy; ignored agriculture to help foreign grain exporters; betrayed national interests by allying with Israel and the West against the Arabs and the Third World; and mimicked the West in order to destroy national identity and transform Iran into what at best would be a second-rate European state. Furthermore, they could neither forget nor forgive the regime for receiving British and American assistance in 1921 and 1953, respectively; for overthrowing Mossadeq, their political hero; and for making a mockery of the 1906 constitution which, in their eyes, was the main achievement of modern Iran. Thus they were eager for a revolution that would overthrow the regime and the wealthy families, and radically alter the country's economic, cultural, and international policies.

Like Shari'ati, many of the young intelligentsia questioned ideologies that had inspired the previous generations. They rejected Marxism—even though they borrowed heavily from Marxist classics—partly because it originated in the West and consequently smacked of gharbzadegi; partly because it was considered to be anti-Islamic; partly because communist states had failed to build "just societies"; and partly because the communist countries, notably China and the Soviet Union, maintained cordial relations with the shah. At the same time, they spurned the previous form of nationalism that found inspiration in pre-Islamic Iran, especially in its ancient monarchy, imperial glory, and racial mythology. They spurned this nationalism both because it lacked roots among the popular masses, and because it was exploited extensively by the regime to legitimize the monarchy. Any attraction this nationalism may have had for the young intelligentsia was shattered by the extravagant show the shah put on in 1971 to celebrate the 2500-year anniversary of the Iranian monarchy.

Finally, many young members of the intelligentsia agreed with Shari'ati that true Islam, especially Shi'i Islam, was a revolutionary movement having nothing in common with the conservative doctrine preached by the traditional 'ulama. For the intelligentsia, true Shi'ism had little to do with rituals and ablutions, hadith interpretations, ecclesiastical jurisprudence, scholastic education, religious nostrums, pious spirituality, seeking of answers in the golden age, hairsplitting over sacred texts, mumbo-jumbo over esoteric issues, and meticulous study of handbooks (*rasalehs*) written by the most prestigious clergymen (*maraje'-i taqleds*). On the contrary, for Shari'ati's followers true Shi'ism was a dynamic religion that, on the one hand, spoke the language of the masses and could inspire them to revolt against the shah, the upper class, and the imperialists; and, on the other hand, could enable Iran to move rapidly toward the future, and adopt Western technology and even Western social science without losing its national identity—that is, to modernize itself without becoming Westernized. In short, Shari'ati produced exactly what the young intelligentsia craved: a radical layman's religion that disassociated itself from the traditional clergy and associated itself with the secular trinity of social revolution, technological innovation, and cultural self-assertion. It is significant that Shari'ati did not even pose the major question that was to trouble his disciples during the Islamic Revolution—the question of whether one could initiate a rebellion under the banner of religion and yet keep the leadership of that rebellion out of the hands of the traditional-minded religious authorities.

CLERICAL OPPOSITION (1963-1977)

In the years after the 1963 crisis, three fluid, overlapping, yet identifiable groups formed within the religious establishment. This division helps explain why no single marja'-i taqled emerged after Boroujerdi's death. The first group, probably the largest of the three, consisted of the scrupulously apolitical 'ulama. Headed by the highly respected Ayatallah Khoi Najafi, Ayatallah Ahmad Khurasani, and Ayatallah Marashi Najafi, this group felt that the clergy should avoid the dirty business of politics and should concentrate on spiritual concerns, preaching the word of God, studying within the seminaries, and training the future generation of theologians. Despite their aloofness, the apolitical clergy were eventually dragged into politics when in 1975-1977 the government initiated the onslaught against the bazaars and the religious establishment. They were willing to leave the regime alone, but that did not mean that the regime was willing to leave them alone. Moreover, they were increasingly perturbed by the inability or unwillingness of the authorities to curb what they saw as a precipitous decline in public morality. The abrupt, unplanned, and uncontrolled influx of young migrants into the cities had created sprawling shanty towns. These, in turn, had produced a vast social problem with its typical symptoms—prostitution, alcoholism, drug addiction, delinquency, suicides, and, of course, a crime wave. Shocked by these, the ʿulama reacted like clergymen anywhere in the world: they argued that moral laxity had produced the social problem, and that the only way to solve the problem was strictly to enforce the religious laws. In early industrial England, unplanned and rapid ur-banization created John Wesley and his Methodist movement. In con-temporary Iran, the same pressures helped create the Khomeini phe-nomenon and the Islamic Revolution. After the revolution, Ahmad Khomeini—the ayatallah's influential son—admitted that the vast majority of the akhunds (clergy) had been apolitical until the mid-1970s, neither opposing the shah nor openly supporting him, but had eventually joined the revolutionary movement mainly because the regime had failed to attack moral decadence and clean the streets of the "unseemly social filth."[47]

The second group can be described as the moderate clerical op-position. It was headed by Ayatallah Muhammad Reza Golpayegani, Ayatallah Muhammad Hadi Melani in Mashad, and, most important of all, Ayatallah Kazem Shariʿatmadari, the senior theologian in Qum, and as the leading Azeri mujtahed, the unofficial spokesman of the Azerbaijani clergy. Also associated with the group in Tehran was Ayatallah Zanjani, an eighty-year-old Azeri cleric who had supported both Mossadeq and the National Resistance Movement, and who re-tained close contacts with the secular National Front as well as the religious-minded Liberation Movement. Although this group op-posed the regime, especially on the questions of women's suffrage and land reform, it preferred to keep open channels of communi-cation to the shah, use these channels to moderate government pol-icies, and lobby as much as possible behind the scenes to protect the vital interests of the religious establishment. This group was also mod-erate in that it did not call for the overthrow of the monarchy, but merely the proper implementation of the 1905-1909 fundamental laws and thereby the establishment of a genine constitutional mon-archy. In appealing to the 1905-1909 laws, no doubt some moderate clergymen hoped to establish some day—for the first time—the "su-preme committee" of five mujtaheds as stipulated in the constitution to ensure that all bills passed by Parliament conformed to the holy shariʿa. The position of the moderate clerical opposition became ob-

[47] A. Khomeini, "Don't Treat the Clergy as if It Was One Group," *Ittilaʿat*, 23 Sep-tember 1979.

viously untenable in 1975-1977 when the shah slammed shut the doors, mounted the assault on the bazaars and the seminaries, and, through the Resurgence party, pressed to take over the entire religious establishment.

The third group can be described as the militant clerical opposition. Headed by Ayatallah Khomeini in Iraq, the group had an informal secret network within Iran. Ayatallah Hussein Montezari, one of the group's older members, was a former student of Khomeini and was himself a leading teacher of Islamic jurisprudence at Qum. Born in 1922 in Isfahan, he studied at the local seminary before moving onto the Fayzieh school, where he met Khomeini. Imprisoned in 1963-1964, in 1974, and again in 1975-1978, he had the reputation of being an uncompromising opponent of the regime. Ayatallah Muhammad Beheshti, the most politically astute member of the group, was also a former student of Khomeini. After graduating from Fayzieh, he retained close links with Khomeini even while studying languages in Europe, writing textbooks for the Ministry of Education, and heading the government-financed mosque in Hamburg. Ayatallah Morteza Mottaheri, the group's leading intellectual, was another former student of Khomeini. Born in Khurasan, he studied in Qum, taught theology at Tehran University, and helped set up the Husseinieh-i Ershad. He also wrote a number of books that stressed the relevance of Islam to the modern world. Hojjat al-Islam Akbar Hashemi Rafsanjani, the group's main organizer, came from a landed family in Rafsanjan near Kerman. Having studied under Khomeini, he had been imprisoned briefly in 1963-1964, 1967, 1972, and 1975-1977. Finally, Hojjat al-Islam ʿAli Khamenehi, the group's youngest organizer, was a junior lecturer at the Fayzieh seminary. Born in 1939 into a clerical family in Mashad, he had studied with Melani at the local seminary as well as with Boroujerdi and Khomeini in Qum. He had also written books on Muslims in India and on the Western threat to Islam. Thus almost all the leaders of the group came from the Persian-speaking provinces and had studied with Khomeini at Qum. All were to play important roles in the forthcoming revolution.

Khomeini's group can be described as extremist for a number of reasons. Unlike members of the second group, Khomeini lived in exile, had burned his bridges, and therefore had no reason to mute or moderate his opposition to the regime. He openly denounced the shah, comparing him to Yazid, the caliph that had murdered Hussein, and exhorted the faithful to overthrow the Pahlevi regime. Unlike the second group, Khomeini aimed not at the reestablishment of the constitutional monarchy, but the establishment of a new form of Islamic government. Even though in this period he still shied away from the term republic, it was clear what he wanted was not reform but political revolution. And unlike the second group, Khomeini envisaged an ideal polity in which the ʿulama would be active in all important spheres of society, interpreting and implementing the shariʿa, teaching and guarding the mellat (community), supervising and controlling the politicians. Thus he sought the creation of not just an Islamic government, but a clerical Islamic government. For Shariʿatmadari, the highest duty of the ʿulama was to protect the shariʿa and the community against the inherently corrupting dawlat (state). But for Khomeini, the highest duty of the ʿulama was to gain control of the state and to use political power to implement the shariʿa and create a truly Islamic community.

Khomeini laid out the essentials of his political theory in a series of lectures delivered at the main seminary in Najaf during the late 1960s. Entitled *Velayat-i Faqih: Hukomat-i Islami* (The Jurist's Trusteeship: Islamic Government), these lectures developed to their logical conclusion some of the arguments expounded by many of the nineteenth-century Shiʿi ʿulama. These theologians had argued that the Twelfth Imam had given the responsibility of protecting the community to the mujtaheds. They had also argued that the mujtaheds should keep their distance from the state and should tolerate states as necessary evils, since without kings and rulers society would disintegrate into utter chaos. According to this theory, the ʿulama had ultimate political authority but could exercise it only when the government grossly transgressed the shariʿa and thereby endangered the Islamic community. This qualification had been accepted by Khomeini in his earlier years. As he had stated in 1943 in his first major work, *Kashf-i Asrar* (Secrets Revealed),

The mujtaheds have never rejected the system of government nor the independence of Islamic governments. Even when they have judged certain laws to be against God's regulations and particular government to be bad, still they have not opposed the system of government. Nor will they. Why not? Because a decayed government is better than none at all. Consequently, the [practical] power of the mujtaheds excludes the government and includes only simple matters such as legal rulings, religious judgements, and intervention to protect the property of minors and the weak. Even when rulers are oppressive and against the people, they [the mujtaheds] will not try to destroy the rulers.[48]

The 1963 crisis, however, must have swept away Khomeini's restraint. For in his Najaf lectures he argued that since God intended the community to observe the shariʿa, since governments had been

[48] R. Khomeini, *Kashf-i Asrar* (Secrets Revealed) (Tehran, n.d.), p. 186.

created to implement the shariʿa, and since the ʿulama—in the absence of the Imams—were the only true interpreters of the shariʿa, the government should be entrusted to the clergy—especially to the faqih (jurists). In his own words,

the [Koranic] phrase "the jurists are the representatives of the prophets" does not mean that the authority of the jurists is limited to interpreting what the prophets said. On the contrary, the most important purpose of the prophets was to establish a just society and to implement the laws. This can only be done by a government that enforces the laws. In the same way the government is embodied in the Prophet, it is also embodied in the Imams and their successors—the jurists.

Since the rule of Islam is the rule of law, only the jurists, and no one else, should be in charge of the government. They are the ones who can undertake what the Prophet intended. They are the ones who can govern as God ordered.

The contemporary jurist is the heir to the Prophet's authority. Whatever was entrusted to the Prophet has been entrusted by the Imams to the jurists. The jurists have authority on all matters. They have been entrusted with the power to govern, rule, and run the affairs of the people.

The jurist should have authority over the state administration and over the machinery for spreading justice, providing security, and dispensing just social relations. The jurist possesses the knowledge to ensure the people's liberty, independence, and progress. . . . I am certain that you [the clergy] are capable of running the state when the foundations of injustice, tyranny, and oppression are destroyed. All the regulations you need are found in Islam, whether laws relating to state administration, taxes, rights, punishments, or laws relating to other matters.[49]

In arguing his point, Khomeini took to task both the apolitical clergy and the moderate clerical opposition. He denounced the former for abdicating their duties, taking refuge in seminaries, and accepting the false notion of secularism imported by the "imperialists." As he stated,

Do not allow the Westerners and their lackeys to dominate you. Teach the people true Islam so that they will not think that the clergy in Qum and Najaf believe in separation of church and state and spend all their time thinking about issues of childbirth and menstruation. The colonialists have spread the insidious idea that religion should be separated from politics and that men of religion are not qualified to act in political and social matters. In the Prophet's times, was the church separate from the state? Were theologians distinct from politicians?[50]

[49] R. Khomeini, *Velayat-i Faqih: Hukomat-i Islami* (The Jurist's Trusteeship: Islamic Government) (n.p., 1976), p. 89, 93, 106-107, 190.

[50] Ibid., p. 23.

Khomeini was more circumspect in his criticisms of the moderate clerical opposition. He argued that the only way to eliminate tyranny, corruption, and treason was through an Islamic political revolution. He insisted that the whole of the judicial system must be returned to the clergy both because the ʿulama were the true interpreters of the shariʿa, and because secular courts wasted years, sometimes decades, discussing simple cases. He also insisted that, although technocrats could be used to draft economic plans and administer the government ministries, ultimate power should reside in the clergy. He argued— for the first time—that the institution of monarchy was anti-Islamic since the Prophet had denounced hereditary kingship as satanic and paganistic.[51] What is more, he claimed that the clerical leaders of the Constitutional Revolution had been fooled by secular intellectuals into accepting non-Islamic institutions. In a section reminiscent of the ultraconservative Shaykh Fazallah Nouri, who had been executed by the constitutionalists, Khomeini argued,

During the Constitutional Revolution British agents deceived the people by importing foreign laws in order to undermine the shariʿa. When the revolutionaries sat down to draft the country's constitutional laws, these agents resorted to the Belgian embassy and used Belgian laws. These agents—I prefer not to name them—copied the Belgian laws, added some others from England and France, and then camouflaged them with Islamic terms. Consequently, the constitution is an import from Europe and has nothing to do with Islam.

The Islamic government we want will be constitutional and not despotic. But it will be constitutional not in the usual sense of the term—that laws will be made by an elected parliament. It will be constitutional in that the state will strictly observe the rules and regulations laid down in the Koran, in the Sunna, and in the Islamic shariʿa.[52]

In his lectures to theology students, Khomeini advocated the establishment of a clerical state. But in his proclamations to the public, he soft-pedaled the theocratic theme—the term *velayat-i faqih* was scrupulously avoided—and instead continued his 1963-1964 strategy of attacking the regime at its weakest points.[53] He accused the shah of selling the country to American imperialists and helping Israel against the Arabs; violating the constitution and trampling on the fundamental laws; favoring the rich and exploiting the poor; destroying national culture; encouraging corruption and wasting precious re-

[51] Ibid., pp. 41, 14, 15-16, 12-13.
[52] Ibid., pp. 11, 52-53.
[53] For Khomeini's proclamations during 1964-1973 see, *Khomeini va Jonbesh* (Khomeini and the Movement) (n.p., 1973), pp. 1-103.

sources on palaces, luxuries, and weapons; ruining the farmers and thereby increasing Iran's dependence on the West. In offering an alternative, Khomeini did not publicly refer to his work on Islamic government; on the contrary, his entourage later disclaimed this work, arguing that it was either a SAVAK forgery or the rough notes of a student listener.[54] Nor did Khomeini commit himself to precise proposals and specific plans; as one journalist later observed, "imprecision was a way of life" for his entourage.[55] Instead Khomeini talked in generalities of throwing out the imperialists, making the country fully independent, bringing "Islamic justice" to the poor, helping the farmers, protecting the working masses, raising the standard of living, eliminating corruption, safeguarding basic freedoms, and establishing a genuine Islamic state, one that would be "democratic" and different from the other self-styled Islamic states.[56]

Moreover, Khomeini worked to rally behind himself all opposition groups—with the exception of the "atheistic Marxists"—while taking care not to be identified too closely with any particular group. For example, in 1968 when Ayatallah Mottaheri, his leading disciple in Tehran, resigned from the Husseinieh-i Ershad to protest Shari'ati's anticlerical lectures, and asked Najaf for support against "that so-called Islamic expert," Khomeini, knowing the latter's popularity, refused to take sides.[57] Instead he kept silent on the quarrel, and, without citing Shari'ati by name, continued to use stock phrases that the Husseinieh-i Ershad lectures had popularized—phrases such as the "mostazafin" (the wretched), "the rubbish heap of history," and "religion is not the opiate of the masses." Hearing these phrases but ignorant of the Najaf lectures, many members of the intelligentsia jumped to the conclusion that Khomeini agreed with Shari'ati's interpretation of revolutionary Islam. Thus Khomeini intentionally propagated a vague populist message and refrained from specific proposals, and thereby created a broad alliance of social forces ranging from the bazaars and the clergy to the intelligentsia and the urban poor, as well as of political organizations varying from the religious Liberation Movement and the secular National Front to the new guerrilla groups emerging from Shari'ati's followers in the universities. Khomeini has often been described as the traditional mulla. In fact, he was a major innovator in Iran both because of his political theory and because of his religious-oriented populist strategy.

[54] Cited by J. Cockroft, "Iran's Khomeini," *Seven Days*, 23 February 1979, pp. 17-18.
[55] *Iran Times*, 2 February 1979.
[56] "Interview with Imam Khomeini," *Khabarnameh*, Special Number 21 (November 1978), pp. 27-28.
[57] "Who Was Mottaheri?" *Iranshahr*, no. 27 (4 May 1979), p. 4.

GUERRILLA ORGANIZATIONS (1971-1977)

On the cold winter eve of February 8 (Bahman 19), 1971, thirteen young men armed with rifles, machine guns, and hand grenades attacked the gendarmerie post in the village of Siakal on the edge of the Caspian forests. With this attack, later to become famous as the "Siakal incident," they sparked off eight years of intense guerrilla activity and inspired many other radicals, Islamic as well as Marxist, to take up arms against the regime. In the period between the Siakal incident and October 1977, when the Islamic revolution began to unfold in the streets of Tehran, 341 guerrillas and members of armed political groups lost their lives. Of these, 177 died in gun battles; 91 were executed, some without trial, others after secret military tribunals; 42 died under torture; 15 were arrested and never seen again; 7 committed suicide to avoid capture; and 9 were shot "trying to escape"—after the revolution their jailors admitted that they had been murdered in cold blood. Moreover, some 200 others suspected of being guerrillas were sentenced to terms ranging from fifteen years to life imprisonment.

In terms of social background, almost all the dead guerrillas came from the ranks of the young intelligentsia. Next of kin and the guerrilla organizations have provided information on the occupations of 306 of the 341 who were killed. Of the 306, 280 (91 percent) can be described as members of the intelligentsia (see Table 10). The other 26 (9 percent) consisted of 22 factory workers, 3 shopkeepers, and 1 low-ranking clergyman. The victims were mostly young: only 10 of the 306 were over thirty-five years old when they died. Among the total 341 dead, there were 39 women; they included 14 housewives, 13 college students, 9 school teachers, 2 doctors, and 1 office employee. It should be noted that the guerrilla movement emerged at a time of middle-class prosperity, rising salaries, and employment opportunities for college graduates. Thus they took up arms not because

TABLE 9
Dead Guerrillas

	Feda'-i	Islamic Mujahedin	Marxist Mujahedin	Other Marxist	Other Islamic	Total
Killed fighting	106	36	16	11	8	177
Executed	38	15	10	12	16	91
Tortured to death	10	18	1	9	4	42
Missing	6	1	2	6		15
Suicide	5	1	1			7
Murdered in prison	7	2				9
Total	172	73	30	38	28	341

TABLE 10
Occupations of Dead Guerrillas

	Feda'-i	Islamic Mujahedin	Marxist Mujahedin	Other Marxist	Other Islamic	Total
College students	73	30	15	14	7	139
High school students	1				7	8
Teachers	17	5	3	1	1	27
Engineers	19	14	2	1		36
Office workers	7	4		1	8	20
Doctors	3			3		6
Intellectuals	4			1		5
Other professionals	11	6	2	1		20
Housewives	8	3	2	1		14
Conscripts	5					5
Shopkeepers		2			1	3
Clergymen		1				1
Workers	12	2	1	7		22
Not known	12	6	5	8	4	35
Total	172	73	30	38	28	341
(Women)	(22)	(7)	(8)	(2)	(0)	(39)

NOTE: This information has been compiled from interviews and from the following newspapers: *Bakhtar-i Emruz*, 1970-1976; *Mujahed*, 1972-1978; *Khabar-nameh*, 1969-1979; *Mardom*, 1970-1979; *Setareh-i Surkh*, 1971-1979; *Ittila'at*, 1971-1980; *Kayhan*, 1978-1979; and *Ayandegan*, 1978-1979.

of economic deprivation, but because of social discontent, moral indignation, and political frustration.

In terms of political background, the guerrillas can be divided into five groupings:

1. the Sazaman-i Cherikha-yi Feda'i Khalq-i Iran (The Organization of the Iranian Peoples' Guerrilla Freedom Fighters), known in short as the Marxist Feda'i;

2. the Sazman-i Mujahedin-i Khalq-i Iran (The Organization of the Iranian Peoples' Freedom Fighters), generally referred to as the Islamic Mujahedin;

3. the Marxist offshoot from the Mujahedin, known simply as the Marxist Mujahedin;[58]

4. small Islamic groups on the whole limited to one locality: Gorueh-i Abu Zarr (Abu Zarr Group) in Nahavand, Gorueh-i Shi'iyan-i Rastin (True Shi'i Group) in Hamadan, Gorueh-i Allah Akbar (Allah Akbar Group) in Isfahan, and Gorueh-i al-Fajar (al-Fajar Group) in Zahedan;

5. small Marxist groups. These included both independent groups, such as the Sazman-i Azadibakhsh-i Khalqha-yi Iran (Organization for the Liberation of the Iranian Peoples), Gorueh-i Luristan (Luristan

---

[58] After the Islamic Revolution, the Marxist Mujahedin took the title of Sazman-i Paykar dar Rah-i Azadi-i Tabaqeh-i Kargar (The Fighting Organization on the Road for the Liberation of the Working Class). It became known as Paykar.

Group), and Sazman-i Arman-i Khalq (Organization for the People's Ideal); and cells belonging to political parties advocating armed struggle—the Tofan group, the Revolutionary Organization of the Tudeh party, the Kurdish Democratic party, and a New Left organization named Gorueh-i Ittehad-i Komunistha (Group of United Communists). Moreover, some of the Feda'is had at the time of their death joined the Tudeh party.

Of these five groupings, the Marxist Feda'i and the Islamic Mujahedin were by far the largest. Of the 341 dead, 172 (50 percent) belonged to the Feda'i; 73 (21 percent) to the Islamic Mujahedin; 38 (11 percent) to the small Marxist groups; 30 (9 percent) to the Marxist Mujahedin; and 28 (8 percent) to the small Islamic groups. What is more, of the many guerrilla organizations only the Feda'i, the Islamic Mujahedin, and the Marxist Mujahedin survived to play a role in the Islamic Revolution.

Although its first major operation took place in February 1971, the origins of the guerrilla movement reached back to 1963. The ability of the armed forces to crush the Muharram demonstrations of that year, the efficiency of SAVAK in rooting out the underground parties, and the reluctance of the main opposition organizations—especially the Tudeh and the National Front—to give up nonviolent means of resistance, all combined to persuade the younger members of the opposition to look for new methods of struggle. Not surprisingly, in the next few years university students formed small secret discussion groups to study the recent experience of China, Vietnam, Cuba, and Algeria, and to translate the works of Mao, Giap, Che Guevara, and Fanon. In the words of one such group,

The bloody massacres of 1963 were a major landmark in Iranian history. Until then, the opposition had tried to fight the regime with street protests, labor strikes, and underground networks. The 1963 bloodbath, however, exposed the bankruptcy of these methods. After 1963, militants—irrespective of their ideology—had to ask themselves the question: "What is to be done?" The answer was clear: "guerrilla warfare."[59]

This period of study produced a number of small Marxist and Islamic groups advocating armed struggle. But most of them were discovered by SAVAK before they could initiate any serious armed actions. In 1964, fifty-seven youngsters, many of them college and high-school students, were arrested in Tehran for buying weapons and forming a secret Hizb-i Mellal-i Islam (Party of the Islamic Nation). In 1966, seven doctors, teachers, and other professionals in Enzeli, Tehran, and Kerman were arrested for advocating violence,

[59] "Armed Struggle," *Mujahed*, 2 (November 1974), 5-6.

translating pamphlets on Cuba, and setting up a secret organization named Jebʿeh-i Azadibakhsh-i Mell-i Iran (Front for the Liberation of Iran). This organization later became known under its acronym JAMA, and its founder, Dr. Kazem Sami, a devout Muslim and psychologist from Kerman, was to become the first minister of health in the Islamic republic. In 1969, some two hundred Tudeh members, dissatisfied with their party's decision to avoid violence, formed a Sazman-i Inqilab-i Komunistha-yi Iran (Revolutionary Organization of Iranian Communists) and robbed a bank in Isfahan to finance future guerrilla operations. However, they were all arrested before it had the chance to launch any such operations. Similarly in 1969, eighteen young professors and university students—some of whom had been in the Tudeh or in Khalel Maleki's Marxist group—were caught trying to cross the Iraqi border to join the PLO. Since none of these groups had physically assaulted the authorities they received relatively mild treatment. Their rank and file members were given prison terms varying from one to ten years; their leaders were given terms varying from ten years to life. The flood of death sentences was to come soon, however, with the emergence of the Feda'i and the Mujahedin.

The Feda'i. This organization, which did not adopt its name until March 1971, was formed of two separate groups that traced their origins back to the early and mid-1960s.[60] The first group had been established in late 1963 by five Tehran University students: Bezhan Jazani, ʿAbbas Sourki, ʿAli Akbar Safaʾi Farahani, Muhammad Ashtiyani, and Hamid Ashraf. Jazani, the circle's central figure, was a student of political science who had been in and out of prison since the mid-1950s. Born in 1937, he had completed high school in his home town, Tehran, and had been active in the youth section of the Tudeh before leaving the party and forming his own secret group. In later years, while serving a fifteen-year prison sentence, he wrote a series of pamphlets for the Feda'i, including *Nabard ba Diktator-i Shah* (Struggle against the Shah's Dictatorship), *Tarikh-i Siy Saleh-i Iran* (Thirty-Year History of Iran), and *Chehguneh Mobarezeh-i Mas-*

[60] For short histories of the Feda'i see: *Kar* (Work), the organ of the Feda'i after the 1979 revolution; *Nabard-i Khalq* (People's Struggle), the theoretical journal of the Feda'i after the 1979 revolution; Feda'i Organization, *Hasht Sal Mobarezeh-i Masale-haneh* (Eight Years of Armed Struggle) (Tehran, 1979), pp. 1-29; Feda'i Organization, *Tarikhcheh-i Sazman-i Cherikha-yi Feda'i* (Short History of the Feda'i Organization) (Tehran, 1969), pp. 1-28; Feda'i Organization, *Tahlil-i Yek Sal-i Mobarez* (Study of One Year of Struggle) (n.p., 1974), pp. 1-24; Y. Zarkar, *Khaterat-i Yek Cherik dar Zendan* (Memoirs of A Guerrilla in Prison) (Tehran, 1973), pp. 1-241; A. Dehqani, *Hamaseh-i Moqavemat* (Epic of Resistance) (n.p., 1974), pp. 1-248.

alehaneh Tudeh-yi Meshavad (How the Armed Struggle Will Be Transformed into a Mass Struggle). Sorouki, another student of political science and former Tudeh member, had grown up in Mazandaran before moving to Tehran to enter the university. Safa'i Farahani, a student of engineering, was a native of Gilan but had met the others in Tehran University. In later years, he wrote a handbook for the Feda'i entitled *Ancheh Yek Inqilabi Bayad Bedanad* (What a Revolutionary Must Know). Ashtiyani, a law student, had been born in Tehran in 1934. By far the oldest, he had completed his military service and was therefore able to train his colleagues in the use and upkeep of light arms. Most of the later Feda'i recruits, however, did not need this training, since they had already served in the armed forces. Thus the shah and his rapid expansion of the military ironically helped the guerrilla movement. Finally, Ashraf, the youngest of the original group, was a student of engineering. Born in Tehran in 1946, he had as a high-school student joined Khalel Maleki's party and in 1964 entered the university, where he had met the others. All five, as well as many other students who later joined them, came from middle-class backgrounds.

Four years after the group was formed, SAVAK infiltrated it and arrested fourteen members, including Jazani and Sourki. Ashraf, however, avoided arrest and found enough recruits to keep the group alive. Meanwhile, Safa'i Farahani and Ashtiyani escaped to Lebanon, spent two years with al-Fatah, and receiving assistance from Radmanesh (the First Secretary of the Tudeh and the director of the party's operations in the Middle East) returned home to rejoin Ashraf. When the Tudeh Central Committee heard of this unauthorized assistance, it recalled Radmanesh and elected Iraj Iskandari as the party's First Secretary. Others of the original Jazani group, including Jazani himself and Sourki, were kept in prison until April 1975, when they were shot "trying to escape." Although Jazani did not actually organize the Feda'i, he is considered to be its "intellectual father."

The second group that formed the Feda'i was led by two university students who had come to Tehran from Mashad. Mas'oud Ahmadzadeh, the main personality, came from an intellectual family well known in Mashad for its opposition to the Pahlevis since the early 1920s, its staunch support of Mossadeq since 1949, and its continued close associations with the National Front and the Liberation Movement. While at high school in Mashad, Ahmadzadeh formed an Islamic Student Club, joined the National Front, and participated in religious demonstrations against the shah. But while studying mathematics in Aryamehr (Industrial) University in Tehran during the mid-1960s, he turned toward Marxism, and in 1967 formed a secret circle to discuss the works of Che Guevara, Regis Debray, and Carlos Marighella, the Brazilian revolutionary who developed the theory of urban guerrilla warfare. In 1970 Ahmadzadeh wrote one of the main theoretical works of the Feda'i, a pamphlet entitled *Mobarezeh-i Aslehaneh: Ham Estrategi Ham Taktik* (Armed Struggle: Both a Strategy and a Tactic).

Amir Parvez Poyan, Ahmadzadeh's close associate, had a very similar background. Born in 1946 in Mashad, he studied in the local high schools, where he joined the National Front and took part in religious clubs. But while studying literature in the National University in Tehran during the mid-1960s, he was drawn to Marxism, especially to the example of Castro, and wrote a book entitled *Zarurat-i Mobarezeh-i Masalehaneh va Rad-i Teor-yi Baqa* (The Necessity of Armed Struggle and the Rejection of the Theory of Survival).

The two groups merged in the course of 1970, with the former constituting the new organization's "rural team" and the latter its "urban team." In negotiating the mergers, the Jazani group—most of whose leaders were former Tudeh members—stressed the importance of building a viable organization, but the Ahmadzadeh group, many of whom were from the National Front, emphasized the roles of mass spontaneity and heroic deeds. As Ashraf's summary of the Feda'i strategy shows, the latter group won out:

After much deliberation we reached the conclusion that it was impossible to work among the masses and create large organizations since the police had penetrated all sectors of society. We decided that our immediate task was to form small cells and mount assaults on the enemy to destroy the repressive "atmosphere" and to prove to the masses that armed struggle was the only way to liberation.[61]

Similarly, Poyan argued:

The defeat of the anti-imperialist movement has enabled the reactionaries to establish a fascist state, destroy the opposition organizations, and coopt opportunistic elements. In a situation where there are no firm links between the revolutionary intelligentsia and the masses, we are not like fish in water, but rather like isolated fish surrounded by threatening crocodiles. Terror, repression, and absence of democracy have made it impossible for us to create working-class organizations. To break the spell of our weakness and to inspire the people into action we must resort to revolutionary armed struggle. . . . To liberate the proletariat from the stifling culture, to cleanse its mind of

[61] H. Ashraf, *Jam'iband-i Seh Saleh* (An Evaluation of Three Years) (Tehran, 1979), p. 92.

petty bourgeois thoughts, and to arm it with ideological ammunition, it is necessary to shatter the illusion that the people are powerless.[62]

Thus the central thesis of the Feda'i was astonishingly simple: guerrilla warfare and more guerrilla warfare. After the constant defeats of the Tudeh and the National Front, the victories of Castro, Giap, and Mao, as well as the newborn confidence of the Latin American guerrillas had an exhilarating effect upon the young Iranian intelligentsia. In formulating their simple strategy, the Feda'is developed critiques of other political organizations. They dismissed the National Front and the Liberation Movement as petty bourgeois paper organizations still preaching the false hope of peaceful change.[63] They accused the pro-Chinese groups, especially the Revolutionary Organization, of applying Mao to Iran "mechanically," dogmatically refusing to accept the fact that in the last decade Iran had been transformed from a feudal society to a capitalist society fully dependent on the West, uncritically accepting the notion that the Soviet Union rather than America was the major threat, and talking much about armed struggle but invariably postponing that struggle on the grounds that first a viable political party had to be formed.[64]

Their criticism of the Tudeh was even more extensive.[65] Although they respected the Tudeh for organizing the working class during the 1940s and producing many national martyrs during the 1950s, they accused the party of blindly following the Soviet Union, of hastily denouncing Stalin, and of underestimating the "national question," especially in Azerbaijan and Kurdistan. The Feda'i asserted that the Tudeh had held back the peasant movement in the 1940s, had overestimated the importance of the national bourgeoisie, and had thereby reached the false conclusion that the forthcoming revolution would be "national democratic" rather than "people's democratic." Above all, claimed the Feda'i, the Tudeh favored a political struggle over an armed struggle, trade unionism over revolutionary militancy, organizational survival over heroic action, and parliamentary reformism over radical communism. The Tudeh retorted that all socialists had

---

[62] A. Poyan, *Zarurat-i Mobarezeh-i Mashalehaneh va Rad-i Teor-yi Baqa* (The Necessity of Armed Struggle and the Rejection of the Theory of Survival) (n.p., 1972), pp. 7-9.

[63] B. Jazani, *Tarikh-i Siy Saleh-i Iran* (Thirty-Year History of Iran) (Tehran, 1979), pp. 69-89.

[64] "The Thoughts of Mao and Our Revolution," *Nabard-i Khalq,* no. 2 (March 1974), pp. 38-48.

[65] Jazani, *Tarikh-i Siy Saleh,* pp. 8-67; Feda'i Organization, *I'dam-i Inqilab-i 'Abbas Shahriyar* (The Revolutionary Execution of 'Abbas Shahriyar) (n.p., 1974), pp. 71-142; 'A. Nabdel, *Azerbaijan va Masaleh-i Melli* (Azerbaijan and the National Question) (n.p., 1973), pp. 18-32.

the duty to support the Soviet Union—the "bastion of Marxism"—and that talk of quickly transforming a national bourgeois revolution into a socialist working-class revolution smacked of Trotsky's notion of "permanent revolution." The Feda'i, they argued, underestimated the Iranian bourgeoisie and consequently misunderstood the true nature of the forthcoming revolution. According to the Tudeh analysis, the Feda'i discounted the class consciousness of the industrial proletariat, and thereby overlooked the possibilities of waging a successful political struggle. Most important of all, the Tudeh viewed the guerrillas as having more in common with Bakunin and the nineteenth-century anarchists who advocated "Long Live Death" and "Propaganda by the Deed," than with Marx, Lenin, and the Bolsheviks, who always stressed that an armed struggle should be initiated only when there was a disciplined revolutionary party present and when the "objective" conditions were ripe.[66]

Undeterred by such arguments, the Feda'i made preparations for guerrilla warfare and sent the "rural team" to Gilan to establish a base in the local mountains. They chose Gilan partly because the rugged mountains were inaccessible to heavy armor; partly because the forests—the jangals—provided thick cover against air attacks; but mainly because the local peasantry had a radical tradition reaching back to the Jangali movement of the 1920s, if not to the Babi uprising of the 1850s. The original plans of the "rural team" called for extensive preparations, living with the mountain shepherds, establishing contact with the villagers, and recruiting fighters from the local population. But these plans had to be scrapped in early February 1971 when the gendarmes in the village of Siakal arrested one of the Feda'i sympathizers. Afraid that torture would be used to extract vital information, the guerrillas took the fateful decision to attack the gendarmerie post and release their colleague. On learning of the attack, the shah reacted with determination and sent his brother to head an expeditionary force of commandos, helicopters, and police agents. After a massive manhunt lasting three weeks, the military authorities announced the elimination of the whole guerrilla band and the execution of its thirteen members. Although the affair was a military fiasco, the Feda'i took it as a great propaganda victory in that they had shown the public that a small band of determined men could frighten the whole Pahlevi regime. Not surprisingly, Bahman 19 (Feb-

---

[66] F. Javan, *Cherikha-yi Khalq Cheh Megunyand* (What Are the Guerrillas Saying?) (n.p., 1972), pp. 1-33; E. Tabari, "This Is Not Marxism-Leninism," *Donya*, 12 (Autumn 1971), 31-41; N. Kianouri, "On Methods of Struggle," *Donya*, 1 (July 1974), 1-10; "A Message to the Feda'i," *Donya*, 1 (November 1974), 1-7.

ruary 8), the day of the Siakal incident, has gone down in Iranian history as the birth of the guerrilla movement.

As if to confirm the importance of the Siakal incident, the regime followed up the executions with a series of dramatic measures. It launched a major propaganda war against the guerrillas, accusing them of being atheists, Tudeh agents, and tools of the PLO and the Arab imperialists. It rounded up fifty-one left-wing intellectuals in Tehran, none of whom had Feda'i connections; granted a week's unscheduled vacation to the universities in Tehran; and outlawed as an international conspiracy the Confederation of Iranian Students based in Europe and North America. It also increased government salaries, decreed the current year to be the Civil Servants' Year, raised the minimum wage, and declared that in the future May 1 would be celebrated throughout Iran as Workers' Day.

During the nine months after Siakal, SAVAK, in a series of armed encounters, managed to arrest or kill amost all the founding members of the Feda'i. Nevertheless, the survivors, notably Hamid Ashraf, were able to continue the fight. Having found eager recruits, they established new cells, mostly in Tehran, Tabriz, Rasht, Gurgan, Qazvin, and Enzeli; started two underground papers—*Bahman 19* (February 8) and *Nabard-i Khalq* (People's Struggle); and organized a number of student strikes and demonstrations to coincide with the first anniversary of Siakal. They also carried out a series of armed operations: holding up five banks; assassinating two police informers, a millionaire industrialist, and the chief military prosecutor; and bombing the embassies of Britain, Oman, and the United States, the offices of International Telephone and Telegraph, Trans World Airlines, and the Iran-American Society, and the police headquarters in Tehran, Tabriz, Rasht, Gurgan, Mashad, and Abadan.

By late 1975, it was clear that a stalemate had been reached in the struggle between the regime and the Feda'i. The former had succeeded in hunting down many guerrillas, waging an aggressive propaganda war on "atheistic terrorists," and, most important of all, restricting the movement to the university campuses. The latter, on the other hand, had succeeded in replenishing its heavy losses, harassing the authorities, and accomplishing numerous heroic feats. But five years of struggle had still not ignited the "people's revolution." In debating on how to end the stalemate, the Feda'i divided into two factions. The majority, headed by Hamid Ashraf until his death in mid-1976, insisted on continuing the armed confrontations until they sparked off a mass uprising. The minority faction, however, argued in favor of avoiding armed confrontations, increasing political activity, especially among factory workers, and establishing closer links with the Tudeh party. In mid-1976, this group affiliated with the Tudeh, denounced the theory of "propaganda by the Deed" as an aberration of Marxism, and formed the Gorueh-i Munsh'eb az Sazman-i Cher-ikha-yi Feda'i Khalq Vabasteh Beh Hizb-i Tudeh-i Iran (Group Sep-arated from the Feda'i Guerrillas and Attached to the Tudeh Party of Iran)—known in short as the Feda'i Munsh'eb.[67] Both factions kept their weapons, and as soon as the revolution began, surfaced as experienced armed organizations eager to challenge the military might of the Pahlevi state.

The Mujahedin. Like the Feda'i, the Mujahedin had its origins in the early 1960s. But whereas the Feda'i developed mostly out of the Tudeh and the Marxist wing of the National Front, the Mujahedin evolved predominantly from the religious wing of the National Front, especially from the Liberation Movement.[68] The organization was founded in 1965 by six former members of the Liberation Movement and recent graduates of Tehran University: Muhammad Hanifne-zhad, Sa'id Mohsen, Muhammad 'Asgarizadeh, Rasoul Moshkinfam, 'Ali Asghar Badi'zadegan, and Ahmad Reza'i.

Hanifnezhad, the oldest, was an agricultural engineer. Born in 1938 into a clerical family in Tabriz, he completed high school in his home town and then moved to Tehran to enter the Agricultural College. There he formed an Islamic Club, joined the Liberation Movement, and, as a result of the 1963 riots, spent a short spell in prison, where he met Taleqani and Bazargan. After his release, Hanifnezhad com-pleted his degree, volunteered for military service, and spent a year in the Isfahan garrison reading as much as he could on the recent revolutions in Cuba, Algeria, and Vietnam. Finishing national service in 1965, he returned to Tehran, gathered together some former class-mates who felt that the Liberation Movement was too moderate, and thereby formed the nucleus of the Mujahedin.

[67] T. Haydar-Begundi, *Teor-yi "Tabligh-i Masalehaneh" Enheraf Az Marksism-Leninism* (The Theory of "Armed Propaganda" Deviates from Marxism-Leninism) (n.p., 1978), pp. 1-81; Feda'i Munsh'eb, *Zindehbad Hizb-i Tudeh* (Long Live the Tudeh Party) (Tehran, 1978), pp. 1-15.

[68] For short histories of the Mujahedin see: *Mujahed* (Freedom Fighter), the organ of the Mujahedin after the Islamic revolution; and the following works by the Muja-hedin Organization: *Sharh-i Tasis va Tarikhcheh-i va Vaqa'eh-i Sazman-i Mujahedin* (Ac-count of the Formation, Short History, and the Major Events of the Mujahedin) (Teh-ran, 1979), pp. 1-87; *Tarikhcheh* (Short History) (Tehran, 1979), pp. 1-40; *Az Zendig-yi Inqilabiun Dars Begirim* (Let Us Learn from the Lives of Revolutionaries) (n.p., 1974), pp. 1-32; *Sazmandi va Taktikha* (Tactics and Organizational Issues) (n.p., 1972), pp. 1-29; *Qesmati az Dafa'at-i Mujahedin* (Extracts from the Defense Speeches of Mujahedin Martyrs) (n.p., 1972), pp. 1-29.

Moshen, a civil engineer, was another Azerbaijani who had studied in Tehran University. From an impoverished clerical family in Zanjan, he won a state scholarship to the Engineering College, where he joined the Liberation Movement and the Islamic Student Club. After being imprisoned eight months after the 1963 riots, he finished his degree and entered the army for military service. ʿAsgarizadeh, a graduate of the Business College, was one of the few Mujahedin who came from a working-class family. Born in Arak in central Iran, he grew up partly in his home town and partly in Tehran, where he won a state scholarship to the university. Completing his degree, he worked in Tehran and Tabriz for a machine manufacturing company. Moshkinfam, another agricultural engineer, came from a middle-class family in Shiraz. After graduating from Tehran University, he was drafted into the army and sent to Kurdistan, where he learned Kurdish and compiled for himself a detailed report on the impact of commercial agriculture on the local peasantry. The Mujahedin later published this report under the title of *Rusta va Inqilab-i Sefid* (The Countryside and the White Revolution). Badiʿzadegan, a young professor of chemistry, came from a middle-class family in Isfahan. After graduating from Tehran University, he was conscripted into the army and stationed in the main arms manufacturing plant in Tehran. Finally, Rezaʾi—the group's main intellectual—was one of the few Mujahedin who had been born in Tehran. From a small merchant family living in northern Tehran, he joined the Liberation Movement while in high school, met Hanifnezhad while in the army, and entered his secret discussion circle while teaching in a Tehran high school. Later Rezaʾi, his two younger brothers, and a teenage sister were all killed fighting the police.

This nucleus in Tehran gradually expanded into the provinces and established cells in Isfahan, Shiraz, and Tabriz. At the same time, Badiʿzadegan, Moshkinfam, and four new recruits went to Jordan to receive guerrilla training from the PLO. What is more, the discussion group, especially Hanifnezhad and Rezaʾi, followed the Liberation Movement in reinterpreting Islam, and reached conclusions similar to that of Shariʿati. In fact, the ideas of Shariʿati and the Mujahedin were so close that many concluded that the former had inspired the latter. The Mujahedin had, however, already formulated their ideas before Shariʿati came to the Husseinieh-i Ershad in 1967. But whatever the exact relationship between the two, it is clear that in later years Shariʿati indirectly helped the Mujahedin with his prolific works focusing on the revolutionary aspects of Shiʿism.

The first major theoretical work of the Mujahedin was entitled *Nahzat-i Husseini* (Hussein's Movement). Written by Rezaʾi, the book argued that the Nezam-i Towhid (Monotheistic Order) sought by the Prophet was a commonwealth fully united both because it worships only one God and because it is a classless society that strives for the common good. Reza'i further argued that the banner of revolt raised by the Shi'i Imams, especially Hussein, was aimed against feudal landlords and exploiting merchant capitalists as well as against usurping caliphs who had betrayed the true cause of the Nezam-i Towhid. For Reza'i and the Mujahedin it was the duty of all Muslims to continue this struggle to create a classless society and destroy all forms of oppression, which, in the modern age, included imperialism, capitalism, despotism, and conservative clericalism. The Mujahedin summed up their attitude toward religion in these words:

After years of extensive study into Islamic history and Shi'i ideology, we have reached the firm conclusion that Islam, especially Shi'i Islam, will play a major role in inspiring the masses to join the revolution. It will do so because Shi'ism, particularly Hussein's historic act of martyrdom and resistance, has both a revolutionary message and a special place in our popular culture.[69]

The Mujahedin began their military operations in August 1971. Their first operations were designed to disrupt the extravagant celebrations of the 2500-year anniversary of the monarchy. After bombing the Tehran electrical works and trying to hijack an Iran Air plane, nine Mujahedin were arrested. Under torture, one of the nine gave information that led to the arrest of another sixty-six members. In the subsequent months, the group lost the whole of its original leadership through executions or street battles. Despite these heavy losses, the group survived and found new members. They obtained financial assistance from the Liberation Movement, helped the Husseinieh-i Ershad, published an underground paper *Jangal* (Forest), sent five volunteers to help the Zhoffar rebels in Oman, and, in the next four years, carried out a succession of violent attacks. These included the robbing of six banks, the assassination of a U.S. military adviser as well as the chief of the Tehran police, and the bombings of Reza Shah's mausoleum and the offices of El Al, Shell, British Petroleum, and British Overseas Airways. By mid-1975, fifty Mujahedin had lost their lives. Over 90 percent of them came from the intelligentsia.

Although the membership of both the Mujahedin and the Feda'i was drawn from the young generation of the intelligentsia, there were nevertheless subtle differences in their social composition. While most Mujahedin—with the notable exception of a few of their founders—came from the central provinces, especially Isfahan, Fars, and Hamadan, most Feda'is came from the northern cities, particularly Teh-

[69] Mujahedin Organization, *Sharh-i Tasis*, p. 44.

ran, Tabriz, Rasht, Gurgan, Qazvin, and Mashad. Many Mujahedin were sons of religious-minded merchants, bazaar traders, clergymen, and other members of the traditional middle class; many Feda'is, on the other hand, were children of secular-minded teachers, civil servants, professionals, and other members of the modern middle class. All Mujahedin without exception were from Shi'i families; but a few of the Feda'is came from non-Shi'i backgrounds—from Sunni, Armenian, and Zoroastrian families. The Mujahedin could count only seven women among their dead; but the Feda'is could count as many as twenty-two. The Mujahedin recruited predominantly from students specializing in the physical sciences—from Tehran Polytechnic, the engineering college, the agricultural college, and the Aryamehr (Industrial) University. By contrast, the Feda'is recruited mostly from students of the arts, humanities, and social sciences—from the colleges of Art, Literature, Economics, Political Science and Teacher Training. Finally, whereas the Mujahedin failed to make inroads among the industrial proletariat, the Feda'is drew a few members from the urban working class: the Mujahedin dead included only two workers, the Feda'i as many as twelve.

Although the Mujahedin was Islamic, its revolutionary interpretation of Islam produced an ideology not very different from that of the Marxist Feda'i. It argued that Iran was dominated by imperialism, especially American imperialism, that the White Revolution had transformed Iran from a feudal society to a bourgeois one heavily dependent on Western capitalism, and that the country was threatened by cultural imperialism as well as by military, economic, and political imperialism. The Pahlevi regime, it asserted, had little social support outside the comprador bourgeoisie, and ruled mainly through terror, intimidation, and propaganda. The only way to shatter this atmosphere of terror was through heroic acts of violence. It also argued that when the regime collapsed the revolutionaries would carry out radical changes, ending the dependence on the West, building an independent economy, giving a free voice to the masses, redistributing wealth, and in general creating the classless Nezam-i Towhid. In fact, these ideas were so close to those of the Feda'i that the regime labeled the Mujahedin "Islamic Marxists" and claimed that Islam was merely a cover to hide their Marxism. The Mujahedin retorted that although they "respected Marxism as a progressive method of social analysis" they rejected materialism and viewed Islam as their inspiration, culture, and ideology.[70] In a pamphlet entitled *An Answer to the Regime's*

[70] Mujahedin Organization, *Dafa'at-i Naser Sadeq* (The Defense Speech of Naser Sadeq) (n.p., 1972), p. 24.

Latest Slanders, the Mujahedin summed up their attitude to both Marxism and Islam.

The shah is terrified of revolutionary Islam. This is why he keeps on shouting a Muslim cannot be a revolutionary. In his mind, a man is either a Muslim or a revolutionary; he cannot be both. But in the real world, the exact opposite is true. A man is either a revolutionary or not a true Muslim. In the whole of the Koran, there is not a single Muslim who was not a revolutionary. . . . The regime is trying to place a wedge between Muslims and Marxists. In our view, however, there is only one major enemy—imperialism and its local collaborators. When SAVAK shoots, it kills both Muslims and Marxists. When it tortures, it tortures both Muslims and Marxists. Consequently, in the present situation there is organic unity between Muslim revolutionaries and Marxist revolutionaries. In truth, why do we respect Marxism? Of course, Marxism and Islam are not identical. Nevertheless, Islam is definitely closer to Marxism than to Pahlevism. Islam and Marxism teach the same lessons, for they fight against injustice. Islam and Marxism contain the same message, for they inspire martyrdom, struggle, and self-sacrifice. Who is closer to Islam: the Vietnamese who fight against American imperialism or the shah who helps Zionism? Since Islam fights oppression it will work with Marxism which also fights oppression. They have the same enemy: reactionary imperialism.[71]

The Mujahedin became even more interested in Marxism after 1972. By the end of 1973, they were reading extensively on the Cuban, Vietnamese, Chinese, and Russian revolutions. By mid-1974, they were sending organizers into the factories. By early 1975, some of their leaders were talking of the need to synthesize Marxism and Islam. And by May 1975, the majority of their leaders who were still free voted to accept Marxism and to declare the organization to be Marxist-Leninist. In a pamphlet entitled *Manifesto on Ideological Issues*, the central leadership declared that after ten years of secret existence, four years of armed struggle, and two years of intense ideological rethinking, they had reached the conclusion that Marxism, not Islam, was the true revolutionary philosophy. According to the manifesto, they had come to this conclusion because they had found that Islam was the "ideology of the middle class" whereas Marxism was the "salvation of the working class."[72]

This transformation was vividly described by Mujtabi Taleqani, the son of Ayatallah Taleqani. In a moving letter to his father, he declared,

It is now two full years since I left home, went underground, and lost contact with you. Because of my deep respect for you and because of the many years

[71] Mujahedin Organization, *Pasokh Beh Etemat-i Akher-i Rezhim* (An Answer to the Regime's Latest Slanders) (n.p., 1975), pp. 10-13.

[72] Mujahedin Organization, *Biyanyeh-i E'lam-i Movaz'-i Iydolozhek* (Manifesto on Ideological Issues) (n.p., 1975), pp. 1-246.

we spent together fighting imperialism and reaction, I feel the need to explain to you why I and my adopted family decided to make major changes in our organization. . . . From my earliest days at your side, I learned how to hate this bloodthirsty tyranny. I always expressed my hatred through religion— through the militant teaching of Muhammad, ʿAli, and Hussein. I always respected Islam as the expression of the toiling masses fighting oppression. . . . In the past two years, however, I have started to study Marxism. Before I thought militant intellectuals could destroy the regime. Now I am convinced we must turn to the working class. But to organize the working class we must reject Islam, for religion refused to recognize the main dynamic of history— that of class struggle. Of course, Islam can play a progressive role, especially in mobilizing the intelligentsia against imperialism. But it is only Marxism that provides a scientific analysis of society and looks toward the exploited classes for liberation. Before I thought that those who believed in historical materialism could not possibly make the supreme sacrifice since they had no faith in the afterlife. Now I know that the highest sacrifice anyone can make is to die for the liberation of the working class.[73]

This ideological about-turn caused a sharp split within the Mujahedin. While some members, mostly in Tehran, supported the change, others, particularly in the provinces, remained Islamic, refused to give up the Mujahedin label, and accused their rivals of engineering a coup, murdering one of their leaders, and betraying others to the police. Thus, after May 1975 there were two rival Mujahedins, each with its own publication, its own organization and its own activities. The exploits of the Islamic Mujahedin included a bank robbery in Isfahan, a bombing of a Jewish emigration office in Tehran, and a strike in the Aryamehr University to commemorate the anniversary of the executions of their founders. Those of the Marxist Mujahedin included the bombing of the offices of International Telephone and Telegraph and the assassination of two American military advisers. In the course of the next two years, thirty members of the Marxist Mujahedin lost their lives. Among those executed was a woman from Tehran University—the first woman to be placed before a firing squad in Iranian history.

By early 1976, the two Mujahedin, like the Fedaʾi, had suffered such heavy losses that they began to reconsider their tactics. The Islamic Mujahedin stepped up its campus activities, circulated its own and Shariʿati's works, and established contact with the Islamic Student Society in North America and Western Europe. Meanwhile, the Marxist Mujahedin intensified its labor activities, called for the establishment of a new working-class party, started a paper called *Qiyam-i Kargar* (Worker's Revolt), and formed links with Maoists among the

[73] M. Taleqani, "Letter to My Father," *Mujahed*, no. 6 (July 1976), pp. 131-44.

Confederation of Iranian Students in Western Europe. It also entered negotiations with the Feda'i to merge the two Marxist organizations, but soon broke off the talks on the grounds that the latter remained tied to "its Castroist roots," refused to denounce "Soviet social imperialism," and secretly flirted with such "dubious entities" as the Tudeh and the National Front.[74] For its part, the Feda'i accused the Marxist Mujahedin of blindly accepting Maoism, and, avoiding polemics on the nature of Islam, backed off from associating with an organization that had shed the blood of Islamic Mujahedins and had openly denounced Islam as a "petty bourgeois ideology."[75]

The guerrilla movement, like the opposition organizations that came before it, failed to bring down the regime. But its work was not entirely in vain, for when the revolutionary upsurge began in late 1977 all four guerrilla organizations—the Feda'i, the pro-Tudeh Feda'i Munsh'eb, the Islamic Mujahedin, and the Marxist Mujahedin—were well placed to take advantage of the situation. All four had kept intact their underground organizations, storing weapons, recruiting new members, and publishing manifestos, leaflets, and journals. All four had gained not only armed experience but also a valuable mystique of revolutionary heroism. And all four had enough cadres—especially after the release of many political prisoners in late 1978—to move into action when the regime began to crumble. In fact, it was these four guerrilla organizations that on February 9-11, 1979—almost on the eighth anniversary of the Siakal incident—delivered the regime its coup de grâce.

[74] Mujahedin Organization, *Masa'el-i Had-i Jonbesh-i Ma* (Critical Problems of Our Movement) (n.p., 1977), pp. 1-392.

[75] Feda'i Organization, *Nashrieh-i Vazheh-i Bahas Darun-i Dow Sazman* (Special Documents on the Debate between the Two Organizations) (n.p., 1977), pp. 1-76.

ELEVEN

The Islamic
Revolution

The most indubitable feature of a revolution is the direct interference of the masses in historic events. In ordinary times, the state, be it monarchical or democratic, elevates itself above the nation, and history is made by specialists— kings, ministers, bureaucrats, parliamentarians, journalists. But in revolutions, the masses break over the barriers excluding them from the political arena, sweep aside the established representatives, and create by their own interference the initial groundwork for a new regime. Whether this is good or bad we leave to the judgment of moralists. . . . The history of revolution is for us first of all the forcible entry of the masses into the political arena.
—L. Trotsky, *The Russian Revolution* (New York, 1959), p. ix.

MIDDLE-CLASS PROTEST (MAY 1977-JUNE 1978)

In the mid-1970s the shah's regime seemed as durable as the massive dams he built and proudly named after his relatives. A vast army, equipped with ultramodern weapons and helped by an efficient secret police, appeared to have the capacity to stamp out rebellions as far away as Oman. An immense bureaucracy, bolstered by the well-financed patronage network, claimed to have the power not only to control the economy but also to radically restructure the whole society. And an enormous income derived from the oil industry provided the means to buy off potential opposition and further expand the instruments of social control. This led most observers to conclude that the regime was so firmly grounded that it was indestructible. Even the scarce few who were less sanguine about the stability of the regime and more aware of the social tensions rising behind the facade expected the system to last until the late 1980s, when the oil revenues would fall. They felt that even though the regime had no foundations in the social fabric and no channels for releasing the mounting tensions, yet its institutional pillars were strong enough to withstand the pressures exerted by uneven development and lopsided modernization. In their estimate, cracks would appear not in the late 1970s, but in the late 1980s and early 1990s.

These calculations, however, were dashed by two unexpected crises: an economic crisis in the form of acute inflation; and an institutional crisis produced by foreign pressures on the shah to relax police controls and observe the human rights of political dissenters. Inflation, which had almost disappeared from the Iranian scene during the second half of the 1960s, reappeared with a vengeance in the early 1970s, raising the cost-of-living index from 100 in 1970 to 126 in 1974, further to 160 in 1975, and further to over 190 in 1976.[1] The rise was even steeper for such essentials as food and housing, especially in the cities. For example, a report published by the London *Economist* in 1976 estimated that rents in residential parts of Tehran rose 300 percent in five years, and that by 1975 a middle-class family could be spending for housing as much as 50 percent of its annual income.[2] A complex combination of factors caused this inflation: the lack of housing and influx of over 60,000 well-paid foreign technicians; the failure of agricultural production to keep up with the rising population; the sudden jump in food prices on the world markets; the crash industrialization program and the continued growth in the military establishment, which created labor shortages, raised wages in the rural sector, drained labor from the rural sector, and thus further aggravated the agricultural problem; and, most important of all, the overheating of the economy once the oil billions were poured into ambitious development projects—in 1974-1975 the government tripled its development investments and increased the money supply by over 60 percent.[3] When economists warned of the dangers of overheating, the shah declared that statesmen should never listen to economists.

However complex the causes of inflation, the regime found a simplistic solution: it placed the blame squarely on the shoulders of the business community. In the words of the London *Economist*, "inflation began to gain momentum in 1973, and by the summer of 1976 had reached such alarming proportions that the Shah, who tends to look at economic problems in military terms, declared war on profiteers."[4] At first, the regime took aim on big businessmen, arrested with much fanfare "industrial feudalists" such as Elqanian and Vahabzadeh, and thereby frightened many others to transfer capital to safer territories.

[1] The Plan and Budget Organization of Iran, *Salnameh-i Amar-i Keshvar* (Annual Statistics for the State) (Tehran, 1977).

[2] M. Field, ed., *Middle East Annual Report* (London, 1977), pp. 150-58.

[3] "Iran's Miracle that Was," *Economist*, 20 December 1975.

[4] Field, *Middle East Annual Report*, p. 14.

As an American journal noted, "the rich voted with their money long before they voted with their feet."[5] And a foreign correspondent aptly stated that the "anti-profiteering campaign" caused schizophrenia among rich entrepreneurs: on one hand they benefited from the socioeconomic system, especially the development plans; on the other hand they suffered from the political system, which placed their wealth and futures in the hands of one man.[6]

Discovering that the war on rich entrepreneurs did not end inflation, the regime took aim on shopkeepers and small businessmen. The central government imposed strict price controls on many basic commodities, and imported large quantities of wheat, sugar, and meat to undercut local dealers. Meanwhile, the Resurgence party organized some 10,000 students into vigilante gangs called "inspectorate teams" and dispatched them into the bazaars to wage a "merciless crusade against profiteers, cheaters, hoarders, and unscrupulous capitalists."[7] Similarly, the so-called Guild Courts set up hastily by SAVAK gave out some 250,000 fines, banned 23,000 traders from their home towns, handed out to some 8,000 shopkeepers prison sentences ranging from two months to three years, and brought charges against another 180,000 small businessmen.[8] By early 1976, every bazaar family had at least one member who had directly suffered from the "anti-profiteering campaign." One shopkeeper told a French correspondent that the White Revolution was beginning to resemble a Red Revolution. Another told an American correspondent that "the bazaar was being used as a smokescreen to hide the vast corruption rampant in government and in the bosom of the royal family."[9] The formation of the Resurgence party had been an affront to the bazaars; the anti-profiteering campaign was a blatant invasion of the bazaars. Not for the first time, the bazaar community increasingly turned to its traditional ally, the ʿulama, for help and protection.

This economic crisis coincided with external pressures on the shah to relax police controls. In early 1975, the London-based Amnesty International, which in the past had focused on political prisoners in the Soviet bloc, turned its attention to noncommunist countries and discovered that Iran was one of the world's "worst violators of human

[5] Mansur, "The Crisis in Iran," *Armed Forces Journal International*, January 1979, p. 29.

[6] E. Rouleau, "Iran: Myth and Reality," *The Guardian*, 31 October 1976.

[7] A. Masʿoud, "The War against Profiteers," *Donya*, 3 (January 1976), 6-10.

[8] P. Balta, "Iran in Revolt," *Ittilaʿat*, 6 October 1979.

[9] *Iran Times*, 8 December 1978; E. Rouleau, "Iran: Myth and Reality," *The Guardian*, 31 October 1976; N. Cage, "Iran: Making of a Revolution," *New York Times*, 17 December 1978.

rights." The more conservative International Commission of Jurists in Geneva took the regime to task for "systematically using torture" and "violating the basic civil rights of its citizens." Likewise, the UN-affiliated International League for Human Rights sent an open letter to the shah in which it accused the regime of intensely abusing human rights and called upon him to "rectify the deplorable human rights situation in Iran."[10]

While international organizations were criticizing the regime, groups of Iranian exiles formed their own human rights committees to publicize SAVAK atrocities. For example, in London graduate students who had contacts with the Labour party and the British trade union movement formed the Committee against Repression in Iran. In New York a similar group of students received help from American writers to establish the Committee for Artistic and Intellectual Freedom in Iran. In Paris the Third National Front worked closely with French lawyers and intellectuals such as Jean Paul Sartre to publicize the plight of political prisoners in Iran. And throughout Western Europe and North America, the Iranian Student Confederation and the Islamic Student Society constantly organized street demonstrations to expose the regime's unpopularity and to tarnish the favorable image the shah had meticulously projected over the years through the Western mass media.

These activities brought results, encouraging influential newspapers that had previously praised the shah to criticize his police methods. For example, the highly respected *Sunday Times* of London ran a series of exposés on SAVAK and concluded that "there was a clear pattern" of torture used not only against active dissidents but also against intellectuals who dared whisper criticisms of the regime.[11] Even more serious for the shah, American Congressmen began to question the wisdom of selling so much sophisticated weaponry to a regime that depended entirely on one man; Washington insiders began to refer to the regime as a "one-bullet state." After hearing evidence presented by Amnesty International and the International Commission of Jurists, the chairman of the House of Representative's Subcommittee on International Organizations declared that the Iranian regime could not be considered stable until it permitted "popular input," created proper parliamentary structures, and allowed the freedom of press,

[10] Amnesty International, *Annual Report for 1974-75* (London, 1975); International Commission of Jurists, *Human Rights and the Legal System in Iran* (Geneva, 1976), pp. 1-72; J. Shestack, Letter to H.I.M. the Shah, 17 June 1977.

[11] P. Jacobson, "Torture in Iran," *Sunday Times*, 19 January 1975.

discussion, and assembly.[12] Similarly, a Subcommittee on Arms Sales, after receiving information from the State Department, the CIA, and the Defense Department, concluded that it was potentially dangerous to sell so many weapons to such a repressive regime.[13] Finally, Jimmy Carter, in the 1976 presidential primaries, championed the cause of human rights throughout the world, and, in the last stages of the presidential election, specifically named Iran as one of the countries in which America should do more to protect civil and political liberties. Although it is not clear that the new administration in Washington actually pressed the regime to liberalize, Carter's election certainly had an immediate impact on both the shah and the opposition. The former felt that the new president expected him to display at least some respect for political liberties. The latter also felt that the White House—for the first time since Kennedy's administration—was willing to protect moderate dissenters from SAVAK onslaughts. As Bazargan put it after the revolution, Carter's election made it possible for Iran to breathe again.[14]

The shah had a number of reasons for responding positively to external pressures. He did not want to jeopardize his "special relations" with Washington and his access to American arms. He was reluctant to lose the image of a forward-looking modernizer eager to bring the advantages of Western civilization to Iran—an image he had cultivated at great expense in Europe and America, especially on Madison Avenue. Moreover, he was convinced that his reforms were so popular that he could relax controls without endangering the whole regime; decades of propaganda had managed to fool the ruler if not the ruled. As he confidently told foreign correspondents in early 1975, the opposition was limited to a handful of nihilists, anarchists, and communists.[15] Furthermore, the death of the more realistic and experienced politicians—notably 'Alam, 'Ala, Eqbal, Sa'id, Hakimi, Bayat, Sayyid Ziya, Qavam, Soheily, and the elder Zahedi—had reduced the shah's circle of advisers to a small group of younger yes-men competing to tell their monarch what he wanted to hear. Thus the shah began to walk toward the abyss of revolution, with court advisers inadvertently helping him to pull down the crown further over his eyes.

The program to relax police controls began in early 1977, and picked up pace in the summer of that year. In February, the regime

---

[12] U.S. Congress, Subcommittee on International Organizations, *Human Rights in Iran* (Washington, D.C., 1977), p. 25.

[13] Cited by Rouleau, "Iran: Myth and Reality."

[14] M. Bazargan, "Letter to the Editor," *Ittila'at*, 7 February 1980.

[15] Cited in "Iran towards Unity," *Khabarnameh*, no. 42 (June 1975), p. 1.

amnestied 357 political prisoners. In March, it allowed the International Commission of the Red Cross to visit twenty prisons and see some 3,000 prison inmates. In April, it permitted foreign lawyers to observe the trial of eleven dissidents accused of terrorism; this was the first time since the early 1960s that outside lawyers had been allowed into a military tribunal. In early May, the shah gave a private audience to a representative of Amnesty International and promised to improve prison conditions. In late May, he gave a similar audience to a representative of the International Commission of Jurists, and, after complaining that the "Jewish controlled press in America" was maligning him, agreed to amend court procedures to better protect the rights of political detainees.[16] In early June, the Resurgence party announced that it welcomed free discussions and constructive criticisms. In July, the shah dismissed Hoveida, who had headed the government for the previous twelve years, and gave the premiership to Jamshid Amouzegar, a fifty-one-year-old American-educated technocrat who headed the more liberal "progressive wing" of the Resurgence party. And in August, the government decreed the court reforms promised earlier to the International Commission of Jurists. These reforms, entitled Rules of Procedure in Military Courts, introduced four significant changes: civilians brought before military tribunals could choose nonmilitary lawyers to be their defense attorneys; detainees were to appear before magistrates within twenty-four hours of their detention; defense lawyers could not be prosecuted for statements made in court; and trials were to be open unless such publicity endangered public order. In decreeing these reforms, the shah privately promised the International Commission of Jurists that in future trials would be in civilian rather than in military courts. This proved to be as big a blunder as his 1949 decision to permit free elections in Tehran.

This slight loosening of controls encouraged the opposition to raise its voice. In May 1977, fifty-three lawyers—many of whom had supported Mossadeq—sent an open letter to the imperial palace and thereby initiated an intense campaign of protests through public communiques.[17] Their letter accused the government of interfering in court proceedings and announced the formation of a special commission to protect the judiciary from the legislative branch. This was

---

[16] W. Butler, "Memorandum to the International Commission of Jurists on Private Audience with the Shah of Iran," 30 May 1977.

[17] For the open letters sent in 1977 see: *Jonbesh* (Movement), a newsletter edited by Hajj Sayyid Javadi; *Buletin-i Khabari* (Bulletin of News), the organ of the Writers' Association; and *Khabarnameh* (Newsletter), the organ of the Union of the National Front Forces.

the first time since 1963 that a group inside Iran had dared to denounce the regime publicity. In June, the three leading personalities of the National Front—Sanjabi, Foruhar, and Bakhtiyar—wrote a more daring letter addressed to the shah, pointedly avoiding use of the royalist calendar and the title Aryamehr, and accusing the regime both of wrecking the economy through inflation and neglect of agriculture, and of violating international law, human rights, and the 1905-1909 constitution. The letter concluded as follows:

The only way to restore national unity and individual rights is to abandon despotism, respect the constitutional laws, observe the Universal Declaration of Human Rights, abolish the one-party system, permit the freedom of press and assembly, release political prisoners, allow exiles to return home, and establish a government that enjoyed public confidence and respected the fundamental laws.

Also in June, forty prominent poets, novelists, and intellectuals sent an open letter to Premier Hoveida and revived their Writers' Association, which had been suppressed since 1964. The letter denounced the regime for violating the constitution, demanded an end to censorship, protested that SAVAK stifled all cultural, intellectual, and artistic activity, and argued that many citizens were in prison for the "crime" of reading books disapproved by the police. The forty signatories covered a wide spectrum of political opinion. They included Behazin, the veteran pro-Tudeh novelist; Baqer Momeni, a Marxist intellectual who had left the Tudeh in the mid 1950s; Hussein Malek, a professor of sociology and since the death of his brother Khalel Maleki the country's leading non-Tudeh Marxist theorist; Manoucher Hezarkhani, another independent Marxist essayist; Naser Pakdaman, a young professor of economics and early member of Khalel Maleki's Society of Iranian Socialists; Homa Nateq, a young French-educated professor of history sympathetic to feminist causes and to the left wing of the National Front; Simin Daneshvar, a novelist, feminist, and widow of the famous writer al-Ahmad; Dr. Ghulam Hussein Sa'edi, a trained psychologist who had become the country's leading playwright and had been arrested in 1975 for publishing depressing literature; Fereydoun Adamiyat, a prominent secular liberal intellectual who had written the best-known histories of the constitutional movement; and 'Ali Asghar Hajj Sayyid Javadi, a popular essayist who began his political career in the early 1940s within the Tudeh, in the 1950s joined Khalel Maleki's group, in the 1960s wrote on socialist and Islamic themes, and by the 1970s had a large following among lay religious readers.

The opposition grew more vocal during the summer of 1977. In early July, a number of writers and publishers formed a Group for Free Books and Free Thought. In a letter sent to journals published in exile, they gave detailed cases of writers who had been tortured and whose works had been censored.[18] In late July, sixty-four prominent lawyers met openly in a Tehran hotel and drafted a strongly worded manifesto. The manifesto accused the government of violating the constitution, demanded the immediate abolition of all extra-constitutional tribunals, and argued that since the legal profession was the "guardian of the fundamental laws" they would assume the responsibility of defending the independence of the judiciary. These lawyers were headed by Nazeh of the Liberation Movement; 'Abdul Karim Lahiji, a young European-educated lawyer sympathetic to the National Front; and Hedayatallah Matin-Daftari, a grandson of Mossadeq, an important member of the Second National Front, and a veteran human rights lawyer who had been badly beaten up by SAVAK in 1964 for trying to give legal counsel to political prisoners.

The opposition grew even more vocal during the autumn. The Writers' Association elected Behazin as its chairman and obtained the signatures of ninety-eight prominent intellectuals on another open letter to the government. This letter accused the regime of hypocrisy, arguing that SAVAK continued to censor the media while the shah was telling the world that he was liberalizing. Meanwhile, fifty-four judges sent an open letter to the High Court complaining that the government had grossly violated the constitution, especially the independence of the judiciary. Twenty-nine opposition leaders, including Bazargan, Sanjabi, Bakhtiyar, Matin-Daftari, Lahiji, Ayatallah Zanjani, Nazeh, and Hajj Sayyid Javadi formed the Iranian Committee for the Defense of Freedom and Human Rights. In their first act, they sent an open letter to the secretary general of the United Nations detailing how the regime had systematically used torture, military tribunals, and arbitrary arrest to intimidate the opposition. One hundred twenty lawyers, led by Nazeh, Lahiji, and Matin-Daftari, formed the Association of Iranian Jurists, demanded immediate implementation of the constitutional laws, and announced that since their previous requests had not been met they would set up a working group with a newsletter to monitor prison conditions and publicize SAVAK abuses. Similarly, a group of professors formed the National Organization of University Teachers to fight for academic freedom, while merchants in the Tehran bazaar established the Society of Merchants, Traders, and Craftsmen to curtail the activities of the Resurgence party. Even

---

[18] Group for Free Books and Free Thought, "An Open Letter," Payam-i *Daneshjow* (Student Message), 4 (August 1977), 51-94.

more important, theology students in Qum formed an Educational Society and demanded the return of Khomeini, the end of censorship, the reopening of Fayzieh seminary and Tehran University—both of which had been closed recently because of student protests, freedom of press and assembly, dissolution of the Resurgence party, independence of the judiciary, help for agriculture, "true sovereignty for Iran," and the "end of ties with imperialistic powers."[19]

Seeing that these professional and human rights groups were able to function, old and new political organizations began to emerge. Sanjabi, Foruhar, Bakhtiyar, a bazaar merchant, and representatives from the Society of Socialists revived the National Front, calling it the Union of National Front Forces (Ittehad-i Niruha-yi Jebʿeh-i Melli). They also started a paper called *Khabarnameh* (Newsletter), and demanded from the government dissolution of SAVAK, trials in civilian courts for civilian defendants, release of all political prisoners, return of all exiles, end of censorship, freedom for all political parties, and removal of restrictions on guilds and trade unions. In announcing these demands, Sanjabi stressed that the National Front would continue to pursue the course set by the late Mossadeq: make Iran truly independent in foreign affairs, and establish genuine democracy at home by fighting for individual rights, social freedoms, and the constitutional laws.[20]

Similarly, Bazargan revived the Liberation Movement, worked closely with the National Front and the bazaar community, and called for the implementation of the 1905-1909 constitution. Meanwhile, Rahmatallah Moqadam Maraghehi, a French-educated liberal intellectual from a prominent Azerbaijani family with close ties to Ayatallah Shariʿatmadari, brought together a group of like-minded secular professionals to form a new party called the Radical Movement (Nahzat-i Radikal). Finally, the Tudeh party reemerged from its underground existence, revived some of its cells, especially in Tehran, Abadan, and Rasht, and, helped by ex-Fedaʾi members, started publishing in Tehran a newspaper named *Nuyid* (Harbinger). It is significant that in this early stage of the revolution none of the major opposition parties openly called for the establishment of either a republic or an Islamic republic. On the contrary, they all stressed that their immediate goal was to reestablish the 1906-1909 fundamental laws that had created a constitutional monarchy.

Until mid-November 1977, the opposition focused its energies on indoor activities: writing letters, forming new groups, reviving old

---

[19] Educational Society of Qum, "Demands," *Mujahed*, 6 (January 1978), p. 5.
[20] K. Sanjabi, "Speech," *Khabarnameh*, 24 August 1977.

ones, drafting manifestos, and publishing newspapers. After mid-November, however, the opposition overflowed into the streets. This marked the start of a new stage in the revolutionary process. The turning point came on November 19, when, after nine evenings of peaceful poetry-reading sessions organized by the Writers' Association in the Iranian-German Cultural Society and in Aryamehr University, the police attempted to disband the tenth session with its full-capacity audience of some 10,000 students. The attempt promptly incited an angry crowd to march out of the campus into the streets shouting antiregime slogans. In the ensuing clash with the police, one student was killed, over seventy were injured, and some one hundred were arrested. The next ten days saw more student demonstrations and the closure of the main Tehran universities in protest over the blood-shed of November 19. And during the course of the following week, the country's major universities struck to commemorate Azar 16—the unofficial student day—and the demonstrators arrested in the previous disturbances were acquitted after brief trials in civilian courts. These trials were a clear sign to the country that SAVAK could no longer use military tribunals to intimidate dissenters. Liberalization, which had been introduced as a political tranquilizer, was proving to be a potent stimulant.

Street protests multiplied in January 1978. On January 7, *Ittila'at* published a diatribe against the antiregime clergy, calling them "black reactionaries" and accusing them of secretly working with international communists to undo the achievements of the White Revolution.[21] The article also charged that Khomeini was really a foreigner who in his youth had worked as a British spy, led a licentious life, and, to top it all, had written erotic Sufi poetry. The article outraged Qum. The seminaries and the bazaar closed down, demanding a public apology; and some 4,000 theology students and their sympathizers clashed with the police as they took to the streets, shouting "we don't want the Yazid government," "we want our constitution," and "we demand the return of Ayatallah Khomeini." According to the government, two were killed in the clash; according to the opposition, seventy were killed and over five hundred were injured.

The casualty figures may have been in dispute, but the repercussions were unambiguous. The following day, Khomeini called for more demonstrations, congratulated Qum and the progressive (*motaraqi*) clergy for their heroic stand against paganism (*taghot*), and accused the shah of collaborating with America to undermine Islam, destroy Iranian agriculture, and turn the country into a dumping ground for

[21] "Iran and the Black and Red Reactionaries," *Ittila'at*, 7 January 1978.

foreign goods.[22] Meanwhile, Shari'atmadari, in a rare interview with foreign correspondents, complained that the government had slandered the 'ulama, the police had behaved in an un-Islamic manner, and said that if wanting the constitution was a sign of "black reaction" then he had to confess to being a staunch "black reactionary."[23] He also threatened to personally convey the bodies of the dead demonstrators to the palace gates in Tehran unless the government immediately stopped its attacks on the 'ulama. Moreover, Shari'atmadari, together with eighty-eight clerical, bazaar, and other opposition leaders, called upon the country to observe the fortieth day of the Qum massacre by staying away from work and peacefully attending mosque services. Thus began three cycles of forty-day upheavals. Journalists, later searching for the spark of the revolution, latched onto the *Ittila'at* article and its subsequent outburst in Qum. But in actual fact, the beginnings of the revolution were more complex and the first spark can be pushed back to the poetry-reading sessions and their subsequent upheavals in Aryamehr University. These two crises not only reflect the complexities of the whole revolution but also epitomize the two divergent forces present in the revolutionary movement: the salaried middle class and its hotbed of political discontent—the modern universities; and the propertied middle class and its centers of sociopolitical organization—the traditional seminaries and the old-fashioned bazaars.

The fortieth day of the Qum massacre fell on February 18. To mourn the dead, the major bazaars and universities closed down. The clergy held memorial services in most large towns. And peaceful demonstrations took place in twelve cities, including Tehran, Qum, Isfahan, Mashad, Ahwaz, Shiraz, and Rasht. In Tabriz, however, the demonstration turned violent after an irate police officer shot dead a teenage student protestor. Incited by the scene, the demonstrators marched onto the police station, and, finding that the authorities were not willing to shoot, took over much of the city, attacking police stations, Resurgence party offices, banks, luxury hotels, and cinemas that specialized in sexy films. In the Tabriz upheaval, as in most upheavals throughout the revolution, demonstrators, however angry, rarely indulged in physical attacks on persons and private property. On the contrary, they invariably avoided persons, focusing instead on particular types of property—police stations and Resurgence party offices because they symbolized the Pahlevi state; luxury hotels because they catered to the affluent rich, both native and foreign; "pornographic"

[22] R. Khomeini, "Proclamation," *Mujahed*, 6 (January 1978), 1-2.
[23] Cited in *Khabarnameh*, no. 54 (January 1978), pp. 1-2.

movie houses because they violated the puritanical mores of the bazaar middle class; and banks, partly because they transgressed the Islamic taboo against usury, partly because they discriminated against small businessmen, but mainly because they were owned by the royal family, the state, and the wealthy entrepreneurs. Small banks owned by bazaar entrepreneurs were often left untouched, and, as European eyewitnesses in Tabriz reported, all the large banks that were attacked lost all their records but "not a single" cent from their tills. These demonstrators, which the government press denounced as "greedy mobs," were interested more in making a political point than in lining their pockets. The Tabriz uprising lasted two full days, subsiding only when the government rushed in military reinforcements, including tanks, helicopter gunships, and armored troop carriers. After the uprising, the total dead were estimated as 6 by the government, as over 300 by the opposition, and as nearly 100 by the European eyewitnesses.[24] Whatever the real figure, this was the largest public protest since 1963. The religious leaders and the National Front asked the country to honor the dead by attending mosque services on the fortieth day after the upheaval.

The fortieth day came on March 29. On that day and the following two days, most bazaars and universities closed down, while large memorial processions were organized in fifty-five urban centers. Although most of these processions were orderly, in Tehran, Yazd, Isfahan, Babol, and Jahrom they turned violent, attacking not only banks, party offices, luxury hotels, and select movie houses, but also police cars, royal statues, and liquor stores. In Yazd, where the most violent of these confrontations took place, some ten thousand mourners, after listening to a fiery preacher just released from prison, marched out of the bazaar mosque and headed for the main police station, shouting "Death to the shah," "Greetings to Khomeini," and "Long live the martyrs of Qum and Tabriz." Before they reached their destination they were intercepted by a volley of police bullets. The nationwide three-day crisis did not end until the shah rushed back from naval maneuvers in the Persian Gulf and took personal command of the antiriot police forces. According to the regime, five demonstrators were killed in the three days of rioting. But according to the opposition, over one hundred were killed in Yazd alone. As before, Khomeini, Shari'atmadari, and other religious as well as lay opposition leaders asked the country to show their disgust with the government by peacefully attending fortieth-day services.

[24] N. Albala, "Mission to Iran" (unpublished report submitted to the Court of Appeals in Paris, March 1978), p. 9.

The next fortieth day fell on May 10. Again bazaars and major teaching institutions went on strike. Again mosque services and memorial processions were organized in many towns. And again some of these processions—this time as many as twenty-four—turned violent. In Tehran, the shah hurriedly canceled a visit to Eastern Europe and ordered two thousand troops to cordon off the city's bazaar and use tear gas to break up a meeting held outside the main mosque. In Qum, the disturbances lasted a full ten hours and subsided only when the army intervened, closing off the city's electricity and shooting indiscriminately into the crowds. In breaking up these crowds, troops chased a group of demonstrators to the doorstep of Shariʿatmadari's home, and, violating the traditional right to take sanctuary in the houses of religious leaders, broke in and shot dead two theology students. According to the government, the three cycles of forty-day riots had left 22 dead and some 200 injured.[25] According to the opposition, they had left 250 dead and over 600 injured.[26] Observers may question these figures, but they cannot dispute the fact that serious cracks had begun to appear in the formidable-looking Pahlevi regime.

To deal with the crisis, the regime adopted a complicated three-pronged strategy. First, it tried to physically intimidate the leaders of the secular opposition. Creating an Underground Committee of Revenge, SAVAK sent threatening letters to the lawyers and writers prominent in the human rights movement; circulated leaflets accusing these lawyers and writers of being stooges of American imperialism; kidnaped and badly beat up Homa Nateq and another member of the Writers' Association; and bombed the offices of Sanjabi, Bazargan, Matin-Daftari, Nazeh, Foruhar, Lahiji, Moqadam Maraghehi, and Hajji Moinian, a bazaar merchant closely identified with the National Front. Similarly, the Resurgence party set up a vigilante force called the Resistance Corps, staffed it with policemen in civilian clothes, and attacked meetings organized by student groups, the Writers' Association, and the National Front. In one such attack, the Resistance Corps, pretending to be irate workers, seriously injured thirty people who were celebrating ʿAyd-i Qurban (Day of Sacrifice) in the private gardens of a National Front leader. Moreover, the shah, when asked by the press if he would negotiate with the secular opposition, rejected any such possibility on the grounds that the National Front was "even more traitorous than the Tudeh party."[27]

[25] Compiled from *Ittilaʿat*, February-June 1978.

[26] Compiled from *Mujahed*, the organ of the Liberation Front published in North America.

[27] Cited in *Iran Times*, 21 July 1978.

Second, the regime abandoned some of the policies that had aroused the wrath of the bazaars and the moderate clergy. It called off the anti-inflation war against small businessmen, dissolved the notorious "inspectorate teams," amnestied shopkeepers imprisoned for profiteering, ended plans for establishing a grand state-owned market, and permitted the Tehran bazaar to form a Society of Merchants, Traders, and Craftsmen. Moreover, the government publicly apologized to Shari'atmadari for the attack on his home; banned "pornographic" films; promised to open the Fayzieh seminary; and allowed 184 journalists to publish an open letter that criticized the state-controlled media for portraying peaceful religious processions as hooligan mobs led by outside agitators and Marxist-Islamic lunatics. Furthermore, the shah made a well-publicized pilgrimage to the Imam Reza shrine in Mashad; increased the annual quota of pilgrims to Mecca; issued a code of ethics for the imperial family, ordering his fifty relatives to end all their business activities; and replaced General Nasiri, the notorious chief of SAVAK for the previous twelve years, with General Moqadam, a respected professional officer whose Azerbaijani family had close ties to Shari'atmadari. The shah also promised to make the forthcoming Majles elections "100 percent free"; encouraged a circle of liberal intellectuals around Empress Farah to form a Study Group on Iran's Problems; and announced that he was willing to negotiate with the religious leaders, since "some of them are not that bad."[28]

Third, Premier Amouzegar tried to slow down the spiraling cost of living—the main economic cause of middle-class discontent—by slowing down the economy. Unable to persuade the shah to reduce the military budget, Amouzegar cut drastically civilian expenditures, especially the development plan. He eliminated $3.5 billion from the Five Year Plan, stretched the remaining three years of the Five Year Plan to four-and-a-half years, tightened credit, shelved plans for a subway system in Tehran, eliminated eighteen of the twenty proposed nuclear plants, postponed the building of many new factories, hospitals, and housing projects, and, most important of all, sharply reduced the number of government contracts given to the booming construction industry. As one American businessman noted, "the Iranian spending spree is over."[29] These cuts had an immediate effect. The GNP, which had been rising at the rate of 15 to 20 percent per annum in the previous years, increased only 2 percent in the first half of 1978. The urban construction industry, which had grown as much as 32 percent in the previous year, increased only 7 percent in the first

[28] Cited ibid., 8 July 1978.
[29] Cited by Y. Ibrahim, "Behind Iran's Revolution," *New York Times*, 4 February 1979.

nine months of 1978. Conversely, the cost-of-living index, which had spiraled at the rate of 30 to 35 percent in the previous years, rose only 7 percent in the first nine months of 1978. The government had managed to control inflation by engineering a mild recession.

The government strategy appeared to work. By the summer of 1978 the streets were remarkably quiet, no major disturbances occurred for two full months, and, even more significant, the fortieth day of the May 10-12 massacres passed without any new bloodshed. In preparation for the fortieth day, Shari'atmadari and the moderate clergy beseeched the faithful to attend mosque services but scrupulously to avoid street demonstrations. Shari'atmadari also told the press that he "did not care whether the shah went or stayed but he did want the return of the constitution."[30] Khomeini, on the other hand, exhorted the country to continue protesting until the "pagan regime" was overthrown.[31] The fact that in June the public heeded Shari'atmadari rather than Khomeini led many to conclude that the regime had weathered the storm. As Amouzegar confidently declared in early June, "the crisis is over."[32] In fact, the crisis had only just begun, and the summer quiet turned out to be the lull before the final storm.

MIDDLE- AND WORKING-CLASS PROTESTS (JUNE 1978-DECEMBER 1978)

During the upheavals of early 1978, the urban wage earners had been conspicuous by their absence. With the notable exception of Tabriz, where workers from small private factories had joined the uprising, most demonstrations had taken place around the universities, bazaars, and seminaries, and their participants had been drawn predominantly from the traditional and the modern middle classes. The situation changed drastically after June, however, when the urban poor, especially construction laborers and factory workers, started to join the street demonstrations. Their participation not only swelled the demonstrations from tens of thousands of marchers to hundreds of thousands and even millions, but also changed the class composition of the opposition and transformed the middle-class protest into a joint protest of the middle and working classes. Indeed, the entry of the working class made possible the eventual triumph of the Islamic Revolution.

[30] *Iran Times*, 2 June 1978.
[31] R. Khomeini, "A Message," *Mujahed*, 7 (June 1978), 1-3.
[32] Quoted in "Step by Step toward the Iranian Revolution," *Mardom*, 11 February 1980.

The working-class protests were triggered by the economic recession. Before the government engineered the recession, the ambitious development projects had eliminated urban unemployment and had even created local labor shortages. These shortages, in turn, had pushed up the wages of unskilled as well as skilled workers. Between 1970 and 1977, the rise in urban wages outpaced the 90 percent rise in consumer prices. For example, the daily minimum wage set by the government jumped from 80 rials in 1973 to 210 rials in 1977.[33] The daily income of unskilled construction laborers went up at the rate of 33 percent per year, rising from the equivalent of $1.20 in 1970 to over $5.50 in early 1977. The average wage in twenty-one key industries climbed 30 percent in 1974-1975 and 48 percent in 1975-1976.[34] The rise in the standard of living was most noticeable among skilled factory workers. In 1971, manufacturing workers in Tehran earned on average 220 rials a day—170 rials in basic pay, 31 rials in overtime, and 19 rials in profit-sharing. But by 1977, machine-tool workers in Arak were earning as much as 850 rials in basic pay alone and 150 rials in overtime.[35]

The rise in real wages directly effected the number of strikes occurring in the main industries. During the middle-class upheavals of October 1977-June 1978, there had been only seven major industrial strikes.[36] The number rose sharply after June, however, when the recession began to take its toll, especially in the construction industry, and the government further cut expenditures by placing a ceiling on wage increases and canceling the annual bonuses usually given to all state employees. By midsummer, real wages started to fall, unemployment rose from almost nothing to nearly 400,000, and take-home pay in the construction industry slumped as much as 30 percent.[37] Moreover, the shah used a televised press conference to launch a campaign against high wages and low productivity. Arguing that the "welfare state" had covered workers with "soft wool," he declared,

This is intolerable. Those who do not work, we shall take them by the tail and throw them out like mice. He who does not do his job properly is betraying not only his own conscience but also his patriotic duty. . . . I remember a few

[33] International Labor Office, *Employment and Income Policies for Iran* (Geneva, 1973), p. 79; *Iran Times*, 21 March 1978.

[34] R. Graham, *Iran: The Illusion of Power* (New York, 1979), pp. 89, 90; E. Rouleau, "Iran: Myth and Reality," *The Guardian*, 31 October 1976.

[35] International Labor Office, *Employment and Income Policies for Iran*, p. 80; "Factory Conditions," *Mujahed*, 4 (August 1975), 4.

[36] Compiled from *Mujahed, Khabarnameh, Mardom*, and *Setareh-i Surkh*.

[37] W. Branigan, "Little Joy Greets Shah's Anniversary," *Washington Post*, 20 August 1978.

years ago a mason—who is now so much in demand that people have to flatter him—was prepared to work a whole day for a mere meal and he never had enough work. But today, in this period of transition, we are in need of more workers and have to run after them in supplication.[38]

The shah ended the interview with the pronouncement that the people had to work harder, make more sacrifices, tighten their belts, and lower their economic aspirations. *Keyhan International* described that interview as historic. It proved to be more historic than anyone could have expected.

The get-tough policy toward labor sparked off a series of industrial strikes. In June, the employees of the electrical works in Tehran and the southern cities, of the water system in Tehran, and of a large industrial plant near Tehran stopped work in protest over the cancellation of the annual bonuses. In early July, over 600 sanitation workers in Abadan struck, demanding health insurance, annual bonuses, and a 20 percent wage increase to compensate for the year's inflation. In late July, 1,750 textile workers in Behshahr stopped work and called for higher wages and free union elections. In August, some 2,000 employees of the machine tool factory in Tabriz stayed away from work for two weeks demanding annual bonuses, higher wages, and better housing. And in September, major strikes over economic grievances broke out in the paper mill of Fars, in the car assembly plants of Tehran, and in the water works and the machine tool factory in Ahwaz.

Workers showed their discontent not only through strikes but also through demonstrations. The first major demonstration that drew large numbers of workers occurred in Mashad on July 22. On that day, a funeral procession for a local Hojjat al-Islam who had died in a car accident turned violent after some of the mourners threw rocks at the police, and the police in return fired into the crowd. By conservative estimates, the dead numbered over forty. This was the first bloody incident since early May. More were to follow in rapid succession. On the seventh day after the Mashad massacre, large memorial services were held in almost every major town. In Tehran, Tabriz, Qum, Isfahan, and Shiraz, the services escalated into street clashes. Even worse violence erupted during the month of Ramazan, which began on August 5. In the first few days of Ramazan, violent demonstrations took place in Tabriz, Mashad, Shahsaver, Ahwaz, Behbehan, Shiraz, and Isfahan. In Isfahan, where the worst incidents occurred, angry demonstrators—some armed with pistols—took over

[38] "Historic Interview with His Imperial Majesty," *Keyhan International*, 26 October 1976.

much of the city and released a highly respected ayatallah who had just been arrested. The government did not regain full control of Isfahan until two days later, when it declared martial law, rushed in army contingents, and shot down over one hundred demonstrators. This was the first time since 1953 that martial law had been imposed on a provincial capital. Amouzegar, in shifting economic gears, thought he was dealing with a Western-style society where recessions can be turned on and off without major upheavals. By mid-August, he had discovered that Iran lacked the political stability of the West, and that government-engineered recessions could very well arouse working-class protests without alleviating middle-class discontent.

After the Isfahan upheavals, the government braced itself for another cycle of forty-day riots. But before the cycle could begin, the country was shaken by a calamity that dwarfed all previous ones. On August 19, coinciding with the twenty-fifth anniversary of the 1953 coup, a suspicious fire burned to death over four hundred men, women, and children trapped inside a cinema in the working-class district of Abadan. The government promptly accused the opposition of responsibility, citing the recent mob attacks on movie houses. The opposition, on the other hand, accused SAVAK of arranging a "Reichstag fire," locking the cinema doors, and sabotaging the local fire department. It also noted that demonstrators attacked only cinemas that were empty and specialized in foreign sex films, whereas the Abadan cinema was showing an Iranian film containing veiled criticisms of contemporary society. Whatever the truth, it was clear that the 10,000 relatives who gathered next day for a mass funeral blamed SAVAK. Marching through the city, the mourners shouted: "Burn the shah. End the Pahlevis. Soldiers, you are guiltless. The shah is the guilty one." The correspondent of the *Washington Post* commented that the Abadan demonstration, like the riots of the previous eight months, had one simple message: "The shah must go."[39]

The shah tried to deal with the heightened crisis by giving more concessions to the opposition. This time, the beneficiaries included the moderate secular opposition, especially the National Front. On the anniversary of the Constitutional Revolution, the shah announced that the country would soon have a "Western-styled democracy," and that all parties except the Tudeh would be free to campaign in the forthcoming parliamentary elections. He also amnestied another 261 political prisoners; continued to send arrested demonstrators to civilian courts, where they were invariably acquitted; allowed the press

[39] W. Branigin, "Abadan Mood Turns Sharply against the Shah," *Washington Post*, 26 August 1978.

to carry information on labor disputes and opposition parties; removed military guards from the universities; declared that deputies were free to leave the Resurgence party if they wished; and permitted Derekhshesh and Pezeshkpour to revive their teachers' union and Pan-Iranist party, respectively. What is more, on August 27 the shah replaced Amouzegar with Sharif Emami, who had been premier briefly in 1960, and gave him carte blanche to negotiate with the moderate clergy. Of all the court politicians, Sharif Emami was best suited for this task: he came from a clerical family, maintained friendly ties with some of the high-ranking ayatallahs, and for years had served as host to visiting religious dignitaries from the Arab countries.

Forming a new government, Sharif Emami took immediate steps to woo the religious establishment. He rescinded the imperial calendar; released many of the high-ranking clerics imprisoned since 1975; cut off state subsidies to the Resurgence party; closed down fifty-seven gambling casinos owned by the Pahlevi Foundation; asked the more corrupt members of the royal family to take extended vacations abroad; and, abolishing the post of minister for women's affairs, set up a Ministry of Religious Affairs. Moreover, Sharif Emami started a well-advertised campaign against prominent figures alleged to be Baha'is: Hoveida was removed from his post of court minister; Yazdani, the wealthy entrepreneur, was arrested for grand larceny; and two generals, the shah's personal physician, and the director of Iran Air were purged from their position on the grounds that they were Baha'i.

Sharif Emami's overtures seemed to work. Shari'atmadari announced that the country should give the new premier three months to implement the constitution. And in preparation for 'Ayd-i Fetr (day ending the Ramazan fast), Sharif Emami reached a settlement with Sanjabi, Bazargan, Foruhar, and other opposition leaders. Sharif Emami issued demonstration permits for that day and promised to place the military in the side streets. In return, the opposition leaders agreed to keep to a prescribed route, avoid slogans that attacked the shah personally, marshal the crowds with their own men, and discourage demonstrations on the following days. 'Ayd-i Fetr, which fell on September 4, was celebrated as planned. In almost every town, large crowds gathered for outdoor prayers. In Tehran, over 100,000 converged from the major mosques and Husseiniehs onto the spacious Shahyad Square shouting, "the army is part of the nation"; "free all political prisoners"; "we want Khomeini back"; "brother soldiers, why do you kill your brothers?" In the words of a foreign observer, the vast crowd was friendly and contained incongruous elements: dissident students in jeans, traditional women in chadours, workers in overalls, merchants in suits, and, most conspicuous of all, bearded mullas in black robes.[40]

ʿAyd-i Fetr passed without a hitch, but the following three days saw a drastic deepening of the crisis. Crowds continued to pour into the streets even though the opposition leaders called for restraint and the government banned all outdoor meetings. Moreover, the crowds grew bigger, and by September 7 the demonstration in Tehran attracted more than half a million participants. This was the largest meeting ever held in Iran. Furthermore, the crowds began to raise more radical slogans, shouting "death to the Pahlevis," "the shah is a bastard," "throw out America," "Hussein is our guide, Khomeini is our leader," "independence, freedom, and Islam," and, for the first time in the Tehran streets, "we want an Islamic republic." The radical demand for an Islamic republic had superceded the moderate call for the return of the 1905 constitution.

Convinced that the situation was getting out of hand, the shah tried to act decisively. On the evening of September 7, he forced the cabinet to decree martial law in Tehran and eleven other cities—Karaj, Qum, Tabriz, Mashad, Isfahan, Shiraz, Abadan, Ahwaz, Qazvin, Johram, and Kazerun. This was the first time since 1963 that martial law had been imposed on Tehran. To add bite to the decree, the shah gave the military governorship of the capital to General Oveissi, who, as governor during the riots of 1963, had earned the nickname, "butcher of Iran." The shah also banned all street demonstrations and issued warrants for the arrests of Sanjabi, Bazargan, Foruhar, Moinian, Lahiji, Behazin, Matin-Daftari, and Moqadam Maraghehi.

The inevitable confrontations took place on the following morning, Friday, September 8. The worst clashes occurred in southern Tehran, where the working-class residents set up barricades and threw molotov cocktails at army trucks; and in Jaleh Square at the heart of the bazaari residential areas in eastern Tehran, where some five thousand residents, many of them students, staged a sit-down demonstration.[41] In the southern slums, helicopter gunships were used to dislodge the rebels. According to one European correspondent, these helicopters left a "carnage of destruction."[42] In Jaleh Square, commandos and tanks surrounded the demonstrators, and, unable to persuade them to disperse, shot to kill. In the words of a European correspondent,

[40] "The Shah's Divided Land," *Time*, 18 September 1978.

[41] For detailed eyewitness accounts of the Jaleh Square massacre, see: I. Aminzadeh, "September 8: Day of Martyrdom," *Ittilaʿat*, 6 September 1979; and "I Witnessed the September 8 Massacre," *Mardom*, 11 February 1980.

[42] J. Gueyras, "Liberalization Is the Main Casualty," *The Guardian*, 17 September 1978.

the scene resembled a firing squad, with troops shooting at a mass of stationary protestors.[43] That night the military authorities announced that the day's casualties totaled 87 dead and 205 wounded. But the opposition declared that the dead numbered more than 4,000 and that as many as 500 had been killed in Jaleh Square alone.

Whatever the true figures, September 8 became known as Black Friday and left a permanent mark on Iran. It placed a sea of blood between the shah and the people. It enflamed public emotions, intensified popular hatred for the regime, and thereby further radicalized the population. It also undermined moderates who called for the 1905 constitution and sought a compromise with the monarchy. In the words of a French journalist, the "biggest casualty of Black Friday was the liberalization program."[44] In short, Black Friday ended the possibility of gradual reform and left the country with two simple choices: a drastic revolution or a military counterrevolution.

Four major reasons explain the failure of the year-old experiment to relax police controls. First, the quarter-century of repression had effectively destroyed all free labor unions, all independent professional associations, and all opposition parties with grass-root organizations. Thus when the shah tried to negotiate with the leaders of the moderate secular opposition, he discovered to his dismay that these leaders had neither the personal following nor the political organizations needed to restrain popular emotions. In short, acute political underdevelopment made it impossible for the shah suddenly to change course and initiate institutional reforms. Second, the sudden change of course coincided with an equally sudden economic recession that produced a mass of indignant unemployed workers. They were indignant not only because of unemployment, poverty, and economic insecurity, but also because of the fifteen years of broken promises. They had first been promised land, then proper wages in agriculture, and finally a decent life in the booming cities. They had received, however, none of these. Not surprisingly, they concluded that they had much to gain and nothing to lose in overthrowing the regime.

Third, the barrage of demonstrations polarized the situation by shifting the arena of politics from the drawing rooms and the negotiating tables to the streets and the slums. Each bullet fired, each dead demonstrator, and each massacre diminished the chances of a negotiated settlement. As one religious leader in Abadan stated after the cinema fire, "the majority of the people are against the shah. He

[43] Quoted ibid.
[44] Ibid.

must go. That is the only thing that will satisfy the people."[45] Finally, Khomeini continued his campaign against the modern-day "Yazid," and rejected any form of compromise with the "devil" who had sold Islam and Iran to the foreigners and whose hands were "seeped in innocent blood." As his proclamation on the eve of ʿAyd-i Fetr declared, it was the duty of all Muslims to stand fast against the regime, reject false promises, win over the troops, and persevere in the struggle until the "looting tyrant" was thrown out of Iran.[46]

Black Friday set off a whirlpool of events. In the afternoon of September 8, Shariʿatmadari gave shelter to Bazargan and five other leaders of the Committee for the Defense of Freedom and Human Rights, and, insisting that his own views did not differ from those of Khomeini, declared that he would not even contemplate negotiating with the government until the constitutional laws were fully implemented. The same evening, the Association of Jurists declared that the martial law decree was illegal, since it did not have the prior approval of the Majles; ʿAli Amini, who had been acting as a go-between for the palace and the opposition, announced that the crisis would not be resolved until the shah resigned; and National Front leaders who had escaped arrest told foreign correspondents that the indiscriminate killings had made reconciliation with the regime impossible.[47]

On September 9, some 700 workers in the Tehran oil refinery went on strike to demand higher wages and protest the imposition of martial law. On September 11, workers in the oil refineries of Isfahan, Shiraz, Tabriz, and Abadan joined the strike. On September 13, cement workers in Tehran struck, calling for better wages, removal of martial law, and freedom for all political prisoners. On September 18, employees of the Central Bank published a list of 177 prominent individuals who they claimed had recently transferred over $2 billion out of the country. The list claimed that Sharif Emami had transferred some $31 million, General Oveissi $15 million, Namazi $9 million, Amouzegar $5 million, General Moqadam $2 million, the mayor of Tehran $6 million, the minister of health $7 million, and the director of the National Iranian Oil Company over $60 million.

The wave of strikes gathered force in the latter half of September. By early October, blue- and white-collar workers demanding political as well as economic concessions had closed down not only many of

[45] W. Branigan, "Abadan Mood Turns Sharply against the Shah," *Washington Post*, 26 August 1978.

[46] R. Khomeini, "Proclamation for ʿAyd-i Fetr," *Khabarnameh*, special no. 20 (September 98), pp. 1-2.

[47] Gueyras, "Liberalization is the Main Casualty."

the oil refineries, but also most of the oil fields, the petrochemical complex in Bandar Shahpour, the National Bank, the copper mines near Kerman, and forty other large industrial plants. The strike wave grew even more powerful during the course of the next month, especially after October 6, when Khomeini was forced out of Iraq into Paris, and October 16—the fortieth day after Black Friday—when more blood was shed in the major cities. By the third week of October, a rapid succession of strikes crippled almost all the bazaars, universities, high schools, oil installations, banks, government ministries, post offices, railways, newspapers, customs and port facilities, internal air flights, radio and television stations, state-run hospitals, paper and tobacco plants, textile mills, and other large factories. In effect, the working class had joined the middle classes to bring about a massive and unprecedented general strike. Moreover, the possibility of ending the crises seemed remote as long as the strikers—especially the 5,000 bank clerks, 30,000 oil workers, and 100,000 government employees—coupled their economic demands for higher wages and better fringe benefits with such sweeping political demands as the abolition of SAVAK, the lifting of martial law, the release of all political prisoners, the return of Khomeini, and the end of tyrannical rule. The shah faced not just a general strike but a political general strike.

While strikes crippled the economy, demonstrations continued unabated, spreading from the larger cities to smaller towns such as Sari, Arak, Qazvin, Amol, and Sanandaj. The street disturbances reached a new climax in early November, when troops fired into a crowd of students trying to pull down the shah's statue inside Tehran University. Early next morning, students who had gathered for the funeral of their thirty dead colleagues rampaged through the streets, shouting "death to the shah," attacking banks, luxury hotels, and foreign air line offices, and, after escorting personnel out of a section of the British embassy, burning down that section. Foreign correspondents described it as the "day Tehran burned."

In face of the deepening crisis, the shah vacillated and moved back and forth from one extreme position to another. On one hand, he followed up Black Friday with a series of measures designed to intimidate the opposition. He extended martial law to other cities, ordered the army to take over the major newspapers, locked up National Front leaders, and pressed the Iraqi government first to place Khomeini under house arrest and then to deport him. Similarly, after the street upheavals of early November, the shah replaced Sharif Emami with General Ghulam Reza Azhari, the commander of the Imperial Guard, and gave six ministries to other high-ranking military officers. The new minister of labor, General Oveissi, promptly imposed martial law on Khuzistan, arrested the strike committee elected by the refinery workers, and threatened to sack oil company employees who did not return to work.

On the other hand, the shah offered an olive branch to the opposition. He amnestied 1,126 political prisoners, including Ayatallah Taleqani, Ayatallah Montazeri, and eight Tudeh members who had been in jail since 1955; ended press censorship and withdrew the military officials from the newspaper offices; arrested 132 former government leaders, including Hoveida and Nasiri; dismissed many of the governors-general; set up a commission to investigate the Pahlevi Foundation; and dissolved the Resurgence party. Ironically, the dissolution of the party that had caused so much discontent passed almost unnoticed. Moreover, he canceled arms contracts totaling $4 billion; gave tax exemptions to low-paid civil servants; and met many of the economic demands made by government employees and industrial workers. Furthermore, he sent the empress on a pilgrimage to Karbala; declared that all exiles, including Khomeini, were free to return home; and announced over national television that he heard his people's "revolutionary message," would hold free elections soon, and would make up for "past mistakes."[48] This erratic swing from one extreme to another led some to conclude that the shah was having a nervous breakdown. Others claimed that he had lost touch with reality because he could not bring himself to read newspapers, which had all dropped his imperial titles and now referred to him simply as "the shah." Yet others argued that he could not make firm decisions because Washington would one day reiterate its commitment to human rights and the next day would stress the need for stability and would reemphasize America's special relations with the shah.[49]

The shah's behavior became even more erratic when the opposition rejected the olive branch. Shari'atmadari announced that negotiations were impossible, since the shah had imposed martial law and formed a military government. Khomeini, from his Paris exile, declared that if the shah had really heard the "revolutionary message" he would promptly abdicate and face an Islamic trial. He also declared that there was no room for compromise, that anyone joining the government would be betraying Islam, and that the public should continue

[48] *New York Times*, 7 November 1978.

[49] When it was later revealed that the shah had cancer, some commentators concluded that he had acted indecisively in 1978 because of the psychological side effects of his anticancer drugs. But as the events of 1951-1953 and 1960-1963 had shown, the shah was capable of acting decisively only when he could fully rely on his army and the United States. Whenever these two factors were missing he vacillated and showed signs of "psychological insecurity."

protesting until the "despicable monarchy" was dumped onto the rubbish heap of history. When European journalists asked what should replace the monarch, Khomeini—for the first time—substituted the term Islamic republic (jumhuri-yi Islami) for his usual answer Islamic government (hukomat-i Islami).[50] He was clearly trying to speak in the language of the secular opposition, especially the militants from the Liberation Movement, National Front, and various student organizations that immediately rallied around him on his arrival in Paris.

In early November, Sanjabi and Bazargan were able to leave Tehran to visit Khomeini. After his audience with Khomeini, Sanjabi declared on behalf of the National Front that "the present monarchy did not fulfill the requirements of the laws and the shari'a because it was tyrannical, corrupt, incapable of resisting foreign pressure, and systematically violated the fundamental laws."[51] He also called for a referendum to establish a "national government based on the principles of Islam, democracy, and national sovereignty." At the same time, Bazargan, on behalf of the Liberation Movement, declared that "the mass demonstrations of the previous year had shown that the people followed Ayatallah Khomeini and that they wanted the monarchy to be replaced by an Islamic system of government."[52] Using slightly different terminology, the secular National Front and the devout but lay Liberation Movement had allied themselves openly with Khomeini. In fact, Sanjabi's and Bazargan's historic pilgrimage to Paris revived the secular-religious alliance that had brought about the Constitutional Revolution of 1905-1909.

As the opposition leaders cemented their alliances, the struggle in the streets and work places intensified. On November 12, the bazaars, universities, and ministries that had just reopened struck again to protest the arrest of Sanjabi after his return from Paris; they remained on strike until the revolution triumphed. On November 15, violent clashes took place in the Kurdish areas, especially in Mahabad, Kermanshah, and Sanandaj. On November 16, the oil workers returned to work but declared that they would produce only what was required for home consumption and for foreign revenues needed to buy essential goods. As one refinery worker said, there is no need to produce more, since the surplus goes into the "pockets of Ali Baba and his

[50] For Khomeini's pronouncements of October-November 1978, see *Khabarnameh*, special number (November 1978), pp. 1-87.

[51] K. Sanjabi, "Proclamation," *Khabarnameh*, special number 23 (9 November 1978), p. 1.

[52] M. Bazargan, "Proclamation," ibid.

forty thieves."[53] And in the last week of November, violent demonstrations broke out in over fifty towns, including some such as Bandar 'Abbas and Ardakan that had been relatively quiet until then.

Far more violent demonstrations, however, were to take place in December, during Muharram. In anticipation of the holy ten days, Azhari warned that foreign enemies were plotting disturbances, and declared that martial law authorities would strictly enforce night curfew and would not issue any demonstration permits. Shari'atmadari replied that the people did not need government permission to commemorate the martyrdom of Hussein and his family. Taleqani asked the faithful to go on rooftops at night and shout "God is Great." The National Front and the Liberation Movement called for a general strike on the first and the last day of the mourning period. And Khomeini exhorted the public to make more sacrifices until blood triumphed over the sword and Islam over the "pagan" Pahlevis. He also exhorted the people to win over the soldiers, and the clergy to go into the villages to convince the peasants that "Islam was against big landlords and big capitalists."[54]

Muharram began on December 2 with three days of violence. In Tehran, hundreds of thousands spent the nights on their rooftops shouting "God is Great," while thousands wearing white shrouds to show their willingness to be killed violated the night curfew and poured into the streets. An estimated seven hundred died. In Qazvin, 135 were killed when tanks rolled over demonstrators. In Mashad, some two hundred—many of them high-school students—were fatally shot when they defied the ban on demonstrations and gathered outside the home of a local religious leader. Similar incidents occurred in many other cities.

Fearful that even worse incidents would occur on Tasua and 'Ahura, the climactic final days of the mourning period, the regime backtracked and sought a settlement similar to that obtained on the eve of 'Ayd-i Fetr. It released Sanjabi, Foruhar, and another 470 political prisoners, allowed religious processions to be held in all the urban centers, and agreed to keep the military and police out of the main streets. In return, the opposition leaders promised to restrain their followers, lead the marches personally, keep to prescribed routes, and avoid direct attacks on the shah. Although some violence broke out

[53] Y. Ibrahim, "Despite Army's Presence Iranian Oil Town Is Challenging the Shah," *New York Times*, 19 November 1978.

[54] R. Khomeini, "Proclamation for Muharram," *Khabarnameh*, special number 24 (27 November 1978), pp. 1-4.

in Isfahan, Hamadan, Mashad, Arak, and Tabriz, the massive demonstrations in the other cities were peaceful. What is more, for the first time these urban rallies drew large numbers of peasants from neighboring villages. In Tehran, the Tasua march was led by Taleqani and Sanjabi, and attracted over half a million people. The ʿAshura march, also led by Taleqani and Sanjabi, was even bigger, lasting a full eight hours and drawing nearly two million people. Although opposition leaders had authorized sixty slogans, none of which attacked the shah, the march marshals were unable to prevent radical groups, particularly the Fedaʾi, Mujahedin, Tudeh, and the pro-Tudeh Fedaʾi Munshʿeb, from joining the demonstration with such banners as "death to the shah," "hang the American puppet," and "arms to the people." At Shahyad Square, where the rally ended, the crowd ratified by acclamation a manifesto endorsing Khomeini's leadership and calling for the overthrow of the monarchy, the establishment of an Islamic government, the return of all exiles, the protection of the religious minorities, the revival of agriculture, and the delivery of "social justice" to the deprived masses.[55] The *Washington Post* reported that "the disciplined and well organized march lent considerable weight to the opposition's claim of being an alternative government." The *New York Times* wrote that the two days had one important lesson: "The government was powerless to preserve law and order on its own. It could do so only by standing aside and allowing the religious leaders to take charge. In a way, the opposition has demonstrated that there already is an alternative government." Similarly, the *Christian Science Monitor* reported that "a giant wave of humanity swept through the capital declaring louder than any bullet or bomb could the clear message: 'The Shah must go.' "[56]

In the two weeks after ʿAshura, the shah's position deteriorated further. Three factors account for this rapid deterioration. First, the opposition battered away with demonstrations, strikes, and even takeovers of offices and factories. By December 20, street violence was a daily occurrence, with youth gangs—many of them from the slums—setting up barricades, taunting the military, and throwing molotov cocktails at army trucks. And by December 25, a series of general strikes had again brought the whole economy to a grinding halt, and

[55] "Resolution Passed at the ʿAshura Rally in Tehran," *Khabarnameh*, special number 26 (15 December 1978), pp. 1-2.

[56] J. Randall, "In Iran, a Throng Votes No," *Washington Post*, 12 December 1978; R. Apple, "Reading Iran's Next Chapter," *New York Times*, 13 December 1978; T. Allway, "Iran Demonstrates," *Christian Science Monitor*, 12 December 1978.

grass-root strike committees had occupied many large factories, government ministries and communication centers. In the oil industry, exports ceased when most of the refinery workers resigned rather than continue producing under the control of the martial-law authorities. As one refinery worker later said, we will export oil only after we have exported the shah and his generals.[57] What is more, the guerrilla organizations, which had been revitalized by the release of the members from prison, carried out a number of armed operations, assassinating an American oil director, blowing up two electrical plants, and bombing the American embassy as well as the Grumman company offices in Isfahan. These attacks prompted many Americans to leave the country.

The second factor that further weakened the shah was the clear sign that the army rank and file, formed entirely of conscripts, was no longer willing to shoot down fellow workers, students, shopkeepers, peddlers, and slum dwellers. The *New York Times* reported that the military had decided to backtrack during Muharram because hundreds of soldiers in Mashad and Qum had deserted, and other conscripts threatened to "follow the orders of religious leaders rather than those of their officers." The *Washington Post* disclosed that in the week after ʿAshura troops in Qum refused to fire on demonstrators, five hundred soldiers and twelve tanks in Tabriz joined the opposition, and three Imperial Guards fired a hail of bullets into their officers' mess hall, killing an unknown number of royalists.[58] Similarly, *Nuyid*, the underground pro-Tudeh newspaper, reported that soldiers in many towns were joining the demonstrators and that garrison troops in Hamadan, Kermanshah, and other provincial cities were secretly distributing weapons to the local population.[59] As one senior general later told a foreign correspondent, the officers could no longer rely on their men and had to do much of the street shooting themselves.[60]

The third factor weakening the regime was Washington's loss of confidence in the shah. Until November, the Carter administration openly supported the shah's efforts to remain in power. For instance, shortly after Black Friday, President Carter wrote to Tehran and reiterated America's support for the shah. After November, however, Carter asked George Ball, a former under secretary of state and liberal critic of the shah, to prepare a report on the Iranian crisis for the

[57] *Iran Times*, 12 January 1979.

[58] R. Apple, "Shah's Army Is Showing Stresses," *New York Times*, 19 December 1978; W. Branigin, "Army Subordination Reported in Iran," *Washington Post*, 19 December 1978.

[59] Cited in "Step by Step toward the Iranian Revolution," *Mardom*, 11 February 1980.

[60] R. Apple, "A Lull in the Battle for Iran," *New York Times*, 3 February 1979.

White House. Not surprisingly, Ball reported that the shah would not survive the crisis unless he took immediate steps to dilute his power and establish a broad-based civilian government.[61] Even a more serious warning was sent to Washington by the French government, which, unlike the CIA, retained an effective intelligence service within Iran. The French reported that the shah could not possibly survive, and that the West could work with Khomeini, since the latter was deeply anticommunist in general and anti-Russian in particular. For his part, Khomeini began a propaganda campaign against the left. He claimed that the Tudeh was cooperating with the shah, accused Marxists of wanting to stab Muslims in the back, and denounced Russia as a greedy superpower.[62] He also declared that once the shah was overthrown Iran would become a reliable oil supplier to the West, would not ally with the East, and would be willing to have friendly relations with the United States.[63]

Responding to the new mood in Washington, in late December the shah began negotiating with Sanjabi and other leaders of the National Front. But these negotiations, which remain shrouded in mystery, soon broke down, probably because Sanjabi refused to head a government of national reconciliation unless the shah agreed to resign as commander-in-chief of the armed forces, leave the country, and remain in exile until a national referendum determined the fate of the monarchy. Sanjabi, the veteran politician who remembered how the shah had used the army to undermine Qavam, Mossadeq, and Amini, was unlikely to accept any settlement that would leave the military under the control of the royal family. The experiences of October 1946, July 1952, August 1953, and July 1962 were forever inscribed in the minds of the National Front leaders. The shah's previous victories were now serving to bring about his final downfall.

Although the veteran members of the opposition were haunted by the past, Bakhtiyar, a younger and less experienced leader of the National Front who feared the clergy more than the military, offered to head a civilian government if the shah merely took a vacation abroad, promised to reign rather than rule, and exiled fourteen diehard generals, including Oveissi. Grabbing at the offer, on December 30 the shah appointed Bakhtiyar prime minister.

[61] R. Burt, "U.S. Pressing Shah to Compromise," *New York Times*, 16 December 1978; S. Armstrong, "The Fall of the Shah," *Washington Post*, 25-30 October 1980.

[62] *Iran Times*, 20 October 1978; *Washington Post*, 2 January 1979; *Iran Times*, 2 February 1979.

[63] *Washington Post*, 2 and 18 January 1979.

THE FALL OF THE SHAH (JANUARY-FEBRUARY 1979)

Bakhtiyar took office with a series of grand gestures designed to win over the opposition. Appearing on national television with a picture of Mossadeq in the background, he talked of his years in the National Front, announced that the shah would soon take a "vacation," and promised both to lift martial law and to hold free elections. In the following week, he canceled $7 billion worth of arms contracts, stopped the sale of oil to Israel and South Africa, and announced that Iran would withdraw from CENTO and cease to be the policeman of the Persian Gulf. He also arrested a number of former ministers and released more political prisoners; promised to dismantle SAVAK; froze the assets of the Pahlevi Foundation; and, describing Khomeini as the "Gandhi of Iran," announced that he was free to return home. Khomeini, with his strong Islamic convictions and detailed knowledge of modern India, could hardly have been flattered by such a description. Finally, he set up a Regency Council to fulfill the shah's constitutional functions while the monarch took an extended "vacation" in Europe. In making these gestures, Bakhtiyar repeatedly warned that if the opposition sabotaged his efforts to create a constitutional government, the generals would follow the example of Chile and establish a brutally repressive military dictatorship.

The opposition leaders reacted in different ways to Bakhtiyar's solicitations. On one hand, Shariʿatmadari and the more moderate religious leaders declared that they would support the new premier and that if his efforts failed the country would fall into the abyss of utter chaos. On the other hand, Sanjabi and Foruhar expelled Bakhtiyar from the National Front, insisting that there would be no peace until the shah abdicated. Meanwhile, Khomeini called for more strikes and demonstrations, declared that any government appointed by the shah was illegal, and warned that obedience to Bakhtiyar was equivalent to obedience to his master—Satan.

Clearly, the militant call of Khomeini and the National Front struck the right chord among the public. The work stoppages, after a brief interval in late December, began anew, causing food and fuel shortages, and paralyzing most of the ministries, bazaars, universities, high schools, oil installations, industrial factories, and transport systems. The daily bonfires and street skirmishes went on unabated, further demoralizing the military and prompting more desertions. What is more, the masses continued to come out in large numbers to demonstrate not only against the shah but also against Bakhtiyar. On January 5, hundreds of thousands marched in the main cities to demand Bakhtiyar's removal. On January 8, equally large crowds, including an estimated half million in Mashad, took part in religious processions mourning those who had been killed in the previous month. On January 13, an estimated two million marched in thirty cities—including Shari'atmadari's hometown Tabriz—to demand Khomeini's return, the shah's abdication, and Bakhtiyar's resignation. On January 16, when the shah flew to Cairo, hundreds of thousands poured into the streets to celebrate the historic occasion and to demand the abolition of the monarchy. On January 19, when Khomeini called for a street "referendum" to determine the fate of both the monarchy and the Bakhtiyar administration, over a million responded in Tehran alone. On January 27-28, twenty-eight people were killed in Tehran protesting the closure of the airport to prevent Khomeini's return. And on February 1, some three million turned out into the streets of Tehran to hail Khomeini's triumphant return. Khomeini, the prophet and strategist of the revolution, had come home to take personal command of his revolution.

When Khomeini returned to claim his revolution, the Pahlevi state had already collapsed. Battered by sixteen months of street clashes, six months of mass rallies, and five months of crippling strikes, the three pillars that held up the state and at one time looked formidable now lay in utter ruins. The armed forces, despite their large numbers and ultrasophisticated weapons, were traumatized by having to go out into the streets day in and day out to shoot down unarmed fellow citizens shouting religious slogans. The vast patronage system was now not a lucrative asset but a political liability. Moreover, the gigantic bureaucracy no longer functioned: the Resurgence party had faded away; former ministers were either in exile or in prison, and current ministers, such as Bakhtiyar, were physically immobilized; and the central as well as the provincial administration had been crippled by large-scale civil service strikes. In fact, by joining the general strikes, the civil servants placed institutional interests behind their class sentiments and proved that they viewed themselves not as clogs in the state machinery but as members of the discontented middle classes. Thus the torrent of middle-class and working-class protests had come together to burst asunder the Pahlevi dam, tearing apart its pillars, and washing away most of its foundations.

As the state disintegrated, power passed into the hands of local ad hoc organizations known as Komitehs (Committees). Many of the Komitehs, especially in the Shi'i Persian-speaking central provinces, were headed by local clergymen who followed Khomeini. For example, in Isfahan Ayatallah Khademi, a ninety-year-old cleric who had opposed the shah since 1949, set up a Komiteh in the last week of January and controlled much of the city by the first week of February. He was helped by diverse groups: wealthy bazaar merchants provided financial assistance; small shopkeepers volunteered to sell goods to the poor at discount prices; some clergymen opened up their mosques to distribute fuel and food to the needy; other clergymen recruited nearly one thousand young men, most of them from the slums, to form an armed militia that later became known as the revolutionary guards (*pasdaran*); teachers, headed by a junior professor, established a Teachers' Association and organized a parallel militia of some 350 armed volunteers; sympathizers in the military, especially among air force technicians, distributed weapons; devout groups that usually organized Muharram processions now marshaled political demonstrations; and bazaar guilds as well as the many strike committees that had sprung up in the large factories coordinated their activities with the city Komiteh. In effect, the Komiteh ruled the city, distributing food, setting prices, policing the streets, and, most significant of all, reviving the old shari'a-styled courts to enforce law and order.

Whereas in the central cities the Komitehs were controlled by pro-Khomeini clergy, in the outer provinces the situation was much more complex. In Azerbaijan, many of the Komitehs were led by clerics, who although outwardly pro-Khomeini, in fact supported Shari'atmadari. In Kurdistan, local power passed into the hands of town Shawras (Councils) formed of intellectuals from the Kurdish Democratic party and clerical followers of Shaykh 'Ezaldin Husseini, the main religious figure in Mahabad. In the Turkoman areas, Sunni mullas and intellectuals from the recently formed Cultural and Political Society of the Turkoman People established local authorities and encouraged peasants to expropriate lands belonging to the royal family. Similarly, in the Baluchi areas Sunni mullas and university-educated teachers who had created the Islamic Unity party set up their own Komitehs. Finally, in the Arab districts of Khuzistan, power was picked up by the newly created Cultural, Political, and Tribal Organization of the Arab People, and by local clerics who, although predominantly Shi'i, supported not so much Khomeini as their own religious mentor Ayatallah al-Shabir Khaqani. Significantly, many of these ethnic organizations demanded not just an Islamic republic but a democratic Islamic republic, and sought guarantees for the provinces, the non-Shi'i communities, and the linguistic minorities.

On his return to Tehran, Khomeini announced that the demonstrations would continue until Bakhtiyar resigned. He also assigned Bazargan the task of forming a provisional government; set up his own Komiteh near Jaleh Square to coordinate the many local Komitehs and to dissolve unreliable ones; and even more importantly, appointed a secret Revolutionary Council (Shawra-yi Inqilabi) to negotiate directly with the chiefs of staff, bypassing Bakhtiyar. It was not until a year later that it was revealed that the original members of this Revolutionary Council included Bani Sadr—Khomeini's chief lay adviser from Paris; Bazargan, Yazdi, and Qotbzadeh—the three most influential spokesmen of the Liberation Movement; and Ayatallah Beheshti, Ayatallah Mottaheri, Hojjat al-Islam Rafsanjani, and Hojjat al-Islam Muhammad Bohanar—four former students of Khomeini from Qum.[64]

While the Revolutionary Council was secretly negotiating with the chiefs of staff, the guerrilla organizations and the Tudeh party delivered the regime its coup de grâce.[65] The final drama began in Tehran on the evening of Friday, February 9, when the Imperial Guard tried to crush a mutiny among air force technicians and cadets at a large military base near Jaleh Square. As soon as the fighting started, the guerrilla organizations rushed to help the besieged cadets and technicians. After six hours of intense fighting, the rebels forced the Imperial Guards to withdraw, distributed arms to the local population, set up street barricades, and, in the words of Le Monde, converted the district of Jaleh Square into a new "Paris commune."[66]

Early next morning, the guerrillas and the air force rebels drove truck loads of weapons to Tehran University. And helped by hundreds of eager volunteers, they spent the day leading a series of successful assaults on nine police stations and the city's main arms factory. By the end of the day, the city had been flooded with weapons. As one Tehran newspaper observed, "guns were distributed to thousands of people, from ten-year-old children to seventy-year-old pensioners." Similarly, the correspondent of the New York Times reported that "for the first time since the political crisis started more than a year ago, thousands of civilians appeared in the streets with machine guns and other weapons."[67]

[64] M. Bohanar, "The Report Card of the Revolutionary Council," Ittila'at, 14 September 1980.

[65] The Tudeh party, which for thirty-eight years had opposed armed adventures, changed policy in mid-January 1979. Convening an emergency meeting in Eastern Europe, the Central Committee elected Kianouri, the leader of the party's left wing, as its First Secretary, and, arguing that the objective situation was ripe for revolution, called upon its members to prepare for an armed uprising. See the editorial in Mardom, 6 (February 1979), 1.

[66] P. Balta and D. Pouchin, "L'Action décisive des groupes de guerilla," Le Monde, 13 February 1979.

[67] Kayhan, 11 February 1979; Y. Ibrahim, "Scores Dead in Iran," New York Times, 11 February 1979.

The fighting reached a climax the following day, Sunday, February 11. Helped by thousands of armed volunteers, the four main guerrilla organizations, the Tudeh, and defectors from the military mounted successful assaults on more police armories, on the barracks of the Imperial Guards, on Evin prison—the notorious SAVAK interrogation center—on the military academy, and on the main army garrison, which they found completely unguarded. At 2 P.M., the chief of general staff announced that the military would not take sides in the struggle between Bakhtiyar and the Revolutionary Council. And at 6 P.M., the city's radio station declared: "This is the voice of Tehran, the voice of true Iran, the voice of the revolution." The two days of intense fighting had brought the Islamic revolution to completion and the 2,500-year monarchy to utter destruction.

Conclusion

Those intellectuals who say that the clergy should leave politics and go back to the mosque speak on behalf of Satan.

—Ayatallah Khomeini, "Speech to University Students," *Ittila'at*, 22 September 1979

Twentieth-century Iran has experienced two major revolutions—that of 1905-1909 and of 1977-1979. The first saw the triumph, albeit brief, of the modern intelligentsia, who, inspired by such Western ideologies as nationalism, liberalism, and socialism, drafted a predominantly secular constitution and hoped to recreate their society in the image of contemporary Europe. The second revolution, on the other hand, has brought to the fore the traditional 'ulama, who, inspired by the "golden age" of Islam, have sealed their victory by drawing up a thoroughly clerical constitution, replacing the state judiciary with shari'a courts, and denouncing Western concepts such as democracy as heretical. In fact, the Islamic Revolution is unique in the annals of modern world history in that it brought to power not a new social group equipped with political parties and secular ideologies, but a traditional clergy armed with mosque pulpits and claiming the divine right to supervise all temporal authorities, even the country's highest elected representatives.

The paradox is compounded by the fact that in the intervening period between the Constitutional Revolution and the Islamic Revolution Iran underwent a major socioeconomic transformation. The processes of urbanization and industrialization, the expansion of the educational and communication systems, and the creation of a centralized bureaucratic state all served to swell the ranks of the modern classes, especially the intelligentsia and the industrial proletariat, and to reduce the relative size of the traditional classes, notably the bazaar petit bourgeoisie and its clerical allies. What is more, the same socioeconomic changes on the one hand undermined patrimonial ties between traditional patrons and their clients, and on the other hand strengthened class consciousness among the modern sectors of the population—especially among the intelligentsia and the urban proletariat. In short, the horizontal ties of class tended to supplant the vertical sentiments of clan, tribe, sect, and locality.

The paradox is further compounded by the fact that in 1941-1953—the only extensive period in recent history in which Iran has enjoyed an open political system—it was not the clergy but the intelligentsia that organized the masses against the power structure. In sharp contrast to the ʿulama, who confined themselves to their bazaar strongholds, the secular organizations—first the Tudeh and later the National Front—went into the public arena and successfully mobilized the discontented classes, particularly the urban wage earners and the salaried middle class. In effect, what inspired the discontented masses during 1941-1953 was not Islam but socialism and secular nationalism.

The prominent role played by Islam in the 1977-1979 revolution not only creates a paradox in Iranian history, but also seems at first glance to debunk the generally held notion that modernization brings secularization, and that urbanization strengthens the modern classes at the expense of the traditional ones. Thus the observer is confronted with two interrelated questions: how can the paradox be explained? and does the Islamic Revolution destroy the conventional theory that modernization inevitably helps secularization? The same questions can be posed in another way: why did the 1977-1979 revolution, whose content was predominantly social, economic, and political, take an ideological form that was undoubtedly religious? And are the factors that gave the revolution its Islamic form temporary or permanent?

These questions cannot be answered without taking into account the decisive role played by Khomeini. In fact, Khomeini is to the Islamic Revolution what Lenin was to the Bolshevik, Mao to the Chinese, and Castro to the Cuban revolutions. Two factors explain Khomeini's decisive role and widespread popularity. The first was his personality, especially his simple way of life and his refusal to compromise with the "satanic tyrant." In a country in which most politicians lived in luxury, Khomeini led a life as austere as that of a Sufi mystic, and as devoid of material opulence as that of the common people. In an environment in which political leaders were wheeler-dealers, influence peddlers, and incorrigible nepotists, Khomeini adamantly rejected compromise, even when compromise seemed expedient; insisted that he would execute his own children if they deserved such punishment; and acted like a "man of God" who sought not worldly power but spiritual authority. Similarly, in a decade notorious for cynical, bland, corrupt, defeatist, and inconsistent politicians, Khomeini appeared to be thoroughly sincere, defiant, dynamic, consistent, and, most important of all, incorruptible. In brief, he was a charismatic revolutionary leader at a time when such leaders were in short supply and in great demand.

The second factor that explains Khomeini's prominence is his astuteness, in particular his ability to rally behind him a wide spectrum of political and social forces. In his fifteen years of exile, he carefully avoided making public pronouncements, especially written ones, on issues that would alienate segments of the opposition—issues such as land reform, clerical power, and sexual equality. Instead, he hammered the regime on topics that outraged all sectors of the opposition: the concessions granted to the West, the tacit alliance with Israel, the wasteful expenditures on arms, the rampant corruption in high places, the decay of agriculture, the rise in the cost of living, the housing shortage and the sprawling slums, the widening gap between the rich and the poor, the suppression of newspapers and political parties, the creation of a vast bureaucratic state, and the gross violations of the constitutional laws. In denouncing the regime, Khomeini promised to liberate the country from foreign domination; extend freedom to all political parties, even "atheistic" ones; guarantee the rights of all religious minorities, except those of the "heretical" Baha'is; and bring social justice to all, particularly to the bazaaris, the intelligentsia (*rushanfekran*), the peasantry (*dehqanan*), and, most mentioned of all, the dispossessed masses (*mostazafin*). These promises, especially the populist and anti-imperialist themes, succeeded in winning over a wide range of political forces, from the followers of the late Ayatallah Kashani and remnants of the Feda'iyan-i Islam at one end of the spectrum, to the Liberation Movement and the National Front at the center, and to the Tudeh, Mujahedin, and the Marxist Feda'i at the other end of the spectrum.

Even more important, by vigorously championing a multitude of popular grievances, Khomeini won over diverse social groups, each of which saw in him their long-awaited savior. To the petty bourgeoisie, he was not only the sworn enemy of the dictatorship but also the guardian of private property, of traditional values, and of the hard-pressed bazaars. To the intelligentsia, he appeared, despite his clerical garb, to be a militant nationalist who would complete Mossadeq's mission of liberating the country from the twin burdens of foreign imperialism and domestic fascism. To the urban workers, he was a man of the people, eager to enforce social justice, redistribute wealth, and transfer power from the rich to the poor. To the rural masses, he was the man who would bring land, water, electricity, roads, schools, and health clinics—the material goods the White Revolution had failed to deliver. And to all, he appeared to embody the spirit of the Constitutional Revolution and to rekindle the hopes the earlier revolution had raised but failed to realize.

The backbone of Khomeini's movement, however, was the traditional middle class, especially the bazaaris and the clergy. He won their staunch allegiance in part because he spoke their language; in part because he appeared to personify the virtues of Imam 'Ali— courage, honesty, and political astuteness; and in part because the regime, by declaring war on the bazaars and the religious establishment, had driven the moderate opposition and even the apolitical clergy into his arms. The only sectors of the society still independent of the state, the bazaars and the religious establishment provided Khomeini not only with generous financial support but also with a nationwide organizational network. In short, by the eve of the revolution the state had shattered all political parties and silenced their main organs; but it had not yet taken over the bazaars, the mosques, and their pulpits. It was therefore not surprising that the bazaar became the focal point of the revolution.

Whereas the traditional middle class provided the opposition with a nationwide organization, it was the modern middle class that sparked off the revolution, fueled it, and struck the final blows. Lawyers, judges, and intellectuals began the campaign to publish open letters and form human rights associations. University students started the street demonstrations. White-collar workers, especially bank clerks, civil servants, and customs officials, crippled the economy. Finally, guerrilla fighters, most of whom were college students, brought the revolution to a successful completion.

Why was the modern middle class, which in the past had deeply distrusted the clergy, willing to follow Khomeini? There were three reasons. First, the shah refused to negotiate with the secular opposition, notably the National Front and the Liberation Movement, until December 1978. But by then the revolutionary movement had turned into a vast torrent that threatened to wash away not only the regime but also any politician suicidal enough to latch onto the shah. Second, Khomeini made timely statements to woo the secular opposition and to assure all that the autocracy would not be superseded by a theocracy. For example, the day after Black Friday, Khomeini warned that the shah planned to grind into dust not only the 'ulama but also the intelligentsia (rushanfekran) and the honest politicians (siyasiun).[1] In November, he told the press that the future government would be

[1] R. Khomeini, "Proclamation," *Khabarnameh*, special number 21 (9 September 1978), p. 1.

"democratic" as well as Islamic.[2] Also in November, he solicited help from "all organizations,"[3] and assured the public that neither he nor his clerical supporters harbored any secret desire to "rule" the country.[4] In December, he declared that in an Islamic society women would be able to vote and have the same rights as men.[5] And in January 1979, he proclaimed that the constitution of the Islamic republic would be drafted by a "freely elected Constituent Assembly."[6] Not surprisingly, intellectuals well versed in the history of the Constitutional Revolution tended to see Khomeini not as another "reactionary" Shaykh Fazallah Nouri—whom he admired for rejecting Western systems of government—but as another "progressive" Ayatallah Tabatabai or Behbehani—whom he despised for being "led astray" by Westernized politicians.

The third reason for Khomeini's success among the modern middle class was the phenomenal popularity of Shari'ati among the young intelligentsia. Although Shari'ati's works contain a great deal of anticlericalism, Khomeini was able to win over his followers by being forthright in his denunciations of the monarchy; by refusing to join fellow theologians in criticizing the Husseinieh-i Ershad; by openly attacking the apolitical and the proregime 'ulama; by stressing such themes as revolution, anti-imperialism, and the radical message of Muharram; and by incorporating into his public declarations such "Fanonist" terms as "the mostazafin will inherit the earth," "the country needs a cultural revolution," and the "people will dump the exploiters onto the garbage heap of history." By late 1978, such was Khomeini's popularity among Shari'ati supporters that it was they—not the clergy—who took the somewhat blasphemous step of endowing him with the title of Imam, a title that in the past Shi'i Iranians had reserved for the Twelve Holy Imams. Lacking both the theological concerns of the 'ulama and the sociological sophistication of their late mentor, Shari'ati's followers argued that Khomeini was not just an ordinary ayatallah but a charismatic Imam who would carry through the revolution and lead the community (Ummat) toward the long-awaited classless society (Nezam-i Towhid). After the 1905-1909 revolution, the 'ulama had protested that they had been fooled by the

---

[2] Committee to End U.S. Intervention in Iran, *Excerpts from Ayatallah Khomeini's Interviews* (Mountview, Cal., 1978), p. 14.

[3] Quoted in *Iran Times*, 24 November 1978.

[4] Committee to End U.S. Intervention in Iran, *Excerpts*, p. 14-15.

[5] Ibid., p. 19.

[6] R. Khomeini, "Proclamation," *Khabarnameh*, special number 27 (17 January 1979), p. 1.

intelligentsia. After the 1977-1979 revolution, it was the intelligentsia who claimed to have been fooled by the ʿulama.

If the two middle classes were the main bulwarks of the revolution, the urban working class was its chief battering ram. Oil workers pushed the state to the verge of bankruptcy. Transport and factory workers brought industry to a halt. Moreover, slum dwellers provided much of the youth that defiantly challenged the military authorities, many of the martyrs that died in the major massacres, and the bulk of the vast crowds that tenaciously marched in the streets.

A combination of elements helps explain why Khomeini managed to mobilize the urban wage earners. First, his promise to bring social justice contrasted sharply with the regime's inability to satisfy the public's rising expectations. Second, the regime, despite its distrust of the high-ranking ʿulama, had not tried to prevent the low-ranking mullas from working among the urban poor, organizing passion plays, funeral ceremonies, flagellation processions, and neighborhood prayer meetings. As one Majles deputy told a foreign social psychologist in 1973, religious ceremonies, especially Muharram plays, were politically useful in that they channeled social frustrations away from communism into harmless directions.[7] By 1978, no doubt, the same deputy would have discovered that the former part of his argument contained some truth, but the latter part of the argument was thoroughly unsound. Whatever the merits of the argument, however, it was clear that the religious networks in the shanty towns provided the clerical opposition with the means not only of disseminating information but also of organizing demonstrations and distributing food, fuel, and even clothing.

Third, religion provided the slum population with a much-needed sense of community and social solidarity—something they had lost when they left their tightly knit villages for the anomic atmosphere of the sprawling new shanty towns. As one American anthropologist discovered in the early 1970s, when comparing a stable village with a new urban slum, where the villagers took religion with a grain of salt and even ridiculed visiting preachers, the slum dwellers, who were all recently dispossessed peasants—used religion as a substitute for their lost communities, oriented social life around the mosque, and accepted with zeal the teachings of the local mulla.[8] In much the same way as early industrialization helped the growth of the Methodist movement in England, so the haphazard urbanization of the 1970s

[7] M. Good "Social Hierarchy and Social Change in a Provincial Iranian Town" (Ph.D. dissertation, Harvard University, 1976), p. 231.

[8] Goodell, "The Elementary Structures of Political Life" (Ph.D. dissertation, Columbia University, 1977), pp. 426-84.

strengthened the popular roots of the Iranian clergy. Thus, paradoxically, modernization helped bolster a traditional group.

The fourth element explaining Khomeini's success among the urban working class was the vacuum created by the regime when it systematically destroyed all secular opposition parties. Whereas the clergy were permitted to go to the poor, the opposition parties were constantly prevented from establishing any form of labor unions, local clubs, or neighborhood organizations. Twenty-five years of repression placed a heavy handicap on the secular opposition. Moreover, in sharp contrast to the clergy, who could speak in the language of the masses and portray Khomeini as an Imam Hussein willing to sacrifice himself and his family for the holy cause, the intellectuals leading the political parties were handicapped by the fact that the urban poor viewed them as kravatis (tie-wearers), dawlatis (government officials), and gharbzadehs (blind imitators of the West). Even the term *rushanfekr* (intelligentsia) was sometimes used by the public and the clergy to mean a pampered "egg-head." Thus class consciousness among the poor did undermine the regime but it did not necessarily strengthen the radical intelligentsia. Of the many secular parties active in the last stages of the revolution, only the Tudeh managed to make any inroads into the working class—especially in the textile mills of Isfahan, the oil installations of Khuzistan, and the large industrial plants of Tehran.

Although the revolution was predominantly urban, this did not mean that Khomeini had no impact on the rural masses. On the contrary, as the revolution unfolded and as Muharram of 1978 approached, many clergymen heeded Khomeini's call to go into the countryside to mobilize the rural population. Ironically, their task was made easier by the socioeconomic changes of the previous era—especially those of the White Revolution. For these changes had freed the peasants and tribesmen from the tight control of their landlords and tribal chiefs, placed the countryside in direct confrontation with the state, drawn the villages into closer commercial contact with the towns, and transformed the rural mullas from spokesmen of the large magnates into allies of the bazaar petit bourgeoisie. In the era after the Constitutional Revolution, clerical power had been restricted not only by the urban intelligentsia but also by the rural magnates who could shepherd their peasants, tribesmen, and household clients into the polling booths. After the Islamic Revolution, however, the clergy had the field to themselves, since recent socioeconomic developments had dissolved the traditional ties between rural magnates and their clients, between landlords and their peasants, and between tribal chiefs and their tribesmen. Again modernization had played the ironic role of strengthening the traditional 'ulama. It is significant that in 1979

Khomeini faced major difficulties mostly in the backward Turkoman, Baluchi, and Kurdish areas where local khans, as well as Sunni mullas and radical intellectuals, were able to establish their own ethnic organizations.

It is thus a combination of permanent and temporary forces that have brought the clergy to power. The permanent ones include the Shi'i culture of the urban masses, the historic links between the bazaars and the religious establishment, and the recent socioeconomic changes that have swept away the powerful tribal chiefs, the large landlords, and the other rural magnates. It should be remembered, however, that during the 1940s the same popular culture did not prevent the Tudeh from mobilizing the urban working class, including the bazaar wage earners. It should also be noted that although Iran will never again see tribal chiefs and rural magnates marching into power—as they did in 1909—the possibility still exists that in future nonclerical groups will be able to mobilize the rural masses. Modernization has struck a death blow to the tribal magnates and the large landlords; it has not given the clergy permanent control over the tribal and peasant populations.

The temporary factors that account for clerical ascendency include the charismatic personality of Khomeini, the intense aversion felt by the public for the shah, and the organizational handicaps that the regime had for a quarter of a century placed on the secular political parties. The clergy are unlikely to produce another Khomeini. For, while some of his disciples have his revolutionary credentials and others have his political astuteness, none combines both to be able to emerge as a successful revolutionary leader. Similarly, the clergy are unlikely to find another public enemy as unpopular as the shah against whom they can rally the whole population—unless, of course, a foreign enemy invades the country and threatens the existence of the entire nation. Finally, the clergy will gradually lose their organizational monopoly once the secular forces catch their breath and start establishing roots among the discontented classes, especially among the intelligentsia, the urban proletariat, and the rural lower classes. But whether it will be the older organizations, notably the Tudeh and the National Front, or those of more recent origin, such as the Feda'i and the Mujahedin, or even elements within the shattered military, that will attract the discontented classes is a question left to posterity.

Glossary

akhund	low-ranking clergyman; synonymous with mulla
anjuman	society, association, organization
asnaf	(sing. senf) guilds
a'yan	notables
ayatallah	high-ranking clergyman; synonymous with mujtahed
'Aydi-Qurban	Day of Sacrifice
bast	sanctuary
boneh	agricultural production team
chadour	long veil
chaqukesh	thug
darbar	court
darugheh	overseer of bazaar guilds
dawlat	state
faqih	religious jurist
farman	royal decree
fatwa	religious decree
feda'i	fighter, devotee, armed volunteer
firqeh	party
fraksiun	parliamentary caucus
hakem	governor
hizb	political party
hojjat al-islam	middle-ranking clergyman
ilkhan	top tribal chief
imam jom'eh	head of the Friday prayer
kadkhuda	village headman
kalantar	bailiff; also used for head of a tribal section
khan	chief
luti	thug, wrestler-acrobat
madraseh	seminary
majles	parliament; council, meeting
mahallat	(sing. mahalleh) district
maktab	traditional elementary school

mellat	community; in modern times used for "nation"
Muharram	Shi'i month of mourning
mujahed	(plural mujahedin) freedom fighter
mujtahed	high-ranking clergyman; synonymous with ayatallah
mulla	low-ranking clergyman; synonymous with akhund
mustawfi	traditional tax collector and accountant
qanat	underground irrigation canal
ra'iyat	common people, subjects, peasants
rushanfekran	intelligentsia
sayyid	descendant of the Prophet
shagerd	apprentice, student
shari'a	religious law
shaykh al-islam	the nominal head of the religious community in the main cities, usually appointed by the Qajars
tabaqeh	(plural tabaqat) group, class
tayifeh	clan
tireh	section, tribal branch
tuyul	fief
tuyuldar	fief holder
'ulama	(sing. 'alem) clergymen
ustad	master, guild elder
va'ez	preacher
vakil	representative, deputy
vali	town governor
vaqf	(plural awqaf) religious endowment

Bibliography

This is not intended to be a comprehensive bibliography on modern Iran. It is merely a selected list of English- and Persian-language books that relate to the politics of modern Iran and are available in major libraries. For more comprehensive bibliographies of articles as well as books in Persian, English, and other Western languages, see the first section below.

BIBLIOGRAPHIES

Afshar, I. *Fehrist-i Maqalat-i Farsi* (Bibliography of Persian Articles). Tehran: Jebi Press, 1959-1971. 3 vols.
————. *Fehristnameh-i Ketabshenasiha-yi Iran* (A List of Bibliographies on Iran). Tehran: Tehran University Press, 1961.
Behn, W. *The Iranian Opposition in Exile: An Annotated Bibliography*. Wiesbaden: Harrassowitz, 1979.
Handley-Taylor, G. *Bibliography of Iran*. Chicago: St. James, 1969.
Moshar, Kh. *Fehrist-i Ketabha-yi Chap-i Farsi* (Bibliography of Published Books in Persian). Tehran: Bongah-i Tarjomeh Press, 1971. 3 vols.
Nawabi, Y. *A Bibliography of Iran*. Tehran: Iran Cultural Foundation, 1969. 2 vols.
Pakdaman, N., and Abdolhamid, A. *Bibliographie française de civilization iranienne*. Tehran: Tehran University Press, 1972-1974. 3 vols.
Ravasani, S. *Sowjet Republic Gilan*. Berlin: Basis-Verlag, 1973.
Sverchevskaia, A. *Bibliografia Irana*. Moscow: Navak, 1967

Much of the unpublished materials I have used from the British Foreign Office can be found in London in the Public Record Office listed under the numbers from *F.O. 371*/Persia 1906/34-106 to *F.O. 371*/ Persia 1948/34-68750. They can also be found in the India Office Library in London filed under L/P and S/10, and L/P and S/12.

NINETEENTH CENTURY

Adamiyat, F. *Amir Kabir va Iran* (Amir Kabir and Iran). Tehran: Khwarazmi Press, 1969.
————, and Nateq, H. *Fekr-i Ijtima'-i va Siyas-i va Iqtesad-i dar Asar-i Montash-*

erashudeh-i Dawreh-i Qajar (Social, Political, and Economic Ideas in Unpublished Qajar Documents). Tehran: Agah Press, 1978.

Algar, H. *Religion and State in Iran, 1785-1906.* Berkeley and Los Angeles: University of California Press, 1969.

Arfaʿ al-Dawleh, M. *Iran-i Diruz* (Yesterday's Iran). Tehran: Ministry of Education Press, 1966.

Ashraf, A. *Movaneʿ-i Tarikh-i Rushd-i Sarmayehdari dar Iran* (Historical Obstacles to the Development of Capitalism in Iran). Tehran: Payam Press, 1980.

Bakhash, S. *Iran: Monarchy, Bureaucracy and Reform under the Qajars.* London: Ithaca Press, 1978.

Browne, E. *A Year amongst the Persians.* London: Black, 1893.

Curzon, G. *Persia and the Persian Question.* London: Longmans, 1892. 2 vols.

Entner, M. *Russo-Persian Commercial Relations, 1828-1914.* Gainsville: University of Florida Press, 1965.

Farmanfarmaian, H., ed. *Khatirat-i Amin al-Dawleh* (The Memoirs of Amin al-Dawleh). Tehran: Amir Kabir Press, 1962.

Fasa'i, H. *History of Persia under Qajar Rule.* Translated by H. Busse. New York: Columbia University Press, 1972.

Issawi, C., ed. *The Economic History of Iran, 1800-1914.* Chicago: University of Chicago Press, 1971.

Iʿtimad al-Saltaneh, M. *Ruznameh-i Iʿtimad al-Saltaneh* (The Diaries of Iʿtimad al-Saltaneh). Tehran: Amir Kabir Press, 1967.

Jamalzadeh, M. *Gang-i Shayegan* (Abundant Treasure). Berlin: Kaveh Press, 1956.

Kasravi, A. *Tarikh-i Pansad Saleh-i Khuzistan* (Five Hundred-Year History of Khuzistan). Tehran: Payam Press, 1950.

Kazemzadeh, F. *Russia and Britain in Persia, 1864-1914.* New Haven: Yale University Press, 1968.

Keddie, N. *Sayyid Jamal al-Din "al-Afghani."* Berkeley and Los Angeles: University of California Press, 1972.

Malcolm, J. *History of Persia.* London: Murray, 1829. 2 vols.

Mirza Hussein Khan (Tahvildar-i Isfahan). *Jughrafiya-yi Isfahan* (Geography of Isfahan). Tehran: Tehran University Press, 1963.

Mustawfi, ʿA. *Sharh-i Zendigani-yi Man* (My Life). Tehran: ʿElmi Press, 1943-1945. 3 vols.

Nafisi, S. *Tarikh-i Ijtimaʿi va Siyasi-yi Iran dar Dawreh-i Muʿaser* (Social and Political History of Iran in the Contemporary Era). Tehran: Foroughi Press, 1956. 2 vols.

Nateq, H. *Az Mast keh Bar Mast* (No One to Blame but Ourselves). Tehran: Agah Press, 1978.

Qodsi, H. *Kitab-i Khatirat-i Man ya Tarikh-i Sad Saleh* (Book of My Life or History of One Hundred Years). Tehran: Abu Rihan Press, 1963. 2 vols.

Safa'i, I. *Asnad-i Siyasi* (Political Documents). Tehran: Sharq Press, 1967.

———. *Namehha-yi Tarikhi* (Historical Letters). Tehran: Sukhan Press, 1969.

Shamim, ʿA. *Iran dar Dawreh-i Saltanat-i Qajar* (Iran during the Qajar Dynasty). Tehran: Ibn Sina Press, 1964.

Sykes, P. *A History of Persia*. London: Macmillan, 1930.

CONSTITUTIONAL REVOLUTION

Adamiyat, F. *Fekr-i Azadi va Moqadimeh-i Nahzat-i Mashrutiyat-i Iran* (The Concept of Freedom and the Beginnings of the Constitutional Movement in Iran). Tehran: Sukhan Press, 1961.

———. *Fekr-i Demokrasi-yi Ijtema'yi dar Nahzat-i Mashrutiyat-i Iran* (The Concept of Social Democracy in the Iranian Constitutional Movement). Tehran: Payam Press, 1975.

———. *Iydolozhi-yi Nahzat-i Mashrutiyat-i Iran* (The Ideology of the Constitutional Movement in Iran). Tehran: Payam Press, 1976.

Algar, H. *Mirza Malkum Khan*. Berkeley and Los Angeles: University of California Press, 1973.

Amir-Khizi, I. *Qiyam-i Azerbaijan va Sattar Khan* (The Uprising of Azerbaijan and Sattar Khan). Tabriz: Shafaq Press, 1960. 2 vols.

Baqer-Vajieh, M. *Balva-yi Tabriz* (The Tabriz Turbulence). Tehran: Amir Kabir Press, 1977.

Browne, E. *The Persian Crisis of December, 1911*. London: Cambridge University Press, 1912.

———. *The Persian Revolution of 1905-1909*. London: Cambridge University Press, 1910.

Dawlatabadi, Y. *Hayat-i Yahya* (The Life of Yahya). Tehran: Ibn Sina Press, 1949. 4 vols.

Fakhrayi, I. *Gilan dar Jonbesh-i Mashrutiyat* (Gilan during the Constitutional Movement). Tehran: Sepehr Press, 1977.

Fathi, N. *Zendiginameh-yi Shahid Shaykh al-Islam Tabrizi* (The Life of Martyr Shaykh al-Islam of Tabriz). Tehran: Amir Kabir Press, 1974.

Fumani, 'A. *Tarikh-i Gilan* (History of Gilan). Tehran: Foroughi Press, 1974.

Great Britain. Parliament. *Correspondence Respecting the Affairs of Persia*. London: Government Printing Office, 1909. 2 vols.

Hairi, A. *Shi'ism and Constitutionalism in Iran*. Leiden: Brill, 1977.

Heravi-Khurasani, M. *Tarikh-i Paydayesh-i Mashrutiyat-i Iran* (History of the Genesis of the Iranian Constitution). Tehran: n.p., 1953.

Javid, S. *Fedakaran-i Faramushshudeh* (Forgotten Heroes). Tehran: Sharq Press, 1966.

———. *Nahzat-i Mashrutiyat-i Iran* (The Constitutional Movement of Iran). Tehran: Sharq Press, 1968.

Jowdat, H. *Tarikh-i Firqeh-i Demokrat* (History of the Democrat Party). Tehran: Derakhshan Press, 1969.

Kasravi, A. *Tarikh-i Mashruteh-i Iran* (History of the Iranian Constitution). Tehran: Amir Kabir Press, 1961.

Keddie, N. *Religion and Rebellion in Iran: The Tobacco Protest of 1891-1892*. London: Cass, 1966.

Kermani, A. Majd al-Islam. *Tarikh-i Inqilab-i Mashrutiyat-i Iran* (History of the Iranian Constitutional Revolution). Isfahan: Isfahan University Press, 1972. 3 vols.

Kermani, Nazem al-Islam. *Tarikh-i Bidari-yi Iranian* (History of the Awakening of Iranians). Tehran: Farhang Press, 1967. 2 vols.

McDaniel, R. *The Shuster Mission and the Persian Constitutional Revolution*. Minneapolis: Bibliotheca Islamica, 1974.

Malekzadeh, M. *Tarikh-i Inqilab-i Mashrutiyat-i Iran* (History of the Constitutional Revolution of Iran). Tehran: Suqrat Press, 1949. 5 vols.

———. *Zendigani-yi Malek al-Motakallemin* (The Life of Malek al-Motakallemin). Tehran: 'Elmi Press, 1946.

Mujtahedi, M. *Rejal-i Azerbaijan dar Asr-i Mashrutiyat* (Politicians of Azerbaijan in the Constitutional Era). Tehran: 'Elmi Press, 1948.

———. *Tarikh-i Zendigani-yi Taqizadeh* (History of Taqizadeh's Life). Tehran: 'Elmi Press, 1942.

Safa'i, I. *Asnad-i Nowyafteh* (Recently Found Documents). Tehran: Sukhan Press, 1970.

———. *Rahbaran-i Mashrutiyat* (The Leaders of the Constitution). Tehran: Sharq Press, 1965.

Tafresh-Husseini, A. *Ruznameh-i Akhbar-i Mashrutiyat* (A Diary of the Constitutional Revolution). Tehran: Amir Kabir Press, 1972.

Taherzadeh-Behzad, K. *Qiyam-i Azerbaijan dar Inqilab-i Mashrutiyat-i Iran* (The Revolt of Azerbaijan in the Constitutional Revolution of Iran). Tehran: Eqbal Press, 1953.

MODERN PERIOD

Akhavi, S. *Religion and Politics in Contemporary Iran*. Albany: State University of New York Press, 1980.

Al-Ahmad, J. *Gharbzadegi* (Drunk with the West). Tehran: n.p., 1962.

———. *Rushanfekran* (The Intelligentsia). Tehran: Khwarazmi Press, 1979.

American University. *Iran: A Country Study*. Washington, D.C.: U.S. Government Printing Office, 1978.

Amirsadeghi, H., and Ferrier, R., eds. *Twentieth-Century Iran*. London: Heinemann, 1977.

Aramesh, A. *Haft Sal Dar Zendan-i Aryamehr* (Seven Years in Aryamehr's Prison). Tehran: 'Am Press, 1979.

Arasteh, R. *Man and Society in Iran*. Leiden: Brill, 1963.

Arfa', H. *Under Five Shahs*. London: Murray, 1964.

Arsanjani, H. *Yaddashtha-yi Siyasi* (Political Memoirs). Tehran: Atesh Press, 1956.

Aryanpour, Y. *Az Saba to Nima* (From Saba to Nima). Tehran: Sepehr Press, 1975. 2 vols.

Ashraf, A. *Shakhesha-yi Ijtima'i-yi Iran* (Social Indicators of Iran). Tehran: Tehran University Press, 1976.

Avery, P. *Modern Iran*. London: Benn, 1965.

Azeri, 'A. *Qiyam-i Khiabani* (The Revolt of Khiabani). Tehran: Safi 'Ali Shah Press, 1950.

———. *Qiyam-i Kolonel Taqi Khan Pesyan dar Khurasan* (The Revolt of Colonel Taqi Khan Pesyan in Khurasan). Tehran: Tajaddod Press, 1950.

Bahar, Malek al-Shua'ra. *Tarikh-i Ahzab-i Siyasi-yi Iran* (History of Political Parties in Iran). Tehran: Rangin Press, 1944.

Bahrami, 'A. *Khatirat* (Memoirs). Tehran: Mazaheri Press, 1966.

Bamdad, M. *Tarikh-i Rejal-i Iran* (History of Iranian Statesmen). Tehran: Bazargan Bank Press, 1968-1972. 6 vols.

Banani, A. *The Modernization of Iran, 1921-1941.* Stanford: Stanford University Press, 1961.

Bharier, J. *Economic Development of Iran, 1900-1970.* London: Oxford University Press, 1971.

Bill, J. *The Politics of Iran: Groups, Classes, and Modernization.* Columbus, Ohio: Merrill, 1972.

Binder, L. *Iran: Political Development in a Changing Society.* Berkeley and Los Angeles: University of California Press, 1962.

Chubin, S., and Zabih, S. *The Foreign Relations of Iran.* Berkeley and Los Angeles: University of California Press, 1974.

Cottam, R. *Nationalism in Iran.* Pittsburgh: University of Pittsburgh Press, 1964.

Davoudi, M. *Qavam al-Saltaneh.* Tehran: Baha Press, 1947.

Eagleton, W. *The Kurdish Republic of 1946.* New York: Oxford University Press, 1963.

Ehteshami, A. *Bazigaran-i Siyasi* (Politicians). Tehran: 'Elmi Press, 1949.

Elwell-Sutton, E. *A Guide to Iranian Area Study.* Ann Arbor: American Council of Learned Societies, 1952.

―――. *Persian Oil.* London: Lawrence and Wishart, 1955.

English, P. *City and Village in Iran.* Madison: University of Wisconsin Press, 1966.

Faroughi, A. *Iran Zed-i Shah* (Iran against the Shah). Tehran: Amir Kabir Press, 1979.

Farrukh, M. *Khatirat-i Siyasi-yi Farrukh* (The Political Memoirs of Farrukh). Tehran: Sahami Press, 1969.

Fateh, M. *Panjah Saleh-i Naft-i Iran* (Fifty Years of Iranian Oil). Tehran: Chehr Press, 1956.

Fischer, M. *Iran: From Religious Dispute to Revolution.* Cambridge: Harvard University Press, 1980.

Garakani, M. *Siyasat-i Dawlat-i Shawravi dar Iran* (The Policy of the Soviet Government in Iran). Tehran: Mazaheri Press, 1947.

Graham, R. *Iran: The Illusion of Power.* New York: St. Martin's, 1979.

Great Britain. Cabinet. *Documents on British Foreign Policy 1919-1939.* London: Government Printing Office, 1963. Series I. Vols 3 and 13.

Hakim-Ilah'i, H. *Zendigi-yi Aqa-yi Sayyid Ziya* (The Life of Mr. Sayyid Ziya). Tehran: n.p., 1944.

Halliday, F. *Iran: Dictatorship and Development.* New York: Penguin, 1979.

Hariri, N. *Moshahebeh ba Tarikhsazan-i Iran* (Interviews with Makers of Iranian History). Tehran: Amir Kabir Press, 1979.

Hunarmand, M. *Pahlevism: Falsafeh-yi Siyasi, Iqtesadi va Ijtema'i* (Pahlevism:

Philosophy of Politics, Economics, and Social Issues). Tehran: Gilan Press, 1966.

Iranian Government. National Assembly. *Mozakerat-i Majles-i Shawra-yi Melli* (The Proceedings of the National Consultative Assembly). Tehran: Majles Press, 1909-1954. 1st Majles to 18th Majles.

Iranian Government. Plan and Budget Organization. *Salnameh-i Amar-i Keshvar* (Annual Statistics for the State). Tehran: Government Printing Office, 1977.

Jacqz, J., ed. *Iran: Past, Present and Future*. New York: Aspen Institute, 1976.

Kamshad, H. *Modern Persian Prose Literature*. Cambridge: Cambridge University Press, 1966.

Kasravi, A. *Tarikh-i Hejdah Saleh-i Azerbaijan* (Eighteen-Year History of Azerbaijan). Tehran: Amir Kabir Press, 1967.

———. *Zendigani-yi Man* (My Life). Tehran: Payam Press, 1946.

Khajeh-Nouri, I. *Bazigaran-i Asr-i Tala'i* (The Politicians of the Golden Age). Tehran: Zarbakhsh Press, 1944.

Khomeini, R. *Kashf-i Asrar* (Secrets Revealed). Tehran: n.p., n.d.

———. *Velayat-i Faqih: Hukomat-i Islami* (The Jurist's Trusteeship: Islamic Government). N.p., 1976.

Kuhi-Kermani, H. *Az Shahrivar 1320 ta Faj'eh-i Azerbaijan* (From August 1941 to the Disaster of Azerbaijan). Tehran: Mazaheri Press, 1946. 2 vols.

Lambton, A. *Landlord and Peasant in Persia*. London: Oxford University Press, 1953.

———. *The Persian Land Reform, 1962-1966*. Oxford: Clarendon, 1969.

Lenczowski, G. *Iran under the Pahlavis*. Stanford: Hoover Institute, 1978.

———. *Russia and the West in Iran, 1918-48*. Ithaca: Cornell University Press, 1949.

Mahmud, M. *Tarikh-i Ravabet-i Siyasi-yi Iran va Englis* (The History of Anglo-Iranian Relations). Tehran: Khudkar Press, 1949-1953. 5 vols.

Makki, M. *Tarikh-i Bist Saleh-i Iran* (Twenty-Year History of Iran). Tehran: Majles Press, 1944-1945. 3 vols.

Maleki, A. *Tarikhcheh-i Jeb'eh-i Melli* (A Short History of the National Front). Tehran: Taban Press, 1954.

Millspaugh, A. *The American Task in Persia*. New York: Century, 1925.

———. *Americans in Persia*. Washington, D.C.: Brookings Institution, 1946.

Musahib, Gh. *Tabaqa-yi Hakima-yi Iranra Beshenasid* (Get to Know the Iranian Ruling Class). Tehran: Chehr Press, 1945.

Nirumand, B. *Iran: The New Imperialism in Action*. New York: Monthly Review, 1969.

Oberling, P. *The Qashqa'i Nomads of Fars*. The Hague: Mouton, 1974.

Ra'in, I. *Faramushkhaneh va Framasuneri dar Iran* (The House of Oblivion and Freemasonry in Iran). Tehran: Amir Kabir Press, 1968. 3 vols.

Ramazani, R. *The Foreign Policy of Iran, 1500-1941*. Charlottesville: University of Virginia Press, 1966.

———. *Iran's Foreign Policy 1941-1973*. Charlottesville: University of Virginia Press, 1975.

Razmara, ʿA., ed. *Jughrafiya-yi Nezami-yi Iran* (The Military Geography of Iran). Tehran: Government Printing Office, 1941-1944. 16 vols.

Rubin, B. *Paved with Good Intentions*. New York: Oxford University Press, 1980.

Saikal, A. *The Rise and Fall of the Shah*. Princeton: Princeton University Press, 1980.

Shafaq, R. *Khatirat-i Majles va Demokrasi Chist?* (Majles Memoirs and the Question What Is Democracy?). Tehran: Shafaq Press, 1955.

Shajiʿi, Z. *Nemayandegan-i Majles-i Shawra-yi Melli dar Bist-u-Yek Dawreh-i Qanunguzari* (Members of the National Consultative Assembly during Twenty-One Legislative Sessions). Tehran: Tehran University Press, 1965.

Shariʿati, ʿA. *Majmueh-i Asar* (Collected Works). Tehran: Husseinieh-i Ershad Press, 1979-1980. 8 vols.

Shayan, A. *Mazandaran: Rejal-i Moʿaser* (Mazandaran: Contemporary Politicians). Tehran: n.p., 1948.

Shifteh, N. *Rejal Bedun-i Mask* (Politicians Unveiled). Tehran: Muzaffar Press, 1952.

Taqizadeh, H. *Maqalat* (Articles). Tehran: Farhang Press, 1943.

United States. Department of State. *Foreign Relations of the United States*. Washington, D.C.: Government Printing Office, 1958-1979). 1940, Vol. 3; 1941, Vol. 3; 1942, Vol. 4; 1943, Vol. 4; 1944, Vol. 5; 1945, Vol. 8; 1946, Vol. 7; 1947, Vol. 5; 1948, Vol. 5; 1949, Vol. 6.

Upton, J. *The History of Modern Iran: An Interpretation*. Cambridge: Harvard University Press, 1968.

Wilber, D. *Contemporary Iran*, New York: Praeger, 1963.

———. *Riza Shah Pahlavi: The Resurrection and Reconstruction of Iran*. New York: Exposition Press, 1975.

Yar-Shater, E., ed. *Iran Faces the Seventies*. New York: Praeger, 1971.

Zonis, M. *The Political Elite of Iran*. Princeton: Princeton University Press, 1971.

TUDEH PARTY

Akbar-Akbari, ʿA. *Elal-i Zaʾef-i Tarikh-i Bourzhuazi-yi Iran* (Historical Reasons for the Weakness of the Iranian Bourgeoisie). Tehran: Tabesh Press, 1979.

ʿAlavi, B. *Panjah-u-Seh Nafar* (The Fifty-three). Tehran: n.p., 1944.

———. *Varaq Parehha-yi Zendan* (Torn Prison Notes). Tehran: n.p., 1942.

ʿAlavi, F. *Shekasht-i Ahzab-i Siyasi dar Intekhabat-i Dawreh-i Chahardahum* (The Defeat of the Political Parties in the Fourteenth Majles Elections). Tehran: Eqbal Press, 1946.

Amidi-Nouri, ʿA., ed. *Azerbaijan-i Demokrat* (Democratic Azerbaijan). Tehran: Dad Press, 1946.

Anonymous. *Gozashteh, Cheragh-i Rah-i Ayandeh Ast* (The Past Is the Light for the Future). Paris: Front for the Liberation of the Iranian People Press, 1966.

Anonymous. *Haqayeq-i Goftani* (Truths that Must Be Said). Tehran: Shu'levar Press, 1947.

Anonymous. *Rah-i Hizb-i Tudeh Iran* (The Road of the Tudeh Party of Iran). Tehran: Shahlevar Press, 1947.

Anonymous. *Tabaqeh-i Kargar Cheh Mikhuahad? Hizb-i Tudeh Cheh Miguyad?* (What Does the Working Class Want? What Does the Tudeh Party Say?). Tehran: n.p., 1946.

Anonymous. *Tahlil az Avza'-yi Hizb* (Study on the Party's Conditions). Tehran: Shu'levar Press, 1947.

Anonymous. *Tarikhcheh-i Nahzat-i Demokratik-i Azerbaijan* (A Short History of the Democratic Movement of Azerbaijan). Rome: Babak Press, 1978.

Eprim, E. *Cheh Bayad Kard?* (What Is To Be Done?). Tehran: n.p., 1947.

———. *Hizb-i Tudeh-i Iran Sar-i Dow Rah* (The Tudeh Party of Iran at the Crossroads). Tehran: n.p., 1947.

Hashtrudiyan, R. *Mas'aleh-i Melliyat* (The National Question). Tehran: n.p., 1945.

Iranian Government. Interior Ministry. *Iqdamat-i Ghayreh Qanuni* (Illegal Activities). Tehran: Interior Ministry Press, 1947.

Iranian Government. Military Governor of Tehran. *Ketab-i Siyah* (The Black Book). Tehran: Kayhan Press, 1956.

———. *Seyr-i Komunism dar Iran* (The Evolution of Communism in Iran). Tehran: Kayhan Press, 1957.

———. *The Evolution of Communism in Iran*. Tehran: Kayhan Press, 1958.

Ivanov, M. *Tarikh-i Novin-i Iran* (The New History of Iran). Translated by H. Tisabi and H. Qayempanah. Stockholm: Tudeh Press, 1977.

Kambakhsh, 'A. *Nazari Beh Jonbesh-i Kargari va Komunisti dar Iran* (Comments on the Workers' and Communist Movement in Iran). Stockholm: Tudeh Press, 1975. 2 vols.

Keshavarz, F. *Man Mottaham Mikunam* (I Accuse). Tehran: Ravaq Press, 1979.

Kianouri, N. *Mobarezat-i Tabaqati* (Class Struggle). Tehran: Azar Press, 1948.

———. *Pursesh va Pasukh* (Questions and Answers). Tehran: Tudeh Press, 1979.

Kuhi-Kermani, H. *Sosiyalism va Iran* (Socialism and Iran). Tehran: Atesh Press, 1952.

Maleki, Kh. *Hizb-i Tudeh Cheh Miguyad va Cheh Mikard* (What the Tudeh Party Says and What It Did). Tehran: Shahed Press, 1951.

Mani, Sh. *Tarikhcheh-i Nahzat-i Kargari dar Iran* (A Short History of the Labor Movement in Iran). Tehran: n.p., 1946.

Mazdak. *Afsaneh "Khalqha-yi" Iran* (The Myth of "Nationalities" of Iran). Florence: Mazdak Press, 1969.

———. *Asnad-i Tarikhi-yi Jonbesh-i Kargari, Sosiyal Demokrat, va Komunisti-yi Iran* (Historical Documents from the Workers', Social Democratic, and Communist Movement in Iran). Florence: Mazdak Press, 1972-1978. 7 vols.

———. *Karnameh-i Mossadeq va Hizb-i Tudeh* (The Record of Mossadeq and the Tudeh). Florence: Mazdak Press, 1979.

Montazam. *Mellat va Melliyat* (Nation and Nationality). Tehran: Qiyam Press, 1948.

Namvar, R. *Rezhim-i Teror va Ekhtenaq* (Regime of Terror and Strangulation). N.p.: Tudeh Press, 1962.

———. *Yadnameh-i Shahidan* (Martyrs' Memorial). N.p.: Tudeh Press, 1964.

Ovanessian, A. *Farhang-i Loghat va Estelahat-i Siyasi va Ijtema'i* (Dictionary of Social and Political Terms). Tehran: Tudeh Press, 1946.

———. *Osul-i Tashkilati-yi Hizb* (The Fundamentals of Party Organization). Tehran: Tudeh Press, 1943.

Pasyan, N. *Marg Bud Bazgasht Ham Bud* (There Was Both Death and Retreat). Tehran: n.p., 1947.

Qassemi, A. *Hizb-i Tudeh-i Iran Cheh Miguyad va Cheh Mikhuahad?* (What Does the Tudeh Party of Iran Say and Want?). Tehran: Tudeh Press, 1944.

———. *Jam'ehra Beshenasid* (Get to Know Society). Tehran: Tudeh Press, 1948.

———. *Qanun Chist?* (What Is Law?). Tehran: Tudeh Press, 1943.

Rouzbeh, Kh. *Eta'at-i Kurkuraneh* (Blind Obedience). Tehran: n.p., 1946.

Saferi, H. *Vaza'i Konuni-yi Iqtesadi-yi Iran* (The Present Economic Condition of Iran). Stockholm: Tudeh Press, 1977.

Tabari, E. *Jahanbiniha va Jonbeshha-yi Ijtima'i dar Iran* (World Outlooks and Social Movements in Iran). Stockholm: Tudeh Press, 1975-1979. 3 vols.

Tudeh Party. Akherin Defa'-i Khosrow Rouzbeh (The Last Defense of Khosrow Rouzbeh). N.p.: Tudeh Press, 1970.

———. *Barnameh-i Hizb-i Tudeh-i Iran* (The Program of the Tudeh Party of Iran). N.p.: Tudeh Press, 1975.

———. *Barnameh va Asasnameh-i Hizb* (Program and Statutes of the Party). N.p.: Tudeh Press, 1960.

———. *Darbareh-i bist-u-Hasteh-i Mordad* (Concerning August 19th). N.p.: Tudeh Press, 1963.

———. *Tudehiha dar Dadgah-i Nezami* (Tudeh Members before the Military Tribunal). N.p.: Tudeh Press, 1968.

Yavari, A. *Darbareh-i Ba'zi az Masa'el-i Hizb-i Tudeh-i Iran* (Concerning Some Problems of the Tudeh Party of Iran). Paris: n.p., 1969.

Zabih, S. *The Communist Movement in Iran*. Berkeley and Los Angeles: University of California Press, 1966.

SUPPLEMENTARY BIBLIOGRAPHY

Bani Sadr, A. *Sad Maqaleh* (A Hundred Articles). Tehran: Inqilab-i Islami Press, 1981.

Behn, W. *Islamic Revolution or Revolutionary Islam in Iran: A Selected Bibliography*. Berlin: Druck Press, 1980.

Hooglund, E. *Reform and Revolution in Rural Iran*. Austin: University of Texas Press, forthcoming.

Katouzian, H. *The Political Economy of Modern Iran*. New York: New York University Press, 1981.

Kazemi, F. *Poverty and Revolution in Iran*. New York: New York University Press, 1980.

Keddie, N. *Iran: Religion, Politics and Society*. London: Cass, 1980.

————, and Bonine, M. *Modern Iran: The Dialectics of Continuity and Change*. Albany: State University of New York Press, 1981.

————. *Roots of Revolution: An Interpretive History of Modern Iran*. New Haven: Yale University Press, 1981.

Kedourie, E., and Haim, S. *Towards A Modern Iran*. London: Cass, 1980.

Ledeen, M., and Lewis, W. *Debacle: The American Failure in Iran*. New York: Random House, 1981.

Said, E. *Covering Islam*. New York: Pantheon, 1981.

Sayyid Javadi, ʿAli Askhar Haj. *Daftarha-yi Inqilab* (Notebooks on the Revolution). Tehran: Jonbesh Press, 1980.

Index

Library of Congress Cataloging in Publication Data

Abrahamian, Ervand, 1940-
    Iran between two revolutions.

  (Princeton studies on the Near East)
  Bibliography: p.
  Includes index.
    1. Iran—Politics and government—20th century.
2. Iran—Social conditions.   I. Title.   II. Series.
DS316.6.A27   955′.05   81-47905
ISBN 0-691-05342-1   AACR2
ISBN 0-691-00790-X (pbk.)